Envision In Depth

READING, WRITING AND RESEARCHING ARGUMENTS

SECOND EDITION

Christine L. Alfano and Alyssa J. O'Brien
Stanford University

Longman

Boston • Columbus • Indianapolis • New York • San Francisco
Upper Saddle River • Amsterdam • Cape Town • Dubai • London • Madrid • Milan
Munich • Paris • Montreal • Toronto • Delhi • Mexico City • Sao Paulo • Sydney
Hong Kong • Seoul • Singapore • Taipei • Tokyo

Executive Editor: Lynn M. Huddon
Senior Development Editor: Virginia L. Blanford
Senior Marketing Manager: Sandra McGuire
Senior Supplements Editor: Donna Campion
Media Supplements Editor: Stefanie Liebman
Production Manager: Stacey Kulig
Project Coordination, Text Design, and Electronic Page Makeup: PreMedia Global
Senior Cover Design Manager: Nancy Danahy
Cover Designer: Nancy Sacks
Cover Images: Official White House Photo by Pete Souza; Iain Crockart / Getty Images; © Alex Segre / Alamy
Photo Researcher: Julie Tesser
Senior Manufacturing Buyer: Dennis Para
Printer and Binder: R.R. Donnelley and Sons
Cover Printer: Coral Graphics, Inc.

For permission to use copyrighted material, grateful acknowledgment is made to the copyright holders on pp.585–590, which are hereby made part of this copyright page.

Library of Congress Cataloging-in-Publication Data

Alfano, Christine L.
Envision In depth : reading, writing, and researching arguments / Christine L. Alfano and Alyssa J. O'Brien. — 2nd ed.
p. cm.
ISBN 978-0-205-75846-3
1. English language—Rhetoric. 2. Persuasion (Rhetoric) 3. College readers. 4. Report writing. 5. Visual communication. 6. Visual perception. I. O'Brien, Alyssa J. II. Title.
PE1431.E56 2010
808'.0427—dc22

2010036451

Copyright © 2011, 2008 by Pearson Education, Inc.

All rights reserved. No part of this publication may be reproduced, stored in a retrieval system, or transmitted, in any form or by any means, electronic, mechanical, photocopying, recording, or otherwise, without the prior written permission of the publisher. Printed in the United States.

Longman
is an imprint of

www.pearsonhighered.com

ISBN-13: 978-0-205-75846-3
ISBN-10: 0-205-75846-0

4 5 6 7 8 9 10—DOC—13 12

Contents

Chapter 3 Composing Arguments 45

PART II RESEARCH ARGUMENTS 73

Chapter 4 Planning and Proposing Research Arguments 74

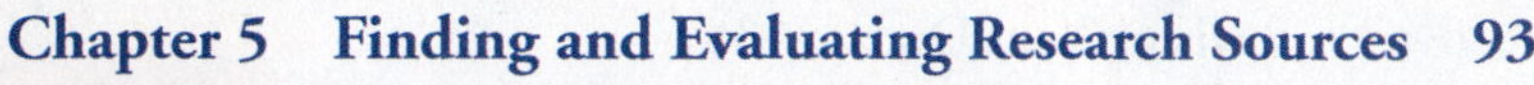

Chapter 5 Finding and Evaluating Research Sources 93

Chapter 6 Organizing and Writing Research Arguments 114

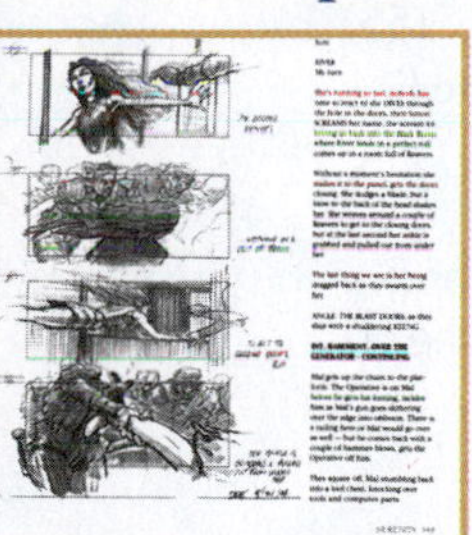

Creativity

CAN SHE BRIDGE THE GAP?

FOOD, INC.

Preface

Students today are surrounded by words and images—both online and in print—that try to persuade them to see the world in a certain way, buy particular products, play specific video games, and understand political realities from diverse perspectives. Our purpose with *Envision In Depth* is to teach students how to understand, analyze, research, and compose arguments about all these kinds of texts. We aim to enable students to develop the skills, confidence, and enthusiasm for writing, research, and effective communication about issues that matter to them.

In *Envision In Depth*, we provide a writing pedagogy that leads students through the steps for analyzing and researching verbal and visual compositions, such as images, ads, films, speeches, and multimedia displays. We complement this instruction with chapters containing readings on topics of interest to students and teachers today. To develop students' understanding of texts of all kinds, we offer guidance in the writing process, from analysis to argumentation, research writing, and presentation. We walk students through interactive lessons on crafting thesis statements, structuring argumentative essays, developing research topics, evaluating sources, integrating quotations, revising papers, and, finally, designing and presenting effective presentations and writing projects. At the same time, students learn key rhetorical concepts for effective communication, such as attending to audience, understanding rhetorical appeals and fallacies, practicing the canons of rhetoric, and differentiating levels of decorum. In the reading chapters, we offer lessons in observation, analysis, and writing about visual and verbal texts on an array of compelling topics.

Each chapter focuses on both words (print materials and articles) as well as writing about images and other contemporary media (ads, photographs, films, video games, tweets). In this way, the book teaches critical literacy about all kinds of texts. Moreover, we provide numerous student writing examples and professional, published readings—both with annotations—in order to demonstrate the writing lessons presented in each chapter and to show students how to successfully implement rhetorical strategies in their own texts. Our goal is to help students accomplish specific writing tasks as they encounter, analyze, research, and produce a range of texts.

To extend the lessons of the book, *Envision In Depth* offers an entire section with a rich range of readings (Part IV). These selections cover today's most engaging and important topics, including debates over the food industry, environmental rhetoric, new writing technologies and social media, gaming, body image and social markers, sports culture, news representations, immigration, and border crossing. Our hope with these extensive chapters is to offer students readings, images, questions and writing prompts so that they can explore issues in more depth, sharpen their skills of analysis, and study models of research and develop expertise in writing on subjects that matter to them. Each chapter provides a topic overview, diverse perspectives on the subject, and a rich pedagogical apparatus. For instance, the "Reflect and Write" questions about the readings provide opportunities for written composition and even launch research projects on topics that interest students today. The collaborative challenge boxes enable in-class work with the readings, and the "Perspectives on the Issue" or "From Reading to Research" prompts at the end of the question often point students to a rich array of resources on the *Envision* Website.

As we revised these chapters and the writing pedagogy for the second edition of *Envision In Depth*, we held on to our hope that this book might accomplish two goals: first, to give teachers the confidence and resources to lead students in an engaging, rhetorically sound pedagogy using an accessible writing instruction to focus on texts that matter most to students; and, second, to interest students while empowering them to become knowledgeable and skilled writers, researchers, and producers of well-composed rhetorical texts for a range of audiences.

What's New in the Second Edition

We have made a number of exciting changes to this edition of *Envision In Depth* based on feedback from both instructors and students. These include:

- Significantly expanded guidance for integrating quotations, paraphrases, and summaries in Chapter 6, because students find this particularly challenging
- A new section on the Toulmin model for analyzing arguments, in Chapter 3
- New sections, called "The Writer's Process," at the end of Chapters 1–9, provide a summary of the step-by-step composing tips discussed in the chapter and return the focus to the student's own work and writing process
- New activity prompts at the end of Chapters 1-9, called "Prewriting with the *Envision* Website," where we point to specific resources available through our extensive Companion Website: www.pearsonhighered.com/envision
- A new placement for the material on avoiding plagiarism and documenting sources, which now appears as Chapter 7, an integral part of Part II on Research Arguments, and which includes current MLA guidelines for documentation
- New readings Part IV—almost 50 percent new to this edition—including selections by danah boyd, Michael Pollan, Al Gore, Thomas Friedman, and Michelle Obama, as well as images by award-winning photographers James Nachtwey, Alex Webb, and more
- A completely new chapter in Part IV called "Fueling Ourselves" that looks at Food Culture, the Green Movement, and environmental rhetoric
- A heavily revised Chapter 11, "Culture 2.0," that focuses on several aspects of contemporary digital culture: gaming, remix culture, and social media
- Revised focus on "Marked Bodies" and "Sports Culture" in Chapters 12-13
- A sharper focus on technologies for photographing ordinary life in Chapter 14, and a timely attention to recent international events in "Images of Crisis"
- A significantly revised Chapter 15, now entitled "Crossing Cultures", with a new focus on immigration and border crossings both along the American border and elsewhere, in addition to an engaging and sharp focus on "McDonaldization" as a case study in globalization

Preview of the Readings in Part IV

In "Fueling Ourselves" (Chapter 10), we've selected a spectrum of readings that touch on both the proliferation of food culture (from food blogging online to the locavorism versus organic debate) and the controversies surrounding the rhetoric of global warming and the Green Movement.

"Culture 2.0" (Chapter 11) looks at culture in the digital age. We start in "Social Lives and Social Media" by considering how technologies such as Facebook and Twitter have reshaped our understanding of ourselves in the world we live in. In "Virtual World and Gaming Lives," we offer students a variety of perspectives on gaming culture, from the creation of avatars in immersive environments such as Second Life, to gender politics in online gaming, and finally how video games can be used as a persuasive tool. Finally, in "Remix Culture," we provide students with an introduction into the ways in which technological advances have forced us to reimagine the limitations of copyright protection to keep pace with an increasing emphasis on read–write culture.

In Chapter 12, "Marked Bodies," we explore how the media shapes our notions of the ideal body as well as what this means for visual representations of gender and cultural identity. We also look at how people seek to control the way society looks at them through making a fashion statement with body art, tattoos, religious clothing or jewelry, and other signs of a self-crafted identity.

"Sports and Media" (Chapter 13) speaks to our American cultural obsession with sports, first asking students to consider what it means to engineer the "ideal" athlete, then inviting them through a selection of articles and visual texts to think about the stereotypes created and perpetuated by the media coverage of sports.

The focus on media continues in Chapter 14, "Representing Reality," as we examine the power of persuasion in photographs—whether taken by Pultizer-Prize winning journalists or by "citizen Paparazzi" with cell phones; the chapter examines both images of local "ordinary" life in America as well as in times of crisis around the world, such as when embedded journalists cover war or "citizen journalists" capture breaking news events and post images on photo-sharing social media Websites.

Finally, in "Crossing Cultures" (Chapter 15), we look at border crossings both within America and across the globe, considering a range of articles and photo essays on the immigration debate, rise of racism, and condition of migrants, as well as they way in which American culture travels outward through franchises such as McDonald's but also through Disney, hip hop, and other cultural practices that spread American values through globalization.

With our choice of texts throughout the revised Part IV, we seek to capture and sustain student interest by using contemporary examples from a variety of media: academic journal articles, newspaper editorials and letters, interviews, radio broadcasts, advertising reviews, and even social media such as blog entries, twitter feeds, and YouTube videos.

In all these chapters, we ask students to analyze the arguments of each text, and we provide writing prompts, activities for collaborative work, and ideas for developed research projects. In this way, we hope to help students become confident and enthusiastic writers, researchers, and communicators about issues that matter to them.

Structure and Sequence of Assignments

Students who are using *Envision In Depth* can develop best as writers through following the sequencing of chapters, moving from analysis to argument, bringing in research, and then ending with presentations. However, teachers can use chapters and assignments in any order.

Part I: Analysis and Argument

Chapters 1 through 3 encourage students to become proficient, careful readers of rhetorical texts and to learn practical strategies for writing thesis statements, rhetorical analysis essays, and synthesis essays incorporating various perspectives. Students learn how to analyze the forms of persuasion in verbal and visual texts—from short articles to political cartoons, ads, and photos—with an emphasis on rhetorical conventions.

Part II: Research Arguments

Chapters 4 through 7 focus on strategies of research argument for sustained writing projects. The writing lessons in this section of the book take students through the research proposal; techniques for keeping a research log; locating sources; integrating visuals; methods of outlining, drafting, and revising; best practices for integrating sources in writing; and the complexities of evaluating and documenting sources. Students can consult sample proposals, outlines, and drafts as well as examples of articles, propaganda posters, and film trailers. They learn how to locate, evaluate, and incorporate research into their own arguments while avoiding plagiarism and accomplishing successful documentation of sources.

Part III: Design and Delivery

Chapters 8 and 9 encourage students to present their writing in effective ways. Students learn about document design—both for academic papers and for visual arguments such as op-ads and photo essays—as well as how to translate written work into effective oral and multimedia presentations. Students gain guidance on how to design memorable and compelling writing projects for a range of academic and professional purposes, including service-learning courses.

Part IV: Readings

Chapters 10 through 15 offer readings for analysis, discussion, and writing prompts. We ask students to think critically about each text in "Reflect and Write" boxes at the end of each verbal or visual reading, and we offer synthesis questions at the end of each chapter called "Perspectives on the Issue" and "From Reading to Research" in which students might conduct a comparative analysis or use the readings as a springboard for a larger research project.

Sequence of Assignments

Throughout the book, we've delineated examples of steps in the writing process: Chapter 1 shows students how to construct a thesis statement; Chapter 2 looks at strategies of argumentation, Chapter 3 focuses on organizational strategies for argument as well as the writing tasks of drafting powerful titles, introductions, and conclusions; Chapter 4 spends time instructing students on writing a proposal and keeping a research log; Chapter 5 offers lessons in annotated bibliographies; and Chapter 6 includes two outlines, a draft, and a revised paper. Chapter 7 takes students through proper documentation practices, and Chapters 8 and 9 cover document design and presentation strategies. In this way, the sequence of the book takes students through all the necessary components for effective writing—from generating an idea, to implementing rhetorical appeals and evidence, to crafting effective transitions, to acknowledging sources using proper MLA style and without risking plagiarism, to conventions of document design. Since the way a paper is formatted represents a type of visual rhetoric, we've also taken time to instruct students in both academic conventions (from papers and abstracts) and in innovative forms (for service-learning projects and visual arguments such as op-ads, photo essays, and Websites).

We base our writing assignments for all these learning goals on lessons from classical rhetoric but we offer a media theme for each chapter—such that we teach students to analyze a range of texts from cartoons, ads, and news photos to propaganda posters, film trailers, and student presentations. To meet our goal of teaching writing skills in analysis, research, and argument through use of verbal, visual, and multimedia examples, we've devised our assignments to meet specific learning objectives delineated by the WPA, as shown in the accompanying table.

MAJOR ASSIGNMENTS AND LEARNING OBJECTIVES

Chapter Title	Chapter Learning Goals	Major Assignments	Media Focus
1: Analyzing Texts	■ Understanding the rhetorical situation ■ Considering relationships between audience, text, and purpose ■ Textual analysis ■ Developing thesis statements	■ Personal narrative essay ■ Rhetorical analysis essay	Cartoons, comic strips, and editorial cartoons
2: Understanding Strategies of Persuasion	■ Strategies of argumentation ■ Understanding rhetorical appeals: *logos, pathos, ethos* ■ Abuses or exaggerated uses of rhetorical appeals ■ Importance of context and *kairos*	■ Contextual analysis essay ■ Analysis of rhetorical appeals and fallacies ■ Comparison/contrast essay	Advertisements
3: Composing Arguments	■ Introductions and conclusions ■ Arrangement and structure of argument ■ Considering various perspectives on argument ■ Developing persona and rhetorical stance ■ Addressing opposing opinion in an argument ■ Effective titles	■ Position paper ■ Multiple sides of argument assignment ■ Argumentative essay incorporating diverse viewpoints ■ Synthesis essay	Photographs, photo essays
4: Planning and Proposing Research Arguments	■ Generating and narrowing research topics ■ Prewriting strategies ■ Developing a research plan ■ Drafting a formal proposal	■ Research log ■ Informal research plan ■ Research proposal	Propaganda posters
5: Finding and Evaluating Research Sources	■ Research strategies ■ Evaluating sources ■ Distinguishing between primary and secondary sources ■ Locating sources ■ Conducting field research ■ Best practices for note taking	■ Critical evaluation of sources ■ Annotated bibliography ■ Field research contact assignment	Magazine and journal covers, Websites
6: Organizing and Writing Research Arguments	■ Organizing and outlining arguments ■ Importance of multiple drafts and revision ■ Writing and peer response ■ Quoting from sources	■ Formal outline ■ Peer review and response ■ Using visual evidence ■ Integrating sources ■ Writing the research argument	Film and movie trailers
7: Documentation and Plagiarism	■ Best practices in documenting sources ■ MLA style rules ■ Avoiding plagiarism	■ Ethical note-taking exercises ■ Citation practice	

(*continued*)

Chapter Title	Chapter Learning Goals	Major Assignments	Media Focus
8: Designing Arguments	■ Understanding the conventions of academic writing ■ Writing abstracts ■ Adopting appropriate voice and tone ■ Considering different genres of argument ■ Relationship between rhetorical situation and types of argument ■ Formatting and genre considerations	■ Writing an abstract ■ Visual argument—opinion advertisement or photo essay ■ Creating electronic arguments using multimedia (audio and visual)	Op-ads, photo essays, Websites, and multiple media
9: Delivering Presentations	■ Using technology to address a range of audiences ■ Transforming written arguments into visual or spoken texts ■ Strategies of design and delivery ■ Conducting field research	■ Conversion assignment—written to oral discourse ■ Fieldwork assignment ■ Multimedia presentation ■ Collaborative conference presentation	Presentations, poster sessions, PowerPoint and other slide software, Multimedia writing

Resources For Teachers and Students

Envision Companion Website

From John Dewey to Cynthia Selfe and Paolo Freire, researchers in rhetoric and composition have shown the advantages of student-centered classrooms and active, student-focused pedagogy. As a result, we have designed a comprehensive, multilayered Companion Website (www.pearsonhighered.com/envision) to accompany this book that offers students additional resources through an *active learning* model.

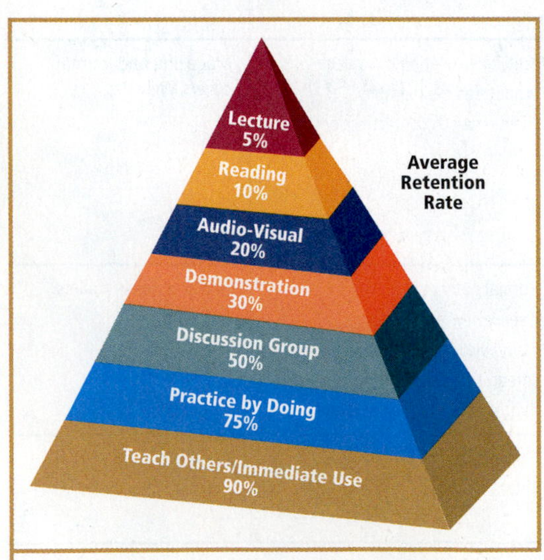

FIGURE 1 The Learning Pyramid shows the benefits of interactive pedagogy.

Envision In Depth is designed around the pedagogical philosophy that students learn more when they interact with the course material and when they are challenged to teach each other than when they simply implement the lessons taught to them. Moreover, the well-known Learning Pyramid depicting student retention rates demonstrates clearly the efficacy of active student engagement in the learning process (see Figure 1).

The *Envision* Website contains an extensive collection of materials designed to facilitate learning, including links to writing, research, and rhetoric resources, supplemental readings designed to complement those found in the book itself, additional writing activities, and over 250 student writing projects to serve as models for student writing, including updated and new samples for this revised edition of the book.

Instructors will also find invaluable resources available on the Website, designed to help you with everyday practical instruction in the classroom, including lessons plans, additional classroom activities, sample syllabi, expanded assignment guidelines, annotated classroom readings, resources for teaching students with disabilities, and chapters of the Instructor's Manual. See the *Envision* Website at www.pearsonhighered.com/envision.

Instructor's Manual

The Instructor's Manual for *Envision In Depth* provides teachers with pedagogical advice for each of *Envision In Depth*'s chapters, including chapter overviews, teaching tips for working with the main concepts and reading selections in the chapter, suggestions for classroom exercises and writing assignments, and strategies for integrating the resources on the *Envision* Website into your classroom. The Instructor's Manual also offers sample syllabi and suggested ways of organizing the reading and exercises according to days of the week. The Instructor's Manual is available on the *Envision* Website at www.pearsonhighered.com/envision.

Social Media Resources

Join us to create an online community around your course. For additional teaching tips and other resources and announcements, please visit Pearson's Facebook fan page for this book (www.facebook.com/envisionseries)

A Note of Thanks

In our chapter on documentation, we emphasize the importance of acknowledging your debts as a writer to those who made your ideas and work possible. We'd like to offer our own note of thanks to those who made possible the writing of this book. We are grateful to the reviewers whose comments informed our decisions about both the first edition and this revised edition: Steve Adkison, Idaho State University; Cora Agatucci, Central Oregon Community College; Scott Earle, Tacoma Community College; Courtney Edwards, Red Rocks Community College; Christopher Eisenhart, University of Massachusetts-Dartmouth; Catherine Gouge, West Virginia University; Sibylle Gruber, Northern Arizona University; Dan Holt, Lansing Community College; Brooke Hessler, Oklahoma City University; Rebecca Ingalls, University of Tampa; Dawnelle Jager, SUNY ESF, Syracuse University; Joseph Jones, University of Memphis; Tina Hultgren, Kishwaukee College; Jeraldine R. Kraver, University of Northern Colorado; Michael Lueker, Our Lady of the Lake University; Randy D. Nichols, Clemson University; Rachela Permenter, Slippery Rock University; Sarah Quirk, Waubonsee Community College; Andrew Scott, Ball State University; Gayatri Sirohi, Highline Community College; Julie Wakeman-Linn, Montgomery College; and Lynda Walsh, New Mexico Tech.

In addition, we would like to extend our thanks to our colleagues here at Stanford who have supported and encouraged us in our revisions to *Envision In Depth*, particularly Paul Bator, Julia Bleakney, Kimberly Moekle, and Kelly Myers, whose scholarship and inspiring pedagogy helped enrich our approach to many of the contemporary issues found in Part IV. We would also like to thank our team at Pearson who continue to support our *Envision* projects: our development editor, Ginny Blanford; assistant editor Rebecca Gilpin; Kristy Zamagni, our project editor at PreMedia Global; and our editor, Lynn Huddon, who has been with us since our very first discussions about the need for this kind of textbook.

We would also like to thank you for your interest in *Envision In Depth*, and we welcome suggestions and feedback. Working on this book has been a collaborative process from the beginning, and we hope that you, too, will join the conversation.

Finally, we extend our greatest appreciation to those who have envisioned our accomplishment and rallied us all the way through: our friends and families. Thank you.

Christine L. Alfano and Alyssa J. O'Brien

Part I

ANALYSIS AND ARGUMENT

Rhetoric's classic definition as the art of persuasion suggests a power. So much of what we receive from others—from family and friends to 30-second blurbs on TV—is intended to persuade. Recognizing how this is done gives greater power to choose.

—Victor Villanueva, Jr.

CHAPTER 1

Analyzing Texts

Chapter Preview Questions

- How do we read and analyze texts rhetorically?
- How do we write about visual texts?
- How can we generate thesis statements for arguments?
- How can we draft rhetorical analysis essays?

Everywhere around us, words and images try to persuade us to think about the world in certain ways. From "Got Milk?" ads to political campaign posters, words and images combine to move us, convince us to buy something, shape our opinions, or make us laugh. Living in such a world requires us to pay attention and to think critically and analytically about all the texts we encounter every day. We can see this persuasive power especially in visual texts, such as the political cartoons and comics you might find on your favorite Weblog or in the campus newspaper.

FIGURE 1.1. Beeler's cartoon from the 2008 election uses visual references to classical catastrophes to make a point about the climate facing the candidates during the election.

Source: © 2009 Nate Beeler, *Washington Examiner*, and PoliticalCartoons.com

Consider the political cartoon by Nate Beeler shown in Figure 1.1. How do the words and the images work together to persuade audiences to think, feel, or act a certain way? Beeler's cartoon conveys through words and images the atmosphere around the first presidential debate between Barack Obama and John McCain. With the collapsing columns and the twin towers in the background, the cartoon offers a powerful message about how America today struggles under many issues or "calamities." Notice that the presidential candidates don't say anything—their faces show consternation while their silence suggests they are overwhelmed by the issues. The cartoon is ironic since when we think of rhetoric, we often think of political rhetoric—or "empty rhetoric." Indeed, rhetoric began as a skill men learned in order to speak in public, often in courts of law where they had to represent themselves. The falling classical columns in the cartoon evoke this history while showing us how "rhetoric" today has expanded to mean any communication that seeks to persuade a specific audience in a certain situation, whether the text be written, visual, auditory, or multimedia.

We can understand how this cartoon works by asking questions about its argument, audience, and author. We can analyze its elements carefully and then come up with our interpretation of the text. When we ask questions and make our own argument about how a text works, we are analyzing how texts can be **rhetorical**, how they aim at persuading particular audiences through the careful choices made by the writer in composing the text. When we make arguments about a text—in writing or in speech or with visual compositions—we are using rhetoric as a practical art.

As you launch into the art of rhetoric and the skills of analyzing and writing in this chapter, you'll learn about comics and political cartoons. By studying these texts, you'll develop skills as both a reader and a writer, learn how to analyze rhetoric, and begin to create powerful arguments about the texts you encounter every day. In the process, you'll come to appreciate how writing as we know it is changing, causing us to approach it with a new set of eyes and a necessary set of rhetorical tools.

Understanding Texts Rhetorically

To approach texts rhetorically means to ask questions about how the text conveys a persuasive message or *argument,* how the text addresses a specific *audience,* and how the writer operates within a *specific context* or *rhetorical situation.*

You encounter many kinds of texts every day, even in just walking across campus. Once you recognize how these texts function *rhetorically*—once you see how texts try to shape your mind about the world—then you can decide whether or not to agree with the many messages you encounter on a regular basis.

FIGURE 1.2.

To grasp this concept, let's follow one hypothetical student—we'll call her Alex—as she walks to class and note the rhetorical texts she sees along the way.

First stop: the dorm room, your average institutional room, which Alex and her roommate have decorated with Altoids ads they've ripped from magazines (Figure 1.2). There's also a large poster for the women's basketball team on one wall and a small Snoopy comic taped above the computer screen.

Alex walks down the hall, past the rooms of other students who have photos and graffiti on their doors, pausing in the lounge where several of her friends are watching a rerun of *The Daily Show* with Jon Stewart and his famous smirk and strategic gestures on a large flat-screen TV (Figure 1.3). She watches until the show breaks for a commercial for Nike shoes, then she continues, down a stairwell decorated with student event flyers—a charity dance for the victims of a recent earthquake, a rally against immigration laws, a dorm meeting to plan the ski trip—and she pushes her way out into the cool autumn air. Outside the student newspaper has a political cartoon on the front designed to grab her attention and she pauses to look at the image of student apathy in the past election (Figure 1.4). The cartoon argues that students prefer popular culture over politics.

FIGURE 1.3.

FIGURE 1.4.

Source: © Tribune Media Services, Inc. All Rights Reserved. Reprinted with permission

She only has two minutes to get to class, so she walks briskly past the student union with its bulletin boards covered with notices of upcoming events, such as one for the Students for a More Just Society (Figure 1.5), which uses eye-catching design to grab the attention of passersby. Alex walks over the school

FIGURE 1.5.

crest in the walkway and past students outside the administration building, waving signs that protest the conditions of janitorial workers. She turns left, weaving along the back of a cluster of gleaming steel and brick buildings that constitute the engineering quad. She passes a thin metal sculpture called *Knowledge and Life* that guards the entrance to the library. Finally, she reaches her destination: the English department. As Alex climbs the stone steps, she stops to scan the photos and headlines on the campus paper before heading down the hall. Into the classroom she rushes, but she's late. The professor has started the PowerPoint lecture already. Alex picks up the handout from the TA and sits down in the back row.

Now that we've seen Alex safely to her seat, how many rhetorical texts did you notice along the way? Ads, posters, cartoons, Websites, textbooks, television shows, flyers, statues, signs, newspapers, PowerPoint slides, even architectural design: each can be seen as an example of rhetoric. Once you begin to look at the world rhetorically, you'll see that just about everywhere you are being persuaded to agree, act, buy, attend, or accept an argument: rhetoric permeates our cultural landscape. The next time you walk to class, pay attention to the rhetoric that you find along the way. Recognizing the power of rhetoric to persuade is an important part of learning to engage in contemporary society. Learning how to read texts rhetorically is the first step in thinking critically about the world.

Student Writing

See examples of several students' visual rhetoric narratives.

www.pearsonhighered.com/envision/04

Understanding Rhetoric

In one of the earliest definitions, ancient Greek philosopher Aristotle characterized **rhetoric** as *the ability to discern the available means of persuasion in any given situation.* Essentially, this means knowing what strategies will work to convince your audience in a given situation. As shown in Figure 1.6, this involves assessing and attending to the **rhetorical situation**—that is, to the relationship between writer, text, and audience. Think of

- the politician who might argue the same political platform but in strikingly different ways depending on what part of his constituency he's addressing;
- the various ways mothers, students, or police officers might convey the same anti-drug message to a group of middle school students;
- the clothing retailers who adapt their marketing messages to suit the media in which they're advertising—magazines, TV, or the Internet.

In each case the *argument* has been determined by the unique relationship between the writer, the audience, and the text.

In constructing your own arguments every day, you also need to evaluate your rhetorical situation.

- When you want to persuade your coach to let practice out early, you probably make your case face to face, rather than through a formal letter.
- When you ask for an extension on a paper, you most likely do so in a well-crafted email rather than a hasty after-class appeal.

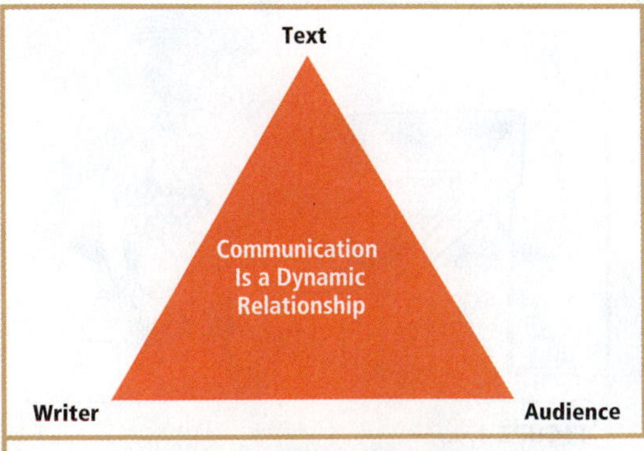

FIGURE 1.6. The rhetorical situation is a dynamic relationship between writer, text, and audience.

- When you apply for a job or internship, you send a formal résumé and cover letter to indicate the seriousness of your interest.

Here we see that the success of your argument depends at least in part on your choice of text (verbal plea, written email, cover letter) in relation to the audience (coach, professor, potential employer) that you're addressing. All these examples are rhetorical acts in the form of oral and written arguments.

Seeing Connections
Consider how Michael Eisner, former CEO of Disney, took his rhetorical situation in account in his Address Before Members of the United States Congress on the dangers of copyright infringement on page 357.

Understanding Visual Rhetoric

Yet persuasion happens through visual means as well: how you stand and make eye contact, how you format your professional documents, even how you capitalize or spell words in an email. Moreover, when you insert an image in an essay, create a poster to advertise a club sport, or draw a cartoon spoofing university policy, you are moving into the realm of **visual persuasion**—"writing" with images. From photographs to Websites, political cartoons to advertisements, these visual texts use rhetorical means to persuade an audience. Although some images may be more aesthetic than argumentative, many convey either inherent or explicit persuasive messages. Think about brochures, movie trailers, flyers, commercial Websites, and even comics; these are all created as arguments to convince audiences.

Since such strategies of persuasion occur through images—either alone or combined with words—rather than merely through words, they are called **visual rhetoric**. Additional examples of visual rhetoric include:

- A documentary produced to suggest a point of view
- An illustration in a children's book provided to shape the meaning of a story
- Sequential cartoons of a comic strip to offer powerful commentary on society or culture

In each example, the writer chooses the best visual representation for the message of the text. In this way, the study of visual rhetoric provides you with the means to understand how and why such choices are made, and what the significance of these decisions is in the larger culture in which we live. In the process of studying such texts, you will develop an essential life skill called **visual literacy**—how to read, analyze, understand, and even produce texts that are primarily visual in nature and powerful as compact messages about culture.

Strategies for Analyzing Texts Rhetorically

Think of your favorite comic strips, political cartoons, or cartoon animations. Although they may seem merely informative about current events, or just plain funny, they do serve as an important mode of communicating ideas and making statements about society. For example, the comic antics in *Calvin and Hobbes, xkcd* (a Web comic of romance, sarcasm, math, and language), or *The Boondocks* may not appear to carry any strong arguments about human relations or political events. However, if you look closely at the details—the address to a specific audience, the words of the characters in the cartoons, and the message made through combination of image and text—then you can gain a deeper understanding of the cartoon's argument. This is what we mean by analyzing texts rhetorically.

In fact, sometimes images can be even more powerful than words at reaching audiences. This is the argument made by Scott McCloud in his book, *Understanding Comics*:

> When pictures are more abstracted from "reality," they require greater levels of perception, more like words. When words are bolder, more direct, they require lower levels of perception and are received faster, more like pictures.

McCloud tells us we need to develop "greater levels of perception," or visual literacy, in order to *read with a critical eye*. In effect, we can look to the brief passage quoted here as an example of a persuasive use of written rhetoric, in which McCloud makes very deliberate choices to strengthen his point. Notice how his words use comparison-contrast (pictures versus words), qualified language ("reality"), and parallel structure (both sentences move from "When" to a final phrase beginning with "more like") to persuade his audience of the way pictures and words can operate in similar ways. Such attention to detail is the first step in rhetorical analysis—looking at the way the writer chooses the most effective means of persuasion to make a point.

Seeing Connections

For examples of graphic novels that function as powerful, rhetorical texts, see "Bound By Law?" on page 351 and an excerpt from Marjan Sartrapi's *Persepolis* on page 419.

What's interesting about McCloud's rhetoric, though, is not just his written strategies but also the way he uses a combination of words and images to make his point. To fully appreciate McCloud's rhetorical decisions, we need to consider the passage in its original context. As you can see in Figure 1.7, McCloud amplifies his argument about comics by using the form of the graphic novel, creating what we call a hybrid text—a strategic combination of words and images.

This complex diagram relies on the visual-verbal relationship itself to map out the complicated nature of how we understand both written text and pictures. The repetition and echoes that we found in the quoted passage are graphically represented in Figure 1.7; in fact, translated into comic book form, the division between word and image breaks down. It becomes a visual continuum that strongly suggests McCloud's

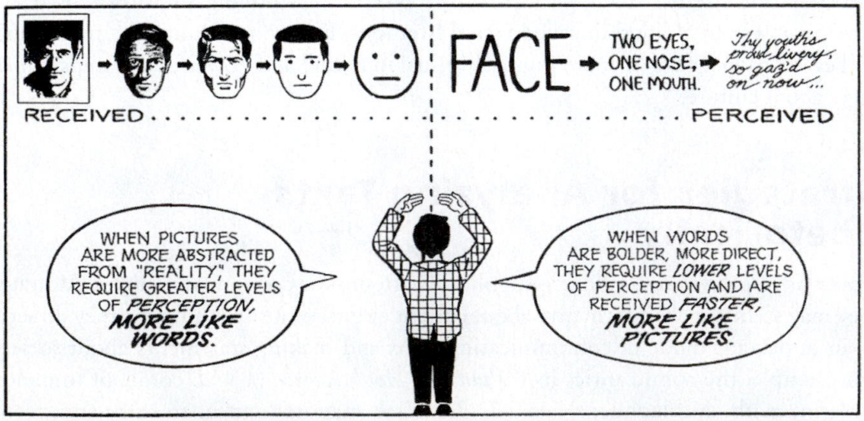

FIGURE 1.7. Scott McCloud writes in the medium of cartoons to explain comics.
Source: Courtesy of Scott McCloud

vision of the interrelationship between these rhetorical elements. The power of this argument comes from McCloud's strategic assessment of the rhetorical situation: he, the **author**, recognizes that his **audience** (people interested in visual media) would find a **text** that relies on both visual and verbal elements to be highly persuasive.

McCloud's example is also instructive for demonstrating the way word and image can collaborate in modern arguments. Today more than ever, rhetoric operates not just through word choice but also through choice of multimedia elements—images in a TV commercial, the audio of a viral ad on the Internet, the design choices of a Website or flyer, even the layout strategies of your textbooks. Therefore, we need to develop skills of analysis for all rhetorical texts. We need to understand argument *as writing across diverse media* and in turn develop **multimedia literacy**, or a careful way of reading, analyzing, and understanding media (visual, verbal, and other rhetorical texts).

One way to develop multimedia or visual literacy is to understand how cartoonists "write" through certain tools. The cartoon in Figure 1.8a shows the writing studio of *New Yorker* cartoonist Marisa Acocella Marchetto. Notice how Marchetto shows her many drafts, her tools of recording devices, and her pens and pads (see Figure 1.8b). As this cartoon reveals, writing is changing today so that audio recordings and graphic novels or cartoon books are becoming legitimate forms of researching and writing arguments about the world.

Analyzing a Comic Strip

As you can tell from Marchetto's drawing of her writer's studio, comic strips are an important form of rhetoric. They can serve as a productive starting point for examining how the rhetorical situation and composition strategies work together to produce powerful texts.

In "The Hipness Threshold," from the *Penny Arcade*, drawn by cartoonist Jerry Holkins (Figure 1.9), you see Gabe and Tycho as they accompany their friend Charles into an Apple Computer store. Notice the elements of the cartoon: images, words, characters, layout, and action. Observe facial expression, body postures, and the changes between the panels. Now try to determine: Who might be the audience? What is the writer's message? Then put it all together and ask yourself: What persuasive statement does the cartoon convey? What is its argument? In this way, you are analyzing visual rhetoric.

Seeing Connections
See Randall Munroe's xkcd cartoon, "Seismic Waves," on page 312 for another example of a powerful argument made through the sequential panels of a comic strip.

Now read the following excerpt from one of the cartoonist's blog posts that accompanied the online publication of this comic. In it, Holkins makes an argument very similar to that made in the cartoon—but this time in words. In what ways does this different rhetorical situation (blog versus Web comic) influence the way he makes his argument?

> The way Apple projects its brand, however, has nothing to do with the underlying technology. It could not be more divorced from it. So if they want to create largely empty stores staffed exclusively by young hardbodies in ill-fitting t-shirts, it's open season. It's possible that each manifestation of this chain does not resemble the others, that each one is not populated with the scrubbed, tousled young things of the sort one sees in serious teen dramas. You'll forgive me if I don't believe that. I'd say it's far more likely that there is a single Apple Store, connected by a series of geographically distinct portals.
>
> I don't put this out there to imply that the places I have to go to get technology or software are somehow superior, because they aren't. They're horrid. But at least I never feel underdressed.

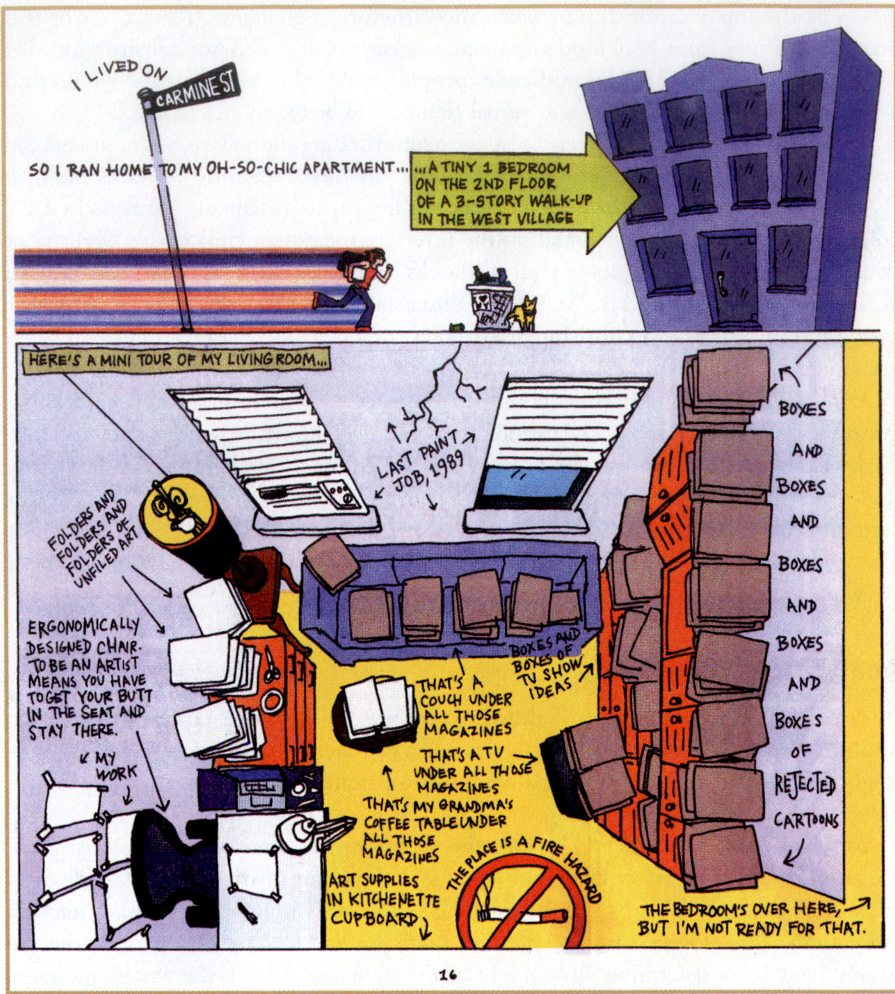

FIGURE 1.8a. Marchetto combines annotation with visual rhetoric in this "tour" of her writing studio.

Observe how Holkins uses visual metaphors in his writing to convey his social critique about Apple Stores. He mentions the tousled hair and hardbodies—visual signs of particular trends in society, reminiscent of Abercrombie & Fitch, for instance, and the physical "look" of Apple store staffers. His words echo the visual design of his cartoon argument. In his writing, he makes his point in the last paragraph by moving his argument to focus "the places I have to go to get technology" and ending with a sarcastic line about not worrying about being "underdressed." The sharp tone parallels the dejected stares of his characters. His persuasive writing strategies thus span both visual and verbal media. Understanding how both work rhetorically will give you the ability and confidence to analyze and produce similar texts of your own.

As these examples demonstrate, we can gather a tremendous amount of information from a seemingly simple comic strip. As we learn to develop our *visual literacy,* we can make more and better-informed interpretations of such intriguing visual

FIGURE 1.8b. Marchetto's writing tools include a tape recorder and drafting pads—with these tools she can compose her cartoons.

texts. These skills of visual analysis will help you approach other kinds of texts rhetorically: political speeches, scholarly articles, letters to the editor about timely issues, even instant messaging and—as we just learned—blog posts. At the same time, approaching visual texts rhetorically will help you develop your skills to participate in and respond to powerful multimedia arguments shaping the world around you.

FIGURE 1.9. The Hipness Threshold cartoon depicts the adventures of Gabe and Tycho as they accompany their friend Charles into an Apple Computer store.

Source: Penny Arcade, Inc. www.penny-arcade.com

"[Cartoons] provide alternative perspectives at a glance because they are visual and vivid and often seem to communicate a clear or obvious message."

—*Matthew Diamond,* "No Laughing Matter" (270)

CREATIVE PRACTICE

Using the comic strip shown in Figure 1.9, create your own version. Change the symbol of Microsoft from inside the box of the panel and put in something different—words or images. Then, write down your point just as Holkins did for his blog entry. When you are done, move into a small group and share your work—both your written analysis and your hybrid text. Discuss what you have learned in producing oral, written, and cartoon texts, and how each text conveys your argument.

Seeing Connections

See page 435 for examples of cartoons that make powerful visual arguments about steroid use in professional sports.

Analyzing Editorial Cartoons

In addition to comic strips, we can look at political cartoons—or **editorial cartoons** as they are also called—for another set of visual arguments to help us further develop effective strategies for analysis and interpretation. Editorial cartoons offer a rich resource for this sort of work.

From the densely symbolic eighteenth-century plates of William Hogarth, to the biting social satire of *Punch*'s illustrators, to the edgy work of political cartoonists such as Ann Telnaes, Mike Luckovich, and Daryl Cagle, the editorial cartoon has emerged as a succinct, powerful tool for writers to contribute to public dialogue on contemporary issues.

FIGURE 1.10. This cartoon by Daryl Cagle uses a striking symbol to make its argument.

Source: Daryl Cagle, Cagle Cartoons, Inc.

In the drawing by Daryl Cagle, for instance (see Figure 1.10), the particular face is recognizable to most twenty-first-century readers: the impish smile, the circular, black-frame glasses, and the prep-school tie identify this figure almost immediately as the young actor who plays Harry Potter in the film series. However, through one strategic substitution, Cagle transforms this image from illustration into commentary; he replaces the famous lightning bolt scar on Potter's forehead with a dollar sign. Cagle's Potter has been branded not by his encounter with a nearly omnipotent wizard but by his face-off with American capitalism. In this way, Cagle uses visual elements in his editorial cartoon to comment on the way this children's book hero has become a lucrative pop culture franchise.

FIGURE 1.11. Doug Marlette received death threats after publishing this cartoon.

Source: Courtesy of Doug Marlette

For a more politically charged example, let's look at a powerful cartoon created by Pulitzer Prize–winning cartoonist Doug Marlette.

In this cartoon (Figure 1.11), Marlette uses the strong reactions against Muslims following the September 11, 2001, attacks as a springboard for lampooning cultural prejudices and fears. His cartoon practices visual and verbal means of persuasion, both of which are important to consider when we are analyzing and writing about a text.

The words of his title, "What Would Mohammed Drive?" echo the famous Christian saying, "What Would

Jesus Do?" as a guideline for behavior, even while the irony of the rewriting asks readers to challenge their assumptions about different religions. Yet, the title suggests a link between the Muslim religion and terrorism by asking what vehicle Mohammed, if fueling terrorist impulses, would drive to conduct the act. The visual drawing positions an Arab man driving a Ryder truck that contains a nuclear warhead. This image echoed fears of "truck bombs" in the wake of the airplane attacks of 9/11. But it also rudely depicts the prophet Mohammed as a terrorist, and many readers view this as blasphemy, insult, or worse. Consider how a negative, demeaning depiction of Jesus might be received by some readers.

The cartoon caused a firestorm of protest from the Muslim community in America, including death threats on the cartoonist. Marlette responded by asserting that "the objective of political cartooning 'is not to soothe and tend sensitive psyches, but to jab and poke in an attempt to get at deeper truths, popular or otherwise'" (quoted in Moore). Marlette's own words reveal that cartoons are not just humorous texts but rather, as we have seen, they are rhetorical—they intend to persuade.

Student Writing

See Jeff Enquist's analysis of a cartoonist's commentary on the media representation of Catholic priests as part of a larger social issue dealing with the place of religion in American culture.

www.pearsonhighered.com/envision/11

Look again at the cartoon and ask yourself *how* it attempts to jab or poke. What elements of composition, framing, shading, and layout suggest to you the target of Marlette's jab? How does the title set up or shape possible readings of the cartoon? How might this cartoon be read differently by an American audience, an Arab audience, and an Arab-American audience? How might it be interpreted in the United States or in the Middle East as conveying a different persuasive message?

Some might argue that the cartoon takes the announced threat of terrorists potentially using trucks to carry out nuclear attacks and reproduces it without irony. Another reader analyzing the cartoon could say that it mocks and belittles the government issuing the warning about post-September 11 terrorists. A third reader could point to the caricature of the driver and state that the cartoon makes fun of people of Arab descent. These varied ways of reading and responding to the text depend on both *audience* and *context*, bringing to light the importance of the rhetorical situation. They also reveal the importance of learning effective means of persuading others to see the text through a certain interpretative lens or way of reading the cartoon.

What we can learn from this practice with rhetoric is that the relationship between interpretation and argument is a complex one. Although the author might intend to produce a certain argument, at times the audience may offer a slightly different interpretation. Our task as readers and writers is both to study a text carefully and to learn how to persuade others to see the text as we see it.

Let's turn now to Doug Marlette's writing to see how he used the art of rhetoric to persuade his many readers to see the cartoon from his perspective. As you read this article, originally published in the *Columbia Journalism Review*, use some of the same strategies of analysis that we've used on comics and cartoons throughout the chapter. Ask yourself: Who is his audience? How does Marlette position himself as author? What is his argument? What evidence does he use to support that argument? Which parts are the most persuasive? Which are the least persuasive? What visual images does he convey with words? Are you persuaded by his argument?

Marlette uses a provocative title to capture his readers' attention.

Marlette begins his article by establishing the context behind it. Notice how he implicitly defends the cartoon by describing how it was intended not just to poke fun at Mohammed but at Christian evangelicals as well. The play on words at the end of this paragraph gives the readers their first taste of the humorous, slightly irreverent tone and the close attention to style that characterize this piece.

In the second paragraph, Marlette uses specific examples of the threats he received to construct a rather unfavorable image of the people offended by his cartoon.

He recounts his response to the protests and comes to one of the most important points of his essay: that he is an equal opportunity offender, having penned cartoons that had enraged many different groups. By moving the question away from an issue of Islam to a larger issue of tolerance, Marlette sets up the issues of censorship and freedom of speech that are the real subjects of this essay.

Notice the way that Marlette also condemns the "murderous fanatics" he describes based on an ongoing pattern of behavior—a rhetorical decision that makes his critique seem less reactionary and more thoughtful.

I WAS A TOOL OF SATAN

Doug Marlette

Last year, I drew a cartoon that showed a man in Middle Eastern apparel at the wheel of a Ryder truck hauling a nuclear warhead. The caption read, "What Would Mohammed Drive?" Besides referring to the vehicle that Timothy McVeigh rode into Oklahoma City, the drawing was a takeoff on the "What Would Jesus Drive?" campaign created by Christian evangelicals to challenge the morality of owning gas-guzzling SUVs. The cartoon's main target, of course, was the faith-based politics of a different denomination. Predictably, the Shiite hit the fan.

Can you say "fatwa"? My newspaper, *The Tallahassee Democrat,* and I received more than 20,000 e-mails demanding an apology for misrepresenting the peace-loving religion of the Prophet Mohammed—or else. Some spelled out the "else": death, mutilation, Internet spam. . . . "What you did, Mr. Dog, will cost you your life. Soon you will join the dogs . . . hahaha in hell." "Just wait . . . we will see you in hell with all jews. . . ." The onslaught was orchestrated by an organization called the Council on American-Islamic Relations. CAIR bills itself as an "advocacy group." I was to discover that among the followers of Islam it advocated for were the men convicted of the 1993 bombing of the World Trade Center. At any rate, its campaign against me included flash-floods of e-mail intended to shut down servers at my newspaper and my syndicate, as well as viruses aimed at my home computer. The controversy became a subject of newspaper editorials, columns, Web logs, talk radio, and CNN. I was condemned on the front page of the Saudi publication *Arab News* by the secretary general of the Muslim World League.

My answer to the criticism was published in the *Democrat* (and reprinted around the country) under the headline *With All Due Respect, an Apology Is Not in Order.* I almost felt that I could have written the response in my sleep. In my thirty-year career, I have regularly drawn cartoons that offended religious fundamentalists and true believers of every stripe, a fact that I tend to list in the "Accomplishments" column of my résumé. I have outraged Christians by skewering Jerry Falwell, Catholics by needling the pope, and Jews by criticizing Israel. Those who rise up against the expression of ideas are strikingly similar. No one is less tolerant than those demanding tolerance. Despite differences of culture and creed, they all seem to share the notion that there is only one way of looking at things, their way. What I have learned from years of this is one of the great lessons of all the world's religions: we are all one in our humanness.

In my response, I reminded readers that my "What Would Mohammed Drive?" drawing was an assault not upon Islam but on the distortion of the Muslim religion by murderous fanatics—the followers of Mohammed who flew those planes into our buildings, to be sure, but also the Taliban killers of noncompliant women and destroyers of great art, the true believers who decapitated an American reporter, the young Palestinian suicide bombers taking out patrons of pizza parlors in the name of the Prophet Mohammed.

Then I gave my Journalism 101 lecture on the First Amendment, explaining that in this country we do not apologize for our opinions. Free speech is the linchpin of our republic. All other freedoms flow from it. After all, we don't need a First Amendment to allow us to run boring, inoffensive cartoons. We need constitutional protection for our right to express unpopular views. If we can't discuss the great issues of the day on the pages of our newspapers fearlessly, and without apology, where can we discuss them? In the streets with guns? In cafes with strapped-on bombs?

In this paragraph, he evokes the First Amendment and ends with an implicit comparison between America, with its civil liberties, and more militaristic and war-torn countries. Notice the power of the rhetorical questions that he uses at the end of the paragraph, asking readers to consider the alternatives to American freedom of speech.

Although my initial reaction to the "Mohammed" hostilities was that I had been there before, gradually I began to feel that there was something new, something darker afoot. The repressive impulses of that old-time religion were now being fed by the subtler inhibitions of mammon and the marketplace. Ignorance and bigotry were reinventing themselves in the post-Christian age by dressing up as "sensitivity" and masquerading as a public virtue that may be as destructive to our rights as religious zealotry. We seem to be entering a Techno Dark Age, in which the machines that were designed to serve the free flow of information have fallen into the hands of an anti-intellectual mobocracy.

Twenty-five years ago, I began inciting the wrath of the faithful by caricaturing the grotesque disparity between Jim and Tammy Faye Bakker's televangelism scam and the Christian piety they used to justify it. I was then working at *The Charlotte Observer,* in the hometown of the Bakkers' PTL Club, which instigated a full-bore attack on me. The issues I was cartooning were substantial enough that I won the Pulitzer Prize for my PTL work. But looking back on that fundamentalist religious campaign, even though my hate mail included some death threats, I am struck by the relative innocence of the times and how ominous the world has since become—how high the stakes, even for purveyors of incendiary doodles.

At this point, Marlette returns to describing his career as an equal opportunity offender, shifting the focus off Islam and instead discussing his troubles with evangelical Christians. By mentioning the death threats he received for his cartoons about the PTL Club (a televangelist show hosted by Jim and Tammy Bakker in the 1980s), he draws an implicit comparison here between Christian fundamentalists and what he calls Islamic "fanatics."

One of the first cartoons I ever drew on PTL was in 1978, when Jim Bakker's financial mismanagement forced him to lay off a significant portion of his staff. The drawing showed the TV preacher sitting at the center of Leonardo Da Vinci's *Last Supper* informing his disciples, "I'm going to have to let some of you go!" Bakker's aides told reporters that he was so upset by the drawing that he fell to his knees in his office, weeping into the gold shag carpet. Once he staggered to his feet, he and Tammy Faye went on the air and, displaying my cartoons, encouraged viewers to phone in complaints to the *Observer* and cancel their subscriptions.

Although he doesn't reproduce his 1978 cartoon here, he offers a clear description to his readers.

Jim Bakker finally resigned in disgrace from his PTL ministry, and I drew a cartoon of the televangelist who replaced him, Jerry Falwell, as a serpent slithering into PTL paradise: "Jim and Tammy were expelled from paradise and left me in charge."

One of the many angry readers who called me at the newspaper said, "You're a tool of Satan."

"Excuse me?"

"You're a tool of Satan for that cartoon you drew."

"That's impossible," I said. "I couldn't be a tool of Satan. *The Charlotte Observer*'s personnel department tests for that sort of thing."

This exchange brings humor back into the piece and demonstrates Marlette's seemingly flippant response to his critics.

Again, Marlette takes time to implicitly defend himself against claims of targeting Islam by describing how he has offended other religious groups as well.

Here Marlette cleverly plays on the idea of cartooning by pausing to assert that the reaction of his critics is "cartoonish" and exaggerated.

Marlette now comes to one of the focal points of his discussion: the way censorship is enforced not by angry critics but by a culture of "niceness" that is afraid to offend.

The reference to the Columbia journalism school would have extra force considering that this piece was originally published in the *Columbia Journalism Review*. Here, also, he clearly articulates the central point of his extended Mohammed story: that the most "disturbing thing" was that critics were able to influence his editors into refusing to run the cartoon.

Confused silence on the other end.

"They try to screen for tools of Satan," I explained. "Knight Ridder human resources has a strict policy against hiring tools of Satan."

Click.

Until "What Would Mohammed Drive?" most of the flak I caught was from the other side of the Middle East conflict. Jewish groups complained that my cartoons critical of Israel's invasion of Lebanon were anti-Semitic because I had drawn Prime Minister Menachem Begin with a big nose. My editors took the strategic position that I drew everyone's nose big. At one point, editorial pages were spread out on the floor for editors to measure with a ruler the noses of various Jewish and non-Jewish figures in my cartoons.

After I moved to the Northeast, it was Catholics I offended. At *New York Newsday*, I drew a close-up of the pope wearing a button that read "No Women Priests." There was an arrow pointing to his forehead and the inscription from Matthew 16:18: "Upon This Rock I Will Build My Church." The *Newsday* switchboard lit up like a Vegas wedding chapel. *Newsday* ran an apology for the cartoon, a first in my career, and offered me a chance to respond in a column. The result—though the paper published it in full—got me put on probation for a year by the publisher. That experience inspired the opening scene of my first novel, *The Bridge*.

* * *

But how do you cartoon a cartoon? It's a problem of redundancy in this hyperbolic age to caricature an already extravagantly distorted culture. When writers try to censor other writers, we're in Toontown. We are in deep trouble when victimhood becomes a sacrament, personal injury a point of pride, when irreverence is seen as a hate crime, when the true values of art and religion are distorted and debased by fanatics and zealots, whether in the name of the God of Abraham, Isaac, and Jacob, the Prophet Mohammed, or a literary Cult of Narcissus.

It was the cynically outrageous charge of homophobia against my book that brought me around to the similarities between the true believers I was used to dealing with and the post-modern secular humanist Church Ladies wagging their fingers at me. The threads that connect the CAIR and the literary fatwas, besides technological sabotage, are entreaties to "sensitivity," appeals to institutional guilt, and faith in a corporate culture of controversy avoidance. Niceness is the new face of censorship in this country.

The censors no longer come to us in jackboots with torches and baying dogs in the middle of the night. They arrive now in broad daylight with marketing surveys and focus-group findings. They come as teams, not armies, trained in effectiveness, certified in sensitivity, and wielding degrees from the Columbia journalism school. They're known not for their bravery but for their efficiency. They show gallantry only when they genuflect to apologize. The most disturbing thing about the "Mohammed" experience was that a laptop Luftwaffe was able to blitz editors into not running the cartoon in my own newspaper. "WWMD" ran briefly on the Tallahassee Democrat Web site, but once an outcry was raised, the editors pulled it and banned it from the newspaper altogether.

The cyberprotest by CAIR showed a sophisticated understanding of what motivates newsroom managers these days—bottom-line concerns, a wish for the machinery to run smoothly, and the human-resources mandate not to offend. Many of my e-mail detractors appeared to be well-educated, recent emigres. Even if their English sometimes faltered, they were fluent in the language of victimhood. Presumably, victimization was one of their motives for leaving their native countries, yet the subtext of many of their letters was that this country should be more like the ones they emigrated from. They had the American know-how without the know-why. In the name of tolerance, in the name of their peaceful God, they threatened violence against someone they accused of falsely accusing them of violence.

Having begun his argument applauding American principles—namely, freedom of speech—he now demonstrates the way that corporate structure and an ideology of tolerance (both hallmarks of American culture) are actually operating in conflict with First Amendment rights.

With the rise of the bottom-line culture and the corporatization of news gathering, tolerance itself has become commodified and denuded of its original purpose. Consequently, the best part of the American character—our generous spirit, our sense of fair play—has been turned against us.

Tolerance has become a tool of coercion, of institutional inhibition, of bureaucratic self-preservation. We all should take pride in how this country for the most part curbed the instinct to lash out at Arab-Americans in the wake of 9/11. One of the great strengths of this nation is our sensitivity to the tyranny of the majority, our sense of justice for all. But the First Amendment, the miracle of our system, is not just a passive shield of protection. In order to maintain our true, nationally defining diversity, it obligates journalists to be bold, writers to be full-throated and uninhibited, and those blunt instruments of the free press, cartoonists like me, not to self-censor. We must use it or lose it.

He ends this paragraph by clarifying his interpretation of the First Amendment, specifically with relation to journalism. He then uses a cliché to emphasize his point.

Political cartoonists daily push the limits of free speech. They were once the embodiment of journalism's independent voice. Today they are as endangered a species as bald eagles. The professional troublemaker has become a luxury that offends the bottom-line sensibilities of corporate journalism. Twenty years ago, there were two hundred of us working on daily newspapers. Now there are only ninety. Herblock is dead. Jeff MacNelly is dead. And most of the rest of us might as well be. Just as resume hounds have replaced newshounds in today's newsrooms, ambition has replaced talent at the drawing boards. Passion has yielded to careerism, Thomas Nast to Eddie Haskell. With the retirement of Paul Conrad at the *Los Angeles Times*, a rolling blackout from California has engulfed the country, dimming the pilot lights on many American editorial pages. Most editorial cartoons now look as bland as B-roll and as impenetrable as a 1040 form.

Notice the analogy he makes between political cartoonists and bald eagles. It operates on two levels, on the one hand emphasizing that they are endangered and on the other hand suggesting that cartoonists represent America's freedoms.

His references on this page to important political cartoonists (Herbert Block, Jeff MacNelly, Paul Conrad) underscore his message about the decline of political cartooning as a genre.

We know what happens to the bald eagle when it's not allowed to reproduce and its habitat is contaminated. As the species is thinned, the eco-balance is imperiled.

In the next paragraph he returns to his metaphor of the bald eagle, developing it into a richer analogy.

Why should we care about the obsolescence of the editorial cartoonist?

Because cartoons can't say "on the other hand," because they strain reason and logic, because they are hard to defend and thus are the acid test of the First Amendment, and that is why they must be preserved.

What would Marlette drive? Forget SUVs and armored cars. It would be an all-terrain vehicle you don't need a license for. Not a foreign import, but American-made. It would be built with the same grit and gumption my

As he moves toward his conclusion, Marlette draws his essay together by echoing and slightly revising the title of the cartoon that started the controversy and demonstrating the way that images carry symbolic weight.

Marlette solidifies his connection to great contributors to American culture by referring to great American writers and trailblazers, from novelist John Steinbeck (the Joads are the family from *The Grapes of Wrath*) to cultural icon Ken Kesey and astronaut Neil Armstrong.

In his final paragraph, Marlette repeats his new catch phrase and uses it to provide a final comment on his vision of America and its inherent freedoms.

grandmother showed when she faced down government soldiers in the struggle for economic justice, and the courage my father displayed as a twenty-year-old when he waded ashore in the predawn darkness of Salerno and Anzio. It would be fueled by the freedom spirit that both grows out of our Constitution and is protected by it—fiercer than any fatwa, tougher than all the tanks in the army, and more powerful than any bunker-buster.

If I drew you a picture it might look like the broken-down jalopy driven by the Joads from Oklahoma to California. Or like the Cadillac that Jack Kerouac took on the road in his search for nirvana. Or the pickup Woody Guthrie hitched a ride in on that ribbon of highway, bound for glory. Or the International Harvester Day-Glo school bus driven cross-country by Ken Kesey and his Merry Pranksters. Or the Trailways and Greyhound buses the Freedom Riders boarded to face the deadly backroads of Mississippi and Alabama. Or the moon-buggy Neil Armstrong commanded on that first miraculous trip to the final frontier.

What would Marlette drive? The self-evident, unalienable American model of democracy that we as a young nation discovered and road-tested for the entire world: the freedom to be ourselves, to speak the truth as we see it, and to drive it home.

In his written argument, Marlette describes the observations he has made about the public's response to his cartoons. Notice how specific Marlette is in describing the reactions to his cartoons and how concretely he conjures up American identity through the imagery of the bald eagle and the driven vehicle. These are *rhetorical moves,* strategic choices he has made as a writer in deciding how best to persuade his readers (especially those outraged by the cartoons) to see his drawing from a different point of view. Just as Holkins picked the most appropriate words and images for inside his *Penny Arcade* cartoon, Marlette picked the most appropriate words and metaphors to use in his article.

Practicing Rhetorical Analysis

We've learned that rhetoric works as a means of persuading an audience to accept the argument of the author. This is also true for the arguments you make about a text. In other words, rhetoric also applies to the texts you craft to persuade someone to accept your interpretation of a specific cultural or political text.

Your task is to argue convincingly and persuade your audience to see the text the way you see it. Your challenge as a student of writing and rhetoric is not only to identify the argument contained by a text but also to craft your own interpretation of that text. This involves a careful assessment of the ways in which the elements of the rhetorical situation work together to produce meaning in a text. In many cases your analysis will also address the interplay of words and images. Your analysis can take many forms: a written essay, an oral report, a visual argument, or a combination of these.

AT A GLANCE

Selecting a Visual Rhetoric Image

When choosing a visual text for analysis, ask yourself the following questions:

- Does the image attempt to persuade the audience?
- Are there sufficient elements in the image to analyze?
- What do you know about the author or the intended audience?
- What's your own interpretation of this image?

Selecting Texts for Analysis

As you select a text for analysis, think back to the cartoons or comics you found most striking in this chapter—perhaps the election cartoon, Scott McCloud's strip, or Doug Marlette's cartoon. Each of these texts conveys a powerful message through words and images, verbal and visual rhetoric. When you choose your own text for rhetorical analysis, make sure you pick one that offers a persuasive point about society or an issue. It is harder to write about a text that is not meant to make a social or political point, one that is not meant to persuade.

Developing a Thesis Statement

Once you have selected the image for analysis, then the most important part of your writing will be your **thesis statement**, the concise statement of your interpretation about your chosen text. To understand thesis statements, let's work through an example. Imagine, for instance, that you want to write an argument about the editorial cartoons in Figures 1.12 and 1.13. Both cartoons comment on recent debates about immigration policy. How might you develop a thesis statement that persuasively conveys your interpretation of how these cartoons contribute to the debate surrounding the status of undocumented immigrants?

FIGURE 1.12. Cartoon by Daryl Cagle.
Source: Daryl Cagle, Cagle Cartoons, Inc.

Start by jotting down what you see; make close observations about these cartoons. Then use questions to bring your argument into focus and to make a specific claim about the images. The end product will be a *working thesis.* The process of developing your thesis might look like this:

1. **Write down your observations.**

   Close observations: Both pictures focus, literally or symbolically, on the border between the United States and Mexico and on the way that we set up fences (or vault doors) to keep illegal immigrants out. Both also show holes in those barriers: one focuses on people running through a hole in the fence; the other shows a small door in the vault that looks as if it's been propped open from the inside. The words are interesting, too. In the Cagle cartoon, the big sign says "Keep out," while the smaller signs are designed to draw people in. In the Ramirez cartoon, the small sign says "Cheap labor welcome," contradicting the message of the large, high-security door that blocks access to the United States.

FIGURE 1.13. Cartoon by Michael Ramirez.
Source: Michael Ramirez and Copley News Service

2. **Work with your observations to construct a preliminary thesis statement.**

   First statement: Both cartoons focus on the contradiction in American border policy.

3. **Refine your argument by asking questions that make your statement less general.**

   Ask yourself: How? What contradications? To what effect? How do I know this?

4. **Revise your preliminary thesis statement to be more specific; perhaps include specific evidence that drives your claim.**

   Revised statement: The cartoons in Figures 1.12 and 1.13 focus on the contradictions in American border policy by showing that on the one hand, the American government wants to keep illegal immigrants out, but on the other hand, economic forces encourage them to enter the United States illegally.

5. **Further polish your thesis by refining your language and asking questions about the implications of your working thesis statement.**

   Ask yourself: What do you find interesting about this observation? How does it tap into larger social or cultural issues?

6. **Write your working thesis to include a sense of the implications of your claim. Sometimes we call this the "So What?" of your claim.**

   Working thesis: The political cartoons in Figures 1.12 and 1.13 offer a pointed commentary on the recent immigration debate, suggesting ways the official government stance against illegal immigration is undermined by economic forces that tolerate, if not welcome, the entry of undocumented workers into the United States.

Seeing Connections
To further explore the topic of border policy, see the "Borderlands" section of Chapter 15 and Alex Webb's photos on pages 528–529.

A strong, argumentative thesis does more than state a topic: it makes a claim about that topic that you will develop in the rest of your paper. Let's look at one more example to further consider ways to produce sharp, clear, and persuasive thesis statements. The examples that follow are a series of thesis statements about Mike Thompson's cartoon in Figure 1.14, published in 2006 in reaction to rising gas prices.

FIGURE 1.14. Cartoon by Mike Thompson.
Source: Mike Thompson and Copley News Service

Thesis 1: Mike Thompson's cartoon is very powerful.

Assessment: *This thesis relies too heavily on subjective opinion; the author offers no criteria for evaluating the cartoon or a context for understanding the statement.*

Thesis 2: Mike Thompson's drawing shows his opinion about SUVs.

Assessment: *This thesis statement rests too much on a broad generalization rather than specific analysis.*

Thesis 3: In response to rising gas prices, Mike Thompson draws a powerful editorial cartoon about the relationship between driving SUVs and consuming fossil fuels.

Assessment: This thesis statement merely states a fact and makes a broad claim rather than offering a focused interpretation of the cartoon. It needs to explain how the cartoon was powerful.

Thesis 4: In his 2006 editorial cartoon "Aptly Named," Mike Thompson persuasively plays with the term *fossil fuel* to suggest that SUVs and the "wanton consumption" of gasoline represent an outdated approach to transportation that needs to recognize its own imminent extinction.

Assessment: Of the four examples, this thesis provides the most provocative and specific articulation of the author's interpretation of the significance of Thompson's cartoon.

A strong argument, driven by a strong thesis statement, is at the heart of any successful rhetorical analysis essay.

AT A GLANCE

Testing Your Thesis

Do you have a specific and interesting angle on your topic?

- Does it offer a statement of significance about your topic?
- Is the thesis sharp enough (not too obvious)?
- Could someone argue against it (or is it just an observation)?
- Is it not too dense (trying to compact the entire paper) or too simplistic (not developing your point thoroughly)?

Analyzing a Student's Writing Sample

Let's look at how one student, Cyana Chilton, combines effective strategies of analysis with a carefully crafted thesis statement to compose her own rhetorical analysis of a recent editorial cartoon.

Student Writing

See examples of other students' rhetorical analysis essays.
www.pearsonhighered.com/envision/19

Chilton 1

Cyana Chilton
Dr. Alyssa J. O'Brien
Rhetorical Analysis Essay

Drugs to Death in a Political Cartoon:
An Oversimplification?

Cyana's title refers to the image she has chosen.

As the more stable counterpart to a volatile southern neighbor, the United States has always had a wary outlook towards Mexico. In recent years, the increase in illegal immigration, the unpredictable economies in both countries, and the issues resulting from drug use and trade have added tension to the already taut relationship. Blame flows easily and lands on various subjects—each government, drug cartels, drug users, and more. However, in a recent political cartoon posted by Daniel Kurtzman (see Fig. 1), various rhetorical strategies are used to portray the

The essay begins by setting up the context for the cartoon. Into this rhetorical situation, Cyana introduces the visual text.

By including the cartoon in her first paragraph, Cyana makes a much more powerful argument than if she had simply appended it to the end of her paper.

The actual thesis emphasizes how rhetoric works to offer an argument about the drug cartels and the government by pointing to specific concrete elements of the cartoon.

Chilton 2

Figure 1. A cartoon by Nate Beeler about Mexican drug cartels and their effect on Mexican society, posted by Daniel Kurtzman. Source: http://z.about.com/d/politicalhumor/l/0/e/2/mexican-pinata.jpg

cartoonist's opinion that blame should be limited to one party: the drug cartels. Through the use of color, stereotypes, and the images of death, the cartoonist blames the violent Latin American drug cartels for Mexico's problems and undermines the legitimacy of the attempts of the Mexican government, as represented by the immobile piñata, to solve the drug issue.

Cyana then develops this thesis by suggesting the significance or "so-what" of her observations—that they cast the drug cartels as dangerous.

In the cartoon, the drug cartels are represented by the figure on the right, with a dark black shirt and a menacing face and stance. The color scheme of the figure, as compared to the gaudy piñata and the white, ethereal skulls, makes the drug cartels an image of destruction and danger.

Cyana uses background knowledge to fill in the rhetorical situation for the reader.

The sheer physical size of the figure also exaggerates the responsibility of those cartels for the destruction to Mexico. The cartoon ignores the presence of the approximately 25 million people in the United States who are illicit drug users and thus create a market for the products of the drug cartels (marijuana and cocaine, for example), instead perhaps over-simplifying the situation to portray the drug problem as a one-dimensional, clear-cut, and violent issue. This message, however, is inaccurate. It may be easier for an American audience, the original audience for the cartoon, to accept an opinion that completely ignores the blame due to the consumers of the drugs sold by the cartels or other potential recipients like corrupt police forces. The oversimplification is also dangerous because it clearly separates Mexico from the United States and does not acknowledge the mutual dependence and interaction, for better or for worse, between them. By creating a foreign, violent-looking figure as "Mexican," there is no attempt to foster a sense of complicity, unity, or responsibility in the audience.

She refers to the term in her title several times to develop her argument.

Each paragraph takes an aspect of the visual text and analyzes it in detail. Notice how her writing becomes fluid and descriptive—matching her discussion of the landscape.

The color scheme and setup of the background for the cartoon are also strategic choices on the part of the cartoonist. The landscape is barren, marked primarily by a dead and blasé tree, two indistinct cacti, and the dry ground. Even the sky is ominous; the clouds converge over the drug cartel

Chilton 3

figure, and the colors are hazy and smoky, as if rising from the dusty ground. The infertility of the landscape and the obvious lack of abundant natural resources occurring at the same time as the drug cartel's mutilation of the piñata lends many negative connotations and associations to the drug cartel, further implicating the figure in Mexico's issues. This rhetoric, however, is a fallacy; although the barren landscape and the drug cartels coincide, the correlation does not necessarily imply causation. Although the drug cartel figure may appear to be at fault for the destruction of the piñata figure and, by extension, the environment of the political cartoon, in reality there is no evidence provided that fairly places all blame on the drug cartels.

The cartoon also, besides overtly placing blame on the drug cartels for the generalized problems and violence in Mexico, underestimates the extent and power of the Mexican government to battle the acknowledged power of the cartels. The imagery associated with "Mexico," in the figure of the piñata, is the most obvious connection to belittling the effects of the Mexican government against the drug cartels. The piñata is immobile, tied to a tree. It hangs suspended in the air, as if it cannot control its own motion or defenses. Its face is blank and that of a donkey—a stupid, impotent animal—suggesting a lack of intelligence or even intense feeling like that seen in the face of the drug cartel figure. This blankness seems wrong because tiny skulls are pouring out of the figure, whose stomach has just been savagely punctured, but no reactive emotion is exhibited. Ironically, piñatas are usually used as lighthearted games at birthday parties for children. The lack of a typical mask on the drug cartel figure's face makes the destruction intentional and more malicious. The implication of the destruction being an easy, game-like pursuit for the drug cartels further attempts to persuade the audience to see the culpability of the drug cartels in comparison to the weakness of the government in Mexico.

Moving to the center image, Cyana takes the time to offer her own interpretation of the piñata, using persuasive force in her own writing.

The vacant gaze of the piñata is mirrored by the blankness of the landscape. The dead, nondescript plant life and the brown earth are seemingly disconnected from the free-hanging Mexico piñata, suggesting that the government has no control or direct connection with the country at large. In fact, however, Mexico's president, Felipe Calderón, has taken the

Notice the transition— from a paragraph talking about a piñata to the Mexican countryside under President Calderón.

Her language becomes strong here as she seeks to persuade her readers to view the cartoon through her interpretation.

Cyana includes a section on the writer or cartoonist.

Each paragraph ends with a strong summary line that reinforces the main point of her thesis.

As the essay begins to wrap up, Cyana broadens out to consider other problems and the larger significance of this visual rhetoric. One final point about the cartoon drives home the thesis and makes the paper a successful argument.

Chilton 4

first step against the pervasiveness of drug violence that no president has dared to take in the past. He has cracked down on drug dealers by jailing them, sending them to the United States to be jailed, and decriminalizing small quantities of drugs in an effort to lower profits for the cartels. These efforts, while perhaps unpopular and not always effective, are the first attempts to fight back against the power of cartels and the violence that erupts as a result of the drug trade. Their reduction in this cartoon to a donkey with a flat affect suspended and isolated in midair is an exaggeration and a miscommunication of the truth.

Furthermore, Mexico is homogenized by various images in the cartoon. An overly commercialized and Americanized symbol, the piñata, deemphasizes Mexican culture's diversity and vitality. By characterizing an entire, diverse country as a small, powerless object, the cartoonist constructs *ethos*, or credibility, for himself by apparently being able to make large generalizations about complex issues, implying that he has an authoritative and encompassing grasp of the subject.

The mound of skulls further serve to homogenize the Mexican population. The skulls have a shimmering halo around them, portraying them as martyr figures and innocent deaths, pouring out of Mexico's belly without being able to stop. This imagery further demonizes the hulking drug cartel figure, but it does not acknowledge that many, if not a majority, of the deaths associated with the drug war are actually those directly involved: members of opposing cartels, policemen or hospital workers, for example. The cartoonist uses *pathos,* or an appeal to emotion, in portraying the skulls—the idea of violent death and the loss of one's individuality is frightening and sobering. The rhetorical device is similar to pictures of devastation from natural disasters or genocides: widespread and indiscriminate death as represented through an image. The victimized and non-individualized skulls characterize the entire Mexican population as weak and victimized. The fact that the skulls fall out of the piñata suggest that the death already existed in Mexico but was just hidden by gaudy colors and flimsy covering; this condescending criticism of Mexico has no evidence in the cartoon and thus seems unfounded. Also, there are a host

Chilton 5

of other problems at large in Mexico: a faltering economy, the swine flu epidemic, and immigration issues as always. The cartoonist's choice to ignore those issues and to focus on the inability of the government to stop just one (admittedly, a large one), is overly reducing the responsibilities of the government and the various nationwide problems that exist.

In this visually simple but subtly complex image from Nate Beeler, many stereotypes and oversimplifications are used as rhetorical strategies by the cartoonist. The color scheme of the piñata, the drug cartel figure, the landscape, and the pile of skulls all serve to place blame for Mexico's troubles solely on the drug cartels. The use, and perhaps misuse, of *pathos*, *ethos*, and logical fallacies all aid the cartoonist in refusing to acknowledge some legitimacy on the part of the Mexican government in bravely—and sometimes successfully—attempting to eradicate drug turf wars from the country. Such a large task cannot be accomplished quickly or cleanly, and one hulking figure cannot possibly hold all the blame for creating a heartrending pile of haloed skulls. The cartoonist, and the world, must look elsewhere in an effort to truly begin to solve this international problem.

As she concludes the essay, Cyana restates the cartoonist's name in full and the key terms of her title and thesis. She offers a summary and then a final point for the reader to consider.

The last line offers a memorable call to action and ends the essay powerfully.

Chilton 6

Works Cited

Beeler, Nate. Cartoon. About.com.: Political Humor. *about.com*, 22 March 2009. Web. 4 April 2009.

United States Center for Disease Control. *FASTATS*. Web. 1 July 2009.

Cyana responsibly attributes the research she conducted to help her write this paper.

Student Writing

See Cyana's research paper generated from this rhetorical analysis essay.

www.pearsonhighered.com/envision/23

Referring to Images in Your Writing

When you follow this example and write about a visual text that interests you, consider the strategic placement of your image. Should you insert it in the paper or append it at the end with your bibliography? If you want to create a true hybrid composition—one that integrates words and images—include the image right in your essay. Make sure to refer to it in your writing as we do in our discussion of cartoons in this chapter. Then, below the image, include a caption and a figure number. This will show you have the proper training as a writer and rhetorician in presenting your ideas.

The Writer's Process

As you turn now to write your rhetorical analysis of a text, you'll be putting into practice all the skills you've learned so far in this chapter. You'll need to write down your observations of the text; spend time discussing them in detail, as we have done with the many examples we've worked on so far; and use these observations as evidence to make an argument that will persuade others to see the text the way you see it.

In composing your analysis of this text, you need to use the same process we have worked through for the analysis of comic strips and cartoons:

- First, look carefully at all the elements in the text. Create a list of your observations or use the prewriting checklist at the end of this chapter to help you read the text more closely.
- Then, speculate about the meaning of each element. How does it contribute to the whole?
- Next, complete the rhetorical triangle (see Figure 1.6) for the text, assessing who the author is, who the intended audience is, what form the text takes, and what the argument is, based on your observations of the details.
- Finally, put all these elements together and develop your argument about the message and meaning of the visual text.

It's crucial to remember that when you write a rhetorical analysis, you perform a rhetorical act of persuasion yourself. Accordingly, you need to include the key elements of analytical writing: (1) have a point of interpretation to share with your readers, (2) take time to walk readers through concrete details to prove your point, and (3) lead your readers through the essay in an engaging and convincing way. But of all these, the most important is your argument, your interpretation of or position on the text—your *thesis.*

In writing your analysis paper, keep in mind the need to begin with observations, but avoid simply describing the elements you notice. Instead, zoom in on specific details and think hard about their meaning. Make a persuasive argument by using *specific* evidence to support your analysis of how the text succeeds at convincing an audience to see an issue in a particular way. Spend some time working on your thesis before composing the entire draft. Make sure your angle is sharp and your interpretation takes into account audience, writer, and message as well as concrete points of visual and verbal composition. This is the key to crafting a persuasive and effective rhetorical analysis.

AT A GLANCE

Visual Rhetoric Analysis Essays

- Do you have a sharp point or thesis to make about the visual text?
- Have you selected key visual details to discuss in support of your main point?
- Do you lead readers through your analysis of the text by discussing important details in sequence? These include:

    Visual composition, layout, and imagery

    Verbal elements in the text

    Color, shading, and arrangement of items

    Caption or title of the image

- Do you have an effective title, main point, introduction, body, and conclusion?
- Have you included the image in the essay?

PREWRITING CHECKLIST

Focus on Analyzing Comics and Cartoons

- ❑ **Topic:** What key issue is the comic or cartoon addressing?
- ❑ **Story:** On the most basic level, what is happening in the cartoon?
- ❑ **Audience:** In what country and in what historical moment was the cartoon produced? In what type of text did it first appear? A journal? A newspaper? Online? Was this text conservative? liberal? radical? feminist? How does it speak to this audience?
- ❑ **Author:** What do you know about the artist? What kinds of cartoons does he or she regularly produce? Where does he or she live and publish? What kinds of other writing does this person do?
- ❑ **Argument:** What is the cartoon's message about the issue? Is there irony involved (does the cartoon advocate one point of view, but the cartoonist wants you to take the opposite view)?
- ❑ **Composition:** Is this political cartoon a single frame or a series of sequential frames? If the latter, how does the argument evolve over the series?
- ❑ **Word and image:** Does the cartoon rely exclusively on the visual? Or are word and image both used? What is the relationship between the two? Is one given priority over the other? How does this influence the cartoon's overall persuasiveness?
- ❑ **Imagery:** What choices of imagery and content does the artist make? Are the drawings realistic? Do they rely on caricatures? Does the artist include allusions or references to past or present events or ideas?
- ❑ **Tone:** Is the cartoon primarily comic or serious in tone? How does this choice of tone create a powerful rhetorical impact on readers?
- ❑ **Character and setting:** What components are featured by the cartoon? A person? An object? A scene? Think about how character and setting are portrayed. What are the ethnicity, age, socioeconomic class, and gender of the characters? Do they represent actual people? Are they fictional creations? How are these choices rhetorical strategies designed to tailor the cartoon and its argument to its intended audience?
- ❑ **Cultural resonance:** Does the cartoon implicitly or explicitly refer to any actual people, events, or pop culture icons? What sort of symbolism is used in the cartoon? Would the symbols speak to a broad or narrow audience? How does the cultural resonance function as a rhetorical strategy in making the argument?

PREWRITING WITH THE *ENVISION* WEBSITE

For one way to begin writing about cartoons as powerful rhetorical acts, go to the *Envision* Website. Follow a link to one of the cartoon collections. Compare how different cartoon artists craft persuasive visual arguments about the same issue with remarkably divergent messages. Pick two cartoons, write an analysis of each cartoon, and prepare to share your interpretations with the rest of the class. Be sure to describe elements of the visual text in detail, present the key components of the rhetorical situation (audience, writer, message), and discuss how each contributes to the overall argument of the cartoon.
www.pearsonhighered.com/envision/25

WRITING PROJECTS

1. **Personal Narrative:** Recall Alex's observations of rhetoric on her way to class; conduct a similar study of the rhetoric in your world. Write your reflections into a *personal narrative essay.* Discuss which types of visual, verbal, bodily, or architectural rhetoric were most evident, which were most subtle, and which you found the most persuasive. Conclude with a statement or argument about these images—what do they collectively say about your culture or community? How do these texts try to shape readers or viewers with certain specific messages?

2. **Rhetorical Analysis:** Choose a political cartoon or comic strip on a current issue and write a *rhetorical analysis*. You might find an appropriate text in a recent issue of *Newsweek*, in a collection such as Charles Brooks's *Best Editorial Cartoons of the Year*, or online through the *Envision* Website resource page for Chapter 1. Use the prewriting checklist to help you write a rhetorical analysis of the cartoon. If you choose to analyze more than one cartoon on the same issue, introduce all your texts in the opening paragraph, and spend some time analyzing each one in detail. Make sure that your writing supports a thesis about elements and messages of all the texts you are analyzing.
www.pearsonhighered.com/envision/26

3. **Comparative Rhetorical Analysis of Text and Image:** After you've begun project 2, search through recent newspapers, newsmagazines, or a library news database like LexisNexis to find an article that addresses the same issue. Write a *comparative analysis of the text and the political cartoon*. What is each one's argument, and what rhetorical strategies does each one use to effectively make that argument? You may want to use the prewriting checklist in looking at the political cartoon. If you want to take a historical approach to this assignment, choose both a political cartoon and an article that span the historical spectrum but focus on one issue, such as racial profiling, immigrant workers, or what's "hip" in the entertainment industry. Be sure to include specific details about each text, shape your observations into a thesis, and don't forget a title for your essay. Look back to the examples in this chapter on how to analyze both images and texts, and see how you can make your argument about social values.

Visit www.pearsonhighered.com/envision for expanded assignment guidelines and student projects.
Visit www.mycomplab.com for additional general writing and research resources.

CHAPTER 2

Understanding Strategies of Persuasion

Chapter Preview Questions

- What specific strategies of argumentation work as persuasion?
- What role do the rhetorical appeals of *logos, pathos,* and *ethos* play in persuasion?
- What is the effect of exaggeration in these appeals?
- How does context (*kairos*) shape texts by time, place, and culture?
- How can you incorporate strategies of persuasion in your own writing?

What convinced you to buy that new cell phone, to try that new sports drink—or even to decide which college to attend? Chances are that some combination of words and images—a printed ad or brochure, a TV commercial, a billboard—influenced your decision.

What strategies of persuasion does the iPod ad use (see Figure 2.1)? Notice, for example, the simple design, the contrast between dark silhouette and bright background, and the placement and gleaming white color of the iPod itself, which draws your eye to the logo and slogan at the top. Does this ad use a logical appeal, emphasizing technical features of the iPod? Or does it appeal to your enthusiasm for music or dancing?

FIGURE 2.1. This eye-catching iPod ad draws the audience immediately into its argument.

Source: © Alyssa J. O'Brien, 2006

Think of other ads you've seen. How do these ads make you pause and pay attention? Perhaps a magazine ad includes a photo of a celebrity or simply a good-looking person, someone you are attracted to or can identify with emotionally. Perhaps a TV ad tells a compelling story or provides a memorable example. Perhaps a brochure offers impressive statistics or supporting evidence for its claims. Often it is not one but a combination of factors that we find persuasive—and often these factors are so subtle that we hardly recognize them. Techniques used to move and convince an audience are called **rhetorical strategies**.

Ads offer us a productive means of analyzing rhetorical strategies because they represent arguments in compact forms. An ad has little room to spare; persuasion must be locked into a single frame or a brief 30-second spot. Advertisements represent one of the most ubiquitous forms of persuasion. The average adult encounters 3000 of these compact, powerful arguments—that is, advertisements—every day (Twitchell, *Adcult* 2). Consider all the places ads appear nowadays: not just in magazines or on the television or radio but also on billboards and computer screens; on the sides of buses, trains, and buildings; in sports stadiums and movie theaters; on T-shirts and caps; and even spray-painted on sidewalks.

As citizens of what cultural critic James Twitchell calls "Adcult USA," we are constantly exposed to texts that appeal to us on many levels. In this chapter, you'll gain a working vocabulary and concrete strategies of rhetorical persuasion that you can use both to become a savvy reader of advertisements and also to produce your own persuasive texts.

Analyzing Ads as Arguments

By analyzing advertisements, we can detect the rhetorical choices writers and artists select to make their points and convince their audiences. In this way we realize that advertisers are rhetoricians, careful to attend to the *rhetorical situation.* We can find in advertisements specific strategies of argumentation that you can use to make your case in your own writing. Advertisers might use:

Seeing Connections
See the strategies of argumentation in David Pogue's piece about Photo Sharing, page 498, or in Cynthia Gorney's article, "Mexico's Other Border," on page 540.

- **Narration** to sell their product—using their ad to tell a story
- **Comparison-contrast** to encourage the consumer to buy their product rather than their competitor's
- **Example** or **illustration** to show how their product can be used or how it can impact a person's life
- **Cause and effect** to demonstrate the benefits of using their product
- **Definition** to clarify their product's purpose or function
- An **analogy** to help make a difficult selling point or product—like fragrance—more accessible to their audience
- **Process** to demonstrate the way a product can be used
- **Description** to show you the specifications of a desktop system or a new SUV
- **Classification and division** to help the reader conceptualize how the product fits into a larger scheme

These strategies are equally effective in both visual and written texts. They can be used effectively to structure both a small unit (part of an ad or, in a more academic text, a paragraph or section of an essay) and a larger one (the entire ad or, in an academic paper, the argument as a whole).

Even a single commercial can be structured around multiple strategies. The famous "This Is Your Brain on Drugs" commercial from the late 1980s used *analogy* (a comparison to something else—in this case comparing using drugs and frying an egg) and *process* (reliance on a sequence of events—here, how taking drugs affects the user's brain) to warn its audience away from drug use. In this 30-second spot, the spokesperson holds up an egg, saying, "This is your brain." In the next shot, the camera focuses on an ordinary frying pan as he states, "This is drugs." We as the audience begin to slowly add up parts A and B, almost anticipating his next move. As the ad moves to the visual crescendo, we hear him say, "This is your brain on drugs": the image of the egg sizzling in the frying pan fills the screen. The final words seem almost anticlimactic after this powerful image: "Any questions?"

These strategies function just as persuasively in print ads. For example, look at the advertisement for Rusk hair spray in Figure 2.2, an ad designed to draw the viewer's eye through the visual argument. What the reader notices

FIGURE 2.2. This problem-solution ad for Rusk hairspray uses several strategies of argumentation.

first are the striking pictures of the golden-haired model, somewhat flat hair on one side and voluminous curls on the other, exemplifying the powerful *comparison-contrast* strategy that is echoed in many levels of the ad. The entire ad is bisected to reflect this structure, opposing "problem" to "solution" and literally dividing the main caption—"Go from ordinary . . . to Extraordinary"—in half. What bridges the divide, both literally and figuratively, is the strategically positioned can of hairspray, tilted slighted toward the right to reinforce emphasis on the *example/illustration* of a satisfied Rusk-user. By centralizing the red-capped canister in this way, the ad therefore also establishes a persuasive *cause-and-effect* argument, implicitly suggesting that using this hairspray allowed this girl to overcome the perceived challenges of limp hair.

Seeing Connections

For an alternative model of using comparison-contrast as a rhetorical strategy, see the excerpts from Robbie Cooper's *Alter Ego* on page 323.

Within written texts, the use of such strategies provides a similar foundation for a persuasive argument. As you read the following online article from Slate.com, look carefully to see which strategies author Seth Stevenson utilizes to make his argument about recent iPod commercials.

YOU AND YOUR SHADOW

The iPod ads are mesmerizing. But does your iPod think it's better than you?

Seth Stevenson

The Spot: Silhouetted shadow-people dance in a strenuous manner. Behind them is a wall of solid color that flashes in neon shades of orange, pink, blue, and green. In each shadow-person's hand is an Apple iPod.

As part of his online series "Ad Reportcard," Stevenson uses a format not usually associated with academic writing—notice here he sets up the commercial under discussion in a separate section before even starting his essay.

Stevenson's chatty voice is very appropriate for his online audience.

I myself own an iPod, but rarely dance around with it. In part because the earbuds would fall out (Does this happen to you? I think I may have narrow auditory canals) and in part because I'm just not all that prone to solitary rump-shaking. It's a failing on my part. Maybe if I were a silhouette I might dance more.

All that said, these are very catchy ads. I don't get sick of watching them. And yet I also sort of resent them, as I'll later explain.

Notice the way Stevenson defers his thesis, although he gives us a sense of his approach toward the ads (resentment).

First, let's talk about what the ads get right. For one, the songs (from groups like Jet and Black Eyed Peas) are extremely well-chosen. Just indie enough so that not everybody knows them; just mainstream enough so that almost everybody likes them. But as good as the music is, the visual concept is even better. It's incredibly simple: never more than three distinct colors on the screen at any one time, and black and white are two of them. What makes it so bold are those vast swaths of neon monochrome.

In this section, Stevenson relies on **description** to set up the foundation for his discussion of the ads; yet, notice that he is somewhat selective, emphasizing the elements that are most important for his analysis—namely, the way the use of silhouettes emphasizes the product.

This simplicity highlights the dance moves, but also—and more importantly—it highlights the iPod. The key to it all is the silhouettes. What a brilliant way to showcase a product. Almost everything that might distract us—not just background scenery, but even the actors' faces and clothes—has been eliminated. All we're left to focus on is that iconic gizmo. What's more, the dark black silhouettes of the dancers perfectly offset the iPod's gleaming white cord, earbuds, and body.

The rhetorical question here points to the turn in his piece from description to analysis, the point where the reader will come closer to understanding his resentment.

This all sounds great, so far. So what's not to like?

At this point in the article, Stevenson moves to **description** and **example** to set up the powerful **comparison-contrast** strategy that he develops further in the next paragraphs.

For the longest time, I couldn't put my finger on it. And then I realized where I'd seen this trick before. It's the mid-1990s campaign for DeBeers diamonds—the one where the people are shadows, but the jewelry is real. In them, a shadow-man would slip a diamond ring over a shadow-finger, or clasp a pendant necklace around a ghostly throat. These ads used to be on television all the time. You may recall the stirring string music of their soundtrack, or the still-running tagline: "A Diamond Is Forever."

By **comparing** the iPod commercials to the DeBeers campaign, Stevenson can clearly articulate his ambivalent feelings about Apple's ads.

Like the iPod ads, these DeBeers ads used shadow-people to perfect effect. The product—in this case, diamonds—sparkles and shines on a dusky background. But what bothered me about the spots was the underlying message. They seem to say that we are all just transient shadows, not long for this world—it's our diamonds that are forever. In the end, that necklace is no overpriced bauble. It's a ticket to immortality!

In his semihumorous interjection, Stevenson returns to the **contrast** between himself and the Apple silhouettes with which he started the article.

My distaste for these ads stems in part from the fact that, with both the iPod and the diamonds, the marketing gives me a sneaking sense that the product thinks it's better than me. More attractive, far more timeless, and frankly more interesting, too. I feel I'm being told that, without this particular merchandise, I will have no tangible presence in the world. And that hurts. I'm a person, dammit, not a featureless shadow-being! If you prick me, do I not write resentful columns?

Notice how he builds on his **comparison** by opening his concluding paragraph with an **analogy**, using a simile ("Like diamond jewelry") that reminds the reader of the connection he has established between the two campaigns.

Like diamond jewelry, the iPod is designed and marketed to draw attention to itself, and I think (I realize I'm in a minority here) I prefer my consumer goods to know their place. If I did it over, I might opt for an equally functional but slightly more anonymous MP3 player. One that deflects attention instead of attracting it. Because I'm the one with the eternal soul here—it's my stuff that's just transient junk.

Grade: B–. Perfectly executed. Mildly insulting message.

Slate.com and Washingtonpost. Newsweek Interactive. All rights reserved.

Understanding the Rhetorical Appeals

Seeing Connections
To see how *pathos, logos,* and *ethos* factor into the development of an advertising campaign, read Susie Orbach's "Fat is an Advertising Issue" on page 386 or see Michel Martin's blog post about racism on page 550.

The rhetorical strategies we've examined so far can be filtered through the lens of classical modes of persuasion dating back to 500 BCE. The formal terms are ***logos, pathos,*** and ***ethos.***

Each type of rhetorical appeal represents a mode of persuasion that can be used by itself or in combination. As you might imagine, a text may employ a combined mode of persuasion, such as "passionate logic"—a rational argument written with highly charged prose, "goodwilled *pathos*"—an emotional statement that relies on the character of the speaker to be believed, or "logical *ethos*"—a strong line of reasoning employed by a speaker to build authority. Moreover, a text may use rhetorical appeals in a combination that produces an *overarching effect,* such as irony or humor. You might think of humor as one of the most effective forms of persuasion. Jokes and other forms of humor

AT A GLANCE

Rhetorical Appeals

- ***Logos*** entails rational argument: appeals to reason and an attempt to persuade the audience through clear reasoning and philosophy. Statistics, facts, definitions, and formal proofs, as well as interpretations such as syllogisms or deductively reasoned arguments, are all examples of means of persuasion we call "the logical appeal."
- ***Pathos,*** or "the pathetic appeal," generally refers to an appeal to the emotions: the speaker attempts to put the audience into a particular emotional state so that the audience will be receptive to and ultimately convinced by the speaker's message. Inflammatory language, sad stories, appeals to nationalist sentiments, and jokes are all examples of *pathos*.
- ***Ethos*** is an appeal to authority or character; according to Aristotle, *ethos* means the character or goodwill of the speaker. Today we also consider the speaker's reliance on authority, credibility, or benevolence when discussing strategies of *ethos*. Although we call this third mode of persuasion the "ethical appeal," it does not strictly mean the use of ethics or ethical reasoning. Keep in mind that *ethos* is the deliberate use of the *speaker's character* as a mode of persuasion.

are basically appeals to *pathos* because they put the audience in the right emotional state to be receptive to an argument, but they can also involve reasoning or the use of the writer's authority to sway an audience.

Since they appear so frequently in combination, you might find that conceptualizing *logos, pathos,* and *ethos* through a visual representation helps you to understand how they relate to one another (see Figure 2.3).

As you read this chapter, consider how each text relies on various rhetorical appeals to construct its message.

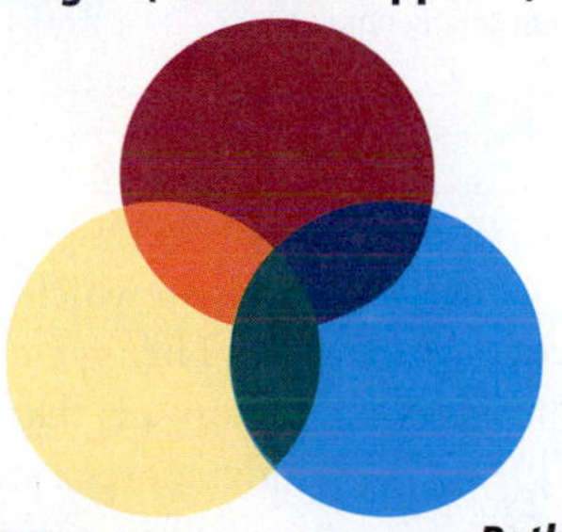

***Logos* ("Rational Appeal")**

***Ethos* ("Ethical Appeal")**

***Pathos* ("Pathetic Appeal")**

FIGURE 2.3. Rhetorical appeals can be understood as intersecting strategies of persuasion.

Appeals to Reason: *Logos*

As a writer, you use *logos* when you construct an essay around facts and reason; in general, an argument based on *logos* will favor the use of logic, statistical evidence, quotations from authorities, and proven facts. In the opening pages of this chapter, for instance, we used *logos*—quotations and statistics about advertising—to persuade you about the omnipresence of advertising in today's culture. Scholars often rely on *logos* in this way to make persuasive academic arguments. Consider, for instance, the way Laurence Bowen and Jill Schmid use *logos* as a strategy of persuasion in this passage from "Minority Presence and Portrayal in Mainstream Magazine Advertising: An Update":

> Some might argue that the small number of minorities featured in mainstream magazine advertising may be due to a very deliberate media strategy that successfully targets minorities in specialized and minority media. However, each of the magazines analyzed does have a minority readership and, in some cases, that readership is quite substantial. For example, according to *Simmons 1993 Study of Media and Markets,* the Hispanic readership of *Life* is 9.9%, yet the inclusion of Hispanics in *Life*'s advertisements was only .8%. *Cosmopolitan* has a 11.3% Black readership, yet only 4.3% of the advertisements

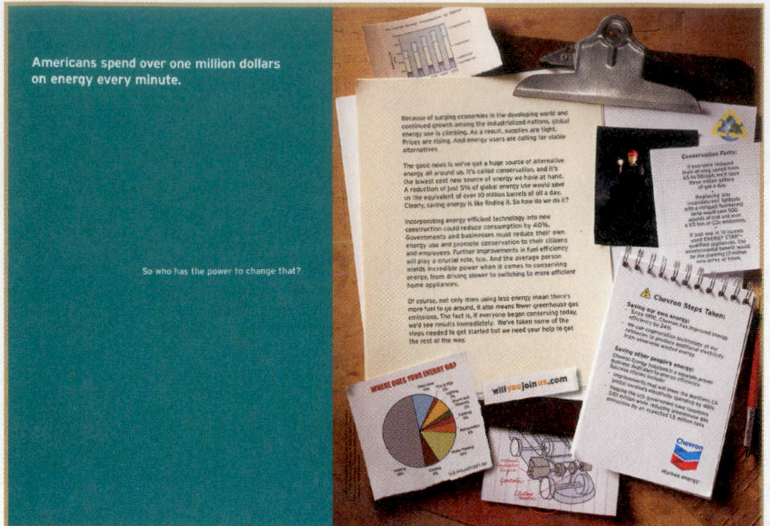

FIGURE 2.4. The Chevron ad relies on a logical argument to persuade the reader. The written text on the left side, set against a vivid background, uses a striking statistic and poses the question that governs the rest of the ad. A variety of research-based evidence on the right side, including a memo, a fact sheet, a pie chart, a schematic, and a bar chart, provides a persuasive abundance of evidence, suggesting that the ad's argument is based in fact rather than simply opinion.

included Blacks; 13.3% of the magazines' readership is Hispanic and only .5% of the advertisements use Hispanics.

Notice how the authors drive their point home through reference to their research with mainstream magazines as well as to statistical data that they have both uncovered and analyzed. The inclusion of this concrete information and examples makes their argument much more convincing than had they provided a more general rebuttal to the statement that begins their paragraph. In this way, appeals to logic can take on many forms, including interpretations of "hard evidence," such as found in syllogisms (formal, structured arguments), reasoned arguments, closing statements in law, inferences in the form of statistical models, and appeals to "common sense" or cultural assumptions.

In advertising, the mode of persuasion we call *logos* often operates through the written text; significantly, the Greek word *logos* can be translated as "word," indicating the way in which we, culturally, often look to words as repositories of fact and reason.

Seeing Connections

For an effective use of *logos* to drive an argument, see Harrison Pope's "Evolving Ideals of Male Body Image as Seen through Action Toys" on page 395.

The type of *logos*-based reasoning found in the Chevron ad in Figure 2.4 appears in many ads that you may also be familiar with: think, for instance, of a computer ad that juxtaposes a striking photo of a laptop with a chart detailing its processor type, memory capacity, screen size, and graphics features; a car ad that offsets a glossy showroom photo with safety ratings and positive reviews from *Car & Driver* and *Motor Trend*, or a commercial for a bank that features a smiling agent listing the reasons to open a checking account at that branch. In each case, the advertisement drives its point through facts, evidence, and reason.

In fact, some might argue that *logos* as an appeal underlies almost all advertising, specifically because most advertising uses an implicit *causal argument:* if you buy this product, then you or your life will be like the one featured in the ad. Sometimes the associations are explicit: if you use Pantene shampoo, then your hair will be shinier; if you buy Tide detergent, then your clothes will be cleaner; if you buy a Volvo sedan, then your family will be safer driving on the road. Sometimes the *cause-and-effect* argument is more subtle: buying Sure deodorant will make you more confident; drinking Coke will make you happier; wearing Nikes will make you perform better on the court. In each case, *logos*, or the use of logical reasoning, is the tool of persuasion responsible for the ad's argumentative force.

The ad for Crest Whitening Strips in Figure 2.5 offers us a useful example of how *logos* can operate in more subtle ways in an ad—through visual as well as verbal argumentation. When we first look at the ad, our eyes are drawn immediately to the model's white smile,

FIGURE 2.5. In this Crest Whitening Strips advertisement, inset images offer visual evidence for the ad's argument.

positioned near the center of the two-page spread. Our gaze next moves up to her eyes and then down again to the two juxtaposed close-up shots of her teeth.

> **Student Writing**
> Fred Chang analyzes Apple Computer's reliance on *logos* in its advertising battle with Intel.
> www.pearsonhighered.com/envision/33

These two before-and-after close-ups carry the force of the argument. The contrast between the two images makes a deliberate *logos* appeal by constructing a cause-and-effect argument, and the captions confirm the message imparted by the images and solidify the visual promise of the ad. The final small box insert is our last visual stop; it shows the product and suggests the solution to the logical equation at work in this ad. The fact that the ad's words, "Your new smile," appear beneath the photo of the product—as the conclusion of the logical argument—reinforces the persuasive message that Crest indeed will give its users such white teeth. To put the logic plainly: if people brush with this product, then they too will achieve this result. In this way, the ad relies on *logos* to attract and convince its audience.

Logical Fallacies. When crafting your own written analysis of advertisements, be careful not to rely on mistaken or misleading uses of *logos*, commonly called **logical fallacies**. The causal strategy underlying most advertising can be seen as an example of faulty logic, for surely it is fraudulent to suggest that wearing a certain brand of clothing will make you popular or that drinking a certain beer will make you attractive to the opposite sex. In classical rhetoric, this fallacy of causality is called a ***post hoc ergo propter hoc fallacy***—namely, the idea that because something happened first (showering with an aloe-enhanced body gel), it is the direct cause of something that happened afterward (getting great grades on your midterms). A similar effect can be produced by the ***cum hoc ergo propter hoc fallacy***, often called a correlation-causation fallacy. According to this model, because two

AT A GLANCE

Logical Fallacies

- ***The post hoc fallacy:*** confusing cause and effect
- ***The cum hoc fallacy:*** interpreting correlation as causation
- ***The hasty generalization:*** drawing a conclusion too quickly without providing enough supporting evidence
- ***The either-or argument:*** reducing an argument to a choice between two diametrically opposed choices, ignoring other possible scenarios
- ***Stacking the evidence:*** offering proof for only one side of the issue
- ***Begging the question:*** using an argument as evidence for itself
- ***The red herring:*** distracting the audience rather than focusing on the argument itself

unrelated events happen at the same time (are correlated), they are interpreted as cause and effect. For instance, the following is an example of a *cum hoc fallacy*: (1) a teenager plays his varsity basketball game wearing his new Air Jordans; (2) the teenager makes many key rebounds and jump shots while playing the game; (3) the Air Jordans caused his success in the game. You can probably think of many commercials that rely on these two particular logical fallacies.

However, in those same commercials, we see more and more cases of advertisers guarding themselves against claims of false causality. For instance, consider the typical weight-loss advertisement. "I lost 31 pounds in 3 months using this nutritional plan!" one happy dieter exclaims on camera. The camera shows an old video clip of the subject at her previous weight, and then it moves to the newly trimmed-down version, usually with a trendy hairstyle and tight-fitting clothes—a clear before-and-after strategy. However, more and more often, you now find these images captioned with one telling phrase: "These results not typical." This disclaimer points to advertisers' recognition that they, like other rhetoricians, need to be careful in their use of *logos* as an argumentative appeal.

Appeals to Emotion: *Pathos*

Roughly defined as "suffering" or "feeling" in its original Greek, the term *pathos* actually means to put the audience in a particular mood or frame of mind. Modern derivations of the word *pathos* include *pathology* and *pathetic,* and indeed we speak of *pathos* as "the pathetic appeal." But *pathos* is more a technique than a state: writers use it as a tool of persuasion to establish an intimate connection with the audience by soliciting powerful emotions. For instance, consider the way the following paragraphs foster an emotional reaction from the reader:

> Dorsey Hoskins' father Bryan felt a tingling in his arm. The diagnosis—an inoperable brain tumor. Six months later, he died at the age of 33, leaving his wife to raise Dorsey and sister Hattie.
>
> Fortunately, Bryan bought life insurance when he married, and again when his daughters were born. Thanks to Bryan's foresight, Dorsey, Hattie, and their mom are taken care of.
>
> Are you prepared should the very worst happen?

This passage relies on a *pathos* appeal on many levels. Clearly, the very premise of the piece—moving from tragedy, to a sense of tempered relief, to personal identification—is designed to evoke a sympathetic response. Looking more closely, however, suggests that even the more subtle stylistic choices also contribute to the emotional appeal. Notice, for example, the power of word choice: the author initially introduces Bryan as "Dorsey Hoskins' father," establishing him from the first in terms of his daughter and, ultimately, her loss; the author withholds Bryan's age for three sentences, at which point he can disclose it to accentuate the tragedy of his early death; finally, after the powerful opening anecdote, the author uses the second person to draw the audience itself into the piece through the pointed rhetorical question.

It shouldn't be a surprise to discover that this passage is in fact taken from an advertisement for life insurance or that the *pathos* of the text is echoed by the emotional charge of a close-up photograph of 5-year-old Dorsey, which serves as the background for the advertisement. We encounter ads that rely on *pathos* all the time, and indeed, the visual composition of an ad often taps our emotions in ways we barely recognize.

Let's look closely at another advertisement that relies on creating an emotional connection with the audience to sell its product. In the spring of 2006 Volkswagen launched a new marketing campaign aimed at pitching safety rather than sportiness; the "Safe Happens" commercials revolve around an unexpected collision and its surprisingly reassuring aftermath (see Figure 2.6). In this commercial, the viewer finds herself transported into the interior of an automobile. At this point, there is no clue as to the car's make or model; the camera shots are all of the car's occupants, a group of friends in their late twenties or early thirties in the middle of a friendly, light-hearted conversation. The camera focuses on each face in turn, creating a bond between the characters and the viewer. The exchange is informal and comfortable, the mood light.

FIGURE 2.6. The final frame from a Volkswagen commercial reinforces the audience's identification with the occupants of the damaged vehicle and extends the *pathos* appeal of the ad's narrative.

The commercial cuts the characters off midsentence with a screech of brakes, blinding headlights, and the sound of a collision. The viewer, an invisible passenger in the car, feels the same surprise and horror as the main characters. The camera focus abruptly changes and moves us outside the vehicle; we become bystanders, watching a nondescript SUV plow into the white sedan that we identify as *our* car, the power of the collision captured with harsh accuracy. As the screen goes black, suddenly silence prevails, except for the uneven clatter of a rolling hubcap.

After a couple of seconds, the image reappears, and we see our former companions, unharmed, standing outside the battered vehicle. This first moment of product identification is captioned by an unusual voice-over; the camera zooms in on one of the female passengers, who looks with disbelief at the wreck and whispers, "Holy. . . ." The implied expletive is silenced by a quick cut to a more traditional car-commercial shot: the Jetta, in a spotless white showroom, slowly revolving on a turntable. Even here, beyond the end of the commercial's central narrative, the *pathos* appeal is reinforced. The rotating car is clearly not a showroom model; the dented driver's side door identifies it once again as *our* car, the one that kept the main characters safe. The written caption reinforces this association, proclaiming "Safe Happens" (playing with the female character's final words) and then announcing that Jetta has received the government's highest safety rating. This moment becomes doubly persuasive because of the viewer's emotional engagement with the commercial: we feel that we ourselves have survived the crash and look to the Jetta as the reason.

Student Writing

Cyrus Chee's rhetorical analysis reads the appeals to *pathos* in two poster ads for contemporary films about the Holocaust.

www.pearsonhighered.com/envision/35

Pathos does not only operate through triggering the highs and lows of emotion in its audience; sometimes the appeals, though still speaking to the visceral more than the rational, are more subtle. Patriotism, indignation, excitement—all these effects can be linked to the *pathos* appeal. Consider the Porsche commercial showing a sleek red car speeding along a windy mountain road, the Ford Escape TV spot featuring the rugged SUV plowing through a muddy off-road trail, or the Mini Cooper ad using uniqueness as a selling point for the little car. Each of these ads uses *pathos* to produce a specific feeling in viewers: I want to drive fast, wind in my hair; I want to get off the beaten path, forge a new frontier; I want to stand out in a crowd, make a statement.

You are probably even more familiar with another type of *pathos* appeal—the appeal to sexuality. Clearly, "sex sells." Look at Victoria's Secret models posed in near nudity or Abercrombie & Fitch poster displays featuring models more likely to show off their toned abs than a pair of jeans, and you can see how advertisers tend to appeal more to nonrational impulses than to our powers of logical reasoning. Perfume and cologne advertisers in particular often use the rhetoric of sexuality to sell their fragrances, whether it be Calvin Klein's Obsession, Armani's Acqua Di Gio, or even Axe's cologne ads, which demonstrate the "Axe effect" by showing cologne-wearers being mobbed by bikini-clad women. Such ads work cleverly to sell perfume, not on the merits of the scent or on its chemical composition but through the visual rhetoric of sexuality and our emotional responses to it.

"Humos is the rhetorical appeal to humor."

—*David Baron,* Stanford student.

Looking at Figure 2.7, we can see yet another typical use of *pathos* to drive an argument: humor, or what some students call *humos.* By using a bald man as a spokesperson for shampoo, this advertisement pokes fun at the stereotype of the lush-haired shampoo spokesmodel to create a memorable and comic argument for its audience.

If you think about it, as a culture we tend to be quite persuaded by humor; against our more rational impulses, the ads that make us laugh are usually the ones we remember. To prove this point, you need only think back to last year's Superbowl ads: Which ads do you remember? Which ads did you talk over with your friends during and after the game? Probably most of those memorable commercials relied on humor. The arguments these ads make may not always be the most logically sound, but the way they foster a connection with the audience makes them persuasive nonetheless.

FIGURE 2.7. This shampoo ad uses humor as a *pathos* appeal to promote its product.

Exaggerated Uses of Pathos. Although these strategies of persuasion successfully move audiences, sometimes advertisers exaggerate the appeal to emotion for more dramatic effect. Many consider the "This-is-your-brain-on-drugs" commercial, described on page 28 as a classic example of the **scare tactic** in the way it builds on its audience's fears to make its argument about the effects of drug usage. The Partnership for a Drug Free America, which originally created this ad, took it one step further in 1997. In this revision, actress Rachel Leigh Cook relies on the familiar props of an egg and a frying pan to demonstrate her point. However, this time instead of frying the egg, she uses the pan to smash the egg dramatically on the counter. Holding up the pan with egg dripping from it, she says, "This is what happens to your brain after snorting heroin." She then continues, "It's not over yet." Wielding her frying pan as a weapon, she destroys the kitchen, shatters plates, glasses, and even the wall clock to demonstrate the effect of snorting heroin on a user's friends, family, and job. What we see here is a dramatic enactment of a **slippery slope** argument—one that suggests that one act leads to a chain of events that results in an undesirable conclusion. More specifically, we can see how the commercial suggests through its dramatic analogy that any heroin use will result in total devastation.

You might be even more familiar with another type of exaggerated *pathos*: the creation of a **false need**. In these cases, a company exaggerates the severity of an existing problem or defines a new one (e.g., thin eyelashes; garbage bags that are difficult to close; even bad breath), then offers up their product as a solution. Take a moment to recall times in your life when you may have been motivated to purchase a product through *false need:* Have you ever bought a razor specifically designed for a man or a woman? Curved sole shape-up or toning sneakers? An angled toothbrush? Curl-enhancing mascara? A transparent Band-Aid? 'Smart' water? What other examples of false needs or exaggerated *pathos* can you recall?

AT A GLANCE

Exaggerated Uses of *Pathos*

- ***Over-sentimentalization:*** distracting the audience from evidence or relevant issues
- ***The scare tactic:*** capitalizing on the audience's fears to make a pitch
- ***The false need:*** amplifying a perceived need or creating a completely new one
- ***The slippery slope fallacy:*** suggesting that an event or action will send the audience spiraling down a "slippery slope" to a serious consequence

Appeals to Character and Authority: *Ethos*

The last of the three appeals that we'll look at in this chapter is *ethos*—literally, "character." Perhaps you have used *ethos* in other disciplines to mean an argument based on ethical principles. But the *rhetorical* meaning of the term is slightly different: according to Aristotle, *ethos* works as a rhetorical strategy by establishing the goodwill or credibility of the writer or speaker. In fact, as a writer you use *ethos* every time you pick up a pen or proofread your essay—that is, you construct an argument in which your power to persuade depends on credibility, your word choice, your tone, your choice of examples, the quality of your research, your grammar and punctuation. All these factors contribute to your *ethos* as an author.

Seeing Connections
Look at the role *ethos* plays in the Corn Refiners Association ad on page 240 and in Paul Mitchell's essay "Faith and Fashion" on page 416.

Ethos can be a very powerful tool for establishing trust and therefore facilitating the persuasiveness of an argument. Companies have long recognized the persuasive power of *ethos*. In fact, a brand logo is in essence *ethos* distilled into a single symbol: it transmits in a single icon the entire reputation of a company, organization, or brand identity. From the Nike swoosh to McDonald's golden arches, the NBC peacock, or the Apple computer apple, symbols serve to mark (or brand) products with *ethos*.

Yet the power of the brand logo as a seat of *ethos* relies on the company's overall reputation with the consumer—a reputation that the company carefully cultivates through advertising campaigns. Many companies, for instance, trade on *ethos* by using celebrity endorsements in their advertising campaigns. Although a rational appeal is at work behind some endorsements—having basketball superstar LeBron James sell basketball shoes, for instance, makes sense—many campaigns rely not only on the celebrity's suitability for selling a product but also on the person's star appeal, character, and goodwill. Consider the power of the famous "Got Milk?" campaign. Here's the argument: if this celebrity likes milk, shouldn't we? Indeed, when we see famous people sporting the trademark milk moustache, we find the ad persuasive because these celebrities are vouching for the product. We look to their goodwill as public figures, to their character as famous people putting their reputation on the line.

However, ad campaigns based upon celebrity endorsements can backfire. The various troubles that confronted Tiger Woods in the late fall of 2009 left advertisers from investment houses to high-end watchmakers to various golf suppliers scrambling to distance themselves from their premier spokesman.

While the impact of a celebrity spokesperson can be a powerful use of *ethos*, sometimes the *lack* of fame can be an effective strategy. The Mac/PC television ads ("I'm a Mac," and "I'm a PC") made a huge initial impression partly because the spokespeople—hip-looking Justin Long as the Mac and slightly schlubby John Hodgman as the PC—were relatively unknown but easy to identify with. It was pretty clear which one you'd like to be. But Microsoft countered with a series of ads showing "ordinary" people using PCs (and Microsoft software) successfully. The most popular of these, showing an adorable 4-year-old girl sending photos to her grandparents using Microsoft products, made us think again about who we actually are and what we want from our computers—rather than who we would like to be.

CREATIVE PRACTICE

With a partner, look at Figures 2.8 and 2.9 below. What specific argumentative strategies and rhetorical appeals does each use to make its argument? Choose one ad and brainstorm with your partner about how the company might market the same car by using a different strategy or appeal. Sketch out your hypothetical ad—including both image and copy—and share it with the class. Talk about how the shift in appeal (audience, context) affects your understanding of the rhetorical situation and the effectiveness of the ad.

FIGURE 2.8. An advertisement for a Saab.

FIGURE 2.9. An advertisement for the Ford Escape hybrid.

Sometimes an ad features a corporate *ethos* to establish that company's credibility. The most obvious of these are the various oil company ads that have appeared over the last few years. Battling the perception that Big Oil, heedless of its role in global warming, is motivated only by ever-increasing profits, these ads inform us endlessly of each company's "green" policies and efforts to give back to the earth.

In contrast to ads that promote a corporate *ethos*, many ads sell products through appeals to the potential consumer's character. In Figure 2.10, for example, a Longines watch ad makes its pitch through words and images: the line, "Elegance is an Attitude," suggests that both the company and the wearer of the company's product can share in elevated *ethos*. The visual image reinforces this idea through the representation of a well-dressed man standing confidently in a black jacket and pin-striped shirt. He looks directly out at the viewer, potentially catching the eye of possible viewers.

FIGURE 2.10. Longines sells its watches through appeals to character.
Source: © Alyssa J. O'Brien, 2006

***Misuses of* Ethos.** One consequence of relying on *ethos*-driven arguments is that sometimes we come to trust symbols of *ethos* rather than looking to the character of the product itself. This tendency points us to the concept of **authority over evidence**—namely, the practice of overemphasizing authority or *ethos* rather than focusing on the merits of the evidence itself, a strategic exaggeration of *ethos* that helps entice audiences and sell products.

The most prominent examples of *authority over evidence* can be found in celebrity endorsements; in many commercials, the spokesperson sells the product not based on its merits but based on the argument, "Believe what I say because you know me, and would I steer you wrong?" However, the American public has become increasingly skeptical of such arguments. Living in a world where rumors of Pepsi-spokesperson Britney Spears's preference for Coke circulate on the Internet, Tiger Woods's $100 million deal with Nike makes front page news, and a star like former Sprite spokesperson Macaulay Culkin publicly announces, "I'm not crazy about the stuff [Sprite]. But money is money" (Twitchell, *Twenty* 214), the credibility of celebrity endorsements is often questionable.

Seeing Connections
For a powerful example of an *ad hominem* argument, see Stephen Steinlight's response to Thomas Friedman's stance on Immigration, page 550.

Often, companies deliberately attempt to undermine the *ethos* of their competition as a way of promoting their own products. You probably have seen ads of this sort: Burger King arguing that their flame-broiled hamburgers are better than McDonald's fried hamburgers; Coke claiming its soda tastes better than Pepsi's; Visa asserting its card's versatility by reminding consumers how many companies "don't take American Express"; and of course the ubiquitous, Mac versus PC commercials. The deliberate *comparison-contrast* builds up one company's *ethos* at another's expense. At times, however, this technique can be taken to an extreme, producing an ***ad hominem*** argument—that is, an argument that attempts to persuade by attacking an opponent's character. We see *ad hominem* at work most often in campaign advertisements, where candidates end up focusing less on the issues at hand than on

AT A GLANCE

Misuses of *Ethos*

Authority over evidence: placing more emphasis on *ethos* than on the actual validity of the evidence
Ad hominem: criticizing an opponent's character (or *ethos*) rather than the argument itself

FIGURE 2.11. This TheTruth.com antismoking ad attacks *ethos* through parody.

Student Writing
Amanda Johnson, in her analysis of a Barbie parody ad, and Georgia Duan, in her reading of cigarette advertising, explore the construction of body image in the media and the use of parody in ads.
www.pearsonhighered.com/envision/40

their opponents' moral weaknesses, or in commercials where companies attack each other for the way they run their businesses rather than the quality of their products. In other words, this strategy attempts to persuade by reducing the credibility of opposing arguments.

Another strategy of persuasion is attacking *ethos* through **parody**, or the deliberate mocking of a text or convention. We can see this at work in the Truth ad in Figure 2.11 that uses the conventions of a typical cigarette ad to argue against smoking. As we can see, parody can be an effective rhetorical strategy for making a powerful argument.

Considering Context: *Kairos*

Seeing Connections
See Mir-Hossein Mousavi Khameneh's tweets from Iran (page 317) to further explore the relation between *kairos* and persuasion.

As you can tell from examining ads in this chapter, a successful argument must take into account not only the *rhetorical situation* but also the context, or the right time and place. That is why promotional trailers for the ABC series *Invasion*—featuring big-budget scenes of a Florida hurricane—could captivate audiences in the early summer of 2005 but horrify and outrage that same audience two months later in the wake of hurricanes Katrina and Rita. In ancient Greece rhetoricians called this aspect of the rhetorical situation ***kairos***—namely, attention to the right time and place for an argument.

In your own writing, you should consider *kairos* along with the other aspects of the rhetorical situation: audience, text, and writer. It is important to recognize the *kairos*—the opportune historical, ideological, or cultural moment—of a text when analyzing its rhetorical force. You undoubtedly already consider the context for persuasive communication in your everyday life. For instance, whether you are asking a friend to dinner or a professor for a recommendation, your assessment of the timeliness and the appropriate strategies for that time probably determines the shape your argument takes. In essence, by picking the right moment and place to make your case, you are in fact paying attention to the *kairos* of your argument.

Consider, Coca-Cola's ad campaigns. Coke has exerted a powerful presence in the advertising industry for many years, in part because of its strategic advertising. During World War II, Coke ran a series of ads featuring servicemen and inspiring slices of Americana that built its beverage campaign around the contemporary nationalistic sentiment and responded to a specific cultural moment.

FIGURE 2.12. This Coca-Cola ad used *kairos* to create a powerful argument for its World War II audience.

Look at Figure 2.12, an advertisement for Coke from the 1940s. This picture uses *pathos* to appeal to the audience's sense of patriotism by featuring a row of seemingly carefree servicemen, leaning from the windows of a military bus, the refreshing Cokes in their hands producing smiles even far away from home. The picture draws in the audience by reassuring them on two fronts:

- It builds on the nationalistic pride in the young, handsome servicemen who so happily serve their country.
- It is designed to appease fears about the hostile climate abroad: as both the picture and the accompanying text assure us, Coca-Cola (and the servicemen) "goes along" and "gets a hearty welcome."

The power of this message relates directly to its context. An ad such as this one, premised on patriotism and pride in military service, would be most persuasive during wartime when many more people tend to support the spirit of nationalism and therefore would be moved by the image of the young serviceman shipping off to war. It is through understanding the *kairos* of this advertisement that you can appreciate the strength of the ad's rhetorical appeal.

An awareness of *kairos* likewise helps us see how a more current coke ad (Figure 2.13) is tailored to today's culture, addressing the viewer as an individual and audience of one. The visual composition of the ad includes the words "hello you" in big font reminiscent of computer type, as if the ad is an online dating message or IM line. In contrast to the nationalism and group solidarity of the earlier Coke ad, this one engages the viewer's attention as an individual, by appealing to *kairos*—the idea that here and now in America the individual reigns supreme. The fuzzy background and soft lighting also suggest today's spirit of fun and exploration of digital environments—our world is very different here and now than it was for the soldiers on the train in the earlier Coke ad. Attending to *kairos* enables us to attend to these differences, to learn how ads and other visual rhetoric texts make use of the present moment and place, and finally, to learn how we can optimally make use of *kairos* when composing our own arguments.

FIGURE 2.13. A 2009 Coke ad points directly to the reader.

Ads convey complex cultural meanings. Recognizing their persuasive presence everywhere, we realize the need to develop our ability to make more-informed interpretations. You can pursue your study of ads by conducting your own careful rhetorical analyses of these visual-verbal texts. You'll find over and over again that ads are a microcosm of many of the techniques of persuasion. From billboards to pop-ups on the Internet, ads employ *logos*, *pathos*, and *ethos* to convey strong messages to specific audiences. We've learned how compact and sophisticated these texts are. Now it's time to apply those insights in your own writing.

The Writer's Process

As you begin to perform your individual analyses of advertisements, consider the way your own writing, like the ads we've discussed, can "sell" your argument to the reader. Consider the rhetorical situation and the specific *kairos* of your argument. What *strategies of argumentation* and *rhetorical appeals* would be most effective in reaching your target audience? Do you want to use narration, a humorous analogy, or a stirring example to forge a connection with your readers based on *pathos*? Or is your analysis better suited to *logos*, following a step-by-step process of reading an ad, drawing on empirical evidence, or looking at cause and effect? Perhaps you will decide to enrich your discussion through cultivating your *ethos* as a writer, establishing your own authority on a subject or citing reputable work done by other scholars. It is probable that in your essay you will use many strategies and a combination of appeals; as we saw in the advertisements presented earlier, from the Crest Whitening Strips ad to the Coca-Cola campaign, a successful argument uses various rhetorical strategies to persuade its audience.

While focusing on the individual strategies, don't forget to keep an eye on the composition of your argument as a whole. Just as an ad is designed with attention to layout and design, so you should look at the larger organization of your essay as key to the success of your argument. As you approach the organization of elements in your essay to maximize your persuasiveness, even a question like "Where should I insert my images?" has profound implications for your argument. Consider the difference between an essay in which the image is embedded in the text, next to the paragraph that analyzes it, and one with the image attached as an appendix. In your writing, use the persuasive power of visual rhetoric more effectively by allowing the reader to analyze the images alongside the written explanations. Use similar careful attention to organization, placement, and purpose as you begin your own analysis and craft your own rhetorical argument.

PREWRITING CHECKLIST

Focus on Analyzing Advertisements

- ❑ **Content:** What exactly is the ad selling? An object? an idea? both?
- ❑ **Message:** How is the ad selling the product? What is the persuasive message that the ad is sending to the audience?
- ❑ **Character and setting:** What is featured by the ad? An object? a scene? a person? How are these elements portrayed? What are the ethnicity, age, socioeconomic class, and gender of any people in the advertisement? How do these choices relate to the ad's intended audience and reflect deliberate rhetorical choices?
- ❑ **Theme:** What is the underlying message of the ad (beyond "buy our product")?
- ❑ **Medium:** What medium was the advertisement produced in? Television? print? radio? How did this choice suit the rhetorical purpose of the ad and accommodate the needs of a particular audience?

- ❑ **Historical context:** In what country and at what historical moment was the advertisement produced? How do the demands of context shape the persuasive appeals at work in the ad? How does the ad reflect, comment on, challenge, or reinforce contemporary political, economic, or gender ideology? How does this commentary situate it in terms of a larger trend or argument?
- ❑ **Word and image:** What is the relationship between the word (written or spoken) and the imagery in the ad? Which is given priority? How does this relationship affect the persuasiveness of the advertisement?
- ❑ **Layout:** How are the elements of the ad arranged—on a page (for a print ad) or in sequence (for a television or Internet commercial)? What is the purpose behind this arrangement? How does the ad's organization lead the reader through—and facilitate—its argument?
- ❑ **Design:** What typeface is used? What size? What color? How do these decisions reflect attention to the ad's rhetorical situation? How do they function in relation to the ad's rhetorical appeals?
- ❑ **Voice:** What voice does the text use to reach its audience? Is the language technical, informal, personal, authoritative? Is the voice comic or serious?
- ❑ **Rhetorical appeals:** How does the advertiser use the images to work in conjunction with rhetorical appeals? For instance, does the image reinforce an appeal to reason? Is it designed to produce an emotional effect on the audience? Does the use of a certain style, such as black-and-white authority, contribute to the *ethos* of the ad?
- ❑ **Strategy of development:** Narration? definition? comparison-contrast? example or illustration? classification and division? process? analogy? cause and effect? How do these strategies contribute to the ad's persuasive appeal?
- ❑ **Cultural resonance:** Does the ad use famous events or places or recognizable symbols to increase its persuasiveness? If so, how does that establish audience or a relationship to a cultural moment?

PREWRITING WITH THE *ENVISION* WEBSITE

To get started writing your analysis of an ad, you might visit an online repository of commercials, such as those linked through the *Envision* Website. With a partner, browse through several commercials, selecting two or three in particular that you find persuasive. Discuss what strategies of argumentation you see at work in these visual rhetoric texts. Try to find an example of each approach listed earlier in the chapter. Write a short paragraph analyzing one of the commercials; compare your interpretation with a partner. Then share your work with the rest of the class.
www.pearsonhighered.com/envision/43

WRITING PROJECTS

1. **Rhetorical Analysis:** Choose two or three ads for the same product and analyze the strategies of persuasion these ads use to reach specific audiences. To find your ads, you might visit an ad archive such as those linked through the Chapter 2 resources on the *Envision* Website, or look at magazines. Select ads that showcase an exaggeration of rhetorical appeals, such as logical fallacies, exaggeration of *pathos,* misuse of *ethos,* or parody. Use the prewriting checklist to help you

analyze the appeals in the ads and to help you develop your argument. Be sure to address how strategies of persuasion operate and what the effects are on the audience as well as a description of context: where and when was the ad published and to whom?

2. **Contextual Analysis:** Write a contextual analysis on the *kairos* of the Coca-Cola campaign. Examine, for instance, another Coke ad from the 1940s through the Adflip link on the *Envision* Website. Do some research and read about this era: explore the time, place, and culture in which the ad appeared. How do the rhetorical choices of the ad you selected reflect an awareness of this context? How does the ad use *logos, pathos,* and *ethos* to comment on or criticize this cultural moment? www.pearsonhighered.com/envision/44

3. **Historical Analysis:** Working in groups, look at several ads from different time periods produced by the same company, such as ads for cigarettes, cars, hygiene products, and personal computers. Each member of your group should choose a single ad and prepare a rhetorical analysis of its persuasive appeals. Share your analyses to explore how this company has modified its rhetorical approach over time. Collaborate to write a paper in which you chart the evolution of the company's persuasive strategies and how that evolution was informed by *kairos.*

4. **Cultural Analysis:** Write a paper in which you compare two ad campaigns and examine the ideology behind specific constructions of our culture. Does one campaign portray gender- or race-specific ideas? How do the tools of persuasion produce each message? What message is conveyed by the reliance on such cultural ideals or notions of identity? What representations of sexuality, gender roles, or class are presented by these ads? Present your findings to the class, holding up examples of the ads to discuss in support of your analysis.

Visit www.pearsonhighered.com/envision for expanded assignment guidelines and student projects.
Visit www.mycomplab.com for additional general writing and research resources.

CHAPTER 3

Composing Arguments

Chapter Preview Questions

- What are the canons of rhetoric, and how do they help us to understand arguments?
- How can you create strong introductions and conclusions?
- What roles do persona and rhetorical stance play in arguments?
- How do photographs function as both visual evidence in arguments and as visual arguments themselves?
- How do writers synthesize multiple perspectives on an issue in an argument?

Imagine that it is September 2005 and the United States is still reeling from the aftermath of Hurricane Katrina. As you click through several news sites, you pause to look at the images they display. One features a striking photo of a military helicopter dropping supplies to the citizens of New Orleans (see Figure 3.1). Another shows an African-American mother clutching two small children and wading through waist-deep water. Yet another displays the image of a mob of angry people, packed together and arguing as they try to evacuate the city. A final site uses the picture of a child's dirt-smeared doll, swept into a pile of debris on the road, as its poignant commentary on natural disaster.

Based on these images, which site would you click back to? How does each image make a different argument about exactly what happened? How might the words that accompany the photo shape your interpretation of the visual texts? How does the choice of a particular visual-verbal combination present a specific point of view?

Photographs and captions on news sites or in newspapers work through the tools of persuasion that we examined in earlier chapters. In this chapter, we'll continue to explore how visual rhetoric shapes our reality in particular ways by focusing on photographs. We will also move forward in our understanding of analysis and argument by learning effective ways to create arguments. We'll become acquainted with the canons of rhetoric—five classifications of argument from ancient Greece—and we'll work through the process of creating an argument: coming up with ideas, structuring those ideas, and developing a style for your own compositions.

FIGURE 3.1. A photograph of supplies being dropped to New Orleans survivors of Hurricane Katrina.

Understanding the Canons of Rhetoric

In ancient Greece, all communicative acts were classified into five categories, or what scholars call the **canons of rhetoric**. These are the principles by which all writing, speaking, or visual arguments operate: **invention** (coming up with ideas), **arrangement** (organizing ideas in effective ways), **style** (expressing those ideas in an

AT A GLANCE

Canons of Rhetoric

- ***Invention:*** creating and constructing ideas
- ***Arrangement:*** ordering and laying out ideas effectively
- ***Style:*** developing the appropriate expression for those ideas
- ***Memory:*** retaining invented ideas, recalling additional supporting ideas, and facilitating memory in the audience
- ***Delivery:*** presenting or performing ideas with the aim of persuading

appropriate manner), **memory** (accessing learned materials), and **delivery** (presenting crafted ideas to an audience).

Each of these canons is necessary for persuasive communication, whether that be through spoken word, written discourse, or, more recently, multimedia texts. For our discussion of composing arguments in this chapter, we'll focus on the first three canons (you can look to Chapter 9 for discussion of the last two canons).

Invention in Argument

When you craft language with the purpose of persuading your audience, you are **inventing** an argument. That is, you are generating ideas about a topic. Aristotle defined *invention* as methods for "finding all available arguments." Methods you might use to "invent" arguments include:

- **Definition:** What does the text *mean*? What are other examples?
- **Division:** What *parts* are comprised within the text?
- **Comparison:** Does the text mean something new versus years ago? How does the text *compare* to other texts?
- **Classification:** What is the *purpose* of the text? Cause and effect? Consequence?
- **Testimony:** What do *others* say about the text?

Invention is the "discovery of valid or seemingly valid arguments to render one's cause probable."

—Cicero, *De Inventione,* I.vii

To develop ideas, you can use a range of rhetorical strategies: invoking *pathos,* using *ethos* or good character, or employing *logos* to reason calmly with your readers or listeners. Your task as a writer is to forge a powerful text that argues a point, to convince others to see a particular perspective, usually your own. In composing arguments, you can look for examples in both writing as well as verbal-visual texts all around you.

We might think a photograph provides a window on another person's reality. But in fact photographs, like written texts, are artifacts of rhetorical invention. The "reality" that photographs display is actually a *version* of reality created by a photographer's rhetorical and artistic decisions: whether to use color or black-and-white film; what sort of lighting to use; how to position the subject of the photograph; whether to opt for a panorama or close-up shot; what backdrop to use; how to crop, or trim, the image once it is printed. In effect, when we see photographs in a newspaper or art gallery, we are looking at the product of deliberate *strategies of invention.* In photography, these strategies include key elements of composition, such as selection, placement, perspective, and framing. In written texts, the same elements—selection, placement, perspective, and framing—are critical to making an argument.

Figure 3.2, an image captured by photojournalist Margaret Bourke-White, shows a line of homeless African Americans, displaced by the 1937 Louisville flood, waiting in line to receive food and clothing from a local Red Cross center. Does the photo merely document a moment in the history of Kentucky? Or have the choice of subject, the cropping, the angle, the background, and the elements within the frame been selected by the photographer to make a specific argument about race and American culture during the first half of the twentieth century?

FIGURE 3.2. Margaret Bourke-White, "At the Time of the Louisville Flood," 1937.

In your own writing, you could look to this photograph as inspiration for invention. You could use this image to support a historically focused argument, perhaps one that examined the catastrophic 1937 Louisville flood and its impact on the local community. Or you could refer to this photograph as visual evidence in a paper that examines the link between social status, race, and disaster relief, perhaps drawing a connection to the Katrina tragedy. Either argument could draw on the power of photographs like this one, a power created by the invention strategies of the artist.

Let's look more closely at how invention factors into the way photographers and writers compose arguments. Consider two famous photographs by Dorothea Lange (see Figures 3.3 and 3.4 on the next page), which offer very different representations of migrant workers during the Great Depression. In each case, we see a migrant family huddled inside a tent. The subjects seem to be poor, hungry, and struggling to make a living. Their material conditions are bleak.

Seeing Connections

For other examples of how photographers use careful composition and arrangement in creating powerful photographs, see Carlos Serrao's "Anything You Can Do" on page 458, the phtographs from "America 24/7" on page 492, and David Leeson's photographs on page 423.

But notice the effects of the different perspectives. In Figure 3.4, we get an intimate look inside this woman's eyes, where we can see her concern. The lines on her face, visible in this close-up, are evidence of her hard life and worries. The photograph in Figure 3.3 has a wider frame that encompasses the tent and the barren ground. This perspective makes a different kind of argument, one that addresses the condition of the soil, the landscape, the living quarters. We can hardly make out the woman huddled in the darkness of the tent. When we look for visual evidence of the living conditions of migrant workers in the American West during the 1930s,

FIGURE 3.3. Dorothea Lange's wide shot gives a stark sense of the experience of migrant farmers.

FIGURE 3.4. The close-up focuses on the struggles of the migrant mother.

each photograph offers different angles on our argument. Which one would we use to support a thesis about the labor conditions of migrant workers? Which one would we use to argue that the human body is scarred by hardship? Depending on our purpose, we would choose one photograph over the other. Each one makes an argument that we can in turn select as evidence for our claims about the Great Depression. Each photograph uses a particular strategy of invention, creating and constructing ideas in visual form about the "reality" of life for migrant workers. We can, in turn, invent different arguments based on our starting point: which photo do we use as evidence for our thesis?

In written documents, different perspectives on the same topic can yield different arguments. Commentary on Lange's *Migrant Mother* photographs exposes the variety of perspectives not only on the photographs' status as "documentary" evidence from the Great Depression but also on the way our historical understanding of that period itself is constructed by the invention or arguments of others. For instance, the following excerpt from historian James Curtis's article "Dorothea Lange, Migrant Mother, and the Culture of the Great Depression" demonstrates the way in which Lange's photos are often interpreted as windows into that period:

> In addition to being a timeless work of art, *Migrant Mother* is a vital reflection of the times. Examined in its original context, the series reveals powerful cultural forces of the 1930s: the impact of the increasing centralization and bureaucratization of American life; the anxiety about the status and solidarity of the family in an era of urbanization and modernization; a need to atone for the guilt induced by the destruction of cherished ideals, and a craving for reassurance that democratic traditions would stand the test of modern times.

For Curtis, the images function both as what he calls elsewhere in the article "a timeless and universal symbol of suffering in the face of adversity" (1) as well as the key to understanding Lange's relationship to the evolving genre of documentary photography. For journalist Geoffrey Dunn, however, Lange's series prompts a different response:

> The photographs taken by Lange and her colleagues at the Resettlement Administration (later to become better known as the Farm Security Administration) have been widely heralded as the epitome of documentary photography. The eminent photographer and curator Edward Steichen called them "the most remarkable human documents ever rendered in pictures."
>
> In recent years, however, the FSA photographs have come under a growing criticism. Many view them as manipulative and condescending, to the point of assuming a "colonialistic" attitude toward their subjects. Still others have argued that they are misleading and disingenuous, and in some instances, fabricated.
>
> In a compelling essay entitled "The Historian and the Icon," University of California at Berkeley professor Lawrence Levine has argued that the FSA photographers focused their lenses on "perfect victims," and in so doing, rendered a caricatured portrait of the era.
>
> "Americans suffered, materially and physically, during the years of the Great Depression to an extent which we still do not fully fathom," Levine asserted. "But they also continued, as people always must, the business of living. They ate and they laughed, they loved and they fought, they worried and they hoped . . . they filled their days, as we fill ours, with the essentials of everyday living."
>
> With the notable exception of FSA photographer Russell Lee, and later, Marion Post Wolcott, whose largely overlooked bodies of work actually capture the dimensions of "everyday living," Lange and her colleagues focused almost exclusively on human suffering. That is most certainly the reason that people like Florence Owens Thompson [the mother in these photographs]—and many others who appeared in FSA images—resented their photographic portrayal.
>
> "Mother was a woman who loved to enjoy life, who loved her children," says Thompson's youngest daughter, Norma Rydlewski, who appears as a young child in Lange's classic photograph. "She loved music and she loved to dance. When I look at that photo of mother, it saddens me. That's not how I like to remember her."

Like Curtis, Dunn uses the photographs as the basis for an argument about Lange's practice of documentary photography; however, Dunn considers first-person accounts from other witnesses of that historical moment and arrives at a different argument. He concludes that the series exemplifies not reflection but misrepresentation.

Seeing Connections

For another viewpoint on the dangers of photography as misrepresentation, see Lenore Skenazy's "Don't Smile for the Camera" on page 486.

All texts—whether written accounts or photographs—are actually shaped by individual perspective and point of view. Texts are "invented" for a specific audience. Your own writing is a text informed by your invention strategies, your purpose, and your point of view. In your writing, you are like a photographer, making important compositional decisions: What will be the subject of your text: an individual, a group, an institution? How will you pose that subject to best convey your own perspective? Should you zoom in, focusing on one particular example as a way of addressing a larger concern? Or should you take a step back, situating your argument in relation to the broader context that surrounds the issue? The choices you make will determine the ultimate impact of your argument: like photographs, effective writing persuades the viewer to look at a topic through the lens of the author's interpretation.

CREATIVE PRACTICE

Examine the picture in Figure 3.5, taken by photographer Todd Heisler, of a soldier's coffin returning home on a civilian flight into Reno, Nevada, being draped with the American flag prior to being unloaded from the plane. What argument is Heisler making about Americans' response to the Iraq war and casualties? Now consider this image as the foundation for your own process of invention: What types of arguments might you construct that would use this image as visual evidence? What other sorts of images or evidence would you use to develop your argument?

FIGURE 3.5. Photograph of the arrival of a soldier's coffin in Reno, Nevada.

Arrangement in Argument

After invention, arrangement becomes your key consideration because the way in which you present material on the page will shape a reader's response to the ideas. In many cases, attention to *arrangement* takes the form of the way you order elements in your argument—whether that be the layout of images and text on a newspaper front page or the way you structure a written argument in a more academic paper. It is the arrangement of an argument that gives it structure or that separates a free-form reaction from a carefully developed and proven argument.

Therefore, when we refer to "arrangement" in a written argument, we often are referring to the underlying structure of the essay itself. Although unifying an essay with a smooth flow of ideas is important, it is just as important that the structure of the essay not simply move from one idea to the next through the process of free association. Here are some common organizational strategies you might choose in composing your own arguments:

- **Chronological structure:** Chronology relies on examples across time, such as the transformation in the Apple computer marketing campaign from the Macintosh to the iPad.

- **Cause-effect:** Show how one event causes another. An essay confronting the issue of sexist imagery in rap music videos might start by exploring how women are represented in popular rap videos (*cause*) and then conclude by discussing the impact of this representation on the self-esteem of young girls (*effect*).
- **Problem-solution:** Define the problem, then offer a solution. A paper about violence and video games might devote the first half of the paper to exploring the *problem* of desensitization and then focus in the second half of the paper on proposing a possible *solution*.
- **Block structure:** Work your way systematically through a series of examples or case studies—such as individual James Bond films in a paper about the relationship between real-world political climates and spy narrative.
- **Thematic structure:** Focus on thematic relationships. A paper on reality TV might include sections on voyeurism, capitalism, and Darwinism (*the themes*), integrating examples from *Survivor, American Idol,* and *America's Next Top Model* as evidence in each section.
- **Deferred thesis:** Substitute a thesis question for a thesis statement at the beginning of your essay, such as "How did images featured in the news define our understanding of the impact of hurricanes Katrina and Rita?" Place your thesis at the end of your paper as a way of synthesizing the evidence explored in the paper itself.

FIGURE 3.6. Picture 1 from "Prepare."

Let's look to photography to see the way a successful argument relies on strategies of arrangement. Figures 3.6 through Figure 3.9 offer a selection of photographs from Jane Gottesman's photo essay *Game Face,* a work devoted to redefining the concept of the modern female athlete. A veteran sportswriter, Gottesman spent years accumulating photographs of amateur and professional women athletes of all ages, races, and socioeconomic backgrounds, a collection that was a museum exhibit and both a print and online photo essay. It is not surprising to find that she gave extra care to strategies of arrangement in composing her visual argument.

Looking at this version of *Game Face*, we can see from the top menu bar that it is divided into four sections: "Prepare," "Compete," "Finish," and "Achieve." Clearly, this is an example of an argument *organized by theme.* This arrangement gives a logical structure to the text: the argument moves along a continuum, from pre-game, to game play, to post-game. Within each of these sections (which roughly approximate the sections of a book or written essay), Gottesman includes several examples (which we might correlate to paragraphs in traditional academic writing). Looking at the individual images, we can see how arrangement plays a strong role in constructing an

FIGURE 3.7. Picture 1 from "Compete."

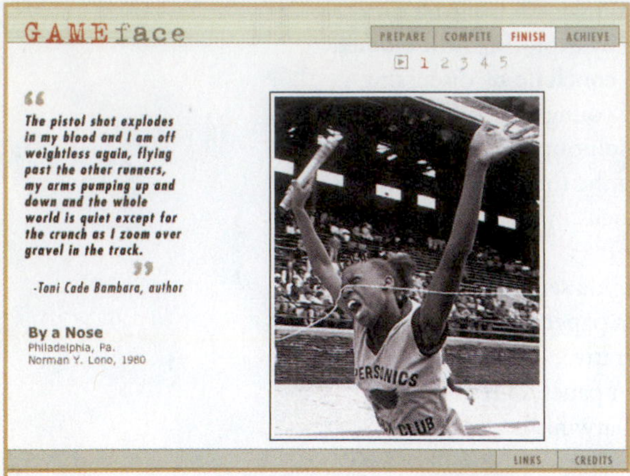

FIGURE 3.8. Picture 1 from "Finish."

FIGURE 3.9. Final picture from the photo essay.

argument; each page makes its commentary on women's athletics by juxtaposing a powerful photo with a descriptive caption and a relevant quotation from a female athlete. The recurring structure gives the overall photo essay coherence and consistency, despite its variety of examples.

Let's take a closer look at the way the pictures reinforce the underlying structure produced by the section headers; we can do so by carefully examining the lead images for the various sections. The lead image (Figure 3.6), for instance, centers on an inspirational event: the moment in 1968 when a woman, for the first time, lit the Olympic flame. As the first image in the photo essay, this picture of Norma Basilio symbolizes accomplishment, possibilities, a global perspective, and even more importantly, an auspicious beginning to the argument, the same way in which the lighting of the flame itself marks the beginning of an auspicious event.

The next image (Figure 3.7), which heads the "Compete" section, offers a similarly strong statement but shifts perspective from the international to the local, capturing the first moments in a 1994 Pennsylvania triathlon. In this image, as much as we see individual competitors, we also see community—a theme that reappears at many different points in that particular section.

The next photograph (Figure 3.8), from the "Finish" section, moves us from the start of competition to its conclusion, focusing on the victory of the female athlete. The series of photographs in this section, from the victorious track star to the weary but triumphant soccer team, celebrate the rewards that come from following through on one's dreams. In the last section, "Achieve," the images escalate in strength, culminating with the inspirational picture of a young girl swinging powerfully toward the stars (Figure 3.9).

Using Toulmin to Arrange or Analyze an Argument

As we've seen, Gottesman makes strategic choices in structuring her photo essay to create a visually and conceptually striking argument. Another powerful way to arrange an argument is to follow the model developed by British philosopher Stephen Toulmin (*The Uses of Argument,* 1969). Toulmin suggests that a logical argument has several parts: claim, grounds, warrants, backing, rebuttal, and response. Let's look at how Toulmin's approach might help a student construct an argument about images such as the one shown in Figure 3.5. Here's the context: until 2009, the Pentagon banned the publication of photographs (and other media coverage) showing the caskets of American soldiers who had been killed in the Middle East. Coming into office, President Obama was faced with the decision about whether to lift the ban. Here's the question: should the media be allowed to publish such images?

- The **claim** is the thesis, or central argument. In other words, the claim is a statement that you are asking your audience to accept as true.

  Claim: The Pentagon should not ban publication of photographs of fallen American soldiers.

- The **grounds** are the reasons you think the claim should be believed and the evidence that supports those reasons (statistics, expert testimony, etc.).

  Grounds: The Constitution guarantees freedom of speech and of the press.

- The **warrants** are assumptions that explain *how* the grounds support the claim. If the warrants are not clear or are implied, they may also need supporting evidence, called **backing**.

  Warrants: Freedom of speech and the press imply a right to *listen* to and *read*—that is, to access information.

- The rebuttal is a listing of anticipated counterclaims, and your response. Arguments can be both written and analyzed following this model.

  Rebuttal: Publishing images of fallen Americans could negatively affect public morale during wartime.

  Response: People have a constitutional right to access information, and openness about American casualties is necessary to produce transparency in government as well as to provide opportunities to memorialize those who sacrificed their lives for our country.

As you can see, working through the Toulmin model provides a framework that helps you think through the complexities of your claim and produce a more nuanced argument. You can use the Toulmin method to compose a claim of your own, to support it with appropriate evidence, and to explain clearly how and why that evidence does in fact prove, or support, your claim. Conversely, you also will find this approach extremely useful in analyzing arguments made by others.

Style in Argument

Inventing a thesis or main idea and *arranging* the elements of your writing are two steps in completing your task of written persuasion. You need also to spend some time considering how you are going to *present* that idea to your audience. This is where *style*—the third canon of rhetoric—enters the scene. Style concerns choosing the appropriate expression for the ideas of your argument; these choices relate to language, tone, syntax, rhetorical appeals, metaphors, imagery, quotations, level of emphasis, and nuance. We'll look more closely at style and the levels of decorum in Chapter 8; for now, let's consider how this canon operates in relation to the writer's voice.

We often translate *style* into *voice* to indicate a writer's unique persona and rhetorical stance as it is manifested in word choice, syntax, pacing, and tone. To construct a successful argument, you need to be able to employ the voice or style that best meets the needs of your rhetorical situation. Consider the following two examples of style, both focused on the persona of President Obama. The first is from a *Sports Illustrated* piece:

> Obama's erect carriage and lefthandedness led me to think of Lionel "Train" Hollins, who commanded the Portland Trail Blazers' backcourt when the kid then known as "Barry O'Bomber" was making his way through high school.

Using basketball lingo ("backcourt") and casual vocabulary ("the kid" and "making his way") helps writer Alexander Wolff construct his persona as someone who speaks the language of popular readers—what classical rhetorician Cicero would have called "plain style." Moreover, the naming of famous players gives credibility to Wolff's persona as someone who knows the players and even their nicknames, and another indication of this level of style.

In contrast, a writer from the academic journal *Rhetoric & Public Affairs* uses what Cicero called high style, or elevated diction, in making a critique of President Obama's persona:

> While Obama's rhetoric of *consilience* approximates dialogic coherence, it nonetheless falls short of the discursive demands of racial reconciliation.

By using sophisticated concepts familiar only to a highly educated academic audience, such as "dialogic coherence" and "discursive demands," writer Mark McPhail forges a persona for himself as an erudite and complex-thinking member of the intellectual class. His "backcourt buddies" are the colleagues who understand that "dialogic coherence" and "discursive demands" refer to ways of speaking and writing.

Similarly, your persona and your stylistic choices contribute to building your *ethos* and persuading your audience. Consider your choices carefully as you will both create a persona and determine which audience will respond to you best. Therefore, if you are wondering, how do you move from invention and arrangement to developing your own style? The answer lies in careful attention to developing *persona* and *rhetorical stance* in your writing.

Constructing Persona

When you select a certain image, a set of words, or a written phrase to shape your argument and try to persuade your audience, you are constructing a **persona** for yourself as a writer and rhetorician. Your persona is *a deliberately crafted version of yourself as writer.* A public figure will often use *persona* as a purposeful rhetorical tool. President Barack Obama might choose to give a speech about war flanked by a group of military men and women, and a speech about health care surrounded by doctors, as we see in Figure 3.10.

The same principle governs the writing process. When you compose a text (written, verbal, or visual), you decide how to use language to present a particular persona to the

FIGURE 3.10. President Barack Obama talks about health care surrounded by white coated medical personnel.

audience you wish to address. You create a portrait of yourself as the author of your argument through tone (formal or informal, humorous or serious); word choice (academic, colloquial); sentence structures (complex or simple and direct); use of rhetorical appeals (*pathos, logos, ethos*); and strategies of persuasion (narration, example, cause and effect, analogy, process, classification, or definition). Creating a persona requires care. A well-designed one can facilitate a strong connection with your readers and therefore make your argument more persuasive. However, a poorly constructed persona—one that is, for instance, biased, inconsistent, or underdeveloped—can have the opposite effect, alienating readers and undercutting your text's overall effectiveness.

Seeing Connections
To consider alternate ways of creating a rhetorical persona, see Mark Stephen Meadows' *I, Avatar* on page 321 and the excerpts from Robbie Cooper's *Alter Ego* on page 323.

Choosing a Rhetorical Stance

To be persuasive, you must assume a persona that responds appropriately to your specific rhetorical situation. Wayne Booth, one of the most important revivalists of classical rhetoric, defined the writer's position in relation to the rhetorical triangle as the **rhetorical stance** and claimed that it is the most essential aspect of effective communication. He argued that communication failed between people (or a text failed to persuade a reader) if the writer assumed a position that ignored the balance of the rhetorical triangle.

We see examples of inappropriate rhetorical stances constantly: the TV evangelist who moves his congregation with a polished sermon that completely distracts them from flaws in his moral character; the used-car salesman who pads his sales pitch with offers of free gifts, rebate specials, and low percentage rates; the actor who uses her celebrity status to drive a product endorsement, rather than clearly articulating the merits of that product itself. In each case, the *rhetorical triangle*—the relationship between author, audience, and text—is out of balance, and the argument itself, ultimately, is rendered less persuasive. In your own writing, therefore, you need to pay special attention not only to the persona you create but also to the stance you assume in relation to your specific rhetorical situation.

AT A GLANCE

Three Rhetorical Stances That Lead to Communication Failure

- ***The pedant or preacherly stance:*** the text is paramount and both the audience's needs and the speaker's character are ignored.
- ***The advertiser's stance:*** the effect on the audience is valued above all, ignoring the quality of the text and the credibility of the speaker.
- ***The entertainer's stance:*** the character of the speaker is elevated above the text and the audience.

Titles, Introductions, and Conclusions

In writing, you signal your persona and rhetorical stance through your word choice, sentence structure, tone, and strategies of persuasion. Let's zoom in for a moment on three key elements of the written argument to see the way each operates as an important site for these stylistic choices.

Title. Your reader's first encounter with your topic and argument comes through your title; in this way, the title itself operates as a rhetorical act that provides a frame and sets up the argument. Let's return for a moment to Figure 3.1. Many newspapers featured this image on their front pages on September 2, 2005—but with different headlines. Figures 3.11 and 3.12 are two examples. Consider how each paper signals its rhetorical stance through the visual-verbal arguments contained on its front page.

How does the headline "City desperate for help" read in combination with the helicopter image suggest a different argument than "Rising rage: Descent into anarchy" coupled with

Fresno-area home prices witness the 19th-largest increase in the nation. Business, C1

LATE FINAL EDITION

The Fresno Bee

50 cents

FRIDAY, SEPTEMBER 2, 2005

City desperate for help

► Evacuation turns 'explosive' ► Hospital patients stranded ► Refugees clamor for aid

Valley cracks $3 mark at pump

Gasoline prices are likely to keep rising, observers say.

Gas prices

As horror intensifies, Louisiana officials decry lack of federal assistance.

Doctors plead for help amid violent chaos

Fresno agency seeks more eminent domain power

INSIDE

'Transporter 2'

Victory for gays

Sunny and warm

FIGURE 3.11. Front page of the *Fresno Bee*, September 2, 2005.

Source: © THE FRESNO BEE, 2006

INSIDE

Fall movies offer thrills, chills, laughs and tears WEEKEND W1

Utah's 8.9% rise in home prices ranks 31st in U.S. BUSINESS D12

Time for a new Itty Bitty Salt Lake City contest LIFE C1

DESERET Morning News

Rising rage

Descent into anarchy

Video links London bombings to al-Qaida

Al-Jazeera tape shows terrorists praising blasts

Chaos spreads as law breaks down

Utahns rally to aid victims of hurricane

Utahns race to pumps as prices soar

INSIDE

deseretnews.com

New public-housing complex may allow convicted killers

FIGURE 3.12. Front page of the *Deseret Morning News*, September 2, 2005.

the same image? The difference in tone, perspective, and rhetorical stance apparent from these contrasting examples underscores the role a headline—and, relatedly, a title—plays in forming a reader's expectations for the argument that follows. In effect, a title is often the first step in writing an interpretation or making an argument.

In writing your own papers, you should spend some time brainstorming your titles. Some writers find constructing a powerful title to be a useful brainstorming activity to start their composition process and help them with invention; others construct the title only after completing the first draft of their paper, as a way of synthesizing the argument by bringing it into sharper focus. As you work with a title, think about its role in setting up your stance on your topic, indicating to your readers not only the scope of your analysis but also your angle on it. Try to play with language, linking the title to your main point, to a key image you discuss, to an underlying metaphor or motif, or to the larger issue raised by your argument. Test your working title by sharing it with a partner in class.

Seeing Connections
See Thomas L. Friedman's "America's Real Dream Team" (page 548) for an example of a powerful introduction that showcases his distinctive writing style.

Introduction. Like your title, your introduction offers your readers insight into the persona and rhetorical stance that will characterize your essay as a whole. In these opening paragraphs (an introduction may be more than one paragraph), you establish your voice (informal? formal?), your tone (measured? firm? angry? cautious?), your persona, and your topic through careful attention to word choice, sentence structure, and strategies of development.

Most introductions also provide the first articulation of your argument as well, moving from a general statement of topic to a more focused statement of your thesis.

However, perhaps even more importantly, the introduction is the moment in which you capture the attention and interest of your reader, often through a device that we call a rhetorical "hook." For instance, looking back at Jane Gottesman's photo essay, we can see how she hooks her online readers in her opening image (Figure 3.6) by framing the 1968 Olympics as a landmark event for women athletes. The reader is drawn in by the *ethos* of the Olympics and intrigued by the fact that it was only as recently as the late 1960s that women first participated in the torch-lighting ceremony. This hook prompts readers to wonder what other "firsts" they might not be aware of, what other facts about women athletes Gottesman might reveal. This is the hook that gets readers interested—and prompts readers to continue reading.

In written texts, you can use your introduction to hook your readers through one of several methods:

- Defining your terms (especially if you're writing on a subject that not everyone may be familiar with)
- Including a significant quotation or a startling statistic or fact
- Presenting an overview of the issue you're discussing
- Using an anecdote or narration
- Incorporating a vivid example
- Drawing on a relevant analogy or metaphor
- Using the second-person pronoun (*you*) to invite readers to make personal connections

Your choice of hook will depend to a large extent on your broader stylistic decisions about your essay and the way in which you want to develop your argument.

Let's look at how one student, Michael Zeligs, took the canon of style into consideration while composing his introduction to a rhetorical analysis of Robert Frank's photography:

> "Robert Frank, Swiss, unobtrusive, nice, with that little camera that he raises and snaps with one hand he sucked a sad poem right out of America onto film, taking rank among the tragic poets of the world."
>
> In his introduction to Robert Frank's *The Americans*, Jack Kerouac captures the photographer's responsible position as a concerned observer of his time, as the first person to sweep away dominating prejudice and expose what post-World War II America really represented. In his book, Frank pushes the limits of traditional art photography—limits that required clear foregrounds and backgrounds, clear subject and exposure and level tilt—and this enables him to focus more on scenes that dominate his eye and inspire emotional arguments. The America that Frank addresses, however, is not one of fulfilled dreams and two-car garages. It is a struggling foreground for change, founded in the two beautifully conflicting scenes of "Charleston, South Carolina," and "Trolley," where unique photographic elements merge to advance a critique of racial inequality during America's post-war crisis of identity.

What hooks the reader first is the quotation that heads the introduction: an abstract, lyrical statement that refuses to sacrifice its vision by adhering to conventional punctuation. This quote announces the essay's topic at the same time that it provides a sharp contrast for the writing style of the main body of the introduction that follows. By comparison, Michael's voice seems crisp, focused, and academic, establishing a persona that is both informed on his subject (he clearly not only has analyzed Frank's photographs but has read the introduction to the book as well) and is also able to discuss it articulately. Michael fashions his first sentence to serve as a bridge between his opening hook and the rest of the paragraph. Rather than using the epigraph simply as a snappy device to capture the reader's attention and then abandoning it, Michael creates an *ethos* appeal by identifying the quotation's author (Jack Kerouac, an iconic critic of American culture) and then restates the meaning of the quote in a way that pulls it in line with his own argument about Robert Frank's photography. The rest of the paragraph moves from general (a description of the project of Frank's larger book, *The Americans*, and a definition of traditional photographic methods) to specific (clarification of the two images Michael is most interested in), ending ultimately with a clear articulation of Michael's rhetorical stance and thesis statement.

Seeing Connections
For an example of a powerful conclusion, see the final paragraph of Elizabeth Kolbert's "Can America Go Green?" (page 262).

Conclusion. If the introduction offers the writer the opportunity to hook the audience's readers while articulating a personal stance on a subject, the conclusion provides the final opportunity to reinforce an essay's argument while making a lasting impact on readers. For this reason, although a conclusion by its nature should include some elements of summary (synthesizing the key points from the essay), it should also have a rhetorical power of its own. Let's look at how Michael concluded his essay on Frank's photographs:

> Robert Frank, in his images from *The Americans*, takes compelling pictures of a socially conflicted south to expose the growing struggle of race in 1950's America. His images spark from a new ideology of the photographer—a lack of concern for absolute photographic perfection allows him to document situations that really *mean* something. He chooses conflicting lives, black and white together on the page but unequal, his film subtly showing sympathy for the downtrodden worker and the weary traveler. Careful lines and deliberate tones show two opposing worlds where skin color can change the appearance of an entire backdrop, where stark white prison bars show us the walls we have erected within ourselves. These are not simple pictures of ordinary people. They are an artist's whisper about the elusiveness of equality, how in the war against bigotry, we are not done yet.

While offering a summary of his evidence, Michael takes care to make his conclusion as stylistically sophisticated as his introduction. Notice his careful use of word choice ("takes compelling pictures," "expose") that works in tandem with the subject of his essay; his return to the task of redefining American photography that he began in his introduction; his implicit reference to his analysis of the images themselves in the main body of his paper ("downtrodden worker and weary traveler," references to "lines" and "tones"); and, finally, the way he broadens his topic to touch on larger, ongoing issues of race relations. His conclusion leaves readers with more than a simple summary of points, prompting them to reflect on the ongoing state of race relations in America.

Consider ways to make your own conclusion a powerful part of your argument.

- Use a key quote, example, or reference that either epitomizes or summarizes your points.
- Return to an opening example or analogy, offering a slightly different, perhaps more informed perspective on it to connect introduction and conclusion as a frame for your argument.
- Use a chronological structure to move from the past to recent times, perhaps ending with a projection into the future.
- Use your conclusion to suggest broader implications that could increase the reader's sense of personal connection to the topic or its urgency.

No matter which strategy you choose, remember to maximize the persuasive potential of your conclusion as a means of reaffirming the strength of your argument with your readers.

Crafting a Position Paper

One way to experiment and put into practice these concepts—invention, arrangement, and style—is to draft a position paper on your topic. By definition, a **position paper** presents one side of an issue, allowing you the opportunity to construct a strong thesis statement and actively argue your main points. A position paper also can be an ideal medium for developing your own particular style, persona, and rhetorical stance. Angela Rastegar, for instance, experimented with persona during a project on photographic coverage of the war in Iraq. She tried out two very different ways of writing. First she composed an argument about the issue from the perspective of an unnamed academic or journalistic commentator. Then she revised the argument by writing a short paper representing an extreme position on the toppling of a Saddam Hussein statue by U.S. troops. Her first "position" offers the academic voice with an ostensibly objective perspective. Notice that there is no obvious "I" speaking, and yet an argument about the power of the media clearly emerges.

Rastegar 1

Angela Rastegar

Academic Position Paper

Imagine a chaotic world in which you cannot trust the media—newspapers, television reports, and magazines are full of lies about the world and politics. Picture trying to decipher current events or important situations without knowing whom to turn to or what to believe. Sounds far-fetched? Unfortunately, this is not far from the truth. Current newspapers are filled with subtle, clever methods used to deceive the public.

As you look at photographic images in widely respected newspaper articles, consider the techniques used to deceive the public. Concerning one incident—the April 9th destruction of Saddam Hussein's monument in Baghdad—the actual events of this day have been carefully concealed from the public. Although the media portrayed a "heroic" destruction of Saddam's symbol by American forces and mobs of Iraqi supporters, this event was essentially staged by the media.

We must use a cautious eye when viewing news stories and alert ourselves to subtle biases. The media has been called the "fourth branch of the government" because of the undeniable power it yields over the American public. No other source of information is so readily and unquestionably accepted. The government realizes this, and it often takes great measures to work with the media to create effective, captivating stories that not only portray Americans in a positive light but will also

Rastegar 2

sell papers. Examples of the media's influence are not by any means limited to this single event; however, wars provide the perfect opportunity for the media to influence the public. They open wounds in all Americans, leaving viewers vulnerable, easily influenced, and starving for more information. As a result, studying the media's influence on any war opens a vast field of controversy. In this time of crisis, we must read the news with a wary eye.

Seeing Connections
For examples of other position papers, see "Two Opinions on McDonaldization" (page 570) and "Can Biotech Food Cure World Hunger?" (page 250).

Finding this voice to offer too much of the "advertiser's stance," Angela then experimented with first person to shape her argument into an analysis of a specific photograph (see Figure 1 in her letter to the editor). She developed this position paper as an examination of the image and named her persona "Elizabeth Grant," a concerned media activist.

Rastegar 1

Angela Rastegar

Writing a Letter to the Editor as "Elizabeth Grant,"

Left-Wing Media Watchdog

I am writing in response to the astonishing display of deceit attempted by President G. W. Bush and the American government on Thursday, April 10th. President Bush's public address began with the words, "Iraqi citizens support overthrowing Saddam," which was illustrated by the enclosed photograph. It depicts an American marine tying the Iraqi flag around the neck of Saddam Hussein's 15-foot monument. Seconds later, U.S. troops connected the ropes and cables to the statue's neck and brought it crashing to the ground.

The photograph, which contains a brightly colored red and white Iraqi flag in the center, focuses the viewer's attention on this emblem. Did the Iraqi citizens request to use this flag? We don't know, but we can see how the government attempted to appeal to those watching by having a soldier tie Iraq's own flag to the chains.

The flag falsely suggests that the Iraqi people were behind the destruction of the monument and that America can work in harmony with the people of Iraq to overthrow Saddam. This message drastically distorts

Rastegar 2

the truth; in fact, the soldier originally held an American flag, but his commanding officers ordered him to tie this particular flag to the chains. Thus, the government's use of logos in this photo subtly attempts to convince the public that Iraq wanted to bring down Saddam's statue—when, in reality, the citizens there had nothing to do with it.

Figure 1. Laurent Rebours, Associated Press. "Scenes from Baghdad." *New York Times.* New York Times, 9 Apr. 2003. Web. 14 Apr. 2003.

In this photograph, the picture also appeals to the viewers' emotions by placing a rope and chains around the neck of Saddam's image. In this sense, it evokes the American hatred for Saddam and creates a clear, understandable aim. The military is able to put a noose around the neck of a symbolic Saddam, displaying the government's ability to destroy him. The government draws on these emotions from the viewers to increase patriotism. Bush applies these same tactics to his public speeches, focusing on American strength to justify our intervention.

In addition, the photo strategically includes a U.S. marine to add to the photo's visual credibility. This symbol of America—a solider in uniform—forces the viewers to place more trust in the photographer and what we see here. My greatest fear is that the average American will hear Bush speak and see this photo without realizing that their goal is to convince the world of Iraqi support for American intervention. They claim that they are fighting to "free Iraq," but in reality, our government simply ties Iraq's fate to Saddam and destroys them both.

In her first position paper, Angela writes about the power of photographs from a generalized, academic perspective, the voice of analytical assessment. But in her subsequent paper, she explores a specific point of view about media coverage of international politics. The persona of Elizabeth Grant—whose style Angela develops through careful attention to word choice, rhetorical appeals, and prose style—relies on the use of "I" and repeated use of strong language. As you can tell, the experimentation with *voice* itself was the most important product of her revisions: it allowed her both to reach into her topic and to examine differences in *style* and *rhetorical stance,* in particularly powerful ways. As she moved into the final stages of her project, she brought the power of this writing to bear on her longer researched argument; although she wrote the final paper from her own perspective, working with the pro and con points of view enabled her to construct a sharper thesis statement and a more persuasive approach to the photographs she was discussing.

Writing Multiple Sides of an Argument

Angela Rastegar's project opens up some interesting possibilities for developing your own persuasive arguments. Sometimes when we write from our own points of view, we get so locked into our individual perspectives that we fail to take into account the diverse or multiple sides of our topics. Such limited vision can weaken our persuasiveness; if we fail to consider or acknowledge alternative positions on our topics, we produce one-sided arguments that lack complexity or credibility with our readers. Recall our earlier discussion of photographs: each photograph suggests a different angle, a unique "version" of an event, and the perspective of a particular persona. When we bring these different sides to light, we find that suddenly an incident or issue that seems polarized—or "black and white"—is actually much more complex. The same holds true for the issues we confront every day as writers and rhetoricians: it is only through exploring the multiple sides of our argument that we can engage it persuasively and effectively.

Begin experimenting with inventing diverse perspectives to achieve a thorough understanding of a complex situation. Although you may be tempted to think of these various perspectives in oppositional terms—as the "pro" or "con" of an issue—such a point of view closes off the richer complexity of the issue. Try to think of arguments not in terms of right or wrong but rather as a spectrum of differing perspectives. As you turn to write your own arguments, consider how you can explore different viewpoints by trying out personas; by inventing diverse responses to your own point of view; and by exploring various writing strategies through experimentation with diction, syntax, style, image selection, arrangement of argument, and voice.

Student Writing

Read Aisha Ali's complete project and other student multiple sides projects.
www.pearsonhighered.com/envision/62

When writing arguments, you might choose to explore more than one *persona* or *rhetorical stance* to see different sides of an issue. Student Aisha Ali, for instance, developed her project on the conflict in the Middle East by creating three articles, or sides, around a single photograph (see Figure 3.13). Using the image as the foundation for each discussion, she assumed the personas of an African photojournalist, an Israeli soldier, and a Palestinian boy. Aisha's contrasting personas offered a series of riveting snapshots of the Palestinian conflict. To create this effect, she took extra care with word choice, sentence structure, and the development of her arguments. In her first side, she opens the piece by exploring the context of the Middle Eastern situation and then moves with fluid and articulate language to the central narrative: the freeing of the doves in front of an oncoming tank. Her second side adopts a different approach: using direct, informal speech, and biased language suitable to a soldier hardened by armed conflict, this persona launches immediately into the narrative itself. The last side also presents the story of the doves' release; however, as the excerpt from her work shows, the voice is clearly that of a child.

Using simple sentence structures and word choices to build a narrative with an underlying *pathos* appeal, Aisha has brought to life the perspective of the young boy forced to free his doves in the shadow of military occupation.

Together, the variety of perspectives in Aisha's writing enabled her to avoid producing a simplistic argument about the violence in the Middle East, and instead to demonstrate its complexity. Although the photograph Aisha used in her series of articles constitutes a powerful visual argument in itself through its striking juxta-position of fluttering doves (a symbol of peace) and military tanks (a symbol of war), she was able to convey the meaning of the image for diverse viewers through powerful writing. You can try this strategy of writing multiple sides of an argument in your own compositions.

FIGURE 3.13. The powerful image of doves in front of a tank in the Middle East offers multiple interpretations.

Writing a Synthesis Paper

Although experimenting with writing in different styles from the perspectives of different personas, incorporating diverse strategies of arrangement for each piece, and inventing opposing arguments allow you to develop a deeper understanding of the complexity of an issue, in many academic contexts you will be asked to **synthesize** these perspectives into a single, thesis-driven text. The task then is to incorporate discussion of multiple perspectives (including positions you might find through research) in a way that reveals the complexity of the issue but ultimately advances your own, final rhetorical stance on the topic at hand.

We find an outstanding example of successfully balancing multiple perspectives with a clear, authorial thesis in Nora Ephron's article "The Boston Photographs," published in *Scribble, Scribble: Notes on the Media* (1978). This essay offers a useful model of the canons of rhetoric we've been discussing so far—invention, arrangement, and style.

Ephron offers us insight into the constant struggles that newspaper editors face in selecting photographs for publication—in this case, deciding whether or not to print the "sensationalist" images of a woman and child falling from a fire escape during a 1976 apartment fire (Figure 3.14). Ephron brings into her article at least three perspectives, each embodying a unique rhetorical stance: from her own perspective to those of Stanley Forman, photographer, and Charles Seib, the *Washington Post* ombudsman (the editor who

Boston Herald American

Complete AP, UPI and New York Times News & Feature Services
Largest Morning Circulation in New England

LATE COMPLETE

House Keeps Oil Price Controls

Exclusive Photo — Safety So Near Then Suddenly...

Ford's Proposal Killed, 262-167

Living Costs Take Biggest Hike Of Year

Girl Dies, Child Hurt in Crash of Fire Escape

Woman Falls to Her Death and Child Is Hurt as Fire Escape Collapses on Marlborough St., Back Bay.

SEE DRAMATIC PHOTO SEQUENCE PAGE 3

Inside Information, Today's Index on Page 2

FIGURE 3.14. The *Boston Herald American* chose to print this disturbing photograph on its front page.

monitors the content of the paper to ensure that it is not offensive to readers). She also represents in miniature other points of view through a series of brief quotations from letters to the editor that appeared shortly after the publication of the controversial photographs. The writers of these letters each get a turn to argue their unique points from the basis of their own rhetorical stance. However, the argument that ultimately is most persuasive is Ephron's own; in this way, she *synthesizes* the arguments to arrive at her own, persuasive conclusion.

THE BOSTON PHOTOGRAPHS

Nora Ephron

Ephron begins with the voice of the photographer, Stanley Forman, using a direct quote to present his perspective.

"I made all kinds of pictures because I thought it would be a good rescue shot over the ladder . . . never dreamed it would be anything else. . . . I kept having to move around because of the light set. The sky was bright and they were in deep shadow. I was making pictures with a motor drive and he, the firefighter, was reaching up and, I don't know, everything started falling. I followed the girl down taking pictures. . . . I made three or four frames. I realized what was going on and I completely turned around, because I didn't want to see her hit."

Her next two paragraphs provide background for Forman's recollections.

Notice Ephron's use of the second person to establish a rapport with her reader built on a sense of shared cultural experience.

Although this section is ostensibly description, look closely at her stylistic choices—especially word choice—to see the way she is setting up her stance on the topic.

You probably saw the photographs. In most newspapers, there were three of them. The first showed some people on a fire escape—a fireman, a woman, and a child. The fireman had a nice strong jaw and looked very brave. The woman was holding the child. Smoke was pouring from the building behind them. A rescue ladder was approaching, just a few feet away, and the fireman had one arm around the woman and one arm reaching out toward the ladder. The second picture showed the fire escape slipping off the building. The child had fallen on the escape and seemed about to slide off the edge. The woman was grasping desperately at the legs of the fireman, who had managed to grab the ladder. The third picture showed the woman and child in midair, falling to the ground. Their arms and legs were outstretched, horribly distended. A potted plant was falling too. The caption said that the woman, Diana Bryant, nineteen, died in the fall. The child landed on the woman's body and lived.

She establishes her *ethos* in the beginning of this paragraph by demonstrating her knowledge of photography.

The pictures were taken by Stanley Forman, thirty, of the *Boston Herald American*. He used a motor-driven Nikon F set at 1/250, f5.6-S. Because of the motor, the camera can click off three frames a second. More than four hundred newspapers in the United States alone carried the photographs: The tear sheets from overseas are still coming in. The *New York Times* ran them on the first page of its second section; a paper in south Georgia gave them nineteen columns; the *Chicago Tribune,* the *Washington Post* and the *Washington Star* filled almost half their front pages, the *Star* under a somewhat redundant headline that read: Sensational Photos of Rescue Attempt That Failed.

While here Ephron finally gives her own assessment of the images (that they "are indeed sensational"), she refrains from a definitive thesis statement at this point.

The photographs are indeed sensational. They are pictures of death in action, of that split second when luck runs out, and it is impossible to look at them without feeling their extraordinary impact and remembering, in an almost subconscious way, the morbid fantasy of falling, falling off a building, falling to one's death. Beyond that, the pictures are classics, old-fashioned but perfect examples of photojournalism at its most spectacular. They're throwbacks, really, fire pictures, 1930s tabloid shots; at the same time they're technically superb and thoroughly modern—the sequence could not have been taken at all until the development of the motor-driven camera some sixteen years ago.

Word choice once again hints at her argument: Notice how the term "sensational" (with slight negative connotations) has become "spectacular," which suggests awe and appreciation.

Most newspaper editors anticipate some reader reaction to photographs like Forman's; even so, the response around the country was enormous, and almost all of it was negative. I have read hundreds of the letters that were printed in letters-to-the-editor sections, and they repeat the same points. "Invading the privacy of death." "Cheap sensationalism." "I thought I was reading the *National Enquirer*." "Assigning the agony of a human being in terror of imminent death to the status of a side-show act." "A tawdry way to sell newspapers." The *Seattle Times* received sixty letters and calls; its managing editor even got a couple of them at home. A reader wrote the *Philadelphia Inquirer:* "*Jaws* and *Towering Inferno* are playing downtown; don't take business away from people who pay good money to advertise in your own paper." Another reader wrote the *Chicago Sun-Times:* "I shall try to hide my disappointment that Miss Bryant wasn't wearing a skirt when she fell to her death. You could have had some award-winning photographs of her underpants as her skirt billowed over her head, you voyeurs." Several newspaper editors wrote columns defending the pictures: Thomas Keevil of the *Costa Mesa* (California) *Daily Pilot* printed a ballot for readers to vote on whether they would have printed the pictures; Marshall L. Stone of Maine's *Bangor Daily News,* which refused to print the famous assassination picture of the Vietcong prisoner in Saigon, claimed that the Boston pictures showed the dangers of fire escapes and raised questions about slumlords. (The burning building was a five-story brick apartment house on Marlborough Street in the Back Bay section of Boston.)

She focuses here on audience reaction to the photographs. The accumulation of quotations increases her *ethos* as a researcher and also gives weight to their outrage, even though it is a reaction that Ephron does not share.

Consider the order in which she arranges the quotes: the last two are the most colorful and memorable.

Her final parenthetical aside slightly undermines the power of this perspective by pointing out an inaccuracy.

For the last five years, the *Washington Post* has employed various journalists as ombudsmen, whose job is to monitor the paper on behalf of the public. The *Post*'s current ombudsman is Charles Seib, former managing editor of the *Washington Star;* the day the Boston photographs appeared, the paper received over seventy calls in protest. As Seib later wrote in a column about the pictures, it was "the largest reaction to a published item that I have experienced in eight months as the *Post*'s ombudsman. . . .

At this point in the essay, she features the *Washington Post* editor who decided to run the photographs in that newspaper. The fact that she follows the reader-response with Seib's reaction is clearly strategic because her own stance most closely resembles his.

"In the *Post*'s newsroom, on the other hand, I found no doubts, no second thoughts . . . the question was not whether they should be printed but how they should be displayed. When I talked to editors . . . they used words like 'interesting' and 'riveting' and 'gripping' to describe them. The pictures told of something about life in the ghetto, they said (although the neighborhood where the tragedy occurred is not a ghetto, I am told). They dramatized the need to check on the safety of fire escapes. They dramatically conveyed something that had happened, and that is the business we're in. They were news. . . .

"Was publication of that [third] picture a bow to the same taste for the morbidly sensational that makes gold mines of disaster movies? Most papers will not print the picture of a dead body except in the most unusual circumstances. Does the fact that the final picture was taken a millisecond before the young woman died make a difference? Most papers will not print a picture of a bare female breast. Is that a more inappropriate subject for display than the picture of a human being's last agonized instant of life?" Seib offered no answers to the questions he raised, but he went on to say that although as an editor he would probably have run the pictures, as a reader he was revolted by them.

In conclusion, Seib wrote: "Any editor who decided to print those pictures without giving at least a moment's thought to what purpose they served and what their effect was likely to be on the reader should ask another question: Have I become so preoccupied with manufacturing a product according to professional traditions and standards that I have forgotten about the consumer, the reader?"

She gently qualifies Seib's argument, asserting the side or perspective while at the same time suggesting her own interpretation of the issue.

It should be clear that the phone calls and letters and Seib's own reaction were occasioned by one factor alone: the death of the woman. Obviously, had she survived the fall, no one would have protested; the pictures would have had a completely different impact. Equally obviously, had the child died as well—or instead—Seib would undoubtedly have received ten times the phone calls he did. In each case, the pictures would have been exactly the same—only the captions, and thus the responses, would have been different.

It is only now, after showcasing these many voices on the issue, that Ephron moves to her own argument.

By using the phrases "all dressed up and cleverly disguised," Ephron exposes her own impatience with some of the reactions elicited by the publication of the photos.

Her clever play on words (puritanism/puritanical) further clarifies her stance.

But the questions Seib raises are worth discussing—though not exactly for the reasons he mentions. For it may be that the real lesson of the Boston photographs is not the danger that editors will be forgetful of reader reaction, but that they will continue to censor pictures of death precisely because of that reaction. The protests Seib fielded were really a variation on an old theme—and we saw plenty of it during the Nixon-Agnew years—the "Why doesn't the press print the good news?" argument. In this case, of course, the objections were all dressed up and cleverly disguised as righteous indignation about the privacy of death. This is a form of puritanism that is often justifiable; just as often it is merely puritanical.

Look at her use of rhetorical questions to make her point and to throw the issue back at her readers.

Seib takes it for granted that the widespread though fairly recent newspaper policy against printing pictures of dead bodies is a sound one; I don't know that it makes any sense at all. I recognize that printing pictures of corpses raises all sorts of problems about taste and titillation and sensationalism; the fact is, however, that people die. Death happens to be one of life's main events. And it is irresponsible—and more than that, inaccurate—for newspapers to fail to show it, or to show it only when an astonishing set of photos comes in over the Associated Press wire. Most papers covering fatal automobile accidents will print pictures of mangled cars. But the significance of fatal automobile accidents is not that a great deal of steel is twisted but that people die. Why not show it? That's what accidents are about. Throughout the Vietnam war, editors were reluctant to print atrocity pictures. Why *not* print them? That's what that was about. Murder victims are almost never photographed; they are granted their privacy. But their relatives are relentlessly pictured on their way in and out of hospitals and morgues and funerals.

I'm not advocating that newspapers print these things in order to teach their readers a lesson. The *Post* editors justified their printing of the Boston pictures with several arguments in that direction; every one of them is irrelevant. The pictures don't show anything about slum life; the incident could have happened anywhere, and it did. It is extremely unlikely that anyone who saw them rushed out and had his fire escape strengthened. And the pictures were not news—at least they were not national news. It is not news in Washington, or New York, or Los Angeles that a woman was killed in a Boston fire. The only newsworthy thing about the pictures is that they were taken. They deserve to be printed because they are great pictures, breathtaking pictures of something that happened. That they disturb readers is exactly as it should be: that's why photojournalism is often more powerful than written journalism.

The use of the first person here marks a moment where Ephron begins to clearly assert her own opinion, rather than reporting on the perspectives of others.

In her conclusion, Ephron ends with a concession to those who were offended and then a strong articulation of her position on the topic that links to larger issues in photojournalism.

How does Ephron present her own argument despite allowing so many voices in her piece? How does she achieve the synthesis of multiple sides while developing her own argument through invention, arrangement, and style?

Let's first determine her main idea, the *invention* in her thesis statement. Where is her thesis? What new perspective on the issue of representing death in photographs has she invented in this essay in order to share it with her reading audience? Look at the final paragraph for the answer.

Now let's analyze the *arrangement* of her essay. As we read through the essay, we see that Ephron strategically allows the multiple viewpoints on the issue to play themselves out in the early part of her article, providing the reader with a firm grounding in the debate, before concluding with her own very strong point of view. By arranging her essay in this way, Ephron focuses the audience reaction to the images and to the editor's decisions to run them through the lens of her own argument. However, Ephron's strategy is just one of many patterns of arrangement that

Seeing Connections

See "The Photo Felt Around the World" on page 509 for another article that talks about the editorial process behind deciding whether run a controversial photograph in a newspaper.

AT A GLANCE

The Arrangement of Ephron's Argument

1. Quotation from photographer (1 paragraph)
2. Background (2 paragraphs)
3. Ephron's general assessment of images (1 paragraph)
4. Reader reaction to photos (1 paragraph)
5. Editor's point of view (4 paragraphs)
6. Qualification of Seib's point of view (1 paragraph)
7. Her own argument (final 3 paragraphs)

Strategies of Arrangement

A Classical Speech or Oration

1. Introduction
2. Statement of facts
3. Division
4. Proof
5. Refutation
6. Conclusion

Option A

Use when you want to ground the reader in your argument before bringing up opposing perspectives.

1. Introduction, identification of rhetorical stance
2. Thesis
3. Statement of background, definition, or context
4. Evidence and development of argument
5. Opposing opinion, concession, qualification, refutation
6. Conclusion

Option B

Establish opposing opinion up front so that the entire piece functions as an extended rebuttal or refutation of that line of argument.

1. Introduction and opposing viewpoint
2. Thesis and identification of rhetorical stance
3. Evidence and development of argument
4. Conclusion

Option C

Treat diverse viewpoints as appropriate during the development of your argument and presentation of your evidence.

1. Introduction, identification of rhetorical stance
2. Thesis
3. Statement of background, definition, or context
4. Evidence, opposing opinion, concession, qualification, refutation
5. Conclusion

take into account incorporating counterarguments while producing a persuasive text. You have multiple options available to you when dealing with opposing viewpoints. You can follow the classical method of arrangement (see table) or select a modified version, depending on your purpose.

Attending to Arrangement in Argument

The models of arrangement in the table are not designed to be rigid parameters. Instead, they should suggest possibilities and potentially productive strategies of arrangement; in your own writing, you will have to select the most productive way to lay out your topic and the diverse opinions that surround it.

You'll need to consider first the strength of the other perspectives on the issue. Do they corroborate your argument? Then you could include them as supporting evidence. Do they offer points of view that you can disprove? Then you might present the opinion and provide a *rebuttal*, or refutation of the points, demonstrating why they are not valid. Do they offer points of view that you can't disprove? Then you might *concede* the validity of their argument but go on to *qualify* their points by showing why your own argument is nonetheless persuasive. The key is to treat these other voices with respect; always represent their points of view fairly and without bias, even if you disagree with them. In a sense, when you are dealing with multiple perspectives, some of which may run counter to your own argument, you face a question of ethics quite similar to that the editors faced with the Boston photographs: How do you present possibly volatile material in a way that is both fair and yet advances your persuasive purpose?

We can see how Ephron herself answered that question by assessing her use of the canon of *style,* specifically in the persona and rhetorical stance she developed in her essay. As a careful analysis of her essay demonstrates, Ephron presents the background on the issue as if through an objective lens; however, her word choice, her selections of quotations, and even the sentence structures themselves collaborate to produce a rhetorical stance that seems all the more persuasive for its earlier objectivity when she moves to the strong statement at the end of her essay. For this reason, when her voice becomes more clearly argumentative in her conclusion, the reader does not automatically resist her argument. Instead, because of Ephron's stylistic choices, readers are more likely to be persuaded by her thesis, "That they [the photographs] disturb readers is exactly as it should be," and to welcome Ephron's fundamental redefinition of the purpose and characteristics of good photojournalism.

AT A GLANCE

Dealing with Multiple Perspectives in Your Arguments

When incorporating other viewpoints into your writing, you can use them in one of three ways:

- ***Evidence:*** you can use the diverse viewpoints to support your own thesis statement.
- ***Concession/Qualification:*** you can admit that the person has a strong point but then explain why it doesn't diminish the persuasiveness or validity of your argument.
- ***Rebuttal:*** you can present an opposing opinion, fairly and respectfully, and then demonstrate why it is not a valid argument in this case.

The Writer's Process

In this chapter, you've learned to harness the canons of rhetoric—invention, arrangement, and style—to compose effective arguments of your own. You've developed strategies for crafting titles, introductions, and conclusions; you've explored the importance of persona and rhetorical stance in argument. You've experimented with developing a position paper, crafting multiple sides of an argument, and then integrating diverse perspectives through a synthesis paper. Now it's time to implement these skills. Practice inventing a position on an issue, arranging claims and evidence for your argument (including working with images as evidence for your points), developing a rhetorical stance, and working on persona through style by crafting your prose with care. You might, for instance, try to rewrite the Nora Ephron piece from the perspective of one of the personas that she mentions in her text: the editor, the photographer, or a disgruntled reader. As you do, incorporate the other perspectives into your argument, experimenting with arrangement and style to produce a piece that synthesizes diverse viewpoints while still making its own strong argument.

PREWRITING CHECKLIST

Focus on Analyzing Photographs

- ❑ **Content:** What, literally, does the photograph depict? Who or what is the subject of the photo? What is the setting?
- ❑ **Cultural context:** What is the historical context of the photograph? If it "documents" a particular event, person, or historical moment, how prominently does this photograph

(continued)

factor into our understanding of this event, person, or place? (For instance, is it the only known photograph of an event, or is it one of a series of pictures taken of the same subject?)

- ❑ **Material context:** Where was this photograph reproduced or displayed (an art gallery, the cover of a magazine, the front page of a newspaper)? If it was published elsewhere originally, does this source credit the original?
- ❑ **Argument:** What, thematically, does the photograph depict? What is its message to the audience? For instance, while the photo might show a group of people standing together, its argument might be about love, family unity across generations, or a promise for the future.
- ❑ **Photographer:** Who took this photograph? What was the person's purpose?
- ❑ **Audience:** Who was the photographer's intended audience?
- ❑ **Purpose:** What is the photograph's purpose? Is it intended to be overtly argumentative and to move its audience to action? Or is the argument more subtle, even to the point of seeming objective or representational?
- ❑ **Rhetorical stance:** How does the composition of the photo convey a sense of the rhetorical stance or point of view of the photographer? Pay attention to issues of focus (what is "in focus"? This may differ from the ostensible "focus" of the picture); cropping (what is "in" the picture, and what has been left "out"?); color (is the picture in black and white? color? sepia?); setting (what backdrop has the photographer chosen?); and perspective (are we looking down? up?).
- ❑ **Representation versus reality:** Does this photograph aspire to represent reality, or is it an overtly abstract piece? Is there any indication of photo manipulation, editing, or other alteration? If so, what rhetorical purpose does this serve—what argument does this alteration make?
- ❑ **Word and image:** Does the photo have a caption? Does the image accompany an article, essay, or other lengthy text? How does the image function in dialogue with this verbal text? Does it offer visual evidence? Does it argue an independent point? Does it provide a counterargument to the print text?

PREWRITING WITH THE *ENVISION* WEBSITE

1. In order to get started with your writing project, download two to three images from MSNBC.com's "Week in Pictures," accessible through the Chapter 3 resources on the *Envision* Website. As a group, select photos that convey different sides of a situation or event. Come up with three personas—the voice of the person in the photo, the voice of the photographer, and the voice of an observer. Now develop a thesis for each side and write a brief description of your imagined persona. Allow each person in the group to contribute a new perspective. Write up each of these sides; format them into a feature article or cover story for a newspaper or magazine, and, when you are done, present your work as a group to the class.
www.pearsonhighered.com/envision/70

2. When we discuss arrangement in reference to photographs like Dorothea Lange's and Jane Gottesman's, we usually refer to the way the photographer stages a shot or orders a series of images. However, in the age of digital photo editing, the canon of arrangement is often used in producing striking arguments in the form of photo illustrations, some of which are even arranged to produce a visual joke, such as the image of a gigantic, great white shark rising from the water to attack a helicopter in the San Francisco Bay, which was virally circulated around the internet. To start pre-writing about visual arguments, break into small groups and visit the following sites, linked through the *Envision* Website.

- ❑ The Hoax Photo Gallery: a collection of doctored photographs from the online Museum of Hoaxes.
- ❑ Frank Van Riper's "Manipulating Truth, Losing Credibility": an article from the *Washington Post* about the Brian Walski photo scandal.
- ❑ Floyd's Website: before-and-after images that demonstrate the dramatic effects of photo editing.
- ❑ "The Case of the Missing Limb": an article from *The Digital Journalist* about how newspaper editors altered a photograph to make it less offensive to readers.

Look through these sites and consider how the canon of arrangement functions in these cases in relation to the ethics of argument. Which altered images are the most convincing? the most disturbing? Why? How do you distinguish between creativity and manipulation? Are there times when photographic manipulation is justified? How can we apply these observations about ethics and arrangement to our consideration of written texts? Use the prewriting checklist above to help focus your analysis of the images.
www.pearsonhighered.com/envision/71

WRITING PROJECTS

1. **Written Argument:** Write an argument about an issue that moves you; base your argument on your analysis of a powerful image; and include your interpretation of the image as part of your writing. Invent a strong thesis, pick your persona, decide on your strategy of arrangement, and write with particular attention to style. You might choose to write a popular article, such as a letter to the editor of the campus newspaper, a Weblog entry, or a newspaper column such as *Newsweek*'s "My Turn."

2. **Three Position Papers:** Write three position papers or articles, with each one commenting on the previous one so that the project forms a coherent whole. Give each persona a name, an occupation, a geographic location, and a strong perspective to argue in words. Each position can offer a new point of view on one image or can develop complexity about an issue by bringing in a new image as visual evidence. You might choose to format your project as a feature article for a specific magazine or reading audience. To do so, first conduct a rhetorical analysis on the features of a chosen publication (*The New Yorker, The Economist,* a national newspaper, or a campus journal) and then format your three arguments as part of that publication. Include a cover page with an introduction by the editor and a closing assessment page, perhaps by a staff writer. You could also format your project as a Website or multimedia text (a flash montage or photo essay).

3. **Multiple Sides Collaboration:** Collaborate on composing multiple position papers by assigning the writing of each argument to a different member of your group. You might, for instance, write about the conflict between your college campus and the surrounding town: have someone interview locals, the sheriff, administrators, and students. Provide a series of arguments from each perspective and images to function as argumentative texts for each side. Be sure to include concession and refutation. Collaborate in the writing of the introduction and the conclusion as well as in the design, arrangement, and style of the project as a whole. The last writer in the group should compose a synthesis paper, incorporating the positions of everyone and providing a closing argument.

Visit www.pearsonhighered.com/envision for expanded assignment guidelines and student projects.
Visit www.mycomplab.com for additional general writing and research resources.

Part II

RESEARCH ARGUMENTS

Research is never completed. . . . Around the corner lurks another possibility of interview, another book to read, a courthouse to explore, a document to verify.

—Catherine Drinker Bowen

CHAPTER 4

Planning and Proposing Research Arguments

Chapter Preview Questions

- How do I generate a productive topic and research questions?
- What prewriting techniques can I use to narrow my topic?
- What are best research practices?
- How do I keep a research log?
- What are the steps in a strong research plan?
- How do I write a formal research proposal?

What's going on in the poster shown in Figure 4.1? Why the juxtaposition of a menacing Soviet officer with a contemporary college student listening to downloaded music? Why the deep red background color and the placement of characters with the officer looking over the student's shoulder? Why is *Communism* so large and visually echoed by the hammer and sickle? At some point, you begin to realize that this poster is intended as a parody and that it pokes fun at recent publicity campaigns by the Recording Industry Association of America (RIAA) to combat file sharing and unauthorized music downloading. These observations will help you begin to make an argument about the poster, but in order to back up or substantiate your claims about its meaning, you would need to do some research. That is, you would need to place the rhetorical elements of the poster in their historical and critical contexts, including the anti-Communist propaganda posters of the cold war 1950s and the current debate about music downloading and copyright law. As you try to grasp the significance of representing the RIAA's position through a parody of anti-Soviet propaganda, you would need to investigate the political and legal controversies surrounding file sharing.

FIGURE 4.1. How does this parody propaganda poster use visual elements to undermine the RIAA's stance on file sharing?

Research can be conducted in any number of ways, including interviews, fieldwork, and the exploration of sources both online and in print. But the starting point of any research effort is to determine what questions to ask, what inquiries to pursue. In this chapter, you will learn the first steps of becoming an active participant in a research community and begin to develop the skills for defining a research question and creating an effective research plan and a solid research proposal.

Asking Research Questions

The discussion in this chapter focuses on a specific subset of persuasive images—propaganda posters—because such texts make very powerful public statements and because, for many of us, to understand the motivations behind a propaganda poster, we have to perform a certain amount of research. Often this research involves pursuing answers to questions we have formulated about the poster. In fact, most research begins with the act of asking questions.

One way you can get started on your research is to pick a text that moves you and start brainstorming questions about it. Let's say that you came across the 1917 American enlistment poster shown in Figure 4.2 in an exhibit on campus or as part of a class discussion about World War I posters. Approaching it for the first time, you and your peers probably will start to analyze the visual rhetoric, much as we did in the earlier chapters of *Envision in Depth.*

FIGURE 4.2. This World War I propaganda poster offers a wealth of detail for historical analysis.

What are your eyes drawn to first, the words or the image? Maybe you look first at the simian figure in the middle, roaring menacingly at you, and then at the swooning, seminaked woman in his arms. In contrast, maybe the person next to you is attracted first to the bold yellow text at the top and then to the bottom, where the words "U.S. Army" in black are superimposed on the imperative "Enlist." In synthesizing various responses to the text, you most likely would find yourself with more questions than answers—a good thing, for those questions can be the beginning of your research inquiry.

You might ask, Is that gorilla King Kong? Your research would allow you to confidently answer, No, since you would discover that the poster was made decades before the movie was released. That same research might produce several books that discuss the wartime practice of casting enemies as subhuman creatures, offering a possible explanation for why the enemy nation is portrayed as a menacing gorilla in this poster. Adding to that your observation that "*culture*" is spelled "Kultur" (on the club the gorilla is holding), you probably would realize that the enemy symbolized here is in fact Germany.

Seeing Connections
To understand how *kairos* factors into an analysis of this sort, see page 40.

Then you might ask: What is the significance of that bloody club? Why is the woman unconscious and partly naked? More research might provide insight on how bestiality emerged as a wartime theme in World War I enlistment posters. If a nation's women were threatened with potential attack by such "monsters," these posters implied, then the men would surely step up to save and protect their wives, daughters, sisters, and mothers.

By asking questions about your text, you can move beyond an initial response and into the realm of intellectual discovery. In fact, your first questions about a text will lead you to ask more pointed questions about the context, political environment, key players, and social trends informing your text. For the propaganda poster in Figure 4.2, such questions might include:

- What conflict was America involved in during 1917?
- What was the meaning of the word on the gorilla's hat, "Militarism," at that time?
- How would an appeal to enlist factor into that historical situation?
- Who is the audience for this poster, and how is this poster part of a series of wartime propaganda images?

If you were to work through these questions, you might begin to develop ideas for a feasible research topic—one that could yield an interesting paper on war propaganda and the relationship between America and Germany in 1917.

As you investigate your research topic, your questions will likely become more specific:

- Do other posters of the same historical period use similar imagery and rhetorical strategies?
- How do the techniques used in early twentieth-century posters differ from those used during World War II?
- How are the rhetorical strategies used in this poster similar to or different from enlistment posters you might encounter today?
- In what ways have enlistment posters changed over time?

In all cases, what these questions lead to is a focused *research topic* and, ultimately, a written project that draws on and contributes to the arguments that others have made about such texts. Generating a range of interesting and productive questions is the first step in any research project; the process of inquiry itself helps you to define a project and make it your own.

AT A GLANCE

Constructing a Research Log

To start your research log, include a variety of entries related to the initial stages of the research process:

- Write freely on possible topic ideas.
- Insert and annotate clippings from newspaper or magazine sources that offer interesting potential topics.
- Paste in and respond to provocative images related to potential topics.
- Write a reaction to ideas brought up during class discussion.
- Insert and annotate printouts from emails or other collaborative work on research ideas.
- Track preliminary searches on the Internet and in your library catalog.
- Develop your research plan.
- Vent anxieties over your project.

Constructing a Research Log

From the very beginning of your research process—as you move from asking questions about a text to identifying a productive topic, to gathering information and taking notes—keep track of your ideas in a research log. This log will help you organize your ideas, collect your materials, chart your progress, and assemble the different pieces of your research.

Your research log can take many forms, from a handwritten journal, to a series of word processing documents, a personal Weblog, or a collection of bookmarked pages from the Web. It can contain primarily written text, or it can include images, video, or audio files as well. The key lies not in what your research log looks like, but in the way you use it to help you develop an interesting and provocative research project that keeps careful track of the sources you encounter along the way.

Generating Topics and Research Questions

If you think back to our discussion of *invention* in Chapter 3, you'll understand that one of the most crucial aspects of starting a research project is selecting a viable and engaging topic. The word *topic*, in fact, comes from the ancient Greek word *topos*, translated literally as "place." The earliest students of rhetoric used the physical space of the papyrus page—given to them by their teachers—to locate their topics for writing. Similarly, your teacher may suggest certain guidelines or parameters for you to follow when it comes to your topic; for instance, you may be given a specific topic (such as representations of race in Dr. Seuss cartoons) or you may be limited to a theme (the rhetoric of political advertisements on television, radio, and the Internet).

In some cases, you may not have any restrictions at all. But regardless of the degree to which your topic has been mapped out for you, you still can—and should—make it your own. You do this partly by generating your own **research questions**, a set of questions that will guide your work and lead you to your final argument. You can generate these questions by responding to the rhetorical situation provided by your assignment and by considering what interests *you* most about the topic. Even if your whole class is writing on the same topic, each person will present a different argument or approach to the issue. Some will use a different stance or persona, some will rely on different sources, some will use different rhetorical appeals, and all will argue different positions about the topic. The way you make a research project your own is by developing powerful research questions.

To see how this works, let's look at one student's project on propaganda posters to see how he moved from a series of images to a more fully developed research topic. When asked to choose a topic for a research paper, student Tommy Tsai found he was interested in propaganda posters from World War II. Looking at a selection of images (see Figures 4.3 through 4.5), Tommy started by asking some questions, such as the ones that follow:

- Who is depicted in these posters? Are these depictions positive or negative?
- What is the purpose of each poster?
- What strategies are these posters using to persuade their audiences?
- How do these posters reveal cultural prejudices?

AT A GLANCE

Screening Questions for Topics

1. ***Am I interested in the topic?*** We write best about ideas, events, and issues that touch us somehow—through curiosity, passion, or intellectual interest.
2. ***Can I argue a position on this topic?*** At this stage, you may not have developed a stand on the issue, but you should see promise for advancing a new perspective on the topic.
3. ***Will I be able to find enough research material on this topic?*** Brainstorm some possible sources you might use to write this paper.
4. ***Does this sort of research appeal to me?*** Since you will be working with this topic for an extended period of time, it is best to have a genuine interest in it and in the type of research that it will require (archival work or fieldwork).

FIGURE 4.3. This Uncle Sam poster from 1917 was reissued for World War II.

FIGURE 4.4. Anti-Nazi propaganda relied on religiously charged rhetoric.

FIGURE 4.5. American war efforts employed extreme visual messages to galvanize support.

Through the process of asking such questions, Tommy was able to identify his preliminary topic as "the rhetoric of World War II propaganda." He wrote in one research log entry that he wanted to analyze these posters in their historical contexts: "In particular, I plan to focus on the propaganda posters that appeared in the three most active countries in that time period: the United States, Germany, and Japan. My research paper will report my findings from the comparison of the different rhetorical strategies employed by the three nations." By generating a set of preliminary research questions, he was able to focus more clearly on the dialogue between those posters and his interest in them. In this way, he was able to turn an overly broad initial topic into one that was more specific and workable.

Student Writing

See Tommy Tsai's research proposal and completed research paper.
www.pearsonhighered.com/envision/78

As you consider your own possible research topics, keep this key principle in mind: successful topics need to interest you, inspire you, or even anger you. Even with assigned topics, you should be able to find some aspect of the assignment that speaks to you. In general, there needs to be a *connection* between you and your topic to motivate you to follow through and transform it into a successful argument.

In addition, while selecting your topic, you might consider the type of research you'll need to do to pursue it; in fact, you might select your topic based mostly on the sorts of research it allows you to do. For instance, a student writing on propaganda of the Prohibition era will work extensively with paper sources, which might involve archival work with original letters, posters, or government documents from that time period. A student writing on visual advertising for ethnic-theme dorms on campus will be more likely to complement paper sources with interviews with the university housing staff, student surveys, and first-person observations. A student writing on sexualized rhetoric in student campaign materials might take a poll, gather concrete examples, and research the newspaper's written coverage of past and present elections. Think broadly and creatively about what kinds of research you might use and what types of research (archival work versus fieldwork involving interviews and survey taking) appeals most to you. A final important consideration is whether you can actually get your hands on the source material you need to construct a persuasive argument.

AT A GLANCE

Looking for the "Perfect" Topic

1. ***Look inward.*** What issues, events, or ideas interest you? Are there any hot-button topics you find yourself drawn to again and again? What topic is compelling enough that you would watch a news program, television special, film, or relevant lecture on it?
2. ***Look outward.*** What are the central issues of student life on campus? Do you walk by a technology-enhanced classroom and see the students busy writing on laptops or using plasma screens? Topic: technology and education. Do you see a fraternity's poster about a "dry" party? Topic: alcohol on campus. Do you see workers outside the food service building on strike? Topic: labor relations at the college.
3. ***Use creative visualization.*** Imagine that you are chatting casually with a friend when you overhear someone talking. Suddenly, you feel so interested—or so angry—that you go over and participate in the conversation. What would move you so strongly?
4. ***Use the materials of the moment.*** Perhaps the *topos* might be closer to the classical Greek model; although not a roll of papyrus, your class reading list or a single issue of a newspaper can house many topics. Scan the front page and opinion section of your school or community newspaper to see what issues people are talking about. Look at the pictures as well. What is gripping the community at large?

Bringing Your Topic into Focus

Once you have settled on a topic and generated some research questions, the next step in the research project involves exploring your knowledge—and the limitations of your knowledge—about it. A productive way to do this is through **prewriting**. Defined literally, prewriting is writing that precedes the official drafting of the paper, but, practically speaking, it can take many forms. Lists, scribbled notes, informal outlines, drawings—all different types of prewriting serve the same goal: to help you focus and narrow your topic.

Brainstorming Topics Visually

The practice of **graphic brainstorming** provides writers with a great way to develop topics. This technique transforms traditional **brainstorming**—jotting down a series of related words and phrases on a topic—into a more visible process. Also called *webbing*, *clustering*, or *mapping*, the goal of *graphic brainstorming* is to help you develop your topic by exploring relationships among ideas. You can brainstorm by hand or on a computer; in either mode, begin by writing a topic in a circle (or square or rectangle, if you prefer). Figure 4.6 shows the first step you might take in brainstorming for a paper generated from various World War I posters.

FIGURE 4.6.

Next, brainstorm ideas and questions about that topic, and then arrange them in groups around your main circle to indicate the relationships among them. As you answer each question and pose more developed ones in response, you begin to bring your topic into focus. You'll notice that Figure 4.7 shows how we might start to do this by writing questions that differentiate between various posters and by grouping them by gender issues. In addition, in our brainstorm, we use various types of notations—including words, phrases, and questions—and insert lines and arrows to indicate the relationship between the concepts. We even use images and color to further emphasize these associations. These techniques help us develop the argument and eventually can lead to a more narrowed topic and perhaps even a preliminary thesis.

As we continue to brainstorm—whether for an hour or over several sessions—it becomes clear why some people call this technique **webbing**. As Figure 4.8 (See next page) shows, our graphic turns into a web of ideas. By using this technique, we have done more than simply develop our topic: we have made it visually apparent that our topic is too broad for a standard research paper assignment. Our web now offers enough ideas for an entire book on the subject. But our diagram also provides us with clues about the direction in which to take our project. We can pick a *subsection* of ideas to focus on in our writing. When you try this technique, pick the subsection that interests *you* most.

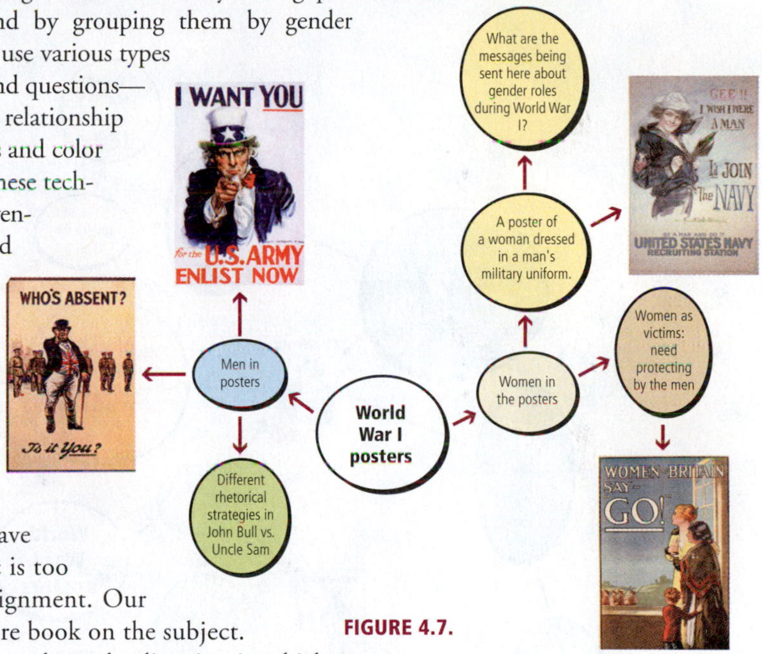

FIGURE 4.7.

Narrowing Your Topic

Let's zoom in on one part of our diagram—the part, color-coded yellow, that asks key questions about representations of women in military posters. Working with this part of the web, we could write a focused paper that examines the implications of the way women are depicted in these texts. We could write about how cross-dressing is used as a deliberate appeal to the audience, or about how military posters evoke the image of wife and mother to mobilize troops. However, to effectively narrow our topic, we should continue to sharpen our questions about these images, such as the one shown in Figure 4.9 (See p. 81).

1. **Write down your topic.**

   Topic formulation: gender roles in World War I.

2. **Work with that topic by asking a pointed question based on close analysis of the text at hand.**

   First question: Is there a sexual undertone to the posters?

3. **Refine the topic by answering that question.**

   Topic narrowing: Yes, in one of the posters, the woman is standing in a provocative pose, looking at the audience in a sexual manner, but in another, the women seem more identified with family (mother, daughter) than with sexuality.

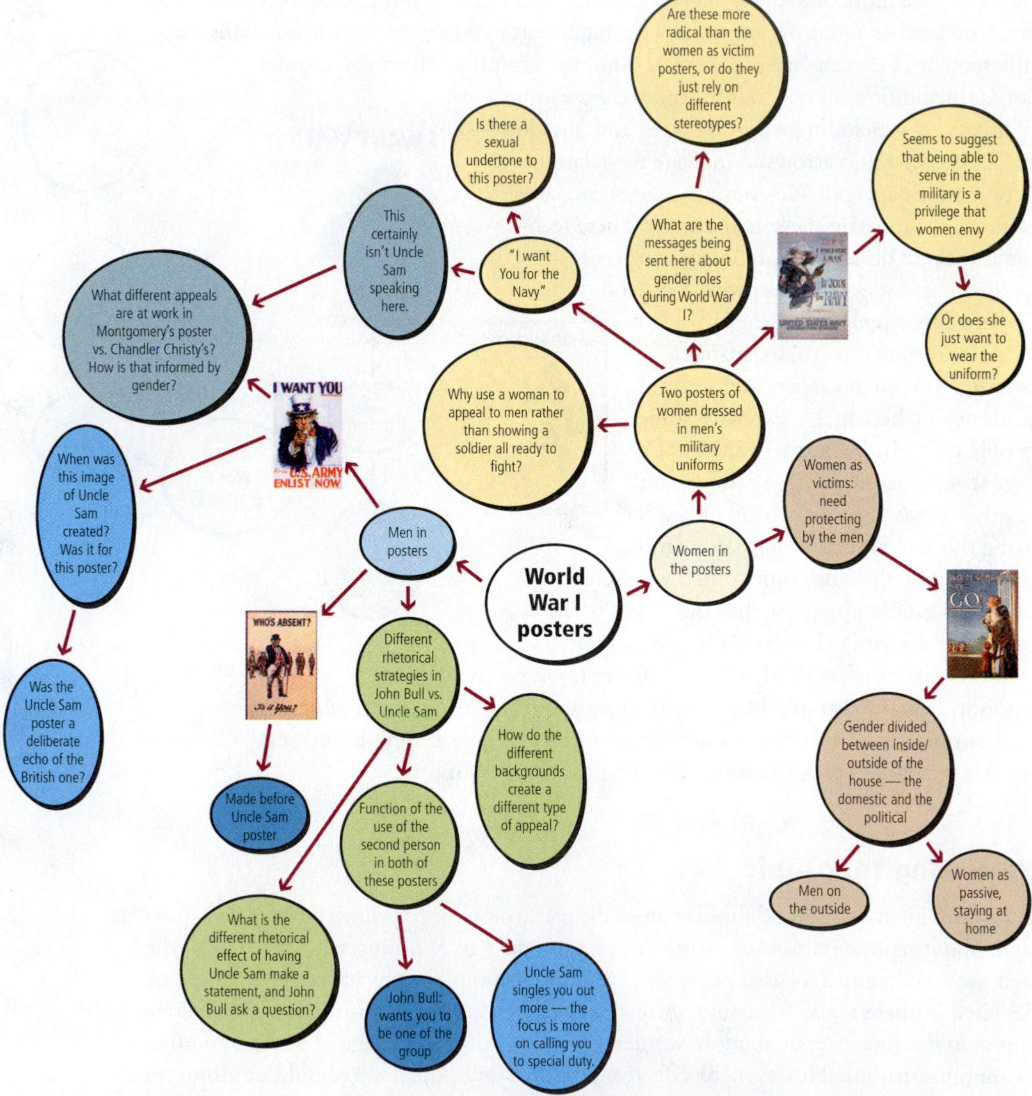

FIGURE 4.8.

4. **Revise the narrowed topic to be more specific.**

   Revised topic formulation: the different constructions of femininity in World War I propaganda posters.

5. **Identify significant aspects of that topic to explore.**

   Second question: How so? In what way? What is the significance?

6. **Use the answers to these questions to focus the topic.**

   Final topic focus: the use of the Madonna-whore stereotype as a persuasive strategy in World War I recruitment posters.

FIGURE 4.9. This 1917 U.S. poster uses a woman in uniform to present its message to enlist.

In working with the webbing process and then asking key questions in this way, we have just completed one of the most important steps in developing a viable research topic: **narrowing** a large subject to a more manageable one. By asking such questions—and we could come up with many others along different lines of inquiry (such as race, sexuality, international representations, and nationalism)—we begin to develop a *focused* topic that will offer us the opportunity for close analysis, rigorous research, and a sharp argumentative stance. That is, we can move from a topic loosely concerned with gender roles in World War I, to one that focuses specifically on a subset of recruitment posters and how they deploy a particular sexist stereotype (the Madonna-whore trope) as a persuasive strategy. With this focused and narrowed topic, we'll be able to contribute a new opinion about war posters and add to the ongoing dialogue that we find in our secondary sources.

CREATIVE PRACTICE

Try out this practice of *narrowing a topic* with a selection of early twenty-first-century posters that protest the U.S. war with Iraq. Examine the posters shown in Figures 4.10 through 4.13, and then complete a *visual brainstorm*

FIGURE 4.10. This recent anti-war poster uses strong language to catch the reader's attention.

FIGURE 4.11. This striking poster implies a connection between the war with Iraq and the oil trade.

(*continued*)

FIGURE 4.12. This poster solidifies the visual argument through a caption.

FIGURE 4.13. Originally composed to protest the Vietnam war, this poster recently re-emerged in reference to the Iraq war.

Student Writing

For a compelling research paper on contemporary recruiting ads, see Maria Mizell's research essay.
www.pearsonhighered.com/envision/82

to develop a feasible topic for your essay. Be sure that you narrow your topic from "anti-war propaganda posters" to a more focused one that you might pursue in a research paper. You might decide during your graphic brainstorm to focus your topic by identifying which images you'd like to write about or by generating key questions to ask about particular texts: What is the significance of the style that is used in the posters? How do the words and images work together in these posters? How do they work against each other? What is the significance of showing people who have been wounded? How does symbolism operate in these posters? The more specific the questions you ask, the more focused your topic will be.

Planning Your Research Through Writing

In completing the "Creative Practice" you most likely constructed a set of web diagrams that, like those in Figures 4.7 and 4.8, alternated between asking and answering questions. This process will narrow your focus and provide you with a direction for your research inquiry. But did you find yourself concerned that you don't have the knowledge necessary to write this essay? Are you worried that the gaps in your own knowledge will prevent you from answering those questions in a satisfactory way? If so, then you are in good company. All researchers and scholars fear the limitations of their knowledge. The key is to use that lack of knowledge as a motivation to develop a **concrete plan** for your research. We'll discuss three ways of planning your research: freewriting about your topic, developing a research hypothesis, and drafting a formal research proposal.

Freewriting About Your Research Topic

One way to start planning your research process is to freewrite about your ideas in your research log. Testing out your research plan in this way will move you from the work you did in narrowing your topic to the work you need to do in gathering sources and developing a research outline. This method also will provide an informal structure for your research, giving it shape and sharper focus as you move deeper into the research process.

In completing your freewrite, you may find it helpful to follow a **three-paragraph model**: in the *first paragraph*, announce your topic and state a preliminary thesis so that you can begin the project with a critical and focused perspective; in the *second paragraph*, identify the sources you plan to use to investigate this topic; in the *third paragraph*, speculate on obstacles or problems you might encounter in your research and how you might avoid or solve these problems. Let's look at a freewrite from student Bries Deerrose, who shaped his research inquiry around questions concerning a piece of contemporary propaganda: a leaflet dropped in Afghanistan by the U.S. military in the 2002–2003 campaign there.

Student Writing
See examples of research freewrites.
www.pearsonhighered.com/envision/83

AT A GLANCE

The Research Freewrite

- Write your ideas in full sentences.
- Use a three-paragraph model to focus your answers:
  - Paragraph 1: Announce the topic and state your hypothesis.
  - Paragraph 2: Identify key sources.
  - Paragraph 3: Anticipate problems.

Research Freewrite

Over the past decade, as America's image fell increasingly under the scrutiny of our allies and enemies alike, President George W. Bush established the Office of Global Communications, the stated purpose of which was "to advise . . . on utilization of the most effective means for the United States Government to ensure consistency in messages that will promote the interests of the United States abroad, prevent misunderstanding, build support for and among coalition partners of the United States, and inform international audiences." In this paper, I will examine how this office fulfilled its mission, especially through visual rhetoric. I will examine how the world, especially the Middle East, responded to such propaganda, and I will examine what image the office portrayed, whether this was an accurate image of America or an example of political rhetoric. Finally, I will discuss whether such marketing was beneficial or detrimental, from both a foreign and American perspective. *Hypothesis:* America has been actively projecting an image of itself using various forms of visual rhetoric; this image responds to the *kairos* of negative scrutiny abroad and uses rhetorieal tactics to try to bring about meaningful, peaceful dialogue between America and the world.

This first paragraph introduces the research topic and describes what Bries thinks the main focus of his paper might be. At the end of the paragraph, he includes a tentative thesis to help him focus his interest and argument as he begins researching this topic.

In the second paragraph, Bries discusses the sources he intends to use. Notice the broad range of possibilities he considers: flyers, television commercials, radio broadcasts, and both American and international sources.

To research this topic, I hope to examine firsthand government-generated materials: flyers, commercials, radio broadcasts, publications, etc. I will also attempt to find any commentaries on this effort as well as on domestic conceptions of what America is and what its image should be. I will compare this with foreign opinions regarding America's image and reactions to the American marketing techniques. To do this, I will need to find foreign commentaries, including visual rhetoric responding to our own visual rhetoric. I will need secondhand sources concerning foreign opinions.

In the third paragraph, Bries anticipates the difficulties he might face and how he can solve them.

The most difficult part of this assignment will be determining foreign opinion, since I am not fluent in other languages. I will also need to form my own opinion about the effectiveness, morality, and accuracy of these rhetorical tactics. Such issues are always sticky, and will require much thought and a wide array of perspectives.

Bries concludes with a concrete example of the visual rhetoric he will use in his research paper, a leaflet dropped in Afghanistan by the United States in the 2002–2003 campaign.

Office of Global Communications leaflet air-dropped in Afghanistan. http://www.psywarrior.com/afghanleaf08.html.

Drafting the Research Hypothesis

Student Writing

For a compelling historical analysis of posters, take a look at Cassandra Atira Richards' project on Vietnam-era propaganda posters and the art projects produced as counter-propaganda against the war.
www.pearsonhighered.com/envision/84

In reading Bries's freewrite, you might have noticed that as he developed his topic, he was simultaneously trying his hand at formulating his argument. For instance, in Bries's first paragraph, he moves from the open-ended language of a proposal ("I will examine," "I will discuss") to a restatement of his subject in terms of a tentative thesis statement at the end of the paragraph. Many times as you draft your research plan, you will find that you enter into your project relying on broad questions ("What do the leaflets that Americans dropped on Afghanistan in 2003 say about our country and our international policy?") or on statements of intention (i.e., "I hope to examine. . ."). However, as we see in the example from Bries, it is also useful to use your research as an opportunity to try freewriting to define your rhetorical stance in relation to that topic.

So how do you make a claim about a topic that you have not yet researched completely? This is a key question, and it is often a frustrating one for many writers.

Realize, however, that you've already taken the first step just by asking pointed questions about your topic. From these questions, you can develop a **hypothesis**, or a working thesis that makes an argumentative claim that you'll attempt to prove. It is crucial for you to try to formulate a tentative *hypothesis* for your research as a way of looking at your project with an analytical eye. Of course, you may revise your hypothesis—and maybe your entire approach to the subject—several times over the course of your research. Indeed, most writers do modify their thesis statements, and this revision process is a natural part of what happens when you actually begin to read your sources and take notes about them in the research log. Nevertheless, trying to state your hypothesis is an important first step in focusing your argument and making the most out of the timeline available to you for research.

Student Writing

See Tommy Tsai's brainstorm about his hypothesis.
www.pearsonhighered.com/envision/85

One way to develop your detailed hypothesis is to rewrite one of your more narrowed questions from the research proposal as a polished declarative statement that you intend to prove. For example, if you, like Tommy Tsai, asked yourself, "How were representations of race used in World War II propaganda?" then you might turn that question into a potential thesis: "Representations of race deployed in World War II propaganda functioned as a way to justify the internment of innocent civilians." As you continue your research, you may come to disagree with that statement, but at least beginning with a tentative hypothesis gives you somewhere to start your research.

This is the process that Tommy himself followed for his paper about World War II propaganda posters. His initial hypothesis, shown below, provided a starting point that allowed him to engage with his texts through the lens of his own argumentative claim. As he continued drafting, his hypothesis narrowed, shifting from a general focus on race in World War II propaganda posters to a compelling criticism of America's use of race in its portrayal of its German and Japanese enemies. Tommy's process underscores that a hypothesis is only the beginning of making a strong, focused research argument.

Seeing Connections

To see how one writer's stance on her topic continued to evolve during her research, see Zoe Flower's "Getting the Girl" on page 329.

Working Hypothesis

I conjecture that German propaganda made use of the *ethos* appeal of its fascist leader Adolf Hitler; that Japanese propaganda utilized the *logos* appeal by continually portraying images of a victorious Japanese army; and that American propaganda for the most part employed the *pathos* appeal by evoking nationalistic feelings and associating war with glory and patriotism (see Figure 1). These conjectures inform my argument that the government of each nation is able to bring its political messages across effectively by employing the appropriate rhetorical appeal in its propaganda posters.

Figure 1. Uncle Sam poster.

Drafting a Research Proposal

In many academic contexts, you will be asked to formalize your research plan through composing a full-length **research proposal**. This type of text is common in many disciplines and professions and is used by writers to develop agendas for research communities, secure funding for a study, publicize plans for inquiry and field research, and test the interest of potential audiences for a given project. In the writing classroom, the research proposal provides a similar formal structure for developing a project, but it also serves another purpose: it is a more structured means of organizing your thoughts to help you solidify your topic and move into the next stages of the research process. For these reasons, the *genre, organization,* and *content* of the research proposal differ in important ways from other kinds of popular and academic writing that you might do. In drafting out your proposal, include the following elements:

Student Writing

See many examples of research proposals on a variety of topics.
www.pearsonhighered.com/envision/86

AT A GLANCE

Key Functions of the Research Proposal

- It introduces the narrowed ***topic***.
- It presents the ***rhetorical stance*** or ***thesis*** that the writer will develop.
- It explains the ***significance*** of the research project.
- It lists possible ***sources*** for investigation.
- It outlines your research ***methods*** or planned approach to the research.
- It delineates a detailed ***timeline*** for investigating the topic.
- It often anticipates any ***difficulties*** that might arise in pursuing this topic.
- It often includes a brief ***biography*** of the researcher (usually a one-paragraph description of the writer's credentials, interests, and motivations).
- It includes, if appropriate, a carefully chosen and analyzed visual rhetoric text as a case study or concrete example of the topic.

- *Background:* What do I already know about my topic? What do I need to find out more about?
- *Methods:* How am I going to research this topic? What research questions are driving my inquiry?
- *Sources:* What specific texts will I analyze? What additional scholarly or popular sources can I reseach to help build my knowledge and my argument?
- *Timeline:* What are my goals for the different stages of research, and how can I schedule my work to most effectively meet these milestones?
- *Significance:* What do I hope to accomplish in my research? What are the broader issues or implications of my research? Why do these matter to me and to my readers?

As this list suggests, your proposal should explain your interest in your chosen subject and establish a set of questions to guide your inquiry. The proposal should delineate the timeline for your research and writing process—a crucial time management strategy.

You should also incorporate an appropriate visual text—a sample propaganda poster to be analyzed or an editorial cartoon that introduces the issue—into your proposal to show readers an example of the materials about which you'll be conducting your research.

Your proposal serves to clarify your research intentions, but it should also *persuade* an audience of the feasibility and significance of your project. In fact, perhaps the most important step in launching your research inquiry is to address the issue of your project's significance or, as some writing instructors call it, the "So What?" part of the project. It is the "So What?"—an awareness of the *significance* of the topic you're addressing and the questions you're asking—that moves the proposal from being a routine academic exercise to a powerful piece of persuasive writing.

When addressing the "So What?" question, consider why anyone else would care enough to read a paper on your topic. Ask yourself:

- What is at stake in your topic?
- Why does it matter?
- What contribution will your project make to a wider community?

Student Writing

Examine Anastasia Nevin's research proposal on the historical mystery of the Romanov assassination, a study of archival photographs and artifacts.

www.pearsonhighered.com/envision/87

Let's look at an example: a research proposal Susan Zhang developed on digital manipulation.

Susan Zhang

Little Photoshop of Horrors?: Digital Manipulation of Media Images

When O. J. Simpson was arrested in the summer of 1994, Newsweek and Time magazines featured his mugshot on their covers. But while Newsweek's photo was unaltered, Time had darkened the color of his skin and reduced the size of his prisoner ID number. To anyone who saw the two magazines on the news rack, the difference was obvious. To some it was even unethical: minority groups protested that the digital manipulation made O. J. look darker and more menacing, thereby presuming his guilt. The Time illustrator who altered the image later claimed that he only "wanted to make it more artful, more compelling." The impartiality of the photography was widely contested.

Susan begins with a specific example to hook the audience and to set up the context for her proposal.

You can't always believe what you read in the news, but a photograph doesn't lie, right? Because the photographer and the camera are perceived to be mere vehicles for converting reality into image, people are more apt to trust a photo, believing it to be the product of a machine rather than a human, and consequently free of bias. But with the advent of digital imaging, that credibility has been compromised. Image-editing programs such as Photoshop make it possible to perform cosmetic touch-ups, graft parts of pictures onto others, even construct a picture entirely from scratch. In many ways, digital imaging has redefined the field of photography. With words like "composograph" and "photoillustration" being coined to describe altered images indistinguishable from the real

In the proposal she turned in for class, Susan also embedded images from the *Newsweek* and *Time* covers in her introduction as visual evidence for her claims. She uses questions to identify common assumptions that her audience might hold about her topic.

She then clearly states her research goals. She suggests some key research questions and then ends with a declarative sentence that underscores her intentions as a researcher. Notice how she mentions the significance—or importance—of the project early on in the proposal.

thing, people have grown wary of deeming the photograph a purveyor of truth.

For my research project, I want to explore how the capacity of image manipulation has affected the way we perceive photos in the news and media. Has it led to a permanent loss of faith? Or, on the flip side, to the establishment of stricter standards for allowable alterations? By examining past incidences of digital manipulation and current guidelines for photographs in the media, and the contexts in which they apply, I hope to gain a better understanding of the credibility of news and media imagery in the digital age.

Susan uses her research questions to structure her "Methods" section: the historical perspective, the audience's perspective, and the photographer's perspective. She carefully thinks through each line of inquiry.

Methods

First, I want to approach my topic through its historical context. I will start with the pre-digital era and look at whether photo manipulation existed then. Surely there were tricked, staged, and doctored photos also? To what extent were photos altered using darkroom techniques? What kind of ethical considerations governed the editing of media images then? By comparing past precedents with the types of digital manipulations commonly used today, I can determine whether digital imaging really has made photo manipulation a bigger and more prevalent problem.

Next, I will look at digital manipulation from the public's point of view. In the past when a digital image was altered, how did the public respond? For example, if a photograph is altered in an obvious or humorous manner, it could be perceived as satire or social commentary, but if it is altered subtly and the change not announced, it could be perceived as deception. How easily can people recognize an altered photo? And when a magazine or newspaper is exposed for digitally manipulating a photo, does this automatically discredit it in the public eye?

I will also consider the photographer's point of view. Do photographers consider photo manipulation a recent development stemming from digital imaging? What are the moral and ethical justifications for manipulated photographs? What kinds of standards exist in the field of photojournalism and media photography? How do these standards regulate the integrity of digital photojournalism?

Sources

To begin my research, I will look at books on the ethics of photojournalism. So far I have checked out Paul Lester's *Photojournalism: An Ethical Approach* and Julianne Newton's *The Burden of Visual Truth: The Role of Photojournalism in Mediating Reality.* These books will help me understand the history of ethical photojournalism, the ways in which a photograph conveys a message, and the public's response to photographs.

Then, moving toward the digital side of media images, I will turn to books such as Thomas Wheeler's *Phototruth or Photofiction?: Ethics and Media Imagery in the Digital Age* and Larry Gross's *Image Ethics in the Digital Age.* The first book examines specific examples of photo manipulation and later provides an ethical framework for considering image manipulation in photojournalism. The second book is a collection of articles on aspects of digital image ethics.

I will also search online databases such as EBSCO and LexisNexis for articles on digital manipulation and recent controversies over digital manipulation. Search terms I might use include "photo manipulation," "digital photojournalism," and "digital image ethics." Through these databases I hope to find authoritative opinions from photojournalists as well as public reactions to altered images in magazines and the news.

As a primary source, I will look at photojournalism Websites. I will visit large news and magazine sites and smaller photojournalism communities, browsing their photographs to see if they use digital manipulation, and if so, how it is addressed. Also, there are many web resources that explain the guidelines that have been development by photojournalists. For example, the National Press Photographers Association's Website features a digital code of ethics. These sites will clarify the guidelines of digital photojournalism and how closely they are being followed.

Timeline

1/20 Research proposal due

1/20–1/22 Search for articles on photojournalism and digital manipulation using online databases

Although this was written before she began serious research, Susan increased her proposal's persuasiveness (and her own *ethos* as a researcher) by including the titles of specific texts she located through a computer search of her library's holdings. She carefully groups her intended sources and also explains briefly why these types of sources would be useful for her research.

By including search terms and specific database names, Susan shows that she is ready to move to actual research.

Susan finishes her discussion of sources with attention to primary sources—the actual photographs themselves—that she intends to find to use in her paper.

In her timeline, Susan lists not only deadlines imposed by her instructor but also key steps in the research process: finding books, evaluating sources, taking notes, constructing a thesis, peer review, a second round of research, drafting, and revising.

With this detailed timeline, Susan shows her careful time management and builds her *ethos* by demonstrating her understanding of the research process; she even uses colored font for due dates to highlight their importance.

1/22–1/27 In-depth research using books

Primary research using photojournalism sites

1/27–1/31 Review notes and write a thesis

Talk with classmates and instructor for advice on my thesis

Evaluate which sources to use

2/1–2/5 Outline paper: decide on the major arguments, draft topic sentences, and choose support for each argument

2/5–2/12 Write first draft of paper

2/12 Research paper draft due

2/15–2/28 Obtain and reflect on feedback

Additional research and revision as necessary

3/3–3/6 Review second draft for polish, errors

3/6 Revision of research paper due

In her conclusion, Susan reasserts the importance of her project, broadening to address the "So What?" that she needs to answer as she enters into her research.

Significance

With advancements in technology, photography has moved from the darkroom to the computer lab, making it possible to alter photographs beyond what is considered ethical. The abuse of this technology has resulted in manipulated photos being passed off as real in the media, and a resulting public skepticism over the reliability of all media images. A closer look at the occurrences of digital manipulation today, as regulated by the evolving guidelines of photojournalism, could reveal to what extent such skepticism is warranted.

The Writer's Process

Seeing Connections
For an example of a modern poster that might likewise provide the basis for a researched argument, see the 2004 Get Real Campaign poster on page 391.

Now that you've learned about the process of generating research questions, narrowing your topic, developing a hypothesis, and then writing up your plans for research in a structured freewrite or a formal proposal, what can you argue about the first propaganda poster of this chapter (Figure 4.1)?

In answering this prompt, you might start to work through the writing projects related to the research process. You might develop a research focus that begins with questions and ends with a "So What?" statement of significance. You might try to incorporate visual images into a proposal that will conclude with a clear statement of your future authority on this topic as a researcher. Try the strategies for keeping track of your ideas and work in progress in a research log, a key tool that you'll be using in the next chapter as we turn to gathering and evaluating sources for your topic. It's time to get started on the research process for writing a persuasive argument about an issue that matters to you.

PREWRITING CHECKLIST

Focus on Analyzing Propaganda Posters

- ❑ What is the underlying message of this poster?
- ❑ What are the specifics of the rhetorical situation informing this piece of propaganda? Who produced the poster? Who was its intended audience?
- ❑ What is the historical context for this poster? What country was it produced in, and what was the social and political situation of the time? How does an understanding of its context affect our understanding of its message?
- ❑ What type of rhetorical appeal does the poster feature? Does it rely primarily on *logos, pathos,* or *ethos* to make its point? How does attention to this appeal manifest itself visually in the poster?
- ❑ Recalling the discussion of exaggerated use of appeals from Chapter 2, does the poster rely on any logical fallacies? any exaggerated use of *pathos*? If so, how do these work to persuade the audience?
- ❑ What is the relationship between word and image in the poster? How do design elements such as color, font, layout, and image selection (photograph or illustration) work as persuasive elements in this text?
- ❑ Does the poster use stereotypes to convey its message? How do stereotypes figure as rhetorical devices in this situation? How does the stereotype place the poster in the context of a larger cultural discussion?
- ❑ What research questions can you develop about this poster?
- ❑ What kinds of sources might you look at to understand better what's going on with this propaganda poster?

PREWRITING WITH THE *ENVISION* WEBSITE

One way to begin approaching your research project is to explore the poster collections available through the *Envision* Website. Come up with a list of three research questions that you might explore based on two to four of the posters. Share your list with classmates and discuss the differences in your questions. Based on your discussions, create three or four concrete research topics that you might want to pursue. Then, you can apply this process to the visual rhetoric of your choice. While you are online, check out the many student models of research available as proposals, plans, and research logs.
www.pearsonhighered.com/envision/91

WRITING PROJECTS

1. **Research Freewrite:** Freewrite about your research ideas by first writing out answers to the questions provided in the "Prewriting Checklist" and then developing them into a three-paragraph *freewrite*. In the first paragraph, introduce your research paper topic and describe what you think the main focus of the paper might be. Include a tentative thesis in this paragraph. In the second paragraph, discuss the sources that you intend to use. In the third paragraph, speculate on what obstacles you foresee in this project and/or what you anticipate to be the most difficult part of the

assignment. If appropriate, use an image to complement your written text. Show your answers to your instructor or your peers for feedback.

2. **Research Proposal:** Write a detailed research *proposal* that discusses your topic, planned method, and purpose in depth. Be sure to cover your topic, your hypothesis, your potential sources and problems, your method, timeline, and, most importantly, the significance of the proposed project. For more specific instruction consult the Writing Guidelines on the *Envision* Website. When you are done with the writing, present your proposal at a roundtable of research with other members of your class. Answer questions from your classmates to help you fine-tune your topic and troubleshoot your future research.
   www.pearsonhighed.com/envision/92a

3. **Peer Review:** Collaboratively peer review your research proposals. Assume that you are on the review board granting approval and funding to the best two proposals of each group. Complete research proposal review letters for each member of your group. When you are done, discuss your letters and what changes you can recommend. Then revise your proposals to make them stronger, better written, and more persuasive. For more specific instructions and for peer review forms for the research proposal, consult the *Envision* Website.
   www.pearsonhighed.com/envision/92b

Visit www.pearsonhighered.com/envision for expanded assignment guidelines and student projects.
Visit www.mycomplab.com for additional general writing and research resources.

CHAPTER 5

Finding and Evaluating Research Sources

Chapter Preview Questions

- What is the best way to locate research sources?
- What is the difference between a primary and a secondary source?
- How do I critically evaluate both print and electronic sources?
- How do I pursue field research for my project?
- What is an annotated bibliography, and how can it help me?
- How should I take notes while researching?

As you move from planning to conducting research, you'll need to investigate resources and evaluate them for your project. You can use your analytical skills to make important distinctions when locating, evaluating, and using sources for your research project. Look, for instance, at the covers in Figures 5.1 and 5.2. Although they focus on the same topic—climate change—the visual rhetoric suggests that the content of each journal will be quite different. The audience for *Time* magazine differs from that of *Science*, and, consequently, the writing styles within the articles will be different as well. The cover of each magazine previews the distinct content inside. Studying the covers can help you look back in history to understand how climate change has been understood in the past. In this way, you are finding and evaluating research sources for your project.

Specifically, the cover of *Time* in Figure 5.1 conveys how the editors chose to represent global warming to their audience in 2006. Ask yourself: What is the argument conveyed by the visual rhetoric of the cover? What is the significance of the choice to use a polar bear as the main character in their image? How is color used strategically? How does the "spotlighting" of the polar bear and

FIGURE 5.1. Cover of *Time*, April 3, 2006.

FIGURE 5.2. Cover of *Science*, March 24, 2006.

the positioning of the image in relation to the words contribute to the rhetorical effect? What kind of stance toward the dangers of global warming does the cover suggest?

In contrast, the *Science* cover (see Figure 5.2) features a photograph of an ice-covered lake. The photo appears to have been taken with a "fish-eye" lens, bringing several ice fragments into prominence in the foreground. How do such different rhetorical strategies appeal to the journal's very scientifically informed audience?

Clearly, the editors deliberately located, evaluated, and used materials for the covers that would reflect their magazine's contents. As a researcher, you can use your skills in rhetorical analysis to help you evaluate sources for your own research project, looking to the different elements of a text—from the cover design, to the table of contents, to the index—to better understand the text's perspective on your topic and its usefulness for your project.

CREATIVE PRACTICE

Working in small groups, compare Figures 5.1 and 5.2 with the cover of the August 26, 2002, issue of *Time* (see Figure 5.3). What contrasts emerge in the use of visual and verbal rhetoric? What stance does the cover suggest that *Time* will take on the topic? How is that stance represented in the cover design? What do these differences suggest to you in terms of how the *conversation* around global warming has changed over the years?

FIGURE 5.3. Cover of *Time*, August 26, 2002.

Now go to the *Envision* Website to find other *Time* covers that have addressed the issue of climate change. What different approaches do these covers take to this issue? How does context seem to inform this approach? Look in the table of contents for each issue; do the article titles seem to support the position suggested by the covers? Finally, as a group, develop your own stance on this issue. Together, sketch a design for a new cover for an upcoming issue of *Science, The Economist*, or *Time*. Use the cover to suggest an argument for a specific perspective on global warming and to provide a visual preview for the contents inside. Share your design and argument with the class.

www.pearsonhighered.com/envision/94

Your task as a researcher is quite similar to that of the editors of *Time* and *Science*. As you begin gathering and evaluating sources for your own research argument, keep in mind that you will need to shape the argument into a paper addressed to a particular audience: your writing class, a group of scientists, a lobbying organization, an advertising firm, or browsers on the Web. To take part in any of these conversations, a researcher needs to learn

- what is being talked about (the *topic*),
- how it is being discussed (the *conversation*), and
- what the different positions are (*research context*).

Visualizing Research

To grasp the specifics of the topic, the conversation, and the research context, it is helpful to take a moment to visualize the research process. When you think of the act of research, what comes to mind? Surfing the Web? Looking through a library? Interviewing experts in the field? All these images represent different research scenarios. The material you gather in each situation will compose the foundation for your research; it will inform your essay, but not all of it will find its way into your final paper. Nevertheless, you need to research widely and thoroughly to be fully informed about your topic and write a compelling research-based argument. One helpful way of visualizing the relationship between the *process* and the *product* of research is through the metaphor of the **iceberg of research** (see Figure 5.4). In essence, your topic or final paper will be only one small part of your research; beneath the surface lie the many different sources you will explore: books, journal articles, Websites, field surveys, historical materials, interviews, multimedia and more. All these constitute the research material. Your task as a researcher is to move beyond a surface knowledge of your topic; you need to gather, assess, keep, throw out, and ultimately use a variety of sources. By exploring such a wide range of material, you will encounter a rich array of scholarly and popular perspectives on your topic. In many ways, your research argument will be, in fact, a discussion with those research sources themselves. You add your voice to theirs. But your final paper may appear as only the "tip of the iceberg" or a result of your careful study of the work of others.

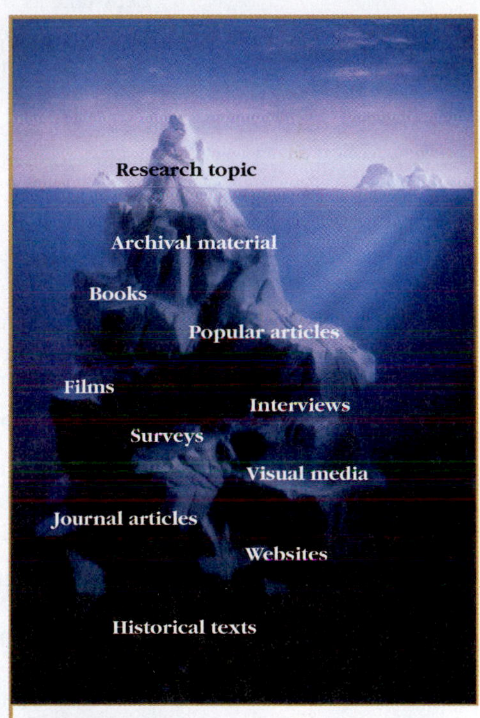

FIGURE 5.4. The iceberg of research.

Sometimes, this process of building on others can be intimidating; we fear that we will have nothing new to add to the conversation. Yet if we think of research sources as texts written by people who were once, like us, struggling to figure out what we are trying to say, then we can see the process of gathering and assessing sources as a very social one, a process in which you *respect* and *acknowledge* the ideas of others and then seek to add your own voice to an ongoing conversation. One way to begin that conversation is to discover what others before you have said, thought, written, and published—and to keep track of that process in your research log, as explained in Chapter 4.

Seeing Connections
For strategies for constructing an effective research log, see page 76.

In this chapter, we'll use the metaphor of the *conversation* to accentuate the point that the research process is an act of *composing a response to an ongoing dialogue about a topic.* By gathering, synthesizing, and sorting the perspectives of others, you begin to shape your own stance on a research topic. By adding your voice as a writer, you are responding to others. Research is a *relationship* that you develop with the source material and the writers you encounter along the way.

Developing Search Terms

The first step in the research process lies in locating relevant and interesting sources to draw into your conversation. This involves finding the best **search terms** to use in looking for sources on your topic. Your search terms will change depending on whether you are searching the Web, an academic database, or a library catalog. You will need to identify the most productive keywords for searching in each of these situations.

Let's take as our example a project about Internet advertising. In a preliminary Web search, specific terms such as "pop-up ads," "Facebook ads," and "ethics & advertising online" probably yield more results than generic terms like "Internet advertising" and "Internet advertisements." If you search a database such as Lexis-Nexis (a resource for news articles as well as legal, medical, and business articles), your keywords might be closer to your preliminary topic. Using the term "Internet advertising" in a database search would provide you with more than 90 citations in popular magazines and journals, while "pop-up ads" might yield fewer than 20 hits—the opposite of your results with a basic Internet search. Finally, you would likely find that a successful search of your library catalog requires still *different terms*—typically more academic terminology, such as "electronic commerce," "social media marketing," or "Internet marketing,"because those phrases appear in scholarly book titles.

Narrowing Your Search

In many initial searches, the list of potential sources returned to you will be much larger than you can efficiently process. Your main task, then, will be to find ways to narrow your search. Experimenting with a range of terms—particularly more limited

AT A GLANCE

Tips for Using Search Terms

- ***Web:*** Use popular or colloquial terminology in your Internet searches because search engines pick up actual terms from pages as they crawl across the Web.
- ***Library:*** The Library of Congress has created a set of terms, called Library of Congress Subject Headings (LCSHs) used by librarians to catalog information. These headings may not always be obvious to you. (For example, the Library of Congress calls the Vietnam War the "Vietnamese Conflict, 1961–1975." A search under "Vietnam War" will produce no results.) You can find the LCSH terms in two ways: by looking at a library record online, or by consulting the print index. By plugging the terms into your library catalog, you can access information for your project more efficiently.
- ***Databases:*** Since databases can house a wide range of materials, from academic publications to popular articles, you will have to customize your language based on the database you have selected. Match your search terms in diction and formality to suit the type of resource you are exploring.

ones—can help you with this task by finding materials specific to your topic. For instance, you might use the narrower term "Internet advertising & law" to eliminate irrelevant sources and focus on the legal aspect of the issue, if that interests you. Through such experimentation you will find the search term that yields the most productive results.

Primary and Secondary Sources

Your initial searches will yield a range of sources—from magazine articles to books, video recordings, and perhaps even manuscripts or a photograph collection. Each of these sources can play a vital role in your research. Scholars divide research into primary and secondary research, and sources, likewise, into **primary sources** (original texts you analyze in your research paper) and **secondary sources** (sources that provide commentary on your primary material or on your topic in general).

Consider, for instance, Tommy Tsai's project, examined in detail in Chapter 4. Propaganda posters were Tommy's *primary sources,* and the articles, books, and transcribed interviews providing analysis of those posters were his *secondary sources.* His paper is now *another* secondary source, one that contributes to an ongoing intellectual discussion about the meaning and power of the posters.

But as you search for your research materials, keep in mind that no sources are *inherently* primary or secondary; those terms refer to *how you use them* in your paper. For instance, if you were working with the topic of Internet advertising, you might use actual Facebook ads and Flash animations as your primary sources, as well as press releases and advertising Websites. For secondary sources you might turn to articles that discuss innovations in social media marketing, a Website on the history of digital advertising, and perhaps even a book by a famous economist about the impact of technology on corporate marketing strategies. However, imagine that you shift your topic slightly, making your new focus the economist's theories about the corruption of traditional advertising by multimedia technology. Now, that same book you looked at before as a *secondary* source becomes a *primary* source for this new topic.

As you can see, your inquiry will determine which sources will be primary and which will be secondary for your argument. In most cases, you will need to use a combination of primary and secondary materials to make a persuasive argument. The primary sources allow you to perform your own analysis, whereas the secondary sources offer you critical viewpoints that you need to take into account in your analysis and integrate into your argument to build up your *ethos.* How you respond to and combine your primary and secondary sources is a matter of choice, careful design, and rhetorical strategy.

AT A GLANCE

Primary and Secondary Sources

- ***Primary sources:*** materials that you will analyze for your paper, including speech scripts, advertisements, photographs, historical documents, film, artwork, audio files, and writing on Websites. Primary sources can also include testimonies by people with firsthand knowledge or direct quotations you will analyze. Whatever is under the lens of your analysis constitutes a *primary source.*
- ***Secondary sources:*** the additional materials that help you analyze your primary sources by providing a perspective on those primary materials; these include scholarly articles, popular commentaries, background materials (in print, video, or interview format), and survey data reinforcing your analysis. Whatever sources you can use as a lens to look at or understand the subject of your analysis constitutes a *secondary source.*

Seeing Connections
To see how one author integrates primary sources (quotations from personal interviews) with secondary materials (references to academic articles on social media), see danah boyd's "Social Network Site Taste Test" on page 293.

Seeing Connections
For an example of an argument was developed principally from research with primary sources (photographs and interviews), see Kate Murphy's "First Camera, Then Fork" (page 222).

Finding Primary Sources

Searching for **primary sources**—original texts you analyze in your research paper—can be challenging, but they can be found in many places: in your library (whether in the general stacks, archives, or multimedia collections); at community centers such as library exhibits, museums, and city hall; or even in online digital archives such as the one maintained by the Library of Congress. These materials can be some of the most exciting sources to work with in your research process and might include:

- Original documents (a handwritten letter by Mahatma Gandhi or Charles Lindbergh's journals)
- Rare books and manuscripts (Roger Manvell's manuscripts on the history of the Third Reich)
- Portfolios of photographs (photos of Japanese-American internment camps or of Black Panther demonstrations from the 1960s)
- Government documents (U.S. censuses and surveys, reports from the Department of Agriculture, or congressional papers)
- Other one-of-a-kind texts (AIDS prevention posters from South Africa, a noted artist's sketchbook, or a series of leaflets produced by the U.S. Psychological Warfare Department)

Student Writing
See James Caputo's annotated bibliography for his research project.
www.pearsonhighered.com/envision/98

In many cases, you can work directly with these materials so you can perform your own firsthand analysis of that piece of cultural history.

Consider the sources that student James Caputo used in his project on media representations of the early years of the NASA space program. James had many fascinating primary resources to work with: John F. Kennedy's inspirational speeches about the formation of the space program; front pages of both American and Russian newspapers detailing the successful completion of the first Apollo mission; publicity shots of the astronauts; the first images—both still and moving—from the moon's surface; and advertisements published after the first moon landing that showed the space program's attempts to win public support through publicity. He chose to focus on multiple magazine covers and images from magazine articles for his primary source materials (see Figures 5.5 and 5.6).

The image in Figure 5.5 originally appeared in an article published in *Collier's* magazine on October 23, 1948, concerning the military applications of space travel. James analyzed it and found that it was intended to warn American readers of the consequences of falling behind in the "space race" with the Russians. Similarly, Figure 5.6, a cover shot from *Time*'s July 25, 1969, issue, relied on *pathos* to persuade the American readers to view the U.S. space program in a certain light. James found that the image, with its strong nationalistic overtones, cast the successful Apollo 11 mission once again in terms of the Cold War and the American-Soviet space race. He placed these primary sources at the center of his research argument, and then he turned to secondary sources to substantiate his own claims about them.

Seeing Connections
See how Pamela Abbott and Francesca Sapsford use secondary sources to develop their argument in "Clothing the Young Female Body" (page 407).

Searching for Secondary Sources

Just as important as your primary materials are your **secondary sources**—texts that provide commentary on your topic and often analyze the texts you have chosen as primary sources. The writers of these texts offer the voices with which you will engage in scholarly conversation as you develop the substance of your argument.

FIGURE 5.5. James used this illustration, "The Rocket Blitz from the Moon," which originally accompanied a 1948 *Collier's* magazine article, as a powerful primary source for his research paper.

FIGURE 5.6. James also analyzed other primary sources, including magazine covers like this one from a 1969 issue of *Time.*

Seeing Connections
For more examples of the argumentative function of primary sources like magazine covers, see the *Sports Illustrated* covers featured on page 467.

Although your instinct may send you directly to the Internet, your first stop in your search for secondary sources should actually be your library's reference area, the home of reference librarians—people trained to help you find what you need—as well as a treasure trove of encyclopedias, bibliographies, and other resource materials. These storehouses of information can be invaluable in providing you with the *foundational sources* for your project, including basic definitions, historical background, and bibliographies. Yet, while such "background" materials are necessary to help you construct a framework for your research argument, they represent only one part of your iceberg of research. For more rigorous analysis, you should turn to books and articles that provide critical analysis and arguments about your specific research subject. To locate these more specific secondary sources, you might search your library catalog for relevant books and films and other published materials.

You can also consult databases and indexes, indispensable research guides that will provide you with bibliographic citations for academic articles on your topic. Databases can come in many forms: collections of electronic journals, Internet resources, or CD-ROMs. Although some databases provide bibliographic citations that you can use to locate the source in your library catalog, many include a detailed abstract summarizing a source's argument, and others link you to full-text electronic copies of the articles you are searching for.

AT A GLANCE

Finding Secondary Sources

- ***Dictionaries, guides, and encyclopedias*** provide helpful background information for your topic.
- ***Library catalogs*** allow you to search the library holdings for relevant books or documentaries.
- ***CD-Rom indexes and bibliographies*** contain vast amounts of bibliographic information.
- ***Electronic databases and indexes*** are available on the Internet through subscription only; many provide access to full-text versions of articles from a range of sources.
- ***Electronic journals and ebooks*** offer access to the full digital versions of books and academic journals from a wide range of disciplines.
- ***Google scholar and Google Books*** can be helpful resources, but should be used in conjunction with academic databases and library catalogues.

AT A GLANCE

Using One Source to Locate Additional Sources

Here's the process for finding sources:

1. Locate one relevant source through the library catalog.
2. Retrieve it from the library stacks.
3. Spend some time looking over books in the same area to discover additional books on the same topic.
4. Assess briefly the applicability of each text to your project, and check out the ones most valuable to you.
5. Look at the bibliographies in the backs of your most useful books to locate sources that were helpful to the authors and may be of use to you.
6. Repeat the process often to build your iceberg of research.

Finally, although databases, catalogs, and search engines provide indispensable tools for conducting your research, remember also that your classmates can serve as secondary sources you might consult or even interview. Ask others who are working on similar topics to share resources, and help each other along the route of your research. This is particularly true for the stage in your research when you produce a **preliminary bibliography**—a working list of the sources for your iceberg of research.

Student Writing

See Vivian Chang's record of her searches in her research log.

www.pearsonhighered.com/envision/100

AT A GLANCE

Recording Searches in Your Research Log

Use your research log to keep careful track of the dates, details, key terms of your searches and to organize your sources and your notes.

- Date each entry in your log to keep track of your progress and show the evolution of your ideas.
- Keep a running list of your sources by call number and title.
- Write down complete identifying information for any source you consult, including images on the Web, articles online, journals or magazines in the library, articles from library databases, and chapters in books.
- Double-check transcribed quotations for accuracy while you still have the source before you, and include page numbers (or paragraph numbers for Website articles).
- Include printouts (or digital copies, if your log is electronic) of relevant articles or database entries, and especially of Web-based articles or Websites that might disappear when their site is updated.
- Annotate the entry by including an evaluation of the source and an indication of how you might use it as part of your final paper.
- If you are using Web sources, be aware that Websites tend to be updated often and sometimes simply disappear. To avoid losing important source material, print out significant Webpages and insert them into your log or download them to your hard drive and include them on a CD-ROM with your research log.

Evaluating Your Sources

Implementing these research strategies to locate primary and secondary materials will provide you with access to many interesting sources, but how do you discriminate among them to find those that are credible, reliable, and authoritative? How do you know which ones will be the most useful for your argument? The key rests in understanding the argumentative perspective, or *rhetorical stance*, of each source. At times, the source's stance may be self-evident: you may automatically gravitate toward experts in the field, well known for their opinions and affiliations. It is just as likely, however, that you may not be familiar with the names or ideas of your sources. Therefore, it is essential to develop a method for evaluating the sources you encounter.

Evaluating Websites

For many of us, when we hear the words "research paper," our first impulse is to log onto the Internet and plug our topic into a search engine such as Google (http://www.google.com) or Bing (http://www.bing.com). That will certainly provide a start, but how do you assess the credibility of the hundreds of sites that may turn up? How do you evaluate the reliability and usefulness of these sites?

To understand how best to evaluate Websites, let's take the example of a research paper on the stem cell debate. An initial Google search on "stem cell research" brings up a list of over 5 million sites. On the one hand, such a plentiful search gives you ample means to "eavesdrop" on the ongoing conversation about your topic; on the other hand, the sheer magnitude of hits can be overwhelming. Even after refining your search terms to get a smaller result, how do you sort through them to identify those most helpful to your research?

First evaluate the author, source, or publisher. For our search, the first hit is quite credible: NIH Stem Cell Information, hosted by the National Institutes of Health of the U.S. government (Figure 5.7).

AT A GLANCE

Evaluating Websites

- Who is the author of the Website? Is it a personal Website or is it institutionally affiliated? What sort of authority does it draw on?
- Does the author take responsibility for the page by offering a place for comments or an email link for feedback?
- Who is the audience?
- What is the purpose?
- What is the rhetorical stance of this Website? Does it deal with both sides of the issue or only one side?
- Does it offer links to other sites on the Web?
- How timely is the page? Does it have a date? Does someone maintain the Website? Are there broken links?
- Is it an archive of primary material? If so, does it cite the original sources in a correct and complete manner?
- Is it easy to navigate? Does it have a search engine?

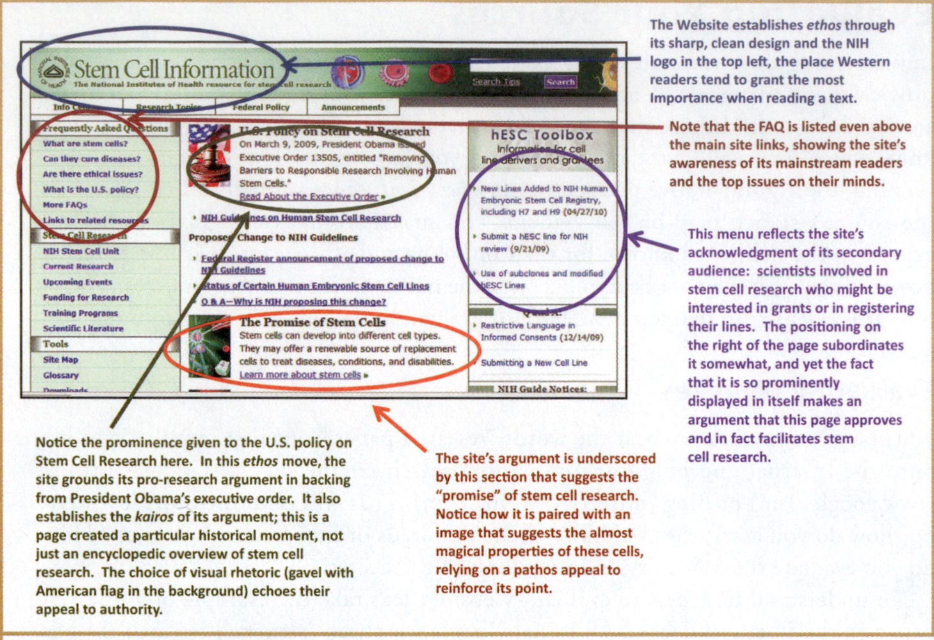

FIGURE 5.7. A screenshot of the NIH Stem Cell Information page.

Second, consider the arrangement, or organization, of material. As you study this Website, you probably notice first the title, Stem Cell Information, at the top of the page, which suggests that this page is intended to be informational—to get the basic facts out. You may also note the small NIH logo next to it. Does the fact that this is a government-sponsored site suggest that it is authoritative? Objective?

Clicking on the first topic listed—U.S. Policy on Stem Cell Research—brings you to a page about executive orders. You may notice that it emphasizes President Barack Obama's executive order, which is titled "Removing Barriers . . ." and, the site notes, revokes an earlier one signed by President George W. Bush. Do you see any rhetorical strategies at work here? Is there any persuasive message embedded in the site?

The next site listed on your Google search, Wikipedia, may provide a good starting point for your search. It contains background information, and the references at the end of the article provide a useful starting point for research. However, Wikipedia itself is often considered a questionable source (since each entry can be edited by anyone), so it is best to substantiate what your learn there by continuing on with your search.

Lower down on your Google results list is another site—Do No Harm: The Coalition of Americans for Research Ethics. The site's title, unlike that of the National Institutes of Health, suggests a point of view: The sponsors of this site believe in ethical research. But how is that defined? Does "ethical research" include or reject research based on embryonic stem cells?

Finding the answer to this requires some careful analysis of the site, shown in Figure 5.8. Looking at the homepage, you may first notice the appeal to authority: the quote from Hippocrates at the top of the page that includes the familiar admonition to the medical profession to do no harm. But initially we don't know how that quote is being interpreted or applied. A quick glance at the page shows that the center frame is given over to news, commentary, and resources, suggesting that it is providing an overview of the topic for its audience. However, as we look closer, the stance becomes more clear. The titles of the links show a clear tendency toward critiquing the use of embryonic stem cells for research. In fact, we can find the organization's position in the upper left quadrant of the page, submerged in the question under the suggestive header "Support Alternatives." As their "Founding Statement" confirms, this group is opposed to embryonic stem cell research as morally unacceptable, but its position is more nuanced than some groups because it endorses what it sees as morally acceptable alternatives—using adult stem cells.

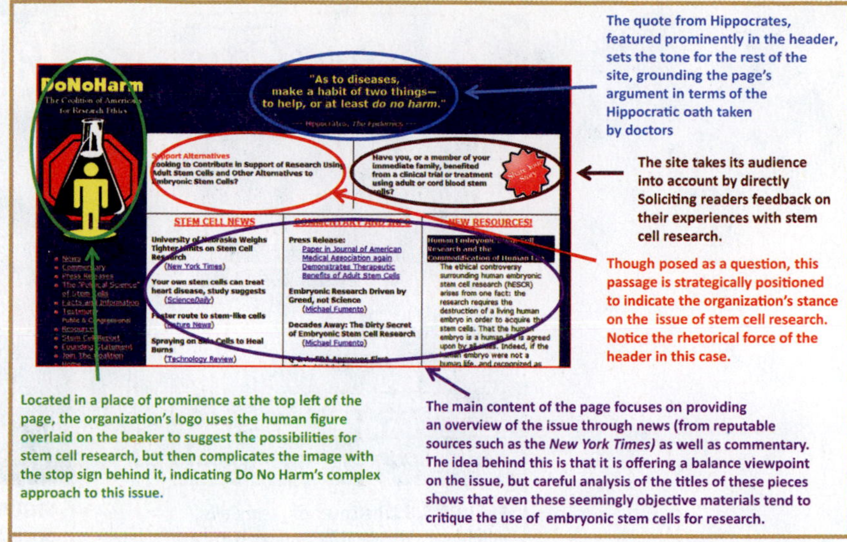

FIGURE 5.8. Homepage for the Do No Harm site.

Having identified the stance, your task as a researcher is not only to take this position into account while reading but also to broaden your research to include many different perspectives on the issue. Identifying the stance or bias of a Website's sponsor or author is critical to evaluating the credibility and usefulness of that site.

As you can see, attention to the visual and verbal rhetoric of a site's homepage—its "cover"—is essential to understanding its argument and therefore its suitability as a research source. After assessing the "cover" pages of each Website, the next step is to move deeper into the site to analyze its content and argument.

Evaluating Library and Database Sources

While Websites can provide sources for a project on stem cells, for almost all college research papers you will need to seek out sources through library shelves and databases since they host scholarly materials that will be more useful for your project.

How might you evaluate library and database sources for a research paper on stem cells? Your first stop is the library's reference area, where you look up foundational information in the *Encyclopedia of Bioethics.* Then you search the library catalog for books, and finally, you might locate journal articles that, you reason, will provide balance to your iceberg of research because they often represent the most current discussions on a topic. To find relevant articles, you begin searching the electronic databases that most closely suit the specific focus of your project: SciSearch, MEDLINE, LegalPeriodical, BIOSIS. You produce an impressive list of citations and even retrieve

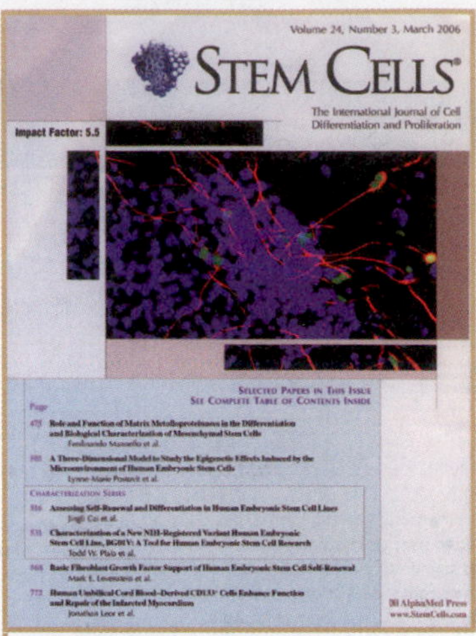

FIGURE 5.9. The cover of *Stem Cells* emphasizes its scientific approach in choices of cover image and text.

FIGURE 5.10. The cover of *Yale Scientific* zooms in on the debate rather than on the science of stem cells.

a few full-text articles. You also search some sources that are more news related, including LexisNexis and ProQuest, to find a selection of references to popular newspaper and magazine articles that will balance the scholarly sources.

Your first search complete, you can now retreat to a quiet space and assess the significance and value of your findings. You can be relatively confident in the quality of the texts you've accumulated because library holdings and scholarly databases tend to contain materials that have been more rigorously screened than those found through an Internet search engine. However, keep in mind that you'll still need to apply the same evaluation criteria to these texts as you would to Websites.

Start by assessing the visual rhetoric of the journal covers, assessing topic, stance, and reliability. You might have come across the two covers found in Figures 5.9 and 5.10. A rhetorical analysis reveals differences in purpose, audience, and focus. *Stem Cells*, by using an actual image of embryonic cells, signals its focus on cellular biology and scientific applications; in addition, by listing its table of contents—complete with authors and article titles—on the front cover, it privileges *ethos* as an appeal. *Yale Scientific* chooses a different approach, using a powerful visual metaphor coupled with the term "Truth" to suggest its engagement with the debate surrounding stem cell research.

However, in many cases you may not be able to use a cover image as a guide to evaluation; many scholarly journals and books have been re-covered in plain library bindings. In that case, the steps you should take to select and evaluate the best sources are outlined in the "At a Glance" box on page 105.

As with evaluating Websites, rhetorical attention to the writing of journal articles and books will help you make good choices as a researcher. You can assess the language, tone, date, context, and stance of the author.

Realize that the most important assessment question is how *useful* a source will be for your project and your potential argument. Then you are on your way to knowing

AT A GLANCE

Evaluating Academic Sources

- Assess the **author**. Perhaps your teacher recommended the author to you or you notice that the author has written many books and articles on the topic. You can look this person up in a bibliography index or on the Web to assess the *ethos* of the writer. If the author turns out to be disreputable or affiliated with an extremist organization, would the source still be an important one to consider? Would the exaggerated stance help you examine extremist positions on your topic?
- Check out the **place of publication**. Is it a university press (suggesting peer-reviewed scholarship) or a trade press (suggesting a commercial venture)? Is it published by a foundation or organization (suggesting a political agenda) or self-published (suggesting the author's struggle to have his or her views accepted for publication)?
- Look at the **date**. Is it a recent contribution or an older study? An older source can provide historical context, but sometimes it can be too outdated to be useful. Usually, you should pick the more recent sources to engage the most timely perspectives on your topic.
- Go beneath the cover of the book or journal. Open it and turn to the **table of contents** and the **index** to see exactly what the book contains. Is it a collection of articles by different authors, or does it reflect the viewpoint of a single author? Now flip through the pages, looking for interesting arguments and judging the quality or complexity of the writing. You may note its **voice** or **tone**: Is it written for specialists in the field or for a popular audience? Does it focus on issues relevant to your research?

how you will use that text from your iceberg of research to craft your own research-based argument on the issue.

Using Field Research

Consider the resources available to you right on your campus. For instance, you might interview faculty members from your university who have written or lectured on subjects related to your topic. This is a great way to make contacts and develop your iceberg of research. In addition to interviewing the faculty member as a secondary source, ask the professor to recommend two or three key books in the field that you might consult as you continue on your research journey.

Seeing Connections
For examples of effective interview style, see "America's Toughest Sheriff' Takes on Immigration" (page 539) and the Interview with George Ritzer (page 569).

Or let's look at a more ambitious approach to fieldwork. Student Vincent Chen used field research quite prominently in his research project about the rhetoric of climate change. Specifically, he included photographs he took while attending the Copenhagen Conference on Climate Change in December of 2009. Included in this conference was a special session on the "15th Conference of the Parties to the UNFCCC (United Nations Framework Convention on Climate Change)," commonly known as "COP15." At the COP15, Vincent conducted impressive field research, such as taking photographs of people milling through the halls, attending talks, and listening to speakers present position statements about the environment. But Vincent's most powerful field research was a single photo, showing the crowds of attendees stopping mid-motion to hear the speech of Mohamed Nasheed, president of the Republic of Maldives. The photo became central to making his argument that Nasheed strongly differentiated himself from other climate leaders at the conference through his inflammatory rhetoric about the danger of rising seas as well as the *logos* argument of his country's small size and

FIGURE 5.11. Vincent Chen's field research includes this powerful photo of Mohamed Nasheed, president of the Republic of Maldives, speaking to a riveted audience at the 2009 Copenhagen Climate conference. © Vincent Chen 2009.

limited economic power. To argue this position, Vincent used a photo he took as visual evidence documenting the power of President Nasheed's conference-stopping speech (see Figure 5.11). He also included additional field research in the form of interviews with other students who attended at the conference and an interview with Professor Stephen Schneider of the Interdisciplinary Environmental Studies Program at his university.

This field research added depth and power to Vincent's argument by allowing him to include his own evidence as strategic argumentative support for his argument. With regard to the photo in Figure 5.11, rather than just asserting his claim to be true, Vincent could allow his readers to *see* the evidence that would support his point that President Nasheed, out of all leaders at the climate conference, made people stop and listen to an argument for action.

AT A GLANCE

Conducting Interviews and Surveys

1. ***Target your population:*** Is the best source for your field research a professor at your college who is expert in this area? a professional from the community? peers in your class, dorm, athletic team, or town?
2. ***Develop questions:*** Review your list of questions with a peer or your instructor. Avoid general questions. Design interview questions to elicit usable quotations; design surveys that balance short, multiple choice questions, which yield primarily statistical data, with short answer questions that will produce more nuanced responses. Keep your survey short; the longer your form, the fewer completed surveys will probably be returned to you.
3. ***Prepare:*** Know your interviewee: read an online biography, read something he or she has written, have some sense of the interviewee's position on the issue. Research the best delivery method for your survey, given your target population.
4. ***Make contact:*** For interviews, explain your purpose, your identity, and your goal for the field research clearly. Offer two or three times. Follow up unanswered requests with polite emails or phone calls. Don't hesitate to persist, but do so respectfully. For surveys, state your deadline clearly, and make sure the respondent knows where and how to return the form.
5. ***Record and document:*** Get written permission from interviewees and survey subjects to use their words in your paper. If you record an interview with a tape recorder or cell phone device, be sure to ask permission first and to create a transcript as soon as possible after the interview. Document all uses of the interview with quotation marks in your paper.
6. ***Follow-up:*** Send a thank-you note to any interviewees and offer a copy of your completed paper. Consider sharing your findings with survey participants, if possible, through a local newsletter or college newspaper article.

Of course, not all fieldwork involves trips around the world. Sometimes you can gather your own evidence for your research project by using resources available within your local community. Consider these possibilities: if you were studying the layout and impact of a new park in your community, you might meet with a city planner or the landscape architect responsible for the project; if you were writing about a city water reservoir, you might visit the site, take photographs, and meet with the site manager; and, if you were writing on the marketing strategies of a local baseball team, you might even write a letter to that team's marketing coordinator. Fieldwork such as this allows you to take your research to the next level and make a truly original contribution of your own.

Student Writing

Look at Sean Bruich's letter he wrote to the marketing coordinator of the Oakland Athletic's baseball team as part of his fieldwork.

www.pearsonhighered.com/envision/107

Evaluating Field Research Sources

When you conduct interviews and surveys, you are looking for materials to use in your paper as secondary sources. But keep in mind the need to evaluate your field research sources as carefully as you assess your Web and print sources. If you interview a professor, a marketing executive, a witness, or a roommate, consider the rhetorical stance of that person. What kind of bias does the person have concerning the topic of your project? If you conduct a survey of your peers in your dorm, assess the value and credibility of your results as rigorously as you would evaluate the data of a published study. Don't fall into the trap of misusing statistics when making claims if you haven't taken into account the need for **statistical significance**, or to paraphrase the social psychologist Philip Zimbardo, the measure by which a number obtains meaning in scientific fields. To reach this number, you need to design the survey carefully, conduct what's called a *random sample*, interview a *large enough* number of people, and ask a *range of different people*. These are complex parameters to follow, but you will need to learn about them to conduct survey research that has reliable and credible results.

"Statistics are the backbone of research. They are used to understand observations and to determine whether findings are, in fact, correct and significant. . . . But, statistics can also be used poorly or deceptively, misleading those who do not understand them."

—Philip Zimbardo (595)

Seeing Connections

How might you evaluate the Pew Research Center's statistics on "Social Media and Young Adults" found on page 291?

As Professor Zimbardo points out, statistics—though we often think of them as Truth—actually function rhetorically. Like words and images, numbers are a mode of persuasion that can mislead readers. You need to be especially vigilant when using a survey or statistics as a supposedly "objective" part of your iceberg of research, particularly if you plan to depend on such materials in your argument.

Take as much care with how you convey information visually as you do with how you convey it in writing. Consider David Pinner's writing project about grade inflation. David accumulated enough quantitative information through fieldwork and primary research to compose his own charts. He discovered a wealth of information in archived faculty senate minutes, which he sorted through during his research. From that work, he came across important statistical data that reflected the change in grade distribution at Stanford over the course of 25 years. In addition to including the numbers in his written text, he created two pie charts (see Figure 5.12), using a

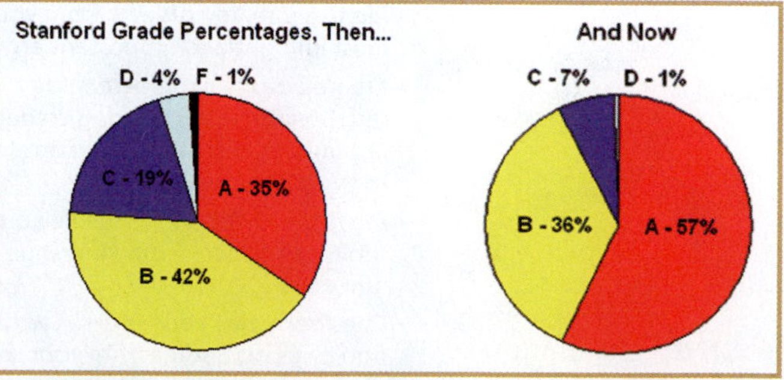

FIGURE 5.12. Student David Pinner created these information graphics from his research data to suggest the difference in grade distribution between 1968 and 1992.

visual comparison of statistics to underscore his point. His argument was more powerful not just because of his impressive field research but also because of how he represented it graphically through responsible use of statistics.

Creating a Dialogue with Your Sources

Seeing Connections
For an example of how sources can be brought in dialogue with one another, see "Playing Unfair" on page 468.

Throughout this chapter we have emphasized that research is social, a conversation with the people whose ideas and writing came before yours. As you gather, assess, and use sources, you are contributing to this conversation, building on the work of others, and adding a new perspective. Indeed, this notion of writing as communal is the reason why you need to use the author's name when citing a quotation or an idea; remember that all your sources are authored sources; each source mentioned in this chapter was composed by a person or a group of people. If you think of these texts as written *by people like you*, you will have an easier time remembering to acknowledge their ideas and integrate their quotations into your essay. In the process, you will go a long way toward avoiding unintentional plagiarism. You can begin this process through an exercise we call a **dialogue of sources**—a fictional conversation among the primary and secondary sources of your research paper designed to help you identify each one's central argument and main idea.

To prepare for her research paper on tobacco advertisements, Amanda Johnson (AJ) wrote this dialogue between several sources she had found: RJ Reynolds Tobacco Co. (RJRT); Larry C. White (LW), author of *Merchants of Death*; and Hugh High (HH), a professor of economics, finance, and law who published a collection of tobacco studies titled *Does Advertising Increase Smoking?* among others, which she presents in a literal dialogue with herself acting as scholarly moderator.

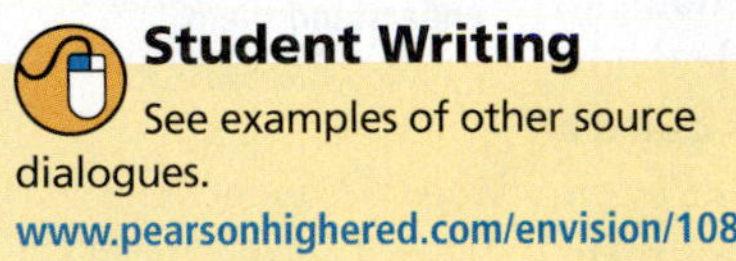

AT A GLANCE

Creating a Dialogue of Sources

- ***Identify the key players*** from your research log and your notes. Which ones have the most influential or important arguments?
- ***Create a cast of characters list*** with a short "bio" for each speaker, including yourself. Describe each person's credentials and rhetorical stance—his or her *ethos* and argument. (You may even want to create identifying icons or pictures to give "faces" to the participants.)
- ***Draft the script.*** Write the key questions you want to ask your sources about your topic. Use quotes from your sources to respond where possible, and include page numbers.
- ***Consider what your sources would say to each other.*** Write their fictional conversation by using quotes from your sources.
- ***Don't just play the "objective" moderator.*** Respond to the sources and, in the process, start to develop your own argument.

Dialogue of Sources [excerpt]

AJ: I would like to thank the panel for joining us this afternoon. We have quite a diverse group of writers, researchers, spokespeople, and a professor here to discuss the focus and objectives of current tobacco advertising. Since I know your comments on this subject vary widely, I suppose I will start off by asking you to talk about what you believe to be the focus of tobacco advertising as it exists today.

RJRT: RJ Reynolds tobacco products are among the best advertised in the industry, and we take pride in our commitment to maintaining honest advertising to the public. We do not intend for our advertising to manipulate nonsmokers into trying our products, nor do we choose to target these audiences. Advertising is simply a method by which we are able to maintain our share of the market and compete with other tobacco manufacturers.

LW: How can you possibly claim to avoid targeting specific audiences and replenishing your older dwindling population with new younger smokers!?! The whole point of advertising is to get more people to buy your product, and, since market shares don't change all that much for large companies like yours, the best way to get more people to buy your product is to increase the number of overall smokers. Youth are your best option because if you can get them hooked now, you will have a steady flow of income for several decades to come.

HH: Mr. White, you make a good point about general economic objectives. However, studies show that advertising does very little to change the number of new smokers. Countries that have banned advertising for tobacco-related products have seen very little decline in the number of consumers that buy their product. As RJRT stated previously, advertising is only successful at making adjustments within the market concerning the relative amounts each company is able to sell.

AJ: I recently reviewed a chart concerning the prevalence of smoking among U.S. adults and found that over the past 40 years since the surgeon general first warned about cigarettes' cancerous effects, the steady decline in smokers has slowed to rest around 25 percent of the population over the age of 18. With the number of people dying each day, it is surprising that this number does not continue to go down. How would you account for the slowed change?

Amanda's complete dialogue begins with a list of speakers and their bios. Then she introduces the topic of her research project. She reproduces the argument of each source, both print and interview, through paraphrase.

By allowing debate to evolve, Amanda begins to see how she might use quotations from these sources in her paper.

Most importantly, she begins to develop her own argument for her research paper in the context of these other perspectives.

She does this by questioning the responses, adding facts from her research, and moving the argument forward as she will need to do in her paper.

Notice how Amanda's work here allows her to write out the process of research *as a conversation* and will help her avoid unintentional plagiarism since she is giving credit to her sources.

Writing an Annotated Bibliography

As you move further into your research, you might want to synthesize your notes in what researchers call an **annotated bibliography**—a list of research sources that provides informational notes about each source and how you might use it as you turn to drafting your paper.

Realize that composing entries in the annotated bibliography involves much more than merely recording information: it is a way for you to synthesize arguments and add your response to what the source has to say about your research topic. Be sure to include quotation marks and page numbers if you quote directly from sources to distinguish between direct quotes and your own paraphrases or commentary; in this way, you can avoid potentially misquoting or plagiarizing sources.

Student Writing
See samples of annotated bibliographies on a variety of topics.
www.pearsonhighered.com/envision/110

As you compose your annotated bibliography, consider including images that you might use as primary or secondary sources as well. In this way, you are crafting a **visual annotated bibliography**—a working list of potential sources in which you include images. This is very helpful if you plan to analyze images in your paper or if your rhetorical analysis covers visual and multimedia texts, such as James Caputo's project on the government's space program.

Consider the excerpt from Carly Geehr's visual annotated bibliography for her research project on the representations of swimming as a gendered sport in the American media throughout history (see Figure 5.13). Both the image of a swimmer from the early 1920s in the secondary source by Douglas Booth and Colin Tatz and the advertising

AT A GLANCE

Composing an Annotated Bibliography

1. Put your sources into alphabetical order; you can also categorize them by primary and secondary sources.
2. For a visual annotated bibliography, include images of your primary and secondary sources (covers, screenshots, photographs, drawings, charts, cartoons, posters) to show each source's stance through visual rhetoric.
3. Provide complete identifying information for each source, including author's name, title, publication, date, page numbers, URLs for Websites, and database information for online sources.
4. Compose a three- to five-sentence annotation for each source:
   - First, summarize the main argument or point of the source; use concrete language. Include quotations if you wish.
   - Next, indicate the writer's stance. How credible or biased is this source?
   - Finally, and most importantly, describe the relevance of this source to your research argument. Will the source be used as background for the opening part of your paper? Does it offer a key counterargument? Will it provide the main authority to back up your claims?

Carly Geehr
Visually Annotated Bibliography

Dr. Alyssa O'Brien
May 13, 2003

The American Media and Swimming: Investigating the "Uphill Battle"

Booth, Douglas and Colin Tatz. *One Eyed: a View of Australian Sport.* Allen and Unwin 2000.

In order to make my argument that swimming could be a more popular sport in the United States, I will need to present strong evidence: this book provides it to me. Booth and Tatz chronicle the history of Australian sports in both society and in the media. From their descriptions of media coverage and the role of gender in sports, I can find out why, culturally and historically, swimming has been able to achieve such a high level of popularity in Australia. Of particular interest to me so far has been their focus on the traditional, accepted role of women in sports-it is drastically different in US history. By comparison to my sources about American sports culture, I will find out the key differences between the two countries and hopefully draw some concrete conclusions as to why swimming is not as popular in the United States as it is in Australia. This photo is the image of a female Australian swimmer whose look and demeanor demand respect, unlike her beautified American counterparts (212). I will be able to compare the Australian images of swimmers with the American images of swimmers, hopefully noting some key differences in visual rhetoric techniques employed—preliminarily, I suspect that the American images will focus much more on aesthetics while Australian images will focus on intensity and ruggedness (more pertinent to the sport itself).

"Duel in the Pool Advertisement." 3 Apr 2003. http://www.usaswimming.org/Duel.

[A little background: USA Swimming recently staged its first "made-for-TV" dual meet versus the Australian national team. The goal was to attract network attention and draw the people who would normally be watching sports on weekend afternoons into watching swimming for a change. According to Mary Wagner, the ratings were good but not exceptional.] This image is one of the advertisements put out by USA Swimming before the event to attract its target audience of teenagers and others (particularly males) who would be watching television on Saturday and Sunday afternoons. It appeals mostly to ethos, citing Michael Phelps as a world record holder, but also appeals more subtly to pathos in using the national colors and the national flag to create a sense of nationalism and passion for the event. However, this image helps me support my claim that USA Swimming's promotions have fallen short of successful in that it is not an exciting image—if the intent was to attract teenagers and adults who typically watch traditional, exciting American sports, then this image fails to create sufficient energy to generate interest or a desire to deviate from watching normal weekend sports on TV.

FIGURE 5.13. Well-chosen images and detailed annotations show Carly Geehr's progress on her research project.

from *U.S.A. Swimming* were key images that Carly analyzed in her paper to make an argument about the feminization of swimming in American sports culture. From this annotated bibliography, it was a short step to generating a full research paper complete with responsible integration of research sources. In this way, you too can make your contribution to the conversation of research.

The Writer's Process

As you begin to articulate your contribution to the research conversation about your topic, use the strategies that you've learned in this chapter. These include visualizing research as a conversation that you are joining and understanding the process of researching your argument as a movement from surface to depth. As you learn to search and locate both primary and secondary sources, you can engage in critical evaluation of these texts in your research log. You can also engage in innovative fieldwork of your own to generate original resource material to use in your argument. In writing your own annotated bibliography, remember that effective annotations and note-taking practices can help you develop the strategies of an academic writer and that these practices will move you toward finalizing your own argument about the topic. By moving from covers to contents, you will watch your iceberg take shape, and you will begin to let your own voice be heard.

AT A GLANCE

Note-Taking Strategies

As you read through your sources, take notes on materials that you could use in your paper:

- Particularly memorable quotations
- Background information
- A well-written passage providing context or a perspective useful to your argument

Be sure to double-check your notes for accuracy, use quotation marks for direct quotes, and include complete source details and page numbers.

Along the way, be sure to take careful notes. This is a crucial step in your writer's process. You can use the dialogue of sources as a note-taking strategy while you work through your research sources. Indeed, many students find this approach to note taking to be the best way to create thorough research logs for their projects, one that keeps their own thesis evident. But honor your own learned techniques, such as taking notes in a software program such as Endnote, on note cards, in a binder, or on your laptop.

PREWRITING CHECKLIST

Focus on Evaluating Covers and Contents

- ❑ What images are featured on the cover? Do the images lend themselves to an appeal to logic? to an appeal to emotion? to an appeal to authority?
- ❑ Do the words included as headings and subheads on the cover contribute to any of these appeals?
- ❑ What do the cover images suggest about the contents of the larger text? Do they suggest a specific rhetorical stance or point of view? What is the effect of each visual choice?
- ❑ How do the words on the cover or homepage work in conjunction with the image to suggest the entire text's rhetorical stance? Do the words complement the image? Do they offer a contrast to the image?

PREWRITING WITH THE *ENVISION* WEBSITE

Visit the Websites listed for "stem cell research" at the *Envision* Website. What rhetorical decisions are apparent from each site's homepage design? How do the images suggest different approaches to the stem cell issue? How does the organization of information, the menu, and the written text contribute to this impression? Follow the site links to explore how the rhetorical stance suggested by the "cover" is reflected in the site's contents. Develop a list of criteria for evaluating Websites.
www.pearsonhighered.com/envision/112

You might include in this list a focus on issues of authority, accessibility, and suitability. You might look at the URL to establish the author or host of a Website, or you might examine the selection of images or the word choice for indications of bias or sensationalism. Look also at the "last updated" note to check the currency of the site or for the "contact" link to evaluate the author's sense of accountability for his or her work. Follow the links to see if the site is self-contained, linking only to its own materials, or whether it contains external links, connecting it to the broader conversation on the topic. Finally, assess the type of material the site contains: primary documents or secondary commentary.

WRITING PROJECTS

1. **Research Log Entries:** Keep a running commentary/assessment of potential research sources for your project. Realize that careful research notes are a crucial part of the process and will help you avoid unintentional plagiarism of material. Include a combination of typed notes, highlighted photocopies, emails, sources from databases, note cards, scanned images, and other means of processing all the information you encounter.

2. **Working with Your Preliminary Bibliography:** Create a *dialogue of sources* or an *annotated bibliography* to showcase the primary and secondary sources you'll employ in the major paper. Be sure that your writing provides a range of primary and secondary sources. Include both print and electronic sources and, if appropriate, include images to demonstrate the kinds of materials you'll be analyzing in the project.

3. **Collaborative Peer Review:** Present your annotated bibliographies to one another in groups. Pull the "greatest hits" from your research log, and tell the class about how your research is going. In other words, *present a discussion of your work in progress.* Identify obstacles and successes so far. You'll get feedback from the class about your developing research project.

Visit www.pearsonhighered.com/envision for expanded assignment guidelines and student projects.
Visit www.mycomplab.com for additional general writing and research resources.

CHAPTER 6

Organizing and Writing Research Arguments

Chapter Preview Questions

- What strategies of organization work best for my paper?
- What are the best ways to get started writing a full draft?
- How do I integrate research sources responsibly and rhetorically?
- How will I know when to quote, paraphrase, or summarize?
- How can collaboration and peer review help me revise?

Constructing a research argument is a complex and ongoing process. From selecting a topic to locating and evaluating sources and taking notes, it involves a series of interrelated steps. This is true of the *drafting* stage as well. In fact, organizing, drafting, and revising information is a prominent part of the process of creating any text—an academic essay, a television commercial, a radio essay, or even a film. Figure 6.1, for instance, lets us glimpse the drafting process behind a film called *Serenity* (2005). In this scene, one of the main characters, River, fights a roomful of Reavers—the cannibalistic bad guys of the film—to protect her brother and friends. What you see in Figure 6.1 are the storyboards for this scene—an artist's draft that lays out the action in chronological increments, mapping out not only the movement of the characters but also the camera angles and thus the audience's experience of the events depicted. Notice the way it captures a sense of motion by rapidly changing perspectives and how it creates a narrative tension in the last panel with the close-up of the Reavers grabbing River to drag her back during her attempted escape. Storyboards like this clearly operate as visual outlines, an organizational strategy that underlies almost all films. The polished final version seen in the theater is actually made possible by drafting steps like this one.

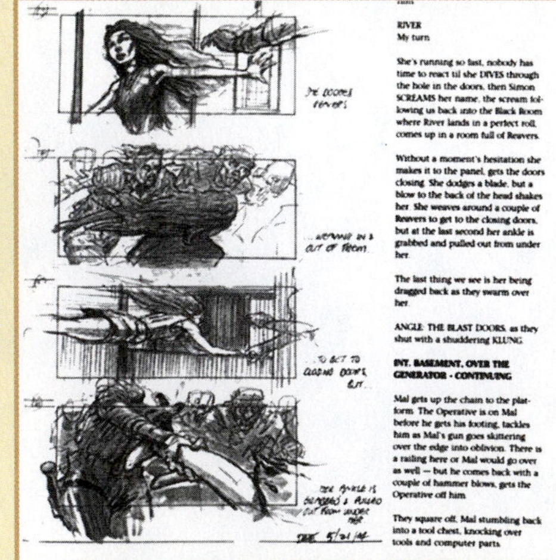

FIGURE 6.1. This storyboard for Joss Whedon's film *Serenity* shows an initial draft for one of the film's climactic action scenes.

In many ways, the process of writing is like film production:

- Both have many small steps that support a grounding vision or main idea
- Both have a carefully planned structure
- Both involve rigorous editing

Because producing a film and producing a research argument share such rich similarities, we'll use the medium of film throughout this chapter to understand the process of writing a research paper: from constructing a visual map and formal outline to integrating sources, key quotations, and evidence. We'll talk about incorporating sources responsibly in a way that sustains the conversation you began in the previous chapter, and we'll walk through the drafting and revision process. Just as filmmakers leave many scenes on the cutting room floor, you too will write, edit, cut, and rearrange much of the first draft of your research paper before it reaches its final form. You'll find that the process of completing your research argument is as collaborative as film production. Additionally, both film and writing involve parameters of length, cost, and time that you need to contend with to produce the best possible text. No matter what your topic, you can think of the way in which film works to help you visualize the final product and move from notes to writing the completed paper.

Organizing Your Draft in Visual Form

It can be quite challenging to turn on the computer and try to crank out a complete draft without first arranging materials into some kind of order. Storyboards like those shown in Figure 6.1, or the bubble webs or graphic flowcharts described in this section, can be productive ways to prewrite through visual means. In fact, filmmakers often begin the production process by visually mapping out movie ideas, key scenes, and plot progressions. You too can use various forms of graphically organizing your research notes and argumentative points in order to sort, arrange, and make connections between ideas.

The most basic way to get organized is physically to stack your research books and materials and then write labels for each pile. This organizational strategy functions as a concrete way of categorizing the resources you have and figuring out, visually, how they relate to one another. Next, you can produce a visual map of these sources by using colored pens and paper or by cutting out shapes and constructing a three-dimensional model for your paper's organization.

Using a computer, you can turn your handwritten visual map into a **bubble web**, in which you arrange your ideas into categories using shapes and colors. You could also try more hierarchical or linear graphic flowcharts as a means of organizing your materials. In **graphic flowcharts**, you list one idea and then draw an arrow to suggest cause and effect and to show relationships among items. Figure 6.2, for example, presents Ye Yuan's graphic flowchart of his ideas about war photography, arranged in a tree structure. This

Student Writing
See examples of visual maps generated by students for their research projects.
www.pearsonhighered.com/envision/115

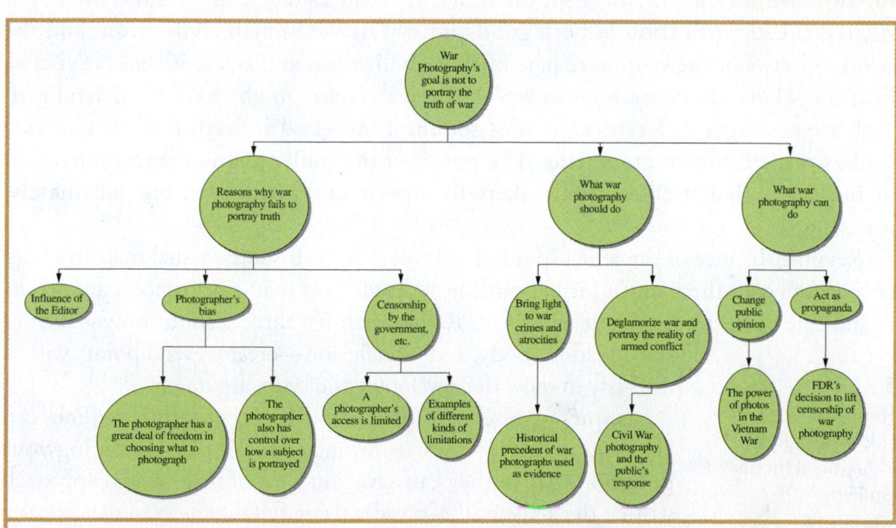

FIGURE 6.2. This graphic flowchart by Ye Yuan, created with the software program Inspiration, allowed him to visualize the sections of his written paper.

Seeing Connections
See an excerpt from Ye Yuan's completed visual argument on this topic on page 184 (Figures 8.9-8.10).

visual hierarchy helped him assess his project by asking questions and checking to see if he had enough research or points to make:

- Is each point developed thoroughly?
- Do I have a balance among the sections?
- Is there a coherent whole?

Learning Outline Strategies

Visual maps can help you sort out your materials and prepare you for the next step: the detailed, written **outline**. For a longer, more complex paper, such as a research-based argument, an *outline* is an extremely useful method of arranging ideas and expediting the drafting process. Outlines offer a plan for your paper and should show the relationships among the various sections in your argument. If your outline simply consists of a list of topics, you won't be able to see the argument of the whole paper, nor will you be able to check for a strong progression between your individual points. In other words, the secret to producing a successful outline—and by extension a successful paper—is to pay special attention to the flow or development of ideas.

It's often hard to know for certain the best way to put together points in an outline. We can learn a lot from films about the ways in which various texts are organized. Consider how a film's **trailer**, or short prerelease video, provides a brief *outline* of the key scenes, the main conflict, the crucial characters, and the message of the movie. Figure 6.3 shows still shots from one of the several theatrical trailers for *Avatar*.

Structured loosely as a narrative, this trailer suggests an outline of the film, moving from an introduction of the human characters, to scenes showing the main avatar (Jake) and his Na'vi girlfriend, to scenes of the final physical conflict between the two civilizations. In doing so, the trailer reproduces one of the central themes of *Avatar*: the identification of both good and evil in the human civilization, and the conflict between the corporate part of that civilization and the spiritual Na'vi civilization. There are many ways in which these elements might have been arranged, each suggesting a different argument for the film—and indeed, different *Avatar* trailers made different arguments. The power of the trailer as an organizational tool or outline is that it allows filmmakers to experiment with order and, ultimately, meaning.

Keeping the idea of the trailer in mind, take your ideas from the visual map you have created and craft them into a **formal outline**, a detailed list that uses numbers and letters to indicate subsections of your argument. Rather than list three sections only—such as Introduction, Body, and Conclusion—create several points within the body to show the development of your argument.

Student Writing

See several examples of research outlines on a variety of topics. Look especially at Chris McCormick's outline on "Artificial Intelligence: Visual Representation in Film."
www.pearsonhighered.com/envision/116

As you organize your ideas, remember that formal outlines can help you work step by step through the process of arguing your position. That is, they can save you a lot of time as you approach writing the essay itself. Consider using full sentences to most clearly articulate your thoughts or inserting sources right into the outline;

FIGURE 6.3. These still shots from one of several trailers for the film *Avatar* transition the viewer from the the human perspective into the world of Pandora, and then into the climactic conflict between the worlds.

these techniques can help you troubleshoot areas where you might need to do supplemental research or expand your argument.

Another benefit of outlining is that it allows you to work with the rhetorical canon of **arrangement** (discussed in Chapter 3), experimenting with different organizational structures. Depending on your topic, you might try several approaches, just as filmmakers rearrange a film to create a variety of trailers. You might start your paper with a question,

AT A GLANCE

Useful Organization Strategies for Writing

- ***Chronological:*** relevant for historical discussions
- ***Thematic:*** helps with diverse case studies
- ***Cause and effect:*** focuses on consequences
- ***Problem-solution:*** useful for social issues papers
- ***Illustrative:*** emphasizes examples of a pattern
- ***Macro to micro:*** moves from the general to the specific
- ***Micro to macro:*** moves from the specific to the general
- ***Narrative:*** employs the personal experience

move through evidence, and then arrive at a declarative thesis statement toward the end of the essay. Alternatively, begin with a firm thesis statement up front, followed by an accumulation of supporting evidence that broadens out to a larger issue. Or, try moving thematically through your research offering a progressive argument. See the "At a Glance" box for additional ways to organize your material in an outline.

Outlines with Argumentative Subheads

Outlines can also help you develop the complexity of your research argument if you incorporate subheads and transitions into your writing. **Subheads**, or labeled headings for each subsection of your outline, are a terrific way to structure your ideas into discrete units to show the progression of your argument and help your readers make sense of a complex argument. Subheads work particularly well for longer, research-based essays. You can transform the key parts of your outline into a short list of **argumentative subheads**, or subheads that indicate the progression of your argument at each point.

Seeing Connections
See how Mark Jacobson and Mark A. Delucchi's "A Path to Sustainable Energy by 2030" (page 281) and Andrew Tilin's "Ready, Set, Mutate!" (page 451) for examples of how authors use subheads to help structure their arguments.

If you were writing a detailed outline, you might insert into the body of your paper subheads that indicate specific parts of your argument. You can feel free to get creative by connecting your subheads thematically or by using a single metaphor to add a rich layer of vivid words to your essay. For a film-marketing paper, for instance, instead of using subheads like "Background," "Movies Online," and "Advertising Movies," you might experiment with "Movies Online Are a Big Splash," "Surfing for Movies," and "The Next Wave in Viral Marketing." After you write a list of working subheads, exchange them with a partner. Suggest modifications and new ideas to each other; keep focused on using subheads to advance the argument of the essay. Look at how Dexian Cai met this challenge by incorporating argumentative subheads into his outline.

As you can see from Dex's example, using an appropriate metaphor in a subhead provides consistency in language that in turn can help the flow of your essay.

AT A GLANCE

Assessing Outlines

- ***Thesis:*** Is it complex, contentious, and interesting?
- ***Argument:*** Is there a fluid progression of ideas? Does each one relate back to the thesis? Is there extraneous information that you can cut? Do more points need to be developed?
- ***Sources:*** Are primary sources identified for analysis in the paper? Are secondary sources listed to provide support and authority for the argument? Are there sufficient sources listed for each point? Are visual texts included as argumentative evidence?
- ***Format:*** Are there argumentative subheads? Do they move the argument of the essay along?

Dexian Cai
PWR1 H-1
Dr. Alyssa O'Brien

Research Paper—Outline

I. Introduction

1. Hook: A brief description of a current McDonald's video advertisement. While ostensibly American and Western, the interesting aspect is that this video is in fact an ad targeting an Asian market.
2. Thesis: McDonald's video advertising in East Asia has evolved over time, adapting to trends and changes in Asian societal values. The paper will argue that McDonald's both shapes and is shaped by these evolving trends, creating a dynamic relationship between the restaurant and consumers.
3. Implications: What are the effects of McDonald's influence on Asian values and societal evolution? Is this a healthy trend or merely a restaurant moving with the times? Are accusations of cultural imperialism or degradation of morals justified?

II. The Background Behind the Arches

- A brief history of McDonald's entry into the various East Asian markets. In particular, research will center on Japan, Hong Kong, Korea, Taiwan, China, and Singapore.
- A summary of McDonald's image and *ethos* in the United States.

III. McDonald's: From Homely to Hip

Then

- Rhetorical analysis of ads from the 1970s and 1980s, when McDonald's first broke into the Asian markets.
- Argument that McDonald's was using *pathos*, attempting to portray itself as a family restaurant that made children feel special. Highlight the fact that the campaigns differed across the various countries because McDonald's tailored each campaign to the specific market's characteristics and perceived needs.
- Compare and contrast with contemporary American campaigns. Family vs. fast food.
- Source: McDonald's Corporation. (Pending the approval of a request sent via e-mail.)
- Secondary Source: Watson, James L. *Golden Arches East*: *McDonald's in East Asia*. Palo Alto, CA: Stanford UP, 1997.

Notice how Dex includes the opening line for his paper, the hook, right in the outline, setting the tone for the paper.

His thesis comprises two sentences since this argument is complex, although he could develop the "how so" part of the thesis more.

He ends the intro with questions to engage the reader.

After a brief background section, Dex moves on to the heart of his argument. The subhead "From Homely to Hip" reflects in words the point Dex will make in this section, namely, that McDonald's has changed its brand image from conservative to trendy. The play on words in the subhead helps keep Dex on track and to interest the reader.

Note that he includes his sources right in his outline so he'll be sure to weave them into his paper.

Since his paper focuses on the visual rhetoric of McDonald's advertising in Asia, it is appropriate for Dex to include images in his outline. These images will serve as evidence for his argument. [Images were removed for copyright purposes but appeared in Dex's original outline.]

Now

- Rhetorical analysis of most recent video ads.
- Argument that McDonald's marketing strategy has evolved to embrace East Asia as an "assimilated market," as the campaign and slogan are standardized the world over. There is no longer a uniquely Asian campaign; instead it is replaced by the homogeneous American set of ads.
- Image of fun and relaxation is interspersed with images of McDonald's products. Using youth to drive the campaign is a clear signal of the target audience and the aim of creating a "cool" and "hip" image for the franchise. This contrasts the familial tone of ads from the "early days." A switch from *pathos* to *ethos*.
- Sources: McDonald's Country Websites

He includes a key research question as a transition into this section. His next subhead again uses language to convey this point in the progression of his argument; with such argumentative subheads, he can be certain that his argument is building in significance.

IV. Getting Behind the Arches

- Key Question: What has brought about this evolution in advertising strategies in East Asia? Why the shift in image?
- Argument: The dynamics of influence are mutual and interactive. Although McDonald's largely responds to perceived societal trends, it also seeks to influence attitudes and sell its version of "hip" or "cool," especially to Asian youth.
- Analyze how the Asian case is reflective of McDonald's marketing strategy internationally. Discuss the moral/ethical implications of such strategies.
- Consider the McDonald's "Culture of Power" argument in Kincheloe's book. Are the claims leveled against the franchise valid?
- Source: Kincheloe, Joe L. *The Sign of the Burger: McDonald's and the Culture of Power*. Philadelphia: Temple UP, 2002.

He is still working on points of the argument, even in the outline, as shown in his question whether to bring in Joe Kincheloe's argument as a secondary source here.

The final section is not titled "Conclusion" but instead uses an argumentative subhead to transition into the closing argument of the paper, namely that the presence of McDonald's is potentially changing distinctions between nations, blurring cultures into a combined identity Dex calls "Amer-Asia."

V. Amer-Asia? A Peek at the Future of Asia

- Summarize/recap the arguments of the paper.

Larger Questions

- Given the trend of increasing global integration, is homogenization under American leadership an inevitable end of modern civilization?
- Discuss ways in which this is not so ("dissenting opinion"). Asia's cultures continue to greatly influence McDonald's, causing wide variations between McDonald's image in Asia and in America.
- Answer these bigger concerns: What are the implications of changing societal trends for Asian youth? How does McDonald's advertising affect and influence these trends? Do the ads exacerbate/speed up the "Americanization" of Asian youth? or do they merely reflect what is already present?

Transitions

You can also enhance the flow of your writing with careful attention to **transitions**—phrases that provide the connections between the paragraphs or sections in your paper. When creating transitions, even during your outlining phase, think about how you can signal the next idea, build on the previous idea, or reiterate the key terms of your thesis as you advance your argument. Many students like to think of the game of dominoes when composing transitions: each domino can only touch another domino with a matching number; two connects with two, three with three. Using this notion of progressive, connecting terms, you can incorporate transitions within sections of your outline to give it overall structure and flow. Then, when you turn to writing the paper, you will avoid big jumps in logic. Instead, by incorporating the transitions from your outline, you will produce a polished piece of written work.

Spotlight on Your Argument

As you turn now from writing an outline to fleshing out the full draft, consider the decision before you concerning what kind of voice or rhetorical stance to take in the language of your prose. Again, we can learn a lot from filmmakers as they face similar decisions.

In his 2007 documentary, *Sicko*, Michael Moore is careful to introduce and acknowledge his sources, but even while he includes many other voices in his film, he ultimately emphasizes his own argument. Of course, the film relies on research as background material, offering the narrator's comments as interview segments, in which a primary or secondary authority speaks directly to the audience, and as quoted material spoken directly by the narrator or through voice-over. But as the poster in Figure 6.4 suggests, Moore's opinion provides the foundation for everything disclosed in the film, making his rhetorical stance a prominent part of the text.

FIGURE 6.4. The promotional poster for *Sicko* reveals the way Michael Moore emphasizes his own argument in the film.

You should also consider diverse ways to present your argument. Think of the power of a casting director on a film set. In a film such as Franco Zeffirelli's version of *Hamlet* (1990), for instance, the entire sexual politics of the narrative was influenced by the decision to cast Glenn Close (age 43 at the time) as Queen Gertrude, mother to Mel Gibson's Hamlet (Gibson was 34). Their close proximity in age set in relief an incest plot at which Shakespeare himself had only hinted. In essence, what audiences watched in the movie theater was less Shakespeare's *Hamlet* and more Zeffirelli's interpretation of it. In your own writing, you have a comparable power; the way you "cast" your sources can influence your reader's understanding of your argument.

In fact, your treatment of your sources will define your approach to your topic. Consider the "objectivity" of a celebrity biography shown on TV: although the text purports to offer no explicit argument, the selection of quotations used, the identities of people interviewed, and the emphasis given to certain stages of the artist's career collaborate to produce not some objective *truth* but a single *version* of that artist's life. Or think about Oliver Stone's *W* (2008) and the controversy it stirred.

The film was in fact an argument: Stone used primary and secondary evidence to create his own interpretation of the events surrounding George W. Bush's life and presidency.

Sometimes you want to put your sources center stage and direct from behind the scenes, and sometimes you will want to step out of the shadows and articulate your argument more explicitly to the audience. Whichever way you go, you should decide what role you, the writer, will play in your paper. The key is to choose the role that will produce the most effective argument on your topic, one that fits the needs of your rhetorical situation. Your voice is your spotlight on your argument; it should have rhetorical purpose and complement the content of your project.

Analyzing a Published Argument

As you outline your research paper and consider ways to bring your sources into your argument, you should study carefully the writing found in articles that you encounter throughout your research project. You can learn a lot about how to organize and spotlight your own argument from a *rhetorical analysis* of the formal properties of your secondary sources. Examine the article by Bret Schulte posted in both the print and online editions of *U.S. News & World Report.* The article provides an excellent snapshot back in time of the rhetorical situation from 2006—when *An Inconvenient Truth* first appeared in cinemas and people were beginning to learn about global warming. Schulte's piece demonstrates many of the writing techniques we've been learning in this chapter, including arranging his points into a progression of ideas and making his own voice quite strong as a spotlight on his argument. Specifically, you'll see that the piece uses interview research and reformats it into an argument that reflects the writer's own perspective on the film. The piece structures itself with subheads that are argumentative, cites interview with quotations, integrates statistics as research, and ends with a memorable conclusion.

Seeing Connections
Compare Bret Schulte's treatment of Al Gore's environmentalism to that found in Bjørn Lomborg's "Inconvenient Truths for Al Gore" (page 259). See also images from *An Inconvenient Truth* on pages 257–258 and Gore's Nobel Peace Prize Lecture on page 276.

SAYING IT IN CINEMA

By Bret Schulte

Posted 5/28/06 *U.S. News & World Report*

President Bush doubts he'll see it, but millions of other people undoubtedly will. Former Vice President Al Gore's docu-horror film about the frightening future promised by global warming—an apocalyptic world of deadly hurricanes, rising oceans, disease, drought, and famine—is pushing the debate to a new level. While tracking Gore's political ascent and contentious loss of the presidency in 2000, the film zeroes in on Gore's newest campaign: to educate the public about the perils of global warming one PowerPoint presentation at a time. Although Gore insists he has no plans

Notice how Schulte's voice emerges immediately when he calls *An Inconvenient Truth* a "docu-horror film."

The alliteration (public–perils–PowerPoint presentation) and exaggerated *pathos* further develop Schulte's rhetorical stance.

to run for national office, the film has thrust him back into the national limelight and sparked an industry of "Al Gore for president" speculation. His well-publicized movie has also provoked critics to run campaign-style ads challenging climate change science. Gore spoke with *U.S. News* about the film, *An Inconvenient Truth*, already playing in select cities and slated for 125 markets by July 4. Excerpts:

Public indifference. We are dumping tens of millions of tons [of carbon dioxide] into the atmosphere every day, and it has literally changed the relationship between the Earth and the sun. It's a challenge to our moral imagination to understand we are now like a bull in the china shop. [And] there has been a very well-organized and lavishly funded effort by a few irresponsible polluters to intentionally confuse the American people by spending millions of dollars a year on pseudo-science reports—the same way the tobacco industry used that technique to stave off action to save the lives of smokers.

Rather than enclosing direct quotations from Gore's interview in quotation marks, Schulte opts for an innovative structure. He pairs a rhetorical subhead of his own (his argument) with an excerpt from interview (his source). The merger of Schulte's and Gore's voice provides a unique rhetorical effect on the reader.

Saving the Earth vs. saving the economy. The companies that are doing well . . . are the ones that have become more efficient. Reducing pollution actually creates jobs and strengthens the economy. Pollution is waste, and the modern approach to pollution reduction dovetails with successful business making higher profits.

Gore's stiff personality. I benefit from low expectations.

At this point, the sarcasm in the subhead "Gore's stiff personality" indicates that you should not take the article as a literal transcription of an interview. Instead, the writer crafts an argument *about Gore* through strong references to history, in this case the 2000 election.

Losing the presidency. I don't cry over spilled milk. It's very difficult in a national campaign for any candidate to be seen and heard without the distortions his or her opponent makes on an hourly basis. I think I've been through a lot since the 2000 campaign, and that old cliche, "What doesn't kill you makes you stronger," is sometimes true.

Global warming and the media. The debate over global warming is over. The slide [in my presentation] people most ask me about is the one that contrasts the massive study of 10 years of peer-reviewed scientific articles on global warming, zero percentage of which disagreed with the consensus, and the study of 14 years of newspaper articles, 53 percent of which expressed doubt about whether the problem is real or not. That is really a striking contrast.

Here, the writer refers to research incorporated by Gore in his film, primarily *logos.*

The Competitive Enterprise Institute's TV campaign. I'm not surprised. They're funded by Exxon Mobil, and they put a lot of money into trying to confuse people. Unfortunately, they have succeeded. I'm hopeful they will soon be recognized for what they are and put in the same category as people who still believe the moon landing was staged in a movie lot.

The references to the TV campaign—and to people not believing the truth of other events—builds the argument.

Looking back on the Senate's turndown of the Kyoto Protocol. I did push as hard as I knew how to. The truth is that Congress was not willing to ratify it. It was already controlled by the Republicans, but if it had been controlled by the Democrats, I dare say at that point, the result would have been nearly the same. I think that is changing.

Lobbying the people, not the politicians. Nothing is going to change in Washington until the sense of urgency felt and expressed by the American people changes. I'm concentrating on that task.

The subtle allusions to steps Gore recommends we take to save the environment serve to build the writer's *ethos*, as they show his strong familiarity with the content. At the same time, these references mock Gore's film.

By ending with humor, the writer packs a memorable punch.

Practicing what you preach. We have a hybrid car and all the new light bulbs. My family is completely carbon neutral. That means reducing as much carbon dioxide as we possibly can and then buying offsets to cancel out the rest.

If Gore were president. One difference is that you might see George W. Bush doing a cold opener on *Saturday Night Live* from an alternate universe.

CREATIVE PRACTICE

Visit the *Envision* Website and follow the link for *The Age of Stupid* (2009). How does this recent film about global warming and climate change make a different argument than Gore's *Inconvenient Truth*? What rhetorical strategies does the filmmaker use to convey his opinion? Notice the voice-over, the images, the narrative, the logical and *pathos* appeals. How does the interplay between image and word construct the argument of the film? How would you characterize the "voice" of the film?

www.pearsonhighered.com/envision/124

Integrating Research Sources

After you decide on your approach to working with sources—as a strong explicit narrator or as the synthesizer of information—you need to start turning your outline into a rough draft. But how will you introduce and weave these other voices (your sources) into your written prose? Specifically, you will need to include your sources not only appropriately (to avoid plagiarism) and rhetorically (to decide on how much of a presence you will have in the paper) but also strategically (to provide a range of quotations and supporting evidence for your paper). We call this process **integrating sources**, and it's a complex process that occurs in three basic ways:

- **Summary:** synthesizing a great deal of information from a source
- **Paraphrase:** putting a source quotation into your own words
- **Direct quotation:** excerpting a specific passage from a source, enclosing it in quotation marks

You'll want to alternate among these methods while incorporating your sources with stylistic variety. This means knowing your options as a writer and selecting the best method for each rhetorical situation within your research essay. Realize that you have many "choices" for how to integrate research sources, and your decisions should be determined by the specific need of each part of your argument as well as the value of the research to build your *ethos*, provide background, offer an alternative perspective, or convey foundational knowledge.

Selecting Summary

A **summary** is a brief version—in your own words—of the overall content of a text. You might want to summarize the plot of a film or a book in a review, or you might want to summarize the basic argument presented by one of your sources in order to respond to it. Summaries are not analyses; you are not exploring your own ideas when you summarize but merely laying out the ideas explored by another writer in another text. You need to make sure that you tell your readers exactly what you are summarizing and provide complete bibliographical information at the end of your paper. For example, a research paper about the Italian films produced after WWII might include a summary that begins:

> In their influential study *Italian Neorealism and Global Cinema*, cultural critics Laura Ruberto and Kristi Wilson provide a concise history of film innovations at the turn of the twentieth century and argue that Italian documentaries allowed international conflicts to seem real to viewers . . .

Your summary would follow, and your list of works cited at the end of your paper would include the following reference:

Ruberto, Laura E. and Wilson, Kristi M. *Italian Neorealism and Global Cinema*. Detroit: Wayne State UP, 2007. Print.

Seeing Connections
See Chapter 7 for a more extended discussion of proper citation form.

If you wanted to include a brief quote within the body of your summary, then you would use quotation marks and a page number, as follows:

> In their influential study *Italian Neorealism and Global Cinema*, cultural critics Laura Ruberto and Kristi Wilson provide a concise history of film innovations at the turn of the twentieth century and argue that Italian documentaries "had a way of making the global seem local" (2).

Note that in this case, you are still writing a summary, but you include a direct quotation because it is rhetorically concise and powerful (with *pathos*-laden language), but also because citing the text gives you more *ethos* or authority as a writer.

Picking Paraphrase

Unlike a summary, a **paraphrase** focuses in and restates one part of a text. While a summary is often shorter than the text it summarizes, a paraphrase may be longer or shorter than the text it paraphrases. You might want to paraphrase a text to help your readers understand it, particularly if the original text is dense or difficult. Or you might simply want to paraphrase to make sure that you understand the source yourself—to offer yourself an opportunity to think clearly about the words you are reading. For instance, you might select the following lines to paraphrase:

> "Film had a way of making the global seem local, and the effect of movement, and, later, sound created an immediacy that still photos and written narratives could not approach" (Ruberto and Wilson 2).

Your paraphrase might read as follows:

> Italian film brought world events home to viewers, especially through moving images and audio (Ruberto and Wilson 2).

Note that you replace all the words, not just some of them, for a paraphrase. When in doubt, put quotes around the words from the original source. This not only allows your reader to see what words come from the text, but it also enables your reader to discern how you are having a conversation with your research sources. You need to be careful that you are using your own words to create a new text, not simply cutting and pasting the words of your source together in a different order. If you follow both the structure and the language of the original source closely, substituting only an occasional synonym to avoid directly quoting, then you are actually plagiarizing—even if you do so accidentally and even if you provide an appropriate citation. You are plagiarizing because you are not informing your reader that the structure, ideas, and much of the language used in your paper were created by someone else.

Seeing Connections
For more guidelines on avoiding unintentional plagiarism, see Chapter 7.

How to avoid this problem? Provide your reader with the appropriate bibliographical information about your source by offering a lead-in phrase ("As Ruberto and Wilson argue in their book *Italian Neorealism and Global Cinema. . .*") and then make sure that you list the complete reference for this source at the end of your paper. Or you can provide a parenthetical citation after the summary or paraphrase including the author's name and, for a paraphrase, the page number where the passage you are paraphrasing appears in the original text (see *Envision* Chapter 7 for guidelines on documentation).

Using Direct Quotations

Quoting directly from a source may seem much simpler than paraphrasing or summarizing, but quotations should be included to accomplish a specific rhetorical purpose, and they must be integrated responsibly so that you give the writer credit. Consider how you might feel if someone took your writing and recycled it without giving you credit. More importantly, realize that naming the author and background of a great passage can build your authority and *ethos* as a writer, so it is a wise move to name your sources in your paper. However, be careful not to swing to the opposite extreme and fill your paper with quotations from others. If a quotation does not fit into any of the categories listed in the "At a Glance" box, consider paraphrasing or summarizing it. What you want to avoid is a paper dominated by unnecessary quotations; in such a case, your argument—what readers expect most in your paper—gets buried. It's similar to what happens in film when the filmmaker splices together too many different scenes—the audience becomes lost in the montage and can no longer follow the narrative.

AT A GLANCE

Reasons to Use Direct Quotations

- ***Evidence:*** the quotation provides tangible evidence for part of your argument.
- ***Ethos:*** the original author is a primary source or an expert on the subject, and including a direct quotation would increase the *ethos* of your argument.
- ***Language:*** the original author used memorable phrasing or has a particular voice that would be lost in paraphrase.

Integrating, Not Inserting, Quotations

Seeing Connections
Look at the various ways in which Clive Thompson integrates direct quotations into his article, "I'm So Digitally Close to You" (page 296).

But how, practically, do you go about *integrating* sources appropriately and effectively rather than simply *inserting* them? To work successfully with quotations, try out various strategies of introducing the quotation listed below.

These examples are from a paper on Al Gore's 2006 film, *An Inconvenient Truth.* Note that these examples do not include page numbers because they refer to an online source without numbered pages, as is true of many of the sources we use today. However, if you are quoting from a print source, your citation should also include the page number where the original material appeared.

- **Use an introductory clause/phrase** that refers to the original author or title of the source:

> Reacting strongly to the environmentalist message, online columnist Joseph Blast argues, "*An Inconvenient Truth* contains very little truth, and a big helping of propaganda."

- **Use an incorporated structure** that seamlessly melds the quotation into your sentence so that it flows smoothly as part of your essay:

  Joseph Blast articulated one of the most common critiques of Al Gore's global warming film in a June 2006 online editorial when he claimed that "*An Inconvenient Truth* contains very little truth, and a big helping of propaganda."

- **Use an interrupted structure,** breaking the quote into two halves and embedding information regarding the author and/or the original text in the middle of the quotation itself:

  "In the style of a previous generation of propaganda films," Joseph Blast argues in his June 2006 editorial, "Gore substitutes vivid images of the alleged effects of global warming for an accurate account of the scientific debate."

- **Use an end comment,** inserting the quotation and then providing an interpretation, or closing comment, that importantly advances the argument:

  Joseph Blast's claim that "*An Inconvenient Truth* contains very little truth, and a big helping of propaganda" exemplifies the critical tendency to undermine the legitimacy of an opposing point of view by categorizing it as "propaganda."

Experiment with these strategies in your own writing to determine which best serves your rhetorical purpose. For instance, if you want to draw attention to the *author* of a quotation to add *ethos* to your argument, you might opt to integrate using an introductory clause; however, if you want to emphasize *information* rather than authorship, an incorporated structure might be more effective. One key to remember is to avoid overusing any one type of integration strategy; in that case, your writing style might become monotonous, like a film that relies too heavily on the same types of shots.

AT A GLANCE

Integrating Sources Appropriately and Effectively

- ***Read.*** Read the source actively and carefully, underlining passages that move you or suggest moments of deep meaning, or passages that might contribute to your argument. If you are working with online texts, cut and paste the citation into a document and note the paragraph number (for Websites) or page number. Always note the page number if you transcribe quotations as you read.

  You'll need this part in order to provide the citation in your own writing.

- ***Record.*** Keep a notebook or an annotated file of citations in which you record your reactions to a particular passage you've read. Does this passage move you? Does it reveal the theme of the text, the climax of a scene, the point of the argument, the purpose of the passage?

  You'll need this part in order to provide your interpretation of the citation.

- ***Relate.*** Place the citation and your interpretation in an appropriate place in your own essay. Think about where in the essay, and in which particular paragraph, the citation should appear. Think about the context—what comes before and after the citation? How is the citation related to the text around it? Never just insert a quotation because it feels like one should be there; use citations (quotations, paraphrases, summaries) strategically to help support your own argument.

  You'll need this part in order to integrate your citations effectively.

Additional strategies for integrating quotations include the following techniques:

- To quote a source within a source, use (quoted in ___) to indicate where *you* found the quotation, for instance:

  Film critic Millicent Marcus argues that "neorealism is first and foremost a moral statement" (quoted in Ruberto and Wilson 7).

- To edit part of a quote, use square brackets as such [ ]. You might do this to get concisely to the heart of the issue in your chosen quotation. For instance, you might edit the Blast quote above:

  Joseph Blast argues in his June 2006 editorial, "Gore substitutes vivid images [. . .] for an accurate account of the scientific debate."

Remember that the purpose of integrating sources is to demonstrate your work as a researcher and to show that you are building your argument on the work of others. Therefore, choose what types of integration strategies work best for each source and for each part of your paper. If you're worried that you have integrated too many sources (and lost your own voice), spend some time reviewing the draft and ask yourself:

- Am I still the moderator of this conversation?
- Is my voice clear, compelling, and original?
- Do I allow my own argument to emerge as foremost in this piece?

In your efforts to integrate sources effectively, keep in mind that source material should *support* your argument, not supplant it.

AT A GLANCE

Check for Integrating Sources

- Did you ***introduce the quote*** in various ways?
- Did you ***link the reference*** to your argument to show the relevance?
- Did you ***comment*** on it afterward to advance your argument?
- Did you ***cite*** it properly using the appropriate documentation style for your subject area?

Documentation During Integration

As you incorporate sources into your draft, be sure to include citations for each quotation or paraphrase. This would also be a good time to begin drafting your works-cited list or bibliography, to save time later. The purpose of this is not only to provide a "list of credits" for your references but also to supply interested readers with the resources to continue learning about your topic. Just as you undoubtedly found certain articles inspiring while investigating your topic and used them as springboards for more focused research, so too might your paper serve as a means of leading your readers to intriguing ideas and articles. You can go back over the correct format for citations in your final edit, following the guidelines in Chapter 7 for documentation to do so.

Drafting Your Research Argument

As you continue to forge ahead with your research argument, turning it from an outline to a full draft or composing sections of your argument in separate time blocks, remember that there are many strategies for getting it done. For each of these ways of working, the key is to start and then just keep writing. Try out one of the many methods described in the "At a Glance" box.

AT A GLANCE

Strategies for Drafting

- ***Following the linear path:*** Start at the beginning, write the introduction, and then move sequentially through each point of argument.
- ***Fleshing out the outline:*** Gradually transform the outline into a full draft, moving from a keyword outline to a prose outline by systematically expanding each of the sections; as you add more detail, the keywords fall away, leaving behind drafted paragraphs.
- ***Writing from the middle:*** Start writing from a point of greatest strength or start with a section you can complete easily; then write around it and fill out sections as you go.
- ***Freewrite and then reverse outline:*** First, freewrite a few pages; then compose a **reverse outline** in which you record the point of each paragraph to assess the argument's flow and structure; and finally, reorder and rewrite the paper until it begins to take the proper form for the argument.

Also realize that to write is to struggle with the process, as noted by Stanford University psychologist David Rasch: "Almost all writers are familiar with the experience of feeling stuck, blocked, overwhelmed, or behind schedule in their writing." What can help? Staying motivated and relying on others.

Keeping Your Passion

As you move deeper into the writing process, integrating quotations and working out the flow of your argument, don't lose sight of your enthusiasm for your subject. Reread your earliest freewrites and your entries in your research log. What goals, what motivations prompted you to begin the project? What aspects of your topic excited you, angered you, or inspired you? What contribution did you imagine yourself making to this discussion? As you begin synthesizing your information and creating a unified argument, you are in effect realizing that initial vision. Remember, your audience will be reading your paper to learn *your* particular point of view on the subject. Your drafts are your shooting scripts, if you will—the versions of your paper that ultimately you will transform, through careful review, editing, and revision, into your "release" of the text into final form.

You should also allow yourself well-needed energy breaks. Brief periods away from the writing process can often recharge and reinvigorate your approach to the paper and help you think through difficult points in the argument. Ironically, a pause in drafting can also help you avoid writer's block by allowing you to remember what interested you about this project in the first place.

Finally, if you are having trouble getting through the draft process, allow yourself to write what Anne Lamott, author of *Bird by Bird,* famously calls the "shitty first draft." In the words of Lamott, "All good writers write them. This is how they end up with good second drafts and terrific third drafts." That is, you should realize that the first version by no means has to be perfect or even close to what the final paper will look like. It is instead simply your first attempt at getting your ideas on paper. Freeing yourself to write something—anything—can help you escape from the weight of perfectionism or the fear of failure that often paralyzes writers. You will have plenty of opportunities to rework the material, show your draft to others, and move forward with the writing process.

Collaboration Through Peer Review

Take advantage of the community of writers in your class to talk through your ideas and share work in progress. You might find your organizational plan confirmed by your peers, or you might be pleasantly surprised by their suggestions for alternative structures, ways of integrating sources, or images to include in the paper. Such discussions can help you get back your fire for your project as well as give you extremely useful advice to implement in the writing of the draft. Moreover, your peers' responses to your work in progress can help you determine if your writing is persuasive or not.

Consider how collaboration works in the film industry. Even though a film is generally recognized as a unified expression of a single idea, in reality it is the product of the collaborative effort of dozens of individuals, from the screenwriter and actors to the key grips and camera operators. But there is another, often less recognized collaborator: the audience. Think about how novels are adapted to the large screen: whether by adding a romantic subplot or substituting a "Hollywood ending" for a less palatable one, many scriptwriters deliberately revise original texts to accommodate the perceived desires of a mass audience. Sometimes an entire narrative is recast to make it more marketable; the 1995 hit, *Clueless*, and the 2001 teen film *O*, are good examples of films in which literary classics (Jane Austen's *Emma* and William Shakespeare's *Othello*) were updated to appeal to a mainstream modern audience.

Sometimes the audience's intervention is more direct. It is common practice for many filmmakers to hold "advance screenings" of major releases, designed to gauge audience reaction. In 1986, a preview audience's reaction to the ending of the film *Fatal Attraction* was so negative that director Adrian Lyne reshot the final scenes (Figure 6.5). When the film was released in the following year, it featured a markedly different conclusion. Similarly, the version of *Blade Runner* released in 1982 was significantly edited in an attempt to increase its box office appeal; however, director Ridley Scott changed the ending yet again years later, premiering his *Blade Runner—The Director's Cut* 11 years after the movie first appeared. In each case, collaboration shaped the final version and made evident the rhetorical triangle between audience, writer, and text. Similarly, writing needs to take into consideration the audience's expectations; we write to show an audience our work, so we need to respond to audience needs when we write and revise our texts.

FIGURE 6.5. When preview audiences saw the original ending for the film *Fatal Attraction,* in which the villainess, Alex, survived, their reactions were so negative that the director Adrian Lyne reshot it, adding a completely new ending in which the young wife stabs her husband's tormentor to death. The film became a huge hit.

As a writer you can benefit from "advance screenings" of your argument; the collaborative work you do on the structure and content of your outlines and drafts should guide you to a revised product that satisfies both you and your audience. But to do so, you need feedback from your audience in the form of peer review; then you will need to revise your draft to accommodate the suggestions you receive.

Analyzing a Student Essay About Film

Let's examine now the draft of Stanford student Wan Jin Park, who developed a research project comparing Gore's film *An Inconvenient Truth* (2006) to Gore's more recent PowerPoint slide show during his talk at TED, a conference organized to showcase the most innovative thinking to date. Wan Jin conducted a range of academic and field research, wrote a detailed outline, and then composed his draft. After feedback from his course instructor and his classroom peers, he revised his first partial draft and outline substantially, as demonstrated later in this chapter. But throughout, Wan Jin kept his passion for his project and his respect for Gore as a leader trying to use rhetoric to persuade people of the importance of attending to the environment. We can study his first draft and conduct a *rhetorical analysis* of his writing strategies to see how you, too, can approach putting your research argument down on paper.

In particular, you'll see that the excerpt from Wan Jin's draft integrates research sources in a variety of ways, begins to showcase Wan Jin's own voice as a writer, and effectively relies on the outline as a prewriting tool.

Wan Jin Park
Working Draft + Outline

Environmental Leadership:
How Al Gore Illuminated an Overlooked Crisis

Rising levels of carbon dioxide emissions do not contribute to global warming. It has become silly and naïve to argue thus even before a group of middle school students. The awareness of the dangers of our carbon addicted lifestyle, however, would not be as widespread as it is today had it not been for the one man spearheading the global movement against climate change: Al Gore. Gore's rise to environmental influence is in large part due to Davis Guggenheim's documentary *An Inconvenient Truth*, which was then followed by a revised presentation at the TED Conference in March 2008. What strikes the audience, however, is not the revision of data and graphics in the slides, but rather, it is the change in Gore's rhetoric. In *An Inconvenient Truth*, Gore focuses on drawing in the audience and persuading them to join the environmental movement through the depiction of himself as a warm, dedicated, but lonely leader in the face of a global crisis; by contrast, at the TED presentation, Gore has garnered huge support, but senses a lack of change in the United States, and thus focuses on pushing the public toward increased initiative through his urgent and passionate rhetoric.

Wan Jin's working title is strong and raises a problem–but in the revision, he will introduce his argument more forcefully.

His organizational strategy is to open with a counterargument, acknowledging that, today, our *kairos* is that even middle-schoolers know about global warming.

Then he introduces the film fully as well as his second primary source: Gore's 2008 TED talk.

Even in a draft, Wan Jin has strongly developed his thesis—this work will sustain him through the rest of the paper. He can use the key terms of the thesis to structure the remaining sections of the essay.

Wan Jin's subheads show his gift for creative language—he uses *pathos* but also indicates this new part of his argument with the subhead.

Gripping the Flames: Gore Leading the Environmental Movement

At the forefront of the global environmental movement against climate change is Al Gore. In fact, The Nielsen Company, a leading global marketing and advertising research company, conducted a survey in conjunction with Oxford University which serves as a testament to Gore's environmental prominence. In a survey of 26,486 people across 47 countries, Gore has been voted as "the most influential spokesperson to champion the global warming debate," even "ahead of former United Nations" Secretary General Kofi Anan (Nielsen).

Already bringing in rerearch, Wan Jin starts with facts and statistics (*logos*) from survey and field research.

Gore has been active with the environmental movement since the beginning of his political career; however, his lasting, and perhaps, most influential contribution did not come until the release of Davis Guggenheim's *An Inconvenient Truth* in May 2006. Although based on lectures "that Gore has been presenting in one form or another for nearly three decades," *An Inconvenient Truth* has achieved levels of popularity and influence unrivalled by those of any other medium employed in the environmental movement (Rosteck). Earning over $49 million, it currently ranks as the fifth-highest-grossing documentary in the history of the United States. Further indicative of the documentary's influence are the results of another survey conducted by The Nielsen Company in April 2007. Of the viewers who have seen *An Inconvenient Truth*, eighty-nine percent reported to have become "more aware of the problem"; sixty-six percent "changed their mind about global warming"; and most importantly, seventh-four percent changed their habits as a result (Nielsen).

Next, he provides background and cites an article from his research (Rosteck).

Considering the fact that *An Inconvenient Truth* is Gore's most influential rhetorical medium, an analysis of the documentary will thus illuminate the key characteristics that define the success of Gore's environmental leadership.

At this point, Wan Jin offers a road map for the rest of his essay, referring back to his title and his thesis in a way that offers powerful coherence for the essay.

Contrasting Images: the Beautiful and the Doomed

An Inconvenient Truth begins with a beautiful depiction of nature. The camera focuses close-up on a branch full of small green tree leaves. The green hue is accentuated by the bright sunlight that is reflected off of the leaf blades. After a few seconds, the camera shifts to the right to reveal a sparkling river. The soft piano music in the background adds to the calm and peaceful mood. Al Gore then narrates in the background, purposefully emphasizing the sibilants as if to imitate the sounds of the river and the rustling leaves:

> You look at that river gently flowing by. You notice the leaves rustling with the wind. You hear the birds. You hear the tree frogs. In the distance, you hear a cow. You feel the grass. The mud gives a little bit on the riverbank. It's quiet; it's peaceful. (Inconvenient)

The first thirty seconds of the film is beautiful. However, Gore interjects and introduces human neglect of nature by stating, "all of a sudden, it's a gearshift inside you and it's like taking a deep breath and going 'Oh yeah, I forgot about this'" (Inconvenient). By using the word "gearshift," Gore metaphorically compares the audience to machines that are equipped with a gear; in essence, Gore argues that we have become the products of our industrial production, and have thus become so separate from our nature that we have completely forgot about it.

The consequences of our neglect are horrifying. After the establishment of our neglect, Gore's presentation shows images of the damages we made to nature. We see images of factories emitting thick black smog that obscures the sun. In one of the images, the hue of the sky is grayish purple; considering how the corpses of formerly sick bodies usually show this hue, this image is suggestive of the damage we have done to nature. Furthermore, as a demonstration of how global warming has aggravated natural disasters, we see footages of the aftermath of Hurricane Katrina. We see footages of crying babies without shelter and caretakers, a bloated dead body lying face down in the water, and a man stroking the forehead of his dead wife. Although Hurricane Katrina has been an American natural disaster, these footages shock even the most foreign audience.

The presentation of these images after Gore's argument that we have forgotten about our nature compels the audience to feel guilt and responsibility. In effect, Gore induces the audience to personalize the issue

As Wan Jin gets into the body of his essay, he takes his evidence one piece at a time, first providing a strong rhetorical analysis of the visual and audio elements of the film, then quoting directly from Gore's voice-over.

With the word, "However," Wan Jin lets us know his view, introducing his argument.

The careful analysis of specific words such as "gearshift" make this rhetorical argument persuasive.

Just as he analyzed the words in the film, Wan Jin carefully analyzes the images, building his argument. His own voice as a writer here becomes adamant and urgent, evoking the mood of the film but also forcing us to take his argument seriously.

This section ends with a mini summary and strong statement of Wan Jin's argument. In this way, he creates an effective organization for his larger paper, and from here can go about completing it one section at a time.

The next sections of the draft show in outline form the content Wan Jin plans to cover: including his main arguments, his section of evidence, and his secondary source citations.

He provides an *ethos*-building introduction for his secondary source.

He will comment on this secondary source with an example of his own.

By selecting and arranging quotes in his draft, Wan Jin can approach the writing with a keen sense of his argument and overall plan for persuading the reader. He has chosen his evidence and uses the draft to sort through it effectively.

of climate change, thereby making us more receptive to Gore's message of change.

The Dedicated Leader

- After fear, Gore portrays himself as a dedicated leader
- autobiographical threads in the documentary
- vulnerable moments in Gore's personal history
- Source: these stories "strengthen[ed] the hero's resolve"
- Secondary source: Kathryn Olson, Director of the Rhetorical Leadership Graduate Certificate Program at University of Wisconsin-Milwaukee, claims the autobiographical threads "persuasively documents Gore's single-mindedness in pursuing his public cause, often at his own expense, through a lifetime of disappointments and sacrificing a comfortable retirement to carry the message globally."
- Gore in a Beijing taxi on way to Tsing Hua University.

Lonely Leader

- personal footages depict Gore as "emotional suffering"
- Senator James Inhofe attacks Gore's ideas
- Secondary Source: Gore "inviting impression that encourages auditors to join him or her in social action" (Olson).

TED Presentation

- More passionate; more religious; his sense of urgency is raised
- His tone of voice, joking, moral issue
- Quote: "The only two countries that didn't ratify—and now there's only one. Australia had an election. And there was a campaign in Australia that involved television and Internet and radio commercials to lift the **sense of urgency** for the people there. And we trained 250 people to give the slide show in every town and village and city in Australia"
    - There has been progress: Gore contributed to the change through his environment
- "The cities supporting Kyoto in the US are up to 780"
- Returning to religious rhetoric, passion, urgency
- Evidence; He does not begin his presentation about how far we have come since 2006, when the documentary film *An Inconvenient Film* was released. Instead, he begins by quoting Karen Armstrong (I believe

she is someone prominent in religious studies) who said "religion really properly understood is not about belief, but about behavior."

- In arguing this, he essentially says that what we lack with our response to climate change is a change in behavior
  - "But, as important as it is to change the light bulbs, it is more important to change the laws. And when we change our behavior in our daily lives, we sometimes leave out the citizenship part and the democracy part."

Seeing Connections
For helpful strategies on composing compelling introductions and conclusions, see Chapter 1, page 58.

As shown by Wan Jin's paper, a working draft should have a strong and well-developed thesis. This will drive the entire argument. Then, you can begin to work through the sections of an outline, providing specific evidence and secondary source support in what in Chapter 5 we called "a conversation with your sources." As you continue, fill in parts of your draft and rely on your peers for support and feedback.

Revising Your Draft

As many professional writers can attest—and Wan Jin would agree with this based on his drafting experience—a text goes through numerous drafts on its way to becoming a polished final product. Even filmmakers produce multiple drafts of their movies before they release their film, experimenting with different sequencing, camera shots, and pacing to create what they consider to be the fulfillment of their artistic vision. We've all seen the results of this process: deleted scenes or *outtakes* from popular film or television programs. What these segments represent are moments of work (writing, producing, and shooting) that, after review and editing, were removed to streamline the film.

As you might imagine, often it's difficult or even painful to reshape your work during revision; it's hard to leave some of your writing behind on the cutting room floor. However, as your project develops, its focus may change: sources or ideas that seemed important to you during the early stages of research may become less relevant, even tangential; a promising strategy of argumentation may turn out to be less suitable to your project; a key transition may be no longer necessary once you reorganize the argument. As you turn to your draft with a critical eye, what you should find is that in order to transform your paper into the best possible written product, you'll need to move beyond proofreading or editing and into the realm of macro changes, or **revision**.

Troubleshooting

Proofreading remains a critical part of the revision process. Careless grammatical and punctuation errors and spelling mistakes can damage your *ethos* as an author, and they need to be corrected. It is very probable that you've been doing such *micro-revision* throughout the drafting process—editing for style, grammar, punctuation, and spelling. However, sometimes it's difficult to do *broader revisions* until you have a substantial part of your paper

AT A GLANCE

Questions for Assessing Your Draft

- ***Argument consistency:*** Are your introduction and conclusion arguing the same points, or have you changed your argument by the end? Either revise the end to be consistent with your original thinking, or embrace your new vision and rework the beginning.
- ***Organization and progression:*** Does your paper flow logically, developing one idea seamlessly into the next? Do you provide important theoretical foundations, definitions, or background at the beginning of the paper to guide the audience through the rest of your argument?
- ***Your voice versus sources:*** Do you foreground your own argument in your paper or do you focus primarily on your sources' arguments, locating your point of view primarily in the conclusion? If the latter is true, bring your voice out more in commentaries on the quotations.
- ***Information:*** Are there any holes in your research? Do you need to supplement your evidence with additional research, interviews, surveys, or other source materials?
- ***Opposition and concession:*** Do you adequately address opposing arguments? Do you integrate your opposition into your argument (i.e., deal with them as they arise), or have you constructed a single paragraph that addresses opposing opinions?

written. It is only once your argument starts coming together that you can recognize the most productive ways to modify it in order to optimize its effectiveness. This is the key to successful revision: you have to be open to *both* microediting and large-scale, multiple revisions. Think of this process as **re-vision**, or seeing it again with new eyes, seeing it in a new light.

Let's look at decisions some students made during the revision process:

- **Content Overload.** Reading over her draft about the propagandistic elements in World War II films, Jennifer realized that she had gotten so caught up in presenting background information that her paper read more like a historical report than an argument.

  Revision: Jennifer sharpened her focus, cut down on some of the background information, and brought her own argument to the forefront.

- **Lack of Reliance on Sources.** Miranda had the opposite problem; in her draft she made a compelling argument about the literary status of graphic novels but did not really quote from or mention any of her sources, so she wasn't showcasing her work as a researcher.

  Revision: She more prominently integrated her source material into her argument, both by referring to specific authors and articles she had read and by using additional direct quotations. In doing so, she greatly increased her *ethos* and the persuasiveness of her argument.

- **Overly Broad Thesis.** After drafting her paper on hip-hop and gender identity, Sharita realized that her thesis was too broad and that in trying to cover both male and female imagery, she wasn't able to be specific enough to craft a really persuasive argument.

  Revision: Realizing that her interest really lay in exploring the conflicted stereotype of powerful, sexualized women in hip-hop videos, Sharita cut large sections of her paper revolving around the male imagery and focused on the female. The result was a provocative argument based on concrete, persuasive examples.

- **Overreliance on Design.** Max, a dedicated Mac user, wrote his draft on the aesthetics of design in the Apple product line. The first version of his paper was visually stunning, detailed, and eloquently written. But it was so one-sided that it read more like a marketing brochure than an academic argument.

  Revision: His task in revision was to provide a more balanced perspective on the Apple computer phenomenon. After further research, he incorporated a greater diversity of perspectives in his paper and softened some of his language to be less biased in favor of Apple products.

AT A GLANCE

Revision Strategies

1. ***Read your essay out loud or have someone read it to you.*** You can hear mistakes and inconsistencies that you unknowingly skipped over when reading silently.
2. ***Gain critical distance.*** Put your essay away for a few hours, or even a few days, and then come back to it fresh.
3. ***Answer peer review questions for your essay.***
4. ***Don't be chained to your computer.*** Print out your draft, making revisions by hand. We conceptualize information differently on paper versus on a screen.
5. ***Look at your writing in different ways.*** Take a paragraph and divide it into distinct sentences, which you line up one under another. Look for patterns (for instance, is the repetition deliberate or accidental?), style issues (is sentence structure varied?), and fluidity of transitions between sentences.
6. ***Take into account feedback even if initially it doesn't seem significant.*** You might not decide to act on the advice, but at least consider it before dismissing it.
7. ***Revise out of order.*** Choose paragraphs at random and look at them individually, or begin at the end. Sometimes our conclusions are the weakest simply because we always get to them last, when we're tired; start revision by looking at your conclusion first.
8. ***Look at revision as a whole.*** As you correct mistakes or prose problems, consider the impact that the revision makes on the rest of the essay. Sometimes it is possible just to add a missing comma or substitute a more precise verb, but often you need to revise more than just the isolated problem so that the sentence, paragraph, or essay as a whole continues to "fit" and flow together.

As these examples indicate, you need to enter into the research process looking not just for mistakes to "fix" but also for larger issues that might relate to your structure, your thesis, your scope, or the development of your ideas.

In addition to your own assessment of your writing, you should take into account **peer evaluations** of your drafts; consider your peer review sessions "advance screenings" with your audience. Sometimes you'll find that your peer reviewers vocalize ideas that echo your own concerns about your draft; other times you may be surprised by their reactions. Do keep in mind that their comments are informed *suggestions*, not mandates; your task, as the writer, is to assess the feedback you receive and implement those changes that seem to best address the needs of both your argument and your audience. Like the filmmaker looking to transform a creative vision into a box office hit, you want to reach your audience without sacrificing your own voice or argument in the process.

One way to facilitate a productive peer session is to use directed peer review questions for one-on-one discussions of your draft, rather than to rely exclusively on oral comments. When exchanging drafts with a peer group, you also may find it helpful to attach a cover memo that points your readers to specific questions you have about your draft so that they can customize their responses to address the particular issues that concern you as a writer.

Analyzing Student Writing

Let's return now to Wan Jin's draft paper and see how he used the peer review suggestions he received to revise his paper and develop it further.

Park 1

Wan Jin Park
Research-Based Argument–Final
March 15, 2010

First, Wan Jin's revised title actually conveys part of his argument—he has traded the general claim "Illuminates" to offer several new terms: soft, passionate, and dynamic rhetoric.

Balancing the Soft and the Passionate Rhetorician:

Gore's Dynamic Rhetoric in His Environmental Leadership

Next, his introduction has a new sense of urgency, shown in short and long sentence variety, strong diction, and sign-posting (the two-part rhetoric).

Moreover, Wan Jin spends a great deal of time advancing a more developed thesis, naming Gore as lonely leader with soft rhetoric and then as passionate leader with dynamic rhetoric. With this thesis, the paper will offer a more forceful argument.

At the forefront of the global environmental movement is one man with the power to blur national boundaries, urge political leaders to adopt reforms, and motivate hundreds of thousands. That man is Al Gore. Gore has been a pivotal leader, attracting unprecedented levels of support for the once overlooked issue, especially through Davis Guggenheim's *An Inconvenient Truth*. The success of the documentary can be attributed to Gore's two-part rhetoric. He first induces fear and guilt in us, the audience, making us more receptive to his message. He then portrays himself as a warm, dedicated, but lonely leader, thereby arousing our desire to join him in social action. Despite the success of his soft rhetoric, Gore sets it aside two years later at the TED2008 Conference and adopts a heightened sense of passion and urgency. The shift in rhetoric mirrors a change in Gore's agenda, and it is this dynamic rhetoric that Gore molds to fit specific goals that defines the success of his leadership. An understanding of Gore's rhetoric offers us invaluable insight on how to use dynamic rhetoric to bring overlooked social issues into the light.

Most importantly, Wan Jin ends the opening with a "So What?" significance statement.

He introduces his own term—one he made up. Wan Jin did not want to use "I" so he speaks in third person but he clearly establishes his own argument in this revision.

His microedits to style and descriptive language make his writing even more vivid and memorable.

Before showing us a change in his rhetoric, Gore uses soft rhetoric in *An Inconvenient Truth*. Soft rhetoric, a newly coined term, refers to a rhetorical tool that draws in a guarded audience, not through impassioned words, but through the appeal to the audience's sense of guilt and the establishment of a warm and inviting *ethos*. Because the public was still guarded toward the issue of climate change before the release of the documentary, Gore shies away from passionate speech that are meant to inspire, and instead focuses on convincing his audience to join him through soft rhetoric.

Contrasting Images: the Beautiful and the Doomed

In the revision, Wan Jin begins with a topic sentence that conveys his *argument*, rather than just launching into the rhetorical analysis of the film's details.

Gore begins his soft rhetoric by inducing fear and guilt in us, the audience, through the juxtaposition of beauty and doom. He first offers us a beautiful depiction of nature. The camera focuses close-up on a branch

Park 2

full of green tree leaves. Bright sunlight reflects off of the leaf blades, accentuating the green hue. After a few seconds, the camera turns to the right to reveal a glistening river. The river is a mix of green and blue, both defining colors of nature. The soft piano music in the background adds to the calm and peaceful mood. Gore then narrates in the background, purposely emphasizing the sibilants as if to imitate the sounds of the river and the rustling leaves:

> You look at that river gently flowing by. You notice the leaves rustling with the wind. You hear the birds. You hear the tree frogs. In the distance, you hear a cow. You feel the grass. The mud gives a little bit on the riverbank. It's quiet; it's peaceful. (*An Inconvenient Truth*)

The sequence of images and narration encapsulates the beauty of nature so well that Professors Thomas Rosteck and Thomas Frentz write in "Myth and Multiple Readings in Environmental Rhetoric: The Case of *An Inconvenient Truth*" that "we experience, visually and through Gore's voiceover, the awe, sublime beauty, and wonder of Earth" (5).

He has also incorporated more research, so he is not over-relying on only one source.

Gore suddenly interrupts the experience and interjects that we have forgotten about nature in spite of its beauty: "all of a sudden, it's a gearshift inside you and it's like taking a deep breath and going 'Oh yeah, I forgot about this'" (*An Inconvenient Truth*). Through the use of the word "gearshift," Gore metaphorically compares us, the audience, to machines that are equipped with a gear; in essence, he argues that we have become so addicted to the industrial age that we have transformed into its products, becoming separate from and oblivious to our nature.

* * *

The images arouse such horror that Bret Schulte, Assistant Professor of Journalism at University of Arkansas, writes that Gore shows us "the frightening future promised by global warming—an apocalyptic world of deadly hurricanes, rising oceans, disease, drought, and famine" (Schulte).

By deliberately introducing the "frightening" images only after his "gearshift" metaphor, Gore compels us to feel not only frightened, but also responsible and guilty for the damages done to nature (Schulte; *An Inconvenient Truth*). The arousal of guilt is crucial in shaping *An Inconvenient*

Here, Wan Jin cites the article analyzed earlier in this chapter. He picks a strong quotation, sets it up by building the *ethos* of the source, and then, most importantly, comments on it in the next paragraph, emphasizing "frightening" and the building on Schulte's reading to develop *his* point about guilt.

Notice here, he offers a strong conversation with many of his sources: Rosteck & Frentz, Olson, and looking back to Schulte.

Most powerfully, he ends with his own point, making sure the spotlight is on *his argument*.

The revised subheads show his advanced thinking and reflect the suggestions of his classmates from peer review.

Wan Jin's essay performs a strong rhetorical analysis of the strategies of the speaker as well as of the film.

He has fleshed out the points from his working draft and outline.

Truth into an effective environmental medium, as it "sets up the rhetorical tension with which Gore will leverage his message" (Rosteck and Frentz). Kathryn Olson, the author of "Rhetorical Leadership And Transferable Lessons For Successful Social Advocacy In *An Inconvenient Truth*," agrees and elaborates on what Gore's message is: "he asks [us] . . . to share the guilt of insufficient action with him and to redeem [our]selves . . . now that [we] grasp the gravity . . . of climate change" (11). The arousal of guilt, the first part of Gore's soft rhetoric, thus draws in a once guarded and reluctant public into the environmental movement.

Dedication Molded by Frustration and Failure

After rendering us more receptive through the appeal to our sense of fear and guilt, Gore portrays himself as a warm, vulnerable, and dedicated leader. Rosteck and Frentz also explore the second part of Gore's soft rhetoric and argue that Gore establishes such *ethos* through "personal images of frustration and failure" that are interspersed throughout the documentary (9). In fact, Gore expresses his frustration right from the beginning of *An Inconvenient Truth*, confessing that "I've been trying to tell this story for a long time, and I feel as if I've failed to get the message across" (*An Inconvenient Truth*). We then meet a naively optimistic Gore who fails to change the world through the first Congressional hearings on global warming; he almost loses his son to a car accident; he loses the presidential election in 2000; and his family, a group of tobacco farmers, loses Gore's sister, Nancy, to lung cancer (*An Inconvenient Truth*).

What these stories of failure and pain have in common are that they "strengthen[ed]" Gore's "resolve" and dedication to the environmental movement (Rosteck 7). His son's near-death-accident taught him how anything taken for granted, even our beautiful environment, can easily vanish. His sister's death taught him the importance of connecting the dots, of connecting our actions to future consequences. His presidential election "brought into clear focus the mission that [he] had been pursuing all these years," convincing him to "[start] giving the slideshow again" (*An Inconvenient Truth*).

Park 4

Because these stories "persuasively [document] Gore's single-mindedness in pursuing his public cause, often at his own expense, through a lifetime of disappointments," Olson also agrees with Rosteck and Frentz that the stories of personal failure and frustration are essential to Gore's portrayal as a human, vulnerable, but dedicated leader (Olson 99). This portrayal places us "in a position to hear demand for action in a more sympathetic light," and when coupled with our sense of guilt, it renders Gore's message irresistible (Rosteck and Frentz 10). And Gore's message is clear. He "shows his evolution from interested observer to committed activist" with the goal of "invit[ing] our own journey of transformation" through the environmental movement (5).

Throughout, Wan Jin is careful to build the conversation among his sources even as he adds his voice to that dialogue.

Gripping the Flames: The Lonely Leader

Rosteck, Frentz, and Olson's arguments have merit. Gore's transformation into a dedicated leader as a result of his frustrations and failures does create an "inviting impression that encourages [us] to join him . . . in social action" (Olson 102). However, they leave unexplored a crucial aspect of Gore's rhetoric. What is more responsible for creating the warm and inviting *ethos* is the portrayal of Gore as a lonely leader (102).

At this point, Wan Jin will credit the research that has come before him and then build upon it.

He sets up his argument by returning to the concept of *ethos*.

* * *

No Longer the Soft Leader

Despite the success of his soft rhetoric in *An Inconvenient Truth,* Gore sets it aside and instead adopts a heightened level of passion and sense of urgency two years later in his follow-up presentation at the TED 2008 Conference. The change reflects a change in Gore's primary agenda. Gore's primary goal is no longer attracting support for the environmental movement, as he already achieved that goal. Gore even acknowledges in his TED presentation the extent of his success. He claims that "68 percent of Americans now believe that human activity is responsible for global warming, [and] 69 percent believe that the Earth is heating up in a significant way" (Gore 9.21). Furthermore . . .

After a significant amount of evidence (excerpted), Wan Jin moves to the next point in his argument. His heading refers to terms in his title, using diction to offer coherence and force in the writing.

He sets up the argument about Gore's 2008 TED talk through citing Gore's own words and leading the reader through the *logos* from his rough draft.

In this revision, Wan Jin took the suggestion of his peers: he analyzes not only the images and words, but also the embodied rhetoric or body language of Gore's persona.

Introducing new concepts such as "honor" and "heroism," Wan Jin increases the power of his words and the significance of his argument. He chooses then to use a direct quote as evidence.

He carefully chooses his lines and concludes with a strong interpretation of their meaning.

Park 5

* * *

Even his body language is imbued with the increased level of passion. As he delivers the line, "we need a worldwide, global mobilization for renewable energy, conservation, efficiency, and a global transition to a low carbon economy," he not only stresses each word, but also moves his hands up and down as he speaks, visually emphasizing each word (Gore, 4.39). He also twists his upper body from left to right, with his arms extended, as he says, "the political will has to be mobilized," visually enacting the word "mobilized" (Gore, 4.57).

The heightened passion in Gore's rhetoric becomes fully manifested near the end of the presentation when Gore appeals to honor and heroism, both qualities we have treasured throughout history, as he stresses the need for a hero generation:

> What we need is another hero generation. We have to . . . understand that history has presented us with a choice. And we have to find a way to create, in the generation of those alive today, a sense of generational mission. (Gore, 17.39)

Gore then alludes to the "hero generation that brought democracy to the planet . . . another that ended slavery . . . and that gave women the right to vote" in order to illustrate the level of passion and dedication that we need to emulate as we fight the climate crisis (Gore, 18.44). The climate crisis is no longer just a global issue, but is now the "opportunity to rise to a challenge that is worthy of our best efforts" (Gore, 20.12). In his last efforts to move the audience toward increased sense of urgency and initiative, Gore closes with the line:

> We are the generation about which, a thousand years from now, philharmonic orchestras and poets and singers will celebrate by saying, they were the ones that found it within themselves to solve this crisis and lay the basis for a bright and optimistic human future. (Gore, 20.47)

The appeal to *pathos,* the appeal to honor, heroism, and love for our children and the ensuing desire to promise them a better future illustrates how Gore sets aside his soft rhetoric and transforms into an impassioned leader, urging his audience to become heroes of our generation.

Park 6

Seesaw: Balancing the Soft and the Passionate Rhetorician

Gore adopts different styles of rhetoric in *An Inconvenient Truth* and in his follow-up presentation for the TED2008 Conference. Gore uses a two-part soft rhetoric in *An Inconvenient Truth* in order to draw in a guarded audience. He first compels us to feel fear and guilt through the juxtaposition of images of the beautiful and the doomed, making us more receptive to his environmental message. He then builds his *ethos* as a warm, dedicated, but still lonely leader, creating the inviting impression that draws us in and encourages us to join him in social action. When Gore delivers his TED presentation, his primary goal changes to motivating increased initiative and political will; he thus sets aside his soft rhetoric and adopts a heightened level of passion and sense of urgency.

This dynamic rhetoric, which Gore molds to fit his specific agenda, is the key to Gore's successful environmental leadership. He can be the warm, authentic, and soft leader when he wants to disarm a guarded audience. He can be the energized leader when he needs to inspire increased initiative in those that look up to him. In light of the recent sufferings caused by earthquakes in Haiti and Chile, the understanding of Gore's rhetoric offers us invaluable insight. In order to bring the countless pertinent but overlooked issues into the light à la Gore, we need to learn how to mold our rhetoric and master the art of balancing the soft and the passionate rhetorician in us.

Moving to his conclusion, Wan Jin explains the final term in his paper: dynamic rhetoric.

He also brings in contemporary events, appealing to *kairos* to make the reader receptive to his argument.

The impassioned tone in Wan Jin's own writing suggests that he is moving toward the end of his paper, and indeed he closes with a compelling call to action.

Park 7

Works Cited

An Inconvenient Truth. Dir. Davis Guggenheim. Perf. Al Gore. Paramount Classics, 2006. DVD.

Gore, Al. "Al Gore's New Thinking on the Climate Crisis." Lecture. *TED: Ideas Worth Spreading*. TED.com, Apr. 2008. Web. 15 Jan. 2010. http://www.ted.com/talks/lang/eng/ al_gore_s_new_thinking_on_the_climate_crisis.html.

The Works Cited, on a separate page, provides proper MLA citation for all the research Wan Jin quoted or paraphrased or summarized in the paper.

MLA suggests that writers include URLs in their Works Cited only when absolutely necessary to find the original source, but this student's professor required that they be included as part of the assignment.

He might also have included field research in the form of interviews with professors or surveys with students who had watched any of Gore's presentations.

He shows a well balanced "iceberg of research"—including scholarly journals, popular articles, videos, and surveys.

Park 8

--- "Al Gore on Averting Climate Crisis." Lecture. *TED: Ideas Worth Spreading*. TED.com, Feb. 2006. Web. 20 Jan. 2010. http://www.ted.com/talks/lang/eng/al_gore_on_averting_climate_crisis.html.

Nielsen Company. *Global Consumers Vote Al Gore, Oprah Winfrey and Kofi Annan Most Influential to Champion Global Warming Cause: Nielsen Survey. Nielsen: Trends & Insights*. 2 July 2007. Web. 18 Jan. 2010. http://nz.nielsen.com/news/GlobalWarming_Jul07.shtml.

Olson, Kathryn M. "Rhetorical Leadership and Transferable Lessons for Succsesful Social Advocacy in Al Gore's An Inconvenient Truth." *Argumentation & Advocacy* 44.2 (2007): 90–109. *Communication & Mass Media Complete*. EBSCO. Web. 24 Feb. 2010.

Rosteck, Thomas, and Thomas S. Frentz. "Myth and Multiple Readings in Environmental Rhetoric: The Case of An Inconvenient Truth." *Quarterly Journal of Speech* 95.1 (2009): 1–19. *Communication & Mass Media Complete*. EBSCO. Web. 24 Feb. 2010.

Schulte, Bret. "Saying It In Cinema." *U.S. News*. 28 Mar. 2006. Web. 17 Jan. 2010. http://www.usnews.com/usnews/news/articles/060605/5warming.b.htm.

Student Writing
See other examples of fully developed research-based arguments.
www.pearsonhighered.com/envision/144

The strong, developed ending of Wan Jin's paper shows how careful revision can help you develop a compelling argument that offers a power fully from beginning to end. Be sure to save some energy for your conclusion: you want your parting words to ring memorably in your reader's ears.

The Writer's Process

In this chapter, you have learned strategies for visual mapping, organizing, outlining, drafting, and revising your research paper. You have explored ways of casting your argument and acquired concrete methods for integrating both written sources and visual texts as evidence for your argument. Chances are you have written the first full draft of your paper. But don't forget revision. Revision shows us the way that all *writing is rewriting.*

Sometimes, when writing, we may continue to revise our papers even after we have "finished." Think back to the earlier *Blade Runner* example and how Ridley Scott revised the film for re-release years after its first showing. Similarly, while you may be satisfied with your final research product when you turn it in, it is possible that you have set the groundwork for a longer research project that you may return to later in your college career. Or you may decide to seek publication for your essay in a school newspaper, magazine, or a national journal. In such cases, you may need to modify or expand on your argument for this new rhetorical situation; you may produce your own "director's cut"—a paper identical in topic to the original but developed in a significantly different fashion. Keep in mind that revision is indeed "re-vision."

As you approach revision—as well as the preceding steps of outlining, drafting, and integrating sources—feel free to be creative by composing a hypertext outline or packaging your research paper electronically with links to visual material such as film clips, advertisement videos, or audio files. Your work as a writer has only just started, and the "premiere" of your project awaits.

PREWRITING CHECKLIST

Focus on Analyzing Film and Documentary

- ❑ Assess the genre of the film (comedy? horror? drama? documentary?) and how this affects the audience's response to its content. Does the film combine elements of different genres? What is the rhetorical effect of this combination?
- ❑ What is the plot of the film? What is the organizational structure?
- ❑ Is this plot arranged chronologically? in parallel sequences? thematically? What is the rhetorical significance of arrangement?
- ❑ What is the message conveyed to readers? Is it persuasive or informative? Is this message conveyed through reliance on *pathos*, *logos*, or *ethos*?
- ❑ How is the *ethos* of the filmmaker conveyed to the audience?
- ❑ What notable types of shots does the filmmaker use? Jot down one or two instances where cinematic techniques (zoom-in, cuts between scenes, fade in/fade out, montage) are used for rhetorical effect.
- ❑ Is there a narrator in the film? voice-over? What is the effect on the audience?
- ❑ Is there any framing—a way of setting the beginning and end in context?
- ❑ How is time handled? Does the film move in chronological order? reverse chronological order? What is the significance of such rhetorical choices on the meaning and power of the film? Are flashbacks used in the film? What effect is achieved through the use of flashbacks?
- ❑ How are *pathos*, *ethos*, and *logos* produced by the different cinematic techniques? For instance, is *pathos* created through close-ups of characters? Is *ethos* created through allusions to famous films or filmmaking techniques? Is *logos* constructed through the insertion of a narrator's viewpoint?
- ❑ What is the audience's point of identification in the film? Is the audience supposed to identify with a single narrator? Does the film negotiate the audience's reaction in any specific ways? How?
- ❑ How is setting used to construct a specific mood that affects the impact of the message of the film?
- ❑ Is the film an adaptation of another work—a play or a novel? To the best of your knowledge, what modifications were made to customize the narrative for a cinematic audience? Does the text as film differ in content or message from the text in its original form? Can you see traces of revision and rewriting?

PREWRITING WITH THE *ENVISION* WEBSITE

One way to get started organizing and writing your argument is to work on these tasks with peers in your class. In groups of three or four, visit the movie trailers site on Apple.com through the *Envision* Website and view two or three trailers, either for the same film or different ones. Write down the main features of each trailer. How does each one function as an outline of the film's key scenes, characters, conflict, and message? What tone or style is conveyed through the selection of imagery, the choice of music, and the emphasis on a particular plot or character? What can you apply to your own outline strategies of arrangement? Together, compose an outline for a potential essay.
www.pearsonhighered.com/envision/146

WRITING PROJECTS

1. **Visual Map or Outline:** Create a visual representation of your argument: a bubble map, flowchart, hierarchal set of bubbles, or handmade construction paper model. Write an annotation for each part of your drawing, model, or storyboard to help you move from mass of material to coherent research-based essay.

2. **Detailed Written Outline:** Working with your research materials and notes, create a written outline of your ideas, using numbers and letters to indicate subsections of your argument. Rather than simply calling the second section "II. Body," create several points within the body to show the development of your argument. You may want to start with a topic outline, but ideally you should aim for argumentative subheadings. Include your working thesis statement at an appropriate place in your outline, and include visuals that you will analyze in the essay itself. After you draft the outline, go back and insert your primary and secondary sources in the outline. Insert actual quotations (with page numbers) from your research where possible, and don't forget to cite your sources for both paraphrase and summary. This outline might easily turn into the paper itself. Use it to check the balance of sources, the progression of ideas, and the complexity of your argument.

3. **Research-Based Argument:** Write a 12- to 15-page argumentative research paper on a topic of your choice. If you wish to analyze and research visual rhetoric, consider the images that shape a debate, tell a certain history, or persuade an audience in a certain way. In other words, address an issue through a visual rhetoric lens. You should integrate research materials that can include articles, books, interviews, field research, surveys (either published or that you conduct yourself), TV programs, Internet texts, and other primary and secondary sources, including visuals. Keep in mind that, because this is a research paper, you need to balance primary and secondary materials. Ultimately, your goal should be proving a thesis statement with apt evidence, using appropriate rhetorical and argumentative strategies.

4. **Reflection Essay:** After you have completed your essay, compose a one-page reflection letter that serves as a self-evaluation. Think back on the development of your argument through research and revision. Include comments on the strengths of the essay, the types of revisions you made throughout your writing process, and how the collaborative process of peer review improved your essay. Conclude by explaining how you might continue to write about this issue in future academic or professional situations.

Visit www.pearsonhighered.com/envision for expanded assignment guidelines and student projects.
Visit www.mycomplab.com for additional general writing and research resources.

CHAPTER 7

Avoiding Plagiarism and Documenting Sources

Chapter Preview Questions

- How can I avoid unintentional plagiarism?
- What is the difference between rhetorical imitation and stealing intellectual property?
- Why is it important to learn the conventions of a documentation style?
- What are the proper methods for in-text citations and bibliographies?

"Creativity always builds on the past." For many writers, the debt to those who have written before them is carefully acknowledged—whether through direct references, parenthetical citations, or a list of sources. Even visual artists and multimedia writers name their sources explicitly to show that they belong to a larger community of writers and that they respect the work of others.

But Justin Cone, a designer and animator based in Austin, Texas, makes this point more emphatically through the multimedia montage shown in Figure 7.1, a short film called *Building on the Past*, which recycles and modifies public-domain film footage to make an argument about the relationship between creativity and legislation. The visuals are accompanied by a musical score and a voice-over that repeats the same sentence intermittently throughout the film: "Creativity always builds on the past." In the scene shown here, which opens the film, Cone re-edited the public-domain footage to run in reverse, showing the children running backward uphill instead of forward downhill, offering a powerful argument about how we rely on others for our own creativity. Cone expresses that idea visually, through his strategy of organization, word choice, and design.

FIGURE 7.1. Justin Cone's film, *Building on the Past*, remixes visuals and sound to emphasize how all our ideas rely on the works of those before us.

Your research project, too, can draw its strength from previous work on the subject. It should be a merger of your argument and the already existing dialogue on the topic. So even as you "re-edit it" to suit the purpose of your paper—by selecting passages to quote, paraphrase, summarize, or even argue against—it is crucial that you let your readers know *where* the ideas originated by providing what we call complete and ethical **source attribution**, or the acknowledgment and identification of your sources.

In this chapter, you'll learn how the **rhetorical art of imitation**—the process by which we all learn to write, compose, speak, and produce texts—differs from the theft of others' ideas, which is called **plagiarism**. We'll discuss intellectual property and why it is important to respect the work of others, and you'll acquire strategies for avoiding unintentional plagiarism. Finally, we'll provide a means of understanding the process of constructing in-text and end-of-paper citations, and we'll explain the logic of MLA, APA, CSE, and Chicago documentation styles.

Rhetorical Imitation and Intellectual Property: Understanding Plagiarism

In ancient times, **rhetorical imitation**, or the practice of taking after others, was a celebrated form of instruction. Students would copy a speech out word by word, studying the word choice, organization, rhythm, and art of the work. Then they would write a rhetorical analysis (as you did in Chapter 1) of the speech to understand figures and tropes, strategies of argument, and organizational choices. Finally, they would use elements of the speeches they studied, including content (words) and form (arrangement), to draft their own speeches. Through this imitation, they learned to be great rhetors. Such imitative exercises helped students learn from models of excellence.

"[Imitation was] the bridge between one's reading and writing (or speaking). . . . Students moved from close imitations of their models to looser sorts, using these models increasingly as starting points for longer, more involved compositions of their own making."

—Gideon Burton

This, too, is your task in your writing class. After analyzing articles and studying argumentative strategies from samples of student writing, at some point you need to move on to create your own text. Yet, in the process, you may wish to refer back to those on whose work you are building. This is where **documentation** comes in—the responsible and correct acknowledgment of your sources and influences.

Today, it is common to talk about ideas, not just in terms of words and thoughts, but also in terms of **intellectual property**, that is, the ideas that belong to someone else. In this increasingly litigious society, you need to understand when to stop imitation and when to start acknowledging your sources so that you preserve the rights of others and protect yourself as an emerging writer.

Plagiarism—using another person's idea as your own—was not a crime in classical times, according to scholars Peter Morgan and Glenn Reynolds. But with the invention of printing technology, copyright law, and a cultural emphasis on the profitability of intellectual concepts came a concern about taking someone else's ideas—and therefore their earning potential—whether intentionally or unintentionally. Consequently, you find a demand for originality in writing in both academic and professional circles today. These days, in colleges and universities, plagiarism can lead to suspension or even expulsion because the perpetrator is charged with literally stealing the ideas of someone else.

But there is another, even more compelling ethical reason for keeping in mind the principle discussed in Chapter 5—that research is always a conversation with those who came before. As you work with sources, realize that the claims you are able to make are in fact based on the foundation provided by others. Identifying your sources thus becomes a writing strategy that you need to implement out of *respect* for those who have come before you. By acknowledging their names, ideas, and words, you contribute to a body of knowledge, graciously extending thanks to those who have paved the way. Therefore, while there are legal issues related to intellectual property, copyright law, and "fair use" that you need to know about, if you keep the *respect principle* in mind, you will rarely fall into the trap of inadvertently "stealing" someone's work.

Seeing Connections
For a better understanding of intellectual property and copyright regulations, see the readings in the "Who Owns Popular Culture?" section of Chapter 11.

Avoiding Unintentional Plagiarism

Plagiarism—or using someone else's ideas without acknowledgement in their original or even altered form—is a serious offense, even if it occurs unintentionally or accidentally. To avoid unintentional plagiarism, or accidentally taking someone else's ideas or words as your own, you might follow two practices.

1. **Always keep in mind that you are contributing to a conversation with other writers.**
   When you are writing a research-based argument using many texts, think of working with sources as responding to people whose works you cite, or quote, as a way of including them in the dialogue. With research papers, you are having a conversation with an entire room of people, introducing each person in turn, and serving as the moderator as well to contributor.
2. **Develop effective ways of note taking while reading through your sources.**
   If you find an interesting quote, don't just underline or highlight it. Copy it into your research log with a notation about how you might use it. Check the quote carefully and be sure to note the source, including complete bibliographic information and page numbers. If you find an intriguing idea, write down the attribution in your research log.

Consider Michael Rothenberg's notations in his research log for a project on the design plans for the Twin Towers Memorial in New York City.

> Source: www.cnn.com/2003/US/northeast/01/12/wtc.skyscrapers/
>
> Category: Safety
>
> "there's no reason to believe the structures that replace the twin towers wouldn't also be targets." CNN? "they're a target forever"—Klemenic, president of an engineering firm Skilling Ward Magnusson Barkshire in Seattle.
>
> Howard Decker, chief curator of the National Building Museum in Washington, DC, said: the other target was the "squat pentagon." He said that shows terrorists choose targets because of their symbolism, not their height. "The desire to build tall buildings is an old one," he said. "The motivations for it are complicated. Commerce. Capitalism. Ego."

Michael first lists his source. Then he organizes his notes by category (safety). He then copies the source directly and writes down the full name and identifying information for the quote. He'll use this to build *ethos* in citing this authority within his paper.

Michael repeats this process for his second note. Here he puts the most interesting words in quotation marks and deliberately uses different words in composing his paraphrase of the source.

This notion of considering your sources as people, as the cast of characters for your research paper, can help you avoid *unintentional plagiarism*, or the phenomenon that happens when we assimilate all the material we have read and then think that the ideas are our own. This can happen for many reasons: fatigue, oversaturation of information, poor memory, or sloppy note taking. Regardless of the circumstances, even the unintentional taking of others' ideas can have very serious consequences. Many colleges and universities have plagiarism policies that do not distinguish between intentional and unintentional plagiarism; the act will bring consequences ranging from a failure in the course to expulsion. When Doris Kearns Goodwin, a widely admired historian, was "caught" using the words and ideas of others in a lengthy book that had taken her many years to research and write, she issued an apology that noted her reverence for her sources, suggested that her note taking strategies early in the research process had been less than meticulous, and promised never to let it happen again.

Student Writing

See Michael Rothenberg's complete research paper and other selected student research papers.
www.pearsonhighered.com/envision/149

AT A GLANCE

Avoiding Unintentional Plagiarism

Remember that you must document your sources when you:

- Quote a source word for word
- Summarize or paraphrase information or ideas from another source in your own words
- Incorporate statistics, tables, figures, charts, graphs, or other visuals into your work from another source

You do not need to document the following:

- Your own observations, ideas, and opinions
- Factual information that is widely available in a number of sources ("common knowledge")
- Proverbs, sayings, or familiar quotations

Citing Sources for Downloaded Images and Multimedia

When you integrate visuals or multimedia in your writing, it is not enough to include just the source and provide the citation for it. You need to spend a few moments thinking about issues of copyright and permissions. Whether you are dealing with images or print quotations, you are using materials produced or prepared by another person, and you must give that person credit for the work. In some cases—particularly if you plan to publish your work—you also need to obtain permission to use it. As you browse through catalogs of images, you need to record in your notes the source of each image you decide to use. If you have copied an image from the Web (by right-clicking and choosing "Save Picture As"), you need to note as much of the full source information as you can find: the Website author, the title, the sponsoring organization, the date. If you have found a visual (photograph, chart, ad) from a print source and scanned it into a computer so you can insert it into your essay, you need to list the print source in full as well as information about the original image (the name of the photographer, the image title, and the date). Listing Google as your source is not sufficient; be sure to find the original source and list it in full. Keep careful track as you locate images, give appropriate credit when you use them in your essay, and ask for permission if necessary by writing the owner of the image.

Understanding Documentation Style

Today, with software programs that can help you format your source attributions into different documentation styles, it may seem confusing or even frustrating to worry about proper documentation style. But realize that different styles are preferred by different communities of writers, as shown in the following table. The format guidelines for each style actually have a rhetorical purpose corresponding to the way that knowledge is constructed for that community. Taking a moment to

Documentation Style	Community of Writers	Defining Features	Purpose of Features	Example
MLA	Modern Language Association (language, literature, writing, philosophy, and humanities scholars and teachers)	Citation begins with author's name (last name first, full first name), then publication information, date, medium of publication (then, if a Website, date you accessed it).	Knowledge advances based on individual author's contributions; thus, names are prioritized over dates; place of publication matters for building *ethos.*	McCloud, Scott. *Understanding Comics.* New York: HarperPerennial, 1994. Print.
APA	American Psychological Association (psychologists and social scientists)	Publication date immediately follows designation of author, multiple authors may be listed (last name and initials), titles are in sentence style (first word capitalized, rest lowercase)	Since knowledge advances based on dated contributions to the field, dates are prioritized; most writing is collaborative, so up to six authors are listed; titles, typically long and technical, are in lowercase.	Bruce V., & Green, P. (1990). *Visual perception: Physiology, psychology, andecology* (2nd ed.). London, England: Erlbaum.
CSE	Council of Science Editors (such as biology and physics)	References include last name and date; often superscript numbers are used	Like APA style, emphasis is on knowledge advancing through studies and scientific research; a heavily cited style of writing	[1]Goble, JL. Visual disorders in the handicapped child. New York: M. Dekker; 1984. p. 265.
Chicago	University of Chicago (business writers, professional writers, and those in fine arts)	Sources are listed as footnotes or endnotes and include page numbers	Knowledge is incremental, and readers like to check facts as they go along	[2]Scott McCloud, *Understanding Comics* (New York: HarperPerennial, 1994), 33.

understand the logic behind the styles will help you practice proper citation without having to look up every instance of how to do it. In the process, you build your *ethos* as a writer by showing that you speak the language of a particular academic community.

For the purposes of this chapter, we focus on MLA style because the writing we've been discussing in this book belongs to disciplines in the humanities. The different styles, methods of organization, modes of argumentation, and conventions for writing in the social sciences, sciences, business, and fine arts communities are not covered in this book, but you can find links to resources through the *Envision* Website for Chapter 7.

Seeing Connections
See the reference section of Harrison Pope's "Evolving Ideals of Male Body Image as Seen through Action Toys" for an example of APA formatting (page 395).

In-Text Citations: Documentation as Cross-Referencing

Documentation is not intended to be some surreptitious way to check up on you; rather, it is part of the research dialogue. The idea is that readers might be inspired enough by your research and your use of materials to want to read some of your sources themselves. In this way, documentation functions as a *road map* for your audience to locate the source—both in your bibliography and in the library or online. Accordingly, the central purpose of in-text documentation is to point readers clearly and explicitly to the list of sources at the end of the paper. We call this *cross-referencing.*

Let's take a look at a citation in Michael Rothenberg's paper on the Twin Towers. We call this an **in-text citation** or reference because it occurs within the body of his paper. MLA style always places such references inside parentheses to set them off from the rest of the writing. Look at how the last name and page number of the citation in parentheses point the reader directly to the author's name in the "Works Cited" list.

> . . . the Twin Towers were so enormous that together they encased a staggering 11 million square feet of commercial space (Czarnecki 31).
>
> * * *
>
> Works Cited
>
> Bravman, John. Personal interview. 13 May 2003.
>
> Bruno, Lisa D. "Studio Daniel Libeskind." *Baltimore Sun*. Baltimore Sun, 6 Nov. 2002. Web. 1 June 2003.
>
> Czarnecki, John E. "Architects at the Forefront as They Show Ground Zero Aspirations." *Architectural Record* Nov. 2002: 31–50. Print.

Notice that Michael has alphabetized the list by authors' last names, which corresponds to MLA style documentation which places author names as most important. Readers need only scan down the page to look for the last name of the source cited earlier. This makes it very easy, and once you understand that this **cross-referencing logic** governs all documentation rules, you can begin to understand how to document a wide range of sources—even new multimedia sources for which there are no set rules of citation.

For instance, Michael needed to document several quotes he obtained from a temporary PDF document posted on the Website of a city review board. By understanding documentation as *cross-referencing*, here's what Michael wrote:

> In particular, they required a memorial that would include both history and memory "such as the Libeskind's below-grade 'ground zero' space," as well as a proposal "that returns a much-lamented presence to the skyline" like Libeskind's tower, and finally, a plan that develops the site in the context of the community (Hutton 3, 12).
>
> * * *
>
> Works Cited
>
> Hutton, Ernest, ed. *Evaluation of Innovative Design Proposals. New York: New Visions.* N.p. 13 Jan. 2003. Web. 25 May 2003.

As you can see, the word within the parenthetical documentation sets up a *cross-reference* to the first word listed in the "Works Cited" list at the end of the paper. This makes it easy to compose a very concise reference within the paper and easy to find that reference at the end of the paper. If there is no author to put in your parentheses, begin with the first word of the source entry on the Works Cited page. Here is an example from Tanner Gardner's paper on the globalization of the NBA, where he quotes an article from the journal *The Economist.* Many of the articles in this journal are collectively written, so no authors are named. In this case, Tanner uses the first words of the title. See how the cross-referencing logic of MLA style helps readers find the source in the Works Cited list at the end of the paper:

Student Writing
Read Tanner Gardner's complete paper on globalization and the NBA
www.pearsonhigheredu/envision/153

> The relationship between Nike and basketball is actually reciprocal, as their promotions actually promote basketball internationally by providing publicity for the sport ("The Yao").
>
> * * *
>
> Works Cited
>
> "The Yao Crowd." *Economist* 9 Aug. 2003: 55. Print.

Tanner used the same technique in other parts of his paper when referring, for instance, to a Website with acknowledged author.

Using Notes for Documentation

Although MLA style relies primarily on in-text citations and a final bibliography—unlike Chicago style, which uses primarily footnotes or endnotes—sometimes you might need to include a note. You'll use notes, for example, when you want to include extra explanatory information but don't want to break the flow of your argument.

Following are two notes from Michael's paper. In the first case, he wanted to define some of the key terms of his argument, but he felt it would be intrusive to pause and explain his terms within the paper itself.

> [1]Those in the public who influenced the design of the new World Trade Center include all of those concerned with the project and not just New York citizens. However, even though the majority of these motivated individuals live in New York, they represent every state and many nations. Hence, the collective group of citizens in the worldwide community who are interested in this project are referred to as "the public" throughout this document, but this phrase should be understood to include primarily New York citizens.

Seeing Connections
For an article with extensive academic notes, see Gerald Jones, "Shooters," beginning on page 334, with notes on page 342.

In the second case, he wanted to add more information from his research log, but again he felt it would break the flow of his argument. In this case, he was able to include direct quotations and statistics from his research; this built his *ethos* and allowed interested readers to learn more about the subject. Notice that he included the source for his research again through the cross-referencing system. A reader would only have to scan down to the *O* section of his bibliography to find the full source for this citation.

> [2]Five thousand people from the New York area participated in a two-week in-depth discussion starting on July 20, 2002. According to their Website, "This historic gathering—called 'Listening to the City'—gave participants an opportunity to help shape the redevelopment of Lower Manhattan and the creation of a permanent memorial to the victims of 9/11." At this gathering, the 5,000 committed individuals responded to many questions and polls. Of the respondents, 60% thought that new towers should be built at least as tall as the originals, 71% thought that adding a "major element or icon" to the skyline was "very important," and 87% thought it was "important" or "very important" to add something unique to the skyline (Online Dialogues).

In addition to providing explanatory information, notes can also point readers to a list of sources you would discuss or include if you had space to do so. In Michael's case, he wanted to discuss mammoth architectural designs more broadly but did not have the space in his paper to do so. His solution was a note pointing the reader to a source on this topic, which happened to be another paper he had written. This note would also be the place for a list of sources about this tangential topic.

> [6]See my paper, "The Two Towers," on the Petronas Towers as the world's tallest, February 2003.

AT A GLANCE

MLA Documentation for Print and Online Sources

For the Works Cited list, follow the order below in listing details about your source:

- Author or authors
- Title of book or article
- If an article, title of journal or book within which it is published
- Place of publication
- Publisher
- Date of publication
- Medium of publication
- If an online source, date you accessed it
- If a printed or PDF article, page span
- If online article from a database, the database or search engine
- The URL for a Website, if your instructor requires it, or if the site would be difficult to find without it

Typically, such notes are formatted as **endnotes**, appearing at the end of your paper, before the bibliography. **Footnotes**, which appear at the bottom or foot of the page, would again break the flow of the argument. But ask your teacher for specific guidance about your own paper.

MLA-Style Works Cited Lists

You've seen how documentation works as a *cross-referencing system,* in which the in-text citation within parentheses points the reader directly to the source in the bibliography. In MLA style, the bibliography is called a **Works Cited** list because it refers explicitly to the works (or sources) you have cited (or quoted) in your paper. Sometimes a Works Cited list is accompanied by another section called a **Works Consulted** list, which names all the other sources you may have read and studied but did not actually quote from in your final revision.

Realize that a reference page is a moment of *ethos* building as well: by listing both works *cited* and works *consulted*, you demonstrate your research process and new knowledge. You also invite your readers to explore the topic in depth with you.

Documentation for Print and Online Sources

MLA style follows a particular logic in ordering information for a citation. Consult the "At a Glance" box and the table below to begin to understand this system. You might also study the list of examples provided in this chapter, but realize that sometimes for less conventional sources (e.g., Facebook wall posts) you may need to improvise the format based on your understanding of MLA style.

Realize that while the latest MLA Handbook suggests that you include a URL only when your instructor requires it, you should always keep track of the URL in your notes or research log. The authors of this book consistently ask their students to include URLs for online sources.

LOGIC OF MLA STYLE

Satrapi, Marjane.	*Persepolis: The Story of a Childhood.*	New York: Pantheon, 2004. Print.
List the author's name first, by last name. If there are multiple authors, include them all, following the order listed on the publication. If there is no author, use the publishing organization (if available) or jump next to the title.	The title comes next. For books and films, italicize the title. For shorter pieces (such as articles, TV shows, songs, etc.), put the title in quotation marks with the larger publication (the collection of essays, TV series, or album) italicized. If you need to refer to the title for in-text citations (and there is no author), use the first few keywords only.	Last comes publication information: place, publisher or company, date, and medium of publication. For shorter pieces, include the complete range of page numbers, followed by a period. For shorter online articles, list the medium of publication (Web) followed by a period. For online texts, conclude with the date of access.

Seeing Connections
Read an excerpt from *Persepolis* on page 419.

Single-Author Book

Satrapi, Marjane. *Persepolis: The Story of a Childhood*. New York: Pantheon, 2004. Print.

Multiple-Author Book

Andrews, Maggie, and Mary M. Talbot, eds. *All the World and Her Husband: Women in Twentieth-Century Consumer Culture*. London: Cassell, 2000. Print.

Introduction, Preface, Foreword, or Afterword in a Book

Gerbner, George. Foreword. *Cultural Diversity and the U.S. Media*. Ed. Yahya R. Kamalipour and Theresa Carillia. New York: State U of New York P, 1998. xv–xvi. Print.

Cohen, Mitchell, and Dennis Hale, eds. Introduction. *The New Student Left*. Boston: Beacon Press, 1967. xvii–xxxiii. Print.

Article in an Anthology

Boichel, Bill. "Batman: Commodity as Myth." *The Many Lives of the Batman*. Ed. Roberta Pearson and William Uricchio. New York: BFI, 1991. 4–17. Print.

Note that for this and all other online sources, the most recent MLA Handbook states "You should include a URL as supplementary information only when the reader probably cannot locate the source without it or when your instructor requires it." (MLA 182)

Article from a Journal

Roberts, Garyn G. "Understanding the Sequential Art of Comic Strips and Comic Books and Their Descendants in the Early Years of the New Millenium." *Journal of American Culture* 27.2 (2004): 210–17. Print.

Article from a Popular Magazine Published Monthly

Maney, Kevin. "The New Face of IBM." *Wired* July 2005. Web. 18 August 2005.

Sontag, Susan. "Looking at War." *New Yorker* 3 Jan. 2003: 43–48. Print.

Article from a Newspaper

Cowell, Alan. "Book Buried in Irish Bog Is Called a Major Find." *New York Times*. New York Times, 27 July 2006. Web. 31 July 2006.

Article from a Database

Chun, Alex. "Comic Strip's Plight Isn't Funny." *Los Angeles Times* 27 Apr. 2006, home ed.: E6. *LexisNexis*. Web. 4 May 2006.

Article from a Website

Yagoda, Ben. "You Need to Read This: How *Need to* Vanquished *Have to, Must* and *Should*." *Slate*. Washington Post Newsweek Interactive, 17 July 2006. Web. 20 July 2006.

Anthology

Herndl, Carl G., and Stuart C. Brown, eds. *Green Culture*. Madison: U of Wisconsin P, 1996. Print.

Anonymous Article

"Hillary's American Dream." *Economist* 29 July 2006: 32. Print.

Definition

"Diversity." *American Heritage Dictionary of the English Language*. 4th ed. Houghton, 2000. Print.

"Greek Mythology." *Wikipedia*. Wikimedia Foundation, 16 April 2010. Web. May 5, 2010.

Letter to the Editor

Tucker, Rich Thompson. "High Cost of Cheap Coal." Letter. *National Geographic* July 2006: 6–7. Print.

Letter or Memo

Greer, Michael. Letter to the authors. 30 July 2006. Print.

Dissertation (Unpublished)

Li, Zhan. "The Potential of America's Army: The Video Game as Civilian-Military Public Sphere." Diss. Massachusetts Institute of Technology, 2004. Print.

Government Publication

United States. Census Bureau. Housing and Household Economic Statistics Division. *Poverty Thresholds 2005*. US Census Bureau, 1 Feb. 2006. Web. 20 May 2006.

Interview

Tullman, Geoffrey. Personal interview. 21 May 2006.

Cho, Ana. Telephone interview. 4 June 2005.

Email

Tisbury, Martha. "Re: Information Overload." Message to Max Anderson. 27 Mar. 2008. E-mail.

Online Posting

Shelly, Ayla. "Visual Rhetoric, Girls, and Ads." *GrlChatSpot*. Google. 5 Nov. 2006. Web. 10 May 2010.

Chat Room Discussion or Real-time Communication

Zhang, Zhihao. "Revision Suggestions." *Cross-Cultural Rhetoric Chat Room*. Stanford U. 25 May 2006. Web. 5 June 2008.

Tweet or Twitter feed

@CarsonDaly. Web log post. Twitter.com. 10 April 2010. Web. 15 May 2010.

Facebook post

The White House. "Spurring Innovation, Creating Jobs." Facebook.com. 5 August 2009. Web. 13 February 2010.

Documentation for Visual, Audio, and Multimedia Sources

Because many of the materials you may work with fall into the category of innovative text produced by new technologies—such as Webmovies, Flash animation, Weblogs, three-dimensional images, storyboards, sound clips, and more—you need to learn how to construct a citation that provides as much detail as possible about the text. Even citing interviews and surveys can be tricky for some because the format does not match conventional books or articles. Just follow the logical steps for citing print and online sources, developing a rubric that works to offer as much information as possible. The key is consistency and adhering as closely as possible to the logic of MLA style.

AT A GLANCE

MLA Documentation for Visual and Multimedia Sources

For the "Works Cited" list, follow the order below in listing details about your source:

- Author or organization
- Title of the image, film, ad, TV series, or document
- If part of a collection, title of the collection
- Place of publication and publisher
- Date of publication
- If online article from a database, the name of the database or search engine
- Medium of publication
- If an online source, date you accessed it
- The URL of an online source, if your instructor requires it, or if the site would be difficult to find without it

Photograph or Visual Image

Golden Gate Bridge, San Francisco. Personal photograph by the author. 23 June 2004.

Goldin, Nan. *Jimmy Paulette & Misty in a Taxi, NYC*. 1991. Photograph. San Francisco Museum of Modern Art, San Francisco.

Sherman, Cindy. *Untitled Film Still*. 1978. Museum of Modern Art. *The Complete Untitled Film Stills of Cindy Sherman*. Web. 7 July 2006.

Advertisement

Nike. "We Are All Witnesses." Advertisement. *Nikebasketball*. 3 Jan. 2006. Web. 15 June 2006.

Film

Beyond Killing Us Softly: The Impact of Media Images on Women and Girls. Dir. Margaret Lazarus and Renner Wunderlich. Prod. Cambridge Documentary Films, 2000. Film.

"A Brief History of America." *Bowling for Columbine*. Dir. Michael Moore. United Artists, 2002. *Bowling for Columbine*, n.d. Web. 13 June 2006.

YouTube

Wesch, Michael. "A Vision of Students Today." YouTube. 12 Oct 2007. Web. 31 March 2010.

Comic Strip or Editorial Cartoon

Wilkinson, Signe. Cartoon. *San Francisco Chronicle*. 1 June 2010: A13. Print.

Pastis, Stephen. "Pearls before Swine." Comic strip. *Comics.com* 18 Apr. 2006. Web. 16 May 2006.

Entire Internet Site

Cartoonists Index. MSNBC, n.d. Web. 4 Nov. 2005.

Individual Webpage from an Internet Site

Stevenson, Seth. "Head Case: The Mesmerizing Ad for Headache Gel." *Slate*. Washington Post Newsweek Interactive, 24 July 2006. Web. 25 July 2006.

Personal Homepage

Corrigan, Edna. Home page. *Ednarules*. N.p., n.d. Web. 24 Oct. 2005.

Cover (Magazine, book, CD, etc.)

Adams, Neil. "Deadman." *Comics VF.com*. Comics VF, 1978. Web. 23 Oct. 2005.

Television Program

"The Diet Wars." *Frontline*. PBS, 2004. Web. 16 Aug. 2006.

Computer Game

Infinity Ward. *Modern Warfare 2*. Activision. 2009. Playstation 3.

Second Life. Your World. Linden Labs, n.d. Web. 7 May 2006.

Screen Shot

"Star Wars Galaxies." Sony Online Entertainment, n.d. Web. 5 Feb. 2005.

Radio Essay

Ydstie, John. "Book Marketing Goes to the Movies." *Morning Edition*. Natl. Public Radio. 18 July 2006. Radio.

Sound Clip or Recording

Reagan, Ronald. "The Space Shuttle *Challenger* Tragedy Address." 28 Jan. 1986. *American Rhetoric*. Web. 5 Mar. 2006.

Class Lecture

Connors, Fiona. "Visual Literacy in Perspective." English 210B. Boston U. 24 Oct. 2004. Lecture.

Speech

Rheingold, Howard. "Technologies of Cooperation." Annenberg Center for Communication. U of Southern California, Los Angeles. 3 Apr. 2006. Speech.

Jobs, Steve. Commencement Address. Stanford U., Palo Alto, 12 June 2005. *iTunes U*. Apple. Web. 27 July 2006.

Painting

Warhol, Andy. *Self Portrait*. 1986. Andy Warhol Museum, Pittsburgh. *The Warhol: Collections*. Web. 3 Aug. 2006.

Map

Hong Kong Disneyland Guide. Map. Disney, 2006. Print.

Performance

Phedre. By Racine. Dir. Ileana Drinovan. Pigott Theater, Memorial Hall, Stanford, 10–13 May, 2006. Performance.

Seeing Connections
See rhetorical analysis and articles on computer games in Chapter 11, the section "Virtual Worlds and Gaming Life."

Student Paper in MLA Style

Stephanie Parker's research paper focuses on how digital communities, such as Soompi (a Korean pop culture Website), have transformed ideas of racial identity. She worked with a wide range of both print and electronic sources in her project.

Student Writing
See Stephanie Parker's full research paper and other student research papers using MLA style.
www.pearsonhighered.com/envision/159

Stephanie heads her paper in proper MLA form, with her name, her instructor's name, the class title, and the date, all flush to the left margin.

Parker 1

Stephanie Parker
Dr. Christine Alfano
PWR 2 Cultural Interfaces
7 December 2008

Soompi and the "Honorary Asian": Shifting Identities in the Digital Age

Every morning at 7:00 AM, Norwegian James Algaard turns on his computer and joins Soompi IRC: a chatroom for members of a Korean Pop Culture discussion forum. James' daily entrance into the chatroom is enthusiastically greeted by online acquaintances who know him as <SeungHo>, a connoisseur of Korean Hip Hop and a collector of limited edition sneakers. Seungho Lee was born in South Korea, but was adopted by a Norwegian family; websites like Soompi are his only connection to Korean culture. Thousands of miles away in Los Angeles, it is 10:00 PM when I, an American with a strong interest in Asia, join the same chatroom to spend time with Seungho and thirty other "Soompiers," people from around the world who have come together to form a strong and tight-knit online community. The chatroom itself [. . .] is visually mundane—a window that gradually fills with text as different users type, but Soompi IRC is an organic and multicultural part of cyberspace where people communicate in English, Korean, Mandarin, Cantonese, Spanish, Norwegian, Swedish, Vietnamese, Japanese, Tagalog, and French about every topic imaginable, 24 hours a day.

Stephanie lists both the author and page number in her citation. Notice that she is citing this source even though she is only paraphrasing his ideas.

We Soompiers are representatives of "Generation I"—we have grown up with the Internet and are using it to define ourselves in a more globalized society (Gates 98). A decade ago, cultural identity for people like Seungho and me was limited by factors like geography, language, and ethnicity; with the emergence of new technology and online communities, we have access to an ever-growing variety of choices for personal expression. Soompi and other cyber communities are at the forefront of a larger movement towards redefining how we culturally relate to one another. This movement will extend past the reach of the Internet and act as a catalyst for cross-cultural interaction and understanding on a level never seen before.

Stephanie closes her introduction with a two-sentence thesis that outlines the claim that she will support through her textual and cultural analysis in the rest of the paper.

* * *

Parker 8

"This Site is My Life": Soompi Addicts and the Asian Fix

For the past decade, most academic research on cyber culture has focused on the type of social interaction that takes place within the digital medium. Scholars Howard Rheingold, Elisabeth Reid, Amy Jo Kim, and Lisa Nakamura have all helped to build the foundations for the study of online group behavior. But there is also another important part of Internet life that is only beginning to develop with the current generation of web users—how membership in an online group affects a person's self-perception in relation to others in real life. Nessim Watson is a Professor of Communication at Westfield State College, and has devoted years to the study of American mass media and cultural representations. After spending two years participating in and studying an online fan club, he concluded that, "those youth formed a community which created not only individual benefits for participants but also a group strength" (102). It is those "individual benefits" that should provide the next source of material for research. The strong allegiance to a web-based group is not something that an Internet user logs in and out of—they take this allegiance with them and it influences their decisions and behavior in the real world: their mode of personal expression, their opinions about other groups, and especially their cultural identity.

Soompi is one of the best venues to observe the brand new phenomenon of people gaining a real sense of culture from an online source. According to Quantcast, a free internet ratings site, Soompi.com has 26 million page views per month, with a full 66% accomplished by "Addicts," or users who log on more than once every day ("Traffic Stats . . ."). For them, Soompi is the most convenient place to get their fix of Asian culture. This makes sense, and is in line with a report published in 2001 by the Pew Internet & American Life Project, "Asian-Americans and the Internet: The Young and Connected." According to the study, English-speaking Asian-Americans "are the Net's most active users . . . and have made the Internet an integral part of their daily lives" (Spooner 2). For hundreds of thousands of people in this demographic, Soompi has definitely become an important force in their personal lives and decisions,

Stephanie's page numbers skip to 8 here since we've abridged her paper.

In this section, midway through her paper, Stephanie synthesizes a variety of different types of sources to make her point.

Stephanie cites the page number for the print source from which she took this direct quote. Notice that because she used the author's name earlier in the sentence, she does not need to include it again in her parenthetical citation.

She cites the source for the statistics she uses. Since her source had no author, she refers to it here with an abbreviation of its title, which she places in quotation marks since it is the title of the article. In the Works Cited, she lists this source by its title as well, so it is easy for the reader to cross-reference.

Even though Stephanie read this as an electronic file, the study was in PDF form and therefore has page numbers that she could refer to in her citations.

This source is a discussion thread from the Website that Stephanie is discussing, but for the purposes of citation, she refers to it by its title, just as she would for an article that had no author listed.

Since Stephanie is working with two different texts written by Nakamura, here she specifies which she is referring to by including the title as well as the author and page number in the citation.

The second time that Stephanie references Nakamura's book, she does not need to include the author or title in the citation since they are exactly the same as in the previous citation.

Since this is from an interview, there is no page number to cite. However, since Stephanie lists more than one source from Shim in her Works Cited, here she includes a citation that makes it clear that this quote was taken from her online interview with him.

and in some cases, is the only website visited besides social utilities like Facebook ("What Would You . . ."). They can use Soompi to build their knowledge of Asian culture, and to form new connections with other people they can relate to around the world. In September of 2008, a discussion topic was posted on the Forums: "What Would You Do Without Soompi?" Certain self-proclaimed "addicts" left replies such as, "I probably wouldn't be so into Asian stuff," and "I would be a lot less knowledgeable about the world" ("What Would You . . ."). For thousands of Soompiers, the Forums are where they learn Asian-specific modes of fashion, style, speech patterns, and other cultural behaviors of expression.

This part of personal development is extremely important in the case of Asian-Americans living in predominantly non-Asian areas, without an "Asian group" of friends to participate in cultural activities with. Prominent scholars in Asian-American studies constantly emphasize the unique relationship between the Asian-American community and New Media, and its power to change traditional ideas about identity, culture, and the potential fluidity of both (Nakamura, *Digitizing Race* 184). Lisa Nakamura recognizes in *Digitizing Race: Visual Cultures of the Internet* that "Interactive media like the Web can question identity while building discursive community in ways that other static media cannot" (184). It allows anyone who wishes to contribute to the evolution of Asian-American culture to effectively "log in" and express their approval, resistance, or creativity in the largest Forum on the planet, all while strengthening the bonds of a real community. Daniel Shim relates his own experience: "I was born in Canada in white communities & I grew up to be like them. Soompi has given me knowledge about Asian culture that I would not get from my school or family" (Online Interview). To follow that point further, in her book, Nakamura argues that the Internet provides a Forum for "questioning a rigid and essentialized notion of Asian American 'authenticity'" (185). This is extremely important—the idea of culture being inextricably linked to ethnicity, language, and geographic location becomes irrelevant in the face of rising online communities, the organic and global nature of which forces the issue of what makes a person "Asian," or "American."

Figure 6. Daniel Shim's parody video, "Wasabi Boy-No Engrish" confronts Asian stereotypes with comedy and has been viewed almost 200,000 times. Author screen shot.

Since Daniel joined Soompi and began to use the Internet as a tool for personal expression, his popularity online has grown enormously: his YouTube videoblog, in which he comments on events in his daily life and makes fun of Asian stereotypes, has almost 30,000 subscribers and is the 4th most popular comedy blog in all of Canada (Shim, "Shimmycocopuffsss's . . ."). Without having grown up around many Asian young people, Daniel has been extremely successful in navigating the cultural landscape with the help of his online community, even producing his own ideas about Asian-American identity as a New Media celebrity (see Figure 6). For young people like Daniel in Toronto and Seungho in Norway, Susan Kang says that "online is pretty much the only place they feel like they can connect to other Asians." Soompi makes it not only possible, but easy for Asians who live in a non-Asian place to immerse themselves in Asian culture and comment on it—an unprecedented step in the separation of culture and a static location.

Stephanie includes a parenthetical reference to Figure 6 to draw her visual evidence into dialogue with her main written argument.

Stephanie once again takes a direct quote from an interview she conducted and so does not cite a page number or author here. The curious reader would look up "Kang" on the Works Cited and discover that the quote came from a personal interview.

This Works Cited represents an abridged version of the much longer Works Cited that Stephanie included with her full paper.

All the sources in the Works Cited listed in alphabetical order by author's last name, or, in the cases where there is no identified author, by title.

Stephanie lists a variety of sources here, from academic journal articles, to books, newspaper articles, advertisements, and even online sources such as Webpages, YouTube videos, and discussion list postings.

Notice the formatting of the entries: the first line of each entry is flush left, with a hanging indent in the wrapped lines so readers can skim the Works Cited easily.

When there is no author, the title is listed first.

Parker 19

Works Cited

Bell, David. *An Introduction to Cybercultures*. London: Routledge, 2001. Print.

Chen, Louie Haoru. Online interview. 16 November 2008.

"Crazy Sale for Korean Fashion." Advertisement. *Yesstyle*. 10 November 2008. Web. 10 November 2008.

Dator, Jim and Seo, Yongseok. "Korea as the wave of a future: The emerging Dream Society of icons and aesthetic experience." *Journal of Futures Studies*, 9:1 (2004): 31–44. Print.

Gates, Bill. "Enter 'Generation I.'" *Instructor*. March 2000: 98. Print.

Gulia, Milena and Wellman, Barry. "Virtual communities as communities: Net surfers don't ride alone." Eds. Smith, Mark A. and Kollock, Peter. *Communities in Cyberspace*. New York: Routledge, 1999. 167–194. Print.

Herring, Susan G. "Questioning the generational Divide: Technological Exoticism and Adult Constructions of Online Youth Identity. " *Youth, Identity, and Digital Media*. Eds. David Buckingham. MIT Press, 2000. 72–95. Print.

Jones, Stephen G. *Virtual Culture: Identity & Communication in Cybersociety*. London: Sage Publications Ltd, 1997. Print.

Kang, Susan. Online interview. 25 October 2008.

Kim, Amy Jo. *Community Building on the Web*. Peachpit Press, 6 April 2000. Web.

Ko, Shu-ling. "GIO looking to take foreign soap operas off prime time TV." *Taipei Times*. 11 January 2006. *AsiaMedia*. 11 January 2006. Web. 20 November 2008.

"Korea Wave Hits Middle East." *Dae Jang Geum* 13 December 2005. Web. 1 November 2008.

Lee, HyukMin. Telephone interview. 15 October 2008.

Nakamura, Lisa. *Cybertypes*. New York: Routledge, 2002. Print.

Parker 20

---. *Digitizing Race: Visual Cultures of the Internet.* Minneapolis, MN: University of Minnesota Press, 2008. Print.

Reid, Elisabeth. "Electropolis: Communications and Community on Internet Relay Chat." Honors Thesis. University of Melbourne, 1991. Print.

Rheingold, Howard. *The Virtual Community: Homesteading on the Electronic Frontier*. Addison-Wesley Publishing Company, 1993. Print.

Shim, Daniel. Online interview. 12 November 2008.

---. "Shimmycocopuffsss's Profile Page" YouTube. 27 November 2008. Web. 28 November 2008.

---. "Wasabi Boy-No Engrish." YouTube. 5 March 2008. Web. 28 November 2008.

Spooner, Tom. "Asian-Americans and the Internet: The Young and Connected." *Pew Internet and American Life Project*. 12 December 2001. PDF file.

"Traffic Stats for soompi.com." Quantcast.com. 1 November 2008. Web. 1 November 2008.

"Wannabe Asians/Wasians" 1721 Posts. *Soompi*. Started 28 July 2006. Web. 1 October 2008.

Watson, Nessim. "Why We Argue About Virtual Community: A Case Study of the Phish.net Fan Community." Jones 102–110. Print.

"What Would You Do Without Soompi?, How would your life be different?" 95 posts. *Soompi*. Started 1 September 2008. Web. 1 October 2008.

"Winter Sonata to be aired in Egypt and Iraq." 5 January 2005. Web. 10 November 2008.

Yang, Jeff. "On top of YouTube: Happy Slip, Choi, KevJumba." *The San Francisco Chronicle*. 6 June 2008. Web. 20 October 2008.

When an author's name appears more than once, three hyphens (---) stand in for the name in the second and subsequent entries, and the entries by the same author are alphabetized by title.

Notice here how in the Watson entry, Stephanie cross-references with the Jones citation above so as not to be redundant.

The Writer's Process

Now that you've learned about the meaning of intellectual property, the dangers of plagiarism, the rhetorical purpose for documentation style, the cross-referencing logic of in-text citations, and the guidelines for MLA Works Cited and Consulted lists, it is time for you to review your own writing. Have you acknowledged all your sources in full? Did you include proper and concise parenthetical attributions in the paper? Does your bibliographic list provide an alphabetized reflection of your research? If so, then you have accomplished a great deal as a writer.

PREWRITING WITH THE *ENVISION* WEBSITE

Visit the *Envision* Website and read Doris Kearns Goodwin's article "How I Caused That Story" from *Time* magazine, January 27, 2002. In this article, Goodwin explains how she unintentionally plagiarized one of her 300 sources; her new technological approach to note taking offers a concrete strategy for preventing this disaster. As a team, develop a "top-ten" list of how to avoid the dangers of plagarism. Write up your answers as a potential article for *Time* magazine and implement these practices into your own work as a writer and researcher.
www.pearsonhigheredu.com/envision/166a

WRITING PROJECTS

1. **Documentation Log:** Develop your own system of note taking to avoid the kind of plagiarism trap that writer Doris Kearns Goodwin fell into.

2. **Peer Review of Citations:** Share your draft paper with a group of peers and have them check to see which sources need citation. Does your paper contain knowledge you must have obtained from a source? If so, you need to acknowledge the source of that knowledge. Do certain passages seem to be common knowledge? If so, you don't need to cite them. What paragraphs could go into notes? What aspects of your paper need more explanation and could use a note?

3. **Writing with Technology:** You might find it helpful to turn to one of the scholarly tools for producing a Work Cited list. These include *Ref Works* and *End Note*. You can find links to these tools on the *Envision* Website. Many researchers and scholars depend on these tools, keeping notes right in the program, inserting all identifying information for a source, and then selecting the documentation format needed for their papers. The technology then produces a list in the proper documentation style. You need to double-check the list, but it can save you time.
www.pearsonhighered.com/envision/166b

Visit www.pearsonhighered.com/envision for expanded assignment guidelines and student projects.
Visit www.mycomplab.com for additional general writing and research resources.

Part III

DESIGN AND DELIVERY

What a shift in the means of delivery does is bring invention and arrangement into a new relationship with each other.

—Kathleen Yancey

Designing Arguments

Chapter Preview Questions

- What are the best ways to design arguments for specific audiences?
- How can I compose an academic abstract and "bio"?
- What is decorum and how does this rhetorical principle govern document design?
- What techniques can you learn for designing your writing in digital and multimedia formats?
- How do visual arguments work, such as opinion advertisements (or op-ads), photo essays, and Websites?

FIGURE 8.1. The cover of Michael Chaitkin's research essay offers a carefully designed visual argument.

This chapter will give you the expertise to design your work for diverse purposes and audiences. We'll provide specific guidelines for academic essays, including line-spacing, margin size, and other formatting considerations. You'll learn how to write an academic abstract, a short biography (bio), and a cover letter. Then we'll examine hybrid document design in the form of newsletters and brochures before turning to visual arguments, such as op-ads, photo essays, and multimedia projects.

Michael Chaitkin, for example, turned the cover of his research paper into a **visual argument**—a graphic representation of a written argument—that served as a compact visual depiction of his thesis (see Figure 8.1). In his paper, Michael explored the significance of Michelle Bachelet becoming Chile's first elected female president; he contended that although she was the daughter of a convicted traitor who was tortured to death by Chilean dictator Augusto Pinochet, she offered the promise of "healing history's wounds" by bridging the political and cultural gap between fighting communities in Chile. Michael encapsulated this argument visually in many ways: by placing the photograph of Bachelet in the center of his collage; by using a picture of Pinochet as a somewhat oppressive top border for the page; by placing images of the Chilean communities on both sides of Bachelet; and by locating his central research question, in blue, between them. In this way, he carefully and deliberately employed the strategies of invention, arrangement, and style to produce a collage that served both as a cover for his written research paper and as an argument in its own right.

Understanding Document Design and Decorum

Let's return to Alex, our hypothetical student from Chapter 1. Her interest in a Health and Society major led her to write an analysis of antismoking advertisements and a research paper on the urban subculture of teenage runaways. She now needs to format her paper for her teacher, and she also is considering submitting it for publication in her college's undergraduate research journal. Moreover, her teacher wants her to convert her paper into a visual argument to appear in a class exhibit. Alex needs to learn appropriate document design for academic audiences, and she wants to explore her choices of media for the visual argument. In each case, she has four key decisions to make: Alex must identify her *argument* (her main point), her *audience* (whom she intends to reach), her *medium* (printed article, abstract, advertisement, photo essay, or multimedia montage), and the specific *form* (the layout and design aspects) for her composition. What governs her choices in each case is a matter of document design strategy, or the choices writers make in formatting their work.

To use terms from classical rhetoric, the decisions you face for document design have to do with **decorum**—a word defined as "appropriateness." In everyday language, someone who exhibits decorum in speaking knows the right kinds of words and content to use given the circumstances and audience. For example, you might swear or whoop in joy at a baseball game, but not on a job interview when talking about how your team won the game. But decorum as a rhetorical principle extends beyond choosing the right words and phrases for the occasion.

In the Roman rhetorical tradition, Cicero separated decorum into three levels of style that he assigned to different argumentative purposes. Cicero defined the *grand style* as the most formal mode of discourse, employing sophisticated language, imagery, and rhetorical devices; its goal is to move the audience. He considered *middle style* less formal than grand style but not completely colloquial; although it uses some verbal ornamentation, it develops its argument more slowly in an attempt to persuade the audience by pleasing them. The final level, *plain style,* mimics conversation in its speech and rhythms, aiming to instruct the audience in a clear and straightforward way. By adding decorum to our rhetorical toolkit, we can make decisions about how to design documents. As demonstrated in the "Levels of Decorum" table below, we can attend to argument, audience, medium, and form by understanding the *level of style* for a particular occasion. Like our classical counterparts, we must understand our rhetorical situation and use a style that best suits the circumstance.

Seeing Connections
For a powerful demonstration of moving from high style to low style in one article, see Michel Martin's "With Immigration, Racism Knows No Borders," on page 546.

LEVELS OF DECORUM

Level	Characteristics	Example: Written Argument for an Antismoking Campaign	Example: Visual Argument for an Antismoking Campaign
Grand or high style	Ornate language; formal structures; many rhetorical devices	Academic paper to be published in a scholarly journal	An antismoking advertisement in the *Journal of the American Medical Association*
Middle style	Some ornamentation; less formal language; argument is developed at a leisurely pace	Feature article or editorial column to be published in the campus newspaper	A photo essay or collage for a school exhibit about effects of smoking or lung cancer
Plain or low style	The least formal style; closest to spoken language; emphasis on clarity, simplicity, and directness	Weblog post on family experiences with cigarette's harmful effects	A Website devoted to the physiology and psychology of nicotine addiction

For the rest of this chapter, we'll look at various models for document design, examining the way in which we need to adjust our choice of style according to the formal and rhetorical demands of each situation.

AT A GLANCE

Characteristics of Academic Writing in Grand Style

- Language should be more sophisticated than ordinary speech
- Use formal structures to organize your paper, including:
  - A complete introduction containing your thesis
  - A transition paragraph predicting your argument
  - Clear subsections for each part of your argument
  - A substantial conclusion

AT A GLANCE

Key Elements of Academic Document Design

- Double-space all pages.
- Provide 1-inch margins on all sides.
- Number pages at the top right; include your last name.
- Use subheads to separate sections.
- Staple or clip the paper together.
- Use in-text citations to acknowledge research sources.
- Use endnotes or footnotes for additional information.
- Include a list of references at the end.
- For specific examples of documentation, see Chapter 7.

Understanding Academic Writing Conventions

From the perspective of decorum, the conventional academic essay falls under either grand or middle style, depending on the preferences of your audience. If your instructor asks you to compose a formal written paper, you will definitely be writing in grand style.

In addition to mastering the content and using grand style for your word choices, you also need to follow the accepted format for designing your essay, as shown in the "At a Glance" box.

An entire scholarly community has reached consensus on format conventions for academic papers, so that everyone knows what information will be provided where. It's similar to the convention of every car in the United States having the steering wheel on the left; the convention fosters a set of shared expectations designed to promote consistency, order, and ease of use.

But there's a deeper *purpose* for these academic-writing conventions. Most have to do with a rhetorical relationship, the fact that people (your instructor and your peers) will be reading your paper, and these reviewers need ample space to provide written comments. By double-spacing your document and providing 1-inch margins on all sides, you leave room for reviewers to comment on lines or paragraphs. You put page numbers and your name in the upper-right corner to enable reviewers to keep track of whose paper it is and to easily refer to your writing by page number in closing comments. The rationale for stapling or clipping is to keep your pages from getting lost.

Integrating Images in Academic Writing

You might want to include visuals in your research paper for many reasons. If, for instance, your topic concerns hybrid cars, you might want to insert a technical diagram to explain the car's mechanics to readers. If you are analyzing advertisement campaigns for hybrid cars, your argument would benefit from showing readers an example through a strategically integrated image. But realize that randomly inserting a picture into your paper does not serve the *purpose* of using images rhetorically in an academic argument. Instead, you need to integrate visual texts into your document design in a rhetorically effective manner.

Carefully consider your strategy of arrangement and the *placement* of your images: Will you put them in an appendix? on your title page? on a separate page? on the same page as your written argument? Each decision is both a stylistic and rhetorical choice. An image placed in an appendix tends to be viewed as *supplementary*, not as integral to an argument; an image on a title page might act as an epigraph to set a mood for a paper, but it is less effective as a specific visual example. If you want to use your images as *argumentative evidence*, you need to show them to your readers as you analyze them; therefore, placing them beside the words of your argument will be most successful.

Once you have determined the placement that best serves your rhetorical purpose, you need to insert the image effectively. Like a quotation, an image cannot be dropped into a text without comment; it needs to be **signposted**, or connected to your argument through deliberate textual markers. You can accomplish this by making explicit **textual references** to the image—for example, "shown in the image at the right" or "(see Figure 3)"—and by taking the time to explain the rhetoric of the image for readers. Just like words quoted from a book or an interview that you might use as evidence, visual material needs *your interpretation* for readers to view it the way you do. Your analysis of its meaning will advance your argument by persuading readers to see the image as you do, and in the process, readers will pause to contemplate the evidence rather than skip over it.

Moreover, it is crucial to draft a **caption** for the image that reiterates the relationship between the point you are making in the paper and the visual evidence you include. In a paper Albert Thomas wrote about the popular sport of *capoeira*, a form of Brazilian martial arts that resembles dancing, he included a still image from the film *Ocean's 12* and wrote an effective caption.

Remember, however, that what is most important is the analysis of the image you include in the body of your paper; don't hide the meaning of the image in the caption. Captions should be concise, but they should not do the work of the written argument.

AT A GLANCE

Including Visuals in a Paper

- Does your paper focus on a visual topic, such as the analysis of ads or films? If so, you probably want to include images or screen shots as evidence and as primary materials to analyze in your writing.
- Does your paper rely on images, such as political campaigns from billboards or Websites, as supporting evidence for your thesis? If so, include images of these materials in your paper.
- If you simply insert an image without comment, readers will skip over it. Make sure you describe its relevance in the text near the image.
- Include a caption with the figure number and a brief description.
- Provide the complete image source in your bibliography.

Figure 1. Vincent Cassel's character in *Ocean's 12* uses *capoeira* to evade this laser grid.

Albert includes a still shot as visual evidence in case his readers haven't seen the film.

His caption includes a figure number, the name of the person and the text (the film), as well as a link to his argument: "Cassel's character . . . uses *capoeira* to evade this laser grid."

A less effective caption would have simply named the film.

Design of Academic Papers

A page from student Allison Woo's paper on Asian-American female stereotypes in contemporary cinema provides an example of both effective academic writing conventions and effective placement and captioning of visuals (see Figure 8.2). Since Allison's project analyzed female stereotypes in two films, *Tomorrow Never Dies* (1997) and *Payback* (1999), she decided to include two images as evidence. Rather than relegating these pictures to an appendix, Allison positioned them in the paper with the text wrapped around it, making the visuals an integral part of her arguments.

Allison's caption lists necessary information—figure numbers, descriptive titles, names of the actresses and films, and the years of release—as well as the sources for the images. Moreover, by paraphrasing the written argument, the caption paraphrases the central point of Allison's paragraph. Through this successful union of words and images, Allison constructs an academic argument effectively and persuasively.

Allison's last name and the page number are in the upper-right corner.

She indents the first line and double-spaces the text.

By embedding the images in the paper, Allison makes readers pause to analyze them as evidence—the way readers would study a poem or a quoted line from a book.

She arranges the visuals so they are in dialogue, reproducing the comparison that is the purpose of her paragraph. In this way, the two figures function effectively as visual evidence for her argument: the striking similarity in pose, costume, and demeanor between actresses Lucy Liu and Michelle Yeoh substantiate Allison's points about the prominence of the "Dragon Lady" stereotype in popular American films.

Woo 9

Meanwhile, the Dragon Lady images of sexuality are equally prevalent in film today. In *Tomorrow Never Dies* (1997), Asian actress Michelle Yeoh plays a seductive Chinese spy, who simultaneously flirts, manipulates, fights, and plays with her costar, James Bond (played by Pierce Brosnan). Screenwriter and novelist Jessica Hagedorn lists Yeoh's character as an archetypical Dragon Lady. Dressed in tight jumpsuit in her favorite color of corruptible black, Yeoh's character double-crosses, connives, and seduces her way through the movie, and it is always unclear whether she is good or evil.

Figs. 8 and 9. Michelle Yeoh in *Tomorrow Never Dies*, 1997 (left); Lucy Liu in *Payback*, 2002 (right). Their common characterization, dress, hairstyle, weaponry, and "dangerous" sexuality illustrate the way Hollywood repackages the same stereotyped characters in different movies.

Bond eventually conquers all, winning sexual access to the Asian woman. In *Payback*, Lucy Liu's character Pearl also double-crosses both sides. Although she only appears in a few scenes, most of them show her seductively whispering a few lines of sexual prompting. Achieving almost orgasmic pleasure from sexually manipulating and dominating men, she thrives in her sexuality and moral corruption. Even Caucasian movie critic Sam Adams recognizes Pearl as a stereotypical "Dragon Lady," as she makes sexual advances on the hero (Mel Gibson) and the villains in the movie. Her Asian heritage is distinguishable from the Caucasian prostitute in the

FIGURE 8.2. In this excerpt from her paper, "Slaying the Dragon," Allison Woo showcases visual and verbal arguments working together.

Tools of Design for Academic Audiences

In addition to the research paper, you might choose to compose supplemental pages, such as a cover page containing an academic *abstract* and research *bio*—a brief biography of the author. We'll discuss these aspects now so you can add them to your toolkit of writing strategies.

Composing an Abstract

Seeing Connections
For an example of an abstract in a popular paper, see Joe Strupp, "The Photo Felt Around the World," page 512.

The **research abstract** is a professional academic genre designed both to present the research topic and to lay out the argument. Abstracts differ depending on the disciplinary audience and the purpose of the writing: When applying to academic conferences in the humanities, for example, academics often must write abstracts that predict the paper's argument, research contribution, and significance, while writers in the sciences or social sciences typically write abstracts *after* the paper has been completed to serve as a short summary of the article. You will encounter abstracts when you begin searching for research articles; they often precede a published paper or accompany bibliographic citations in online databases.

Abstracts can range from a few sentences to a page in length, but they are usually no longer than two paragraphs. The key in writing an abstract is to explain your argument in one brief, coherent unit. As you compose your abstract, you will need to make several rhetorical decisions.

To understand how your answers to the questions listed in the "At a Glance" box will shape your writing, let's consider three student abstracts that each correspond to a different level of decorum, use varying levels of specificity, and implement diverse means of constructing a research persona.

- Molly Cunningham, for her abstract on her paper "Illuminating the Dark Continent: Hollywood Portrayals of Africa," writes in the *grand style* of decorum: she uses complex academic terms and a sophisticated vocabulary, including terminology from her discipline of postcolonial anthropology. In three complex sentences, she conveys her theoretical approach to analyzing film, names the films, and provides her thesis before ending with a statement of broader significance.
- Laura Hendrickson's abstract for her paper titled "Plastic Surgery Among Women in South Korea" uses the *middle style* of decorum by combining the use of "I" with specific terms from her research, such as "Neo-Confucian ideals." She identifies her topic—observations about plastic surgery in Korean female role models—and makes a claim about it—that surgery represents a projected Western standard of beauty.
- David Pinner relies more heavily on *plain style* for his abstract on copyright and the Creative Commons movement (see below). His abstract includes contractions, avoids excessive display, and is written in the first person.

AT A GLANCE

Writing an Abstract

Plan to write one or two paragraphs about your paper, working through these questions:

- What level of decorum or style do you wish to use?
- How will the style predict the tone of your paper and establish your persona as a researcher?
- Do you want to use "I"?
- How much specificity should you include from the paper?
  - Do you want to list the concrete examples you analyze in your writing?
  - Do you want to give an overview of your argument?
  - Should you name sources you use in making your argument?
- How can you be both brief and engaging?

Since the rise of Napster and mp3s, the battle for intellectual property control of artistic works has exploded. Restrictive measures by the RIAA and MPAA threaten to take control of creative works away from both users and creators, to the point where people can't even control the data on their computer. However, a new alternative has emerged: Creative Commons, a copyright license designed for flexibility, readability and ease of use. In my project, I examine the way that Creative Commons is changing the nature of artistic collaboration in a world where art is increasingly created and distributed through electronic means.

Notice the clear, direct style that avoids excessive display or ornamentation.

The use of the contraction *can't* and first person mark this as plain style.

The somewhat informal concluding statement of purpose resists providing a fully developed argument.

Shaping Your Bio

While the abstract offers a concise statement of the argument, the **bio** is a concise paragraph that explains the persona of the writer to the intended audience. The bio functions to persuade readers of the writer's depth of knowledge or connection to the topic. Usually, the bio describes the writer's credentials, interests, and motivations for engaging in research work. Molly Cunningham's bio for her paper on Hollywood depictions of Africa follows this model, resembling the polished "About the Author" paragraph that you might find at the back of a book on the topic or in the headnote of an academic article:

Student Writing
See research abstracts and student bios in a variety of styles.
www.pearsonhighered.com/envision/245

Molly names specific qualifications and experiences she has had that make her an authority in this area.

She ends the bio with her future plans in this area of research that suggest her pursuit of a "research line" or academic path of scholarly inquiry.

> Molly Cunningham is a sophomore planning to double major in Cultural and Social Anthropology and English. After spending time in East Africa, she has become interested in exploring cultural definitions of the orphan within the community and family in light of postcolonialism as well as the AIDS pandemic. She is currently planning a summer research project in Botswana to do ethnographic research on this topic. Cunningham is also interested in the politics of humanitarian aid and the interplay between community and international donors. Involved in fundraising for a Kenyan orphanage, she hopes to deconstruct the meanings and attitudes that shape the nature and determine the amount of foreign aid going into Africa. She has utilized this research project to expand her thinking on this topic while learning to convey her findings to wider audiences.

If you are writing a bio to accompany a research proposal you may feel that, at this point in your project, you have no authority on the topic. Keep in mind that as you explore your sources, you will become more knowledgeable about your topic and be able to contribute to dialogue about your area of research. Thus even at an early stage of your research, you can use language, tone, and style to construct a sense of *ethos*. Look, for example, at David Pinner's bio:

David creates a sense of credibility by using humor: he demonstrates his familiarity with the terms of the debate and refers to some of the prominent "players."

> David Pinner is a sophomore at Stanford University majoring in physics. His father came from a traditional copyrighted background, while his mother's family had long been in the public domain. Being raised in a multilicensed household was difficult, but thanks to the work of Creative Commons and other copyleft organizations, his situation is finally being

recognized by the general public. He enjoys electronic media, sailing, playing music, and Stickin' it to The Man. He is a dues-paying member of the Electronic Frontier Foundation (www.eff.org) and releases his blog under an Attribution-NonCommerical-ShareAlike v2.0 Creative Commons license.

When formatting your own bio, you might decide to include a photograph of yourself. Remember to select your picture carefully, with attention to its rhetorical impact. Many students who choose to write a traditional bio like Molly's opt for a formal photograph such as a school portrait; other students, like David, might choose a more candid or humorous picture to complement the tone of their bios. One student, when writing about online gaming communities, even created a Photoshopped portrait of herself standing next to her onscreen avatar identity to represent the two perspectives she was bringing to her research. As you can tell, the picture works in conjunction with the bio not only to construct a persona for the writer but also to suggest that writer's rhetorical stance.

Combining Visual and Verbal Design Elements

The visual rhetoric of a page matters to an audience: from the paragraph indents to the margins and double-spaced lines, to the rhetorical placement of images—all these design decisions are ways of conveying your level of decorum and your purpose to your specific audience. When we say "first impressions," we often mean how well a writer meets the conventions anticipated by the audience.

When your audience allows you to combine visual and verbal elements, you can produce *a hybrid composition* such as a feature article for a magazine, a newsletter aimed at a community audience, or an online article for diverse readers. Research has shown that in such texts, readers tend to focus on the visual part of a text first, before the words. Whether it's a news article, a traditional academic paper with a visual, or a multimedia collage, the visual grabs the attention first. Perhaps the images in this book engage your interest more immediately than the prose. Indeed, according to Adbusters, an organization devoted to cultural criticism and analysis, the visual part of any page is noticed significantly more than any text on the same page. Adbusters uses this finding to provide advice for creating ads, but we can apply the insight to written compositions combining visual and verbal elements.

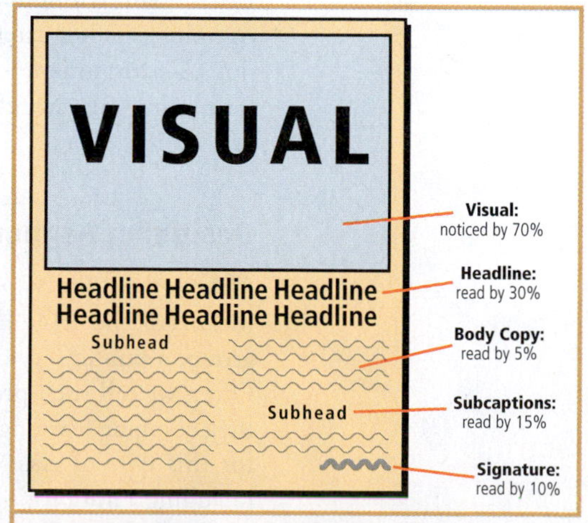

FIGURE 8.3. A graphic representation of what readers notice most on a page: visuals grab attention most.

Figure 8.3 provides a useful diagram for understanding the way readers process information, showing that 70 percent of readers notice visuals and 30 percent pay attention to headlines; much farther down on the attention-grabbing scale are the body, subheads, and the signature. Knowing this, consider

B & M Press

Where the Real Stories Get Presented

Volume 1, Issue 1

October 28, 2003

Ashley Denise Mullen | Editor & Chief

INSIDE THIS ISSUE:

Attacks On American Troops Are Growing... (Washington Post)	2
Misrepresented & Misjudged	6
What about My Defenseless Child?	7
Risky Side Effects	8
Final Thoughts	9

Special points of interest:

- Check out the graphic and personal images in this issue.
- New B&M Press on-site reporter, Sherman Jackson, will wow the readers with his interviewees' emotional responses.
- Advertisements! Advertisements! Advertisements!

There is A Thin Line Between Police Assistance and Police Brutality

Imagine yourself sleeping serenely in a comfortable bed and dreaming about the items that young children often fantasize about. But, instantaneously, your dream is interrupted due to the loud noise of rummaging and ransacking your home. Keep in mind that those who entered your property did so without your permission and are not sympathetic towards your valuable and fragile belongings. An honest and popular reaction from society would be of opposition and others may even feel violated. You, the injured party, may have a different reaction to this scenario but a similar case drew plenty attention. After MSNBC featured a salacious picture of an Iraqi child peacefully sleeping during an intense police raid in his home, the public grew weary and gave disapproving looks at the U.S. Army and the Iraqi police. For years civilians' rights have been fought for, modified, and even questioned. There has not always been a fine line between which police actions are considered ethical or unethical. Where do you actually draw the line? While further investigating the parties involved, the B&M Press was able to find three distinct points of view on the MSNBC image. Since the United States Army and Iraqi police was held accountable for causing distress it seemed only fair to allow them to rationalize their defense. The mother of the child pictured in the photo had an opportunity to express her feelings and respond to the way her child was mistreated. And finally, an experienced child psychologist put in her input on the matter from an outside perspective. As editor, I want to allow each viewpoint to have a voice, and make sure to include each individual's response to the image as well as a featured Washington Post article in to order justify his or her feelings.

Figure 1: Asleep through sweep; **A U.S. soldier and an Iraqi policeman search a room as an Iraqi child sleeps on the bed during a joint raid by the 401st Military Police Company of the U.S. Army and the Iraqi police in Tikrit, about 110 miles northwest of Baghdad**

FIGURE 8.4. Design of Ashley Mullen's hybrid composition.

the importance of visuals as you approach designing your own hybrid compositions. As for your headline—second in importance to viewers—follow a suggestion from Adbusters: "The most important thing to remember here is that your headline must be short, snappy and must touch the people that read it. Your headline must affect the readers emotionally, either by making them laugh, making them angry, making them curious or making them think." Clearly, headlines work through rhetorical appeals: you need to think carefully about which appeal—*pathos, ethos,* or *logos*—would provide the most effective way to engage your audience.

Let's look at the design decisions Ashley Mullen made in formatting her writing project on the topic of police brutality. She created a newsletter that featured a cover story in which she arranged words around a powerful image. In designing this text, Ashley took into account not only the argument she sought to make but also, as Figure 8.4 makes clear, the choices of layout, placement of images, font size, color, and overall design. Her painstaking care with the design of this text is evident in the power of her finished product. Inside the newsletter, Ashley selected several photographs—each functioning as an individual argument—as a graphic way of representing the additional points she wanted to make on the issue: each photo anchored her writing and complemented the diverse perspectives she crafted. We can see here how visual rhetoric functions as a powerful tool of argument for her hybrid composition; it complements her careful attention to style through her word choices, imagery, expressions, and argument for each position. You might do the same in your writing through formatting your work in newspaper columns or as a magazine feature article, Website, or personal letter.

Designing Arguments for Public Audiences

Although Ashley Mullen designed her hybrid composition for an academic audience (her class), she could have easily decided to share this writing project with a community group, a public service organization, or a student group dedicated to social change. Often we call such projects **service-learning** or **community service** projects because they combine learning (or writing) with service to the community. The writing you do for this type of class project is likely to be produced for a nonacademic audience, including a nonprofit agency, a city council, or members of an outreach group.

For these writing projects, you might be asked to produce a grant letter, a newsletter article, a fact sheet, a brochure, or even a Website. Such projects benefit both the nonprofit

FIGURE 8.5. Jonathan Denby and Chris Fedor's poster for Palo Alto Open Space.

organization and the members it serves; in addition, it provides you with experience producing the kinds of texts you'll be asked to write throughout your professional career.

Let's take a look at the design strategies employed in community service writing projects, which are often multilayered, just like many of the professional projects you might encounter outside the university setting. That is, you might be asked to develop not just one flyer, pamphlet, or poster but rather a series of interconnected texts; thus, design becomes a more complicated process of connecting diverse documents according to purpose and audience.

> **Community-based writing—whether it is practical or academic—is *writing for real.* It engages tangible issues, uniting thought and action, and it calls for new approaches to writing.**
>
> —Carolyn Ross and Ardel Thomas, *Writing for Real,* 17

For example, as part of a service-learning project for a nonprofit Open Space organization, Jonathan Denby and Chris Fedor created a poster advising visitors to the local baylands to refrain from feeding the wildlife. As Figure 8.5 shows, the poster draws the audience in through the pairing of its provocative headline ("You are killing us with your kindness!") with a seemingly innocuous picture of a hand feeding bread to a duck. The incongruity of word and image moves the reader to the bolded question "HOW?", and then down into the bottom of the poster that outlines different elements of the argument. Although they used a vertical structure (we read from top down), Jonathan and Chris deliberately distributed the key components across the bottom of their page, using clear subheads to anchor their points and guide their readers through their claims. Notice also the strategic use of subsidiary images to reinforce their points both as visual evidence and as *pathos* appeals. Referring back to Figure 8.3, we can see that much of the success of this poster lies in Jonathan and Chris's understanding of how to effectively design a visually-based argument.

Keep in mind that community service writing projects are often multilayered, just like many of the professional projects you might encounter outside the university setting. That is, Chris and Jonathan might have been asked to create a Website or newletter article to accompany their poster; or for a similar assignment, you might be asked to develop not just a single pamphlet or flyer, but rather a series of interconnected texts. In such situations, design becomes a more complicated process of connecting diverse documents according to purpose and audience.

Formatting Writing for Audiences

Let's look now at a purely verbal or written example of formatting writing for online audiences before we move to the visual arguments in the next section. In the following reading, the author employs many of the elements from the "At a Glance" box on document design that appeared earlier in the chapter. The selection includes a title, subheads, references, and a reference list at the end. But notice how the written argument has been changed or translated into a *hybrid composition* to meet the expectations of the online reading audience.

The title is in plain style and all capital letters, with the subtitle in lowercase. This font decision makes it appealing to online readers.

WHAT'S WRONG WITH THE BODY SHOP?

—a criticism of 'green' consumerism—

REFERENCED VERSION—all the facts and opinions in THE London Greenpeace A5 'Body Shop' leaflet validated. Note: most references are given just by way of example.

The numbers correspond to notes and sources at the end. These notes are *hyperlinked*, so readers can jump there easily while reading on the Web.

The Body Shop have successfully manufactured an image of being a caring company that is helping to protect the environment [1] and indigenous peoples [2], and preventing the suffering of animals [3]—whilst selling 'natural' products [4]. But behind the green and cuddly image lies the reality—the Body Shop's operations, like those of all multinationals, have a detrimental effect on the environment [5] and the world's poor [6]. They do not help the plight of animals [7] or indigenous peoples [8] (and may be having a harmful effect), and their products are far from what they're cracked up to be [9]. They have put themselves on a pedestal in order to exploit people's idealism [10]—so this leaflet has been written as a necessary response.

Companies like the Body Shop continually hype their products through advertising and marketing, often creating a demand for something where a real need for it does not exist [11]. The message pushed is that the route to happiness is through buying more and more of their products. The increasing domination of multinationals and their standardised products is leading to global cultural conformity [12]. The world's problems will only be tackled by curbing such consumerism-one of the fundamental causes of world poverty, environmental destruction and social alienation [13].

FUELLING CONSUMPTION AT THE EARTH'S EXPENSE

The Body Shop have over 1,500 stores in 47 countries [14], and aggressive expansion plans [15]. Their main purpose (like all multinationals) is making lots of money for their rich shareholders [16]. In other words, they are driven by power and greed. But the Body Shop try to conceal this reality by continually pushing the message that by shopping at their stores, rather than elsewhere, people will help solve some of the world's problems [17]. The truth is that nobody can make the world a better place by shopping.

20% of the world's population consume 80% of its resources [18]. A high standard of living for some people means gross social inequalities and poverty around the world [19]. Also, the mass production, packaging and transportation of huge quantities of goods is using up the world's resources faster than they can be renewed and filling the land, sea and air with dangerous pollution and waste [20]. Those who advocate an ever-increasing level of consumption, and equate such consumption with personal well-being, economic progress and social fulfillment, are creating a recipe for ecological disaster [21].

Rejecting consumerism does not mean also rejecting our basic needs, our stylishness, our real choices or our quality of life. It is about creating a just, stable and sustainable world, where resources are under the control of local communities and are distributed equally and sparingly—it's about improving everyone's quality of life. Consuming ever more things is an unsatisfying and harmful way to try to be happy and fulfilled. Human happiness is not related to what people buy, but to who we are and how we relate to each other. LET'S CONSUME LESS AND LIVE MORE!

MISLEADING THE PUBLIC

Natural products? The Body Shop give the impression that their products are made from mostly natural ingredients [22]. In fact like all big cosmetic companies they make wide use of non-renewable petrochemicals, synthetic colours, fragrances and preservatives [23], and in many of their products they use only tiny amounts of botanical-based ingredients [24]. Some experts have warned about the potential adverse effects on the skin of some of the synthetic ingredients [25]. The Body Shop also regularly irradiate certain products to try to kill microbes—radiation is generated from dangerous non-renewable uranium which cannot be disposed of safely [26].

* * *

CENSORSHIP

As the Body Shop rely so heavily on their 'green', 'caring' image, they have threatened or brought legal action against some of those who have criticised them, trying to stifle legitimate public discussion [46]. It's vital to stand up to intimidation and to defend free speech.

The article uses argumentative subheads, as might an academic paper. They convey points of argument being made in the article. Moreover, they keep readers interested.

Notice how the article uses all CAPS to draw the online reader's attention and even begins a new section with a two-word question.

Some sections are very short, a common feature in online writing, where information is "chunked" into accessible packages.

The article uses direct address, the pronoun *you*, to engage readers. This design strategy again indicates the use of the plain style.

WHAT YOU CAN DO

Together we can fight back against the institutions and the people in power who dominate our lives and our planet. Workers can and do organise together to fight for their rights and dignity. People are increasingly aware of the need to think seriously about the products we use, and to consume less. People in poor countries are organising themselves to stand up to multinationals and banks which dominate the world's economy. Environmental and animal rights protests and campaigns are growing everywhere. Why not join in the struggle for a better world? London Greenpeace calls on people to create an anarchist society—a society without oppression, exploitation and hierarchy, based on strong and free communities, the sharing of precious resources and respect for all life. Talk to friends and family, neighbours and workmates about these issues. Please copy and circulate this leaflet as widely as you can.

For more information, contact:
London Greenpeace
5 Caledonian Road
London N1 9DX, UK.
Tel/Fax 0171 713 1269
Tel 0171 837 7557
E-mail: lgp@ envirolink.org

The "More Information" column above is an online design version of the bio; the contact information gives readers more knowledge of the persona while building *ethos* and authority.

REFERENCES

1. See "Fuelling Consumption" paragraphs in the leaflet and associated references.

2. See "Exploiting Indigenous Peoples" paragraphs in the leaflet and associated references.

3. See "Helping Animals?" paragraph in the leaflet and associated references.

4. See "Natural products?" paragraph in the leaflet and associated references.

10. [Numerous publications, statements, advertisements, etc. by the Body Shop.] For example, the company's Mission Statement (1998) says that they are dedicating their business "to the pursuit of social and environmental change" and are trying to ensure that their business "is ecologically sustainable, meeting the needs of the present without compromising the future." "For us, animal protection, human rights, fair trade and environmentalism, are not just fads or marketing gimmicks but fundamental components in our holistic approach to life of which work and business are a part" [Gordon Roddick (Chairman) quoted in 1996 *Body Shop* publication "Our Agenda".] "I'd rather promote human rights, environmental concerns, indigenous rights, whatever, than promote a bubble bath" said Anita Roddick (the *Body Shop* founder and Chief Executive) [speech at 'Academy of Management', Vancouver (Aug 95).]

Since these notes are positioned far down on the page, they can go into more detail because they assume that only very interested readers will be accessing this part of the composition.

Back to 'Beyond McDonald's—Retail' Section

London Greenpeace Press Release
WWW Body Shop FAQ
London Greenpeace reply to Body Shop statement
A5 version of 'What's Wrong With The Body Shop'

From a design perspective, the final series of links for future reading signifies one of the great benefits of writing in a digital environment.

As you can tell from this article, the same strategies of design that shape academic research papers also apply to other modes: what is most important in each is a consideration of *purpose, audience,* and *argument.* Think about how readers will interact with your writing—whether as a print copy handed in for comments (in which case you double-space and follow academic guidelines); as a newsletter (in which case you might open with a powerful image, lay out the writing in columns or boxes, and use an interesting page size); or as a hybrid piece to be read on the Web (in which case you include hyperlinks, single-space, create shorter chunks, and use font strategically).

Designing Visual Arguments

In essence, *visual arguments* are compact multimedia texts that exist as independent creations, such as op-ads, photo essays, Websites, and montages. We can understand these texts through the levels of decorum (outlined earlier in the chapter): someone surfing the Web might find the student Website dedicated to family members who died from smoking cigarettes (our plain-style example); a person browsing through departmental publications might encounter a student's photo essay about the effects of smoking (our middle-style example); or a visitor looking at an exhibit case in a library might see op-ads created by a Writing and Social Issues class and find in this work powerful pieces of visual rhetoric (our grand-style example).

When you construct a visual argument—whether generated for your research project, as a new argument about a issue, or as an assignment for your class—you have the opportunity to experiment with many forms of media to make a powerful argument. You can apply strategies for inventing, arranging, and producing the design of an innovative visual argument that will persuade viewers to agree with your message.

Keep in mind, however, that each medium structures information in a distinct way. A photo essay is set up differently than a Webpage, just as a Webpage is set up differently than a magazine advertisement. Therefore, part of creating a powerful visual argument lies in identifying your chosen medium's conventions of structure and style and adjusting the form of your argument—its layout, design, style, and organization of information—to be the most appropriate choice for your project.

FIGURE 8.6. This Body Shop opinion advertisement relies on a powerful visual argument to shock readers into questioning concepts of beauty.

Crafting an Op-Ad

The **op-ad,** or **opinion advertisement,** is one of the most concise forms of visual argument. Most op-ads promote an opinion rather than a consumer product. Many nonprofit organizations, special interest groups, and political parties find the op-ad a particularly effective way to reach their target audiences. Like all ads, the op-ad is a compact persuasive text, one that uses rhetorical appeals to convey its message. In addition, like other types of ads, an op-ad may rely partially on written text, but it tends to work through the visual components of its argument.

Seeing Connections
For a broader discussion of body image, see the section "Imagining the Ideal Body" in Chapter 12.

In Figure 8.6, for instance, the op-ad makes its point through a strategic combination of visual and verbal elements. The Body Shop has crafted an innovative image that

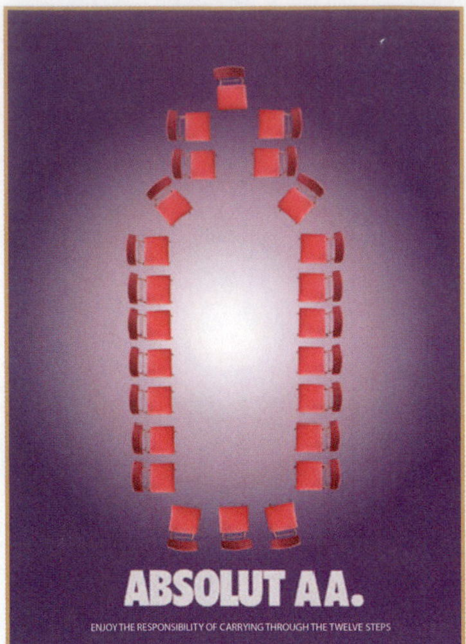

FIGURE 8.7. This Alcoholics Anonymous op-ad parodies the design of the familiar Absolut Vodka ads.

communicates a powerful message: the realistically proportioned doll, set in a confident, casual pose against a natural background of ivy, produces a strong counterstatement against standards of body image in the mass media that promote exceptional thinness for feminine beauty. The words, "There are 3 billion women who don't look like supermodels and only 8 who do," are arranged to reinforce the visual argument of the doll's curvy body. The image creates an argument based on *pathos*, while the statistics draw on *logos*. The design of the op-ad thus works through visual and verbal strategies to make people think twice about body image. The tiny words under the Body Shop name and logo accentuate and confirm the argument of the image: "Know your mind love your body." In this way, the op-ad uses the way readers attend to information on a page: image first, headline second, caption third.

In many ways, the figure of the heavyset Body Shop doll evokes Barbie; op-ads often rely on this rhetorical strategy—**parody**, or the use of one text's formal properties to subvert the meaning of the original and make an independent argument. We can see the power of this strategy in Figure 8.7, a spoof ad from Adbusters. In this example, the parody ad invokes the popular Absolut Vodka ad series with some key differences: the iconic Absolut Vodka bottle has been transformed into a circle of chairs for an AA meeting; and the caption and taglines now reflect the AA agenda.

To understand how to compose your own op-ad, let's look at the process by which one student, Carrie Tsosie, constructed her visual argument. After writing an effective research paper that presented the dangers of allowing uranium mining on or near Navajo reservations, Carrie decided to reformulate her argument as an op-ad to reach a larger audience. Her initial considerations were her visual format and her headline—two elements of her ad that underwent some revision. She explained:

> My first idea was to have an image of a deformed lamb because then the audience would see what radiation poisoning can do. I wanted to use the phrase "Stop mining before it starts," but it seemed like that phrase was overdone, and I don't think that my audience could really relate to the deformed lamb because they do not know how important it is to some Navajo people and their lives. (Tsosie, reflection letter)

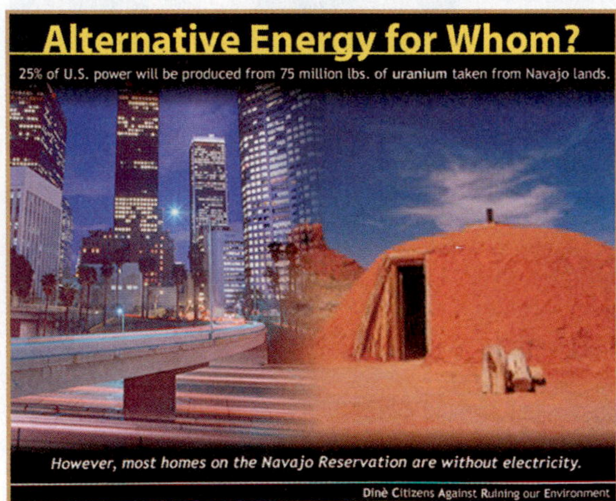

FIGURE 8.8. Carrie Tsosie's op-ad uses visual juxtaposition and a strong headline to make its argument against U.S. mining practices.

As shown in her completed op-ad (Figure 8.8), Carrie decided against the *pathos*-based image of a sick animal.

She opted instead to feature different human environments through her strategic choices of images. In addition, rather than base her ad on a strong imperative such as "Stop Mining," she chose to soften her voice and reach her audience by asking them to question their assumptions about alternative energy. In her final op-ad, she composed a heading with the provocative question "Alternative

AT A GLANCE

Designing an Op-Ad

- Decide on your purpose (to inform, to persuade, to move to action).
- Identify your audience.
- Know your argument.
- Determine which appeals to use (*pathos, logos, ethos*).
- Select key images for your ad.
- Write your print text; decide how it will function in relation to your image(s).
- Draft a gripping headline to complement your image.
- Experiment with layout—arrangement, image size, organization of text—to arrive at the most effective design.

Energy for Whom?" and then followed the words with a striking visual argument. It is here, in the image, that we find the main work of argumentation. Carrie combined an image from the urban landscape with a stereotypical image from the reservation to produce a striking effect, using what we call *visual juxtaposition*, or the combination of multiple images, as a rhetorical device to call attention to the discrepancy between these ways of life and inform readers about her critique.

Seeing Connections
For an example of an Op-Ad poster, see the 2004 Get Real Campaign poster from the National Eating Disorders Association on page 391.

Producing a Photo Essay

Although op-ads offer a concise, forceful argument, you may wish to develop your points more thoroughly than one page allows or use visual space to show the range of material with which you've been working. If so, consider the **photo essay**—a text in which photographs, rather than print text, convey the central argument. In a word-based essay, verbal text takes priority, and images are typically used as supplements. In a photo essay, by contrast, the visual either collaborates with the verbal or becomes the *primary mode* of representation and persuasion.

As a genre, the photo essay first emerged in 1936 with the launching of *Life* magazine, whose mission statement was "to see life; to see the world." Over the 63 years it remained in print, *Life* hosted many of America's most famous photo essays, covering a range of topics from the space race to the Vietnam War, the civil rights movement, and rock and roll. But the photo essay can assume many different forms and use diverse media: it could be a series of documentary photographs and articles about southern sharecroppers published together in book form, such as Walker Evans's and James Agee's *Let Us Now Praise Famous Men* (1941); it could be a book-length photo essay that juxtaposes images with first-person narratives, such as Lauren Greenfield's *Girl Culture* (2002); it could be a striking 27-page color spread in a magazine, such as William Albert Allard's "Solace at Surprise Creek" in the June 2006 issue of *National Geographic*; or it could even be an online arrangement of captioned photos, such as *A Rescue Worker's Chronicle*, created by paramedic Matthew Levy. In each case, the photographs and written text work together, or the images themselves carry the primary weight of the argument.

Seeing Connections
For examples of photo essays, see Jane Gottesmann's "Game Face" (page 51); Chris Rainer's "Tattoos, Piercings, and Body Markings" (page 421); and Peter Menzel and Faith d'Aluisio's "What the World Eats" (page 248).

Today electronic photo essays are essential conveyers of important events, a result of Internet news sources like CNN.com, Time.com, and MSNBC.com, which routinely publish photo essays as "picture stories" on their Websites. Such texts are composed of a series of images and words that work together to suggest an argument about a

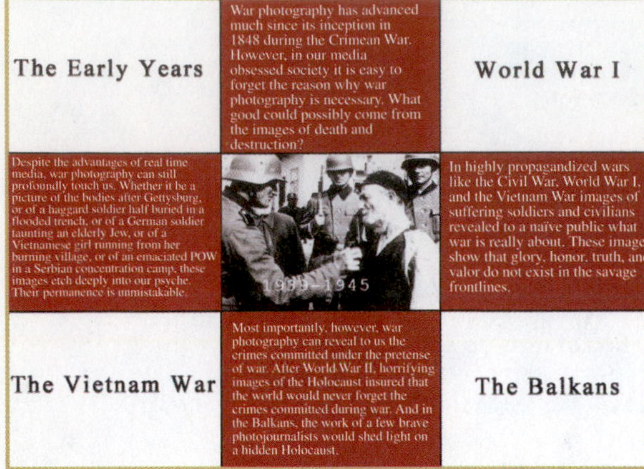

FIGURE 8.9. Ye Yuan's "Looking Through the Lens" photo essay with the rollover graphic activated.

person, event, or story. Each electronic photo essay typically contains (1) a photo, (2) an accompanying caption, (3) an audio option, and (4) a table of contents toolbar that allows readers to navigate through the images. The result is an electronic text that maintains many structural similarities to print text: it offers readers a clear sense of progression from beginning to end while investing its argument with the rhetorical force of multiple media (word, image, sound).

Let's now consider how one student, Ye Yuan, created an online photo essay that uses a dynamic format to give readers control over the way they view the information and the way the argument is assembled.

Figure 8.9 demonstrates this reader-oriented dynamic. The arrangement of information, though it follows a roughly left-to-right, top-to-bottom organization, also opens up the possibility of browsing this photo essay in a less rigidly determined fashion. As you might expect, clicking on a bolded title takes you to a series of sequential images from that time period, offering structure to this broad discussion of war photography. At first glance, this arrangement might seem to rely on a traditional hierarchy of image and word, with the pictures serving as a secondary layer to the word-based introduction. Yet as soon as the reader begins to interact with this photo essay, moving the mouse across the page, this illusion is dispelled. Each bolded title contains a rollover graphic, so that when the reader moves the mouse over the words, a representative image appears. This dynamic relationship between word and image suggests a conjunction of meaning between the two; cooperation between the visual and the verbal is designed to "hook" and move the reader to the next level of the photo essay.

FIGURE 8.10. One of Ye Yuan's linked pages in his photo essay. Each link contains a single photograph with an explanatory caption.

At the subsection level (shown in Figure 8.10), the reader finds a carefully chosen image that represents war photography from that historical period. Here, the photographs function as the arguments, because the heading remains constant for each subsequent image; the pictures change, but the print remains the same.

The photo essay works best if you have a topic that can be effectively argued through an accumulation of visual evidence presented as a sequence of images. Keep in mind that designing a photo essay is like drafting a research paper: you may take pages of notes, but the task of crafting the argument involves sifting through information, deciding between relevant and irrelevant materials, and arranging the most powerful evidence in your finished product. Remember to shape your photo essay around your argument through carefully made rhetorical choices about purpose, audience, and medium.

Composing a Website

If you decide to move your project online and produce a Website, your readers will then encounter your visual argument as **hypertext**, or a series of interlinked Web pages. Hypertext authors construct a framework for an argument through the **homepage** (the site's introduction), the **navigation scheme** (the site's organizational structure), and the contents of individual pages, offering both internal and external links designed to guide readers through the various levels of argument and evidence. In effect, a *hypertext argument* is produced by the collaboration between the author's direction and the readers' participation; in this way, the rhetorical situation of a Website as a visual argument becomes literally interactive, with readers playing an active role in the construction of meaning.

This dynamic determines the argumentative structure for TheTruth.com's Crazyworld page (see Figure 8.11), accessible through TheTruth.com's archives of past pages. The site's target audience might be young people inclined toward smoking. But by appearing on the Internet the site conveys its argument to the broader public, using the carnival motif to suggest what a "crazy world" we live in, where tobacco companies continue to sell—and consumers continue to buy and smoke—cigarettes that contain chemicals like arsenic, benzene, and cyanide. The site's primary *level of decorum* is plain style: through simple language, the carnival metaphor, and engaging visuals, the Website seeks to persuade viewers of the dangers of tobacco usage to both smokers and nonsmokers. This draws readers into the site, where they encounter the more explicitly argumentative indictments of Big Tobacco in the site's subsidiary content pages that reveal statistics, interviews, and indictments of cigarette companies.

The power of this visual argument lies in the flexibility of its design, which allows the audience to explore its many features. Although it resists relying on the sort of linear development typically found in paper texts, it still offers readers a variety of structured and clearly delineated pathways into its central arguments against Big Tobacco. On the surface, the site presents striking graphics and a visual *menu bar*, consisting of links to different aspects of the site. However, its primary *navigation toolbar*, the list of links that provide direct access to the interior of the Website, is actually hidden beneath the clown image. The toolbar only appears when the viewer rolls the mouse over the word *Navigate*, placed beneath the curved arrow that points at the clown. This Website, then, has been composed as a highly interactive piece of digital writing. There is no "right way" to navigate this site, and the writers are able to reach a wide audience and convey a powerful argument about the dangers of smoking.

The process of authoring your own Website may seem daunting at first. However, in many ways drafting text for the Web resembles drafting the complex argument of a long research paper: in both cases, you need to identify the necessary elements of your

AT A GLANCE

Designing a Photo Essay

1. Decide on the argument or thesis for your project.
2. Categorize your images, arranging them within the theme groups.
3. Organize them into different configurations: by chronology, theme, and subject.
4. Draft written text in the form of headings, captions, and paragraphs.
5. Determine your layout by experimenting with ways of formatting the words and images.

FIGURE 8.11. The Crazyworld homepage demonstrates multiple strategies of effective Website composition.

AT A GLANCE

Essential Elements for Composing a Website

- Decide on your target audience.
- Select your content and main argument.
- Determine your purpose (to teach, persuade, or move to action).
- Compose your level of decorum.
- Design your site organization, navigation, and layout.

composition, and then you need to follow a process of careful planning and organization.

In designing your Website, you will need to account for three levels of information: a *homepage* at the **primary level** (which will serve as the introduction to your site); a *series of topic pages* at the **secondary level** (which will contain both content and, sometimes, links to further, more specialized subtopic pages); and the *subtopic pages* at the **deep level** (which will contain content and perhaps even more links). Although most sites contain only one home page, some use a **splash page**—often featuring a single provocative quote, a flash animation, or gripping image—that functions as a hook or **gateway** to a more substantive introductory homepage. There is no limit on the number of topic and content pages you can include; you should determine the scope of your project and number of pages based on your assessment of how to make your argument most effectively.

Seeing Connections
Explore the arrangement of images on the Website created by *TIME* for a special report on The New Frontier / La Nueva Frontera, with photos by Alex Webb, on page 528.

In terms of design, composing a Website resembles the process of outlining a research paper. Yet there are important differences between digital writing and writing for print readers. For a Website:

- *Chunk* your information—or divide it into manageable parts.
- *Strive for consistency* of theme, font, and/or color throughout your site; avoid visual clutter and ineffectual use of images.
- Think about the *relationship between the words and images.*
- *Consider creating* a *template,* or visual precedent, that establishes the key elements for the rest of the site, much as an introduction in a written paper often sets the style and conventions for the rest of the argument to follow.

Let's look at a sample web project on the visual rhetoric surrounding the 1963 March on Washington. The design was intended to encourage readers to engage with the primary texts within the framework of a researched argument.

The homepage for this site (Fig. 8.12) models the composition of the entire project. The most striking element is the photograph, used here to underscore the author's argument. (The photograph is taken from Wikimedia Commons, a repository for public domain photographs, showing the author's careful attention to copyright regulation; since a Webpage is a type of publication, you should not use copyrighted images in public Websites.) Notice the way the homepage

- pairs image with text;
- uses a quote (in blue) as an epigraph for the page;
- explicitly states its argument in bold;
- meticulously cites its sources (with parenthetical, hyperlinked references to the Sources page).

On the subpages, the author supports her researched argument through reference to secondary sources and analysis of the primary texts. For instance, on the "Celebrities" page, she analyzes photographs of Joan Baez, Bob Dylan, Harry Belafonte, Sammy Davis Jr., and Charlton Heston. The homepage also demonstrates the site's attention to organization. The tabbed menu at the top is duplicated by the visual menu

FIGURE 8.12. This project on the 1963 March on Washington uses a carefully designed Website as its medium.

below, where each subpage is assigned a representative image. Color is used strategically in both instances (white font; yellow border) to help the viewers locate themselves in relation to the larger structure of the argument.

As you compose your own Website as a visual argument, be sure to consider **usability**—how user friendly your hypertext is and how accessible to users with disabilities. Even a site with professional design and a state-of-the-art graphic interface is ultimately ineffective if the audience cannot navigate it. You can test your Website for usability through the resources available on the *Envision* Website. Learning to write with attention to diverse readers will make you a more rhetorically savvy and effective communicator.

AT A GLANCE

Designing a Website

- Draft a header; consider including an image in it.
- Map a logical organization for your site to help readers find information easily and understand your purpose and argument.
- Include a navigation tool either below the title or at the left margin.
- Develop clear content using words and images.
- Be consistent in using color, imagery, and font; avoid jarring color combinations or visual clutter.
- Be strategic in your use and placement of images
- Link to subpages and external sites.
- Provide a feedback link for comments.
- Include a "last updated" feature note.
- Test your site for usability—both in terms of its general user friendliness and its accessibility to users with disabilities.
- Use user-friendly online tools (such as Wix, Wordpress, or PBWorks) to help design your site.

Making a Multimedia Montage

In this last section, we'll introduce you to writing projects such as visual collages, multimedia mixes using audio and video, hand-painted murals, self-produced films, startup magazines, and more. We'll call these texts **multimedia montages** because they involve the combination of numerous media (images, sound, writing, digital elements, and more) and because they often consist of nonlinear collections of evidence; the argument occurs in the project as a whole. Although the term *montage* is taken from film studies and refers to a sequence of still images, we'll extend it to refer to any combination of diverse media elements. The key to designing multimedia montages lies in understanding not

Student Writing
Read Yang Shi's reflection letter concerning his design decisions.
www.pearsonhighered.com/envision/266

only your audience, argument, medium, and form but also the purpose for the project.

Consider Yang Shi's decision to construct a visual collage based on his purpose. He began his project with the goal of creating a print photo essay on the subject of Mao Zedong's political impact on China, but he soon found that the photo essay's linear structure seemed to suggest a single definitive interpretation of Mao's influence. Since Yang was interested in exploring the complexity and contradictions inherent to the issue, he found the graphic possibilities of a visual collage preferable since this format allowed for a dialogue between simultaneous, competing images. By juxtaposing and intertwining numerous images from 1960s China, Yang Shi created a powerful, complex argument about the causalities of Mao's Cultural Revolution. Yang recognized that in a collage he could not only exploit the power of numerous images but also crop and arrange those images for rhetorical purpose. Accordingly, he created an overtly chaotic layout, one that he felt reflected the lack of focus of the Chinese Cultural Revolution (see Figure 8.13).

Despite the initial impression of randomness, however, there is an underlying order to Yang's collage: from the portrait of Mao heading the page, to the patriotic children surrounding him, to the statistics at the bottom, and finally to the outline of China as a faint red background at the poster's center in front of the protestors, all the visual elements structure the text's visual argument. In one sense, China encompasses all these representations—struggles and tragedies, ideals and victories. Yet the collage's inclusion of Mao's choice of political imagery—the propaganda drawings of happy workers—suggests that Mao undermined his own anti-West stance by "marketing" himself along the same lines as traditional Western advertising. In this way, Yang's strategic use of the collage form produces a powerful statement through a careful arrangement of images and color.

FIGURE 8.13. Yang Shi's photo collage about Mao Zedong and the Chinese Cultural Revolution.

Think carefully about your purpose, your argument, your audience's familiarity with the topic, the organization of your materials, and the media available to you as you design your own multimedia montage.

- KiYonna Carr paired a sequence of historical and contemporary photographs with her own voice-over narration to create a self-timed slideshow about the enduring legacy of slavery on African-American women's self-image.
- Derrick Jue used a short-film format for an argument about Iraq war protests, arranging a slide show of news photographs showing the war, protest demonstrations, and politicians speaking about the war and adding a soundtrack—the song "Wake Me Up" by Evanescence. The rapid succession of images paired with stirring music provokes an emotional reaction, without need for verbal commentary.
- Jessica Vun used a tactile collage—a handsewn fabric "manners" book—to give readers a "feel" for gender roles in the 1800s.
- Allison Smith stained her own drawings with tea to suggest age for a project on Margaret Sanger's battle for legalized birth control.
- Lauren Dunagan used a 14-foot hand-painted graffiti mural to make an argument about the power of graffiti as a medium for social protest and self-expression.
- Madeline Wright used Google Maps to create a final visual argument for her project on Intelligent Design versus evolution in Texas education, using the geographic interface to support her claim that intelligent design prospers in small towns and rural areas (see Figure 8.14).

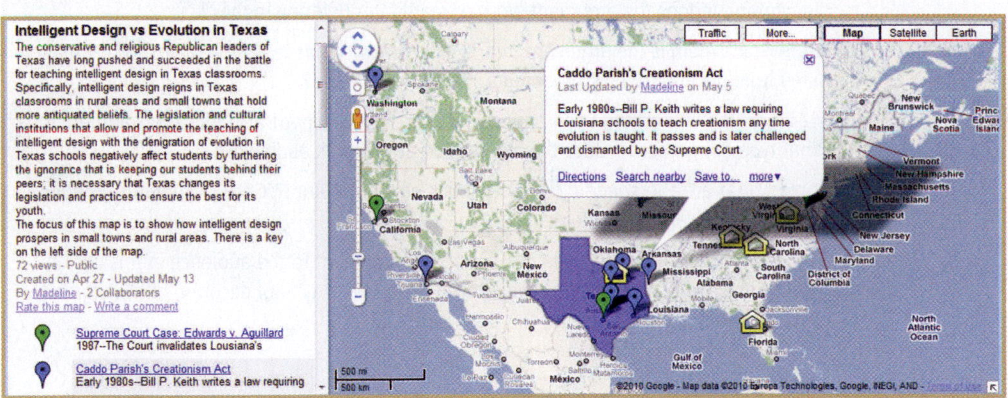

FIGURE 8.14. Madeline Wright used Google Maps to compose her visual argument for her research project.

In all of these cases, the student carefully considered how to use a non-traditional medium (a model, a stained historical document, a mural) to create a rhetorically effective argument. The range of persuasive possibilities presented here suggests the ways writing has changed over time—and how it continues to evolve with the advent of new writing and composing technologies. From Weblogs to interactive multimedia exhibits and collaborative hypertext projects, the way we understand language, argument, and persuasion continues to evolve. With the ever-changing face of modern media, you have an increasing number of choices for designing arguments with purpose, power, and creativity.

The Writer's Process

In this chapter, you've learned how writing offers an opportunity to experiment with designing and producing your texts in ways that meet your purpose and match the expectations of your audience. Often this means knowing, understanding, and adhering to conventions set forth by a community of scholars, readers, or writers. This is the case for the document design of your research paper, cover page, abstract, and bio. At other times, this means exploring innovative approaches to design in multimedia contexts. It is also the case for the document design of hybrid compositions and visual arguments. All modes of design depend on your rhetorical expertise in choosing a level of decorum, in knowing what strategies best work for your situation, in deciding on your medium and your format, and then in having these choices support your purpose in designing your work. By examining academic essays, op-ads, photo essays, Websites, and multimedia montages, you have seen that the rhetorical principles of audience, argument, form, and purpose carry across diverse media. It's time now for you to make your contribution. Write out your brainstorming ideas, and begin to design your own argument.

PREWRITING CHECKLIST

Focus on Analyzing Design in Arguments

- ❑ **Argument:** What is the topic and the argument? What evidence is used to support the argument? What is the rhetorical stance and point of view on the topic? What role does verbal, visual, or multimedia play in persuasion in this text? Are words and images complementary or does the argument work primarily through one means?
- ❑ **Audience:** Whom is the argument intended to reach? What response seems to be anticipated from the audience? sympathetic? hostile? concerned?
- ❑ **Medium:** Is the medium used appropriate for the argument and its target audience? What type of interaction does the medium create with its audience?
- ❑ **Form:** What are the specific characteristics of the medium? Consider layout, images, style, font. How are these elements organized?
- ❑ **Purpose:** What is the purpose in presenting the argument to the audience in this design? To move them to action? inform them? teach them? What type of decorum or style (grand, middle, or plain) is used to realize this purpose?

PREWRITING WITH THE *ENVISION* WEBSITE

Perform a rhetorical analysis of several Websites: first, using the link from the *Envision* Website, look at "Error 404," a parody Webpage created during the U.S. war with Iraq; then compare http://www.whitehouse.org, a parody site, with the official White House site. How does the parody site use rhetoric, organization, style, and decorum to produce an argument? Working collaboratively, draft a sample homepage that makes the same argument as the parody page but without using parody. What rhetorical choices did you make in designing your page?
www.pearsonhighered.com/envision/190

WRITING PROJECTS

1. **Design Elements to Accompany Your Final Revision:** Write an abstract and bio for your final research paper. Check that you have adhered to proper academic document design. Now compose a one-page op-ad featuring the argument from your research project. The op-ad should combine both images and written elements. Keep in mind those elements important to successful advertising, including consideration of audience and purpose; use of space, color, and image; strategies of development; and an appropriate hook. Indicate in a written note the intended audience (who would read it) and context (what magazine or newspaper they would read it in) for your ad. Post all your documents online as a showcase of your work as a writer and researcher.

2. **Visual Argument:** Create a photo essay based on the argument from your research paper or as part of an independent project. The images you use in your photo essay may be from your paper, or you can use a completely new set, particularly if you did not use images in your paper. Your argument may mirror that in your research paper, or you may focus on a smaller portion of your overall argument. The style, arrangement, medium, and rhetorical strategies of your photo essay should match your audience and your purpose. Include written text in your photo essay strategically. Once you have finished, write a one-page reflection on the strategies you used in this project.

3. **Multimedia Argument:** Transform your written essay into an electronic format that uses audio strategically as part of the text's persuasive power. You can match your images to a recorded argument. Alternatively, combine visual images with a soundtrack. Pick your music carefully, and time each image to match a particular mood or moment in the music or select music to match the sequence of your images. If you are transforming a paper essay into an electronic audio version, feel free to modify your organization, arrangement, text selection, and even treatment of images to accommodate this shift in medium. Once you have finished, write a one-page reflection on how the shift in medium affected your argument.

Visit www.pearsonhighered.com/envision for expanded assignment guidelines and student projects.
Visit www.mycomplab.com for additional general writing and research resources.

CHAPTER 9

Delivering Presentations

Chapter Preview Questions

- How can I transform a written argument into a presentation?
- What are the branches of oratory, and how do they shape my presentation options?
- When should I use a speech, a poster session, PowerPoint, or a live performance? What rhetorical choices shape my decision?
- How can the canons of memory and delivery help my presentation?

You've finished your written argument. You've submitted it to your instructor according to proper academic conventions and maybe you have even translated it into a hybrid composition or visual argument. But sometimes you are asked to do more: to present your argument to an audience in the form of a "live" presentation. Both academic and public audiences call for oral or multimedia presentations on occasion, and you need to develop skills and strategies for designing and delivering presentations to take advantage of these opportunities. In this chapter, we'll learn from famous writers and speakers, such as Barack Obama, whose keynote speech at the 2004 Democratic National Convention catapulted him to the forefront for the 2008 presidential race. Obama's rhetorical strategies in this speech laid out the basic themes of his campaign—"[T]here's not a liberal America and a conservative America; there's the United States of America. There's not a black America and white America and Latino America and Asian America; there's the United States of America"; "Do we participate in a politics of cynicism or a politics of hope?"—and offered a powerful argument for hope and unity. But his presentation did not derive solely from his written script. As the image in Figure 9.1 suggests, it was the convergence of well-crafted language, passionate delivery, and deliberate gesture that combined to produce a memorable moment in American history.

FIGURE 9.1. Barack Obama delivers his argument at the 2004 Democratic National Convention.

You might look to Obama and other orators as models for effective presentation strategies as you prepare to shape your writing for oral delivery. As you approach drafting your presentation, take time to explore the many possibilities available to you for this act of effective communication. You will need to base your decisions for picking certain presentation strategies on a solid rhetorical foundation, and to do so, you need to understand the *branches of oratory* as well as how to apply them to particular occasions. In this chapter, you'll learn effective strategies for selecting the appropriate branch of oratory for your rhetorical situation, for translating your written argument into a multimedia presentation, and for scripting and designing a memorable and effective delivery of your argument.

Understanding the Branches of Oratory

As you draft, design, and deliver a compelling presentation, classical rhetoric may provide ways of understanding the needs of your specific writing situation—your own purpose, audience, and persona. Today we turn to rhetoric to shape any verbal or visual argument, but rhetoric originally evolved as a technique in classical Greece for teaching people how to speak both eloquently and persuasively in public. Classical rhetoricians such as Aristotle divided oratory into three **branches** based on time, purpose, and content.

- **Judicial** or **forensic discourse** involves defending or accusing and deals with the past. Think of this as oratory about right and wrong. *You might employ judicial oratory to argue about a past action in debate team, or moot court or law school, using verbal arguments as well as charts, graphs, photos, and other visual evidence arranged and designed to persuade your audience.*
- **Deliberative** or **legislative discourse** concerns politics or policy and typically argues for or against specific actions that might take place in the future. Think of this as oratory about what is benefical or harmful. *You might employ deliberative oratory to exhort or dissuade an audience in promoting the launch of your own business, the development of a new software, or a plan for a fund-raising trip. Your presentation might include memos, a financial plan, and specifications concerning the worthiness of the enterprise; you might employ PowerPoint slides, charts, images, prototypes, models, and animation to support your argument.*

BRANCHES OF ORATORY: CONTEMPORARY EXAMPLES

Judicial or forensic discourse—involves accusing or defending	**Deliberative or legislative discourse**—designed to argue for or against specific actions	**Epideictic discourse**—involves praise or blame
Johnny Cochran's 1995 defense of O. J. Simpson represents a notable instance of forensic discourse when Cochran used powerful visual and verbal rhetoric to clear O. J. Simpson of murder charges.	In his documentary film *An Inconvenient Truth* (2006), Al Gore employs deliberative discourse to advise the audience of the necessary steps for reducing the future impact of global warming.	Eulogies, such as the speeches delivered at Senator Edward Kennedy's funeral in 2009, are a typical form of epideictic discourse in that they center on praising and celebrating people's lives.

Notice the way Cochran makes his point visually by slipping on gloves that had been used in the crime to underscore his point "If it doesn't fit, you must acquit."	*An Inconvenient Truth* features Gore giving a series of lectures, many of which are rendered more powerful by carefully chosen background images and striking photographs.	Although colleagues told funny stories about Ted Kennedy, their remarks were celebratory and their demeanors somber and respectful.

- **Epideictic** or **ceremonial discourse** generally deals with the present. Think of this as oratory about praising or blaming. *You might employ ceremonial oratory in a senior thesis, a company report, an advertising campaign, or even a political party statement designed to praise (or blame) a candidate.*

FIGURE 9.2. U2 leader Bono addresses world financial leaders at the annual symposium in Davos, Switzerland.

As you can tell, although the branches of oratory may be unfamiliar in theory, we see them in practice all the time, from your instructor's PowerPoint lecture defending the inclusion of "intelligent design" in high school science curricula (forensic) to a club member's report about the success of their community outreach program (epideictic). Since strategies differ from one rhetorical branch to another, you'll find it helpful to assess which branch best addresses the demands of your particular situation.

Audience, Purpose, and Persona

The branches of oratory are only one of the resources from classical rhetoric that writers draw on in crafting successful presentations. Concepts such as attention to *audience, purpose,* and *persona,* which we've discussed in relation to written texts, are key elements for oral rhetoric as well. For instance, consider how attention to purpose, audience, and persona determines the presentations shown in Figures 9.2 and 9.3. Notice rock star Bono's trademark sunglasses as he presents his views to world leaders at the Davos economic forum in Figure 9.2. Compare this to Steve Jobs and his very rehearsed presentation at MacWorld 2008, where he stands in his predictable black turtleneck and jeans, gesturing emphatically to underscore his point. In each case, the speaker has chosen presentation strategies—including words, expression, dress, props, and persona—to fit the audience and purpose of his rhetorical situation. Keep this in mind when you need to design a presentation, select words and visual material, and practice a form of delivery that is specific to the rhetorical situation. In each case, you can carefully construct your presentation to be a powerful visual and verbal argument.

FIGURE 9.3. Steve Jobs, Apple CEO, presents a new product at MacWorld 2008.

Consider the many kinds of presentations you encounter as part of your academic experience. Do you attend lectures on specific topics, with a single speaker standing at a podium and delivering a verbal argument? Have you been an audience member for a formal academic panel, where multiple speakers take turns presenting arguments, sometimes providing handouts to the audience or using a projection screen to convey their ideas? Or is your most frequent presentation experience the PowerPoint lecture, in which the speaker provides a point-by-point map of the material, includes images related to the subject matter, and sometimes posts a copy of the slides on a Website for future reading? Although these presentations might differ in

AT A GLANCE

Identifying Your Audience, Purpose, and Persona

1. **What format will my presentation take** (purely oral speech, multimedia slideshow, interactive drama, etc.)?
2. **Who is my audience?** What do they know or not know about this topic already? How receptive will they be to my material?
3. **What is my purpose?** What do I hope to accomplish? What is my ultimate goal with this presentation?
4. **What branch of oratory does my presentation represent?** Is it designed to defend or accuse? To argue a position or policy? To celebrate or condemn?
5. **What persona do I want to convey** to my audience (knowledgeable, friendly, impassioned, concerned, expert, peer, etc.)? How do I visualize myself as a presenter?
6. **What kind of tone do I want to use** in my presentation (fun, serious, informative, sarcastic, concerned, alarmed, practical, etc.)?
7. **What supporting materials do I plan to use** in my presentation (quotes from research, photographs in a PowerPoint slide or on a handout, film or commercial clips, graphs, charts, posters, etc.)?

Seeing Connections
Consider the different audiences, purposes and personae found in Michelle Obama's "Let's Move" speech (page 229), Al Gore's 2007 Nobel Peace Prize Lecture (page 276), and Michael Eisner's address before Congress (page 357).

format, they are similar in that all are designed to meet the needs of their particular audience and rhetorical situation.

In your own work, you may find yourself presenting to your class, to a larger academic audience as part of a conference panel, to college administrators or a university forum, or even to a public audience. In each case, you'll have many choices to make. You can start determining the possibilities for your own presentation by using focusing questions such as those found in the "At a Glance" box above, designed to help you identify your audience, purpose, and persona.

As the final point in the "At a Glance" box suggests, most presentations today include strategically chosen visual texts—what we used to call "visual aids"—that in fact perform a crucial rhetorical function: they collaborate with words to convey the speaker's argument. A photo of extensive crop damage can provide *evidence* in an environmental science lecture, and a chart can communicate economic trends to an audience quickly and effectively. Sometimes, moreover, visuals provide a stronger message than or even contradict the verbal component of the speech. A presenter might use a visual text ironically—for instance, showing a slide listing statistics that refute an opponent's argument or providing an emotional appeal while conveying information in a flat tone of voice. In these ways, visual texts communicate powerful arguments that you can use as part of your overall presentation.

Transforming Research into a Presentation

Whether you are a student preparing for an in-class presentation or a polished public-speaker, creating a compelling oral argument involves a process of planning, scripting, revision, and rehearsal. Figure 9.4 provides us a glimpse into this composition process; shown here are President Obama's handwritten edits of his September 9, 2009, speech

FIGURE 9.4. President Barack Obama's speeches are products of a careful process of drafting and revision, as is apparent in this picture of the President's annotated speech for a September 9, 2009, address to a joint session of Congress.

to Congress about health care reform. Through consultation with his speech writers, the President carefully crafted word choice, sentence structure, example, and organization to produce a compelling polemic on the need for nationalized health care.

Like the President in this example—who drew on a vast corpus of research, statistics, and examples in producing this speech—when composing your presentation, you will need to consider how to best transform your research into a form meant for oral delivery. This process can be quite challenging; you need to take into account scope, content, and style. If you have 15 written pages of argument, this would probably take 40 minutes or more to read out loud. But of course, you would certainly not choose to simply read your written paper; writing meant to be read silently differs from writing meant to be read out loud. Only in certain academic circles is there a preference for complex, written prose as a formal presentation style. In most cases, audiences desire clear, conversational speech that is easy to follow. To achieve this goal, you need to think about transforming your research argument from one kind of writing to another—from writing for readers to writing for listeners. You'll also need to cut down the sheer amount of material you can convey and think about ways to present it in an interesting, memorable way. You can accomplish all these goals through a process of *selection, organization,* and *translation.*

AT A GLANCE

Key Steps in Transforming Your Research Argument into a Presentation

- ***Scope:*** How do you convert 10, 15, or even 20 pages of argument into a 5-, 10- or 15-minute oral presentation?

  Answer: Selection

- ***Content:*** How do you reframe the content so that it makes sense to your audience?

  Answer: Organization

- ***Style:*** How do you change the written word to a spoken, visual, and digital medium?

  Answer: Translation

Selection

Always plan for a shorter presentation time than what you actually have allotted. Most of us speak for longer than we realize; so if you are planning material for a 10-minute presentation, aim for 8; a 15-minute presentation, aim for 12; a 5-minute presentation, aim for 3. One way to keep your time frame manageable is to select a subset of material to present. That is, if your written argument comprises three main areas, plan to cover only one in your presentation. Also, if you plan on speaking extemporaneously (or improvising), be sure that you build this into your schedule for your presentation. Finally, remember to be as selective with your visual evidence as you are with your overall information; if your research relies heavily on images, charts, or graphs, be sure to carefully consider which to include in your presentation. You might opt to use only the most powerful images, or you might decide to center your presentation on a single case study or example and therefore feature only those materials relevant to that narrower focus.

You should find the focusing questions in the "At a Glance" box to the right helpful for moving through the process of selection for your project. Question 1 will help you identify the crux of your presentation. This may be your thesis, but it may also *not* be your thesis. That is, in the course of writing your paper, you may have found that what really matters most is the need to raise awareness about an issue, the need to publicize potential solutions to a problem, or the need to advocate for a particular research agenda. Question 2 will help you narrow your project to a few points designed to convey your project's significance to the audience. Question 3 will help you confirm your purpose and begin to translate your main point into a medium that will persuade your audience: do you want to raise awareness, rally support, propose a change, offer new insights, or suggest avenues of future research? You need to select your materials with these goals in mind.

AT A GLANCE

Questions for Focusing Your Argument

1. What matters most about this project?
2. What two or three points can I make to convey my answer to the above question?
3. What do I want my audience to walk away thinking about when I am done?

Organization

As you move through the process of transforming your research into an oral presentation, you have an opportunity to **reorder** your written argument to meet the needs and expectations of a listening audience. You might, for instance, begin with your conclusion and then convey the narrative of your research. Or you might want to show your visual evidence first, ask questions, and then provide your thesis at the end. In other words, you don't need to create your presentation as a miniature version of your written talk. Be innovative in your choice of organization; think about what structure would be the most effective for your audience.

To help with this process, create a flowchart, outline, or block graphic of each element of your presentation. Don't forget your opening "hook" and closing message as you work on organizing your presentation. Try matching each component to a minute-by-minute schedule to make sure that you are within time limits. And finally, consider creating a **visual outline** by drawing or pasting in images next to your verbal cues to show how and when you will use visual rhetoric as a part of your presentation. Looking at a section of Tommy Tsai's presentation outline (see Figure 9.5) for his oral presentation on World War II propaganda, we can see that he carefully paired the words he intended to speak (on the right) with the slides he would show to his audience (on the left). In this way, he could clearly map

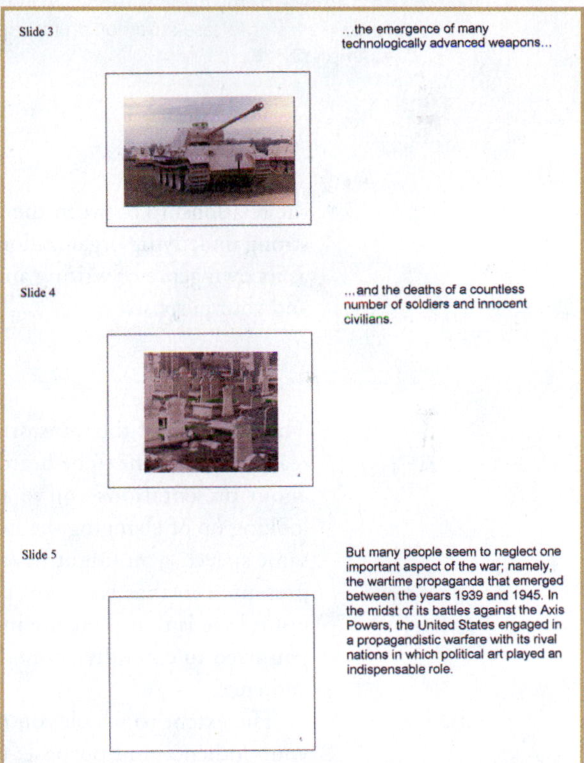

FIGURE 9.5. Tommy Tsai's presentation outline strategically juxtaposed the oral script with the visual evidence he would present in his slides. Note that he includes a blank slide.

Student Writing

See design and content plans for several student presentations.

www.pearsonhighered/envision/197

AT A GLANCE

Key Questions to Shape Your Organization

- **How can I "hook" my audience?** What would be an effective way to open my presentation? Should I appeal to emotion? to reason? Should I establish my authority as a researcher? What parts of my research would help me do so?
- **What strategies can I use to organize my presentation?** Narration? Example? Cause and effect? Problem-solution? Process? Definition? Which strategies would be most useful for conveying my argument clearly and effectively to my audience?
- **What main points do I want to use as the centerpiece** of my presentation? Do I want to focus on a single case study or on multiple examples?
- **At what point do I want to present my thesis?** Do I want to start with a question or line of inquiry and then end with my argument in my conclusion? Or do I want to start strong with my thesis within the first moments of my talk and then prove it with evidence?
- **How do I want to close my presentation?** Do I want to conclude by summing up my points or by pointing to the future or further implications? Do I want to end with a call to action or with a provocative question? What strategy would create the greatest impact on my audience?

the relationship between the visual and verbal elements of his presentation, creating a strong underlying organization for his argument. The key here is to see the presentation as its own genre of writing and draft a text that meets the needs of both your audience and your purpose.

Translation

The final step of the transformation is to translate your writing from text meant to be read to text meant to be heard. This is more important than it may first appear. Think about presentations you've attended where the speaker read from a script without looking up or changing the inflection of his or her voice. If you sat down and read that same speech, you might have found it interesting; however, listening to the material presented in that way, you probably found yourself bored, confused, or both. The point here is that there are important differences between these types of writing, and you need to carefully *translate* your research into a form accessible to your listening audience.

The extent to which you modify your writing as you draft your script depends on your audience and purpose; for instance, if you were trying to persuade your college administrators to endorse a new recycling policy (an example of deliberative discourse), you would adopt a different style and mode of speaking than if you were accusing that same administration of inattention to the recycling issue at a student council meeting (an example of forensic discourse). However, in general, there are some steps you can take to facilitate the translation process.

- **Examine the length of your sentences,** the complexity of your prose, and the sophistication of your diction. Most listeners find shorter sentences, specific language, and clear transitions and prose structures important for understanding oral discourse.

- **Avoid jargon** and define any terms with which your audience might not be familiar.
- **Add clear signposting**—verbal "signs" that indicate the steps of an argument or the structure of your presentation. More often than not, listeners need more explicit signposting than do readers of papers.

Listeners also respond to humor, direct address, concrete examples, and even questions. These strategies are designed to directly engage your audience's attention. As you write your script, annotate your written copy with places where you pause, emphasize words, look up, or laugh. Also include reminders of when to point to visuals or advance your slides.

AT A GLANCE

Signposting

Help listeners by including these terms to structure your argument:

- First
- Second
- Third
- On one hand
- On the other hand
- For example
- Consider
- But
- Yet
- In conclusion

Transformation in Action

Let's take a close look at how one student transformed her written research paper into a multimedia research presentation. As we saw in Chapter 4, Susan Zhang wrote a research proposal on the photo manipulation of media images. After finishing the written proposal, she was asked to present her proposal orally to her class. What follows is the written script for her presentation; as you read through it, you may want to reference her original proposal (see pages 87–90) in order to appreciate the way she transformed her written argument into an oral presentation.

Hi everyone, my name is Susan, and before I begin, a little bit about me.

[cue slide: "About Me"]

Last summer I vacationed with my family in Australia, and that was the beginning of my interest in photography, as you can see. **[cue animation: Mom & me]** And I had a really great time taking pictures of wildlife there, including this one of a duck. **[cue animation: duck]** Well actually that was all a lie. I've never been south of the equator, and that picture of my mom and me is grafted onto the background of Sidney harbor, and that duck is a digital rendering of the animal.

This prompts some unusual questions. If I can pass off a digitally altered photograph as real, why can't others, such as the news and the media for example? Can we trust the pictures that we see in the news?

[cue slide: title slide]

Note how Susan has references to her slides.

Her language is casual and low style. She even uses humor.

And that brings us to the topic of my proposal, which is titled "Little Photoshop of Horrors? Digital Manipulation of Media Images."

Her explicit signposting helps the audience follow her argument.

Let's start by looking at some examples.

[cue slide: OJ] This photo is from 1994 when O. J. Simpson was arrested. *Newsweek* kept his mugshot unaltered, while *Time* darkened the color of his skin. Minority groups protested that this made him look darker and more menacing and therefore presumed his guilt. The photographer claimed that he was only going for a more artful, more compelling image.

[cue slide: Martha Stewart] This is the *Newsweek* cover released last year when Martha Stewart was released from prison. The caption is "Martha's Last Laugh: After Prison, She's Thinner, Wealthier and Ready for Primetime." This may be true, but the slim body pictured is not in fact hers.

[cue slide: Walinski]

This photo was taken in 1994, which is when a British soldier was photographed pointing a gun at an Iraqi citizen. It is actually a composite *[cue animation: original photos]* of these two photos. The photographer later apologized and was fired.

[cue slide: "Introduction"]

She uses rhetorical questions and cuts down the length and complexity of her prose in order to convey her argument effectively to her audience.

What happened? Before digital imaging, people trusted photography to be an honest medium. A photographer and his camera were deemed the unbiased purveyor of reality. How has the capacity for photo manipulation affected the credibility of photos in media? Some hypotheses I have are: **[cue animation: point one]** has it led to a loss of credibility due to more powerful image-editing techniques, or **[cue animation: point two]** has it led to increased credibility due to the evolution of stricter standards?

[cue slide: "Perspectives"]

Some perspectives I plan to take are number one historical. **[cue animation: historical]** I intend to look at photo manipulation before digital imaging to look at whether people doctored photos then and whether the guidelines are stricter then versus now. **[cue animation: public]** Also, I plan to look at the public response to digital manipulation. For example, where is the line drawn? Sometimes when the doctoring is obvious, it could be interpreted as social satire or commentary; however, if it's subtle, people could perceive this as perception. Also, how easily can people recognize altered images? **[cue animation: photographer]** And for the photographer's point of view, what are some of the reasons for our digitally manipulated photographs. Could it be out of respect for the privacy of the subject, or for the sensibilities of the audience? Also, what are the guidelines and the various contexts in which they may apply?

[cue slide: "Methods"]

Some methods that I'll use for my research include books. **[cue animation: books]** I'll start with a kind of general approach to ethical photojournalism. Some books I have include *The Burden of Visual Truth: The Role of Photojournalism in Mediating Reality* and also some books on digital image ethics. I also plan at looking at **[cue animation: databases]** online databases to find some examples of digital image ethics and photo manipulation, some articles on recent controversies over altered photos, authoritative opinions by photojournalists and photographers, and some examples of how their public responded to the incidents.

The ample use of "I" works well in her presentation to convey a confident research persona.

[cue animation: Websites] And also I'll look at some other Websites such as news and media sites online and some smaller photojournalism sites to see how they address image authenticity and to see if they label their images as illustrations or as genuine photographs. And finally I'll look at online guidelines. The National Press Photography Association has a Website for a digital code of ethics, for example.

She invokes specific examples in her script to make her talk persuasive.

[cue slide: "Summary"]

In summary, we find digital imaging has made photo manipulation easier and perhaps more prevalent. For example, you could use aesthetic touch-ups, graft parts of pictures onto others, and even construct a picture entirely from scratch. As a result, there's a lot of public skepticism over the reliability of the images. So my proposal is to explore to what extent this skepticism is really justified.

Her strong and compelling conclusion provides an effective ending to her script.

Reading through Susan's proposal, we can see the effective ways in which she transformed her proposal for oral delivery.

Selection: Although she focused on a single pair of images in her original proposal, Susan used a series of current, recognizable examples of photo manipulation to persuade her audience in her presentation, including some photographs she "altered" herself. She also condensed her sources section and eliminated her timeline altogether, taking into account what information would most interest her listeners.

Organization: Susan's organization in the latter half of her presentation resembles that found in her proposal in moving through methods, to sources, to conclusion. However, her introduction is completely reworked, designed to better capture the attention of a listening—and viewing—audience.

Translation: Throughout, Susan simplified her language and moved to a more colloquial tone that matched the very colloquial introduction she used to hook her audience. Compare, for instance, the final line of her oral presentation with this one, which served as the final sentence for her proposal: "A closer look at the occurrences of digital manipulation today, as regulated by the evolving guidelines of photojournalism, could reveal to what extent such skepticism is warranted." In her presentation, the language is much more direct, clear, and succinct. It is tailored to a listening audience.

Considering Strategies of Design

As you can tell from Susan Zhang's presentation, careful translation can be the key to communicating your argument powerfully and persuasively. Her combination of personal example, a series of persuasive case studies, a strong voice, clear structure, and solid delivery all combined to create a compelling presentation. What other presentation models might you consider?

- Jessica Luo centered her talk about the media coverage of the Tiananmen Square uprising in 1989 on photographs from both Chinese and European presses. She created pairs to demonstrate the arguments made through photos by each media organization. Jessica wanted to move a mainly American student audience into caring about an incident that happened in China more than 20 years ago. Thus, she decided to transform her "objective" writer's voice into a personal narrative and used rhythmic, repetitive terms that explained the rhetorical significance of each image.
- For a project on land mines, Stewart Dorsey showed two PowerPoint presentations side by side on large projection screens. He stood between the two screens to suggest that his argument offered a feasible compromise between polarized camps.
- Max Echtemendy used a mixture of media and interactivity in his research presentation on fantasy violence. First, he set up a table showing horror novels, DVD boxes, articles in magazines, music videos, and many other examples of "fantasy violence all around us." Then he asked students to complete a brief questionnaire, and he worked with their answers as he discussed the key elements of his argument. He ended by showing a clip from *The Lord of the Rings* and asking for audience response.
- Tom Hurlbutt, exploring the implications of Internet surveillance, created a dynamic PowerPoint presentation that linked to Websites, asked students to log

on to Amazon, and revealed code that showed their search history from previous class sessions. In this way, he integrated graphic effects in a rhetorically purposeful way.

- Eric Jung, for a presentation on art and technology, transformed the classroom into a twenty-second-century museum, complete with "exhibits" of technologically produced art. He assumed the role of museum guide and gave the class a "tour" of the exhibit, concluding with a "retrospective" lecture about the early twenty-first-century debate over how digital media changed popular conceptions of art.

These innovative projects suggest the many effective ways to use strategies of selection, organization, and translation to design the most intriguing, powerful, and appropriate presentation for your purposes.

COLLABORATIVE CHALLENGE

Take 10 minutes to brainstorm the design possibilities for your presentation. Complete the following questions:

1. What format will your presentation take?
2. What materials do you plan to use in your presentation?
3. What might be a potential outline for your presentation?

Now peer review your responses with a partner. Have each person suggest changes, new ideas, and alternative ways of designing the presentation. You might also use this time to begin practicing the presentation. Finally, to get a sense of how your presentation will change according to your audience, consider how your answers would change depending on whether you presented to a class audience or a group of friends in the dorm, a review panel at a company, or a potential employer. Experiment to find the most effective ways to design your presentation.

Using Visuals Rhetorically

Presentations can vary greatly in their design and delivery. At times, you may be asked to deliver an exclusively *oral presentation*, in which you make your argument without the use of any visuals. We are most familiar with this form of public speaking: great civil rights leaders, peace activists, and political leaders rarely cue up a PowerPoint slide to make their points. Yet, even the shortest talks can be augmented by strategically chosen visual texts that enhance the persuasiveness of an argument. For your own assignments, you will probably be given the option of using visuals in your presentations, so it is important that you develop strategies for doing so effectively—that is, with rhetorical purpose.

Writing for Poster Sessions

Posters communicate arguments both verbally and visually. The presentation style is used most frequently in the sciences, where **poster sessions** are common at conferences and large conventions. Visitors walk through exhibit halls where hundreds of posters are on

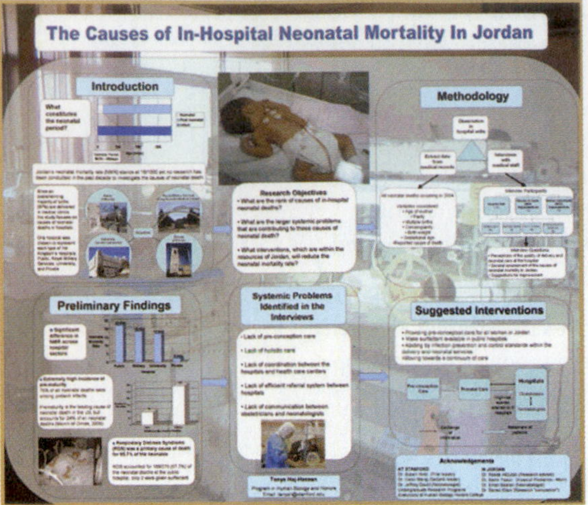

FIGURE 9.6. Tanja Haj-Hassan won awards for this poster, displayed at the 2005 Stanford Symposium for Undergraduate Research in Progress.

display, stopping to read those that interest them and often requesting copies of the complete research paper. If you plan on pursuing a science major, you might want to ask your instructor if a poster presentation is acceptable to report research findings.

To create posters, researchers select salient points from their work and organize the content into short summaries with complementary visuals. The goal of a poster presentation is to produce a visual-verbal display that conveys the research accurately, engagingly, and concisely. Figures 9.6 and 9.7 show examples of award-winning student posters from a Stanford University student research symposium. While clearly the authors of these posters designed them differently, both share certain features:

- Bold headings offering clear titles that are easy to read from a distance
- Clear, vertical hierarchies for information
- Concise written content paired with compelling images

Both posters are designed to engage the interest and understanding of their audience.

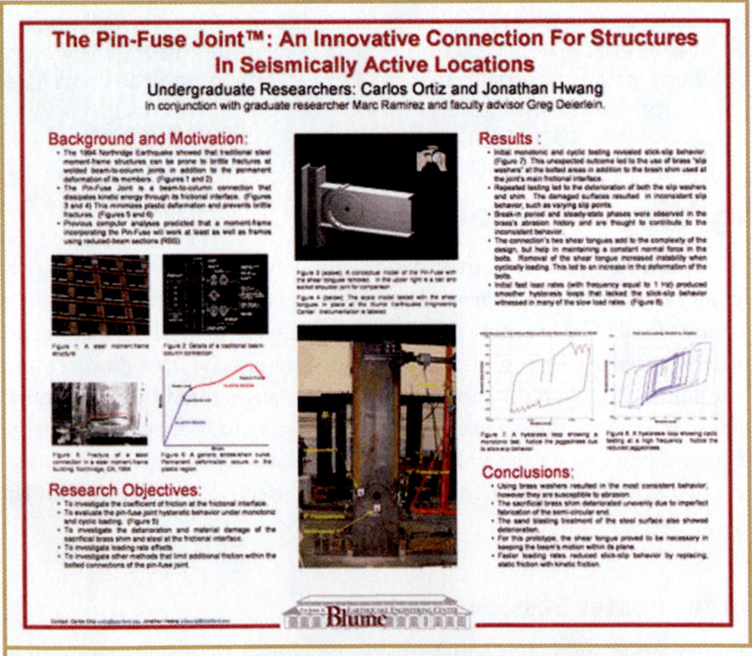

FIGURE 9.7. Co-researchers Carlos Ortiz and Jonathan Hwang transformed their research into this award-winning poster for the 2005 Stanford Symposium for Undergraduate Research in Progress.

AT A GLANCE

Guidelines for Creating Posters for a Poster Session

- Make sure your poster is readable from a distance; size your fonts accordingly.
- Put the poster's title, authors, and academic affiliation at the top.
- Avoid visual clutter; consider using white space to offset various elements, including tables, figures, and written texts.
- Arrange materials in columns, not rows.
- Avoid long passages of texts; rely primarily on visual persuasion.
- Always check with the conference organizers for their specific guidelines.

For more detailed advice, go to the *Envision* Website.

www.pearsonhighered/envision/205

Writing for Multimedia Presentations

In today's increasingly high-tech environment, multimedia presentations have become very popular in both academic and professional contexts. There are a range of options available to today's presenter; PowerPoint, Keynote, or Prezi slideshows; film or audio clips; screencasts; projection of digital images; even live Web browsing. Many factors will influence your choice of multimedia support, including your access to technology, the capabilities of the room in which you are presenting, the requirements of your presentation assignment, and your own technological expertise. However, any time you consider incorporating multimedia into a presentation, be sure to keep in mind the following: these multimedia components are *secondary* to your argument. Start by planning what to say, and then choose the rhetorical tools that will help you craft the most powerful presentation.

Working with Slideshows

For many presenters, the default tool for presentations is PowerPoint. In fact, commonly we overhear students saying, "I have to give a PowerPoint" rather than "I have to give a presentation." The first step in constructing a successful slideshow—whether using PowerPoint, Keynote, Prezi, or other presentation software—is to remember that you need to prioritize your argument, not fonts, templates, design, and graphics.

Seeing Connections
Consider how Michael Eisner integrates multimedia into his Address to Congress about intellectual property (page 357).

This is a rule clearly observed by dynamic presenters, from Steve Jobs to Lawrence Lessig, who successfully integrate slides into their presentations. Increasingly, they have moved away from text-heavy slides filled with bullet lists of information, to a more visually dynamic, minimalist style that balances text with image and that serves as visual evidence (some might even say visual punctuation) to their oral argument.

If you are composing a slide-based presentation, think strategically about how to use those slides to your best advantage. Will you use them to analyze primary sources (images, film clips, information graphics)? To structure your argument, outlining claims and subclaims? To reinforce key terms or concepts? To showcase definitions or key quotations? To feature an in-depth case study or example? To move your audience emotionally through *pathos* or appeal to their intellect through compelling data? Keep in mind, too, that it's not just what slides you create that matters; it's how you use them.

Student Writing

See Morgan Springer's complete presentation as well as examples of other multimedia slideshows.
www.pearsonhighered.com/envision/206

Morgan Springer, for instance, felt that using a map in his slideshow would strengthen his argument on self-determination in Kosovo and East Timor. Having selected one, he customized it to his argument by coloring in red those countries experiencing political wars and military dictatorships. As a final touch, after presenting that slide to the audience, he used the slide animation to circle the two countries that he was going to focus on in his own particular project (Figure 9.8).

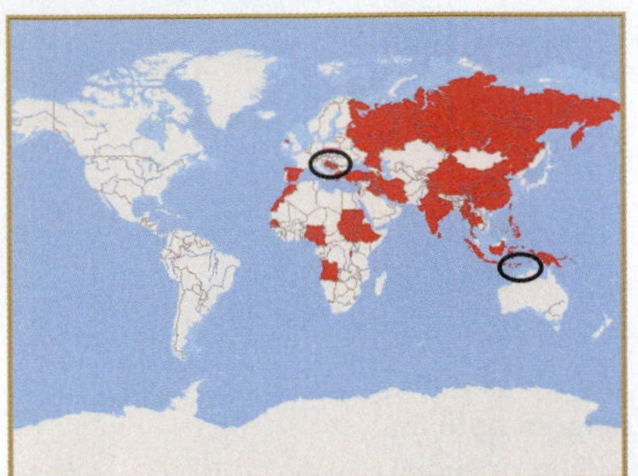

FIGURE 9.8. One of Morgan Springer's map slides from his PowerPoint presentation on self-determination in Kosovo and East Timor.

Similarly, Natalie Farrell had her audience in mind while working with her materials for a project on Yucca Mountain. She wanted the class to guess at the power of a projected nuclear disaster on Yucca Mountain before shocking them with the actual numbers, so she created slides with blanks left in the list of statistics (Figure 9.9). After a moment of audience participation where she invited them to verbally fill in the blanks, she then moved to a slide that revealed the true statistics (Figure 9.10).

For his project, Frank Li decided to embed a screenshot of Yahoo's Fire Eagle press release in his slideshow. However, previewing it, he realized that although the image created a significant visual impact, it was too text-heavy for the audience to read. To solve this problem, he used his slide software to highlight a key quote from the text (Figure 9.11), so his audience would have the benefit of both the primary source and the quotation.

Conversely, Alex Bleyleben's use of slides is notable for his understanding of when *not* to use them. In his presentation about global activism, Alex projected a series of images of the slaughter of the endangered black rhino. To capitalize on the momentum of this *pathos* appeal, Alex dramatically turned the screen after quickly showing a series of gruesome pictures so as to shift the audience's attention back to his own presence at the podium as he delivered the key points of his argument.

These examples suggest many purposeful, rhetorical ways of writing for slide-based presentations that move beyond just using the slides to visually record your

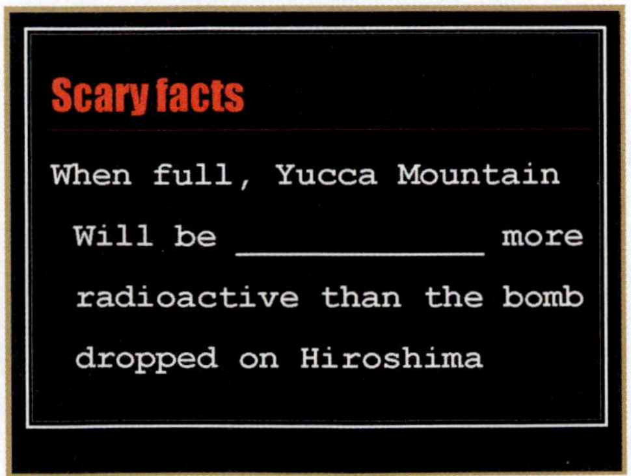

Scary facts
When full, Yucca Mountain
Will be ____________ more
radioactive than the bomb
dropped on Hiroshima

FIGURE 9.9. Natalie Farrell's presentation titled "Yucca Mountain and Nuclear Waste: Gambling with the Future of the Human Race," slide 5.

Scary facts
When full, Yucca Mountain
Will be _1,400,000_ more
radioactive than the bomb
dropped on Hiroshima

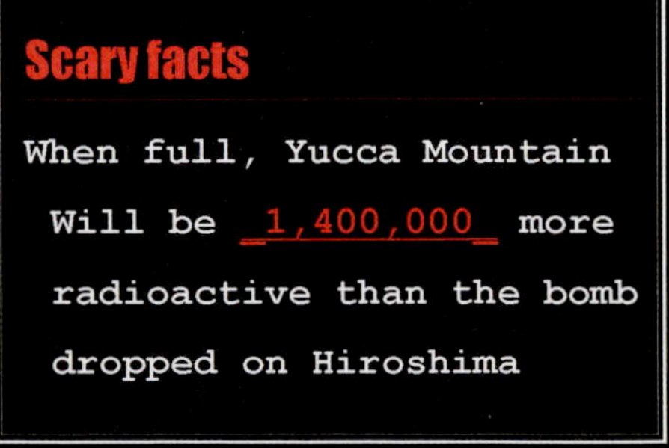

FIGURE 9.10. Slide 6, in which Natalie dramatically fills in the blank.

notes. Rather, they succeed in what cultural critic Stephen Shugart deems is the necessity of "transforming the concept of PowerPoint from 'presenting at' into 'a way of promoting discussion' or to use it in unconventional ways to create more effective learning situations."

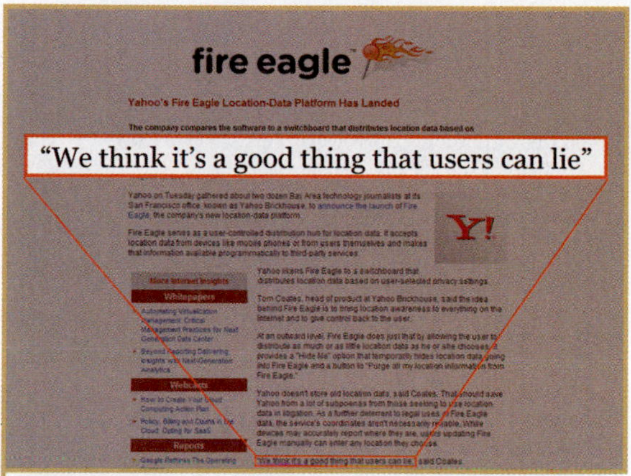

FIGURE 9.11. Frank Li pulls out a key quote from his primary source on his slide.

Beyond the Slideshow

As with all arguments, in deciding how to compose your presentation, you should begin with your purpose and your audience and then design your text to meet your needs. In some cases, that will mean shutting off your slideware and looking into alternate ways to leverage the power of multimedia in your argument. Let's look at some of the innovative ways in which some students used multimedia to support their oral argument:

In her presentation "Redefining the Essay," Caroline Chen embedded audio clips from her interview with rhetoric scholar Andrea Lunsford into her slideshow, reinforcing the key points from their discussion by transcribing select phrases onto the slides for the audience to read as they listened to the audio.

Max Oswald, for his presentation on the effects of technology on modern life, adopted a very unconventional approach. He composed the first eight minutes of his talk as a YouTube-style video, complete with spliced scenes and dramatic camera angles, to make his point about the distancing effect of technology (Figure 9.12). Then, as shown in Figure 9.13, for the final three minutes of his presentation, he turned off the

AT A GLANCE

Writing an Effective Slide-Based Presentation

- Use purposeful visuals, not clip art.
- Plan to spend time discussing the images you use as visual evidence.
- When using a film or audio clip, be selective in how much to show so it doesn't overwhelm your presentation.
- Don't put too much text on each slide or rely too heavily on bullet lists.
- Use slide animation to stagger the amount of information you share with your audience.
- Keep fonts consistent in style, size, and color to avoid distracting the audience.
- Break complicated ideas into multiple slides.
- Consider using clear, interesting headers to help visually structure your argument.
- Tie your slides together with a visual theme, motif, or template that, if possible, reflects the tone or content of your topic.
- Include sound effects and animation rhetorically rather than for flair or flash.
- Give a handout with full quotations or complicated information graphics as necessary.

Find more detailed advice on the *Envision* Website.
www.pearsonhighered/envision/207

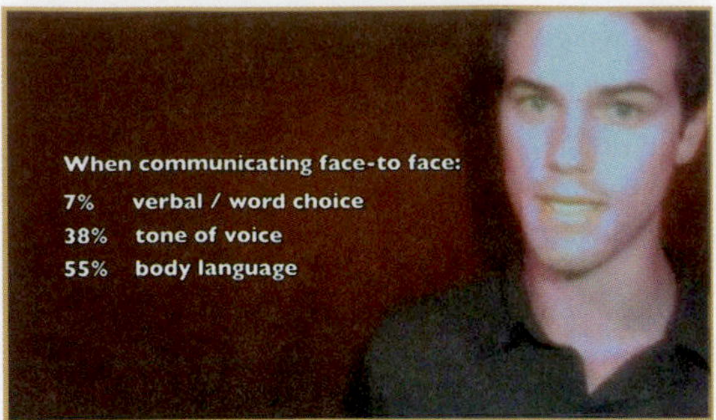

FIGURE 9.12. Max Oswald created a YouTube-type video as the core of his presentation about the distancing effects of modern technology.

FIGURE 9.13. At the end of his presentation, Max underscored his argument by stopping the video and delivering his conclusion live.

video and delivered his conclusion in person, dramatically underscoring his argument about the difference between technologically-mediated and live encounters.

During a presentation on the political applications of Twitter, Luisa Russell took her audience to Venezuelan President Hugo Chávez's Twitter page, pointing out his growing number of followers, then performing a rhetorical analysis of the content of his feed. At the end of the presentation, she then refreshed her screen, pointing to the updated number of followers as a way of emphasizing for her audience the currency of her topic and Twitter's ever-increasing significance as a political platform.

Rather than browsing the internet live during her presentation, Rose Emerson used screen capture software to record a segment of gameplay from *Modern Warfare 2.* She then played the footage in the background as she delivered her argument about hypermasculinization and hypermilitizarization in video games, pausing the recording at pre-designated moments so she could approach the screen and point out key elements to support her argument. She timed her presentation carefully so that she moved toward her conclusion during a particularly brutal moment of the gameplay that culminated in her character's death, delivering her final lines as the screen capture froze on the final image of battle's bloody aftermath.

AT A GLANCE

Delivery with Multimedia

- Practice your timing; experiment with the way you introduce and analyze the media that you present.
- Make eye contact; look at your audience, not the screen.
- If you are using slides, try not to read off them; prepare a separate script to create a dialogue with your audience.
- Always practice a multimedia presentation at least once before giving it live, especially if you are using slides with animations, or film or audio clips.

Choosing Methods of Delivery

As you can tell, the way you present your visual materials is just as crucial as drafting content for that presentation. In other words, after *selection, arrangement,* and *design* of materials, you need to think about ways of *delivering* the presentation. But why is delivery so important? Won't the content carry the persuasiveness of the presentation? If the writing is good, won't the delivery be good? Indeed, the writing must be skillful; the selection, organization, and translation of your argument into an appropriate, audience-centered design are crucial for your success. But you also need to attend to *how* you communicate your argument to your audience. In other words, you need to involve those last two canons of rhetoric, *memory* and *delivery.* In brief:

- **Memory** entails both memorizing one's argument to communicate it to the audience and evoking memorable phrases.
- **Delivery** concerns strategies of presenting your argument to an audience.

We know that memory was crucial for rhetoricians before the invention of the printing press. Speakers would memorize phrases, stories, and histories to pass down from

AT A GLANCE

Some Fundamental Elements of Delivery

- ***Stance or posture:*** also called embodied rhetoric
- ***Gesture:*** use of hands to communicate information
- ***Voice:*** pitch, tone, loudness, softness, and enunciation
- ***Pacing:*** of words, visuals, and argument
- ***Rhetorical appeals:*** use of *logos, pathos, ethos*
- ***Visuals:*** slides, posters, graphics, handouts
- ***Embodied visuals:*** not only stance but dress, appearance, mannerisms
- ***Style:*** elements such as repetition, allusion, metaphor, stories, personal narrative, jokes, and pauses

generation to generation. Significantly, this process occurred through a form of visual organization called an **architectural mnemonic technique**, a method in which you associate a phrase to a room or a part of a house so that as you look around during your presentation you receive visual clues to trigger your memory.

As you think about strategies of presentation, you might want to try memorizing key parts of your speech through this technique by creating a visual map of your script. Also, attend to the way your audience will remember your words, and choose your examples, your diction, and your pacing accordingly. In this way, memory leads naturally into delivery, the last canon of rhetoric.

When asked which three of the five canons of rhetoric he considered most significant, the Greek orator Demosthenes replied, "delivery, delivery, delivery." In other words, so crucial is this fifth canon that it can supersede the rest. One core aspect of the canon of delivery is the *sound* of the presentation: how speakers use tone of voice, pacing, strategic pauses, or changes in volume or inflection to make their arguments memorable and effective.

"[The rhetorician Cicero described mnemonic technique as] a set of visual images like the rooms of a house, which can be associated with the items in a long speech"

—William Covino and David Joliffe (67).

Delivery, as one of the five canons of rhetoric, deals primarily with the effectiveness of a speech's presentation. Oral communication, combined with variations in the presenter's voice and body movements, comprises the delivery of speech. The speaker's ability to manipulate auditory and visual techniques enables him/her to effectively convey his/her argument to the audience.

—Kelly Ingleman

Seeing Connections

To review the other canons of rhetoric (invention, style, and arrangement), see Chapter 3.

Embodied Rhetoric

If you think of some of the most prominent speakers of recent history—Barack Obama, Ronald Reagan, former Congresswoman Barbara Jordan—you probably can hear in your head the rhetorically powerful ways they used the sound of language itself. You can likewise prepare yourself for effective oral delivery by annotating your script to indicate places where you will pause, emphasize a key word, or use the strength of your voice to underscore a point. Written cues like this can help you to deliver a memorable, moving, and convincing oral argument.

However, it is not just the *sound* of delivery that affects the persuasiveness of an oral presentation but the *look* of that presentation as well. How many times have you seen a talk in which the speaker dressed up to make a point or used the rhetoric of his or her body to persuade the audience? This form of presentation is a genre we call **embodied rhetoric**, a presentation in which the body becomes a visual means of communicating the message. In most presentations, you employ the power of embodied rhetoric through the clothes you wear, how you stand, the voice you

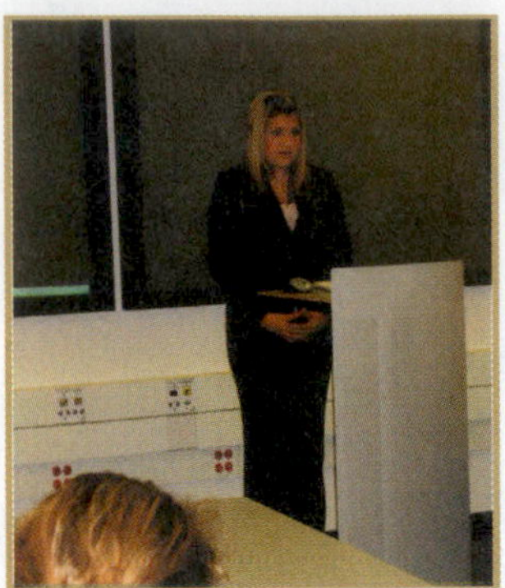

FIGURE 9.14. During her presentation on sexual assault on campus, Liz Kreiner opted against using multimedia, relying instead on her voice and embodied rhetoric to convey the seriousness of her subject.

choose, and even how you hold the materials you use to convey your argument. When Liz Kreiner delivered her presentation on sexual assault on campus, for instance, she made very strategic decisions about her embodied rhetoric: to emphasize the seriousness of her subject, she dressed conservatively and stood absolutely still at the podium as she recounted the disturbing stories of date rape that she had uncovered during her research. Her somber demeanor, reinforced by her serious tone of voice, produced an extremely powerful rhetorical moment (see Figure 9.14).

In most cases, we see embodied rhetoric at work through gesture. Often, when we think about the term *gesture* in relation to public speaking, we think of very overt or intentional hand motions that public speakers make for emphasis, like that made by Jake Palinsky in Figure 9.15, in which he directs the audience's attention by gesturing to the diagram he is describing. Our eyes follow his finger to focus on the part of the diagram he is explaining at that moment.

The gesture is a careful rhetorical move: it has purpose and works effectively as a strategy of communication. Sometimes gestures in public speaking seem less carefully composed, such as the one in Figure 9.16. Here we see the speaker in midsentence, her hands opened as if in an involuntary accompaniment to her words. But notice how the open palm, extended toward members of the audience, invites them to listen; it is tilted down to allow words to travel and open the space between the speaker and the audience. This subtle instance of embodied rhetoric invites the listeners into the argument and demonstrates a moment of explanation and connection.

Although we all use gestures without realizing that we do, we can in fact train ourselves to use the rhetoric of the body more carefully, and even strategically, as an integral part of our overall presentation design. Your purpose in using gestures as part of a presentation should be to harness the power of the body effectively to communicate ideas. Therefore, as you draft and deliver your presentation, remember that your *entire* body—from body language to clothes, posture, expression, and gestures—participates in communicating your ideas and information.

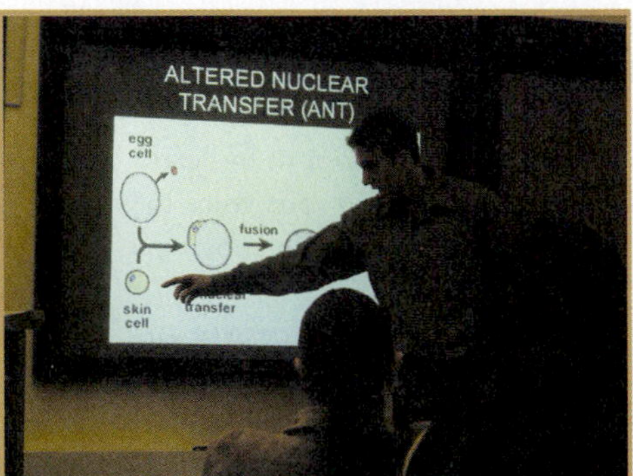

FIGURE 9.15. In his presentation on recent developments in stem cell research, Jake Palinsky used gesture deliberately to help his audience understand a scientific diagram.

FIGURE 9.16. In a moment of explanation, Alina Lanesberg uses a subtle gesture to emphasize her point and draw her audience into her argument.

CREATIVE PRACTICE

Analyze the gestures used by one of the most famous public speakers, Martin Luther King Jr. (see Figure 9.17 and Figure 9.18). Write a brief analysis of the suggested meaning and purpose of each gesture, describing each of the images as you make your argument. Then select the words you might match to the gesture. This exercise will help you explore strategies to use in your own presentations.

FIGURE 9.17. Martin Luther King Jr. gesturing at a press conference.

FIGURE 9.18. Martin Luther King Jr. emphasizes his point at a mass rally in Philadelphia, August 4, 1965.

Winston Churchill could never have stirred the British public as he did were it not for the grave, serious, and controlled tone of voice that he employed in his radio speeches. His faith in the allied powers rang out in stentorian cadences that by their very vibrations instilled belief in the masses. His message was often cliché, but his delivery was never anything but spell-binding. Had he had a feeble voice, perhaps Germany would have fared better.

—Dr. Gideon Burton

Practicing Your Presentation

Speakers like Martin Luther King Jr. dedicate much of their time to practicing their delivery. Similarly, two ideologically opposed political figures, Adolf Hitler and Winston Churchill, relied extensively on practice to develop their delivery.

- Hitler incessantly recorded himself speaking and using hand gestures, then would watch the films over and over again, selecting the motions that he felt were most powerful. Next, he would practice that form of delivery—the tone of voice, the pacing, the bodily stance, and the hand gestures—until he felt it was perfect. Finally, he would destroy the recordings so that no one would know how carefully he practiced. The practice made his delivery seem natural and his power seem real.
- Churchill used voice alone to persuade the British public to withstand the waves of Nazi attacks night after night in the bombing of Britain. Over the radio wires, his practiced and powerful words—delivered with the perfect amount of confidence and encouragement—helped the British persevere during those dark days.

These examples reveal the power of practice in strengthening delivery and its capacity to persuade audiences. Likewise, you should incorporate repeated practice into the process of drafting and revising your presentations. As with any assignment, your argument will benefit from peer review, so consider performing a "dress rehearsal" for a friend or roommate to get his or her feedback on the clarity of your ideas, your use of multimedia or visual aids, and the effectiveness of your delivery. Better yet, become your own peer reviewer by filming your "dress rehearsal" and then critiquing your performance.

Sometimes, by becoming a member of the audience yourself, you can see how to revise your presentation into a truly powerful oral argument.

Anticipating Problems and the Question-and-Answer Session

As you practice your presentation, don't forget to consider problems that might arise, such as faulty technology, a bored or confused audience, or even hecklers. To troubleshoot technology, visit your room and test out your equipment in advance. Make sure you have backup for the technology: save your work on a CD or flash drive, or email it to yourself. But remember, even if your practice session goes smoothly, bring handouts in case your PowerPoint slides don't work, and be prepared to talk without technology if necessary. Also, be ready to cut down or extend the length of your talk by indicating on your script places you might pause or points you might discuss in more detail. Realize that the more comfortable you are with your material, the more you can adapt on the spot to the needs of your audience.

Successful adaptation includes handling the question-and-answer session well; this part of a presentation, usually located at the end, serves as the final opportunity to clarify your argument and convince your audience. A successful presenter anticipates and, in some cases, even sets up the framework for the question-and-answer session. For instance, during his presentation on Marilyn Manson, Ben Rosenbrough realized he didn't have time to develop the link he saw between Elvis Presley and Manson in his formal presentation and so he made only a passing reference to the connection, hoping that the audience would be intrigued and ask about it after his talk. When they did, he advanced his PowerPoint beyond his conclusion slide to one documenting these connections in a powerful way. His surprise preparation for the question-and-answer session made his presentation design exceptionally successful. Similarly, you can anticipate what questions your audience might have by delivering your presentation to a peer group member, seeing what questions your presentation generates and even practicing trial responses. Consider having some new evidence, a stunning visual, or even a handout prepared to answer a question that you hope might be asked after your presentation.

Documenting Your Presentation

Design. Delivery. Practice. What is left? After all your hard work on your presentation, you probably want to leave some kind of trace, a written artifact, or a form of textual memory of the presentation. **Documentation**—*some form of written or visual evidence of your presentation's argument*—is the answer. Documentation serves an important rhetorical function: to inform and persuade. This might take the form of a **handout** that provides additional information in the form of an annotated bibliography, a summary of your key points and thesis, visual rhetoric from your presentation, references for further reading, or a printout of your PowerPoint presentation. You should put your contact information on it so the audience can ask you further questions.

Documentation might also consist of a **text** or **script** for your presentation. This can either be the annotated printout of your PowerPoint presentation, a full speech, or a typed set of notes in outline form with placeholders for your slides or media aids such as shown in Tommy Tsai's visual outline (see Figure 9.5). More innovatively, you might document your presentation with a **creative take-away** that reflects a key

Student Writing

See Courtney Smith's handout, designed to accompany her presentation on Palestinian female suicide bombers, as well as other presentation take-aways.
www.pearsonhighered.com/envision/212

aspect of your presentation. Consider Wendy Hagenmaier's handout for her project on media coverage of the bombing of Hiroshima and Nagasaki (see Figure 9.19). The cover of the *New York Times* from August 1945 is attached to a small candle; Wendy's caption reads, "Light this candle in remembrance of how the August 1945 atomic bombings of Hiroshima and Nagasaki have been remembered by Japanese and American photojournalists. The 'flashes' of its flame will serve to remind you that photojournalistic coverage is often an attempt to shape collective national memory and that remembrance is subjective." Another student, Falco Pichler, presenting his research finding on Nike marketing strategies, created a "backstage pass" to what he called the "Nike Show" and invited students to read his paper online. Aaron Johnson, presenting his research on media representation of athletes who take performance-enhancing drugs, made a mock subscription card with the title "Sports Exaggerated" as creative documentation for his presentation (see Figure 9.20). Using Photoshop, he embedded a cover of *Sports Illustrated* into the subscription card and listed the main points of his argument as "advertising points" for his presentation. Notice his complete contact information at the bottom of the card.

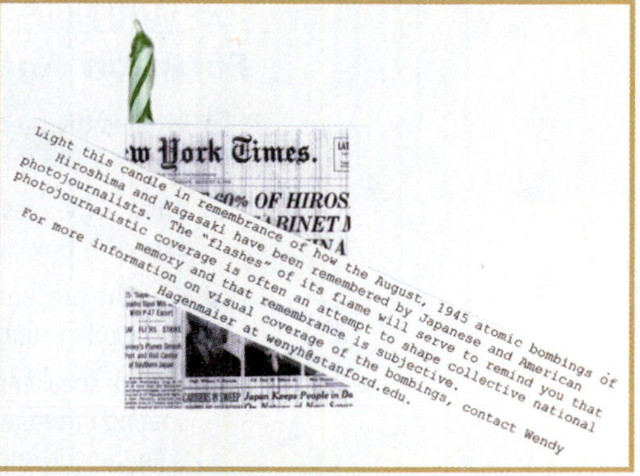

FIGURE 9.19. Wendy Hagenmaier's creative handout on the 1945 atomic bombings of Hiroshima and Nagasaki.

FIGURE 9.20. Aaron Johnson's creative presentation takeaway for his research project on *Sports Illustrated.*

These examples begin to show the range of creative documentation strategies you might pursue as the final part of your presentation. Taking the lead from Aaron, you might even craft an interactive visual take-away such as a graphic montage, a minibook, or other forms of visual argument. The importance of such texts—whether conventional prose handouts or compelling visual creations—lies in their power to make your presentation memorable, convincing, and engaging. So consider your strategies for documentation as carefully as you design your entire presentation.

The Writer's Process

In this chapter, you have explored possibilities for presentations; learned how to convert a written argument into a spoken, visual, multimedia presentation or performance; and worked through the different ways of writing for oral, poster, and PowerPoint presentations. Recall the strategies of design, arrangement, and delivery you have learned, and keep in mind the importance of both gesture and embodied rhetoric as ways of communicating your message and your purpose to your particular audience. Finally, as you begin to craft your own presentation, remember the old adage, "practice makes perfect." Peer review and revision are as important to your presentation as collaboration on drafts and revision are to your written work. They enable you to anticipate problems and harness your creativity as you shape your ideas into a memorable, moving, and persuasive form of rhetorical communication.

PREWRITING CHECKLIST

Focus on Analyzing Presentations

- ❑ What is the presenter's purpose? To inform? persuade? instruct? motivate? initiate discussion? Did the presentation successfully accomplish that purpose?
- ❑ What is the presenter's relationship to the topic he or she discussed? Is the presenter an expert? a novice? fairly well informed?
- ❑ Was the presentation appropriate for the audience? Consider language, organization, and explanation of technical or specialized concepts.
- ❑ Did the speaker present him- or herself as an authority instructing the audience? as a peer sharing information? Did the presenter make eye contact (indicating a direct relationship with the audience) or simply read from a prepared text (indicating a focus on the material rather than the audience)? How did this affect the structure and style of the presentation?
- ❑ How was the presentation structured? Was an outline or summary provided for the audience to follow? Was this done orally, on the board, in a handout, or on a slide? Was the development of the argument clear? Did it follow the designated structure?
- ❑ Did the presenter take into account the audience's reaction? For instance, did he or she notice some confusion in the audience and pause to explain a difficult point?
- ❑ How did the presentation begin? Did the presenter use any effective oral or visual devices to "hook" the audience? Was there a clear conclusion?
- ❑ Were the main points clearly developed? How was the scope of the presentation? Was there too much information? too little?
- ❑ Did the presenter use word choices appropriate to the occasion, audience, and subject matter? Were the sentence structures too complex (as if to be read silently) or more colloquial (as if to be read aloud)? Did the presenter project his or her voice enough? Did he or she speak slowly and clearly or rush through the material?
- ❑ Did the presenter use any formal devices—figurative language, deliberate repetition, literary allusions?
- ❑ Consider the presenter's embodied rhetoric. Did he or she stand or sit? remain stationary, or move around? Did the presenter use gestures, facial expression, or even costume to add to the rhetorical effect of the argument?
- ❑ How did the presenter use visuals? Did he or she show slides, bring in posters, write on a blackboard, distribute handouts, engage in role-playing, pass around books, or bring in material evidence for the presentation? Were the visual components rhetorically purposeful or did they seem an afterthought?
- ❑ If the presenter used posters, were they clear and accessible to the audience? Did they stand alone as arguments, or was their meaning only clear in conjunction with the oral presentation? Were the words large enough to read from a distance? Did the poster avoid visual clutter? Did it contain a clear title and use information graphics effectively?
- ❑ If the presenter used a slide program such as PowerPoint, was the visual design of the slides effective? Did the slides have a unity of theme, color, and layout? Did the presenter avoid visual clutter on the slides? How much text was on each slide? Were placeholders used for emphasis or pacing? Were there innovations in the slideshow, such as using dual screens, animation, or embedded clips or Internet links? Were these effective or distracting? Did the presenter speak to the computer screen rather than the audience? Did the presenter's body block the screen, obscuring the slides?

- ❑ If the presenter used the blackboard or whiteboard, did he or she write clearly and legibly? Were the notations on the board purposeful? Did the presenter block the board, making it difficult to read?
- ❑ If the presenter used technology, were there any technical difficulties? Did the presenter overcome them smoothly (for instance, having a backup plan), or have a difficult time recovering from the glitch, perhaps because of relying more heavily on technology than on the force of argument?
- ❑ Did the presenter finish within the allotted time? How did he or she handle the question-and-answer session?

PREWRITING WITH THE *ENVISION* WEBSITE

Compare the very different styles of two speeches, both given by women, both concerning human rights, but presented to very different audiences and by very different personas: Eleanor Roosevelt's speech entitled "Adoption of the Declaration of Human Rights," delivered December 9, 1948, in Paris, France; and a speech by Cher (played by Alicia Silverstone) from the movie *Clueless* (1995) on "Whether all oppressed people should be allowed refuge in America" (both linked through the *Envision* Website). Look at the written versions of their speeches as you listen to them talk. What characteristics of the spoken word does each piece of writing share? How are they different?
www.pearsonhighered.com/envision/215

WRITING PROJECTS

1. **Field Research on Presentation:** As part of the necessary preparation for writing your own presentation, conduct field research in the form of observing three public speeches, presentations, or oral/multimedia arguments. If possible, take a camera with you and document your observations of each kind of presentation. Type up a brief rhetorical analysis on the delivery, rhetorical strategies, and effectiveness of each one. Then indicate what strategies you plan to use in your own presentation. These presentations can include lectures in any of your classes, speakers visiting campus or your dorms, or the practice presentation of a member of your class.

2. **Formal Presentation:** Create and deliver a timed presentation of your research argument for your class (ask your instructor for the precise time limit). You should include the appropriate media (visual rhetoric, PowerPoint slides, Websites, movie clips, performative or interactive aspects). In addition, the oral delivery of your presentation might include a handout that you distribute to the class to provide information—for example, an annotated bibliography, a summary of your key points and thesis, visual rhetoric from your presentation, references for further reading, or a printout of your PowerPoint presentation—formatted in the proper manner (or in a creative way if that works for your presentation) with your complete contact information on it. Also compose a script for your presentation. This can either be the annotated printout of your PowerPoint presentation, a full speech, or notes in outline form (with placeholders for your slides or multimedia). Include references in the text or script of your presentation to any materials you use (handouts and printouts of multimedia).

3. **Collaborative Presentation:** Work in groups of two to four to design and deliver a presentation to the class. You might want to divide the tasks of selecting material, brainstorming strategies of presentation, and designing your visual materials. Will you take turns speaking throughout the

presentation, or will each person be responsible for a distinct segment of the presentation? Will one person write the script, another person deliver it—perhaps from memory—while a third creates the slides? Choose the strategy that best suits your audience and your purpose. Don't forget to practice together, and when your group is presenting, look at the others who are speaking to keep the class's attention focused on your group presentation.

4. **Community Writing Presentation:** Either in groups or individually, design your presentation for a specific community audience. What happens if you present your research project on performance art to a group of politicians, to school administrators, to the theater department? Think about how your message can reach a broader audience in this way. What if your project is on the educational poster campaign to prevent the spread of AIDS? After you design one presentation for your writing class, rewrite it to meet the audience expectations of a not-for-profit organization, an international amnesty meeting, or an urban center continuing education class.

Visit www.pearsonhighered.com/envision for expanded assignment guidelines and student projects.
Visit www.mycomplab.com for additional general writing and research resources.

Part IV

Photography takes an instant out of time, altering life by holding it still.
—Dorothea Lange

CHAPTER 10

Fueling Ourselves

In 2008, National Geographic Channel aired one of its most ambitious films to date tackling the issue of consumption—that is, how much the average American consumes in his or her lifetime. Entitled *The Human Footprint*, this documentary provided a dramatic visual portrait of American consumerism, as the crew laid out representative quantities of bread, milk, diapers, soda cans, and other common products around the periphery of an iconic American home. The documentary is filled with images such as the ones in Figure 10.1, where 4,376 loaves of bread and 12,129 hamburger buns are symbolically arranged to indicate how much bread an individual consumes over the course of his or her life, and in Figure 10.2, where 28,333 rubber ducks are used to represent the amount of water than an average American will use during that same time. By quantifying consumption in such strikingly visual terms, the film makes a strong statement about the amount of resources it takes to feed and clothe people throughout their lives.

FIGURE 10.1. By arranging the loaves of bread in the shape of an American flag, the producers make a strong statement about how much bread the average American will consume in his or her lifetime.

FIGURE 10.2. *The Human Footprint* uses rubber duckies here to represent the amount of water used by an individual during his or her life.

This question of quantifying, calculating, and confronting our human footprint—our impact on our world—is one that preoccupies many people these days. Every day the news media carries stark forecasts about the implications of climate change, global warming, water and food shortages, the threat of species extinctions, and the depletion of our fossil fuels. Never before have we been so aware of the impact of our individual lives on our environment. Not surprisingly, we've seen the corresponding rise of a new movement of ethical consumerism, namely a push to implement a practice of buying goods and services that were produced with minimal harm to humans, animals, or the environment. Consider for instance, the sign shown in Figure 10.3, displayed in a campus cafeteria. Using bold primary colors and a campy, retro design, this placard operates on the basis of a very simplistic logic: there is a causal relationship between what we eat and what happens to our planet. Asking, "Is my cheeseburger causing global warming?", the sign appeals to the audience on an individual level, implying that even the smallest consumption patterns have large-scale implications. From purchasing carbon offsets for our air travel, to buying produce from local farmers markets, or choosing to carry a reusable water bottle rather than buy disposable plastic, how we fuel ourselves (our cars, our homes, and even our bodies) has become an opportunity for eco-activism.

FIGURE 10.3. This display from a campus cafeteria draws a direct correlation between what we eat and its impact on the environment.

Source: © Christine L. Alfano, 2010

In this chapter, we will explore some of the issues embedded in the decisions we make as consumers. In "You Are What You Eat," we will examine food culture, from trends in food blogging to debates over locavorism versus organic eating, to the use of genetically modified foods to curb world hunger. Then in "Greening Culture," we'll examine the cultural implications of the eco-friendly movement. We'll read articles that wrestle with the different faces of "Going Green," from superficial trendiness, to meaningful activism, to corporate green-washing. We'll dive deeper into the debate surrounding climate change and examine the relationship between environmental rhetoric and scientific data. Finally, we'll conclude this section with a consideration of the future of sustainable energies as we look for alternate, greener ways to fuel ourselves in the decades ahead.

YOU ARE WHAT YOU EAT

We take as the title for this section the phrase "You Are What You Eat" because never before has this simple idiom held such complex meanings. The dinner table has long been a site of negotiation between children and parents, but the conflicts have moved from whether to eat your vegetables and finish what's on your plate to a much larger arena. Food studies as a field has become a battleground between epicureans and nutritionists, ranchers and activists, and local growers and big business. Thinking about food and its impact on the individual, the environment, and the future has become a new obsession.

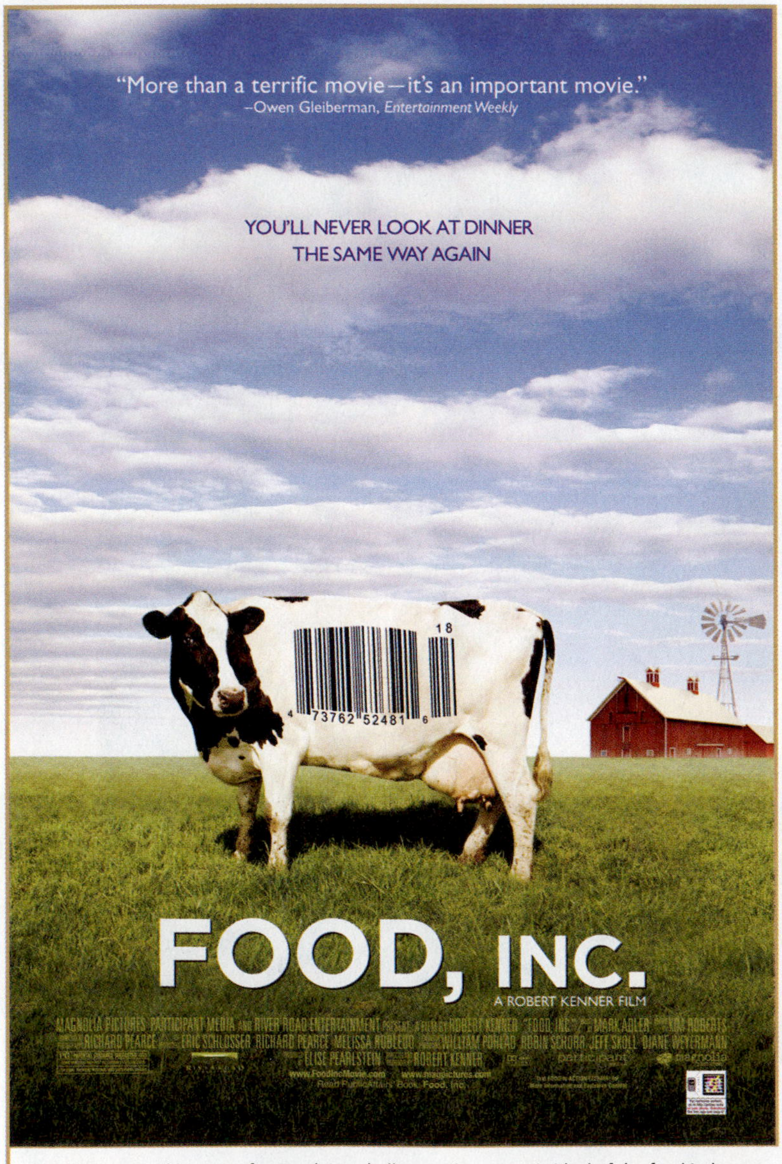

Let's consider the ways that our discussions about food have moved out of the kitchen. Walk into Borders or Barnes and Noble bookstores and you'll find not only glossy-covered gourmet magazines and fully illustrated cookbooks but you'll probably also encounter a display adorned with copies of Maria Rodale's *Organic Manifesto*, Bryant Terry's *Vegan Soul Kitchen*, Peter Singer's *The Ethics of What We Eat*, and numerous copies of Michael Pollan's best-selling *The Omnivore's Dilemma, In Defense of Food*, and *Food Rules*. Feel like watching a film? You can select from a variety of movies that celebrate food, relationships, and community: from *Chocolat*, to *Eat Drink Man Woman, Babette's Feast, The Big Night*, and even *Willy Wonka and the Chocolate Factory*. Perhaps you simply decide to surf the Internet. You're likely to come across a recipe site aggregating family recipes; a food blogger photo-documenting his every meal; or a food activist providing commentary on the latest incursion against processed foods and fast food chains. Turning on the TV will have similar results; shows like *Cake Boss, Ultimate Cake-off, Top Chef*, and *Hell's Kitchen* grow every week in

FIGURE 10.4. This poster for *Food, Inc.* challenges the romantic ideal of the food industry.

popularity, and the Food Network has carved out its own niche on cable TV. Even a stroll down the street will bring food culture in sharp focus, from the rampant spread of Jamba Juices, Starbucks, and McDonald's into the empty nooks and crannies of our consumer spaces to the rise of specialty markets like Trader Joe's and Whole Foods. Food provides more than just sustenance; it increasingly has come to shape and mediate our understanding of ourselves and our culture.

Perhaps because of the omnipresence of food culture, we are also witnessing a growing critique of it. To see this, we need look no further than our local movie theater and the release of several films over the past ten years that have challenged us to reevaluate the role of food in our lives. *Fast Food Nation* and *Supersize Me* began the trend in the mid-2000s by targeting the fast food industry and its deleterious effects on American health. However, more recently, the 2009 film *Food, Inc.* shifted focus from individual eating habits to corporate farming and industrialized agriculture. The theatrical release poster, shown in Figure 10.4, succinctly epitomizes this critique. What we notice first in the poster is the stereotypical scene of bucolic America: a cow, standing in a green field, blue sky and the trademark red barn in the background. However, there is one noticeable addition to the scene that disrupts this idealistic vision: the large barcode branded broadly across the cow's side. This film's goal, the poster argues, is to expose the truth behind our romantic ideal of food culture, to expose the inner workings of this big business industry, and to problematize our understanding of our relationship to our food.

In the readings that follow, you'll be introduced to the range of commentary on food culture today, from the food bloggers who memorialize each meal with a highly pixilated photo and pithy commentary to scholars and activists who draw a link between American food obsession and the rise of obesity and Type 2 diabetes among American children. We'll look carefully at the USDA food pyramids, then dive into the debate about high fructose corn syrup, looking at both sides of the argument. We'll enter into the organic versus local debate, considering how even among healthy eating advocates there is disagreement about the best practices for a healthy lifestyle and agricultural sustainability. Finally, we'll delve into the controversy surrounding genetically engineered crops, looking at their viability as a solution to world hunger. As you read through these selections, we invite you to contemplate your own eating habits and ask yourself: How are food and culture linked? How does what we eat, how we eat, where we eat, and who we eat with shape our ideas of ourselves and our community?

Reflect & Write

- ❑ Notice the subtitle to *Food, Inc.* at the top of Figure 10.4. How does it complement and complicate the argument of the poster's central image and main title?
- ❑ Considering that this film exposes some of the more controversial practices in the food industry, why do you think the poster designers chose this image rather than one that would have more shock value?
- ❑ **Write.** Write a rhetorical analysis of this image that uses a strong thesis statement and specific references to the visual composition of the poster to argue about the significance of this image in relation to the film's title or argument.

Kate Murphy *In this article,* New York Times *journalist Kate Murphy describes the culture of "food blogging," the growing practice of keeping an online food diary, complete with photos. This article originally appeared in the* New York Times *on April 7, 2010.*

First Camera, Then Fork

By Kate Murphy

JAVIER GARCIA, a 28-year-old neuroscientist at the University of California, Irvine, was in the campus pub recently having a grilled cheese sandwich. But before he took a bite, he snapped a digital picture of it, cheese artistically oozing between toasted white bread, just as he has photographed everything he has eaten in the last five years.

Every other week he posts the photos on his Web site, ejavi.com/javiDiet, providing a strangely intimate and unedited view of his life and attracting fans from as far away as Ecuador. The nearly 9,000 photos leave nothing out, not even snacks as small as a single square of shredded wheat.

When he lost his iPhone while visiting New York last month, he pleaded with exasperated friends to take pictures of his food and to e-mail them to him, lest his record be incomplete. "It was a nightmare," Mr. Garcia said, particularly because the unfocused pictures "were not the quality I'm used to."

In 1825, the French philosopher and gourmand Jean Anthelme Brillat-Savarin wrote, "Tell me what you eat, and I will tell you what you are." Today, people are showing the world what they eat by photographing every meal, revealing themselves perhaps more vividly than they might by merely reciting the names of appetizers and entrees.

Keeping a photographic food diary is a growing phenomenon with everything from truffle-stuffed suckling pig to humble bowls of Cheerios being captured and offered for public consumption. Indeed, the number of pictures tagged "food" on the photo-sharing Web site Flickr has increased tenfold to more than six million in the last two years, according to Tara Kirchner, the company's marketing director. One of the largest and most active Flickr groups, called "I Ate This," includes more than 300,000 photos that have been contributed by more than 19,000 members. There would be more, but members are limited to 50 photos a month. The same phenomena can be found on other sites like Twitter, Facebook, MySpace, Foodspotting, Shutterfly, Chowhound and FoodCandy.

Nora Sherman, 28, the deputy director of the City University of New York's Building Performance Lab, which promotes sustainable construction, finds that the pictures she takes of her food are her most popular posts on Facebook, Twitter and on her blog, Thought for Food, (noraleah.com). The immediate and enthusiastic commentary on, say, an arugula and feta salad or a plate of fried okra have given her a sense of connection and community since moving to Manhattan from New Orleans in 2006.

"People I have never met follow my blog and know me through the food I eat," Ms. Sherman said. She was even introduced to her boyfriend through someone she came to know through his comments on the food pictures on her blog, and who thought the two might be a match.

She said she takes pictures of at least half the meals she eats, omitting, for example, multicourse meals when it might "interrupt the flow." But she has noticed lately that it's becoming harder to suppress the urge to shoot. "I get this 'must take picture' feeling before I eat, and what's worse is that I hate bad pictures so I have to capture it in just the right light and at just the right angle," Ms. Sherman said.

She uses a Canon PowerShot S90 and uploads pictures to her Web site daily, sometimes several times a day, which takes at most 30 minutes a day. The camera, she said, is small but works well in low light. She doesn't style her photos, saying, "I like to take shots that no pro would ever take—holding an oyster in my hand about to slurp it down, or a bagel with a bite out of it."

10 Her impulse to photograph her food and do so artistically has made her a more adventurous eater. "It's driven me to seek out interesting, photogenic foods," she said. She is now more likely to eat foods she would have once avoided, like beef tendon, heart and tripe at an Asian shopping mall in Flushing, Queens. And, she said, photographing the food has kept her honest when she has started diets: "When I decided to have salad for dinner during a juice fast, I snapped and posted that."

Photos are also a means of self-motivation for Mr. Garcia, who began photographing his food after he lost 80 pounds. "It's definitely part of my neuroticism about trying to keep thin," he said. "It keeps you accountable because you don't want to have to see that you ate an entire jar of peanut butter."

And, ever the scientist, he hopes to one day use the photographs to calculate how much money he spends to consume a calorie versus how much he spends in gym memberships and sports gear to burn a calorie. "People I have dated haven't been that into it," he said of his food photo-journaling. "But it's never been a deal breaker."

Pamela Hollinger, 36, an independent radio programmer and announcer in Stephenville, Tex., said her husband of eight years is resigned to her taking pictures of her food. "When we were dating, it was like, 'What are you doing?'" she said. "Now it's a quirk he's come to accept."

Her habit began in 1997 as a way to show her mother what she ate on vacations, but she now photographs almost everything she eats, leaving out only insignificant snacks and anything unappealing looking, like a bowl of oatmeal. "I think getting an iPhone had a lot to do with it," Ms. Hollinger said. "It's so easy to just take a quick picture of what I'm eating and no one really notices." Or maybe they think she is just texting at the table.

15 She e-mails the pictures directly from her phone to a few friends and posts some of them on her Facebook page as well as on Chowhound. "I like to show off what I'm eating or something I've made that I'm proud of, like a pork rib-eye roast that became pulled pork sandwiches and then pork tacos and then pork salad," she said. "I get more comments on my food pictures than anything else. Within seconds, I get, 'Oh, I'm jealous,' or 'Hey, can I come over?' "

That some people are keeping photographic food diaries and posting them online does not surprise psychotherapists. "In the unconscious mind, food equals love because food is our deepest and earliest connection with our caretaker," said Kathryn Zerbe, a psychiatrist who specializes in eating disorders and food fixations at Oregon Health and Science University in Portland. "So it makes sense that people would want to capture, collect, catalog, brag about and show off their food."

Photographing meals becomes pathological, however, if it interferes with careers or relationships or there's anxiety associated with not doing it. "I'd have to ask if they would feel O.K. if they didn't do it," said Tracy Foose, a psychiatrist at the University of California, San Francisco, who treats patients with obsessive-compulsive disorders. "Could they resist the urge to do it?"

Joe Catterson, the general manager of Alinea restaurant in Chicago, said that, increasingly, people can't. "One guy arrived with the wrong lens or something on his camera and left his wife sitting at the table for an hour while he went home to get it," he said.

Such compulsion is apparent even at restaurants where the plating is less elaborate. "They've got to take a picture of their pancakes and send it to their friend," said John Vasilopoulos, the manager at the Cup & Saucer, a diner on the Lower East Side. "I don't get it because their food gets cold, but I take it as a compliment."

20 Evidently aware of the trend, manufacturers like Nikon, Olympus, Sony and Fuji have within the last two years released cameras with special "food" or "cuisine" modes, costing around $200 to $600. "These functions enable close-up shots with enhanced sharpness and saturation so the food colors and textures really

pop," said Terry Sullivan, associate editor of digital imaging technologies at Consumer Reports.

This bemuses Tucker Shaw, the food critic for The Denver Post, who made do with a basic point-and-shoot digital camera to take pictures of everything he ate in 2004; he published the photos in his book, "Everything I Ate: A Year in the Life of My Mouth."

"It used to turn heads if you took a picture of your food, and I even got in trouble at a few restaurants," he said. "Now it's ubiquitous and just shows that we are in a spastic food era—we couldn't get more obsessive."

Nonetheless, Mr. Shaw said the year he spent photographing his food (and a year was enough for him) resulted in an achingly honest account of his life that revealed far more than the fact that he ate too few leafy green vegetables: "The pictures, I realize now, are incredibly personal, and by looking at them you can probably deduce the type of person I am." Moreover, the pictures set off memories and emotions in a way a written journal could not. "I remember every single day, who I was with, what I was feeling," he said.

Unlike a picture of a flower or friend, a picture of a meal recalls something smelled, touched, tasted and ultimately ingested. Carl Rosenberg, 52, a Web site developer who divides his time among San Francisco; Austin, Tex.; and Addis Ababa, Ethiopia, photographs his food along the way with a Nikon D3.

25 "You have more of a direct connection with your food, so it forms a more essential memory of an occasion," he said. He often places a small stuffed animal, a sheep, which he calls the Crazy Sheep, next to his food before taking a picture; reminiscent of the globe-trotting garden gnome in the French film "Amélie."

"I think photographing food is a more accurate way to document life," said Mr. Rosenberg, who shares photos with family and friends but does not post them. "Food isn't going to put on a special face when you take a picture of it."

Reflect & Write

- ❑ How does Murphy hook her readers into the article?
- ❑ Visit the original article online through the link on the *Envision* Website and look at the use of visual evidence. What do the images contribute to Murphy's argument? How does it change your experience as a reader? www.pearsonhighered.com/envision/224
- ❑ According to the article, what effect does food photography have on the photographer? In terms of community? In terms of eating habits?
- ❑ Why does Murphy include the opinion of psychiatrists? How does their opinion change your understanding of the practice of food blogging? How would the article have been different if she had omitted that section?
- ❑ **Write.** Murphy quotes one of her sources, Carl Rosenberg, as saying, "I think photographing food is a more accurate way to document life . . . Food isn't going to put on a special face when you take a picture of it." Do you agree that photographs of food document life more accurately than other types of photographs? Why would that be the case? Write a personal essay that draws a connection between your food practices (how you snack; your food addictions or favorite foods; childhood memories associated with food; your grocery shopping habits; when or where you eat) and a larger commentary about who you are and your overall approach to life.

■ *Circulated through social networks like Flickr and Facebook, photographs such as these not only document food, but also are composed in deliberate ways to make a specific argument about that food.*

Food Photographs

FIGURE 10.5. Laura Thal first shared her image of "happy-go-latte" on Facebook.

FIGURE 10.6. Sanctu originally posted this photograph of Mee Siam soup in Singapore through the Flickr group "I Ate This."

FIGURE 10.7. This photograph of a homemade beef mince burger was originally shared on Flickr by member Su-Lin with the caption: ". . . So delicious!"

Reflect & Write

- ❑ Consider the title of Laura Thal's photograph in Figure 10.5: "happy-go-latte". How does the composition of the photo work together with the title? What argument about culture is the photograph making?
- ❑ Look at the perspective of Sanctu's photograph. What impression does the layout, the framing, and the angle make on the audience? What is the photo's argument?
- ❑ What argument is Su-Lin making about her hamburger? How do the caption and the image work together to make that argument? What is it about the photograph that makes that argument persuasive?
- ❑ **Write.** Visit the "I Ate This" pool on Flickr through the links on the *Envision* Website. Select three images that work in dialogue to make a specific argument about food or food consumption: draft a thesis statement that presents your interpretation. Now, working with the canon of Arrangement, order the images strategically in a slideshow to make that claim. Show the slideshow to your classmates and ask them to identify your argument. At the end of your discussion, share your thesis statement with them and discuss to what extent the audience's experiences of the argument were the same as your authorial purpose.
www.pearsonhighered.com/envision/225

Jeffrey Kluger *Jeffrey Kluger is a senior writer at* Time *magazine, who specializes in science writing. He has written broadly and notably on issues such as the Columbia shuttle disaster, the Mars Pathfinder landing, and global warming. He is the author of several books, including* Splendid Solution: Jonas Salk and the Conquest of Polio, Simplexity, *and* Lost Moon: The Perilous Voyage of Apollo 13. *In this article, which was originally published in the June 12, 2008, issue of* Time, *he tackles the issue of childhood obesity, considering it principally as an American phenomenon.*

How America's Children Packed On the Pounds

By Jeffrey Kluger

Americans disagree about a lot of things, but we rarely quarrel when it comes to our food. For a nation built on grand democratic virtues, there is still nothing that defines us quite like our love of chow time.

We have plenty of reasons to fetishize our food—not the least being that we've always had so much of it. Settlers fleeing the privations of the Old World landed in the new one and found themselves on a fat, juicy center cut of continent, big enough to baste its coasts in two different oceans. The prairies ran so dark with buffalo, you could practically net them like cod; the waters swam so thick with cod, you could bag them like slow-moving buffalo. The soil was the kind of rich stuff in which you could bury a brick and grow a house, and the pioneers grew plenty—fruits and vegetables and grains and gourds and legumes and tubers, in a variety and abundance they'd never seen before.

With all that, was it any wonder that when we had a chance to establish our first national holiday, it was Thanksgiving—a feast that doesn't merely accompany a celebration but in effect is the celebration? Is it any wonder that what might be our most evocative patriotic song is *America the Beautiful*, in which an ideal like brotherhood doesn't even get mentioned until the second-to-last line, well after rhapsodic references to waves of grain and fruited plains? "We've defined an American version of what it means to succeed," says neuroscientist Randy Seeley, associate director of the Obesity Research Center at the University of Cincinnati Medical School. "And a big part of that is access to an environment in which there is a lot of food to be consumed."

The problem is, all those calories come at a price. Humans, like most animals, are hardwired not just to eat but to gorge, since living in the wild means never knowing when the next famine is going to strike. Best to load up on calories when you can—even if that famine never comes. "We're not only programmed to eat a lot," says Sharman Apt Russell, author of *Hunger: An Unnatural History*, "but to prefer foods that are high in calories." What's more, the better we got at producing food, the easier it became. If you're a settler, you eat a lot of buffalo in part because you need a lot of buffalo—at least after burning so many calories hunting and killing it. But what happens when eating requires no sweat equity at all, when the grocery store is always nearby and always full?

5 What happens is, you get fat, and that's precisely what we've done. In 1900 the average weight of a college-age male in the U.S. was 133 lb. (60 kg); the average woman was 122 lb. (55 kg). By 2000, men had plumped up to 166 lb. (75 kg) and women to 144 lb. (65 kg). And while the small increase in average height for men (women have remained the same) accounts for a bit of that, our eating habits are clearly responsible for most. Over the past 20 years in particular, we've stuffed ourselves like pâté geese. In 1985 there were only eight states in which more than 10% of the adult population was obese—though the data collection then was admittedly spottier than it is now. By 2006, there were no states left in which the obesity rates were that low, and in 23 states, the number exceeded 25%. Even those figures don't tell the whole story, since they include only full-blown obesity. Overall, about two-thirds of all Americans weigh more than they should.

"Sit down on a bench in a park with a person on either side of you," says Penelope Slade-Royall, director of the U.S. Office of Disease Prevention and Health Promotion. "If you're not overweight, statistically speaking, both of the other people sitting with you are."

If there was any firewall against the fattening of American adults, it was American kids. The quick metabolism and prodigious growth spurts of childhood make it a challenge just to keep up with all the calories you need, never mind exceed them. But even the most active kids could not hold out forever against the storm of food coming at them every day. In 1971 only 4% of 6-to-11-year-old kids were obese; by 2004, the figure had leaped to 18.8%. In the same period, the number rose from 6.1% to 17.4% in the 12-to-19-year-old group, and from 5% to 13.9% among kids ages just 2 to 5. And as with adults, that's just obesity. Include all overweight kids, and a whopping 32% of all American children now carry more pounds than they should. "There's no way to overestimate how scary numbers like this are," says Seeley.

Obese boys and girls are already starting to develop the illnesses of excess associated with people in their 40s and beyond: heart disease, liver disease, diabetes, gallstones, joint breakdown and even brain damage as fluid accumulation inside the skull leads to headaches, vision problems and possibly lower IQs. A staggering 90% of overweight kids already have at least one avoidable risk factor for heart disease, such as high cholesterol or hypertension. Type 2 diabetes is now being diagnosed in teens as young as 15. Health experts warn that the current generation of children may be the first in American history to have a shorter life expectancy than their parents'. "The more overweight you are, the worse all of these things will be for you," says acting U.S. Surgeon General Steven Galson. And, warns Seeley, the worse they are likely to stay: "When you're talking about morbidly obese kids, zero percent will grow up to be normal-weight adults."

It's hardly a secret how American children have come to this sickly pass. In the era of the 64-oz. soda, the 1,200-calorie burger and the 700-calorie Frappuccino, food companies now produce enough each day for every American to consume a belt-popping 3,800 calories per day, never mind that even an adult needs only 2,350 to survive. Not only are adults and kids alike consuming far more calories than they can possibly use, but they're also doing less and less with them. The transformation of American homes into high-def, Web-enabled, TiVo-equipped entertainment centers means that children who come home after a largely sedentary day at a school desk spend an average of three more sedentary hours in front of some kind of screen. Schools have contributed, with shrinking budgets causing more and more of them to slash physical-education programs. In 1991, only 42% of high school students participated in daily phys ed—already a troublingly low figure. Today that number is 25% or less.

10 Washington, too, is dropping the ball. Seven years ago, Congress allocated $125 million for a smart new health campaign dubbed Verb, aimed at getting preteen kids to become more active. Boldface names such as teen star Miley Cyrus and quarterback Donovan McNabb headlined public-service ads, and volunteers set up booths at public events. In the program's first year, up to 80% of kids polled were aware of the Verb message, and communities began sponsoring their own Verb-based activities. But that success could not survive congressional budget cuts, and the program's funding was steadily slashed. By 2007, funds were shut off altogether, and Verb was past tense.

The government insists that the decision was a fiscally prudent one and that local and state programs, like the widely publicized fitness initiatives launched by California governor Arnold Schwarzenegger or the less publicized INShape program begun in 2005 by Indiana governor Mitch Daniels, are a more efficient way to get the message out. "Obesity is not the kind of problem that is going to respond to just the flow of federal funds," says Galson. The fact is, however, that in the case of Verb, responding was precisely what it was doing—even if only a little.

In all of this, there are flickers of hope. In May, epidemiologists were thrilled when the *Journal of the American Medical Association* published a study of 8,165 children, which showed that for the first time in decades, the increase in U.S. childhood obesity had leveled off. It's not certain if the plateau is a sign that public-awareness programs and improved menus in many school cafeterias are producing results or merely that some kind of saturation point has been reached, with most kids genetically susceptible to gaining too much weight having done so. "Whether this is meaningful data, we don't know yet," says Seeley. "But anyone who wants to stick a flag in this and declare victory is just crazy."

Clearly, nobody is going that far. Victory may indeed come, but it will be only after a long, multifront war, one that, as the following stories in this TIME special section show, is at last being joined. Parents are fighting it in the home as they learn how to make healthier meals available to their families, set better examples with their own food choices and manage the critical issues of self-esteem that can be so disabling for overweight kids. Policymakers are fighting it as they study the growing body of research showing how everything from income to race to education plays a role in how much kids weigh and as they craft local solutions to solve these local problems. Doctors are fighting it as they deal daily with the ills associated with childhood obesity and work to repair the damage that's been done. And perhaps most important, teachers, mentors and public role models are fighting it as they help kids navigate a culture that fosters fat but idealizes thin and as they teach them that what truly counts is getting themselves as fit as their body type and genes allow—and then loving that body no matter what.

Do all these things—and do them right—and the national obesity epidemic just might be brought under control before some kids struggling with their weight today even reach middle age. "If we got this way over the last 30 years," says Galson, "it's not going to take us centuries to get back. We could reverse things at the same speed or even faster." Americans will continue to love good food; the trick will be to learn to love good health even more.

Reflect & Write

- ❑ How does Kluger support his implicit claim that Americans are defined by their fetishization of food? How does it affect the argument to provide such a historical and cultural framework at the beginning of his article?
- ❑ Does Kluger anticipate a resistant audience or a sympathetic one? How can you tell from his writing? What changes might he have made to his style or structure if he had anticipated the other type of audience?
- ❑ Where does he bring *logos* into his argument? How would the article have changed if he had introduced his facts and statistical research in the first paragraph?
- ❑ Look at his concluding paragraph. How does it work in conjunction with his introduction?
- ❑ **Write.** Do you agree with Kluger that American culture fetishizes food? Write a response in which you use examples and evidence from your own experience or research to either support, refute, or qualify his claim.

COLLABORATIVE CHALLENGE

How are eaters' relationship to food influenced by the way in which it is offered to them? This is the question you'll answer for the collaborative challenge in which you and a group will visit three types of restaurants: a fast food restaurant, a family style chain restaurant, and an upscale gourmet restaurant. For each one, perform a rhetorical analysis of the menu. How, when, and where is it presented to the eater? How is it designed in terms of color, layout, and even the materials used? What is contained on the menu? Price? Ingredients? Calories? Which information is presented as the most important to the eater? How can you tell? If you have permission from the establishment, take photographs of the menu to use as visual evidence. Having performed your analysis, write a summary of your findings, and present them (with the photographic examples, if you have them) to the class.

According to the official White House press release, the Let's Move Campaign was designed to "combat the epidemic of childhood obesity through a comprehensive approach that builds on effective strategies, and mobilizes public and private sector resources." Spearheaded by First Lady Michelle Obama, Let's Move's mission is to marshal government, educational, and medical resources to support parents in creating healthier eating and lifestyle habits among children, with the goal of solving the problem of childhood obesity within a generation. What follows are the remarks prepared for the First Lady to deliver at the launch in Washington, DC, on February 9, 2010.

Remarks of First Lady Michelle Obama As Prepared for Delivery Let's Move Launch

Washington, DC February 9, 2010

Hello everyone, thank you so much. It is such a pleasure to be here with all of you today.

Tammy, thank you for that wonderful introduction and for your outstanding work in the White House garden.

I want to recognize the extraordinary Cabinet members with us today—Secretaries Vilsack, Sebelius, Duncan, Salazar, Donovan and Solis—as well as Surgeon General Benjamin. Thanks to all of you for your excellent work.

Thanks also to Senators Harkin and Gillibrand, and Representatives DeLauro, Christensen and Fudge for their leadership and for being here today.

5 And I want to thank Tiki Barber, Dr. Judith Palfrey, Will Allen, and Mayors Johnson and Curtatone for braving the weather to join us, and for their outstanding work every day to help our kids lead active, healthy lives.

And I hear that congratulations are in order for the Watkins Hornets, who just won the Pee Wee National Football Championship. Let's give them a hand to show them how proud we are.

We're here today because we care deeply about the health and well-being of these kids and kids like them all across the country. And we're determined to finally take on one of the most serious threats to their future: the epidemic of childhood obesity in America today—an issue that's of great concern to me not just as a First Lady, but as a mom.

Often, when we talk about this issue, we begin by citing sobering statistics like the ones you've heard today—that over the past three decades, childhood obesity rates in America have tripled; that nearly one third of children in America are now overweight or obese—one in three.

But these numbers don't paint the full picture. These words—"overweight" and "obese"—they don't tell the full story. This isn't just about inches and pounds or how our kids look. It's about how our kids feel, and how they feel about themselves. It's about the impact we're seeing on every aspect of their lives.

10 Pediatricians like Dr. Palfrey are seeing kids with high blood pressure and high cholesterol—even Type II diabetes, which they used to see only in adults. Teachers see the teasing and bullying; school counselors see the depression and

low-self-esteem; and coaches see kids struggling to keep up, or stuck on the sidelines.

Military leaders report that obesity is now one of the most common disqualifiers for military service. Economic experts tell us that we're spending outrageous amounts of money treating obesity-related conditions like diabetes, heart disease and cancer. And public health experts tell us that the current generation could actually be on track to have a shorter lifespan than their parents.

None of us wants this kind of future for our kids—or for our country. So instead of just talking about this problem, instead of just worrying and wringing our hands about it, let's do something about it. Let's act . . . let's move.

Let's move to help families and communities make healthier decisions for their kids. Let's move to bring together governors and mayors, doctors and nurses, businesses, community groups, educators, athletes, Moms and Dads to tackle this challenge once and for all. And that's why we're here today—to launch "Let's Move"—a campaign that will rally our nation to achieve a single, ambitious goal: solving the problem of childhood obesity in a generation, so that children born today will reach adulthood at a healthy weight.

But to get where we want to go, we need to first understand how we got here. So let me ask the adults here today to close your eyes and think back for a moment . . . think back to a time when we were growing up.

15 Like many of you, when I was young, we walked to school every day, rain or shine—and in Chicago, we did it in wind, sleet, hail and snow too. Remember how, at school, we had recess twice a day and gym class twice a week, and we spent hours running around outside when school got out. You didn't go inside until dinner was ready—and when it was, we would gather around the table for dinner as a family. And there was one simple rule: you ate what Mom fixed—good, bad, or ugly. Kids had absolutely no say in what they felt like eating. If you didn't like it, you were welcome to go to bed hungry. Back then, fast food was a treat, and dessert was mainly a Sunday affair.

In my home, we weren't rich. The foods we ate weren't fancy. But there was always a vegetable on the plate. And we managed to lead a pretty healthy life.

Many kids today aren't so fortunate. Urban sprawl and fears about safety often mean the only walking they do is out their front door to a bus or a car. Cuts in recess and gym mean a lot less running around during the school day, and lunchtime may mean a school lunch heavy on calories and fat. For many kids, those afternoons spent riding bikes and playing ball until dusk have been replaced by afternoons inside with TV, the Internet, and video games.

And these days, with parents working longer hours, working two jobs, they don't have time for those family dinners. Or with the price of fresh fruits and vegetables rising 50 percent higher than overall food costs these past two decades, they don't have the money. Or they don't have a supermarket in their community, so their best option for dinner is something from the shelf of the local convenience store or gas station.

So many parents desperately want to do the right thing, but they feel like the deck is stacked against them. They know their kids' health is their responsibility—but they feel like it's out of their control. They're being bombarded by contradictory information at every turn, and they don't know who or what to believe. The result is a lot of guilt and anxiety—and a sense that no matter what they do, it won't be right, and it won't be enough.

20 I know what that feels like. I've been there. While today I'm blessed with more help and support than I ever dreamed of, I didn't always live in the White House.

It wasn't that long ago that I was a working Mom, struggling to balance meetings and deadlines with soccer and ballet. And there were some nights when everyone was tired and hungry, and we just went to the drive-thru because it was quick and cheap, or went with one of the less healthy microwave options, because it was easy. And one day, my pediatrician pulled me aside and told me, "You might want to think about doing things a little bit differently."

That was a moment of truth for me. It was a wakeup call that I was the one in charge, even if it didn't always feel that way.

And today, it's time for a moment of truth for our country; it's time we all had a wakeup call. It's time for us to be honest with ourselves about how we got here. Our kids didn't do this to themselves. Our kids don't decide what's served to them at school or whether there's time for gym class or recess. Our kids don't choose to make food products with tons of sugar and sodium in super-sized portions, and then to have those products marketed to them everywhere they turn. And no matter how much they beg for pizza, fries and candy, ultimately, they are not, and should not, be the ones calling the shots at dinnertime. We're in charge. We make these decisions.

But that's actually the good news here. If we're the ones who make the decisions, then we can decide to solve this problem. And when I say "we," I'm not just talking about folks here in Washington. This isn't about politics. There's nothing Democratic or Republican, liberal or conservative, about doing what's best for our kids. And I've spoken with many experts about this issue, and not a single one has said that the solution is to have government tell people what to do. Instead, I'm talking about what we can do. I'm talking about commonsense steps we can take in our families and communities to help our kids lead active, healthy lives.

25 This isn't about trying to turn the clock back to when we were kids, or preparing five course meals from scratch every night. No one has time for that. And it's not about being 100 percent perfect 100 percent of the time. Lord knows I'm not. There's a place for cookies and ice cream, burgers and fries—that's part of the fun of childhood.

Often, it's just about balance. It's about small changes that add up—like walking to school, replacing soda with water or skim milk, trimming those portion sizes a little—things like this can mean the difference between being healthy and fit or not.

There's no one-size-fits-all solution here. Instead, it's about families making manageable changes that fit with their schedules, their budgets, and their needs and tastes.

And it's about communities working to support these efforts. Mayors like Mayors Johnson and Curtatone, who are building sidewalks, parks and community gardens. Athletes and role models like Tiki Barber, who are building playgrounds to help kids stay active. Community leaders like Will Allen who are bringing farmers markets to underserved areas. Companies like the food industry leaders who came together last fall and acknowledged their responsibility to be part of the solution. But there's so much more to do.

And that's the mission of Let's Move—to create a wave of efforts across this country that get us to our goal of solving childhood obesity in a generation.

30 We kicked off this initiative this morning when my husband signed a presidential memorandum establishing the first ever government-wide Task Force on Childhood Obesity. The task force is composed of representatives from key agencies—including many who are here today. Over the next 90 days, these folks will review every program and policy relating to child nutrition and physical activity. And they'll develop an action plan marshalling these resources to meet our goal. And to ensure we're continuously on track to do so, the Task Force will set concrete benchmarks to measure our progress.

But we can't wait 90 days to get going here. So let's move right now, starting today, on a series of initiatives to help achieve our goal.

First, let's move to offer parents the tools and information they need—and that they've been asking for—to make healthy choices for their kids. We've been working with the FDA and several manufacturers and retailers to make our food labels more customer-friendly, so people don't have to spend hours squinting at words they can't pronounce to figure out whether the food they're buying is healthy or not. In fact, just today, the nation's largest beverage companies announced that they'll be taking steps to provide clearly visible information about calories on the front of their products—as well as on vending machines and soda fountains. This is exactly the kind of vital information parents need to make good choices for their kids.

We're also working with the American Academy of Pediatrics, supporting their groundbreaking efforts to ensure that doctors not only regularly measure children's BMI, but actually write out a prescription detailing steps parents can take to keep their kids healthy and fit.

In addition, we're working with the Walt Disney Company, NBC Universal, and Viacom to launch a nationwide public awareness campaign educating parents and children about how to fight childhood obesity.

35 And we're creating a one-stop shopping website—LetsMove.gov—so with the click of a mouse, parents can find helpful tips and step-by-step strategies, including healthy recipes, exercise plans, and charts they can use to track their family's progress.

But let's remember: 31 million American children participate in federal school meal programs—and many of these kids consume as many as half their daily calories at school. And what we don't want is a situation where parents are taking all the right steps at home—and then their kids undo all that work with salty, fatty food in the school cafeteria.

So let's move to get healthier food into our nation's schools. That's the second part of this initiative. We'll start by updating and strengthening the Child Nutrition Act—the law that sets nutrition standards for what our kids eat at school. And we've proposed an historic investment of an additional $10 billion over ten years to fund that legislation.

With this new investment, we'll knock down barriers that keep families from participating in school meal programs and serve an additional one million students in the first five years alone. And we'll dramatically improve the quality of the food we offer in schools—including in school vending machines. We'll take away some of the empty calories, and add more fresh fruits and vegetables and other nutritious options.

We also plan to double the number of schools in the HealthierUS School Challenge—an innovative program that recognizes schools doing the very best work to keep kids healthy—from providing healthy school meals to requiring physical education classes each week. To help us meet that goal, I'm thrilled to announce that for the very first time, several major school food suppliers have come together and committed to decrease sugar, fat and salt; increase whole grains; and double the fresh produce in the school meals they serve. And also for the first time, food service workers—along with principals, superintendents and school board members across America—are coming together to support these efforts. With these commitments, we'll reach just about every school child in this country with better information and more nutritious meals to put them on track to a healthier life.

These are major steps forward. But let's not forget about the rest of the calories kids consume—the ones they eat outside of school, often at home, in their neighborhoods. And when 23.5 million Americans, including 6.5 million American children, live in "food deserts"—communities without a supermarket—those calories are too often empty ones. You can see these areas in dark purple in the new USDA Food Environment Atlas we're unveiling today. This Atlas maps out everything from diabetes and obesity rates across the country to the food deserts you see on this screen.

So let's move to ensure that all our families have access to healthy, affordable food in their communities. That's the third part of this initiative. Today, for the very first time, we're making a commitment to eliminate food deserts in America—and we plan to do so within seven years. Now, we know this is ambitious. And it will take a serious commitment from both government and the private sector. That's why we plan to invest $400 million a year in a Healthy Food Financing initiative that will bring grocery stores to underserved areas and help places like convenience stores carry healthier food options. And this initiative won't just help families eat better, it will help create jobs and revitalize neighborhoods across America.

But we know that eating right is only part of the battle. Experts recommend that children get 60 minutes of active play each day. If this sounds like a lot, consider this: kids today spend an average of seven and a half hours a day watching TV, and playing with cell phones, computers, and video games. And only a third of high school students get the recommended levels of physical activity.

So let's move. And I mean that literally. Let's find new ways for kids to be physically active, both in and out of school. That's the fourth, and final, part of this initiative.

We'll increase participation in the President's Physical Fitness Challenge. And we'll modernize the challenge, so it's not just about how athletic kids are—how many sit-ups or push-ups they can do—but how active they are.

We'll double the number of kids who earn a Presidential Active Lifestyle Award in the next school year, recognizing those who engage in physical activity five days a week, for six weeks. We've also recruited professional athletes from a dozen different leagues—including the NFL, Major League Baseball, and the WNBA—to promote these efforts through sports clinics, public service announcements and more.

45 So that's some of what we're doing to achieve our goal. And we know we won't get there this year, or this Administration. We know it'll take a nationwide movement that continues long after we're gone. That's why today, I'm pleased to announce that a new, independent foundation has been created to rally and coordinate businesses, non-profits, and state and local governments to keep working until we reach our goal—and to measure our progress along the way. It's called the Partnership for a Healthier America, and it's bringing together some of the leading experts on childhood obesity, like The Robert Wood Johnson Foundation, The California Endowment, The Kellogg Foundation, the Brookings Institution, and the Alliance for a Healthier Generation, which is a partnership between the American Heart Association and the Clinton Foundation. And we expect others to join in the coming months.

So this is a pretty serious effort. And I know that in these challenging times for our country, there are those who will wonder whether this should really be a priority. They might view things like healthy school lunches and physical fitness challenges as "extras"—as things we spring for once we've taken care of the necessities. They might ask, "How can we spend money on fruits and vegetables in our school cafeterias when many of our schools don't have enough textbooks or teachers?" Or they might ask, "How can we afford to build parks and sidewalks when we can't even afford our health care costs?"

But when you step back and think about it, you realize—these are false choices. If kids aren't getting adequate nutrition, even the best textbooks and teachers in the world won't help them learn. If they don't have safe places to run and play, and they wind up with obesity-related conditions, then those health care costs will just keep rising.

So yes, we have to do it all . . . we'll need to make some modest, but critical, investments in the short-run . . . but we know that they'll pay for themselves—likely many times over—in the long-run. Because we won't just be keeping our kids healthy when they're young. We'll be teaching them habits to keep them healthy their entire lives.

We saw this firsthand here at the White House when we planted our garden with students like Tammy last Spring. One of Tammy's classmates wrote in an essay that her time in the garden, and I quote, " . . . has made me think about the choices I have with what I put in my mouth . . ."

50 Other wrote with great excitement that he'd learned that tomatoes are both a fruit and a vegetable and contain vitamins that fight diseases. Armed with that knowledge, he declared, "So the tomato is a fruit and is now my best friend."

Think about the ripple effect when children use this knowledge to make healthy decisions for the rest of their lives. Think about the effect it will have on every aspect of their lives. Whether they can keep up with their classmates on the playground and stay focused in the classroom. Whether they have the self-confidence to pursue careers of their dreams, and the stamina to succeed in those careers. Whether they'll have the energy and strength to teach their own kids how to throw a ball or ride a bike, and whether they'll live long enough to see their grandkids grow up—maybe even their great grandkids too.

In the end, we know that solving our obesity challenge won't be easy—and it certainly won't be quick. But make no mistake about it, this problem can be solved.

This isn't like a disease where we're still waiting for the cure to be discovered—we know the cure for this. This isn't like putting a man on the moon or inventing the Internet—it doesn't take some stroke of genius or feat of technology. We have everything we need, right now, to help our kids lead healthy lives. Rarely in the history of this country have we encountered a problem of such magnitude and consequence that is so eminently solvable. So let's move to solve it.

I don't want our kids to live diminished lives because we failed to step up today. I don't want them looking back decades from now and asking us, why didn't you help us when you had a chance? Why didn't you put us first when it mattered most?

So much of what we all want for our kids isn't within our control. We want them to succeed in everything they do. We want to protect them from every hardship and spare them from every mistake. But we know we can't do all of that. What we can do . . . what is fully within our control . . . is to give them the very best start in their journeys. What we can do is give them advantages early in life that will stay with them long after we're gone. As President Franklin Roosevelt once put it: "We cannot always build the future for our youth, but we can build our youth for the future."

That is our obligation, not just as parents who love our kids, but as citizens who love this country. So let's move. Let's get this done. Let's give our kids what they need to have the future they deserve.

Thank you so much.

Reflect & Write

- ❑ Look at the first six paragraphs of the speech. To what extent do they serve a rhetorical purpose in relation to the rest of the speech or in terms of the First Lady's assessment of the audience and rhetorical situation?
- ❑ How does the First Lady establish *ethos* in her speech? What types of authority does she invoke? Find specific phrases or passages where she establishes her credibility. Why does she establish *ethos* in this way? How does it contribute to the persuasiveness of her speech?
- ❑ Where does the call to action begin in the speech? How does she build up to it? Is it an appropriate place in the speech to shift to a call to action? Would you have done it earlier? Later? Why?
- ❑ Analyze the movement in this speech from the focus on the individual, to the community, to the government. How effective is this structure for her argument?

- ❑ Consider the rhetorical repetition of the phrase "let's move." What multiple meanings does it hold?
- ❑ Look carefully at the language and word choice she uses in the conclusion of her speech. What deliberate rhetorical choices did she make to bring her speech to a powerful close?
- ❑ **Write.** Clearly this argument was written to be delivered orally. Condense this speech into a 1½–2 page memo between a local representative of Let's Move and a community's Parent Teacher Organization. What changes in content, development, style, and format do you need to institute to accommodate the shift in rhetorical situation and genre?

■ *The United States Department of Agriculture (USDA) released the first food pyramid in 1992, using an information graphic to represent the recommended daily intact of different food categories. The USDA revises the food pyramid every five years.*

USDA Food Pyramids

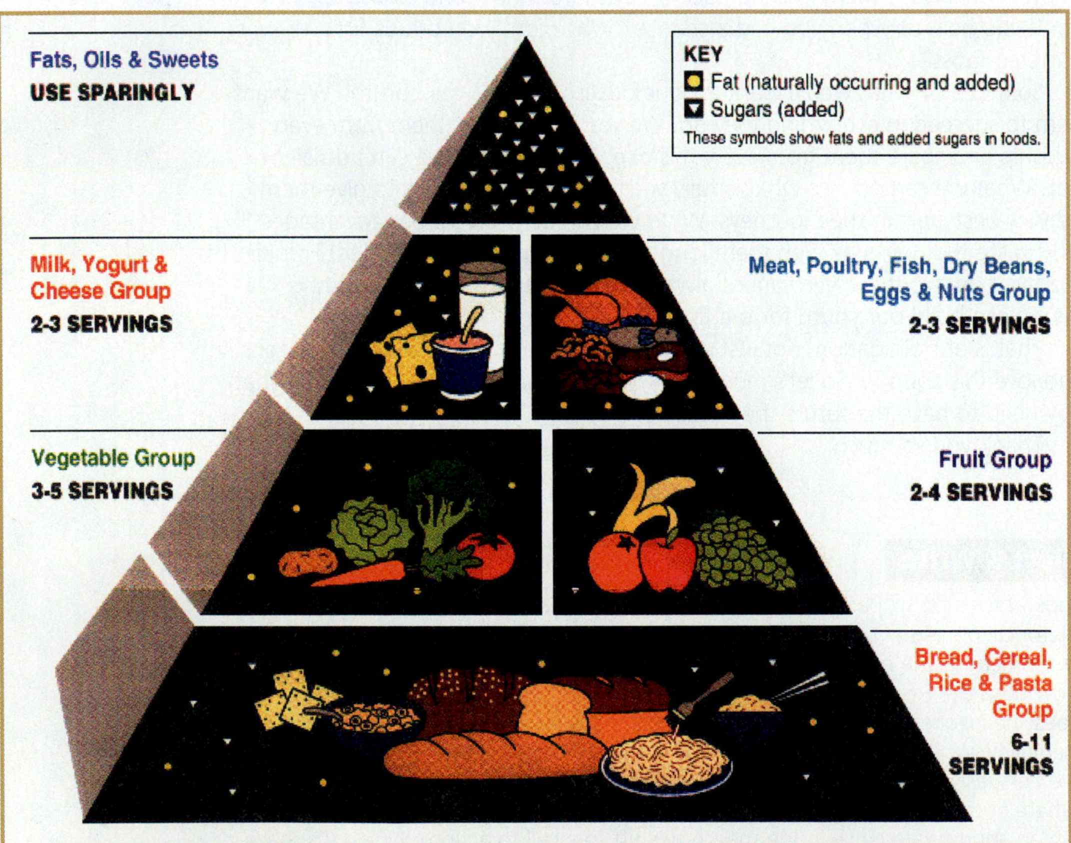

FIGURE 10.8. This food pyramid was the first released by the USDA in 1992 and was based on a similar model published in Denmark in 1978. Many food packages still feature this original pyramid.

FIGURE 10.9. Released in 2005, the MyPyramid graphic revised the pyramid design to reflects shifts in the American approach to "a healthier you."

Reflect & Write

- ❑ How does the original food pyramid make use of the pyramid structure to make its argument?
- ❑ Consider the changes made in the 2005 pyramid, from title, to layout, new elements, omitted elements, and content. How do these revisions change the argument that the USDA is making? How does the shift in *kairos* reflect a similar shift in cultural approaches to eating and health?
- ❑ **Write.** Take the information from the current food pyramid and rework it into two different types of information graphics (for instance, a bar graph or a pie chart). How does the change in the delivery of the argument change the argument itself?

■ **Michael Pollan** *In recent years, Michael Pollan has become one of America's leading writers on food culture. Some of his most notable works include* Food Rules: An Eater's Manual *(2009), a guide to sensible eating;* In Defense of Food: An Eater's Manifesto *(2008), which won the James Beard Award; and* The Omnivore's Dilemma *(2006), which has won numerous awards and was named one of the ten best books of 2006 by both the* Washington Post *and the* New York Times. *In the following op-ed piece, originally published in the June 19, 2002, issue of the* New York Times, *Pollan anticipates his longer works through an examination of how corn dominates both American agriculture and diet.*

When a Crop Becomes King

Michael Pollan

CORNWALL BRIDGE, Conn. —Here in southern New England the corn is already waist high and growing so avidly you can almost hear the creak of stalk and leaf as the plants stretch toward the sun. The ears of sweet corn are just starting to show up on local farm stands, inaugurating one of the ceremonies of an American summer. These days the nation's nearly 80 million-acre field of corn rolls across the countryside like a second great lawn, but this wholesome, all-American image obscures a decidedly more dubious reality.

Like the tulip, the apple and the potato, zea mays (the botanical name for both sweet and feed corn) has evolved with humans over the past 10,000 years in the great dance of species we call domestication. The plant gratifies human needs, in exchange for which humans expand the plant's habitat, moving its genes all over the world and remaking the land (clearing trees, plowing the ground, protecting it from its enemies) so it might thrive.

Corn, by making itself tasty and nutritious, got itself noticed by Christopher Columbus, who helped expand its range from the New World to Europe and beyond. Today corn is the world's most widely planted cereal crop. But nowhere have humans done quite as much to advance the interests of this plant as in North America, where zea mays has insinuated itself into our landscape, our food system—and our federal budget.

One need look no further than the $190 billion farm bill President Bush signed last month to wonder whose interests are really being served here. Under the 10-year program, taxpayers will pay farmers $4 billion a year to grow ever more corn, this despite the fact that we struggle to get rid of the surplus the plant already produces. The average bushel of corn (56 pounds) sells for about $2 today; it costs farmers more than $3 to grow it. But rather than design a program that would encourage farmers to plant less corn—which would have the benefit of lifting the price farmers receive for it—Congress has decided instead to subsidize corn by the bushel, thereby insuring that zea mays dominion over its 125,000-square-mile American habitat will go unchallenged.

5 At first blush this subsidy might look like a handout for farmers, but really it's a form of welfare for the plant itself—and for all those economic interests that profit from its overproduction: the processors, factory farms, and the soft drink and snack makers that rely on cheap corn. For zea mays has triumphed by making itself indispensable not to farmers (whom it is swiftly and surely bankrupting) but to the Archer Daniels Midlands, Tysons and Coca-Colas of the world.

Our entire food supply has undergone a process of "cornification" in recent years, without our even noticing it. That's because, unlike in Mexico, where a corn-based diet has been the norm for centuries, in the United States most of the corn we consume is invisible, having been heavily processed or passed through food animals before it reaches us. Most of the animals we eat (chickens, pigs and cows) today subsist on a diet of corn, regardless of whether it is good for them. In the case of beef cattle, which evolved to eat grass, a corn diet wreaks havoc on their digestive system, making it necessary to feed them antibiotics to stave off illness and infection. Even farm-raised salmon are being bred to tolerate corn—not a food their evolution has prepared them for. Why feed fish corn? Because it's the cheapest thing you can feed any animal, thanks to federal subsidies. But even with more than half of the 10 billion bushels of corn produced annually being fed to animals, there is plenty left over. So companies like A.D.M., Cargill and ConAgra have figured ingenious new ways to dispose of it, turning it into everything from ethanol to Vitamin C and biodegradable plastics.

By far the best strategy for keeping zea mays in business has been the development of high-fructose corn syrup, which has all but pushed sugar aside. Since the 1980's, most soft drink manufacturers have switched from sugar to corn sweeteners, as have most snack makers. Nearly 10 percent of the calories Americans consume now come from corn sweeteners; the figure is 20 percent for many children. Add to that all the corn-based animal protein (corn-fed beef, chicken and pork) and the corn qua corn (chips, muffins, sweet corn) and you have a plant that has become one of nature's greatest success stories, by turning us (along with several other equally unwitting species) into an expanding race of corn eaters.

So why begrudge corn its phenomenal success? Isn't this the way domestication is supposed to work?

The problem in corn's case is that we're sacrificing the health of both our bodies and the environment by growing and eating so much of it. Though we're only beginning to understand what our cornified food system is doing to our health, there's cause for concern. It's probably no coincidence that the wholesale switch to corn sweeteners in the 1980's marks the beginning of the epidemic of obesity and Type 2 diabetes in this country. Sweetness became so cheap that soft drink makers, rather than lower their prices, super-sized their serving portions and marketing budgets. Thousands of new sweetened snack foods hit the market, and the amount of fructose in our diets soared.

10 This would be bad enough for the American waistline, but there's also preliminary research suggesting that high-fructose corn syrup is metabolized differently than other sugars, making it potentially more harmful. A recent study at the University of Minnesota found that a diet high in fructose (as compared to glucose) elevates triglyceride levels in men shortly after eating, a phenomenon that has been linked to an increased risk of obesity and heart disease. Little is known about the health effects of eating animals that have themselves eaten so much corn, but in the case of cattle, researchers have found that corn-fed beef is higher in saturated fats than grass-fed beef.

We know a lot more about what 80 million acres of corn is doing to the health of our environment: serious and lasting damage. Modern corn hybrids are the greediest of plants, demanding more nitrogen fertilizer than any other crop. Corn requires more pesticide than any other food crop. Runoff from these chemicals finds its way into the groundwater and, in the Midwestern corn belt, into the Mississippi River, which carries it to the Gulf of Mexico, where it has already killed off marine life in a 12,000-square-mile area.

To produce the chemicals we apply to our cornfields takes vast amounts of oil and natural gas. (Nitrogen fertilizer is made from natural gas, pesticides from oil.) America's corn crop might look like a sustainable, solar-powered system for producing food, but it is actually a huge, inefficient, polluting machine that guzzles fossil fuel—a half a gallon of it for every bushel.

So it seems corn has indeed become king. We have given it more of our land than any other plant, an area more than twice the size of New York State. To keep it well fed and safe from predators we douse it with chemicals that poison our water and deepen our dependence on foreign oil. And then in order to dispose of all the corn this cracked system has produced, we eat it as fast as we can in as many ways as we can—turning the fat of the land into, well, fat. One has to wonder whether corn hasn't at last succeeded in domesticating us.

Reflect & Write

- ❑ What does Pollan mean by the term "cornification"? How does he build up to this definition? How is it central to the argument of his essay?
- ❑ How does Pollan personify corn? Find at least three places where he uses phrases or terms to describe corn that we usually associate more with people than plants. What is the effect of this personification?
- ❑ Find the place in the essay where Pollan asks a rhetorical question that he then answers by asserting his thesis. Do you find his claim persuasive? Why do you think that he inserted the claim midway through the essay rather than at the beginning or at the end?
- ❑ Is this an argument about the environment? About health? About both? How do these issues interrelate?
- ❑ **Write.** The first paragraph of the op-ed piece invokes a nostalgic picture that is subverted by the final phrase: ". . . this wholesome, all-American image obscures a decidedly more dubious reality." Rewrite this first paragraph and its corn field description to more explicitly reflect Pollan's argument about King Corn in the rest of the essay. Use word choice to make Pollan's distrust of corn even stronger.

In 2008, the Corn Refiners Association (CRA) launched a campaign designed to change the popular perception that high fructose corn syrup, is a less desirable alternative to table sugar. Called "Changing the Conversation about High Fructose Corn Syrup," this campaign involved both commercials and print ads, such as the one below, as well as the development of a multimedia-enhanced Website at SweetSurpise.com. After studying the ad, read the student analysis of this campaign written by student Katherine Disenhof, available on the Envision *Website. www.pearsonhighered.com/envision/240*

FIGURE 10.10. This 2009 print ad was part of a publicity campaign by the Corn Refiners Association.

Reflect & Write

- ❏ How do the choice of text, characters, color, and layout contribute to the ad's argument? What information seems to be the most important? How can you tell?
- ❏ How does the Sweet Surprise campaign use *ethos* as the foundation for its argument? Is this an effective strategy?
- ❏ **Write.** Visit the Sweet Surprise Website, linked through the *Envision* Website, and write a comparative analysis of how the CRA make its argument debunking popular "myths" about high fructose corn syrup in both a commercial and the print ad featured here. Be sure to consider how the difference in medium (static print image versus dynamic film image) affects the rhetorical strategies used to convey this argument.
www.pearsonhighered.com/envision/241

■ **John Cloud** *In recent years, the ethical eating movement in America has polarized between two camps: the Organic Food Movement, which argues for the benefits of consuming pesticide free, organically grown foods; and Locavorism, which advocates purchasing only locally grown foods.* Time *magazine senior writer John Cloud jumps into the center of the local-versus-organic debate with the article below, which was originally published in the March 2, 2007, issue of* Time. *Before you read this piece, consider your own stance on the issue: does it make more sense to eat organic or to eat local?*

Eating Better Than Organic

John Cloud

Not long ago I had an apple problem. Wavering in the produce section of a Manhattan grocery store, I was unable to decide between an organic apple and a nonorganic apple (which was labeled conventional, since that sounds better than "sprayed with pesticides that might kill you"). It shouldn't have been a tough choice—who wants to eat pesticide residue?—but the organic apples had been grown in California. The conventional ones were from right here in New York State. I know I've been listening to too much npr because I started wondering: How much Middle Eastern oil did it take to get that California apple to me? Which farmer should I support—the one who rejected pesticides in California or the one who was, in some romantic sense, a neighbor? Most important, didn't the apple's taste suffer after the fruit was crated and refrigerated and jostled for thousands of miles?

In the end I bought both apples. (They were both good, although the California one had a mealy bit, possibly from its journey.) It's only recently that I had noticed more locally grown products in the supermarket, but when I got home I discovered that the organic-vs.-local debate has become one of the liveliest in the food world. Last year Wal-Mart began offering more organic products—those grown without pesticides, antibiotics, irradiation and so on—and the big company's expansion into a once alternative food culture has been a source of deep concern, and predictable backlash, among early organic adopters.

Nearly a quarter of American shoppers now buy organic products once a week, up from 17% in 2000. But for food purists, "local" is the new "organic," the new ideal that promises healthier bodies and a healthier planet. Many chefs, food writers and politically minded eaters are outraged that "Big Organic" firms now use the same industrial-size farming and long-distance-shipping methods as conventional agribusiness. "Should I assume that I have a God-given right to access the entire earth's bounty, however far away some of its produce is grown?" asks ethnobotanist Gary Paul Nabhan in his 2002 memoir, Coming Home to Eat: The Pleasures and Politics of Local Foods. Nabhan predicted my apple problem when he vacillated over some organic pumpkin canned hundreds of miles from his Arizona home. “If you send it halfway around the world before it is eaten,” he mused, “an organic food still may be ‘good’ for the consumer, but is it ‘good’ for the food system?”

I had never really thought about how my food purchases might affect “the food system.” Even now I don’t share the pessimism and asceticism of the local-eating set. In her 2001 memoir, This Organic Life, Columbia University nutritionist Joan Dye Gussow writes that her commitment to eating locally “is probably driven by three things. The first is the taste of live food; the second is my relation to frugality; the third is my deep concern about the state of the planet.” I don’t have much relation to frugality, and, perhaps foolishly, I’m more optimistic than Gussow about our ability to develop alternative energy sources.

5 But I care deeply about how my food tastes, and it makes sense that a snow pea grown by a local farmer and never refrigerated will retain more of its delicate leguminous flavor than one shipped in a frigid plane from Guatemala. And I realized that if more consumers didn’t become part of the local-food market, it could disappear and all our peas would be those tasteless little pods from far away.

Still, the fact that not all locally grown products are organic had me worried. Even if most Americans wanted to buy locally grown organics, they wouldn’t be able to find many. In a few not-too-dry, not-too-wet, not-too-warm regions—central California is one—it is possible to find abundant organic produce grown locally. But if you live in a humid climate, say, the moisture that encourages bacteria and fungi means that growing without pesticides is much more risky, expensive and rare. Consequently, in the Hudson Valley of New York, near me, it’s very difficult to find fruit that hasn’t been sprayed with chemicals at least once. In other regions, like the upper Midwest, most big farms don’t grow any vegetables for local markets, conventional or organic. Instead, they produce commodity crops like corn and soybeans for sale to food processors. At a large Hugo’s grocery store in Jamestown, N.D., last summer, I noticed only one local product: flour, which is milled in-state from local wheat. But there were organic apples and oranges from out of state.

Farmers’ markets often feature organic produce from nearby farms, but not everyone lives near a farmers’ market—and most products at the markets aren’t organic. “I’ve been to farmers’ markets, and there’s people hauling stuff from the truck that they got at a wholesaler,” says Joseph Mendelson III, legal director of the Center for Food Safety, a liberal Washington group that supports strong organic standards. Mendelson prefers the “gold standard” of locally grown organics, but he is rather frightening on the subject of nonorganic food, whatever its origin. When I asked him whether I should favor local products, he replied, “I don’t know what local means. Do they use local pesticides? Does that mean the food is better because they produce local cancers?”

All of which further tangles my original question: The organic apple or the conventionally grown local one?

It turns out to be a frustratingly layered choice, one that implicates many other questions: What’s the most efficient way to grow food for all? Should farms be big or small, family- or corporate-run? How do your choices affect the planet? What tastes better? And then there’s that little matter of cancer.

10 Let’s get that one out of the way at the start. If scientists could conclusively prove that agricultural chemicals are harmful, we would all go organic. But it’s not clear, for instance, that the low levels of pesticide typically found on conventional produce cause cancer. The risks of long-term exposure to those residues are still undetermined.

Even if conventional foods don’t turn out to be as dangerous as organic advocates claim, several recent studies have suggested that organic foods contain higher levels of vitamins than their conventionally grown counterparts. In a paper published in October in the Journal of Agricultural and Food Chemistry, a team from the University of California, Davis, demonstrates that organically grown tomatoes have significantly more vitamin C than conventional tomatoes. Even so, the same study shows no significant differences between conventional and organic bell peppers.

“We’re just beginning to understand these relationships,” says U.C. Davis food chemist Alyson Mitchell, one of the paper’s authors. “We understand, and have understood for a long time, that there is some relation between soil health and plant quality, but we still don’t have a solid scientific database to link this to nutrition.”

Organic adherents take it on faith that the way food is grown affects its nutritional quality. But advocates of local eating are now making another leap, saying what happens after harvest—how food is shipped and handled—is perhaps even more important than how it was grown. Locavores.com a site popular among local purists, asserts that "because locally grown produce is freshest, it is more nutritionally complete." But Mitchell says she knows of no studies that prove this.

In short, science can't tell you what to eat for dinner. Many of us end up relying on the government to keep food safe, or we just don't think about it. For those who do start to think—nervous new parents, say, or McDonald's burnouts—there are more alternative grocers than ever. There are online purveyors of gourmet health foods (pricey), the old food co-ops (too political for me), and of course those farmers' markets, which—in spite of basic limitations like not being open every day—have grown larger and more sophisticated. (According to Samuel Fromartz's valuable 2006 history Organic Inc.: Natural Foods and How They Grew, there were 3,706 U.S. farmers' markets in 2004, double the number there were a decade earlier.)

15 But for the past few years, the easiest answer for food-baffled Americans has been a single company: Whole Foods Market.

Whole Foods now has 190 locations from Tigard, Ore., to Notting Hill in London. In fiscal 2006 the chain's sales grew 19% (to $5.6 billion), a bit lower than 2005's 22% growth. Fretful about increasing competition from mainstream grocers who are offering more organic products, investors have punished Whole Foods in the past year; its stock price has fallen more than a third since February 2006.

Still, Whole Foods is expanding rapidly. It recently said it would acquire Wild Oats Markets Inc.; the merger would give Whole Foods an additional 112 locations in North America. Already, many Americans have come to see Whole Foods as the repository of both their dietary hopes and fears—the place we can buy not only organic arugula but a decadent chocolate bar too. I have shopped at Whole Foods off and on since 1990, when I had a summer job in Austin, Texas, where Whole Foods began in 1980. If I was going to decide whether to buy organic or buy local, I figured Whole Foods' ceo, John Mackey, could help me. After all, he is vegan, and his politics lean libertarian, so he thinks hard about different paths. And he has made a great fortune by joining two previously antagonistic alimentary impulses—health and excess.

When we spoke last fall, Mackey was at first diplomatic about the organic-local choice. He told me that when he can't get locally grown organics—and even he can't reliably get them—he decides on the basis of taste. "I would probably purchase a local nonorganic tomato before I would purchase an organic one that was shipped from California," he said. He called the two tomatoes "an environmental wash," since the California one had petroleum miles on it while the nonorganic one was grown with pesticides. "But the local tomato from outside Austin will be fresher, will just taste better," he said.

However, he also noted that products like hard squash that can last months in storage don't taste so different for being shipped. In that case, he said, "I might purchase the organic version from California." Mackey acknowledged that organic agriculture is "flawed"; he criticized organic-milk farms where cows are pumped with feed in factory settings just like conventional-milk cows. But he also bristled at criticism from local activists. He noted that just because a farm is near your home doesn't mean it practices sustainable farming. "There's an assumption that small is beautiful and big is industrial, and that's not necessarily the case," he said. Whole Foods could not keep growing without supplies from large international farms, which is one reason the organic-vs.-local debate is a delicate issue for Mackey.

20 At least at my Whole Foods—the one in Manhattan's Union Square, where I shop once or twice a month—most of the available produce comes from California or some other distant land, even during the local growing season. Like all other Whole Foods locations, the store began to push local products more aggressively last summer. A placard was posted above the escalator exhorting customers to BUY LOCAL, and all the cash registers were changed to show photos of area farmers.

These days, in the final weeks of winter, it would be unfair to ask Whole Foods to sell predominantly local produce at my store, because so little can be grown in the Northeast right now. But even during verdant summertime, the vast majority of products sold at my Whole Foods (fresh or otherwise) aren't from the Northeast. Actually, it would be more accurate to say that the packages in which most Whole Foods groceries are sold say nothing about the food's origin. For instance, in the freezer section you can find Whole Foods' Whole Kitchen brand Breaded Eggplant Slices with Italian Herbs. The box tells you a wealth of information about the eggplant slices—that they contain wheat, dextrose and annatto (a dye); that they can be fried, baked or microwaved; that they have no trans fat; that they are "flavorful" and "versatile." But you don't learn where the eggplant comes from.

A Whole Foods spokeswoman told me the eggplant was grown in Florida, which is too bad because eggplant grows easily in the Northeast. But in the company's defense, very few customers care whether their food is local. Most who do, shop at farmers' markets. Also, there's not even a standard definition of what local means. To Nabhan, who inspired many local activists with Coming Home to Eat, it means eating within a 250-mile radius of his Arizona home. Many who blog at a site called eatlocalchallenge.com aim for a stricter "100-mile diet."

My favorite definition of local comes from Columbia's Gussow, a reporter for Time in the 1950s who went on to become a local-eating pioneer. For 25 years, Gussow has lectured on the environmental (and culinary) disadvantages of relying on a global food supply. Her most oft-quoted statistic is that shipping a strawberry from California to New York requires 435 calories of fossil fuel but provides the eater with only 5 calories of nutrition. In her memoir, Gussow offers this rather poetic meaning of local: "Within a day's leisurely drive of our homes. [This] distance is entirely arbitrary. But then, so was the decision made by others long ago that we ought to have produce from all around the world."

On his blog, Whole Foods' Mackey has used a radius of 200 miles to mean local. Measuring from my home, that includes not only much of New York State, New Jersey and Connecticut but also parts of seven other Northeastern states. Such a large food shed produces a great variety of fruits and vegetables, and Whole Foods has said it wants to increase its percentage of local produce. (Of the roughly $1 billion in produce the company sold last year, 16.4% came from local sources, up from 14.9% in 2005.) Last year Mackey announced a $10 million loan program for local farmers.

25 But Mackey also knows that most Americans will never eat a purely local diet. "One of the challenges of being a retailer is you don't want to offend people," Mackey told me. "Some customers want to eat apples year-round, and they're willing to pay more for a New Zealand apple." Finally, he offered a defense of the global food economy: "When I was a little boy—I'm 53 years old—being able to get oranges from Florida or produce from another state was a very big deal because the local-produce availability where I lived in Houston wasn't great. People back then didn't have nearly as diverse a diet as we do now, and you might also point out their life spans weren't as long."

That made me wonder if purely local eating was even possible—or healthy. Could I get everything I needed from the Northeast? What would I have to give up? For gustatory reasons, I long ago stopped eating out of season—I have no interest in those hard Canadian tomatoes my Whole Foods was selling in February. But would I have to forgo coffee? What would replace my breakfast cereal? How much would all this cost? I wasn't sure. So like everyone else, I went to Google.

I mean, I literally went to Google, to the company's Mountain View, Calif., campus.

I had read that one of Google's new cafeterias, Café 150, served only food originating within a 150-mile radius of Mountain View. I knew this radius included a glorious fund of farms, ranches and fisheries, the Salinas Valley food shed that Steinbeck made famous in East of Eden. I also knew that as one of the most successful companies of the era, Google could afford not only to pursue such a whimsical culinary ideal as total locality but also to do so in the form of a fine-dining restaurant. (Café 150 is one of 11 employee eateries on the Google campus, all of which famously charge nothing.)

Still, I wanted to see how Café 150's founding chef, Nate Keller, managed to serve more than 400 purely local meals a day. Most chefs simply place orders with suppliers. Good cooks understand that quality and origin are related because of the toll extracted by transportation, but in the end, if Emeril Lagasse wants to serve wild salmon one night, he can just order it from Alaska. Keller, who recently became the chef at another Google restaurant, couldn't do that. Although just a freckly 30-year-old, he had to plan his menus the way preindustrial cooks did, according to whatever local vendors offered that day.

30 "These guys have to be so flexible with their menus, it's unreal," said Café 150's fishmonger, Tim Zamborelli of Today's Catch in San Jose, Calif. "We have to find out what's coming in on that particular day and let them know so they can change." Café 150, which opened a year ago, can serve no shrimp or scallops, since they can't be found in the area, and tuna was available only from August through October, when currents brought bluefins into the radius. The day I visited, Keller hadn't learned what vegetable he would be serving until the night before. (He got baby red chard.)

It's a radically new way of thinking about cooking because it's so very old. But I was surprised to learn that Café 150 was the brainchild not of some anticorporate artisan but of John Dickman, 51, Google's food-service manager. Dickman not only worked for 14 years at the food giant Marriott—he even trained flight attendants to cook plane food. I was curious how he had created such a radical restaurant.

Dickman says he was inspired by chef Ann Cooper, whose 2000 book, Bitter Harvest, is well described by its subtitle: A Chef's Perspective on the Hidden Dangers in the Foods We Eat and What You Can Do About It. Cooper, who now runs the acclaimed meal program of the Berkeley, Calif., public schools, writes passionately against industrialized farms that "inhabit a flattened landscape dotted not with trees, farmhouses [and] animals . . . but with huge motorized vehicles." After meeting her, Dickman began to go to farmers' markets.

When Dickman arrived at Google in 2004, he says, "organic was the cool thing," and the company's chefs were buying organic whenever they could—even if that meant flying in Chilean nectarines. Dickman worked with the team to write new standards that place local before organic for all Google eateries. "You're using X amount of jet fuel to get it here, and that doesn't make sense," he says. "So forget the nectarines. Buy something local. Get some plums." Of course, this doesn't work in, say, Dublin, where Dickman also helped set up a Google café. ("Everything is flown in there," he said.) When I asked if he thought a restaurant as strictly local as Café 150 would be possible anywhere outside central California, he answered, glumly, "Probably not."

But others are trying. Restaurants from Cinque Terre in Portland, Maine, to Mozza in Los Angeles are run by cooks who strive always to find local products first. Some chefs are not only buying locally but actually growing the food. The two Blue Hill restaurants in New York—one in Manhattan and the other in Pocantico Hills—buy less than 20% of their ingredients from outside the New York region, according to chef Dan Barber. Much of both restaurants' food (including all the chicken and pork) is raised on about 20 acres next to the Pocantico Hills location. In the 3½ years since the farm was launched, Barber has become one of the nation's most eloquent prolocal spokesmen, not least because he makes local eating profitable (and delicious—his restaurants win raves). But his commitment to locality means that Barber can't always serve beef, since the quality and availability of steers in the Northeast are uneven.

40 Café 150 has access to local beef from Bassian Farms in San Jose, Calif., but the restaurant can't obtain everything it needs from the valley. Take salt. "There are salt flats a quarter-mile that way," said Keller, pointing to the horizon, "but they're for industrial purposes." So he buys salt "off the truck," from a food-service deliverer.

Still, apart from such staples, Café 150 is living up to its name. It never serves tropical fruits, and it has planted lemon and lime trees just outside to ensure local citrus. The restaurant grows many of its own herbs and makes its own ketchup. And last fall Café 150 jarred tomatoes and fruit so that even though it's March, Googlers can get a taste of the local harvest every day. Imagine that: a company as ostentatiously hip as Google canning fruit in its kitchens.

Could I do this? Could I operate my own "kitchen 150"?

Following Café 150's lead, I decided to keep basic dry goods like coffee, chocolate and spices. But since I have no interest in gardening (and no yard, for that matter—I live in an apartment), I needed a source of produce. I find farmers' markets inconvenient, if only because you have to pay each farmer separately for items, which can mean a lot of waiting in the cold. Then I heard about the farm shares run by Community Supported Agriculture (csa) programs.

They sounded a little lefty to me at first, but it turns out csas are a wonderfully market-driven idea: you join with others in your community to invest in a local farm. At the beginning of the season, members pay the farmer a lump sum. Each week, or perhaps once a month in the winter, the farm delivers fresh vegetables (and, for more money, items like fruit, eggs and flowers) to a central location. Prices vary widely depending on where you live. The csa in the Mott Haven neighborhood of the Bronx costs just $220 for five months for those with a low income (food stamps accepted). The csa run by Angelic Organics in Caledonia, Ill., starts at $600 for 20 weeks of vegetables and goes north of $1,000 when you add fruit.

There are some lefty aspects: You don't choose what the farmer grows. He does. You might get lettuce one week and then—if, say, a hailstorm hits the lettuce patch—none for several weeks after. Also, you're locked into a fixed amount of food each week, so if you don't feel like cooking for a couple nights in a row, you feel guilty. A farmer sweated over these beautiful ears of corn, and I'm going to throw them out so I can pick up riblets at Applebee's?

The benefit is that the food is affordable—for $40 a month at my csa, I get (to take February as an example) four bunches of winter greens, a head of red cabbage, 5 lbs. of apples, and about 2 lbs. each of beets, onions, carrots, turnips and Yukon Gold potatoes. The stuff is phenomenally fresh. I once discovered a nine-day-old head of lettuce from my CSA farm at the back of the refrigerator. Because it had come to me just 24 hours after being picked, it was still crisp.

But how local was my CSA farm? And was it organic?

Windflower Farm is in Valley Falls, N.Y., 185 miles northeast of my apartment. Mapquest calls it a 3½-hr. drive, but if you leave on a weekday at 5:30 P.M., as Windflower's Ted Blomgren and I did, it can take closer to five hours. That meets Gussow's definition of local—"within a day's leisurely drive"—although our drive through Manhattan wasn't leisurely.

Blomgren runs Windflower with his wife Jan. He is 46, and on the day we rode to the farm, he wore sandals and glasses. Ted, who has a degree from Cornell, is balding and studious, and might pass for a professor if he didn't have so much dirt under his toenails. Ted and Jan—who has lovely bright blue eyes perpetually fixed in a startled expression—have operated Windflower for eight years with their sons Nathaniel, 14, and Jacob, 11. On the day I visited last summer, I watched a barefoot Nathaniel walk to the henhouse to collect eggs in an old white bucket, as he did every day. I had been eating those eggs most days—that's how I had replaced cereal. Seeing Nate carry that bucket into the smelly humidity of the chicken coop, I realized I had never before felt so connected to my food. I had not only seen the chickens that produced my eggs but had also met the person who gathered them.

That's a core goal of CSAS—to remind you that your food originates in some place other than a grocery store. There are now some 1,200 csa farms in the U.S., according to the Robyn Van En Center at Wilson College in Pennsylvania. Van En helped start the first American csa at her Massachusetts farm in 1985 after hearing about the idea of farm shares from a Swiss friend. (You can find a csa near you at sites like localharvest.org.)

So I was finally eating local, and it tasted great. Ted's yellow wax beans last year were so crisp and oniony sweet you could eat them directly from the field. During the winter months, Ted has delivered sturdy vegetables from his cold storage that look as good as anything at Whole Foods and seem to taste better, if only because they remind me of a warm day on the farm. And yet I do worry that the Blomgrens aren't certified by the Federal Government as organic growers. They say they don't use synthetic pesticides or fertilizers, and Ted's policy is that any csa member can come to his farm to check his growing practices. "I couldn't show up at my local Agway and buy a jug of herbicide without it getting told to everybody," he said. Like many small farmers I met, Ted felt that organic certification would be too costly and time consuming.

Having met Ted, Jan and their sons—and having spent the night in their barn—I trust they don't use chemicals. But the Blomgrens don't grow fruit for the CSA. They buy it from other local growers, and most of them use sprays because of the humidity. Ted's hens were free-range—they strutted around eating the grass behind his house. But pastured chickens still require some grain feed, and the grain Ted bought was mostly conventionally grown, industrially processed corn.

I was deflated to hear that I had ingested chemicals with my fruit and eggs. But at this point I threw up my hands. If I wanted total purity, the only option was to grow my own food. Forget it. Farming is dirt-under-the-toenails hard work, and the Blomgrens are by no means making a vast fortune.

But I had arrived at an answer to my question: I prefer local to organic, even with the concessions local farmers must make. I realize there's something romantic about the desire to know exactly where your food is from. Among true agrarians, that desire carries a reactionary strain, a suspicion of modernity. "Instead of relying on the accumulated wisdom of a cuisine, or even on the wisdom of our senses, we rely on expert opinion," journalist Michael Pollan wrote in last year's acclaimed book The Omnivore's Dilemma. "We place our faith in science to sort out what culture once did." But science should trump culture on matters of nutrition. The problem is that science offers no clear guidelines yet on how beneficial organic food is.

When asked years ago whether she preferred butter or margarine, Gussow famously remarked, "I trust cows more than chemists." For my part, I do not. I will still go to Whole Foods to buy the mass-produced Organic Food Bars I eat for breakfast when I don't have time for eggs. I am happy that food scientists are finding ways to produce everyday products like cereal with organic ingredients. (How about organic Froot Loops? I have a weakness for Froot Loops late at night.) But when it comes to my basic ingredients—literally, my "whole" foods rather than my convenience foods—I would still rather know the person who collects my eggs or grows my lettuce or picks my apples than buy 100% organic eggs or lettuce or apples from an anonymous megafarm at the supermarket. Choosing local when I can makes me feel more rooted, and (in part because of that feeling, no doubt) local food tastes better.

Eating locally also seems safer. Ted's neighbors and customers can see how he farms. That transparency doesn't exist with, say, spinach bagged by a distant agribusiness. I help keep Ted in business, and he helps keep me fed—and the elegance and sustainability of that exchange make more sense to me than gambling on faceless producers who stamp organic on a package thousands of miles from my home. I'm not a purist about these choices—I ate a Filet-O-Fish at McDonald's on the way to Ted's farm. But in general, I have decided that you are where you eat.

Reflect & Write

- ❑ How does the Whole Foods supermarket chain function as a character in this article? How does Cloud use references to Whole Foods to support his argument?
- ❑ How does Cloud eventually answer his local-versus-organic question? What motivates his decision?
- ❑ Look at the paragraph where Cloud describes Ted and his farm. What sort of language and imagery does he use? What effect does that have on his argument?
- ❑ Read through a copy of this article with two highlighters in hand. Highlight Cloud's primary research in yellow and his secondary research in blue. When does he use each type of research to advance his argument? Which seems to play a larger role in what he finally decides at the end of this article?
- ❑ **Write.** Read through the article and list out the pros and cons of locavorism and the organic food movement. Use that information to create an information graphic to accompany this article. Where would you put it in the structure of the essay? To what extent would visual evidence like this fit with the style that Cloud adopts in this essay?

Peter Menzel *and* **Faith d'Aluisio** *In 2005, photojournalist Peter Menzel and his wife, writer Faith d'Aluisio, published* Hungry Planet, *an extensive look at eating habits around the world through photographs and essays. This work received numerous awards, including the 2006 James Beard Foundation award for Book of the Year and the 2006 Harry Chapin World Book of the Year award from the World Media Foundation. A selection of the images from* Hungry Planet *were published by* Time *magazine as a photo essay called "What the World Eats," with the subtitle "What's on family dinner tables around the globe?" The images and captions below are taken from that photo essay.*

FIGURE 10.11. United States: The Revis family of North Carolina
Food expenditure for one week: $341.98
Favorite foods: spaghetti, potatoes, sesame chicken

FIGURE 10.12. China: The Dong family of Beijing
Food expenditure for one week: 1,233.76 Yuan or $155.06
Favorite foods: fried shredded pork with sweet and sour sauce

FIGURE 10.13. Mexico: The Casales family of Cuernavaca
Food expenditure for one week: 1,862.78 Mexican Pesos or $189.09
Favorite foods: pizza, crab, pasta, chicken

FIGURE 10.14. Chad: The Aboubakar family of Breidjing Camp
Food expenditure for one week: 685 CFA Francs or $1.23
Favorite foods: soup with fresh sheep meat

Reflect & Write

- ❑ Look carefully at the captions, reproduced as they originally appeared in the *Time* photo essay. What information is included? Judging by this information, what types of comparisons does the photo essay encourage the readers to make between the different families?
- ❑ Consider the staging of the food and the use of space. How do these elements contribute to each photograph's argument?
- ❑ Which photograph surprised you the most? Why? Did any of them seem to reinforce common stereotypes? Did any of them resist those stereotypes?
- ❑ **Write.** First, choose one of the pictures above and write a rhetorical analysis of its argument, referring to specific elements in the photo and caption as evidence. Then, find a copy of *Hungry Planet* in your local library or bookstore. Look through the book to find the photo you selected and examine it within this different context, reading through the text that accompanies it in *Hungry Planet* as well. Now, as an addendum to your initial analysis, write a reflection on how your understanding of the argument of the photograph changes with the different rhetorical situations. Be sure to take into account the issue of audience, purpose, and genre (book versus online photo essay) in your writing.

Seeing Connections
Look at the Prewriting Checklist on page 69 for strategies for analyzing a photograph.

■ *In the October 26, 2009, edition of the* New York Times, *the editors posed the following questions to foster debate: "What will drive the next Green Revolution? Is genetically modified food an answer to world hunger? Are there other factors that will make a difference in food production?" Below are excerpts from the responses received from a select group of nutritionists, economists, activists, and scholars.*

Can Biotech Food Cure World Hunger?

By The Editors

Carla Gottgens/Bloomberg A crop of genetically modified canola grows in a field in Lake Bolac, in the Western District of Victoria, Australia, Sept. 29, 2009.

With food prices remaining high in developing countries, the United Nations estimates that the number of hungry people around the world could increase by 100 million in 2009 and pass the one billion mark. A summit of world leaders in Rome scheduled for November will set an agenda for ways to reduce hunger and increase investment in agriculture development in poor countries.

What will drive the next Green Revolution? Is genetically modified food an answer to world hunger? Are there other factors that will make a difference in food production?

- Paul Collier, economist, Oxford University
- Vandana Shiva, activist and author
- Per Pinstrup-Andersen, professor of nutrition and public policy, Cornell
- Raj Patel, Institute for Food and Development Policy
- Jonathan Foley, University of Minnesota
- Michael J. Roberts, economist, North Carolina State University

Put Aside Prejudices

Paul Collier *is a professor of economics at Oxford University and the director of the Center for the Study of African Economies. He is the author of "The Bottom Billion: Why the Poorest Countries Are Failing and What Can Be Done About It."?*

The debate over genetically modified crops and food has been contaminated by political and aesthetic prejudices: hostility to U.S. corporations, fear of big science and romanticism about local, organic production.

Refusing genetic modification makes a difficult problem more daunting.

Food supply is too important to be the plaything of these prejudices. If there is not enough food we know who will go hungry.

Genetic modification is analogous to nuclear power: nobody loves it, but climate change has made its adoption imperative. As Africa's climate deteriorates, it will need to accelerate crop adaptation. As population grows it will need to raise yields. Genetic modification offers both faster crop adaptation and a biological, rather than chemical, approach to yield increases.

Opponents talk darkly of risks but provide no scientific basis for their amorphous expressions of concern. Meanwhile the true risks are mounting. Over the past decade global food demand has risen more rapidly than expected. Supply may not keep pace with demand, inducing rising prices and periodic spikes. If this happens there is a risk that the children of the urban poor will suffer prolonged bouts of malnutrition.

African governments are now recognizing that by imitating the European ban on genetic modification they have not reduced the risks facing their societies but increased them. Thirteen years, during which there could have been research on African crops, have been wasted. Africa has been in thrall to Europe, and Europe has been in thrall to populism.

Genetic modification alone will not solve the food problem: like climate change, there is no single solution. But continuing refusal to use it is making a difficult problem yet more daunting.

The Failure of Gene-Altered Crops?

***Vandana Shiva** is the founder of Navdanya, the movement of 500,000 seed keepers and organic farmers in India. She is author of numerous books, including "The Violence of the Green Revolution" and "Soil, Not Oil."*

Food security over the next two decades will have to be built on ecological security and climate resilience. We need the real green revolution, not a second "Green Revolution" based on genetic engineering.?

We need biodiversity intensification that works with nature's nutrient and water cycles, not against them.

Genetic engineering has not increased yields. Recent research by Doug Gurian-Sherman of the Union of Concerned Scientists published as a study "Failure to Yield" has shown that in a nearly 20 year record, genetically engineered crops have not increased yields. The study did not find significantly increased yields from crops engineered for herbicide tolerance or crops engineered to be insect-resistant.

The International Assessment of Agricultural Science and Technology for Development carried out by 400 scientists over four years has also concluded that genetic engineering does not hold much promise. Instead, small farms based on principles of agriecology and sustainability produce more food.

That is why I an so disappointed that the Gates Foundation in its global development program is supporting the use of genetically modified crops in Africa.

Green revolution technologies and strategies, reliant on monoculture and chemical fertilizers and pesticides, have destroyed biodiversity, which has in many places led to a decline in nutrition output per acre.

As I have shown in my book "Soil, Not Oil," industrial systems of food production are also a major contributor to greenhouse gas emissions and climate change. Industrial monocultures are more vulnerable to climate change since they reduce soil organic matter which is vital for moisture conservation and resilience to draught.

The claim by the genetic engineering industry that without genetically modified food we cannot respond to climate change is simply false. Climate resilient traits in crops have been evolved by farmers over centuries. In the community seed banks that I have helped create through the Navdanya movement, we have seeds for drought resistance, flood resistance and salt tolerance. This is the biological capital for the real green revolution.

The gene giants are now pirating and patenting the

collective and cumulative innovation of Third World farmers. Patent monopolies on seed cannot create food security. They can only push small farmers in debt.

20 The green revolution that we are building through Navdanya is based on conserving biodiversity and conserving water while increasing food production per acre. What we need is biodiversity intensification, not chemical intensification. What we need is to work with nature's nutrient cycles and hydrological cycle, not against them. It is time to put small farmers, especially women, at the heart of this process.

When Cheap Water and Oil Disappear

***Raj Patel** is a fellow at the Institute for Food and Development Policy, and author of "Stuffed and Starved".*

The U.S. leads the world in genetically modified agricultural technology, yet one in eight Americans is hungry. Last year, with bumper harvests, more than a billion people ate less than 1,900 calories per day. The cause of hunger today isn't a shortage of food—it's poverty.

> Agriculture will need to be much more regionally controlled and locally adapted.

Addressing that will require not new agricultural technology, but a political commitment to making food a human right.

We do, however, need to transform the way we farm. Today's industrial agriculture depends on fossil fuels and abundant water. The growing and processing of food for the average American every year takes the equivalent of more than 500 gallons of oil. The future will see both cheap water and oil disappear.

25 So how should we farm tomorrow? To answer this, we'll need the very best independent and peer-reviewed science. In 2005, the World Bank's chief scientist, Robert Watson, brought together leading natural and social scientists, representatives from government (including the U.S.), private sector and non-governmental organizations to ask how we'd feed the world in 2050, when there will be nine billion of us.

Over three years, more than 400 experts worked on a sobering report which has recently been published as "Agriculture at a Crossroads."

The scientists concluded that genetically modified crops had failed to show much promise in feeding the world. Instead, the study suggested that to feed the world, we need both political and technological change. Tomorrow's agriculture will need to be much more regionally controlled and locally adapted, and will need a diversity of approaches to meet the challenges of climate change and resource scarcity.

Among the farming techniques endorsed by the report is agroecology, which builds soil, insect and plant ecology. The result is a farming system that uses water frugally, sequesters vast amounts of carbon and doesn't require external inputs.

This is cutting edge science, but it isn't terribly profitable for large U.S.-based agricultural corporations. Perhaps that explains why, despite strong support for this report among governments overseas, the U.S. government last year refused to endorse it.

The Third Way

***Jonathan Foley** is the director of the new Institute on the Environment at the University of Minnesota. His research is focused on global land use, agriculture and climate.*

The future of agriculture must address several goals simultaneously. First, it now appears that we will have to double world food production in the next 40 years given continued population growth, increasing meat consumption and pressure from biofuels.

> You're either with Michael Pollan or you're with Monsanto, but neither paradigm can fully meet our needs.

We will also have to dramatically reduce the environmental impacts of our farming practices, which have caused widespread damage to soils, ecosystems, watersheds and even the atmosphere. In fact, agriculture's impacts rival climate change as a top environmental concern.

We will also have to improve food security for the world's poor. While the Green Revolution of the 1960s made it possible to feed hundreds of millions more people than in earlier eras, the number of undernourished in the world has started to rise again.

30 Finally, we will have to increase the resilience of agriculture. Today, our high-efficiency, globalized world has many benefits, but it is vulnerable to disruption, whether from drought, disease or price spikes.

We must start building more resilience into food systems to better insulate us from future shocks.

Currently, there are two paradigms of agriculture being widely promoted: local and organic systems versus globalized and industrialized agriculture. Each has fervent followers and critics. Genuine discourse has broken down: You're either with Michael Pollan or you're with Monsanto. But neither of these paradigms, standing alone, can fully meet our needs.

Organic agriculture teaches us important lessons about soils, nutrients and pest management. And local agriculture connects people back to their food system. Unfortunately, certified organic food provides less than 1 percent of the world's calories, mostly to the wealthy. It is hard to imagine organic farming scaling up to feed 9 billion.

Globalized and industrialized agriculture have benefits of economic scalability, high output and low labor demands. Overall, the Green Revolution has been a huge success. Without it, billions of people would have starved. However, these successes have come with tremendous environmental and social costs, which cannot be sustained.

Rather than voting for just one solution, we need a third way to solve the crisis. Let's take ideas from both sides, creating new, hybrid solutions that boost production, conserve resources and build a more sustainable and scalable agriculture.

There are many promising avenues to pursue: precision agriculture, mixed with high-output composting and organic soil remedies; drip irrigation, plus buffer strips to reduce erosion and pollution; and new crop varieties that reduce water and fertilizer demand. In this context, the careful use of genetically modified crops may be appropriate, after careful public review.

A new "third way" for agriculture is not only possible, it is necessary. Let's start by ditching the rhetoric, and start bridging the old divides. Our problems are huge, and they will require everyone at the table, working together toward solutions.

Reflect & Write

- ❑ In their commentaries, Collier and Shiva present opposing viewpoints. Which is the most persuasive? Why? Does it have to do with facts? Evidence? Reasoning? Structure of argument? Voice? *Pathos* appeal? *Ethos*? Other factors?
- ❑ How does Shiva rely on *ethos* to bolster her argument? To what end? Find at least two points in her piece where she does so.
- ❑ How does Patel establish a different focus in his opening paragraphs from Collier and Shiva? How is this difference in focus maintained throughout his commentary? Is this more likely or less likely to appeal to his audience? Why?
- ❑ What does Foley mean by "the third way"? What debate is he tapping into? What are his solutions?
- ❑ **Write.** Choose one of the four selections from this debate and choose the point of view with which you least agree. Write a response to that stance in which you articulate your own position and complicate the writer's original argument. Be sure to use direct quotes from the text in your response.

PERSPECTIVES ON THE ISSUE

1. In Kluger's essay, he looks specifically at how American children suffer from a culture of poor eating practices. On his blog, Raj Patel wrote an entry with a similar premise, but which he took in a different direction. Read his April 9, 2010 post, "Down with the Clown," linked through the *Envision* website. Then write a response to his post that links your assessment of his call to action with the material contained in the Kluger and Obama reading you did in this chapter.
www.pearsonhighered.com/envision/253

2. Visit food bloggist Nora Sherman's Website, linked through the *Envision* Website, and look at examples of posts and photos from her food blog. Now, keep your own food blog for a week, writing entries and taking photos styled on Sherman's work. After a week, share your blog posts with the class and write a brief reflection about the process of food blogging and what you learned about yourself and your relationship to food by this experience.
www.pearsonhighered.com/envision/254a

3. Watch the video of Michelle Obama delivering her announcement of the Let's Move Project, linked through the Envision Website. As you watch, take notes, comparing it to the content and composition of the Let's Move Launch speech you read in this chapter. How is the rhetorical situation of the two pieces different? How did Obama modify her script for the Website version? What did she emphasize more or less in her revision? Think also about her delivery and the staging of the Website video. What images were chosen, how were they arranged, and how do they complement oral delivery? Use these notes to produce a comparative analysis essay of the two videos.
www.pearsonhighered.com/envision/254b

FROM READING TO RESEARCH

1. Working in small groups, create your own contribution to the "What the World Eats" series by taking a "What the American College Student Eats" photograph. Consider the following: Who should be in the photo? What location should you use? What foods should you represent? How should you arrange and stage them? After taking your photograph, write a caption similar to the ones found on the pictures above. Print out your photo and mount it and the caption on foam board for a class exhibit. Tour the exhibit with your class and then compare your different interpretations of the typical college diet. Discuss the results of your field research with the class.

2. Do your own primary research about American food culture by considering the visual rhetoric of food advertisements. Using the links through the *Envision* Website and the questions found in Chapter 2, collect a set of ads and analyze the way in which they produce an argument about food consumption to their audience. Your ads should have a clear relationship to one another, for instance: ads for a single brand or type of food spanning several decades; contemporary food ads aimed at children (fast food, cereal, even vitamins); ads from a single food industry, such as dairy farmers or the meat industry; or even weight-loss program ads. Write a rhetorical analysis in which you make a strong claim about how these ads use specific rhetorical strategies to make an argument to the consumers about the food they eat.
www.pearsonhighered.com/envision/254c

3. One term that the scholars in "Can Biotech Food Cure World Hunger?" avoid is commonly used by those who criticize genetically modified foods: "Frankenfood." Research this term to develop an understanding of the larger controversies about genetically modified foods. Identify the most prominent contributors to this scholarly conversation and read one article by each one to get an overview of the controversy. Now, using the structure found in Debatepedia as a model (linked through the *Envision* Website), write a brief summary of the controversy, and then use a two-column format to list out some of the most common claims for and against the use of genetically modified foods. Be sure to include references to your sources to support each claim. You should have at least four pros and four cons in your chart.
www.pearsonhighered.com/envision/254d

GREENING CULTURE

How green are you? In today's culture, more and more people are inscribing everyday actions with a series of choices that directly speak to what *National Geographic*'s Green Guide calls "your eco-smarts." Do you use paper or plastic? Or do you bring your own bag? Do you drive alone? Rideshare? Take the bus or train? Ride a bicycle? Drive a hybrid? An electric car? An SUV? Do you eat local or organic? Do you eat seasonal? Do you turn off your lights when you leave the house? Do you use compact fluorescent bulbs? The list of choices is endless, the pressure to choose green increasing every day. As Alex Steffan argues in the article reproduced in this section, "Green has become the new black," and it is fashionable to do the "green thing". But, as many of the authors found in this section ask, is being green so trendy that it empties these actions of any meaningful environmental impact? Are you really doing good by going green?

It is not just the individual who is making such choices. In the larger community, we find retailers, public services, and organizations pushing the same environmental agenda. Consider the snapshot from daily life shown in Figures 10.15–10.17. Perhaps you might have seen reminders spray-painted in public areas, such as the one in Figure 10.15 from a parking lot in Palo Alto, California, encouraging shoppers to use their own

FIGURE 10.15. The public works department in Palo Alto, California, provides downtown shoppers with a reminder to go green.

Source: © Christine L. Alfano, 2010

FIGURE 10.16. This Starbucks container encourages its customers to act green.

Source: © Christine L. Alfano, 2010

bags for their purchases. In the same community, people are reminded by colorful stenciling over sewer grates that what goes down there "flows to the bay," as a means of discouraging people from dumping toxins or garbage into the sewer. Or perhaps you see your restaurants going green. Some campus dining halls have moved to corn-based utensils and away from plastic takeout containers to attack waste products, encouraging recycling and composting with separate trash receptacles. One Starbucks in Connecticut took an even more aggressive step toward reducing waste, setting up a collection container, seen in Figure 10.16, where customers could place their paper waste so employees could recycle the paper or reuse the coffee sleeves instead of just contributing to landfill. Even public utilities and city organizations participate in the Green Movement. Gas and electric companies across the United States provide rebates for buying Energy Star-certified appliances. Many states feature "carpool lanes" on highways to encourage ride sharing that even single-passenger hybrids are allowed to use as a reward for being environmentally friendly. In encouraging their consumers to make eco-friendly choices, such organizations tap directly into the rhetoric of the Green Movement, as we can see exemplified in Figure 10.17, a public service advertisement from a side of a bus that connects using public transit with stopping global warming.

In the section that follows, we will look carefully at the "greening" of American culture, both in terms of the environmental issues driving it and the controversies and contradictions embedded within it. We'll read authors like Al Gore who cast the fight against global warming as a moral imperative; then we'll compare Gore's stance to that of his critics, such as Bjørn Lomborg, who suggests that contemporary environmentalist rhetoric often misdirects attention away from important facts, short-circuiting realistic ways to address climate change. We'll distinguish between green advertising and "greenwashing," namely the way that companies clothe themselves in the rhetoric of environmentalism as a way of improving *ethos* without really substantially changing their practices. We'll examine Earth Day, both as a way to celebrate our relation to the Earth and as a platform for Big Business to assume an environmentally friendly pose. Lastly, we'll look to the future, toward new solutions for sustainable energies and practices designed to curb climate change and move people toward a healthier coexistence with their environment.

FIGURE 10.17. This public service advertisement, found on the side of a local bus, relates the rider's transportation choices to a larger green agenda.

Source: © Christine L. Alfano, 2010

Reflect & Write

- ❑ What sort of appeal drives the ad shown in Figure 10.15? How would its argument have changed if it had been designed to rely on a different appeal?
- ❑ The sign shown in Figure 10.16 was created by the barristas at the local Starbucks, not the company itself. If Starbucks were to endorse this sort of recycling campaign, how would you suggest a revision of this sign to incorporate more of the corporate *ethos* and branding?
- ❑ **Write.** Write a memo to a public organization or retailer in which you suggest a sign that promotes a green practice such as the one in Figure 10.17. Be sure to include a sketch for the design of the sign as well as a rationale for why that organization would benefit from encouraging eco-friendly behavior from its patrons.

Al Gore *In 2006, former vice president Al Gore's long-time crusade against global warming was brought to the big screen by director Davis Guggenheim, who transformed the PowerPoint slideshow that Gore had presented over a thousand times across the United States into a full-length documentary entitled* An Inconvenient Truth. *That year, Gore also published a book by the same title, which included additional data and analysis, from which the figures below are taken.*

Information Graphics from An Inconvenient Truth

This is what would happen to Florida.

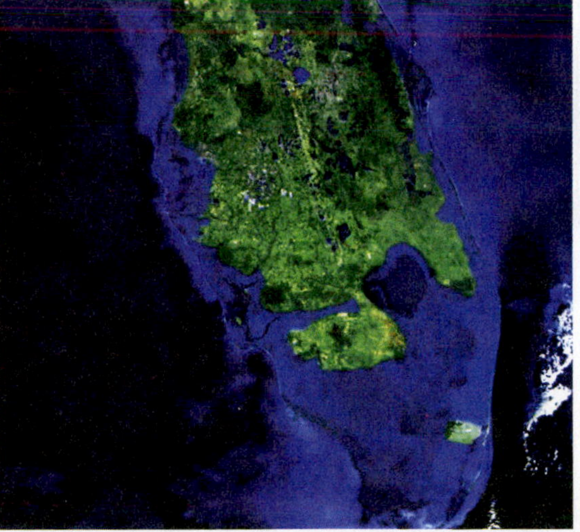

FIGURE 10.18. These satellite images represent a before-and-after projection of how a marked increase in sea levels due to global warming could impact Florida's coastlines and topography.

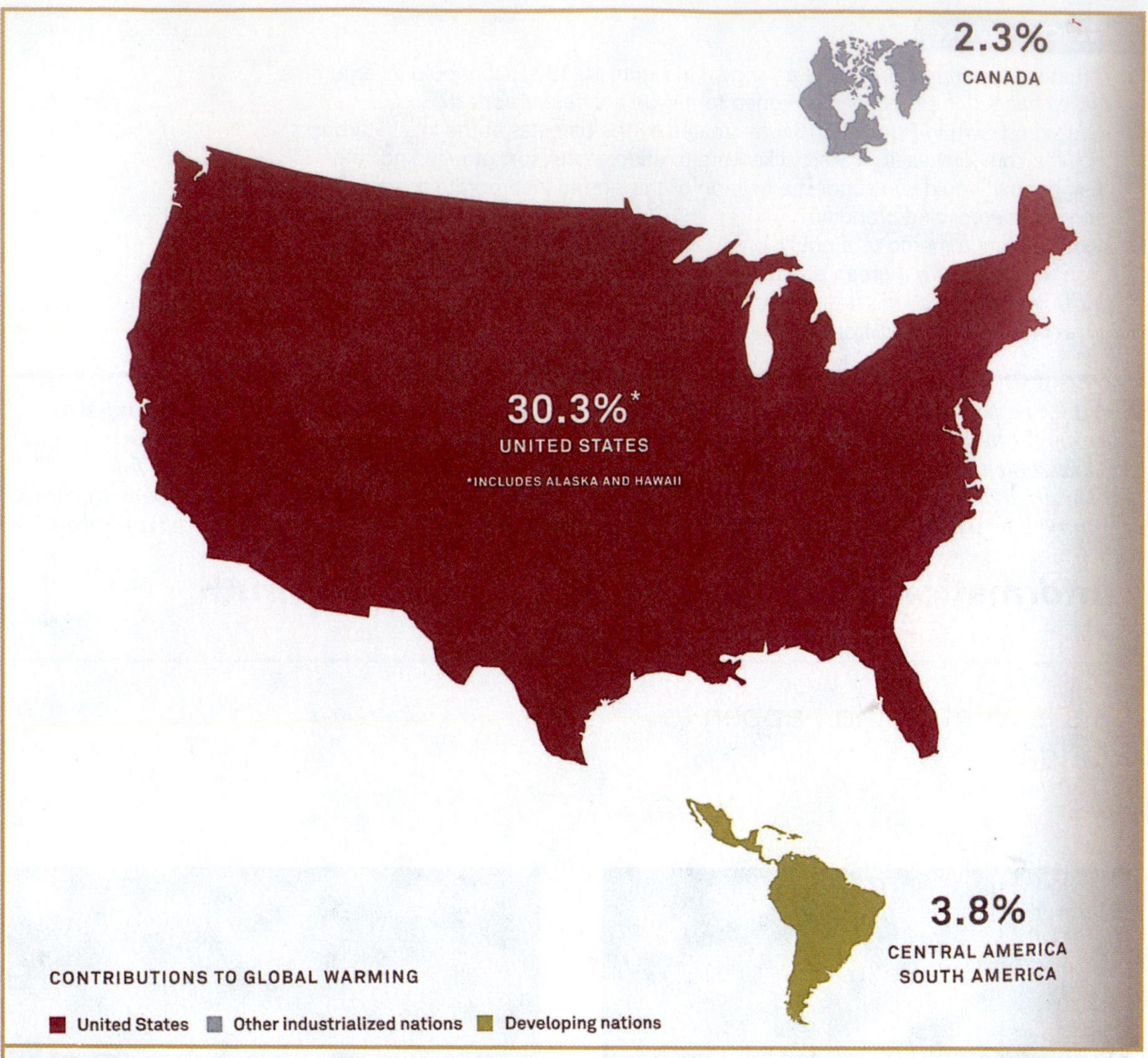

FIGURE 10.19. This graphic maps contribution to global warming by nation and region.

Reflect & Write

- ❑ How does the map in Figure 10.18 construct its argument about every nation's relative contribution to global warming? Consider the use of layout, color, text, scale, and perspective. Who is the central protagonist of this visual argument? How can you tell?
- ❑ Look carefully at the satellite image in Figure 10.19. How does the before-and-after structure underscore the point Gore is trying to make with his rendering of what Florida might look like after a rise in sea level? How does his choice to use satellite imagery rather than an illustration such as seen in Figure 10.18 reflect a strategic decision? How would this argument have been different if it had been made through a drawn map or if there had been no comparative image?

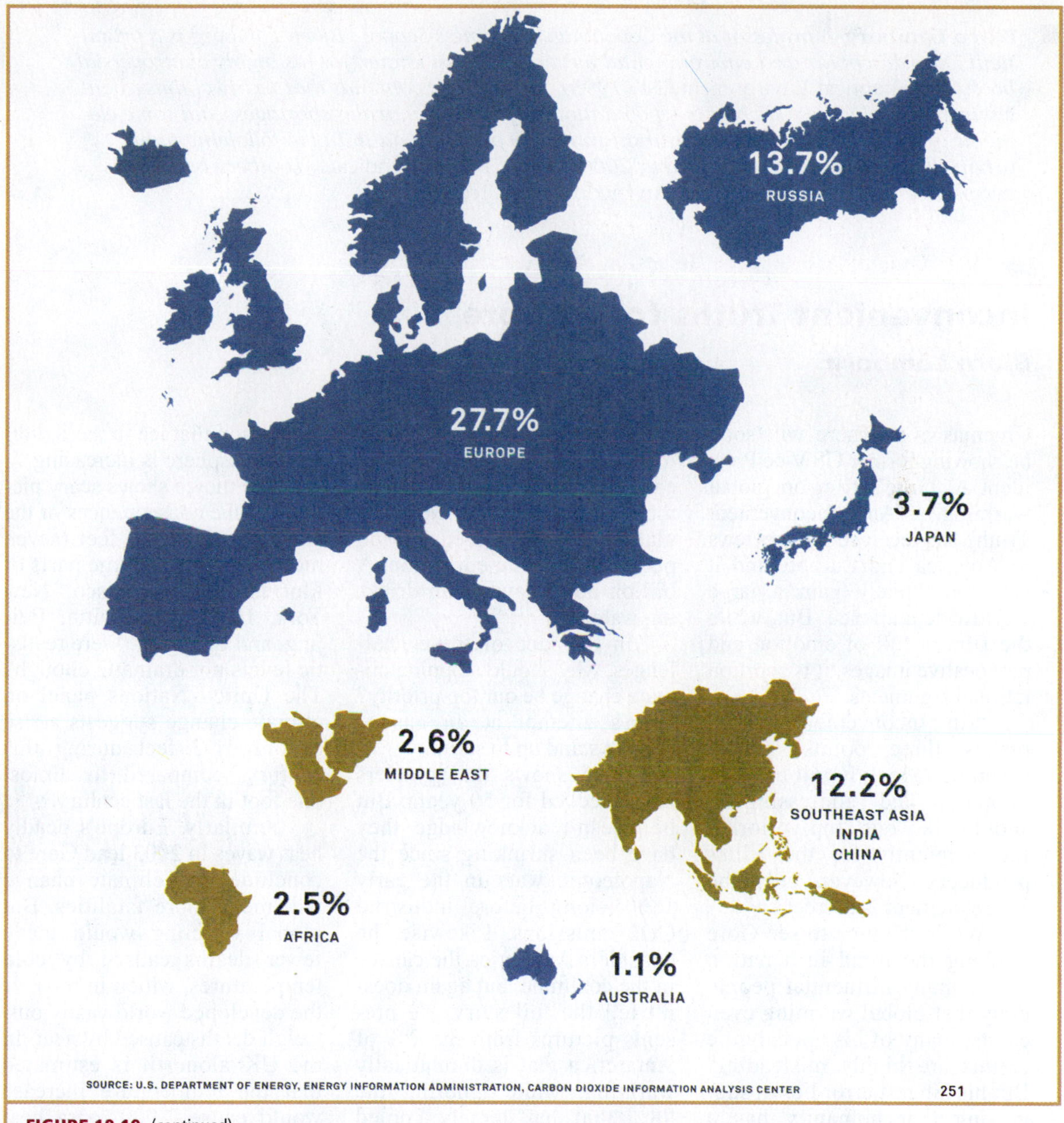

FIGURE 10.19. (continued)

- ❑ **Write.** Take the data found in Figure 10.18 and render it in a different form—as a bar graph, pie chart, line graph, or other information graphic. Then also convert it into a paragraph that uses the data compellingly to spotlight the United States' contributions to global warming. How do these different modes of delivery change the way you construct the argument? Which one would have the greatest impact on the audience? In what context?

Bjørn Lomborg *A professor at the Copenhagen Business School , Bjørn Lomborg is a prominent Danish scholar and environmental writer. He is best known for his highly controversial book,* The Skeptical Environmentalist *(1998), in which he contends that many claims about environmental issues (such as overpopulation, deforestation, water shortages, and some elements of global warming) are unsubstantiated by pertinent data. In the following piece, originally published in the September 2006 issue of* Project Syndicate, *Lomberg brings this perspective to bear on Gore's film,* An Inconvenient Truth.

Inconvenient Truths for Al Gore

Bjørn Lomborg

Cinemas everywhere will soon be showing former US Vice President Al Gore's film on global warming. "An Inconvenient Truth" has received rave reviews in America and Europe, and it will most likely gain a large worldwide audience. But, while the film is full of emotion and provocative images, it is short on rational arguments.

"An Inconvenient Truth" makes three points: global warming is real; it will be catastrophic; and addressing it should be our top priority. Inconveniently for the film's producers, however, only the first statement is correct.

While it's nice to see Gore bucking the trend in a nation where many influential people deny that global warming even exists, many of his apocalyptic claims are highly misleading. But his biggest error lies in suggesting that humanity has a moral imperative to act on climate change because we realize there is a problem. This seems naïve, even disingenuous.

We know of many vast global challenges that we could easily solve. Preventable diseases like HIV, diarrhea, and malaria take 15 million lives each year. Malnutrition afflicts more than half the world's population. Eight hundred million people lack basic education. A billion don't have clean drinking water.

5 In the face of these challenges, why should stopping climate change be our top priority? Gore's attempt at an answer doesn't stand up to scrutiny.

Gore shows that glaciers have receded for 50 years. But he doesn't acknowledge they have been shrinking since the Napoleonic wars in the early 1800's–long before industrial CO2 emissions. Likewise, he considers Antarctica the canary in the coalmine, but again doesn't tell the full story. He presents pictures from the 2% of Antarctica that is dramatically warming, while ignoring the 98% that has largely cooled over the past 35 years. The UN climate panel estimates that Antarctica's snow mass will actually increase during this century. And, whereas Gore points to shrinking sea ice in the Northern Hemisphere, he fails to mention that ice in the Southern Hemisphere is increasing.

The movie shows scary pictures of the consequences of the sea level rising 20 feet (seven meters), flooding large parts of Florida, San Francisco, New York, Holland, Calcutta, Beijing, and Shanghai. Were realistic levels not dramatic enough? The United Nations panel on climate change suggests a rise of only 1-2 feet during this century, compared to almost one foot in the last century.

Similarly, Europe's deadly heat waves in 2003 lead Gore to conclude that climate change will mean more fatalities. But global warming would mean fewer deaths caused by cold temperatures, which in most of the developed world vastly outweigh deaths caused by heat. In the UK alone, it is estimated that the temperature increase would cause 2,000 extra heat deaths by 2050, but result in 20,000 fewer cold deaths.

Financial losses from weather events have increased dramatically over the past 45 years, which Gore attributes to global warming. But all or almost all of this increase comes from more people with more possessions living closer to harm's way. If all hurricanes had hit the US with today's demographics, the biggest damage would have been caused not by Katrina, but by a hurricane in 1926. Allowing for changes in the number of people and their wealth, flood losses have actually decreased slightly.

10 The movie invites viewers to conclude that global warming caused Hurricane Katrina, with Gore claiming that the warm Caribbean waters made the storm stronger. But when Katrina made landfall, it was not a catastrophic Category 5 hurricane; it was a milder Category 3. In fact, there is no scientific consensus that global warming makes hurricanes more destructive, as he claims. The author that Gore himself relies on says that it would be "absurd to attribute the Katrina disaster to global warming."

After presenting the case for the potentially catastrophic effects of climate change, Gore unveils his solution: the world should embrace the Kyoto Protocol, which aims to cut carbon emissions in the developed countries by 30% by 2010.

But even if every nation signed up to Kyoto, it would merely postpone warming by six years in 2100, at an annual cost of $150 billion. Kyoto would not have saved New Orleans from Hurricane Katrina. But improved levees and maintenance could have. While Gore was campaigning for Kyoto in the 1990's, a better use of resources would have been to bolster hurricane defenses.

Indeed, the real issue is using resources wisely. Kyoto won't stop developing countries from being hardest hit by climate change, for the simple reason that they have warmer climates and fewer resources. But these nations have pressing problems that we could readily solve. According to UN estimates, for $75 billion a year—half the cost of implementing the Kyoto Protocol—we could provide clean drinking water, sanitation, basic health care, and education to every single human being on Earth. Shouldn't that be a higher priority?

Recent hurricanes killed thousands in Haiti, and not in Florida, because Haiti is poor and cannot afford even basic preventive measures. Combating disease, hunger, and polluted water would bring immediate benefits to millions and allow poorer countries to increase productivity and break the cycle of poverty. That, in turn, would make their inhabitants less vulnerable to climate fluctuations.

15 At the climax of his movie, Gore argues that future generations will chastise us for not having committed ourselves to the Kyoto Protocol. More likely, they will wonder why, in a world overflowing with "inconvenient truths," Gore focused on the one where we could achieve the least good for the highest cost.

Reflect & Write

- ❑ Find the part of Lomborg's essay where he summarizes Gore's film and then moves to critique. Is this a rhetorically effective moment in the essay?
- ❑ What strategy does Lomborg use to undermine the credibility of *An Inconvenient Truth*? Look for structural repetition in how he addresses different aspects of his argument. What purpose does such a repetition serve?
- ❑ Some might argue that Lomborg's essay intends less to critique Gore than to provide Lomberg with a means to advance his own political opinions. Do you agree with this claim? What parts of the essay either support or negate it?
- ❑ **Write.** Lomborg writes that "[Gore's] biggest error lies in suggesting that humanity has a moral imperative to act on climate change because we realize there is a problem." Write a brief response to this argument. Where does morality fall in discussions of environmental issues? Do you think that humanity has a moral imperative to act on climate change?

Seeing Connections

For another perspective on Al Gore's Inconvenient Truth, see Bret Schulte's "Saying it in Cinema" (pages 122–124).

Elizabeth Kolbert *A staff writer for* The New Yorker, *Elizabeth Kolbert has written extensively on environmental issues and climate change. In fact, her series* "The Climate of Man," *which addresses the issue of global warming, won many awards, including the 2006 National Magazine Award for Public Interest and the 2006 National Academics Communication Award. Her other work on this subject includes* Field Notes from a Catastrophe: Man, Nature, and Climate Change *(2006). In the following article, which was published in the June 19, 2006, issue of the* New Statesman, *Kolbert uses Al Gore's* An Inconvenient Truth *as a starting point for discussing whether "going green" is antithetical to American culture.*

Can America Go Green?

Elizabeth Kolbert

In *An Inconvenient Truth*, perhaps the world's first film based on a PowerPoint presentation, Al Gore plays himself: a sometimes brooding, sometimes funny ex-politician come to deliver a message about "a planetary emergency". He gives an impressive performance, one that the American press—a group that never before seemed terribly sympathetic to the former vice-president—has greeted with almost universal enthusiasm. (In two fairly representative examples: the *New York Times* described Gore as "the surprisingly engaging vehicle for some very disturbing information", while *USA Today* called the documentary a showcase for his "dedication, warmth and, yes, charm".) *An Inconvenient Truth* has prompted a great deal of discussion in the United States about what might have happened had Gore revealed a few more of the qualities of his on-screen persona while out campaigning in 2000, and even more speculation about whether he is preparing to run again in 2008.

Perhaps not surprisingly, the strongest claims about the film's reception have come from the star himself. Speaking last month on the popular public radio show *Fresh Air*, Gore said that recent events had made him "optimistic" that American attitudes towards global warming were finally changing. The US political system, he further observed, "shares one thing in common with the climate system. It's non-linear. It can appear to move at a glacier's pace and then, after crossing a tipping point, it can suddenly move rapidly into a completely new pattern. I've seen that happen."

Certainly, there are few questions more urgent than how—and how quickly—the US will react to climate change. As is well known, Americans represent less than 5 per cent of the world's population, and yet they produce roughly 25 per cent of its carbon-dioxide emissions. The country is one of only two industrialised nations that has rejected the Kyoto Protocol and, with it, mandatory emissions cuts. (The other is Australia.) Even as European leaders are pushing for negotiations to begin on a post-Kyoto treaty, the US has refused to participate. And on and on. At this point, it is almost impossible to imagine how the world will avoid disastrous climate impacts without a fundamental, and prompt, change in US policy.

Gore's professed optimism that such a change is at hand, which is shared, at least for the purposes of public consumption, by many of the country's leading environmentalists, rests on what might be called the democratic (with a small "d") imperative. As Gore points out, accurately enough, companies such as ExxonMobil and General Motors, working in concert with right-wing think-tanks such as the George C Marshall Institute, have spent millions of dollars trying systematically to obscure the facts. (Indeed, as if on cue, the Competitive Enterprise Institute greeted the première of Gore's movie with a pair of 60-second TV ads full of jumping gazelles and kids skipping rope, carrying the tag line: "Carbon dioxide: they call it pollution; we call it life.") Add to this an American press corps axiomatically devoted to the notion of "balance", and the result has been confusion. But as soon as Americans understand "the inconvenient truth" about climate change, Gore has asserted, they'll do the right thing.

5 Making generalisations about an entire nation is always a dubious enterprise, and this is especially true of the US. The modern environmental movement was born in America and enjoyed its first successes there. Even under George W Bush—perhaps the most polluter-

friendly president in the nation's history—the country still spends more money than any other on environmental science; as the president likes to boast, this year alone, the federal government will spend roughly \$2bn on climate research and monitoring. Britain's Met Office has the Hadley Centre: the US supports three climate modelling teams—one at Nasa, the second at the National Oceanic and Atmospheric Administration (NOAA) and the third at the National Centre for Atmospheric Research (NCAR).

All around the country there are towns and cities and state governments that are actively working to reduce their emissions in spite of—or perhaps one should say because of—federal inaction. In February 2005 the mayor of Seattle, Greg Nickels, began to circulate the "US Mayors Climate Protection Agreement", which calls on cities to "strive to meet or beat the Kyoto Protocol targets in their own communities"; as of this month, 243 mayors, representing communities as diverse as Miami, Racine in Wisconsin and Charleston, South Carolina, had signed on. New York, New Jersey and several other north-eastern states have pledged to freeze their power-plant emissions at current levels and, eventually, to begin to roll them back. Even Governor Arnold Schwarzenegger, the Hummer collector, has joined in the effort: an executive order he signed last year calls on California to reduce its greenhouse—gas emissions to 2000 levels by 2010 and to 1990 levels by 2020. "I say the debate is over," Schwarzenegger declared before signing the order. "We know the science. We see the threat. And we know the time for action is now." The California Public Utilities Commission recently launched a \$2.9bn rebate programme aimed at installing solar-power arrays on one million rooftops.

Ballooning house sizes. If you focus on efforts such as these, it's tempting to conclude that the US is ready to shift course and, indeed, to some extent is already doing so. Look elsewhere, however, and it's far less clear. Consider what has happened to the average new home built in the country. Even as average household size has declined, the size of the average house has ballooned. It was 1,000 square feet in 1950 and is nearly 2,500 square feet today. New homes, meanwhile, now routinely feature a gamut of energy-intensive conveniences, such as outdoor kitchens, professional-sized appliances and heated towel racks.

Or consider what has happened to the American automobile. At the same time Americans were being presented with ever more compelling evidence of global climate change, they were also, in ever greater numbers, purchasing cars like GM's Yukon Denali, which has a 335-horsepower engine, weighs 7,000lb, comes equipped with heated leather seats, and gets 13 miles to the gallon. On average, passenger vehicles purchased in the US last year got 21.0 miles to the gallon; this was a worse gas mileage than the average passenger vehicle got 20 years earlier. In many parts of the country George Bush's recalcitrance isn't representative, but in others his equivo-cations look positively progressive: Senator James Inhofe, Republican of Oklahoma, who chairs the Senate committee on environment and public works, has famously called global warming the "greatest hoax ever perpetrated on the American people". Every year Senator John McCain, the Republican Party's most vocal proponent of action on climate change, brings to the floor a bill that would impose federal limits on CO_2 emissions. Every year it's a foregone conclusion that the bill will be defeated. It is worth noting that all the way back in 1992, Gore published a book, *Earth in the Balance*, which eloquently laid out the dangers of global warming. The book became a bestseller. Gore became the vice-president. And still nothing happened.

Are such patterns really the result of disinformation? Do Americans drive around in 7,000lb cars because somehow they missed the many thousands of news stories and scientific studies documenting record high temperatures, rising sea levels and shrinking ice caps? As an American, I'd like to believe this is so. But it's hard to.

10 Life in the United States, more than just about anywhere else save perhaps some of the oil-producing Gulf states, depends on cheap and plentiful energy. This is a fact of American culture and also of the American economy. Really addressing the problem of climate change will require many small-scale adjustments (no more heated towel racks) and also a great many more substantial ones: changes in energy consumption, energy production, patterns of land use, transportation systems, international relations. Rather than assume that Americans haven't done anything about global warming because they are sceptical about the threat, one could just as plausibly argue that they are sceptical about the threat because they don't want to do anything.

Shortly after Gore was elected vice-president, he proposed a tax on energy—specifically on the energy content of fossil fuels. It was defeated ignominiously, even though the Demo-crats still controlled Congress. Gore never raised the prospect of an energy tax again. Four years later he flew to Japan to salvage the Kyoto Protocol when negotiations seemed on the verge of breaking down. The Clinton administration eventually signed the protocol but never presented it to the Senate for ratification. Though Gore knew that the very future of the planet was at stake, he apparently concluded that pressing for action was hopeless, or politically inexpedient, or both. Talk about an inconvenient truth.

Beyond the tipping point

At this point, midterm elections in the US are just five months away. Recent polls suggest that control of both houses of Congress is up for grabs. It's possible that the Democrats will win a majority in at least one, in which case the chairmanships of certain important committees will shift to less openly anti-science members. On the other hand, it is also possible that the Republicans will retain their majorities, in which case they are likely to interpret the results as a mandate for staying the course. Two years from now is a presidential election. Among the current leading contenders are some of the most passionate advocates of action—Gore and McCain—and also some of the leading obstructionists, such as Senator Chuck Hagel, Republican of Nebraska. (Hagel was among the chief opponents of Kyoto.) Whoever wins in 2008 will face an American public that still expects the government to respond to rising energy prices by cutting gasoline taxes.

Such is the inexorable nature of global warming that, at some point or other, even the US will be forced to acknowledge the scale of the problem. As McCain has observed: "This is clearly an issue that we will win on over time because of the evidence." The tragedy is: we don't have more time. The earth's climate system is vast and hugely inertial, and so already we are much further along the path to catastrophe than it appears. The rapid melting of mountain glaciers, the accelerating flow off the Greenland ice sheet, the 2003 heatwave in Europe, the 2005 hurricane season in the US—these are just the first faint harbingers of changes that have, by now, already become inevitable.

If we continue on our present course, at a certain point, truly terrible climatic disasters—the disintegration of the Greenland or the West Antarctic ice sheet, for instance—will become similarly unavoidable. These disasters may take centuries to play out fully, but once the process begins, it will become self-reinforcing and therefore virtually impossible to stop. This "tipping point" could be reached 20 years from now, or ten years from now, or, if truth be told, it could have already been reached ten years ago. Of course the US can go green. The question is: will it do so before it is too late?

15 *Elizabeth Kolbert is a writer for the New Yorker. Her book "Field Notes from a Catastrophe: climate change-is time running out?" is published by Bloomsbury (£14.99)*

Reflect & Write

- ❏ Consider the author's opening characterization of *An Inconvenient Truth:* "the world's first film based on a PowerPoint presentation." How might that influence the way that the reader thinks about the film? What other ways might Kolbert have introduced the film that would have produced a different perception?
- ❏ At one point in her argument, Kolbert asserts, "Rather than assume that Americans haven't done anything about global warming because they are skeptical about the threat, one could just as plausibly argue that they are skeptical about the threat because they don't want to do anything." Which side of this argument does she seem to support? How can you tell?
- ❏ Look carefully at Kolbert's conclusion. Is it a call to action? What is the effect of her last two sentences and of her ending with a rhetorical question?
- ❏ **Write.** Throughout her piece, Kolbert tends to talk broadly about "American culture," occasionally referring to "Americans." Rewrite the section where she addresses the issue of new home size and the automobile purchases to be a direct address to the American audience. Use the second person to make this a forceful indictment of American approaches to green practices. How does your revision change the tone of Kolbert's argument?

■ *Since 2007, TerraChoice Environmental Marketing has released a biannual report to inform consumers about how companies in the United States, UK, Canada, and Australia use misleading green-based ad campaigns and marketing to increase sales. Defining this practice as "Green-washing," TerraChoice also developed its list of the Seven Sins of Green-washing, reproduced below, to help its audience recognize the false claims made by many companies. In their 2009 study, Terrachoice reported that 98 percent of the companies it surveyed had committed at least one of its seven sins.*

The Seven Sins of Green-washing

Green-wash (green'wash', -wôsh')—verb: the act of misleading consumers regarding the environmental practices of a company or the environmental benefits of a product or service.

The Seven Sins of Green-washing

Sin of the Hidden Trade-off

A claim suggesting that a product is 'green' based on a narrow set of attributes without attention to other important environmental issues. Paper, for example, is not necessarily environmentally-preferable just because it comes from a sustainably-harvested forest. Other important environmental issues in the paper-making process, such as greenhouse gas emissions, or chlorine use in bleaching may be equally important.

Sin of No Proof

An environmental claim that cannot be substantiated by easily accessible supporting information or by a reliable third-party certification. Common examples are facial tissues or toilet tissue products that claim various percentages of post-consumer recycled content without providing evidence.

Sin of Vagueness

A claim that is so poorly defined or broad that its real meaning is likely to be misunderstood by the consumer. 'All-natural' is an example. Arsenic, uranium, mercury, and formaldehyde are all naturally occurring, and poisonous. 'All natural' isn't necessarily 'green'.

Sin of Worshiping False Labels

A product that, through either words or images, gives the impression of third-party endorsement where no such endorsement exists; fake labels, in other words.

Sin of Irrelevance

An environmental claim that may be truthful but is unimportant or unhelpful for consumers seeking environmentally preferable products. 'CFC-free' is a common example, since it is a frequent claim despite the fact that CFCs are banned by law.

Sin of Lesser of Two Evils

A claim that may be true within the product category, but that risks distracting the consumer from the greater environmental impacts of the category as a whole. Organic cigarettes could be an example of this Sin, as might the fuel-efficient sport-utility vehicle.

Sin of Fibbing

Environmental claims that are simply false. The most common examples were products falsely claiming to be Energy Star certified or registered.

Reflect & Write

- ❏ Considering that TerraChoice also releases a detailed, 25+ page report on green-washing, why do you think they developed this Seven Sins List? Consider the rhetorical situation and purpose.
- ❏ Why do you think that TerraChoice did not just call their list: "Seven Ways that Companies Green-wash Their Products"? Why call them the "Seven Sins"?
- ❏ What do the images add to the list? To what extent are they a rhetorically effective part of the argument?
- ❏ Do the Sins seem to be organized in a deliberate order? What is the argument made by the arrangement of these elements?
- ❏ **Write.** Transform this list into a paragraph that describes these sins to the reader. Be sure to revise the language and development as you translate this information from an itemized list into a coherent, fluid paragraph.

COLLABORATIVE CHALLENGE

With your group, go online or visit your library and look for environmentally themed ads for big oil companies (such as Chevron, ExxonMobil, or BP) from the last ten years. Select three and access to what extent they represent any of the Seven Sins of Green-washing. Create a poster that pairs each ad with a caption or brief paragraph that describes how it green-washes the company. Display your poster in a class exhibition.

Seeing Connections
For guidelines for creating effective posters, see page 203.

In April 1970, U.S. Senator Gaylord Nelson founded Earth Day (April 21), a day dedicated to encouraging appreciation for the environment. It is currently celebrated by more than 175 countries, although it sometimes has been received with skepticism over the years. This sentiment is reflected in Alex Steffen's blogpost "On Earth Day," which was appeared on Earth Day 2006 on the blog for the organization, Worldchanging. This nonprofit media organization, based in Seattle, has been ranked as the second-largest sustainability Website by Nielson, has won the Utne Independent Press award, and has been nominated for both the Webbys and the Bloggies (both online awards) for its articles featuring innovative problem-solving for many environmental issues. **Alex Steffen** *is the co-founder and executive editor of* WorldChanging. *He has been a featured speaker at Harvard, Yale, and Stanford, has delivered presentations at the TED talks, and has appeared on the* Today Show *and NPR.*

On Earth Day

Alex Steffen

Green is the new black. No buzz-phrase better sums up both the excitement many of us feel about the blooming environmental and social consciousness around us and the essential hollowness of the answers being promoted by many newly-minted eco-pundits.

The flood of environmental magazine cover stories, documentaries and advertisements has pushed us over a public-opinion threshold, which is great. But the solutions being touted by many of our new-found allies are themselves creating a new kind of problem—people who should know better are selling a muddle-headed, style-over-substance, "lite green" environmentalism at a time when we need to be rebuilding our civilization to avoid disaster. To be blunt, we're being sold out.

People are being told to buy organic cotton T-shirts, keep their tires inflated and recycle their beer bottles. But the reality of the situation is that the impacts of these sorts of actions are totally out whack of with the magnitude of the planetary problems bearing down upon us. Those of us who care about the future of the planet need to reclaim this moment from those who would have people think that our biggest challenge is picking the most stylish vegan shoes.

With every passing day, we are discovering that things are worse than we thought. Our climate is ripping apart at the seams at a rate that's surprising even the so-called alarmists. Natural systems are collapsing. The ocean seems headed towards a series of catastrophic tipping points. Economic inequity is producing a planet of billionaires and a billion desperate people. Our political systems are suffering a massive crisis of legitimacy, while insane fundamentalists, violent criminals and two-bit dictators (wearing both uniforms and Armani suits) are stealing or destroying everything they can get their hands on. Everywhere on the planet we find an empty consumer culture so accepted we barely speak of it, except perhaps to make an ironic joke. We have placed a Great Wager on the future of humanity, and the odds are getting worse.

5 In the face of this reality, recycling a bottle is an act so insignificant as to be merely totemic. Paper or plastic? Who the hell cares?

In the developed world, few of us, essentially none of us, currently live a "one-planet life." The vast majority of us, even of those of us who have committed ourselves to change, consume more resources and energy than our sustainable share: indeed, it is very, very difficult to live an individually sustainable life, because the very systems in which we are enmeshed—which enfold and make possible our lifestyles—are themselves insanely unsustainable. We're driving our hybrid SUVs down the highway to the Collapse.

Most of the harm we cause in the world is done far from our sight, created through the workings of vast systems whose workings are often intentionally hidden from us, and over which we have very little influence as single individuals. Alone, we are essentially powerless to change anything that matters. We can't shop our way to sustainability.

I believe we are bombarded with messages encouraging us to take the "small steps" precisely because those steps are a threat to no one. They don't depress sales of fashionable crap we don't need. They don't bring people into the streets or sweep corrupt politicians from office. They certainly don't threaten the powerful, entrenched interests who are growing fantastically rich off keeping us locked into the systems that make our lives such a burden on the planet and impoverish our brothers and sisters elsewhere.

Buying a hemp hoodie is not a blow for better world, it's at best a mere gesture towards the idea that the world ought to better. And, here in the Green Spring of 2006, we *must* finally admit to ourselves that gestures are no longer enough. That to be focused on lifestyle tweaks and attitudinal adjustments at this moment in history is like showing up with a teaspoon to help bail out a sinking ship. If the New Green degenerates into handing out more stylish spoons, we're screwed.

10 We don't need more carpool lanes. We need to eliminate fossil fuels from our economy. We don't need more recycling bins. We need to create a closed-loop, biomimetic, neobiological industrial system. We don't need to attend a tree-planting ceremony. We need to become expert at ecosystem management and gardening the planet. We don't need another unscented laundry detergent. We need to ban the vast majority of the toxic chemicals upon which our livestyles currently float and invent a completely non-toxic green chemistry. We don't need lite green fashions. We need a bright green revolution.

To really change the world we need to hand out real tools: rugged, free, collaborative tools for understanding the world and our role in it, for seeing the systems in which we are trapped; tools for learning how to work together to either transform those systems or destroy them completely and bioremediate the rubble. Tools that help us as people make meaningful changes in both our own lives and the world. We need to make people participants, not consumers. We need answers that address peoples' lives, not their lifestyles.

We need to take back the ballot box. With the exception of a couple small nations like Finland, most governments on earth are now seething messes of corruption, oppression and entrenched privilege, and our government here in the U.S. is worse than many. We need transparency, accountability, genuine equity, real democracy and human rights. No environmental or social issue transcends the need for worldwide political reform, and none of our huge planetary problems can be solved without it.

We need to seize the trading floor. Most large corporations, and most of the markets we've established through regulation, incentive and tradition, demand that we participate (as employees, consumers or investors) in ecological destruction, unfair labor practices and an assault on the public realm. We need to grab hold of these economic systems, strip them down to their component parts and rebuild them anew. That means supporting (or becoming) clean energy entrepreneurs, green builders, sustainable product designers, socially-responsible investors, and so on. We need a new generation uncompromisingly innovative and determined regulators, planners, bankers, insurers. We need to take back business as a realm of service and do away with the dinosaurs who dominate it today, and we need an army of people ready to put their careers and investments on the line to do it.

We need to share. There is no sustainable future without a vigorous and lively public realm. We need to defend the commons, from the air we breath to the culture we create together. That commons is everywhere under attack from those who would privatize it for profit and stifle innovation to protect the status quo, the way, for instance, that the music and film industries are trying to take away our ability to freely (and legally) share our own music and videos, because they're worried not only that someone might illegally share some of their music or videos, but because the explosion of free music and video we're seeing threatens their out-of-date business models. We must counter-attack, supporting open culture and public ownership, and working everywhere to redistribute the future.

15 We need better mousetraps. The stuff that surrounds us is crap: toxic, wasteful, unjust, ugly. We need innovation everywhere, real innovation, stuff that isn't just marginally better or superficially green, but stuff that is actually, right now or as soon as possible, an order of magnitude more efficient, completely non-toxic and closed-loop. We need to support the folks out there trying to design these things. We need to laud their efforts, invest in their inventions, and generally do everything we can to get better design, technology and thinking applied to every aspect of our lives. Then we need to help regular people separate the bright green from the greenwashed.

We need to grow new systems. The systems which surround us are awful. Some of them we can hack. Some of them simply need to be replaced. Suburban sprawl, for instance, is simply wrong: there's no way to make it sustainable. We should simply bring it to a halt. Farming, on the other hand, needs to be reformed—and through conscious buying, political activism and ethical leadership, we can help steer agriculture away from petrochemical factory farming and towards innovative local sustainable farms. Some of our choices nurture changed systems—those are the choices we need to show people how to make.

We need to help each other. Consumer-based approaches and "simple things" lists tend to reinforce our sense that the only sphere in which we can act is our own little private lives, and that isolates us. But the isolation we all sometimes feel in the face of the magnitude of the problems is itself a major part of the problem. None of us can change the world single-handedly: as Wendell Berry says, "to work at this work alone is to fail." We need to organize, mobilize, join together, act in concert. We need to seek out our allies and get their backs when they need us. That happens through applied effort, not impulse buying.

We need to admit that we're at war over the definition of the future. There are a lot of powerful interests spending a lot of money to keep people ignorant, make them uncertain, postpone action, encourage cynicism and apathy, and lock them in the mental prison of thinking that no better future is possible. To the extent they are successful, nothing we advocate can happen. We need to fight back. We need to speak clearly, intelligently, and, if possible, with humor and passion. We need to label our opponents (from climate denialists to apologists for the status quo) what they are—enemies of the future. We need to make the nature of our times crystal-clear for all to see. We need to hew to the demanding standards our actual real situation imposes on us—that we achieve measurable sustainability, honest-to-goodness one-planet living, for everyone, within our lifetimes—and scorn the mental tyranny of small goals. We need to break through the meaningless chatter around environmental and social issues, and point to genuine alternatives, hold real conversations, and create a culture that speaks to the soul of our times.

We need, above all else, to show that another world is possible, indeed, it's here all around us, though we do not see it. We need to inspire not only our fellow citizens but ourselves with visions of what we're beginning to accomplish together, visions of what a planet brought back to sanity will look and feel like, visions of how we will live in a bright green future. That future should be beautiful and stylish, dynamic and creative, but it must before all else be genuinely sustainable, or it's not much of a future at all, is it?

20 The world is listening. It's our obligation to tell it a better story.

Reflect & Write

- ❑ How does the opening line "Green is the new black" set the tone for the rest of the argument? What cliché is Steffen appropriating here? What does it suggest about the Green Movement?
- ❑ In this piece, Steffen uses a very strong personal voice and assumes an unapologetically opinionated stance. How does this manifest itself in his writing and structure? To what extent does it alienate the reader? To what extent does it make his argument more persuasive?
- ❑ Consider the paragraph that begins "We don't need more carpool lanes." Note how Steffen moves toward a higher level of decorum. What patterns or structures

do you see that are representative to this shift to high style? Why do you think he makes this rhetorical move at this point in the essay? How effective is it?

❑ **Write.** At one point in his blogpost, Steffen states, "In the face of this reality, recycling a bottle is an act so insignificant as to be merely totemic. Paper or plastic? Who the hell cares?" Do you agree? Are recycling, bringing your own bag to the grocery store, biking to work, washing your clothes in cold water, and changing to compact fluorecent bulbs pointless actions? Write a response to this passage in which you either argue for the importance of individual acts or concur with his assessment through use of your own evidence and examples. Adopt the tone of an opinion piece, similar to that found in Steffen's article.

■ **Geoffrey Johnson** *Geoffrey Johnson originally published this article in the April 22, 2004, issue of the* New York Times. *At the time of its publication, he was the program coordinator for the nonprofit environmental group Green Life.*

Marking Earth Day Inc.

Geoffrey Johnson

Welcome to Earth Day 2004, brought to you by petroleum powers, big-box developers, old-growth loggers and chemically dependent coffee companies trying to paint their public image green.

Let's start with Sierra Pacific, a benefactor of northern Nevada's celebration of Earth Day. The timber company is involved in a lawsuit aimed at weakening the Sierra Nevada Framework, which protects the region's forests. Marathon Oil is Earth Day's sponsor down in Houston. Behind closed doors in Texas, Marathon worked on voluntary emissions regulations that have helped give Houston some of the worst air quality in the country.

The Earth Day cleanup and restoration program held by the California State Parks Foundation is financed by corporations with poor environmental records in the state: ChevronTexaco, which recently agreed to a $275 million settlement over air pollution from five of its California refineries; Wal-Mart, which lobbied unsuccessfully for a ballot initiative in Inglewood to exempt a proposed supercenter from environmental restrictions; and Pacific Gas and Electric, whose illegal dumping of carcinogenic chemicals near the town of Hinkley was memorialized in the movie "Erin Brockovich."

In New York City and other areas, Starbucks has its own events, centered around its latest slogan, "More than our logo is green." Yet the company will neither label nor remove genetically modified ingredients in its products. And while it promotes its "origins" line of coffees as a symbol of its commitment to sustainable coffee farming, the origins varieties account for just a sliver of the coffee that Starbucks sells.

5 Some might argue that there is nothing wrong with corporations acting as a friend of Earth Day, no matter how unfriendly their everyday operations may be. Perhaps they are just showing solidarity with the millions of Americans who support Earth Day each year to combat the necessary environmental evils of their year-round lifestyles. But the reality is that sponsorship is often intended not as atonement for misdeeds against nature, but as a distraction from them.

Through concerted marketing and public relations campaigns, these "greenwashers" attract eco-conscious consumers and push the notion that they don't need environmental regulations because they are already environmentally responsible. Greenwashing appears in misleading product labels like "all natural" and "eco-friendly"; in television commercials showing S.U.V.'s rolling peacefully through the wilderness; and in the co-opting of environmental buzzwords like "sound science" and "sustainability"—which corporate executives render meaningless through relentless repetition.

Earth Day events are select venues for greenwashers, allowing them to communicate with their target audience of green consumers. They also amount to a public relations bargain. BP spent $200 million rebranding itself from British Petroleum to "beyond petroleum." Major corporations pay hundreds of thousands of dollars for environmentally themed advertisements in high-circulation magazines like National Geographic and Time. In contrast, at most Earth Day festivities, a few hundred to a few thousand dollars will get a company marquee exhibition space and a prominent place for its logo on publicity materials.

It would be a shame to let the high-flying banners of greenwashers distract Earth Day participants from the environmental advocates, community associations and government agencies that work to protect the environment throughout the year. But it is also incumbent upon those same groups—many of which are in the position of choosing who sponsors these events—to adopt a strict screening process to separate the genuinely green businesses from the greenwashers. Finally, let's not forget the most charitable patron of all. Earth Day, like every day, is brought to us by the generosity of none other than the planet itself.

Seeing Connections

For another perspective on corporate green-washing, see "What's Wrong with the Body Shop?" (pages 178–180)

Reflect & Write

- ❑ Considering that Senator Gaylord Nelson originally founded Earth Day as a way to draw attention to the importance of the environment, how does Johnson argue that it has changed in the 30+ years since the first Earth Day celebration?
- ❑ Does Johnson at all showcase the positive side of Earth Day? If so, where and to what extent? How does this rhetorical decision affect his argument?
- ❑ This article is driven principally by the strategy of example. Review the strategies of argumentation found in Chapter 2. What other strategies might Johnson have used to make his point, but perhaps in a different way? How would that have changed the delivery and force of the argument?
- ❑ **Write.** At one point, Johnson contends that "the reality is that sponsorship is often intended not as atonement for misdeeds against nature, but as a distraction from them." Do you agree with this claim? Write a one-page response paper in which you discuss how corporate sponsorship complicates the experience, practice, and message of Earth Day.

■ **Jared Diamond** *A professor of geography and physiology at the University of California at Los Angeles, Jared Diamond is a scientist and author best known for his award-winning books* The Third Chimpanzee *(1992),* Guns, Germs, and Steel *(1997), and* Collapse *(2005). He published the following op-ed piece in the December 6, 2009, edition of the* New York Times.

Will Big Business Save the Earth?

Jared Diamond

THERE is a widespread view, particularly among environmentalists and liberals, that big businesses are environmentally destructive, greedy, evil and driven by short-term profits. I know—because I used to share that view.

But today I have more nuanced feelings. Over the years I've joined the boards of two environmental groups, the World Wildlife Fund and Conservation International, serving alongside many business executives.

As part of my board work, I have been asked to assess the environments in oil fields, and have had frank discussions with oil company employees at all levels. I've also worked with executives of mining, retail, logging and financial services companies. I've discovered that while some businesses are indeed as destructive as many suspect, others are among the world's strongest positive forces for environmental sustainability.

The embrace of environmental concerns by chief executives has accelerated recently for several reasons. Lower consumption of environmental resources saves money in the short run. Maintaining sustainable resource levels and not polluting saves money in the long run. And a clean image—one attained by, say, avoiding oil spills and other environmental disasters—reduces criticism from employees, consumers and government.

5 What's my evidence for this? Here are a few examples involving three corporations—Wal-Mart, Coca-Cola and Chevron—that many critics of business love to hate, in my opinion, unjustly.

Let's start with Wal-Mart. Obviously, a business can save money by finding ways to spend less while maintaining sales. This is what Wal-Mart did with fuel costs, which the company reduced by $26 million per year simply by changing the way it managed its enormous truck fleet. Instead of running a truck's engine all night to heat or cool the cab during mandatory 10-hour rest stops, the company installed small auxiliary power units to do the job. In addition to lowering fuel costs, the move eliminated the carbon dioxide emissions equivalent to taking 18,300 passenger vehicles off the road.

Wal-Mart is also working to double the fuel efficiency of its truck fleet by 2015, thereby saving more than $200 million a year at the pump. Among the efficient prototypes now being tested are trucks that burn biofuels generated from waste grease at Wal-Mart's delis. Similarly, as the country's biggest private user of electricity, Wal-Mart is saving money by decreasing store energy use.

Another Wal-Mart example involves lowering costs associated with packaging materials. Wal-Mart now sells only concentrated liquid laundry detergents in North America, which has reduced the size of packaging by up to 50 percent. Wal-Mart stores eventual goal is to end up with no packaging waste.

One last Wal-Mart example shows how a company can save money in the long run by buying from sustainably managed sources. Because most wild fisheries are managed unsustainably, prices for Chilean sea bass and Atlantic tuna have been soaring. To my pleasant astonishment, in 2006 Wal-Mart decided to switch, within five years, all its purchases of wild-caught seafood to fisheries certified as sustainable.

10 Coca-Cola's problems are different from Wal-Mart's in that they are largely long-term. The key ingredient in Coke products is water. The company produces its beverages in about 200 countries through local franchises, all of which require a reliable local supply of clean fresh water.

But water supplies are under severe pressure around the world, with most already allocated for human use. The little remaining unallocated fresh water is in remote areas unsuitable for beverage factories, like Arctic Russia and northwestern Australia.

Coca-Cola can't meet its water needs just by desalinizing seawater, because that requires energy, which is also increasingly expensive. Global climate change is making water scarcer, especially in the densely populated temperate-zone countries, like the United States, that are Coca-Cola's main customers. Most competing water use around the world is for agriculture, which presents sustainability problems of its own.

Hence Coca-Cola's survival compels it to be deeply concerned with problems of water scarcity, energy, climate change and agriculture. One company goal is to make its plants water-neutral, returning to the environment water in quantities equal to the amount used in beverages and their production. Another goal is to work on the conservation of seven of the world's river basins, including the Rio Grande, Yangtze, Mekong and Danube—all of them sites of major environmental concerns besides supplying water for Coca-Cola.

These long-term goals are in addition to Coca-Cola's short-term cost-saving environmental practices, like recycling plastic bottles, replacing petroleum-based plastic in bottles with organic material, reducing energy consumption and increasing sales volume while decreasing water use.

15 The third company is Chevron. Not even in any national park have I seen such rigorous environmental protection as I encountered in five visits to new Chevron-managed oil fields in Papua New Guinea. (Chevron has since sold its stake in these properties to a New Guinea-based oil company.) When I asked how a publicly traded company could justify to its shareholders its expenditures on the environment, Chevron employees and executives gave me at least five reasons.

First, oil spills can be horribly expensive: it is far cheaper to prevent them than to clean them up. Second, clean practices reduce the risk that New Guinean landowners become angry, sue for damages and close the fields. (The company has been sued for problems in Ecuador that Chevron inherited when it merged with Texaco in 2001.) Next, environmental standards are becoming stricter around the world, so building clean facilities now minimizes having to do expensive retrofitting later.

Also, clean operations in one country give a company an advantage in bidding on leases in other countries. Finally, environmental practices of which employees are proud improve morale, help with recruitment and increase the length of time employees are likely to remain at the company.

In view of all those advantages that businesses gain from environmentally sustainable policies, why do such policies face resistance from some businesses and many politicians? The objections often take the form of one-liners.

We have to balance the environment against the economy. The assumption underlying this statement is that measures promoting environmental sustainability inevitably yield a net economic cost rather than a profit. This line of thinking turns the truth upside down. Economic reasons furnish the strongest motives for sustainability, because in the long run (and often in the short run as well) it is much more expensive and difficult to try to fix problems, environmental or otherwise, than to avoid them at the outset.

20 Americans learned that lesson from Hurricane Katrina in August 2005, when, as a result of government agencies balking for a decade at spending several hundred million dollars to fix New Orleans's defenses, we suffered hundreds of billions of dollars in damage—not to mention thousands of dead Americans. Likewise, John Holdren, the top White House science adviser, estimates that solving problems of climate change would cost the United States 2 percent of our gross domestic product by the year 2050, but that not solving those problems would damage the economy by 20 percent to 30 percent of G.D.P.

Technology will solve our problems. Yes, technology can contribute to solving problems. But major technological advances require years to develop and put in place, and regularly turn out to have unanticipated side effects—consider the destruction of the atmosphere's ozone layer by the nontoxic, nonflammable chlorofluorocarbons initially hailed for replacing poisonous refrigerant gases.

World population growth is leveling off and won't be the problem that we used to fear. It's true that the rate of world population growth has been decreasing. However, the real problem isn't people themselves, but the resources that people consume and the waste that they produce. Per-person average consumption rates and waste production rates, now 32 times higher in rich countries than in poor ones, are rising steeply around the world, as developing countries emulate industrialized nations' lifestyles.

It's futile to preach to us Americans about lowering our standard of living: we will never sacrifice just so other people can raise their standard of living. This conflates consumption rates with standards of living: they are only loosely correlated, because so much of our consumption is wasteful and doesn't contribute to our quality of life. Once basic needs are met, increasing consumption often doesn't increase happiness.

Replacing a car that gets 15 miles per gallon with a more efficient model wouldn't lower one's standard of living, but would help improve all of our lives by reducing the political and military consequences of our dependence on imported oil. Western Europeans have lower per-capita consumption rates than Americans, but enjoy a higher standard of living as measured by access to medical care, financial security after retirement, infant mortality, life expectancy, literacy and public transport.

25 NOT surprisingly, the problem of climate change has attracted its own particular crop of objections.

Even experts disagree about the reality of climate change. That was true 30 years ago, and some experts still disagreed a decade ago. Today, virtually every climatologist agrees that average global temperatures, warming rates and atmospheric carbon dioxide levels are higher than at any time in the earth's recent past, and that the main cause is greenhouse gas emissions by humans. Instead, the questions still being debated concern whether average global temperatures will increase by 13 degrees or "only" by 4 degrees Fahrenheit by 2050, and whether humans account for 90 percent or "only" 85 percent of the global warming trend.

The magnitude and cause of global climate change are uncertain. We shouldn't adopt expensive countermeasures until we have certainty. In other spheres of life—picking a spouse, educating our children, buying life insurance and stocks, avoiding cancer and so on—we admit that certainty is unattainable, and that we must decide as best we can on the basis of available evidence. Why should the impossible quest for certainty paralyze us solely about acting on climate change? As Mr. Holdren, the White House adviser, expressed it, not acting on climate change would be like being "in a car with bad brakes driving toward a cliff in the fog."

Global warming will be good for us, by letting us grow crops in places formerly too cold for agriculture. The term "global warming" is a misnomer; we should instead talk about global climate change, which isn't uniform. The global average temperature is indeed rising, but many areas are becoming drier, and frequencies of droughts, floods and other extreme weather events are increasing. Some areas will be winners, while others will be losers. Most of us will be losers, because the temperate zones where most people live are becoming drier.

It's useless for the United States to act on climate change, when we don't know what China will do. Actually, China will arrive at this week's Copenhagen climate change negotiations with a whole package of measures to reduce its "carbon intensity."

30 While the United States is dithering about long-distance energy transmission from our rural areas with the highest potential for wind energy generation to our urban areas with the highest need for energy, China is far ahead of us. It is developing ultra-high-voltage transmission lines from wind and solar generation sites in rural western China to cities in eastern China. If America doesn't act to develop innovative energy technology, we will lose the green jobs competition not only to Finland and Germany (as we are now) but also to China.

On each of these issues, American businesses are going to play as much or more of a role in our progress as the government. And this isn't a bad thing, as corporations know they have a lot to gain by establishing environmentally friendly business practices.

My friends in the business world keep telling me that Washington can help on two fronts: by investing in green research, offering tax incentives and passing cap-and-trade legislation; and by setting and enforcing tough standards to ensure that companies with cheap, dirty standards don't have a competitive advantage over those businesses protecting the environment. As for the rest of us, we should get over the misimpression that American business cares only about immediate profits, and we should reward companies that work to keep the planet healthy.

Reflect & Write

- ❑ What rhetorical appeals does Diamond draw on in his first paragraphs? Why does he make this choice? How do the appeals contribute to the persuasiveness of his argument?
- ❑ How does he use example to drive his argument? Why might he name Wal-Mart in particular? Compare Diamond's use of example to Geoffrey Johnson's in the previous article. What are the differences in the ways that each author leverages this strategy to make his point?

- ❑ Find places in the essay where economic concepts provide a framework for the argument. What types of models does Diamond use in other parts of the article? A moral framework? Scientific? A cultural critique? How does he weave these together to create a persuasive argument?
- ❑ **Write.** In this title, Diamond asks: Will Big Business Save the Earth? What do you think is his answer? Now write a blog post in which you respond to Diamond. Do you agree with his "nuanced" view of big business's role in greening America?

■ *In 2006, former U.S. Vice President* **Al Gore** *released his film,* An Inconvenient Truth, *which launched the issue of climate change into the public awareness, earning $49 million at the box office and an Academy Award in the process. The subsequent year, Gore and the U.N.'s Intergovernmental Panel on Climate Change were awarded the Nobel Peace prize for their work on this global problem. What follows is the acceptance speech that Gore delivered on December 10, 2007, in Oslo, Norway.*

The Nobel Peace Prize 2007

Al Gore

Seeing Connections
To see one student's draft and revision of a research paper on Al Gore's environmental rhetoric, see Chapter 6, page 131 and page 138.

Nobel Lecture, Oslo, 10 December 2007.

Your Majesties, Your Royal Highnesses, Honorable members of the Norwegian Nobel Committee, Excellencies, Ladies and gentlemen.

I have a purpose here today. It is a purpose I have tried to serve for many years. I have prayed that God would show me a way to accomplish it.

Sometimes, without warning, the future knocks on our door with a precious and painful vision of what might be. One hundred and nineteen years ago, a wealthy inventor read his own obituary, mistakenly published years before his death. Wrongly believing the inventor had just died, a newspaper printed a harsh judgment of his life's work, unfairly labeling him "The Merchant of Death" because of his invention—dynamite. Shaken by this condemnation, the inventor made a fateful choice to serve the cause of peace.

5 Seven years later, Alfred Nobel created this prize and the others that bear his name.

Seven years ago tomorrow, I read my own political obituary in a judgment that seemed to me harsh and mistaken—if not premature. But that unwelcome verdict also brought a precious if painful gift: an opportunity to search for fresh new ways to serve my purpose. Unexpectedly, that quest has brought me here. Even though I fear my words cannot match this moment, I pray what I am feeling in my heart will be communicated clearly enough that those who hear me will say, "We must act."

The distinguished scientists with whom it is the greatest honor of my life to share this award have laid before us a choice between two different futures—a choice that to my ears echoes the words of an ancient prophet: "Life or death, blessings or curses. Therefore, choose life, that both thou and thy seed may live."

We, the human species, are confronting a planetary emergency—a threat to the survival of our civilization that is gathering ominous and destructive potential even as we gather here. But there is hopeful news as well: we have the ability to solve this crisis and avoid the worst—though not all—of its consequences, if we act boldly, decisively and quickly. However, despite a growing number of honorable exceptions, too many of the world's leaders are still best described in the words Winston Churchill applied to those who ignored Adolf Hitler's threat: "They go on in strange paradox, decided only to be undecided, resolved to be irresolute, adamant for drift, solid for fluidity, all powerful to be impotent."

So today, we dumped another 70 million tons of global-warming pollution into the thin shell of atmosphere surrounding our planet, as if it were an open sewer. And tomorrow, we will dump a slightly larger amount, with the cumulative concentrations now trapping more and more heat from the sun. As a result, the earth has a fever. And the fever is rising. The experts have told us it is not a passing affliction that will heal by itself. We asked for a second opinion. And a third. And a fourth. And the consistent conclusion, restated with increasing alarm, is that something basic is wrong.

We are what is wrong, and we must make it right.

Last September 21, as the Northern Hemisphere tilted away from the sun, scientists reported with unprecedented distress that the North Polar ice cap is "falling off a cliff." One study estimated that it could be completely gone during summer in less than 22 years. Another new study, to be presented by U.S. Navy researchers later this week, warns it could happen in as little as 7 years.

Seven years from now.

In the last few months, it has been harder and harder to misinterpret the signs that our world is spinning out of kilter. Major cities in North and South America, Asia and Australia are nearly out of water due to massive droughts and melting glaciers. Desperate farmers are losing their livelihoods. Peoples in the frozen Arctic and on low-lying Pacific islands are planning evacuations of places they have long called home. Unprecedented wildfires have forced a half million people from their homes in one country and caused a national emergency that almost brought down the government in another. Climate refugees have migrated into areas already inhabited by people with different cultures, religions, and traditions, increasing the potential for conflict. Stronger storms in the Pacific and Atlantic have threatened whole cities. Millions have been displaced by massive flooding in South Asia, Mexico, and 18 countries in Africa. As temperature extremes have increased, tens of thousands have lost their lives. We are recklessly burning and clearing our forests and driving more and more species into extinction. The very web of life on which we depend is being ripped and frayed.

We never intended to cause all this destruction, just as Alfred Nobel never intended that dynamite be used for waging war. He had hoped his invention would promote human progress. We shared that same worthy goal when we began burning massive quantities of coal, then oil and methane.

Even in Nobel's time, there were a few warnings of the likely consequences. One of the very first winners of the Prize in chemistry worried that, "We are evaporating our coal mines into the air." After performing 10,000 equations by hand, Svante Arrhenius calculated that the earth's average temperature would increase by many degrees if we doubled the amount of CO_2 in the atmosphere.

Seventy years later, my teacher, Roger Revelle, and his colleague, Dave Keeling, began to precisely document the increasing CO_2 levels day by day. But unlike most other forms of pollution, CO_2 is invisible, tasteless, and odorless—which has helped keep the truth about what it is doing to our climate out of sight and out of mind. Moreover, the catastrophe now threatening us is unprecedented—and we often confuse the unprecedented with the improbable.

We also find it hard to imagine making the massive changes that are now necessary to solve the crisis. And when large truths are genuinely inconvenient, whole societies can, at least for a time, ignore them. Yet as George Orwell reminds us: "Sooner or later a false belief bumps up against solid reality, usually on a battlefield."

In the years since this prize was first awarded, the entire relationship between humankind and the earth has been radically transformed. And still, we have remained largely oblivious to the impact of our cumulative actions. Indeed, without realizing it, we have begun to wage war on the earth itself. Now, we and the earth's climate are locked in a relationship familiar to war planners: "Mutually assured destruction."

More than two decades ago, scientists calculated that nuclear war could throw so much debris and smoke into the air that it would block life-giving sunlight from our atmosphere, causing a "nuclear winter." Their eloquent warnings here in Oslo helped galvanize the world's resolve to halt the nuclear arms race.

20 Now science is warning us that if we do not quickly reduce the global warming pollution that is trapping so much of the heat our planet normally radiates back out of the atmosphere, we are in danger of creating a permanent "carbon summer." As the American poet Robert Frost wrote, "Some say the world will end in fire; some say in ice." Either, he notes, "would suffice."

But neither need be our fate. It is time to make peace with the planet.

We must quickly mobilize our civilization with the urgency and resolve that has previously been seen only when nations mobilized for war. These prior struggles for survival were won when leaders found words at the 11th hour that released a mighty surge of courage, hope and readiness to sacrifice for a protracted and mortal challenge.

These were not comforting and misleading assurances that the threat was not real or imminent; that it would affect others but not ourselves; that ordinary life might be lived even in the presence of extraordinary threat; that Providence could be trusted to do for us what we would not do for ourselves.

No, these were calls to come to the defense of the common future. They were calls upon the courage, generosity and strength of entire peoples, citizens of every class and condition who were ready to stand against the threat once asked to do so. Our enemies in those times calculated that free people would not rise to the challenge; they were, of course, catastrophically wrong.

25 Now comes the threat of climate crisis—a threat that is real, rising, imminent, and universal. Once again, it is the 11th hour. The penalties for ignoring this challenge are immense and growing, and at some near point would be unsustainable and unrecoverable. For now we still have the power to choose our fate, and the remaining question is only this: Have we the will

to act vigorously and in time, or will we remain imprisoned by a dangerous illusion?

Mahatma Gandhi awakened the largest democracy on earth and forged a shared resolve with what he called "Satyagraha"—or "truth force."

In every land, the truth—once known—has the power to set us free.

Truth also has the power to unite us and bridge the distance between "me" and "we," creating the basis for common effort and shared responsibility.

There is an African proverb that says, "If you want to go quickly, go alone. If you want to go far, go together." We need to go far, quickly.

30 We must abandon the conceit that individual, isolated, private actions are the answer. They can and do help. But they will not take us far enough without collective action. At the same time, we must ensure that in mobilizing globally, we do not invite the establishment of ideological conformity and a new lock-step "ism."

That means adopting principles, values, laws, and treaties that release creativity and initiative at every level of society in multifold responses originating concurrently and spontaneously.

This new consciousness requires expanding the possibilities inherent in all humanity. The innovators who will devise a new way to harness the sun's energy for pennies or invent an engine that's carbon negative may live in Lagos or Mumbai or Montevideo. We must ensure that entrepreneurs and inventors everywhere on the globe have the chance to change the world.

When we unite for a moral purpose that is manifestly good and true, the spiritual energy unleashed can transform us. The generation that defeated fascism throughout the world in the 1940s found, in rising to meet their awesome challenge, that they had gained the moral authority and long-term vision to launch the Marshall Plan, the United Nations, and a new level of global cooperation and foresight that unified Europe and facilitated the emergence of democracy and prosperity in Germany, Japan, Italy and much of the world. One of their visionary leaders said, "It is time we steered by the stars and not by the lights of every passing ship."

In the last year of that war, you gave the Peace Prize to a man from my hometown of 2000 people, Carthage, Tennessee. Cordell Hull was described by Franklin Roosevelt as the "Father of the United Nations." He was an inspiration and hero to my own father, who followed Hull in the Congress and the U.S. Senate and in his commitment to world peace and global cooperation.

35 My parents spoke often of Hull, always in tones of reverence and admiration. Eight weeks ago, when you announced this prize, the deepest emotion I felt was when I saw the headline in my hometown paper that simply noted I had won the same prize that Cordell Hull had won. In that moment, I knew what my father and mother would have felt were they alive.

Just as Hull's generation found moral authority in rising to solve the world crisis caused by fascism, so too can we find our greatest opportunity in rising to solve the climate crisis. In the Kanji characters used in both Chinese and Japanese, "crisis" is written with two symbols, the first meaning "danger," the second "opportunity." By facing and removing the danger of the climate crisis, we have the opportunity to gain the moral authority and vision to vastly increase our own capacity to solve other crises that have been too long ignored.

We must understand the connections between the climate crisis and the afflictions of poverty, hunger, HIV-Aids and other pandemics. As these problems are linked, so too must be their solutions. We must begin by making the common rescue of the global environment the central organizing principle of the world community.

Fifteen years ago, I made that case at the "Earth Summit" in Rio de Janeiro. Ten years ago, I presented it in Kyoto. This week, I will urge the delegates in Bali to adopt a bold mandate for a treaty that establishes a universal global cap on emissions and uses the market in emissions trading to efficiently allocate resources to the most effective opportunities for speedy reductions.

This treaty should be ratified and brought into effect everywhere in the world by the beginning of 2010—two years sooner than presently contemplated. The pace of our response must be accelerated to match the accelerating pace of the crisis itself.

40 Heads of state should meet early next year to review what was accomplished in Bali and take personal responsibility for addressing this crisis. It is not unreasonable to ask, given the gravity of our circumstances, that these heads of state meet every three months until the treaty is completed.

We also need a moratorium on the construction of any new generating facility that burns coal without the capacity to safely trap and store carbon dioxide.

And most important of all, we need to put a *price* on carbon—with a CO_2 tax that is then rebated back to the people, progressively, according to the laws of each nation, in ways that shift the burden of taxation from employment to pollution. This is by far the most effective and simplest way to accelerate solutions to this crisis.

The world needs an alliance—especially of those nations that weigh heaviest in the scales where earth is in the balance. I salute Europe and Japan for the steps they've taken in recent years to meet the challenge, and the new government in Australia, which has made solving the climate crisis its first priority.

But the outcome will be decisively influenced by two nations that are now failing to do enough: the United States and China. While India is also growing fast in importance, it should be absolutely clear that it is the two largest CO_2 emitters—most of all, my own country—that will need to make the boldest moves, or stand accountable before history for their failure to act.

45 Both countries should stop using the other's behavior as an excuse for stalemate and instead develop an agenda for mutual survival in a shared global environment.

These are the last few years of decision, but they can be the first years of a bright and hopeful future if we do what we must. No one should believe a solution will be found without effort, without cost, without change. Let us acknowledge that if we wish to redeem squandered time and speak again with moral authority, then these are the hard truths:

The way ahead is difficult. The outer boundary of what we currently believe is feasible is still far short of what we actually must do. Moreover, between here and there, across the unknown, falls the shadow.

That is just another way of saying that we have to expand the boundaries of what is possible. In the words of the Spanish poet, Antonio Machado, "Pathwalker, there is no path. You must make the path as you walk."

We are standing at the most fateful fork in that path. So I want to end as I began, with a vision of two futures—each a palpable possibility—and with a prayer that we will see with vivid clarity the necessity of choosing between those two futures, and the urgency of making the right choice now.

The great Norwegian playwright, Henrik Ibsen, wrote, "One of these days, the younger generation will come knocking at my door."

The future is knocking at our door right now. Make no mistake, the next generation *will* ask us one of two questions. Either they will ask: "What were you thinking; why didn't you act?"

Or they will ask instead: "How did you find the moral courage to rise and successfully resolve a crisis that so many said was impossible to solve?"

We have everything we need to get started, save perhaps political will, but political will is a renewable resource.

So let us renew it, and say together: "We have a purpose. We are many. For this purpose we will rise, and we will act."

Copyright © The Nobel Foundation 2007

Reflect & Write

- ❑ Reread the lecture and highlight examples of high style in the text. How does this level of decorum reveal itself in word choice, sentence structure, and rhetorical strategies? To what extent was Gore's choice of this style appropriate to the occasion?
- ❑ Early in the speech, Gore draws a parallel between himself and Alfred Nobel. What purpose does this comparison serve for his argument?
- ❑ Find places where Gore situates himself or global warming in terms of other famous people or in terms of history. What does he accomplish by this? What does it lend to his argument? Why might he quote others so often? Find one example that strikes you as particularly persuasive. Why does it work?
- ❑ Analyze his last line as a key rhetorical moment in the text. What elements make it a powerful conclusion for his speech?
- ❑ **Write.** Watch the video of Gore delivering this speech, linked through the *Envision* Website. Look carefully at how he delivers the speech, considering elements such as vocal intonation, emphasis, pacing, and embodied rhetoric. Now write an essay in which you analyze how the canon of delivery influences the persuasiveness of this speech.
  www.pearsonhighered.com/envision/281

Seeing Connections
See Chapter 9 for a discussion of oral rhetoric and the canon of delivery.

■ **Mark Jacobson** *and* **Mark A. Delucchi** *In anticipation of the December 2009 Copenhagen Environmental Summit, which many looked to as a pivotal moment in defining a global plan to curb climate change,* Scientific American *devoted its entire November 2009 issue to questions of sustainability and environmental issues. This piece, co-authored by Stanford Civil & Environmental Engineering Professor Mark Jacobson and Mark Delucchi, a research scientist from UC Davis's Institute of Transportation Studies, was featured as the issue's cover story and touched on how alternative energy sources could be leveraged to reduce dependence on fossil fuels and provide for the world's energy needs.*

A Path to Sustainable Energy by 2030

Mark Jacobson and Mark A. Delucchi

In December leaders from around the world will meet in Copenhagen to try to agree on cutting back greenhouse gas emissions for decades to come. The most effective step to implement that goal would be a massive shift away from fossil fuels to clean, renewable energy sources. If leaders can have confidence that such a transformation is possible, they might commit to an historic agreement. We think they can.

A year ago former vice president Al Gore threw down a gauntlet: to repower America with 100 percent carbon-free electricity within 10 years. As the two of us started to evaluate the feasibility of such a change, we took on an even larger challenge: to determine how 100 percent of the world's energy, for all purposes, could be supplied by wind, water and solar resources, by as early as 2030. Our plan is presented here.

Scientists have been building to this moment for at least a decade, analyzing various pieces of the challenge. Most recently, a 2009 Stanford University study ranked energy systems according to their impacts on global warming, pollution, water supply, land use. wildlife and other concerns. The very best options were wind, solar, geothermal, tidal and hydroelectric power—all of which are driven by wind, water or sunlight (referred to as WWS). Nuclear power, coal with carbon capture, and ethanol were all poorer options, as were oil and natural gas. The study also found that battery-electric vehicles and hydrogen fuel-cell vehicles recharged by WWS options would largely eliminate pollution from the transportation sector.

Our plan calls for millions of wind turbines, water machines and solar installations. The numbers are large, but the scale is not an insurmountable hurdle; society has achieved massive transformations before. During World War II, the U.S. retooled automobile factories to produce 300,000 aircraft, and other countries produced 486,000 more. In 1956 the U.S. began building the Interstate Highway System, which after 35 years extended for 47,000 miles, changing commerce and society.

5 Is it feasible to transform the world's energy systems? Could it be accomplished in two decades? The answers depend on the technologies chosen, the availability of critical materials, and economic and political factors.

Clean Technologies Only

Renewable energy comes from enticing sources: wind, which also produces waves; water, which includes hydroelectric, tidal and geothermal energy (water heated by hot underground rock); and solar, which includes photovoltaics and solar power plants that focus sunlight to heat a fluid that drives a turbine to generate electricity. Our WWS plan includes only technologies that work or are close to working today on a large scale, rather than those that may exist 20 or 30 years from now.

To ensure that our system remains clean, we consider only technologies that have near-zero emissions of greenhouse gases and air pollutants over their entire life cycle, including construction, operation and decommissioning. For example, when burned in vehicles, even the most ecologically acceptable sources of ethanol create air pollution that will cause the same mortality level as when gasoline is burned. Nuclear power results in up to 25 times more carbon emissions than wind energy, when reactor construction and uranium refining and transport are considered. Carbon capture and sequestration technology can reduce carbon dioxide emissions from coal-fired power plants but will increase air pollutants and will extend all the other deleterious effects of coal mining, transport and processing, because more coal must be burned to power the capture and storage steps. Similarly, we consider only technologies that do not present significant waste disposal or terrorism risks.

In our plan, WWS will supply electric power for heating and transportation—industries that will have to revamp if the world has any hope of slowing climate change. We have assumed that most fossil-fuel heating (as well as ovens and stoves) can be replaced by electric systems and that most fossil-fuel transportation can be replaced by battery and fuel-cell vehicles. Hydrogen, produced by using WWS electricity to split water (electrolysis), would power fuel cells and be burned in airplanes and by industry.

Plenty of Supply

Today the maximum power consumed worldwide at any given moment is about 12.5 trillion watts (terawatts, or TW), according to the U.S. Energy Information Administration. The agency projects that in 2030 the world will require 16.9 TW of power as global population and living standards rise, with about 2.8 TW in the U.S. The mix of sources is similar to today's, heavily dependent on fossil fuels. If, however, the planet were powered entirely by WWS, with no fossil-fuel or biomass combustion, an intriguing savings would occur. Global power demand would be only 11.5 TW, and U.S. demand would be 1.8 TW. That decline occurs because, in most cases, electrification is a more efficient way to use energy. For example, only 17 to 20 percent of the energy in gasoline is used to move a vehicle (the rest is wasted as heat), whereas 75 to 86 percent of the electricity delivered to an electric vehicle goes into motion.

10 Even if demand did rise to 16.9 TW, WWS sources could provide far more power. Detailed studies by us and others indicate that energy from the wind, worldwide, is about 1,700 TW. Solar, alone, offers 6,500 TW. Of course, wind and sun out in the open seas, over high mountains and across protected regions would not be available. If we subtract these and low-wind areas not likely to be developed, we are still left with 40 to 85 TW for wind and 580 TW for solar, each far beyond future human demand. Yet currently we generate only 0.02 TW of wind power and 0.008 TW of solar. These sources hold an incredible amount of untapped potential.

The other WWS technologies will help create a flexible range of options. Although all the sources can expand greatly, for practical reasons, wave power can be extracted only near coastal areas. Many geothermal sources are too deep to be tapped economically. And even though hydroelectric power now exceeds all other WWS sources, most of the suitable large reservoirs are already in use.

The Plan: Power Plants Required

Clearly, enough renewable energy exists. How, then, would we transition to a new infrastructure to provide the world with 11.5 TW? We have chosen a mix of technologies emphasizing wind and solar, with about 9 percent of demand met by mature water-related methods. (Other combinations of wind and solar could be as successful.)

Wind supplies 51 percent of the demand, provided by 3.8 million large wind turbines (each rated at five megawatts) worldwide. Although that quantity may sound enormous, it is interesting to note that the world manufactures 73 million cars and light trucks every year. Another 40 percent of the power comes from photovoltaics and concentrated solar plants, with about 30 percent of the photovoltaic output from rooftop panels on homes and commercial buildings. About 89,000 photovoltaic and concentrated solar power plants, averaging 300 megawatts apiece, would be needed. Our mix also includes 900 hydroelectric stations worldwide, 70 percent of which are already in place.

Only about 0.8 percent of the wind base is installed today. The worldwide footprint of the 3.8 million turbines would be less than 50 square kilometers (smaller than Manhattan). When the needed spacing between them is figured, they would occupy about 1 percent of the earth's land, but the empty space among turbines could be used for agriculture or ranching or as open land or ocean. The nonrooftop photovoltaics and concentrated solar plants would occupy about 0.33 percent of the planet's land. Building such an extensive infrastructure will take time. But so did the current power plant network. And remember that if we stick with fossil fuels, demand by 2030 will rise to 16.9 TW, requiring about 13,000 large new coal plants, which themselves would occupy a lot more land, as would the mining to supply them.

The Materials Hurdle

15 The scale of the WWS infrastructure is not a barrier. But a few materials needed to build it could be scarce or subject to price manipulation.

Enough concrete and steel exist for the millions of wind turbines, and both those commodities are fully recyclable. The most problematic materials may be rare-earth metals such as neodymium used in turbine gearboxes. Although the metals are not in short supply, the low-cost sources are concentrated in China, so countries such as the U.S. could be trading dependence on Middle Eastern oil for dependence on Far Eastern metals. Manufacturers are moving toward gear-less turbines, however, so that limitation may become moot.

Photovoltaic cells rely on amorphous or crystalline silicon, cadmium telluride, or copper indium selenide and surfide. Limited supplies of tellurium and indium could reduce the prospects for some types of thin-film solar cells, though not for all; the other types might be able to take up the slack. Large-scale production could be restricted by the silver that cells require, but finding ways to reduce the silver content could tackle that hurdle. Recycling parts from old cells could ameliorate material difficulties as well.

Three components could pose challenges for building millions of electric vehicles: rare-earth metals for electric motors, lithium for lithium-ion batteries and platinum for fuel cells. More than half the world's lithium reserves lie in Bolivia and Chile. That concentration, combined with rapidly growing demand, could raise prices significantly. More problematic is the claim by Meridian International Research that not enough economically recoverable lithium exists to build anywhere near the number of batteries needed in a global electric-vehicle economy. Recycling could change the equation, but the economics of recycling depend in part on whether batteries are made with easy recyclability in mind, an issue the industry is aware of. The long-term use of platinum also depends on recycling; current available reserves would sustain annual production of 20 million fuel-cell vehicles, along with existing industrial uses, for fewer than 100 years.

Smart Mix for Reliability

A new infrastructure must provide energy on demand at least as reliably as the existing infrastructure. WWS technologies generally suffer less downtime than traditional sources. The average U.S. coal plant is offline 12.5 percent of the year for scheduled and unscheduled maintenance. Modern wind turbines have a down time of less than 2 percent on land and less than 5 percent at sea. Photovoltaic systems are also at less than 2 percent. Moreover, when an individual wind, solar or wave device is down, only a small fraction of production is affected; when a coal, nuclear or natural gas plant goes offline, a large chunk of generation is lost.

20 The main WWS challenge is that the wind does not always blow and the sun does not always shine in a given location. Intermittency problems can be mitigated by a smart balance of sources, such as generating a base supply from steady geothermal or tidal power, relying on wind at night when it is often plentiful, using solar by day and turning to a reliable source such as hydroelectric that can be turned on and off quickly to smooth out supply or meet peak demand. For example, interconnecting wind farms that are only 100 to 200 miles apart can compensate for hours of zero power at any one farm should the wind not be blowing there. Also helpful is interconnecting geographically dispersed sources so they can back up one another, installing smart electric meters in homes that automatically recharge electric vehicles when demand is low and building facilities that store power for later use.

Because the wind often blows during stormy conditions when the sun does not shine and the sun often shines on calm days with little wind, combining wind and solar can go a long way toward meeting demand, especially when geothermal provides a steady base and hydroelectric can be called on to fill in the gaps.

As Cheap as Coal

The mix of WWS sources in our plan can reliably supply the residential, commercial, industrial and transportation sectors. The logical next question is whether the power would be affordable. For each technology, we calculated how much it would cost a producer to generate power and transmit it across the grid. We included the annualized cost of capital, land, operations, maintenance, energy storage to help offset intermittent supply, and transmission. Today the cost of wind, geothermal and hydroelectric are all less than seven cents a kilowatt-hour (¢/kWh); wave and solar are higher. But by 2020 and beyond wind, wave and hydro are expected to be 4¢/kWh or less.

For comparison, the average cost in the U.S. in 2007 of conventional power generation and transmission was about 7¢/kWh, and it is projected to be 8¢/kWh in 2020. Power from wind turbines, for example, already costs about the same or less than it does from a new coal or natural gas plant, and in the future wind power is expected to be the least costly of all options. The competitive cost of wind has made it the second-largest source of new electric power generation in the U.S. for the past three years, behind natural gas and ahead of coal.

Solar power is relatively expensive now but should be competitive as early as 2020. A careful analysis by Vasilis Fthenakis of Brookhaven National Laboratory indicates that within 10 years, photovoltaic system costs could drop to about 10¢/kWh, including long-distance transmission and the cost of compressed-air storage of power for use at night. The same analysis estimates that concentrated solar power systems with enough thermal storage to generate electricity 24 hours a day in spring, summer and fall could deliver electricity at 10¢/kWh or less.

Transportation in a WWS world will be driven by batteries or fuel cells, so we should compare the economics of these electric vehicles with that of internal-combustion-engine vehicles. Detailed analyses by one of us (Delucchi) and Tim Lipman of the University of California, Berkeley, have indicated that mass-produced electric vehicles with advanced lithium-ion or nickel metal-hydride batteries could have a full lifetime cost per mile (including battery replacements) that is comparable with that of a gasoline vehicle, when gasoline sells for more than $2 a gallon.

When the so-called externality costs (the monetary value of damages to human health, the environment and climate) of fossil-fuel generation are taken into account, WWS technologies become even more cost-competitive.

Overall construction cost for a WWS system might be on the order of $100 trillion worldwide, over 20 years, not including transmission. But this is not money handed out by governments or consumers. It is investment that is paid back through the sale of electricity and energy. And again, relying on traditional sources would raise output from 12.5 to 16.9 TW, requiring thousands more of those plants, costing roughly $10 trillion, not to mention tens of trillions of dollars more in health, environmental and security costs. The WWS plan gives the world a new, clean, efficient energy system rather than an old, dirty, inefficient one.

Political Will

Our analyses strongly suggest that the costs of WWS will become competitive with traditional sources. In the interim, however, certain forms of WWS power will be significantly more costly than fossil power. Some combination of WWS subsidies and carbon taxes would thus be needed for a time. A feed-in tariff (FIT) program to cover the difference between generation cost and wholesale electricity prices is especially effective at scaling-up new technologies. Combining FITs with a so-called declining clock auction, in which the right to sell power to the grid goes to the lowest bidders, provides continuing incentive for WWS developers to lower costs. As that happens, FITs can be phased out. FITs have been implemented in a number of European countries and a few U.S. states and have been quite successful in stimulating solar power in Germany.

Taxing fossil fuels or their use to reflect their environmental damages also makes sense. But at a minimum, existing subsidies for fossil energy, such as tax benefits for exploration and extraction, should be eliminated to level the playing field. Misguided promotion of alternatives that are less desirable than WWS power, such as farm and production subsidies for biofuels, should also be ended, because it delays deployment of cleaner systems. For their part, legislators crafting policy must find ways to resist lobbying by the entrenched energy industries.

Finally, each nation needs to be willing to invest in a robust, long-distance transmission system that can carry large quantities of WWS power from remote regions where it is often greatest—such as the Great Plains for wind and the desert Southwest for solar in the U.S.—to centers of consumption, typically cities. Reducing consumer demand during peak usage periods also requires a smart grid that gives generators and consumers much more control over electricity usage hour by hour.

A large-scale wind, water and solar energy system can reliably supply the world's needs, significantly benefiting climate, air quality, water quality, ecology and energy security. As we have shown, the obstacles are primarily political, not technical. A combination of feed-in tariffs plus incentives for providers to reduce costs, elimination of fossil subsidies and an intelligently expanded grid could be enough to ensure rapid deployment. Of course, changes in the real-world power and transportation industries will have to overcome sunk investments in existing infrastructure. But with sensible policies, nations could set a goal of generating 25 percent of their new energy supply with WWS sources in 10 to 15 years and almost 100 percent of new supply in 20 to 30 years. With extremely aggressive policies, all existing fossil-fuel capacity could theoretically be retired and replaced in the same period, but with more modest and likely policies full replacement may take 40 to 50 years. Either way, clear leadership is needed, or else nations will keep trying technologies promoted by industries rather than vetted by scientists.

A decade ago it was not clear that a global WWS system would be technically or economically feasible. Having shown that it is, we hope global leaders can figure out how to make WWS power politically feasible as well. They can start by committing to meaningful climate and renewable energy goals now.

Reflect & Write

- ❑ How do the authors use subheads to structure the argument? What do the subheads add to the text? What changes would the authors have to make if they had decided not to use them?
- ❑ Find the article's thesis statement. Do the authors follow through on this thesis in the rest of the article?
- ❑ To what extent is the development of this article dominated by *ethos*? By *pathos*? By *logos*? What do the authors accomplish through these rhetorical choices?
- ❑ Toward the end, the authors suggest that the obstacles to a mass adoption of alternative fuel sources "are primarily political, not technical." Locate some specific places in the article where they make this point. How persuasive is this claim?
- ❑ **Write.** Convert this article into a short, formal speech in high style that is a call to action. Your speech should be no longer than five minutes in length, so you will need to condense Jacobson and Delucchi's points to accommodate this time frame. Practice your delivery, taking care to consider embodied rhetoric and oral delivery. Deliver your speech to the class, and then discuss which had a more powerful effect on the audience: the *Scientific American* piece or your speech.

Seeing Connections
Review strategies for translating an article into a presentation on page 195.

PERSPECTIVES ON THE ISSUE

1. Compare Al Gore's before-and-after satellite images of Florida in Figure 10.19 to Jill Soubule's song about Global Warming, linked through the *Envision* Website. What different approach does each writer take to showing his or her audience the possible consequences of global warming? In what rhetorical situation would each one be most appropriate? Does one make a more persuasive argument? If so, how?
www.pearsonhighered.com/envision/286
2. Do you think, paraphrasing Kolbert's question, that Americans can go green? Write an essay answering this question, drawing on texts from this section as well as your own experience and examples.
3. Several of these articles offer differing stances on how we should approach climate change on a national or even international level. Using the strategies for writing a dialogue of sources from Chapter 5, choose three or four of the authors and write a fictional dialogue between them in which you highlight their own individual stances. Start by writing key questions to ask the writers; as you have them articulate their positions, use direct quotations from the sources you read above. As you move from the monologue to dialogue, consider what they would say in response to one another. Draft yourself into the conversation as a moderator figure: be sure that you provide an opening frame in which you introduce each of the speakers, that you interject commentary into their conversation, and that you provide closing remarks that synthesize the key points from the conversation.

FROM READING TO RESEARCH

1. In her article, Elizabeth Kolbert calls *An Inconvenient Truth* "the world's first film based on a PowerPoint presentation," and clearly the award-winning film also had a much larger impact than the slide presentation from which it derived. Following that argument, the book *Inconvenient Truth* may be the world's first book based on a PowerPoint presentation. Check out the book from your library and watch the film; then write a comparative analysis in which you look at how the same argument was produced in two different media. Is one more persuasive than the other or more successful (those might not mean the same thing)? Why?

Student Writing

See several examples of student papers about Green Culture.

www.pearsonhighered.com/envision/287

2. Look at some of the environmentally themed ads from Diesel clothing and Denver Water linked through the *Envision* Website. Perform a rhetorical analysis on one or more of the ads, considering the way in which it conveys its argument to the reader.
www.pearsonhighered.com/envision/287

3. Building from "The Path to Sustainable Energy," choose one of the following topics or controversies on which to conduct your own research: wind farms; invasive species; Three Gorges Dam in China; the Mohavi solar array; hydrogen fuel cells; geo-engineering; hybrid car technology; transmission lines in Texas; high altitude wind power. Narrow your topic to so that you can make a strong claim, and use at least eight sources to develop your argument about this controversy or technology in relation to the larger conversation about the development of sustainable energies for the future.

4. Read one or more of Edward Tufte's books on visual design, such as *Envisioning Information*, *Visual Explanations*, and *The Visual Display of Quantitative Information*. Now look again at Gore's use of information graphics in book version of *An Inconvenient Truth.* Would Tufte approve of Gore's use of charts, graphs, and other visual evidence? Why or why not? Use quotes from Tufte and examples from Gore to support your claim.

Visit www.pearsonhighered.com/envision for expanded assignment guidelines and student projects.
Visit www.mycomplab.com for additional general writing and research resources.

CHAPTER 11

Culture 2.0

What does it mean to live in a world defined by "Culture 2.0"? The image in Figure 11.1 offers one perspective. As the image suggests, Culture 2.0 surrounds us with stimulating encounters and interfaces. It is culture literally taken to the next level. As part of Culture 2.0, we read our novels on Kindles and iPads, and we get our news from flash-driven Websites and personalized online RSS subscriptions. However, we not only read material on the Internet; we also create material, post on blogs, edit wikis, and share our photos, videos, and thoughts, as well as our own mash ups and remixes of popular texts. We manage our lives with our BlackBerrys and smartphones, and we measure a carrier's worth by the dimensions of its Wi-Fi coverage. In our cars, our talking TomToms tell us how to get from point A to point B, and advanced GPS technology in our cell phones and even cameras helps us geolocate ourselves, our friends, and all of our photographed experiences. We watch our media on our iPods, our cellphones, on HD tablets, iPads, 50"-plasma TVs, and in the theater in 3-D with digital surround sound. We spend our leisure time in immersive environments and alternate worlds, or gaming with systems that enable multiplayer campaigns or that track our physical movements and translate them to the screen. We create and re-create multiple online identities and profiles for ourselves, and we connect with our friends through pithy 140 character updates, textspeak-laden instant messages, and videochat. In some ways, Culture 2.0 is the future, and we are immersed in it.

FIGURE 11.1. Culture 2.0 surrounds us with many possibilities for virtual experiences that can be seen as either exciting or overwhelming.

Source: http://www.adweek.com/aw/contentdisplay/special-reports/30-anniversary/articles/e3i33bb91d0a29fdfb122d1ae67711847cd.

However, there is a flipside to the Culture 2.0 phenomenon, which is also suggested by the image in Figure 11.1: modern life offers us many opportunities, but it also offers us perhaps too many distractions. In our oversaturated, mediated society, sometimes we can feel a bit like the man in the photo: running to keep up with technological changes, overwhelmed, fragmented, not knowing exactly where to look or what to listen to first. With our advances in culture come new intellectual and ethical questions. How much is too much? Is our reliance on media distorting our understanding of ourselves and our reality? In fact, does our consumption of media change who we are and how we experience the world? How does it change our basic understanding of what culture is and how it is made?

In this chapter, we will explore some of these questions through an in-depth examination of three facets of contemporary culture: social media, gaming, and popular culture. In "Social Media, Social Lives," we will look at how tech-driven advances in how we interact with our network of friends have changed our understanding of ourselves, our relationships, and our possibilities for social action. Then, in "Virtual Worlds and Gaming Lives," we will investigate the world of immersive environments and gaming culture. We'll look at identity construction through avatars, how gender politics are mapped onto game design, how violent game play affects players, and the way persuasive gaming can be used to serve a specific social or political agenda. We'll conclude this chapter by digging deep into the nature of culture creation itself. By asking "Who Owns Popular Culture?" we'll tap into the complex issues of proprietary rights surrounding user-created content. In a read-write world, where pop culture consumers can easily adapt and remix existing texts into fresh creations, where do we draw the line between author and audience? Between theft and creativity? For many, as for the man in Figure 11.1, the experience of Culture 2.0 can be viewed through different perspectives, as exciting or overwhelming. By examining these issues in depth, we hope to draw them into sharper focus.

SOCIAL LIVES AND SOCIAL MEDIA

How has our understanding of ourselves and our relationships with others changed with the rapid growth of social media? That is the question that this section attempts to answer by providing a variety of viewpoints on how our hyperconnected technological lives have changed the way we experience our interactions with our family, our friends, and the world around us.

This is also the question that informs Mick Stevens's cartoon, published in the March 15, 2010 issue of the *New Yorker.* As you can see in Figure 11.2, the scene initially seems a stereotypical one: a hospital nursery, lined with rows of bassinets, and a professional-looking nurse busy with forms to one side. What distinguishes this particular scenario is the center frame: a small pair of hands holding a rectangular shaped object and a

FIGURE 11.2. In this cartoon, artist Mick Stevens provides a humorous commentary on the new wired generation.

speech bubble proclaiming, "OMG! I just got born!" The commentary operates on multiple levels, moving us from a critique of technology to a critique of a generation. The meaning seems clear: Stevens is commenting on the birth of a new generation, one inculcated with technology from the cradle, for whom touch screens are second nature, immediate and constant connectedness is taken for granted, and the very nature of language itself (OMG!) is changing. Even more interesting, however, are the suggestions this cartoon makes about how we are learning to process reality. For this faceless baby, self-awareness is mediated completely by technology: it is as if his or her birth itself only becomes a fact when posted on an anonymous status update—as if private experience can only be legitimated and understood through public announcement.

This may seem like an extreme claim, but think about your own experiences with social media. To what extent have you come to rely on your friend's profiles, status updates, or Twitter feeds to mark events and occurrences in their lives? How much of your social life do you manage in person, and how much do you manage through the devices (cell phones, laptops, netbooks) that increasingly dominate our lives? And how much do the constant advances in those devices—from the release of the iPhone and Google's Nexus One to the proliferation of mobile applications ("There's an App for that!")—further encourage us to move our social life into online spaces? Clearly the shift to technologically mediated relationships is hardly unproblematic. Scholars from many disciplines are just starting to make sense of how such online interactions are changing our lived experience. Communications experts warn of the way that sites like MySpace and Facebook encourage users to create menu-driven identities (What's your favorite TV show? Political stance? School affiliation? Religion?) that curtail true creative self-expression. Linguists and English professors worry about the way that textspeak (LOL) and 140 character limits on status updates are changing language and the way we process and construct information. Legal scholars worry about intentional or unintentional privacy violations. Activists and political scientists ponder the implications of transforming activism into a process of forming online protest groups or microblogging about unfolding current events. In this section, we'll explore different views on the effects of social media on our social lives to better understand the impact of new technologies on the way we understand ourselves, our friends, and the world around us.

Seeing Connections
For another cartoonist's commentary on how technology defines our social identity, see Figure 1.9 (page 9).

Reflect & Write

- ❑ Why do you think Stevens only shows the baby's hands? How would showing the baby's head, face, or body have changed the emphasis of the image?
- ❑ Why include the nurse in the frame? What does she contribute to the cartoon?
- ❑ **Write.** This cartoon makes an argument about one generation's interaction with technology and social media. Sketch either a single-panel or multiple-panel cartoon that provides an argument about an older generation's relationship to technology.

■ *The* **Pew Internet & American Life Project** *conducts studies examining the impact of the Internet on twenty-first-century culture, including families, education, and civic life. The project, which sent out its first survey in 2000, is one of seven projects that comprise the Pew Research Center, an organization focused on investigating the social forces and trends that shape contemporary American life. What follows is a summary of its report on Social Media and Young Adults, which was published in February 2010. The researchers included Amanda Lenhart, the direct of the project's research on teens and their families; Kristen Purcell, the associate director of research; Aaron Smith, a research specialist in the area of teens, family, and the role of technology in civic life; and research assistant Kathryn Zickuhr. The report is based primarily on data they collected between June and September 2009 from teenagers between the ages of 12 and 17.*

Social Media and Young Adults

Summary of Findings

Overview

Since 2006, blogging has dropped among teens and young adults while simultaneously rising among older adults. As the tools and technology embedded in social networking sites change, and use of the sites continues to grow, youth may be exchanging 'macro-blogging' for microblogging with status updates.

Blogging has declined in popularity among both teens and young adults since 2006. Blog commenting has also dropped among teens.

- 14% of online teens now say they blog, down from 28% of teen internet users in 2006.
- This decline is also reflected in the lower incidence of teen commenting on blogs within social networking websites; 52% of teen social network users report commenting on friends' blogs, down from the 76% who did so in 2006.
- By comparison, the prevalence of blogging within the overall adult internet population has remained steady in recent years. Pew Internet surveys since 2005 have consistently found that roughly one in ten online adults maintain a personal online journal or blog.

While blogging among adults as a whole has remained steady, the prevalence of blogging within specific age groups has changed dramatically in recent years. Specifically, a sharp decline in blogging by young adults has been tempered by a corresponding increase in blogging among older adults.

- In December 2007, 24% of online 18–29 year olds reported blogging, compared with 7% of those thirty and older.
- By 2009, just 15% of internet users ages 18–29 maintain a blog—a nine percentage point drop in two years. However, 11% of internet users ages thirty and older now maintain a personal blog.

Both teen and adult use of social networking sites has risen significantly, yet there are shifts and some drops in the proportion of teens using several social networking site features.

- 73% of wired American teens now use social networking websites, a significant increase from previous surveys. Just over half of online teens (55%) used social networking sites in November 2006 and 65% did so in February 2008.
- As the teen social networking population has increased, the popularity of some sites' features has shifted. Compared with SNS activity in February 2008, a smaller proportion of teens in mid-2009 were sending daily messages to friends via SNS, or sending bulletins, group messages or private messages on the sites.
- 47% of online adults use social networking sites, up from 37% in November 2008.
- Young adults act much like teens in their tendency to use these sites. Fully 72% of online 18–29 year olds use social networking websites, nearly identical to the rate among teens, and significantly higher than the 39% of internet users ages 30 and up who use these sites.
- Adults are increasingly fragmenting their social networking experience as a majority of

those who use social networking sites—52%—say they have two or more different profiles. That is up from 42% who had multiple profiles in May 2008.

- Facebook is currently the most commonly-used online social network among adults. Among adult profile owners 73% have a profile on Facebook, 48% have a profile on MySpace and 14% have a LinkedIn profile.[1]
- The specific sites on which young adults maintain their profiles are different from those used by older adults: Young profile owners are much more likely to maintain a profile on MySpace (66% of young profile owners do so, compared with just 36% of those thirty and older) but less likely to have a profile on the professionally-oriented LinkedIn (7% vs. 19%). In contrast, adult profile owners under thirty and those thirty and older are equally likely to maintain a profile on Facebook (71% of young profile owners do so, compared with 75% of older profile owners).

5 Teens are not using Twitter in large numbers. While teens are bigger users of almost all other online applications, Twitter is an exception.

- 8% of internet users ages 12–17 use Twitter.[2] This makes Twitter as common among teens as visiting a virtual world, and far less common than sending or receiving text messages as 66% of teens do, or going online for news and political information, done by 62% of online teens.
- Older teens are more likely to use Twitter than their younger counterparts; 10% of online teens ages 14–17 do so, compared with 5% of those ages 12–13.
- High school age girls are particularly likely to use Twitter. Thirteen percent of online girls ages 14–17 use Twitter, compared with 7% of boys that age.
- Using different wording, we find that 19% of adult internet users use Twitter or similar services to post short status updates and view the updates of others online.
- Young adults lead the way when it comes to using Twitter or status updating. One-third of online 18–29 year olds post or read status updates.

Wireless internet use rates are especially high among young adults, and the laptop has replaced the desktop as the computer of choice among those under thirty.

- 81% of adults between the ages of 18 and 29 are wireless internet users. By comparison, 63% of 30–49 year olds and 34% of those ages 50 and up access the internet wirelessly.
- Roughly half of 18-29 year olds have accessed the internet wirelessly on a laptop (55%) or on a cell phone (55%), and about one quarter of 18–29 year-olds (28%) have accessed the internet wirelessly on another device such as an e-book reader or gaming device.
- The impact of the mobile web can be seen in young adults' computer choices. Two-thirds of 18–29 year olds (66%) own a laptop or netbook, while 53% own a desktop computer. Young adults are the only age cohort for which laptop computers are more popular than desktops.
- African Americans adults are the most active users of the mobile web, and their use is growing at a faster pace than mobile internet use among white or Hispanic adults.

Cell phone ownership is nearly ubiquitous among teens and young adults, and much of the growth in teen cell phone ownership has been driven by adoption among the youngest teens.

- Three-quarters (75%) of teens and 93% of adults ages 18–29 now have a cell phone.
- In the past five years, cell phone ownership has become mainstream among even the youngest teens. Fully 58% of 12-year olds now own a cell phone, up from just 18% of such teens as recently as 2004.

Internet use is near-ubiquitous among teens and young adults. In the last decade, the young adult internet population has remained the most likely to go online.

- 93% of teens ages 12–17 go online, as do 93% of young adults ages 18–29. One quarter (74%) of all adults ages 18 and older go online.

---

[1] Because respondents were allowed to mention multiple sites on which they maintain a profile, totals may add to more than 100%.

[2] The question is asked differently among teens and adults–teens were asked "Do you ever use Twitter?" while adults were asked "have you ever used Twitter or another service where you can update your status online?" which may explain some of the difference in the data between the two groups.

- Over the past ten years, teens and young adults have been consistently the two groups most likely to go online, even as the internet population has grown and even with documented larger increases in certain age cohorts (e.g. adults 65 and older).

Our survey of teens also tracked some core internet activities by those ages 12–17 and found:

- 62% of online teens get news about current events and politics online.
- 48% of wired teens have bought things online like books, clothing or music, up from 31% who had done so in 2000 when we first asked about this.
- 31% of online teens get health, dieting or physical fitness information from the internet. And 17% of online teens report they use the internet to gather information about health topics that are hard to discuss with others such as drug use and sexual health topics.

Reflect & Write

- ❑ Which was the most surprising statistic to you in the summary? Why?
- ❑ The summary begins with a discussion of blogging. Why do you think that the researchers began that way? If you had to suggest an alternate type of social media to feature at the opening of the report, which would it have been?
- ❑ Although there are many information graphics included on the Website and in the full-length report, there are none in the summary. What would information graphics have contributed to this report? How do you think through the information differently without them?
- ❑ **Write.** Select one section of the report (the section on blogging, or on Twitter, for example) and write a paragraph about teenage use of that type of social media that draws on the statistical information to create an engaging, coherent, and cohesive paragraph. Don't forget to use a topic sentence to establish the purpose and claim that the paragraph will develop and to spotlight your own voice, using the source material to support your points.

Seeing Connections

When using statistics in your own work, keep in mind social psychologist Philip Zimbardo's advice (pages 106–107).

---

danah boyd *is a Fellow at Harvard University's Berkman Center for Internet and Society and a Social Media Researcher at Microsoft Research New England. In addition, she is one of the co-authors of* Hanging Out, Messing Around, and Geeking Out: Kids Living and Learning with New Media *(2009). As this title indicates, her research focuses principally on youth and social media, a topic about which she blogs and tweets frequently. The following is an excerpt from "White Flight in Networked Publics? How Race and Class Shaped American Teen Engagement with MySpace and Facebook," which originally appeared on boyd's blog, Apophenia, and is forthcoming in Lisa Nakamura and Peter Chow-White's Digital Race Anthology (Routledge).*

Social Network Site Taste Test: MySpace or Facebook?

danah boyd

For many teens, embracing MySpace or Facebook is seen as a social necessity. Which site is "cool" depends on one's cohort. Milo, an Egyptian 15-year-old from Los Angeles, joined MySpace because it was *"the thing"* in his peer group but another girl from the same school, Korean 17-year-old Seong, told me that Facebook was the preferred site among her friends.

In an environment where profiles serve as "digital bodies" (Boyd, 2008), profile personalization can be seen as a form of digital fashion. Teens' Facebook and MySpace profiles reflect their taste, identity, and values (Donath, 2007). Through the use of imagery and textual self-expressions, teens make race, class, and other identity markers visible. As Nakamura (2008) has argued, even in the most constrained online environments, participants will use what's available to them to reveal identity information in ways that make race and other identity elements visible.

In describing what was desirable about Facebook versus MySpace, teens often turned to talk about aesthetics and profile personalization. Teens' aesthetics shaped their attitudes towards each site. In essence, the *"glitter"* produced by those who *"pimp out"* their MySpaces is seen by some in a positive light while others see it as *"gaudy," "tacky,"* and *"cluttered."* While Facebook fans loved the site's aesthetic minimalism, others viewed this tone as *"boring," "lame,"* and *"elitist."* Catalina, a white 15-year-old from Austin, told me that Facebook is better because *"Facebook just seems more clean to me."*—Catalina. What Catalina sees as cleanliness, Indian-American 17-year-old Anindita from Los Angeles, labels simplicity; she recognizes the value of simplicity, but she prefers the *"bling"* of MySpace because it allows her to express herself.

5 The extensive options for self-expression are precisely what annoy some teens. Craig Pelletier, a 17-year-old from California, complained that,

> *"these tools gave MySpacers the freedom to annoy as much as they pleased. Facebook was nice because it stymied such annoyance, by limiting individuality. Everyone's page looked pretty much the same, but you could still look at pictures of each other. The MySpace crowd felt caged and held back because they weren't able to make their page unique."*—Craig

Craig believes the desire to personalize contributed to his peers' division between MySpace and Facebook.

In choosing how to express themselves, teens must account for what they wish to signal. Teens are drawn to styles that signal their identities and social groups. Due to a technical glitch, MySpace enabled users to radically shape the look and feel of their profiles while Facebook enforced a strict minimalism. To the degree that each site supports profile personalization in different ways, identity and self-presentation are affected. While some are drawn to the ability to radically shape their profiles to their liking, others prefer an enforced cleanness.

Teens who preferred MySpace lamented the limited opportunities for creative self-expression on Facebook, but those who preferred Facebook were much more derogatory about the style of profiles in MySpace. Not only did Facebook users not find MySpace profiles attractive, they argued that the styles produced by MySpace users were universally ugly. While Facebook's minimalism is not inherently better, conscientious restraint has been one marker of bourgeois fashion (Arnold, 2001). On the contrary, the flashy style that is popular on MySpace is often marked in relation to "bling-bling," a style of conspicuous consumption that is associated with urban black culture and hip-hop. To some, bling and flashy MySpace profiles are beautiful and creative; to others, these styles are garish. While style preference is not inherently about race and class, the specific styles referenced have racial overtones and socio-economic implications. In essence, although teens are talking about style, they are functionally navigating race and class.

Taste is also performed directly through profiles; an analysis of "taste statements" in MySpace combined with the friend network reveals that distinctions are visible there (Liu, 2007). The importance of music to MySpace made it a visible vector of taste culture. Youth listed their musical tastes on their profiles and attached songs to their pages. While many genres of music were present on MySpace, hip-hop stood out, both because of its salience amongst youth and because of its racial connotations. Although youth of all races and ethnicities listen to hip-hop, it is most commonly seen as a genre that stems from black culture inside urban settings. Narratives of the ghetto and black life dominate the lyrics of hip-hop and the genre also serves as a source of pride and authenticity in communities that are struggling for agency in American society (Forman, 2002). For some, participating in this taste culture is a point of pride; for others, this genre and the perceived attitudes that go with it are viewed as offensive. Although MySpace was never about hip-hop, its mere presence became one way in which detractors marked the site.

10 Taste and aesthetics are not universal, but deeply linked to identity and values. The choice of certain cultural signals or aesthetics appeals to some while repelling others. Often, these taste distinctions are shaped by class and race and, thus, the choice to mark Facebook and MySpace through the language of taste and aesthetics reflects race and class.

References

Arnold, Rebecca. 2001. *Fashion, Desire and Anxiety: Image and Morality in the 20th Century.* Rutgers, NJ: Rutgers University Press.

boyd, danah. 2008. *Taken Out of Context: American Teen Sociality in Networked Publics.* PhD Dissertation, University of California-Berkeley.

Donath, Judith. 2007. "Signals in Social Supernets." *Journal of Computer-Mediated Communication*, 13(1): article 12. http://jcmc.indiana.edu/vol13/issue1/donath.html

Forman, Murray. 2002. *The 'Hood Comes First: Race, Space, and Place in Rap and Hip-Hop.* Middleton, CT: Wesleyan University Press.

Liu, Hugo. 2007. "Social Network Profiles as Taste Performances." *Journal of Computer-Mediated Communication,* 13(1), article 13. http://jcmc.indiana.edu/vol13/issue1/liu.html

Nakamura, Lisa. 2008. *Digitizing Race: Visual Cultures of the Internet.* Minneapolis: University of Minnesota Press.

Reflect & Write

- ❑ Perform a quick rhetorical analysis of boyd's essay. Where does she rely on *logos*? *Ethos*? *Pathos*? How is each of the appeals used strategically in the essay?
- ❑ How does boyd use quotations, paraphrase and summary in this piece? Which are from primary sources? Which are from secondary sources? How do her choices about working with her sources affect the persuasiveness of her argument?
- ❑ How might boyd have used visual evidence to support her points? How might inserting photographs of teenagers produce a different impact than integrating screenshots from Facebook or MySpace? Which types of visual rhetoric do you think would most strongly underscore her argument?
- ❑ Write a response to danah boyd in the form of a blog comment in which you either confirm, refute, or qualify her concluding point that, "the choice to mark Facebook and MySpace through the language of taste and aesthetics reflects race and class." Refer to specific passages from her article in your response as well as evidence drawn from your own experience.

COLLABORATIVE CHALLENGE

Pull up a random MySpace page. Analyze the visual rhetoric of the page, paying special attention to the layout, use of color, content, design, and organization. How do these elements combine to create an impression about the persona of the page's author? What "argument" is the author making about him or herself, and how does the MySpace interface support it? Now, perform the same analysis, but this time on a random Facebook page. As a group, compare your findings, and develop a claim about the different ways in which MySpace and Facebook help their users construct an online identity.

A writer for the New York Times Magazine, **Clive Thompson** *specializes in writing about technology and society. He is also a columnist for* Wired *magazine and contributes articles to* Fast Company. *Thompson also posts his insights on collisiondetection.net, his blog about technology and culture. In this article, which was published originally in the September 7, 2008, issue of the* New York Times, *Thompson writes about the implications of the integration of the News Feed (a type of microblogging) into Facebook.*

I'm So Totally, Digitally Close to You

Clive Thompson

On Sept. 5, 2006, Mark Zuckerberg changed the way that Facebook worked, and in the process he inspired a revolt.

Zuckerberg, a doe-eyed 24-year-old C.E.O., founded Facebook in his dorm room at Harvard two years earlier, and the site quickly amassed nine million users. By 2006, students were posting heaps of personal details onto their Facebook pages, including lists of their favorite TV shows, whether they were dating (and whom), what music they had in rotation and the various ad hoc "groups" they had joined (like "Sex and the City" Lovers). All day long, they'd post "status" notes explaining their moods—"hating Monday," "skipping class b/c i'm hung over." After each party, they'd stagger home to the dorm and upload pictures of the soused revelry, and spend the morning after commenting on how wasted everybody looked. Facebook became the de facto public commons—the way students found out what everyone around them was like and what he or she was doing.

But Zuckerberg knew Facebook had one major problem: It required a lot of active surfing on the part of its users. Sure, every day your Facebook friends would update their profiles with some new tidbits; it might even be something particularly juicy, like changing their relationship status to "single" when they got dumped. But unless you visited each friend's page every day, it might be days or weeks before you noticed the news, or you might miss it entirely. Browsing Facebook was like constantly poking your head into someone's room to see how she was doing. It took work and forethought. In a sense, this gave Facebook an inherent, built-in level of privacy, simply because if you had 200 friends on the site—a fairly typical number—there weren't enough hours in the day to keep tabs on every friend all the time.

"It was very primitive," Zuckerberg told me when I asked him about it last month. And so he decided to modernize. He developed something he called News Feed, a built-in service that would actively broadcast changes in a user's page to every one of his or her friends.

Students would no longer need to spend their time zipping around to examine each friend's page, checking to see if there was any new information. Instead, they would just log into Facebook, and News Feed would appear: a single page that—like a social gazette from the 18th century—delivered a long list of up-to-the-minute gossip about their friends, around the clock, all in one place. "A stream of everything that's going on in their lives," as Zuckerberg put it.

5 When students woke up that September morning and saw News Feed, the first reaction, generally, was one of panic. Just about every little thing you changed on your page was now instantly blasted out to hundreds of friends, including potentially mortifying bits of news—*Tim and Lisa broke up; Persaud is no longer friends with Matthew*—and drunken photos someone snapped, then uploaded and tagged with names. Facebook had lost its vestigial bit of privacy. For students, it was now like being at a giant, open party filled with everyone you know, able to eavesdrop on what everyone else was saying, all the time.

"Everyone was freaking out," Ben Parr, then a junior at Northwestern University, told me recently. What particularly enraged Parr was that there wasn't any way to opt out of News Feed, to "go private" and have all your information kept quiet. He created a Facebook group demanding Zuckerberg either scrap News Feed or provide privacy options. "Facebook users really think Facebook is becoming the Big Brother of the Internet, recording every single move," a California student told The Star-Ledger of Newark. Another chimed in, "Frankly, I don't need to know or care that Billy broke up with Sally, and Ted has become friends with Steve." By lunchtime of the first day, 10,000 people had joined Parr's group, and by the next day it had 284,000.

Zuckerberg, surprised by the outcry, quickly made two decisions. The first was to add a privacy feature to News Feed, letting users decide what kind of information went out. But the second decision was to leave News Feed otherwise intact. He suspected that once people tried it and got over their shock, they'd like it.

He was right. Within days, the tide reversed. Students began e-mailing Zuckerberg to say that via News Feed they'd learned things they would never have otherwise discovered through random surfing around Facebook. The bits of trivia that News Feed delivered gave them more things to talk about—Why do you hate Kiefer Sutherland?—when they met friends face to face in class or at a party. Trends spread more quickly. When one student joined a group—proclaiming her love of Coldplay or a desire to volunteer for Greenpeace—all her friends instantly knew, and many would sign up themselves. Users' worries about their privacy seemed to vanish within days, boiled away by their excitement at being so much more connected to their friends. (Very few people stopped using Facebook, and most people kept on publishing most of their information through News Feed.) Pundits predicted that News Feed would kill Facebook, but the opposite happened. It catalyzed a massive boom in the site's growth. A few weeks after the News Feed imbroglio, Zuckerberg opened the site to the general public (previously, only students could join), and it grew quickly; today, it has 100 million users.

When I spoke to him, Zuckerberg argued that News Feed is central to Facebook's success. "Facebook has always tried to push the envelope," he said. "And at times that means stretching people and getting them to be comfortable with things they aren't yet comfortable with. A lot of this is just social norms catching up with what technology is capable of."

10 In essence, Facebook users didn't think they wanted constant, up-to-the-minute updates on what other people are doing. Yet when they experienced this sort of omnipresent knowledge, they found it intriguing and addictive. Why?

Social scientists have a name for this sort of incessant online contact. They call it "ambient awareness." It is, they say, very much like being physically near someone and picking up on his mood through the little things he does—body language, sighs, stray comments—out of the corner of your eye. Facebook is no longer alone in offering this sort of interaction online. In the last year, there has been a boom in tools for "microblogging": posting frequent tiny updates on what you're doing. The phenomenon is quite different from what we normally think of as blogging, because a blog post is usually a written piece, sometimes quite long: a statement of opinion, a story, an analysis. But these new updates are something different. They're far shorter, far more frequent and less carefully considered. One of the most popular new tools is Twitter, a Web site and messaging service that allows its two-million-plus users to broadcast to their friends haiku-length updates—limited to 140 characters, as brief as a mobile-phone text message—on what they're doing. There are other services for reporting where you're traveling (Dopplr) or for quickly tossing online a stream of the pictures, videos or Web sites you're looking at (Tumblr). And there are even tools that give your location. When the new iPhone, with built-in tracking, was introduced in July, one million people began using Loopt, a piece of software that automatically tells all your friends exactly where you are.

For many people—particularly anyone over the age of 30—the idea of describing your blow-by-blow activities in such detail is absurd. Why would you subject your friends to your daily minutiae? And conversely, how much of their trivia can you absorb? The growth of ambient intimacy can seem like modern narcissism taken to a new, supermetabolic extreme—the ultimate expression of a generation of celebrity-addled youths who believe their every utterance is fascinating and ought to be shared with the world. Twitter, in particular, has been the subject of nearly relentless scorn since it went online. "Who really cares what I am doing, every hour of the day?" wondered Alex Beam, a Boston Globe columnist, in an essay about Twitter last month. "Even I don't care."

Indeed, many of the people I interviewed, who are among the most avid users of these "awareness" tools, admit that at first they couldn't figure out why anybody would want to do this. Ben Haley, a 39-year-old documentation specialist for a software firm who lives in Seattle, told me that when he first heard about Twitter last year from an early-adopter friend who used it, his first reaction was that it seemed silly. But a few of his friends decided to give it a try, and they urged him to sign up, too.

Each day, Haley logged on to his account, and his friends' updates would appear as a long page of one- or two-line notes. He would check and recheck the account several times a day, or even several times an hour. The updates were indeed pretty banal. One friend would post about starting to feel sick; one posted random thoughts like "I really hate it when people clip their nails on the bus"; another Twittered whenever she made a sandwich—and she made a sandwich every day. Each so-called tweet was so brief as to be virtually meaningless.

15 But as the days went by, something changed. Haley discovered that he was beginning to sense the rhythms of his friends' lives in a way he never had before. When one friend got sick with a virulent fever, he could tell by her Twitter updates when she was getting worse and the instant she finally turned the corner. He could see when friends were heading into hellish days at work or when they'd scored a big success. Even the daily catalog of sandwiches became oddly mesmerizing, a sort of metronomic click that he grew accustomed to seeing pop up in the middle of each day.

This is the paradox of ambient awareness. Each little update—each individual bit of social information—is insignificant on its own, even supremely mundane. But taken together, over time, the little snippets coalesce into a surprisingly sophisticated portrait of your friends' and family members' lives, like thousands of dots making a pointillist painting. This was never before possible, because in the real world, no friend would bother to call you up and detail the sandwiches she was eating. The ambient information becomes like "a type of E.S.P.," as Haley described it to me, an invisible dimension floating over everyday life.

"It's like I can distantly read everyone's mind," Haley went on to say. "I love that. I feel like I'm getting to something raw about my friends. It's like I've got this heads-up display for them." It can also lead to more real-life contact, because when one member of Haley's group decides to go out to a bar or see a band and Twitters about his plans, the others see it, and some decide to drop by—ad hoc, self-organizing socializing. And when they do socialize face to face, it feels oddly as if they've never actually been apart. They don't need to ask, "So, what have you been up to?" because they already know. Instead, they'll begin discussing something that one of the friends Twittered that afternoon, as if picking up a conversation in the middle.

Facebook and Twitter may have pushed things into overdrive, but the idea of using communication tools as a form of "co-presence" has been around for a while. The Japanese sociologist Mizuko Ito first noticed it with mobile phones: lovers who were working in different cities would send text messages back and forth all night—tiny updates like "enjoying a glass of wine now" or "watching TV while lying on the couch." They were doing it partly because talking for hours on mobile phones isn't very comfortable (or affordable). But they also discovered that the little Ping-Ponging messages felt even more intimate than a phone call.

"It's an aggregate phenomenon," Marc Davis, a chief scientist at Yahoo and former professor of information science at the University of California at Berkeley, told me. "No message is the single-most-important message. It's sort of like when you're sitting with someone and you look over and they smile at you. You're sitting here reading the paper, and you're doing your side-by-side thing, and you just sort of let people know you're aware of them." Yet it is also why it can be extremely hard to understand the phenomenon until you've experienced it. Merely looking at a stranger's Twitter or Facebook feed isn't interesting, because it seems like blather. Follow it for a day, though, and it begins to feel like a short story; follow it for a month, and it's a novel.

20 You could also regard the growing popularity of online awareness as a reaction to social isolation, the modern American disconnectedness that Robert Putnam explored in his book "Bowling Alone." The mobile workforce requires people to travel more frequently for work, leaving friends and family behind, and members of the growing army of the self-employed often spend their days in solitude. Ambient intimacy becomes a way to "feel less alone," as more than one Facebook and Twitter user told me.

When I decided to try out Twitter last year, at first I didn't have anyone to follow. None of my friends were yet using the service. But while doing some Googling one day I stumbled upon the blog of Shannon Seery, a 32-year-old recruiting consultant in Florida, and I noticed that she Twittered. Her Twitter updates were pretty charming—she would often post links to camera-phone pictures of her two children or videos of herself cooking Mexican food, or broadcast her agonized cries when a flight was delayed on a business trip. So on a whim I started "following" her—as easy on Twitter as a click of the mouse—and never took her off my account. (A Twitter account can be "private," so that only invited friends can read one's tweets, or it can be public, so anyone can; Seery's was public.) When I checked in last month, I noticed that she had built up a huge number of online connections: She was now following 677 people on Twitter and another 442 on Facebook. How in God's name, I wondered, could she follow so many people? Who precisely are they? I called Seery to find out.

"I have a rule," she told me. "I either have to know who you are, or I have to know of you." That means she monitors the lives of friends, family, anyone she works with, and she'll also follow interesting people she discovers via her friends' online lives. Like many people who live online, she has wound up following a few strangers—though after a few months they no longer feel like strangers, despite the fact that she has never physically met them.

I asked Seery how she finds the time to follow so many people online. The math seemed daunting. After all, if her 1,000 online contacts each post just a couple of notes each a day, that's several thousand little social pings to sift through daily. What would it be like to get thousands of e-mail messages a day? But Seery made a point I heard from many others: awareness tools aren't as cognitively demanding as an e-mail message. E-mail is something you have to stop to open and assess. It's personal; someone is asking for 100 percent of your attention. In contrast, ambient updates are all visible on one single page in a big row, and they're not really directed at you. This makes them skimmable, like newspaper headlines; maybe you'll read them all, maybe you'll skip some. Seery estimated that she needs to spend only a small part of each hour actively reading her Twitter stream.

Yet she has, she said, become far more gregarious online. "What's really funny is that before this 'social media' stuff, I always said that I'm not the type of person who had a ton of friends," she told me. "It's so hard to make plans and have an active social life, having the type of job I have where I travel all the time and have two small kids. But it's easy to tweet all the time, to post pictures of what I'm doing, to keep social relations up." She paused for a second, before continuing: "Things like Twitter have actually given me a much bigger social circle. I know more about more people than ever before."

I realized that this is becoming true of me, too. After following Seery's Twitter stream for a year, I'm more knowledgeable about the details of her life than the lives of my two sisters in Canada, whom I talk to only once every month or so. When I called Seery, I knew that she had been struggling with a three-day migraine headache; I began the conversation by asking her how she was feeling.

Online awareness inevitably leads to a curious question: What sort of relationships are these? What does it mean to have hundreds of "friends" on Facebook? What kind of friends are they, anyway?

In 1998, the anthropologist Robin Dunbar argued that each human has a hard-wired upper limit on the number of people he or she can personally know at one time. Dunbar noticed that humans and apes both develop social bonds by engaging in some sort of grooming; apes do it by picking at and smoothing one another's fur, and humans do it with conversation. He theorized that ape and human brains could manage only a finite number of grooming relationships: unless we spend enough time doing social grooming—chitchatting, trading gossip or, for apes, picking lice—we won't really feel that we "know" someone well enough to call him a friend. Dunbar noticed that ape groups tended to top out at 55 members. Since human brains were proportionally bigger, Dunbar figured that our maximum number of social connections would be similarly larger: about 150 on average. Sure enough, psychological studies have confirmed that human groupings naturally tail off at around 150 people: the "Dunbar number," as it is known. Are people who use Facebook and Twitter increasing their Dunbar number, because they can so easily keep track of so many more people?

As I interviewed some of the most aggressively social people online—people who follow hundreds or even thousands of others—it became clear that the picture was a little more complex than this question would suggest. Many maintained that their circle of true intimates, their very close friends and family, had not become bigger. Constant online contact had made those ties immeasurably richer, but it hadn't actually increased the number of them; deep relationships are still predicated on face time, and there are only so many hours in the day for that.

But where their sociality had truly exploded was in their "weak ties"—loose acquaintances, people they knew less well. It might be someone they met at a conference, or someone from high school who recently "friended" them on Facebook, or somebody from last year's holiday party. In their pre-Internet lives, these sorts of acquaintances would have quickly faded from their attention. But when one of these far-flung people suddenly posts a personal note to your feed, it is essentially a reminder that they exist. I have noticed this effect myself. In the last few months, dozens of old work colleagues I knew from 10 years ago in Toronto have friended me on Facebook, such that I'm now suddenly reading their stray comments and updates and falling into oblique, funny conversations with them. My overall Dunbar number is thus 301: Facebook (254) + Twitter (47), double what it would be without technology. Yet only 20 are family or people I'd consider close friends. The rest are weak ties—maintained via technology.

This rapid growth of weak ties can be a very good thing. Sociologists have long found that "weak ties" greatly expand your ability to solve problems. For example, if you're looking for a job and ask your friends, they won't be much help; they're too similar to you, and thus probably won't have any leads that you don't already have yourself. Remote acquaintances will be much more useful, because they're farther afield, yet still socially intimate enough to want to help you out. Many avid Twitter users—the ones who fire off witty posts hourly and wind up with thousands of intrigued followers—explicitly milk this dynamic for all it's worth, using their large online followings as a way to quickly answer almost any question. Laura Fitton, a social-media consultant who has become a minor celebrity on Twitter—she has more than 5,300 followers—recently discovered to her horror that her accountant had made an error in filing last year's taxes. She went to Twitter, wrote a tiny note explaining her problem, and within 10 minutes her online audience had provided leads to lawyers and better accountants. Fritton joked to me that she no longer buys anything worth more than $50 without quickly checking it with her Twitter network.

"I outsource my entire life," she said. "I can solve any problem on Twitter in six minutes." (She also keeps a secondary Twitter account that is private and only for a much smaller circle of close friends and family—"My little secret," she said. It is a strategy many people told me they used: one account for their weak ties, one for their deeper relationships.)

It is also possible, though, that this profusion of weak ties can become a problem. If you're reading daily updates from hundreds of people about whom they're dating and whether they're happy, it might, some critics worry, spread your emotional energy too thin, leaving less for true intimate relationships. Psychologists have long known that people can engage in "parasocial" relationships with fictional characters, like those on TV shows or in books, or with remote celebrities we read about in magazines. Parasocial relationships can use up some of the emotional space in our Dunbar number, crowding out real-life people. Danah Boyd, a fellow at Harvard's Berkman Center for Internet and Society who has studied social media for 10 years, published a paper this spring arguing that awareness tools like News Feed might be creating a whole new class of relationships that are nearly parasocial—peripheral people in our network whose intimate details we follow closely online, even while they, like Angelina Jolie, are basically unaware we exist.

35 "The information we subscribe to on a feed is not the same as in a deep social relationship," Boyd told me. She has seen this herself; she has many virtual admirers that have, in essence, a parasocial relationship with her. "I've been very, very sick, lately and I write about it on Twitter and my blog, and I get all these people who are writing to me telling me ways to work around the health-care system, or they're writing saying, 'Hey, I broke my neck!' And I'm like, 'You're being very nice and trying to help me, but though you feel like you know me, you don't.' " Boyd sighed. "They can observe you, but it's not the same as knowing you."

When I spoke to Caterina Fake, a founder of Flickr (a popular photo-sharing site), she suggested an even more subtle danger: that the sheer ease of following her friends' updates online has made her occasionally lazy about actually taking the time to visit them in person. "At one point I realized I had a friend whose child I had seen, via photos on Flickr, grow from birth to 1 year old," she said. "I thought, I really should go meet her in person. But it was weird; I also felt that Flickr had satisfied that getting-to-know you satisfaction, so I didn't feel the urgency. But then I was like, Oh, that's not sufficient! I should go in person!" She has about 400 people she follows online but suspects many of those relationships are tissue-fragile. "These technologies allow you to be much more broadly friendly, but you just spread yourself much more thinly over many more people."

What is it like to never lose touch with anyone? One morning this summer at my local cafe, I overheard a young woman complaining to her friend about a recent Facebook drama. Her name is Andrea Ahan, a 27-year-old restaurant entrepreneur, and she told me that she had discovered that high-school friends were uploading old photos of her to Facebook and tagging them with her name, so they automatically appeared in searches for her.

She was aghast. "I'm like, my God, these pictures are completely hideous!" Ahan complained, while her friend looked on sympathetically and sipped her coffee. "I'm wearing all these totally awful '90s clothes. I look like crap. And I'm like, Why are you people in my life, anyway? I haven't seen you in 10 years. I don't know you anymore!" She began furiously detagging the pictures—removing her name, so they wouldn't show up in a search anymore.

Worse, Ahan was also confronting a common plague of Facebook: the recent ex. She had broken up with her boyfriend not long ago, but she hadn't "unfriended" him, because that felt too extreme. But soon he paired up with another young woman, and the new couple began having public conversations on Ahan's ex-boyfriend's page. One day, she noticed with alarm that the new girlfriend was quoting material Ahan had e-mailed privately to her boyfriend; she suspected he had been sharing the e-mail with his new girlfriend. It is the sort of weirdly subtle mind game that becomes possible via Facebook, and it drove Ahan nuts.

"Sometimes I think this stuff is just crazy, and everybody has got to get a life and stop obsessing over everyone's trivia and gossiping," she said.

Yet Ahan knows that she cannot simply walk away from her online life, because the people she knows online won't stop talking about her, or posting unflattering photos. She needs to stay on Facebook just to monitor what's being said about her. This is a common complaint I heard, particularly from people in their 20s who were in college when Facebook appeared and have never lived as adults without online awareness. For them, participation isn't optional. If you don't dive in, other people will define who you are. So you constantly stream your pictures, your thoughts, your relationship status and what you're doing—right now!—if only to ensure the virtual version of you is accurate, or at least the one you want to present to the world.

40 This is the ultimate effect of the new awareness: It brings back the dynamics of small-town life, where everybody knows your business. Young people at college are the ones to experience this most viscerally, because, with more than 90 percent of their peers using Facebook, it is especially difficult for them to opt out. Zeynep Tufekci, a sociologist at the University of Maryland, Baltimore County, who has closely studied how college-age users are reacting to the world of awareness, told me that athletes used to sneak off to parties illicitly, breaking the no-drinking rule for team members. But then camera phones and Facebook came along, with students posting photos of the drunken carousing during the party; savvy coaches could see which athletes were breaking the rules. First the athletes tried to fight back by waking up early the morning after the party in a hungover daze to detag photos of themselves so they wouldn't be searchable. But that didn't work, because the coaches sometimes viewed the pictures live, as they went online at 2 A.M. So parties simply began banning all camera phones in a last-ditch attempt to preserve privacy.

"It's just like living in a village, where it's actually hard to lie because everybody knows the truth already," Tufekci said. "The current generation is never unconnected. They're never losing touch with their friends. So we're going back to a more normal place, historically. If you look at human history, the idea that you would drift through life, going from new relation to new relation, that's very new. It's just the 20th century."

Psychologists and sociologists spent years wondering how humanity would adjust to the anonymity of life in the city, the wrenching upheavals of mobile immigrant labor—a world of lonely people ripped from their social ties. We now have precisely the opposite problem. Indeed, our modern awareness tools reverse the original conceit of the Internet. When cyberspace came along in the early '90s, it was celebrated as a place where you could reinvent your identity—become someone new.

"If anything, it's identity-constraining now," Tufekci told me. "You can't play with your identity if your audience is always checking up on you. I had a student who posted that she was downloading some Pearl Jam, and someone wrote on her wall, 'Oh, right, ha-ha—I know you, and you're not into that.' " She laughed. "You know that old cartoon? 'On the Internet, nobody knows you're a dog'? On the Internet today, everybody knows you're a dog! If you don't want people to know you're a dog, you'd better stay away from a keyboard."

Or, as Leisa Reichelt, a consultant in London who writes regularly about ambient tools, put it to me: "Can you imagine a Facebook for children in kindergarten, and they never lose touch with those kids for the rest of their lives? What's that going to do to them?" Young people today are already developing an attitude toward their privacy that is simultaneously vigilant and laissez-faire. They curate their online personas as carefully as possible, knowing that everyone is watching—but they have also learned to shrug and accept the limits of what they can control.

45 It is easy to become unsettled by privacy-eroding aspects of awareness tools. But there is another—quite different—result of all this incessant updating: a culture of people who know much more about themselves. Many of the avid Twitterers, Flickrers and Facebook users I interviewed described an unexpected side-effect of constant self-disclosure. The act of stopping several times a day to

observe what you're feeling or thinking can become, after weeks and weeks, a sort of philosophical act. It's like the Greek dictum to "know thyself," or the therapeutic concept of mindfulness. (Indeed, the question that floats eternally at the top of Twitter's Web site—"What are you doing?"—can come to seem existentially freighted. What are you doing?) Having an audience can make the self-reflection even more acute, since, as my interviewees noted, they're trying to describe their activities in a way that is not only accurate but also interesting to others: the status update as a literary form.

Laura Fitton, the social-media consultant, argues that her constant status updating has made her "a happier person, a calmer person" because the process of, say, describing a horrid morning at work forces her to look at it objectively. "It drags you out of your own head," she added. In an age of awareness, perhaps the person you see most clearly is yourself.

Reflect & Write

- ❑ What strategy does Thompson use to start his article? To what extent is it successful in drawing the reader in and setting up background for the rest of the essay?
- ❑ What, according to Thompson, is the "paradox of ambient awareness"?
- ❑ How does Thompson use historical context and social sciences to bolster his commentary? How do these choices influence the persuasiveness of his claims?
- ❑ Look for places where Thompson includes personal narrative and experience in the article. How might that be strategic? What do those moments accomplish?
- ❑ **Write.** In the conclusion of the piece, Thompson suggests, "In an age of awareness, perhaps the person you see most clearly is yourself." Over the course of five days, use microblogging as a mode of self-expression. Update your status feed on Facebook or Tweet at least three times a day (you can do more if you like): if you don't have a Facebook or Twitter account, create one, or keep a log of your simulated micro-blogs in a Word document. Use the updates to capture a moment in your day, link to a reading you liked, provide commentary, work through your thoughts, or to contemplate an issue, event, etc. Do not exceed 140 characters in your posts. At the end of the five days, cut and paste all your micro-blogs into a Word document. Read through them, and beneath, write a short reflection about what they say about you. Is Thompson right? Do you see yourself more clearly? Did writing in this way help you process your experiences? Feel free in your reaction to respond directly to the claims found in his article.

■ *This satire was originally published in the May 30, 2007, issue of* The Onion.

MySpace Outage Leaves Millions Friendless

BEVERLY HILLS, CA—An estimated 150 million people continued to be without social lives Tuesday as a massive system failure at MySpace.com entered its third day.

"The problem is taking longer than we anticipated, but rest assured we're working around the clock to get MySpace back online," said David Gundy, a spokesman for the social networking site. "We're hoping to have friendship restored to our users as soon as possible."

The outage, which occurred late Saturday night, is believed to be the result of a complicated wallpaper upload for the page of a former VH1 *I Love New York* contestant, which triggered a chain reaction of web browser crashes and server shutdowns. Although MySpace's emergency-response team has so far been unable to reconnect any of the millions currently

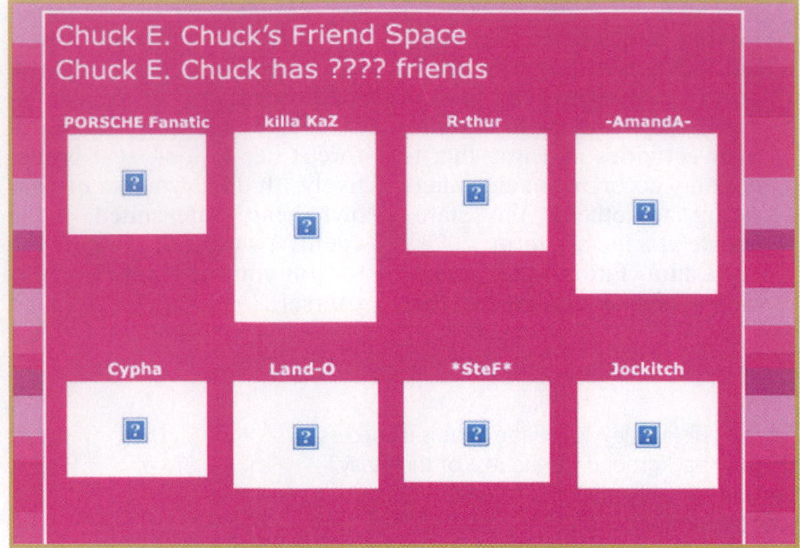

MySpace users now find themselves completely alone in the world.

stranded without access to online companionship, Gundy said he remains hopeful that no profiles have been lost.

However, because the sudden lack of friends has deprived MySpace users of comments, bulletin posts, and searches for elementary school crushes, it is feared that the ordeal could inflict long-term psychological damage. In Chicago alone, an estimated 50,000 people remain trapped in their apartments, with no way of contacting the outside world about new bands, *Adult Swim* cartoons, or the latest video games.

Desperate citizens gather in communal hotspots to check repeatedly if MySpace is back online yet.

5 "I lost 6,456 of my best friends in an instant," said Minneapolis resident Peter Steinberg, 20, who has loyally befriended as many profiles as possible over the past two years. "Nothing can describe how devastated I feel. Some of these people I've exchanged two, even three comments with, and I can't tell you how many ROTFLMAOs we've shared, too."

Steinberg was among the first to suspect something was wrong with MySpace.com Friday when he was unable to send an animated image of TV's ALF chasing a cat to his MySpace group, "Welcome to Bartertown, Bitch."

Other stranded, friendless citizens are doing their best to cope, but are finding it harder and harder to go on.

"I've just been wandering in and out of my cubicle in a daze, not knowing what to say and who to talk to," said Upper Darby, PA data-entry technician Patrick "Smiley457" Mancuso, 31. "I thought about asking someone at work or in my apartment building if they'd join my friend group. But how am I supposed to tell which ones I will like and which ones I won't? It's too overwhelming."

Corey "Aqualad" Friesen, 18, of Danville, IL appeared to share Mancuso's fears about manual and analog socializing. "I vaguely remember trying to make friends pre-MySpace, but in 16 years, I only made three real friends," Friesen said. "If I have to revert back to face-to-face friend gathering, I would be middle-aged before I built that number into the double digits. I'd definitely never get back into the hundreds again."

10 Denver's Marco Imbrescia, known to his MySpace friends as I Smell Tuna, contemplated the existential ramifications of the outage.

"Without an 'About Me' section, I've lost all sense of self," said Imbrescia, 17, who depends on the site to convey his innermost thoughts to millions of extended-network friends. "Do I want kids? How tall am I? What's my body type? These are questions I can't answer anymore. I'd pray to a god for help, but I've lost my religion field."

A handful of relief organizations have begun to offer some assistance to MySpace refugees. The American Red Cross is currently setting up a network of approximately 60 smaller-sized "fill-in" sites, where lonely MySpace users can post abbreviated profiles and receive instant messages from aid workers in half-hour increments. But because it's only intended as a temporary stopgap, user options are austere: MySpace members cannot list hobbies and interests, upload MP3s, or link to favorite YouTube clips, making friendship compatibility and popularity nearly impossible to predetermine.

On Monday, MySpace co-creator Tom Anderson issued an apologetic press release on the website of MySpace's parent company, News Corporation.

"So I know alot [sic] of you couldn't check out your profiles and I just want to say sorry for all the lameness on our end," Anderson wrote. "Rock on. :)"

Reflect & Write

- What makes this article funny? How much does it exaggerate, and where does it seem that it could be reporting an actual public reaction?
- What argument is the article actually making about MySpace users? Find places where this argument is most evident to support your answer.
- Look at the conclusion. How successful is Tom Anderson's final comment as a conclusion to this piece? Why? How does *humos* work here?
- **Write.** Write a similar short news piece about a hypothetical Twitter outage. What might be the public reaction if people could no longer follow, tweet, or re-tweet? Be sure to refer to specific Twitter followers' usage patterns and Twitter features in your article. Add screenshots or photos as visual rhetoric if you like.

A Distinguished Writer in Residence at the New York University Department of Jounalism, **Steven Johnson** *writes extensively on science, technology, and the human experience. He is a columnist for* Discover *magazine, a contributing editor for* Wired, *and has published articles in the* New York Times, *the* Wall Street Journal, *and the* Nation. *His books include* Invention of Air: A Story of Science, Faith, Revolution, and the Birth of America; The Ghost Map; Mind Wide Open *(for which he used himself as a test subject), and* Everything Bad Is Good for You *(2005). He has appeared on* The Daily Show with Jon Stewart, The NewsHour with Jim Lehrer, *and* The Charlie Rose Show. *In this article, which first appeared in the June 5, 2009, issue of* Time *magazine, Johnson looks closely at Twitter and how it is changing the way we interact with each other and information online.*

How Twitter Will Change the Way We Live

Steven Johnson

The one thing you can say for certain about Twitter is that it makes a terrible first impression. You hear about this new service that lets you send 140-character updates to your "followers," and you think, Why does the world need this, exactly? It's not as if we were all sitting around four years ago scratching our heads and saying, "If only there were a technology that would allow me to send a message to my 50 friends, alerting them in real time about my choice of breakfast cereal."

I, too, was skeptical at first. I had met Evan Williams, Twitter's co-creator, a couple of times in the dotcom '90s when he was launching Blogger.com. Back then, what people worried about was the threat that blogging posed to our attention span, with telegraphic, two-paragraph blog posts replacing long-format articles and books. With Twitter, Williams was launching a communications platform that limited you to a couple of sentences at most. What was next? Software that let you send a single punctuation mark to describe your mood?

And yet as millions of devotees have discovered, Twitter turns out to have unsuspected depth. In part this is because hearing about what your friends had for breakfast is actually more interesting than it sounds. The technology writer Clive Thompson calls this "ambient awareness": by following these quick, abbreviated status reports from members of your extended social network, you get a strangely satisfying glimpse of their daily routines. We don't think it at all moronic to start a phone call with a friend by asking how her day is going. Twitter gives you the same information without your even having to ask.

The social warmth of all those stray details shouldn't be taken lightly. But I think there is something even more profound in what has happened to Twitter over the past two years, something that says more about the culture that has embraced and expanded Twitter at such extraordinary speed. Yes, the breakfast-status updates turned out to be more interesting than we thought. But the key development with Twitter is how we've jury-rigged the system to do things that its creators never dreamed of.

5 In short, the most fascinating thing about Twitter is not what it's doing to us. It's what we're doing to it.

The Open Conversation

Earlier this year I attended a daylong conference in Manhattan devoted to education reform. Called Hacking Education, it was a small, private affair: 40-odd educators, entrepreneurs, scholars, philanthropists and venture capitalists, all engaged in a sprawling six-hour conversation about the future of schools. Twenty years ago, the ideas exchanged in that conversation would have been confined to the minds of the participants. Ten years ago, a transcript might have been published weeks or months later on the Web. Five years ago, a handful of participants might have blogged about their experiences after the fact.

But this event was happening in 2009, so trailing behind the real-time, real-world conversation was an equally real-time conversation on Twitter. At the outset of the conference, our hosts announced that anyone who wanted to post live commentary about the event via Twitter should include the word *#hackedu* in his 140 characters. In the room, a large display screen showed a running feed of tweets. Then we all started talking, and as we did, a shadow conversation unfolded on the screen: summaries of someone's argument, the occasional joke, suggested links for further reading. At one point, a brief argument flared up between two participants in the room—a tense back-and-forth that transpired silently on the screen as the rest of us conversed in friendly tones.

At first, all these tweets came from inside the room and were created exclusively by conference participants tapping away on their laptops or BlackBerrys. But within half an hour or so, word began to seep out into the Twittersphere that an interesting conversation about the future of schools was happening at #hackedu. A few tweets appeared on the screen from strangers announcing that they were following the #hackedu thread. Then others joined the conversation, adding their observations or proposing topics for further exploration. A few experts grumbled publicly about how they hadn't been invited to the conference. Back in the room, we pulled interesting ideas and questions from the screen and integrated them into our face-to-face conversation.

When the conference wrapped up at the end of the day, there was a public record of hundreds of tweets documenting the conversation. And the conversation continued—if you search Twitter for *#hackedu,* you'll find dozens of new comments posted over the past few weeks, even though the conference happened in early March.

10 Injecting Twitter into that conversation fundamentally changed the rules of engagement. It added a second layer of discussion and brought a wider audience into what would have been a private exchange. And it gave the event an afterlife on the Web. Yes, it was built entirely out of 140-character messages, but the sum total of those

tweets added up to something truly substantive, like a suspension bridge made of pebbles.

The Super-Fresh Web

The basic mechanics of Twitter are remarkably simple. Users publish tweets—those 140-character messages—from a computer or mobile device. (The character limit allows tweets to be created and circulated via the SMS platform used by most mobile phones.) As a social network, Twitter revolves around the principle of followers. When you choose to follow another Twitter user, that user's tweets appear in reverse chronological order on your main Twitter page. If you follow 20 people, you'll see a mix of tweets scrolling down the page: breakfast-cereal updates, interesting new links, music recommendations, even musings on the future of education. Some celebrity Twitterers—most famously Ashton Kutcher—have crossed the million-follower mark, effectively giving them a broadcast-size audience. The average Twitter profile seems to be somewhere in the dozens: a collage of friends, colleagues and a handful of celebrities. The mix creates a media experience quite unlike anything that has come before it, strangely intimate and at the same time celebrity-obsessed. You glance at your Twitter feed over that first cup of coffee, and in a few seconds you find out that your nephew got into med school and Shaquille O'Neal just finished a cardio workout in Phoenix.

In the past month, Twitter has added a search box that gives you a real-time view onto the chatter of just about any topic imaginable. You can see conversations people are having about a presidential debate or the *American Idol* finale or Tiger Woods—or a conference in New York City on education reform. For as long as we've had the Internet in our homes, critics have bemoaned the demise of shared national experiences, like moon landings and "Who Shot J.R." cliff hangers—the folkloric American living room, all of us signing off in unison with Walter Cronkite, shattered into a million isolation booths. But watch a live mass-media event with Twitter open on your laptop and you'll see that the futurists had it wrong. We still have national events, but now when we have them, we're actually having a genuine, public conversation with a group that extends far beyond our nuclear family and our next-door neighbors. Some of that conversation is juvenile, of course, just as it was in our living room when we heckled Richard Nixon's Checkers speech. But some of it is moving, witty, observant, subversive.

Skeptics might wonder just how much subversion and wit is conveyable via 140-character updates. But in recent months Twitter users have begun to find a route around that limitation by employing Twitter as a pointing device instead of a communications channel: sharing links to longer articles, discussions, posts, videos—anything that lives behind a URL. Websites that once saw their traffic dominated by Google search queries are seeing a growing number of new visitors coming from "passed links" at social networks like Twitter and Facebook. This is what the naysayers fail to understand: it's just as easy to use Twitter to spread the word about a brilliant 10,000-word *New Yorker* article as it is to spread the word about your Lucky Charms habit.

Put those three elements together—social networks, live searching and link-sharing—and you have a cocktail that poses what may amount to the most interesting alternative to Google's near monopoly in searching. At its heart, Google's system is built around the slow, anonymous accumulation of authority: pages rise to the top of Google's search results according to, in part, how many links point to them, which tends to favor older pages that have had time to build an audience. That's a fantastic solution for finding high-quality needles in the immense, spam-plagued haystack that is the contemporary Web. But it's not a particularly useful solution for finding out what people are saying *right now*, the in-the-moment conversation that industry pioneer John Battelle calls the "super fresh" Web. Even in its toddlerhood, Twitter is a more efficient supplier of the super-fresh Web than Google. If you're looking for interesting articles or sites devoted to Kobe Bryant, you search Google. If you're looking for interesting comments from your extended social network about the three-pointer Kobe just made 30 seconds ago, you go to Twitter.

From Toasters to Microwaves

15 Because Twitter's co-founders—Evan Williams, Biz Stone and Jack Dorsey—are such a central-casting vision of start-up savvy (they're quotable and charming and have the extra glamour

of using a loft in San Francisco's SoMa district as a headquarters instead of a bland office park in Silicon Valley) much of the media interest in Twitter has focused on the company. Will Ev and Biz sell to Google early or play long ball? (They have already turned down a reported $500 million from Facebook.) It's an interesting question but not exactly a new plotline. Focusing on it makes you lose sight of the much more significant point about the Twitter platform: the fact that many of its core features and applications have been developed by people who are not on the Twitter payroll.

This is not just a matter of people finding a new use for a tool designed to do something else. In Twitter's case, the users have been redesigning the tool itself. The convention of grouping a topic or event by the "hashtag"—#hackedu or #inauguration—was spontaneously invented by the Twitter user base (as was the convention of replying to another user with the @ symbol). The ability to search a live stream of tweets was developed by another start-up altogether, Summize, which Twitter purchased last year. (Full disclosure: I am an adviser to one of the minority investors in Summize.) Thanks to these innovations, following a live feed of tweets about an event—political debates or *Lost* episodes—has become a central part of the Twitter experience. But just 12 months ago, that mode of interaction would have been technically impossible using Twitter. It's like inventing a toaster oven and then looking around a year later and seeing that your customers have of their own accord figured out a way to turn it into a microwave.

One of the most telling facts about the Twitter platform is that the vast majority of its users interact with the service via software created by third parties. There are dozens of iPhone and BlackBerry applications—all created by enterprising amateur coders or small start-ups—that let you manage Twitter feeds. There are services that help you upload photos and link to them from your tweets, and programs that map other Twitizens who are near you geographically. Ironically, the tools you're offered if you visit Twitter.com have changed very little in the past two years. But there's an entire Home Depot of Twitter tools available everywhere else.

As the tools have multiplied, we're discovering extraordinary new things to do with them. Last month an anticommunist uprising in Moldova was organized via Twitter. Twitter has become so widely used among political activists in China that the government recently blocked access to it, in an attempt to censor discussion of the 20th anniversary of the Tiananmen Square massacre. A service called Sick City scans the Twitter feeds from multiple urban areas, tracking references to flu and fever. Celebrity Twitterers like Kutcher have directed their vast followings toward charitable causes (in Kutcher's case, the Malaria No More organization).

Social networks are notoriously vulnerable to the fickle tastes of teens and 20-somethings (remember Friendster?), so it's entirely possible that three or four years from now, we'll have moved on to some Twitter successor. But the key elements of the Twitter platform—the follower structure, link-sharing, real-time searching—will persevere regardless of Twitter's fortunes, just as Web conventions like links, posts and feeds have endured over the past decade. In fact, every major channel of information will be Twitterfied in one way or another in the coming years:

News and Opinion

20 Increasingly, the stories that come across our radar—news about a plane crash, a feisty Op-Ed, a gossip item—will arrive via the passed links of the people we follow. Instead of being built by some kind of artificially intelligent software algorithm, a customized newspaper will be compiled from all the articles being read that morning by your social network. This will lead to more news diversity and polarization at the same time: your networked front page will be more eclectic than any traditional-newspaper front page, but political partisans looking to enhance their own private echo chamber will be able to tune out opposing viewpoints more easily.

Searching

As the archive of links shared by Twitter users grows, the value of searching for information via your extended social network will start to rival Google's approach to the search. If you're looking for information on Benjamin Franklin, an essay shared by one of your favorite historians might well be more valuable than the top result on Google; if you're looking for advice on sibling rivalry, an article recommended by a friend of a friend might well be the best place to start.

Advertising

Today the language of advertising is dominated by the notion of impressions: how many times an advertiser can get its brand in front of a potential customer's eyeballs, whether on a billboard, a Web page or a NASCAR hood. But impressions are fleeting things, especially compared with the enduring relationships of followers. Successful businesses will have millions of Twitter followers (and will pay good money to attract them), and a whole new language of tweet-based customer interaction will evolve to keep those followers engaged: early access to new products or deals, live customer service, customer involvement in brainstorming for new products.

Not all these developments will be entirely positive. Most of us have learned firsthand how addictive the micro-events of our personal e-mail inbox can be. But with the ambient awareness of status updates from Twitter and Facebook, an entire new empire of distraction has opened up. It used to be that you compulsively checked your BlackBerry to see if anything new had happened in your personal life or career: e-mail from the boss, a reply from last night's date. Now you're compulsively checking your BlackBerry for news from other people's lives. And because, on Twitter at least, some of those people happen to be celebrities, the Twitter platform is likely to expand that strangely delusional relationship that we have to fame. When Oprah tweets a question about getting ticks off her dog, as she did recently, anyone can send an @ reply to her, and in that exchange, there is the semblance of a normal, everyday conversation between equals. But of course, Oprah has more than a million followers, and that isolated query probably elicited thousands of responses. Who knows what small fraction of her @ replies she has time to read? But from the fan's perspective, it feels refreshingly intimate: "As I was explaining to Oprah last night, when she asked about dog ticks . . . "

End-User Innovation

The rapid-fire innovation we're seeing around Twitter is not new, of course. Facebook, whose audience is still several times as large as Twitter's, went from being a way to scope out the most attractive college freshmen to the Social Operating System of the Internet, supporting a vast ecosystem of new applications created by major media companies, individual hackers, game creators, political groups and charities. The Apple iPhone's long-term competitive advantage may well prove to be the more than 15,000 new applications that have been developed for the device, expanding its functionality in countless ingenious ways.

25 The history of the Web followed a similar pattern. A platform originally designed to help scholars share academic documents, it now lets you watch television shows, play poker with strangers around the world, publish your own newspaper, rediscover your high school girlfriend—and, yes, tell the world what you had for breakfast. Twitter serves as the best poster child for this new model of social creativity in part because these innovations have flowered at such breathtaking speed and in part because the platform is so simple. It's as if Twitter's creators dared us to do something interesting by giving us a platform with such draconian restrictions. And sure enough, we accepted the dare with relish. Just 140 characters? I wonder if I could use that to start a political uprising.

The speed with which users have extended Twitter's platform points to a larger truth about modern innovation. When we talk about innovation and global competitiveness, we tend to fall back on the easy metric of patents and Ph.D.s. It turns out the U.S. share of both has been in steady decline since peaking in the early '70s. (In 1970, more than 50% of the world's graduate degrees in science and engineering were issued by U.S. universities.) Since the mid-'80s, a long progression of doomsayers have warned that our declining market share in the patents- and-Ph.D.s business augurs dark times for American innovation. The specific threats have changed. It was the Japanese who would destroy us in the '80s; now it's China and India.

But what actually happened to American innovation during that period? We came up with America Online, Netscape, Amazon, Google, Blogger, Wikipedia, Craigslist, TiVo, Netflix, eBay, the iPod and iPhone, Xbox, Facebook and Twitter itself. Sure, we didn't build the Prius or the Wii, but if you measure global innovation in terms of actual lifestyle-changing hit products and not just grad students, the U.S. has been lapping the field for the past 20 years.

How could the forecasts have been so wrong? The answer is that we've been tracking only part of the innovation story. If I go to grad school and invent a better mousetrap, I've created value, which I can protect with a patent and capitalize on by selling my invention to consumers. But if someone else figures out a way to use my mousetrap to replace his much more expensive washing machine, he's created value as well. We tend to put the emphasis on the first kind of value creation because there are a small number of inventors who earn giant paydays from their mousetraps and thus become celebrities. But there are hundreds of millions of consumers and small businesses that find value in these innovations by figuring out new ways to put them to use.

There are several varieties of this kind of innovation, and they go by different technical names. MIT professor Eric von Hippel calls one "end-user innovation," in which consumers actively modify a product to adapt it to their needs. In its short life, Twitter has been a hothouse of end-user innovation: the hashtag; searching; its 11,000 third-party applications; all those creative new uses of Twitter—some of them banal, some of them spam and some of them sublime. Think about the community invention of the @ reply. It took a service that was essentially a series of isolated microbroadcasts, each individual tweet an island, and turned Twitter into a truly conversational medium. All of these adoptions create new kinds of value in the wider economy, and none of them actually originated at Twitter HQ. You don't need patents or Ph.D.s to build on this kind of platform.

30 This is what I ultimately find most inspiring about the Twitter phenomenon. We are living through the worst economic crisis in generations, with apocalyptic headlines threatening the end of capitalism as we know it, and yet in the middle of this chaos, the engineers at Twitter headquarters are scrambling to keep the servers up, application developers are releasing their latest builds, and ordinary users are figuring out all the ingenious ways to put these tools to use. There's a kind of resilience here that is worth savoring. The weather reports keep announcing that the sky is falling, but here we are—millions of us—sitting around trying to invent new ways to talk to one another.

Reflect & Write

- ❑ Look carefully at the movement in the first few paragraphs of the article. How does Johnson move beyond audience skepticism about Twitter to his main point? Why is this important for him to do at the beginning of the essay?
- ❑ What is the purpose of his including the Hacking Education example? What does it accomplish in relation to his argument?
- ❑ How does Johnson see Twitter as an alternative to Google?
- ❑ What does Johnson mean by "user-end innovation"? How does he see this as an important component of Twitter's current and continued success?
- ❑ **Write.** At one point in the article, Johnson identifies how three different "channels of information" will be "Twitterfied" in upcoming year. Choose one of these "channels" and, building from Johnson's starting point, write a two-page essay that further develops the way that Twitter might influence and augment this mode of communication. Speculate on specific uses and examples in your writing.

■ *A Professor of Communications at Webster University,* **Art Silverblatt** *is best known for his writings on media and communication. His publications include* Media Literacy: Keys to Interpreting Media Messages *(1995);* International Communications *(2004); and* Approaches to Genre Study *(2007). In this article, he links Twitter feeds to Newspeak, the linguistically and conceptually truncated form of writing prophesied by George Orwell in his dystopian novel,* 1984. *This article was originally published in the September/October 2009 issue of the* St. Louis Journalism Review.

Twitter As Newspeak

Art Silverblatt

It can be argued that Twitter has emerged as a legitimate form of communication that could influence how children will spell—and think—in the future. Both Fox News and CNN have adopted the form and syntax of Twitter for their closed-captions, so that Twitter is no longer merely a computer shorthand but has become an integral facet of our mainstream media.

To illustrate: On September 11, 2001, Fox News carried a story about President Bush's immediate response to the terrorists' attacks that adopted Twitter as the style for their closed-caption account (he "did rht thin").

This year, a new keyboard was introduced called "Tweet-board." The traditional keyboard has been reconfigured, so that Twitter symbols assume prominent positions on the top row: @ (reply), # (hashtags), RT (retweet), and via @. Another key is for shortening URLs.

One way to understand the impact of Twitter is to consider another language that is predicated on the elimination and abbreviation of words—the language of Newspeak, found in George Orwell's futuristic novel, 1984. In the Appendix of 1984, Orwell observes that "Newspeak differed from most all other languages, in that its vocabulary grew smaller instead of larger every year."

Reduction of vocabulary was regarded as an end in itself, and no word that could be dispensed with was allowed to survive. Newspeak was designed not to extend but to diminish the range of thought, and this purpose was indirectly assisted by cutting the choice of words down to a minimum . . . The Newspeak vocabulary was tiny, and new ways of reducing it were constantly being devised.

Like Newspeak, the syntax of Twitter is based on economy. Only 140 characters are allowed in a single tweet. Thus, in an online article, entitled "7 Tips to Improve Your Twitter Tweets," the first tip involves ways to cut the copy:

Abbreviate. If you can say it with less letters, do so! . . . There are only 140 characters allowed in a single tweet, so shortening a word or using a bit of slang is completely acceptable. Instead of "are," say "r." the same goes for "you" and "u."

Orwell's comments about the impact of Newspeak on thought may also be applicable to Twitter, in the following respects:

Ideas Are Reduced to Literal Meaning

In these reductive languages, the meaning of words is reduced to a literal level; there is no space to examine the implications of meaning. Orwell explains:

"The A vocabulary consisted of the words needed for the business of everyday life—for such things as eating, drinking, working, putting on one's clothes . . . Their meanings were far more rigidly defined. All ambiguities and shades of meaning had been purged out of them."

To illustrate: Danny Ayalon, the Assistant Foreign Minister of Israel, issues daily Tweets to the public. The problem, of course, is reducing the complexity of a 2500-year religious, cultural, and political conflict to 140 characters. On September 9, Ayalon tweeted, "Dilemma is placed on international community by Iran. Need to turn the tables and place dilemma back on Iran. Only with strong sanctions." This missive provides only surface information, leaving numerous questions unaddressed.

What is the "dilemma"? Why has this dilemma been placed on the international community by Iran? What is meant by "strong sanctions"? How do strong sanctions "place the dilemma" back on Iran? What other options (in addition to sanctions) exist, and what are their relative strengths and weaknesses?

No Context to Information Is Provided

Both Twitter and Newspeak operate in an eternal present; there is no room to discuss ideas within a historical or cultural context. Orwell declares, "When Oldspeak had been once and for all superseded, the last link with the past would have been severed." Thus, Ayalon's tweet leaves unanswered essential background information, such as:

When was this "dilemma" placed on the international community by Iran? Have sanctions been tried before? When, and with what results? What was the role of other countries in this activity—Israel, United States and Western Allies, other Arab nations.

Language Assumes a Neutral Tenor

15 The use of abbreviations eliminates the emotional connotation of content. Orwell explains:

"Even in the early decades of the twentieth century, . . . the tendency to use abbreviations was most marked in totalitarian countries and totalitarian organizations. Examples were such words as Nazi, Gestapo, Comintern, Inprecorr, Agitprop. In the beginning the practice had been adopted as it were instinctively, but in Newspeak it was used with a conscious purpose. It was perceived that in thus abbreviating a name one narrowed and subtly altered its meaning, by cutting out most of the associations that would otherwise cling to it."

One major difference between Newspeak and Twitter, of course, involves function. Newspeak's purpose was ideological; the government of Big Brother instituted this language as a way of controlling the masses. In contrast, the form and format of Twitter is technologically driven; Twitter has been designed to reach targeted groups of people throughout the virtual world instantaneously. But regardless of intention, Twitter is anti-democratic. It helps create a young generation that not only cannot spell but is also incapable of examining the implications of ideas, challenging information, and thinking independently.

Reflect & Write

- ❑ How does Silverblatt see Twitter-style communication permeating popular media? What does he consider to be the larger implications of this stylistic shift?
- ❑ By choosing an Orwellian analogy for Twitter, what type of approach does Silverblatt signal he is taking toward the trend? Why?
- ❑ Who is the audience for Silverblatt's article? How can you tell?
- ❑ Look carefully are Silverblatt's examples. How persuasive are they?
- ❑ **Write.** Do you agree with Silverblatt's assertion that Twitter is helping to create "a young generation that not only cannot spell but is also incapable of examining the implications of ideas, challenging information, and thinking independently"? Write a one-page response to Silverblatt confirming, refuting, or qualifying his statement. Be sure to locate your argument in relation to Twitter—its usage and its style.

■ *Created by software programmer* **Randall Munroe,** xkcd *is a "webcomic of romance, sarcasm, math and language" that has garnered a large cult following and has been reproduced in mainstream publications such as the* New York Times *and the* Guardian.

FIGURE 11.3. Entitled "Seismic Waves," this *xkcd* comic speculates on the reaction of Twitter users to an earthquake.

Reflect & Write

- ❑ What argument is this cartoon making? Write out the claim or thesis as a single paragraph. Write out the claim or thesis as a single sentence.
- ❑ What is represented in the different panels? What is the function of each panel? How do they work together to produce the argument?
- ❑ What is the relationship between text and image? What are the different "voices" or perspectives reproduced in this sequence?
- ❑ Where does the "punchline" of the sequence occur? Would this punchline have been as effective if the cartoonist had created a single-panel comic? Why or why not?
- ❑ **Write.** The style of *xkcd* is very distinctive, with its simple lines and stick-figure characters. Sketch out the same sequence of panels using the characters and style of an alternate comic strip, for instance, *Garfield*, *Doonesbury*, *Calvin and Hobbes*, *Peanuts*, or *Boondocks*. Keep the same basic structure, but alter the characters and their dialogue to better match the comic style you've chosen. Was the argument as persuasive in the alternate form? Why or why not?

Seeing Connections
Refer to Chapter 1 for guidance on analyzing cartoons and composing effective thesis statements

■ **Evgeny Morozov** *is best known for his work as a contributing editor to* Foreign Policy *and for running "Net Effect," the magazine's blog about global politics and the Internet age. Currently a Yahoo! Fellow at Georgetown University's Institute for the Study of Diplomacy, Morozov has published broadly in many venues, including in* The Economist, *the* Wall Street Journal, Newsweek, *the* Times Literary Supplement, *and the* San Francisco Chronicle. *The following article was first posted on September 5, 2009, to the Net Effect blog.*

From Slacktivism to Activism

Evgeny Morozov

Below is the text of a talk about "slacktivism"—a subject that has received considerable attention on this blog and elsewhere—that I delivered at Festival Ars Electronica this morning (the session was dedicated to "cloud intelligence").

As someone who studies how the Internet affects global politics, I've grown increasingly skeptical of numerous digital activism campaigns that attempt to change the world through Facebook and Twitter. To explain why, let me first tell you a story about a campaign that has gone wrong.

If you have been to Copenhagen, you probably have seen the Stork Fountain, the city's famous landmark. A few months ago, a Danish psychologist Anders Colding-Jørgensen, who studies how ideas spread online, used Facebook to conduct a little experiment using the Stork Fountain as his main subject. He started a Facebook group, which implied–but never stated so explicitly–that the city authorities were planning to dismantle the fountain, which of course was NEVER the case. He seeded the group to 125 friends who joined in a matter of hours; then it started spreading virally. In the first few days, it immediately went to a 1000 members and then it started growing more aggressively. After 3 days, it began to grow with over 2 new members each minute in the day time. When the group reached 27,500 members, Jørgensen decided to end the experiment. So there you have it: almost 28,000 people joined a cause that didn't really exist! As far as "clouds" go, that one was probably an empty one.

This broaches an interesting question: why do people join Facebook groups in the first place? In an interview with the Washington Post, Jorgensen said that "just like we need stuff to furnish our homes to show who we are, on Facebook we need cultural objects that put together a version of me that I would like to present to the public." Other researchers agree: studies by Sherri Grasmuck, a sociologist at Temple University, reveals that Facebook users shape their online identity implicitly rather than explicitly: that is, the kind of campaigns and groups they join reveals more about who they are than their dull "about me" page.

5 This shopping binge in an online identity supermarket has led to the proliferation of what I call "slacktivism", where our digital effort make us feel very useful and important but have zero social impact. When the marginal cost of joining yet another Facebook group are low, we click "yes" without even blinking, but the truth is that it may distract us from helping the same cause in more productive ways. Paradoxically, it often means that the very act of joining a Facebook group is often the end—rather than the beginning—of our engagement with a cause, which undermines much of digital activism.

Take a popular Facebook group "saving the children of Africa." It looks very impressive—over 1.2 million members—until you discover that these compassionate souls have raised about $6,000 (or half a penny per person). In a perfect world, this shouldn't even be considered a problem: better donate a penny than not to donate at all. The problem, however, is that the granularity of contemporary digital activism provides too many easy way-outs: too many people decide to donate a penny where they may otherwise want to donate a dollar.

So, what exactly plagues most "slacktivist" campaigns? Above all, it's their unrealistic assumption that, given enough awareness, all problems are solvable; or, in the language of computer geeks, given enough eyeballs all bugs are shallow. This is precisely what propels many of these campaigns into gathering signatures, adding new members to their Facebook pages, and asking everyone involved to link to the campaign on blogs and Twitter. This works for some issues—especially local ones. But global bugs—like climate change—are bugs of a different nature. Thus, for most global problems, whether it's genocide in Darfur or climate change, there are diminishing returns to awareness-raising. At some point one simply needs to learn how to convert awareness into action—and this is where tools like Twitter and Facebook prove much less useful.

This is not to deny that many of the latest digital activism initiatives, following the success of the Obama electoral juggernaut, have managed to convert their gigantic membership lists into successful money-raising operations. The advent of micro-donations—whereby one can donate any sum from a few cents to a few dollars–has enabled to raise funds that could then be used—at least, in theory—to further advance the goals of the campaign. The problem is that most of these campaigns do not have clear goals or agenda items beyond awareness-raising.

Besides, not every problem can be solved with an injection of funds, which, in a way, creates the same problem as awareness-raising: whether it's financial capital or media capital, spending it in a way that would enable social change could be very tough. Asking for money could also undermine one's efforts to engage groups members in more meaningful real-life activities: the fact that they have already donated some money, no matter how little, makes them feel as if they have already done their bit and should be left alone.

Some grassroots campaigns are beginning to realize it: for example, the web-site of "Free Monem", a 2007 pan-Arab initiative to free an Egyptian blogger from jail carried a sign that said "DON'T DONATE; Take action" and had logos of Visa and MasterCard in a crossed red circle in the background. According to Sami Ben Gharbia, a Tunisian Internet activist and one of the organizers of the campaign, this was a way to show that their campaign needed more than money as well as to shame numerous local and international NGOs that like to raise money to "release bloggers from jail", without having any meaningful impact on the situation on the ground.

That said, the meager fund-raising results of the Save the Children of Africa campaign still look quite puzzling. Surely, even a dozen people working together would be able to raise more money. Could it be that the Facebook environment is putting too many restraints on how they might otherwise have decided to cooperate?

Psychologists offer an interesting explanation as to why a million people working together may be less effective than one person working alone. They call this phenomenon "social loafing". It was discovered by the French scientist Max Ringelmann in 1913, when he asked a group of men to pull on a rope. It turned out they each pulled less hard than when they had to pull alone; this was basically the opposite of synergy. Experiments prove that we usually put much less effort into a task when other people are also doing it with us (think about the last time you had to sing a Happy Birthday song). The key lesson here is that when everyone in the group performs the same mundane tasks, it's impossible to evaluate individual contributions; thus, people inevitably begin slacking off. Increasing the number of other persons diminishes the relative social pressure on each person. That's, in short, what Ringelmann called "social loafing".

Reading about Ringelmann's experiments, I realized that the same problem plagues much of today's "Facebook" activism: once we join a group, we move at the group's own pace, even though we could have been much more effective on our own. As you might have heard from Ethan Zuckerman, Facebook and Twitter were not set up for activists by activists; they were set up for the purposes of entertainment and often attracted activists not because they offered unique services but because they were hard to block. Thus, we shouldn't take it for granted that Facebook activism is the ultimate limit of what's possible in the digital space; it is just the first layer of what's possible if you work on a budget and do not have much time to plan your campaign.

So far, the most successful "slacktivist" initiatives have been those that have set realistic expectations and have taken advantage of "slacktivist" inclinations of Internet users rather then deny their existence. For example,

Student Writing

Read Emily Harris's research paper on this topic: "Youth, the Internet, Pop Culture, and Other Frivolous Things: How 'Slacktivist" is Today's Youth Activism?"

www.pearsonhighered.com/envision/316

FreeRice, a web-site affiliated with the UN Food Program, which contains numerous education games, the most popular of which are those helping you to learn English. While you are doing so, it exposes you to online ads, the proceeds of which go towards purchasing and distributing rice in the poor countries (by FreeRice's estimates, enough rice is being distributed to feed 7,000 people daily).

15 This is a brilliant approach: millions of people rely on the Internet to study English anyway and most of them wouldn't mind being exposed to online advertising in exchange for a useful service. Both sides benefit, with no high words exchanged. Those who participate in the effort are not driven by helping the world and have a very selfish motivation; yet, they probably generate more good than thousands of people who are "fighting" hunger via Facebook. While this model may not be applicable to every situation, it's by finding practical hybrid models like FreeRice's that we could convert immense and undeniable collective energy of Internet users into tangible social change.

So, given all this, how do we avoid "slacktivism" when designing an online campaign? First, make it hard for your supporters to become a slacktivist: don't give people their identity trophies until they have proved their worth. The merit badge should come as a result of their successful and effective contributions to your campaign rather than precede it.

Second, create diverse, distinctive, and non-trivial tasks; your supporters can do more than just click "send to all" button" all day. Since most digital activism campaigns are bound to suffer from the problem of diffusion of responsibility, make it impossible for your supporters to fade into the crowd and "free ride" on the work of other people. Don't give up easily: the giant identity supermarket that Facebook has created could actually be a boon for those organizing a campaign; they just need to figure out a way in which to capitalize on identity aspiration of "slacktivists" by giving them interesting and meaningful tasks that could then be evaluated.

Third, do not overdose yourself on the Wikipedia model. It works for some tasks but for most–it doesn't. While inserting a comma into yet another trivia article on Wikipedia does help, being yet another invisible "slacktivist" doesn't. Finding the lowest common denominator between a million users may ultimately yield lower results than raising the barrier and forcing the activists to put up more rather than less effort into what they are doing. Anyone who tells you otherwise is insane. Or, worse, a slacker! Thank you.

Reflect & Write

- ❑ Think carefully about Morozov's choice of his opening example. How would his starting the essay with a positive example of online activism have changed his reader's understanding of the topic?
- ❑ What is "social loafing," and why is it an important concept for Morozov's definition of online activism?
- ❑ Toward the end of the article, Morozov moves from an article focused on example and analysis to one that functions as a call to action. Why did he make that transition? How would the article have been different if he hadn't?

❑ **Write.** Early in his article, Morozov suggests that "Facebook users shape their online identity implicitly rather than explicitly: that is, the kind of campaigns and groups they join reveal more about who they are than on their dull 'about me' page." However, some readers have contended than on a factor missing from Morozov's analysis is the role that peer pressure plays in group- and cause-joining on Facebook, that many times users join a group because a friend has recommended it not because they are deliberately trying to craft an online persona. Using examples from your own Facebook experience or that of friends, write a one-page position paper that assesses Morozov's claim in terms of this idea of social pressure.

Mir-Hossein Mousavi Khameneh *is the former prime minister of Iran and the current leader of its Green Movement. A candidate in the 2009 Iranian presidential election, Khameneh used his Twitter feed to protest the election results, as did many others, with the result that Twitter became one of the primary news sources for the unfolding Iranian election drama and protest in June 2009.*

Tweets from Iran: June 13, 2009

Login Join Twitter!

ALL internet & mobile networks are cut. We ask everyone in Tehran to go onto their rooftops and shout ALAHO AKBAR in protest #IranElection

12:44 PM Jun 13th, 2009 via web

mousavi1388
MirHossein Mousavi

© 2010 Twitter About Us Contact Blog Status Goodies API Business Help Jobs Terms Privacy

FIGURE 11.4. Mir-Hossein Mousavi Khameneh sent this tweet at 12:44 P.M. on the day of the 2009 Iranian presidential elections.

FIGURE 11.5. Khameneh sent this tweet approximately four hours later.

Reflect & Write

- ❑ Look carefully at the time stamps on these tweets. What story do they tell?
- ❑ How does an awareness of audience influence these tweets? How does that distinguish a post on Twitter from other types of communication, such as an editorial, a press release, or an academic article?
- ❑ How do Twitter feeds operate as primary sources? What purpose might they serve in a research-based argument? How reliable are they as sources? Why?
- ❑ Think about the rhetorical choices made by Twitter as a social media system. What are the implications of the name "Twitter"? What are the visual characteristics of these tweets? Based on the design, what information is the most important?
- ❑ **Write.** What are the potential and the limitations of Twitter as political tool? Write a memo to a political figure or organization in which you argue for or against starting a Twitter feed to share information with or to motivate "followers."

PERSPECTIVES ON THE ISSUE

1. In "From Slacktivism to Activism," Evgeny Morozov argues that social activism on social network sites like Facebook has little real impact for social change. Given danah boyd's assertions about "taste and aesthetics" in relation to Facebook and MySpace pages, how much do you think that membership in social activist groups on Facebook amounts to a type of politically correct digital "bling"? Are such memberships simply another way that teenagers construct an online persona, or do they indicate a true commitment to a cause? In answering these questions, be sure to draw on both Morozov's and boyd's points, as well as your own experience.
2. One of the hot topics about Facebook in 2010 was the question of privacy. How do you feel about the privacy controls currently in place on Facebook or the other social networks that you participate in? What are the dangers of lax privacy restrictions? What are the benefits of more public access to information? Building on the model of *The Onion*'s MySpace article contained in this section, draft a short satiric piece in which you convey your stance on the Facebook privacy controversy.
3. As you have seen, many of the authors in this section are skeptical about the effectiveness of Twitter as an agent of social action. Drawing from information in the Morozov article and using the style of *xkcd*, create a three-to-four panel stick figure cartoon in which you argue for—or against—the effectiveness of Twitter as a political medium.

FROM WRITING TO RESEARCH

1. Read the full report on "Social Media and Young Adults," linked through the *Envision* Website, and compare it to the summary that you read in this section. Now, using statistics and information from these two sources, storyboard a short five-minute film on this topic intended to be shown to high school and college students. Change up the title, include visual examples, strategically organize your information, select some direct quotes, and most importantly, identify and develop a claim that you want to make about social media usage. For added challenge, produce your film and share it with your class.
   www.pearsonhighered.com/envision/319
2. Randomly select at least five of your Facebook or Twitter friends and research their status updates or tweets for the last month. For each friend, cut and paste their updates or feeds into a Word document in chronological order, then read through them sequentially, looking for trends in the way they use the microblogging function. Do they use it to narrate their lives? For self-promotion? To advertise causes? To share links? To experiment in poetry? To quote their favorite lyrics or lines from movies? Based on your research, define at least three different categories or "types" of updates and write an analysis that describes each one and then makes a claim for how each one represents a different way of managing online identity and relationships through social media.
3. Although, as the readings in this section indicate, Twitter played a prominent role in the unfolding of the 2009 Iranian presidential election, it has also been a key player in other global venues, including Haiti, Venezuela, and Moldavia. Choose one of these locales and conduct a research project on the influence of Twitter in that region, drawing on both secondary sources (writings by critics such as Morozov) and primary materials (Twitter feeds). Make a claim about to what extent Twitter influenced contemporary events in that case, drawing a connection to Twitter's larger potential as an agent of global action.

VIRTUAL WORLDS AND GAMING LIFE

A 10-year-old boy battles imperial storm troopers in *Lego Star Wars: The Complete Saga*. A second-grade girl gives Barbie a French manicure in *Barbie Fashion Show*. A summer intern plays a quick game of *Plants vs. Zombies* on his iPhone during his lunch-break. A group of high school friends banter while playing in *Halo 3: ODST*. A college student logs in to join fellow guild members across the country to complete a quest in *World of Warcraft*. Each is participating in modern gaming culture; each demonstrates the way that video games have expanded their audience to reach beyond the arcade, into elementary schools, onto university campuses, and beyond.

FIGURE 11.6. One user's screen capture shows the diversity of characters she created playing *The Sims 2* game.

But with the protean reach of video games—from Nintendo DSi to PlayStation 3 to computer screen to cell phone—comes questions about their social implications. Is the gaming world, as games like *Sims 3* suggest (see Figure 11.6), just a simulation, a practice run for reality? What is the relationship between game play and lived experience? How do computer games alternately undermine and reinforce gender stereotypes, both on screen and off? What relationship do video games centered on aggression have to real-life acts of violence? And, more broadly, to what degree do video games provide platforms for education, amusement, and social interaction, and to what extent do they promote social isolation and political apathy?

The key to examining video games in this way is to understand them as a dynamic form of visual rhetoric. In this section, we invite you to consider them through the lens of "Procedural Rhetoric," what game theorist Ian Bogost defines as "the practice of persuading through . . . computational processes[,] . . . a technique for making arguments with computational systems and for unpacking computational arguments others have created." In other words, it is not just in their social effects that video games hold meaning; the very way they are designed (from how you create your avatar, interact with the apparatus, level up, achieve rewards, negotiate conflict) represents a complex web of rhetorical processes designed to have a certain persuasive effect on the player.

In this section, we will bring this perspective to bear on many issues typically associated with gaming culture and virtual worlds. We'll begin by considering what it means to create an online persona, asking, with Mark Stephen Meadows and Robbie Cooper

Robbie and Tracy Spaight, if avatars are a self-portrait or an alter ego. Then, we'll move to investigate the role of gender politics in the design and play of computer games, looking at both the female avatars, like the Sims women in Figure 11.6, who often seem to be pixilated visions of male fantasy, as well as the female players and designers struggling to find their niche in an industry still dominated by men. We'll take on some of the thornier questions surrounding game play, including the controversy over first-person shooters, and we'll conclude with speculating on the power of gaming and simulation to effect positive social change, looking at persuasive games that address topics as various as poverty in Haiti, human rights violations in Guatanamo Bay, and the energy crisis. Taken together, the selections in this section will argue for a more complex and nuanced understanding of video gaming, showing how even "play" can contain embedded significance.

Reflect & Write

- ❑ To what extent does the image in Figure 11.6 represent a realisticially diverse group of people? Who is missing? How would you adapt these characters if you were a player in this game?
- ❑ Think about the implications of playing a "simulation" (where you act out real-life events) compared to playing a fantasy game (where the events are fabricated). Which type of game play are you most drawn to? Why?
- ❑ **Write.** Write a short essay in which you explain which of the characters from Figure 11.6 you would play in *Sims 3* if you had to choose. Does it represent a "simulation" of your real identity? Or does it represent simply an aspect of—or a complete antithesis–to that identity? Why would you choose to represent yourself in that way?

Artist and author **Mark Stephen Meadows** *has spent the last 15 years working with artificial intelligence, virtual worlds, and other interactive technologies. As early as the 1990s, he helped design Well.com and the first open-protocol multiuser environment. Since that time, he has continued his work in this area, at Xerox-PARC, Stanford Research Institute, and in his own companies devoted to artificial intelligence and avatars. In addition, he is an award-winning artist, having received awards from Ars Electronica and the Cooper-Hewitt National Design Museum. In* I, Avatar, *from which the essay "Auto Portraits" is taken, Meadows uses sociology, psychology, history, and his own art to help explore the possibilities for avatar-based identities.*

Auto Portraits

Mark Stephen Meadows

The avatar is a self-portrait

Avatars are, ultimately, interactive self-portraits that we use to represent ourselves. My avatar, Pighed, is one of many avatars that I've made. In the past year, for myself I've made little pig avatars, tall grey aliens, short fat girls, Chinese couples named Wong, Canadian couples named Wright, cherubs, samurai warriors, racecars, and talking buildings. Some of them were linked, somehow, to my personality, and some were not. Every time someone makes an avatar they create a portrait, though it may have little to do with who one is in the real world. But this is nothing new for portraits—portraits have always been combinations of realism and the techniques artists use to communicate the subject's personality.

FIGURE 11.7. Self Portrait (Pighed Stonecutter), one of many avatars by Meadows.

Avatars as portraits can be seen as another step in a historical progression of exhibitionism and narcissism. Royal families in Europe have always hired painters to make portraits of themselves as a means not only to indicate lineage, wealth, and social rank, but also to purchase a kind of immortality. German art historian Hans Belting has called this "painted anthropology" because the portraits give us a good deal of information not only about the person, but how they lived. Paintings outlast their subjects. So do photographs. In fact, when photography was invented, it was mostly used for portraits. People generally use these technologies to make images of people they care about. Most image-based consumer technology, now including video, is used to generate portraits.

Portraits can become more important than their subjects. There are many examples of this in painting, radio, television, film, and the Internet. For example, people used to pray to portraits of Jesus Christ, and in many parts of the world they still do. The very image alone is enough to inspire piety. We don't need to have Baby Jesus and Mother Mary there; all we need are the symbols of the personality to get people praying. There are many contemporary examples, too. Ask someone if they like Oprah Winfrey. They will probably be able to say yes or no (at least). Then ask them if they know Oprah Winfrey. Chances are they will say no. Her image is enough to inspire love or loathing. Oprah, for example, was voted by *Forbes,* in 2007, as the most powerful celebrity in the world. Her portrayal is of massive importance. But Oprah, herself?

Avatars are portraits we make of ourselves. They exist to do all the things that portraits of the past have done, and a few more. Avatars add to the history of portraiture and do all the things that portraits of the past have done as well. Avatars provide us with social rank, immortality, and influence that extends far beyond where we stand. Avatars now, like paintings of the past, are forming a "pixelated anthropology."

Reflect & Write

- ❑ How does reading the article change the way you look at the image—"SelfPortrait (Pighed Stonecutter)"—that accompanies it? As an artist/writer, Meadows deliberately paired the picture of this avatar with this essay. What do you think he was hoping to accomplish?
- ❑ Why does Meadows connect avatar-creation with the historical practice of portraiture? How does that transform the way you think about creating an online avatar?
- ❑ What does Meadows mean when he says "Portaits can become more important than their subjects"? How does he use the Oprah Winfrey example to substantiate this point? To what extent are you convinced by this example?
- ❑ **Write.** If, as Meadows asserts, "The avatar is a self portrait," what does his picture of Pighed Stonecutter say about him? Write an interpretation of Pighed that examines how Meadows' design reflects his statement about his own identity.

The profiles that follow are taken from the book Alter Ego: Avatars and their Creators, *which complicates stereotypes of gaming and virtual identity by exploring the different identities that people create for themselves online. The book is a product of a three-year study by* **Robbie Cooper**, *a photojournalist and video artist, and his co-author, virtual ethnographer Tracy Spaight. It launched simultaneously in bookstores and in the virtual world Second Life in 2007.*

Profiles from *Alter Ego: Avatars and their Creators*

FIGURE 11.8.
Name: Jason Rowe
Born: 1975
Occupation: None
Location: Crosby, Texas, USA
Average hours per week in-game: 80
Avatar name: Rurouni Kenshin
Avatar created: 2003
Game played: *Star Wars Galaxies*
Server name: Radiant
Character type: Human marksman/rifleman
Character level: 55
Special abilities: Ranged weapon specialization

The difference between me and my online character is pretty obvious. I have a lot of physical disabilities in real life, but in Star Wars *Galaxies* I can ride an Imperial speeder bike, fight monsters, or just hang out with friends at a bar. I have some use of my hands—not much, but a little. In the game I use an onscreen keyboard called 'soft-type' to talk with other players. I can't press the keys on a regular keyboard so I use a virtual one. I play online games because I get to interact with people. The computer screen is my window to the world. Online it doesn't matter what you look like. Virtual worlds bring people together—everyone is on common ground. In the real world, people can be uncomfortable around me before they get to know me and realize that, apart from my outer appearance, I'm just like them. Online you get to know the person behind the keyboard before you know the physical person. The internet eliminates how you look in real life, so you get to know a person by their mind and personality. In 2002 at the *Ultimate Online* Fan Faire in Austin, I noticed that people were intrigued by me, but they acted just like I was one of them. They treated me as an equal, like I wasn't even the way that I am—not disabled, not in a wheelchair, you know. We were all just gamers.

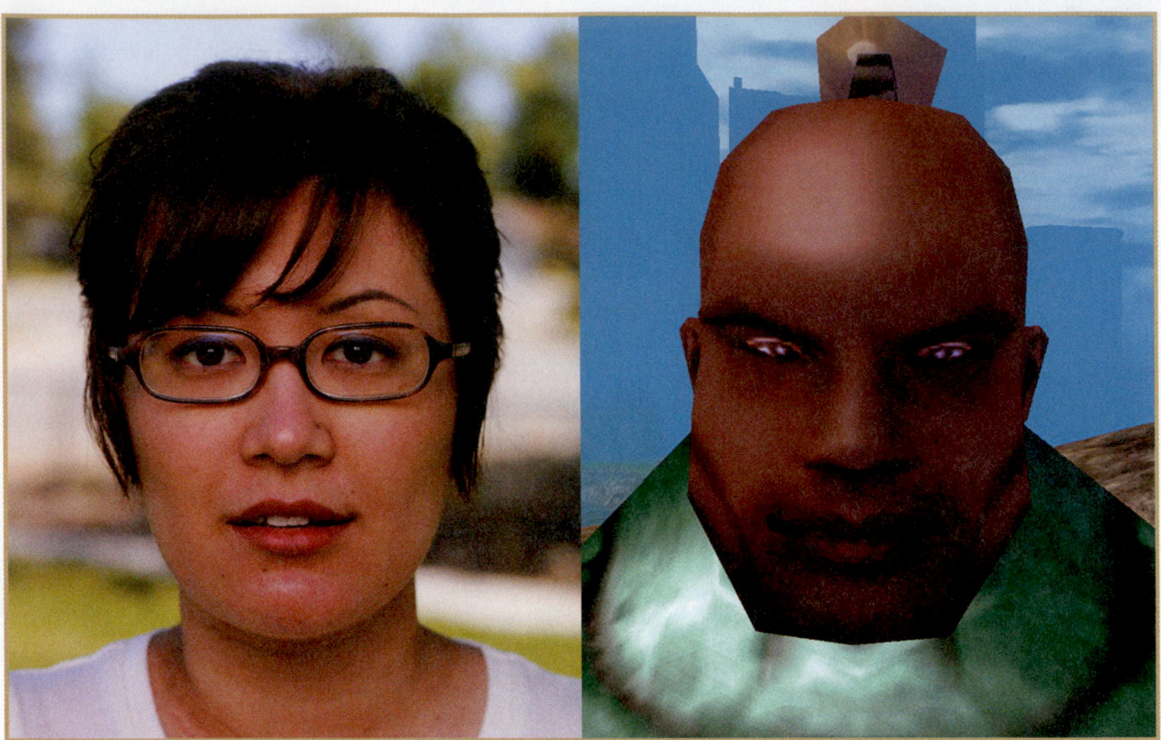

FIGURE 11.9.
Name: Rebecca Glasure
Born: 1980
Occupation: Housewife
Location: Los Angeles, California, USA
Avatar name: Stygian Physic
Avatar created: 2005
Game played: City of Heroes
Character type: Elf

My avatar in *City of Heroes* is my complete opposite. Stygian Physic is big, black, and male. I created him that way because I didn't want to get hit on all the time. I wanted to be noticed for my skills, not my pixel-boobs. By playing as a guy, I found that people treated me differently. Being a guy enabled me to form relationships that I would never otherwise be able to experience. The guys just assume I'm a guy. If I'm the leader, I can make a call and they'll all just follow. And they'll open up about problems with their girlfriends and so on. When I play as a female character, I get challenged a lot more and have to argue about everything. No thanks. I've made some good friends playing as a guy. To this day they don't know I'm really a chick. I don't lie about it. They just assume that I'm a guy and never ask.

I have a six-year-old daughter who's needed more of my attention lately, and because of that I've cut back on my playing hours a lot. I would say that I used to be a 'hardcore' player, because I would spend literally all day sitting at my computer. But now my daughter's getting older, I just don't have that luxury any more. It's my hope that she grows up to like games, so we can all play together. That would blow my mind. My husband and I used to play together for the first year. When we're old and grey our reminiscences will probably consist of things like, 'Remember that time we slaughtered the Hydra and got level 40 at the same time?"

FIGURE 11.10.
Name: Cassien Guier
Born: 1985
Occupation: Student
Location: Lyon, France
Average hours per week in-game: 8
Avatar name: La blonde
Avatar created: 2005
Game played: City of Heroes
Server name: Vigilance
Character type: Human female
Character level: 30

First of all you have to know I'm not a good player. In the game I spend more time and money making my character look good and changing her hairstyle than I do playing. By the way, thanks to all the players for giving me money to make it possible for me to change my hair every day!

I decided to make a superhero reflecting my inner self so I created La blonde, the supra super heroine! She's wonderful, in pink and yellow clothes and splendid shoes. She has the biggest breasts you have ever seen. Just like a real blonde, her wardrobe changes every week. She likes to smile, and people must think she looks pretty stupid because they never take her seriously. Her attitude amazes all the other superheroes! The world can collapse but La blonde will remain optimistic. She often dies. I'm not sure why but the monsters kick her out first. As if a blonde could be dangerous!

I don't really know why people like to have her in their group when fighting the bad monsters. Probably because of her pretty smiley face. Actually she must be the most useless character in the world of MMORPGs.

Reflect & Write

- ❑ How do the people from *Alter Ego* defy or reinscribe common stereotypes about gamers? Mention concrete visual details in answering this question.
- ❑ Perform a rhetorical analysis of these selections. Where are *pathos*, *logos*, and *ethos* located in the different components of the profiles?

- ❑ Consider the gender-crossing found in both Cassien's and Rebecca's choices of avatars. In each case, what do their choices say about their understanding of gender dynamics in virtual environments? How do their choices reflect certain stereotypes?
- ❑ Look carefully at the layout of the profiles. How are the elements of the profiles (photos, demographics, descriptive paragraphs, avatar portraits) arranged to make a specific argument about the relationship between avatars and their creators? What is this argument in each case?
- ❑ **Write.** As the "Reflect" question above suggests, the layout of *Alter Ego* contributes powerfully to its argument. Make a copy of one of the *Alter Ego* profiles and, using scissors and a fresh sheet of paper, cut and paste the words and images into a new layout that is designed specifically to produce a different argument about the relationship between avatars and their creators. You can also use word processing to turn the information on the right side into a formal paragraph if you'd like, or you can use the scaling feature on your copying machine to change the size of the images. Once you are done with your new design, write a short reflection on how your design reflects your argument about avatar identity.

■ **Sheri Graner Ray** *is an award-winning game designer who began her career working on the* Ultima *game series. In 2004, she was listed by the* Hollywood Reporter *as one of the Top 100 Most Influential Women in the Computer Game Industry and in 2005 was recognized for her work on gender and games by the International Game Developer's Association.*

In addition, she has worked on games such as Star Wars Galaxies *and* Nancy Drew *and for several companies including Sony Online Entertainment and Electronic Arts. She is the Executive Chair for Women in Games International, which she helped to found. This selection is the final chapter of her 2003 book,* Gender Inclusive Game Design: Expanding the Market, *an important contribution to the ongoing discussion about women's role in the gaming industry.*

But What If the Player Is Female?

Sheri Graner Ray

When Barbie Fashion Designer (Mattel) showed up on the retail computer game shelves in 1996, it blew away the largest misconception in the game development industry—that girls don't play computer games. The financial success of Barbie® titles soon had publishers scrambling to develop something that would capture a piece of this exciting, new, and lucrative market.

Unfortunately, this did not result in better-designed games or an honest evaluation of what females wanted in computer entertainment. With the exception of a few intrepid developers, it resulted in an industry that simply tried to recreate the Barbie title numbers by cloning these games again and again. Thus, the girls' market came to be defined not so much as a market, but as a genre of shopping, make-up, and fashion games for girls ages 6–10—a market which was then quickly saturated.

When these titles didn't succeed like their progenitor, the industry decided the market was not as lucrative as they thought. So they went back to developing titles for the traditional market of males, ages 13–25.

What the industry overlooks is that this short-sightedness has left a huge hole in the market. Girls that play Barbie games do grow up. With no titles for them to graduate to, they simply spend their money elsewhere. It doesn't have to be this way.

5 By looking at the differences in male and female entertainment criteria, and applying this information to the titles the industry is developing, it is possible to remove the barriers that prevent the female market from accessing those titles. And it is possible to do this without putting Doom into a pink box or making games about fuzzy kittens.

It can be done by looking at some of the basic foundations of game design and recognizing that males and females may deal with game basics in very different ways. From the first contact with a title, their differences in approach can be seen.

The avatar is the first thing a player comes in contact with, usually on the package cover. How the players experience the game through their avatars can be greatly enhanced with an understanding of the importance of avatar presentation and representation. When the female avatar is hypersexualized, it is highly likely the female player won't even consider the title. This 'eye candy' may be pleasing for male players, but they are a barrier for female players.

Also, providing avatars that are gender stereotyped in their roles in the game, or are limited in their scope, serves to push away the female audience. Likewise, if designers know that sexually-oriented humor that contains 'put-downs' of females will cause female players to walk away, they can avoid inadvertently adding content that will drive away a sizeable portion of their sales audience.

Differences in learning styles can affect whether or not a player actually plays the game when they first come in contact with the tutorial and, if it is a demo, whether the player actually buys it. Females want a modeling style of learning, whereas males prefer a more explorative method. If designers keep this in mind, they can work to develop tutorial styles that will best benefit both genders and make game tutorials seamless and natural for all players; the player is encouraged to enter the game, and their level of enjoyment is increased (Gottfried 86).

10 Even the basic concept of the game can be a barrier for some players. The concept of conflict usually serves as the basic premise for any game title. If it is apparent from the game description that the resolution of the conflict is only going to be handled in the traditionally male manner—that is, a confrontational resolution—then this will dissuade those players that would normally choose other resolution styles, such as negotiation or compromise. With the knowledge of how each gender handles conflict, designers can build resolutions into their games that complement both styles and appeal to both audiences.

The stimuli designers use to capture their audience and keep their attention can have an effect on which markets find the title engrossing as well. Males are physically stimulated by visual input. Females may enjoy visual stimulus, however, they do not have a physical response to it. Their response comes from emotional or tactile input. So games that rely on fast movement and visual special effects may not capture the female market as well as they do the male market. By understanding this difference, designers can balance the stimuli they are using for their game and attract and keep a greater percentage of their players.

When the players have actually entered the game, how they are rewarded for their successes can either reinforce a positive game experience or it can demotivate the players. While males prefer punishment for error in a game, females prefer forgiveness. Punishment for errors is the classic method by which games are resolved. The player is given a limited number of 'lives' and has only so many 'chances' to succeed. If they do not succeed, then they are usually returned to the beginning of the level, and all progress on that level is lost.

Forgiveness for error means the loss is not permanent. Instead, it is a temporary loss, or progress toward the final goal is slowed; but it can be regained quickly, normal gameplay resumed, progress can be continued. There is no 'dying' and starting over.

Often for females, the reward of 'winning' or achieving a high level is simply not enough reason to play a game. They want to find a solution that is mutually beneficial and socially significant. They want to accomplish something, rather than 'win.' By understanding this, designers can adapt their reward system and their victory conditions to better accommodate different player expectations.

Even how males and females use computers is basically very different. Males wish to conquer the machine. They want to use it as an expression of physical power. Females want to work with the machine. They want to use it to expand their communications powers. However, because of the limited amount of cross-gender entertainment software, females have come to view computers not so much as an entertainment medium, but as a communications and productivity tool instead (Turkle 98).

Why is it important for females to play games? There are two reasons. One reason is ideological, and the other is economic.

Ideologically, it is vitally important that girls play and enjoy computer games because it increases their comfort level with technology, and this is essential for them to maintain economic parity with males in today's society. If girls are not allowed to have fun with technology today, we cannot expect them to excel with technology tomorrow.

However, the more economic reason is that the game industry must expand to other markets if it wishes to sustain growth. There are only so many males age 13–25 in the world at any given time. If no other audiences are farmed, then the game industry will outgrow its market, resulting in loss of revenue and ultimately a contraction of the industry. Add to that the fact that females control an ever-growing percentage of the disposable income, then it makes sense to appeal to them if this industry wants 'a piece of the action.' However, to do this, designers must be willing to look at play patterns and models that are not necessarily their own. It is going to take producers/publishers who are willing to diversify their workforces by making a concerted effort to seek out qualified female candidates. It also means that those women who are already in the industry must be willing to serve as role models and mentors for the women who want to break into the industry. And overall, it's going to take an industry that is willing to step back, take a look at their titles, and ask themselves, "But what if the player is female?"

References

Gottfried, Allen W. and Catherine Caldwell Brown. *Play Interactions: The Contribution of Play Materials and Parental Involvement to Children's Development.* Mississippi: Lexington Books, 1986. Print.

Turkle, Sherry, "Computational Reticence; Why Women Fear the Intimate Machine." Ed. Cheris Kramarae. *Technology and Women's Voices.* New York: Pergamon Press, 1986. 41–61. Print.

Reflect & Write

- ❑ Does Ray make a persuasive argument? Why or why not?
- ❑ Select some places in the argument where she might have used specific examples—rather than generalizations—to be more persuasive. What examples would you use?
- ❑ Ray is writing for a particular audience here: game designers. How do you see this concern over audience reflected in the structure, tone, and execution of her argument? How does she make her argument matter to this audience?
- ❑ **Write.** Ray provides some concrete advice for game developers about how to create games that appeal to girls. Using her advice, work with a group to draft a proposal for a new game. Include an overview of the game play and story, a description of the main characters, and mock up either an advertisement or a cover for your game. Present your group's proposal and other materials to the class.

■ **Zoe Flower's** *Girlspy column appears biweekly on Gamespy.com, a news site for the gaming community; she has a popular column on the* Official PlayStation Magazine (OPM); *she co-produces with her friend Stephanie Drinnan an action series about female extreme sports athletes called "Hardcore Candy"; and she toured America in 2002 as "GamerGirl," in which role she did TV and radio spots to discuss issues related to the gaming community. She is currently a designer with Slant Six Games. This article, published January 1, 2005, in* OPM, *focuses on her area of specialty: girls and gaming.*

Getting the Girl: The Myths, Misconceptions, and Misdemeanors of Females in Games

Zoe Flower

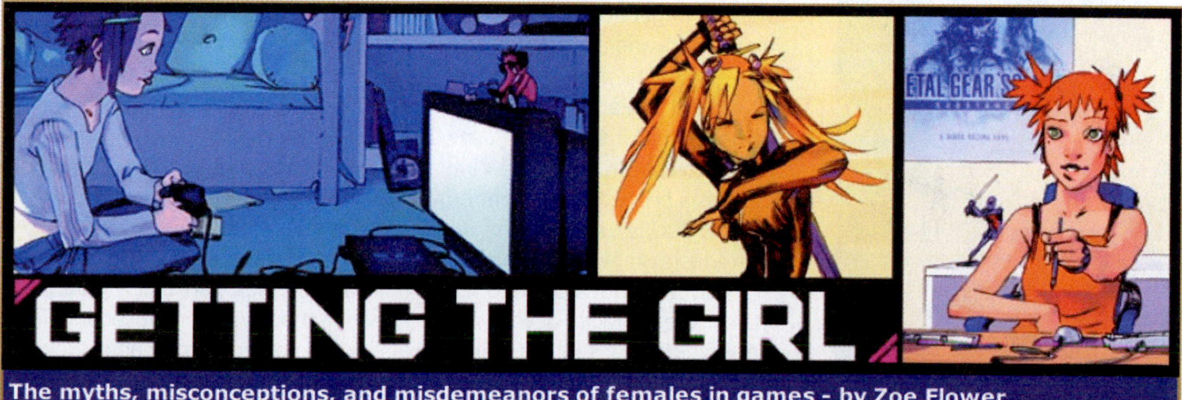

The first identifiable female gaming action hero, Lara Croft has appeared in six games since her debut eight years ago in the original Tomb Raider.

Will Nina's low-cut shorts and thigh-high boots allow her to deliver a more powerful blow in Death by Degrees? The developer wants you to believe so.

It was 1996 when a little development house out of the U.K. finished work on a lush new adventure game featuring a brunette archeologist named Lara Croft. It was a defining moment for me as I watched her strut seductively across my screen and into the sex symbol status that would turn the gaming world on its head. Fast-forward eight years through the evolution of next-gen hardware, multimillion-dollar budgets, and massive acceptance of games in pop culture. Still, Lara Croft continues to personify an ongoing culture clash over gender, sexuality, empowerment, and objectification. It was while standing in my first-ever ladies' room line at E3 2004 as I pondered the Playboy bunnies, the return of Leisure Suit Larry, and the slew of buxom virtual ladies headlining each booth that I questioned whether the industry had evolved at all.

It might seem like a simple puzzle to solve: trying to understand why female representation in videogames—whether it's as characters, developers, or gamers—is important. But it seemed the more questions I asked, the more elusive the answers became. And it wasn't long before my own stereotypes were called into question.

When I requested an interview to discuss Cyberlore's *Playboy: The Mansion,* I never even considered that the senior designer on the Sims-style project might be a woman—one pregnant with twins, in fact. As I expected, Brenda Brathwaite has a lot to say about females in today's games. But I can guarantee it's not what you might expect.

"If you're going to animate breasts, animate them properly," admonishes Brathwaite. "The breasts in the original *Dark Alliance* drove me nuts. If my breasts moved like that, I'd go to the doctor . . . or call an exorcist."

5 While this industry veteran shows a sense of humor and perspective concerning her work, there are many who won't find the idea of creating a *Playboy* magazine simulator funny. "I suspect that those who feel it's a gender controversy have probably not seen an issue of *Playboy* magazine. They have it stereotyped," suggests Brathwaite. "I find that *Playboy* is a celebration of women and goes out of its way to be respectful. On *Playboy: The Mansion*, we were committed to making a good, tasteful game."

I got a similar response regarding Majesco's *BloodRayne*; Rayne, coincidentally, just appeared in *Playboy*'s "Sexiest Game Characters" spread. And here too, the product manager for the goth queen was herself female.

"If you don't have the gameplay to back up the character appeal, T&A will only get you so far," effuses Liz Buckley. "*BloodRayne* resonates very well with our target audience of males ages 17 to 34, but Rayne has a huge female following as well. I think that's attributable to her strength and attitude—it's definitely empowering to play as her."

So if it's all about personality, why bother with the heaving bosom and leather chaps? It turns out Rayne was an ugly duckling before her transformation to voluptuous vixen. "Initially, Rayne had a militant, dark gothic look. She was a brunette with tight buns in her hair and a very severe body line," explains Buckley. And I even found myself admitting I'd rather play the "extreme makeover" version of the vamp.

Maybe it's not a crime to sex up the leading ladies, particularly if they retain some character development. But what about Vivendi's upcoming *Red Ninja,* which claims to incorporate sexuality as a gameplay mechanic, allowing main character Kurenai to seduce unsuspecting guards?

Beyond Good & Evil's Jade bucked the trend of buxom and deadly heroines; the game was critically acclaimed, but sales proved disappointing

Rayne got new, more revealing outfits in the sequel to BlooodRayne; the new game also includes a code that allows players to inflate or deflate Rayne's breasts from their default size.

10 "It's a challenging concept to attempt when body language and atmosphere are confined by things like polygon limits," admits Associate Producer Melissa Miller. "Early on, we conducted a focus test specifically with female gamers. They liked the concept of Kurenai but felt she was showing too much skin with the short kimono. Once we justified the need for some sexiness with the seduction mechanic, they bought into Kurenai completely and were really excited about playing her."

Producer Yozo Sakagami of Namco's *Death by Degrees,* featuring Tekken's Nina, expressed a similar design challenge when trying to achieve what his team calls "functional beauty in combat." It turns out that Nina's bikini and catsuit are more than just eye candy. "The outfit designs were based on ease of movement and variation in appearance," states Sakagami. "Depending on whether an attack connects with bare or clothed skin, the resulting damage differs."

Right. And are female gamers buying into it? "We've received favorable reactions from women toward Nina in this game. We were surprised because these women saw in Nina the character image we had hoped to create but feared we hadn't attained. Intangible elements such as these can easily be obscured while developing a game."

With such a positive response to stereotypical female protagonists, I began to question whether it was possible to design a strong female character without the requisite augmented body and sexual references.

"These types of character designs are not necessary; it is an easy way out," argues Ubisoft's Tyrone Miller. "*Beyond Good & Evil* shows us that you can convey the same strength and likability in a female character without having to use blatant sex appeal."

15 Interestingly enough, *BG&E*'s protagonist Jade is the brainchild of game designer Michel Ancel (*Rayman*, *King Kong*). "Rumor has it that Ancel's wife actually served as the main inspiration and muse for Jade's look and personality," informs Miller. "Ancel wanted to create a realistic lead character with a persona that players could connect to and identify with. As you play the game, you really develop an attachment to her."

So with men designing approachable leading ladies of realistic proportions and women enthusing over the feminine aspects of *Playboy* and goth queens, I realized that the issue might have less to do with gender and more to do with how sexuality is perceived in today's games.

"It's wrong to single out female characters when their male counterparts are usually just as superficial," argues Amy Hennig, game director for Naughty Dog. "We seem to be at that 'naughty' stage, where some developers are testing the limits to see what they can get away with. Games aren't considered just toys anymore, but we haven't matured beyond juvenile titillation."

Karin Yamagiwa, 2D-texture lead for Sucker Punch (*Sly Cooper*). points out, "Sexuality can be powerful, but it depends on how it's used. Games like *Rumble Roses*. . . some of my female friends find them a bit offensive, while others find them hilarious. Is it for boys to ogle? Of course! But I also know plenty of men who are embarrassed by it."

Anna Kipnis, a programmer for Double Fine Studios, adds, "Games can have story elements and amazing gameplay that can appeal to people regardless of gender. I believe that is what game developers should strive for, and perhaps not enough do."

A Konami press release for Rumble Roses states, "Modeled in revealing bikinis, these vicious vixens aren't afraid of getting a little dirty. Delivering realistic mud matches, players will literally see mud sliding off these sexy wrestlers after each takedown in the mud pit."

In order to justify Kurenai's revealing clothing, Red Ninja's developers gave her a move that allows her to seduce her male enemies.

20 Aletheia Simonson of Sony CEA's product evaluation group agrees. "Games for women are there; the hurdle is getting a woman who has never played a videogame to try one. It will probably be some time before the game equivalent of the romantic comedy is a blockbuster hit," she explains.

Well, one developer seems to have combined gender equality with mass appeal. EA Maxis' *The Sims* franchise has laid claim to a whopping 50 percent female audience. And it's not as if this series is without its gender stereotypes and sex appeal. One look at *The Urbz: Sims in the City* reveals a prevalence of thong panties and revealing clothing. So just whom is this game meant for?

"Were we planning to entice the male? Well, it does make them look twice in the office!" jokes Virginia McArthur, lead producer on *The Urbz* Handheld. "But you will find when women play, they tend to choose the hip low-riders, as it really fits in with the culture of the location."

As for the secret of *The Sims*' success, McArthur answers confidently: "When we brought *The Urbz* to consoles, we realized that what keeps females interested in our products is the customization and real-life interactions and scenarios they can play out as an Urb. Female players on consoles wanted to spend more time socializing and unlocking items and outfits; they wanted to spend less time on motives and watching animations."

But isn't it generalizations like those above that have been packaged into the dreaded concept of the "girl game"? "It's silly and patronizing to think there's some magic 'girl game' formula, that if the box is pink and there's shopping in the game, girls will buy it in droves," warns Naughty Dog's Hennig, who believes this stereotyping disenfranchises girls all the more. "In general, I think women prefer games that include exploration, problem-solving, customization, and nonlinear play. When we incorporate these elements into our games—whether it's *GTA* or *The Sims*—we're going to attract a wider demographic."

25 However, despite the recent growth spurt of women making and playing games, there remains a great divide between male and female gamers. Many women report feeling intimidated, whether it's because of an overwhelming amount of product on store shelves or the often aggressive behavior of other gamers. It's no secret that it can be tough to become part of the hardcore online community, even for the most talented players.

In an attempt to bridge the gender gap, Ubisoft has created and funded a fully female gaming team known as the Frag Dolls, a group of hardcore twitch gamers with panache who play *Splinter Cell* and *Rainbow Six.* At first impression, this could be taken as a marketing gimmick by Ubisoft to attract more males to their products. Not true, claims the publisher.

"We're creating role models for a whole legion of girls out there who may have been too intimidated to play games online—or even play at all," explains Ubisoft's online community manager, Nate Mordo. "For those who have bemoaned the fact that in-game heroines have tended to adhere to a certain template, I think that more women playing games means that we'll see more games that cater to this newly diverse audience."

The Frag Dolls are looking to debunk the myths associated with girl gamers and help support other women looking to play. But it's still naive to think that all gamers are treated equally: One visit to the girl team's forums (www.fragdolls.com) demonstrates the uphill battle to convince male gamers that girls are worthy adversaries and teammates.

So it appears, in fact, that publishers are finally accepting the existence of the once mythical female market. However, whether the industry can mature and evolve to capture their interests still remains to be seen. What I can guarantee is a sentiment echoed by every woman I spoke with: The more women that get involved, the more power they have to evoke change from within. It may take time and effort, but I don't know anyone who ever said getting the girl was easy.

Reflect & Write

- ❑ Flower conducted a long interview with Brenda Brathwaite—consider the quotation with which she chose to introduce Brathwaite. Why this particular one? How does it affect the way that the reader initially perceives Brathwaite? How does it affect the way the reader understands the development of Flower's argument?
- ❑ While discussing the character Rayne, Flower admits that she herself would rather play the "extreme makeover" version of this character. How does this personal revelation about her own feelings about female characters affect the persuasiveness of her overall argument?
- ❑ Midway through the article, Flower writes, "I realized that the issue might have less to do with gender and more to do with how sexuality is perceived in today's games." What is the difference between gender and sexuality as Flower constructs it in this article? Do you agree with her statement or not?
- ❑ Analyze Flower's conclusion. What are its strengths? What would you have added or done differently if you were writing this article?
- ❑ **Write.** Look carefully at the images that Flower included in her article, both the banner images at the top (created for this article) as well as the pictures of avatars at the side (from commercial games). Write a brief analysis, drawing on Flower's article, that describes the differences in gendered representation among these female characters. How do they operate differently in relation to the article? What purpose does each type of images serve?

COLLABORATIVE CHALLENGE

Brainstorm a game that would appeal to a female gamer. Storyboard some of the initial action of the game, write an abstract description, and design an ad or box design for the game. Next, create a PowerPoint presentation and marketing pitch aimed at the executives of a successful but relatively conservative gaming company, making a case for why this game would be a hit with its target audience. Deliver your presentation to the rest of the class.

San Francisco-based media critic **Gerard Jones** *has written on sitcoms and the American dream and on the history of comic books. In 2005, he won an Eisner Award for* Men of Tomorrow Geeks, Gangsters, and the Birth of the Comic Book. *He has also contributed text for several comic books, including titles featuring Batman, Superman, and the X-Men. His 2000 book,* Killing Monsters, *argues for the benefits of allowing children to indulge in fantasy violence. The following selection is taken from the section of that book where he turns his focus specifically on violent video games.*

Shooters

Gerard Jones

Most of the experts I know see the value of superheroes, action figures, and slapstick cartoons. But the mere mention of gory video games provokes a very different reaction. After a passionate defense of superheroes at a conference panel, one developmental psychologist paused and then said with special vehemence, "But I don't think video games in which the player is induced to shoot at other human beings are ever good for *anyone.*" A psychiatrist who helped me with my research cringed slightly at the mention of *Quake* and said, "There has to be something wrong with a person who'd want to look at that."

Once, on a cable news channel, I debated a New York state senator who was pushing legislation to ban violent video games for children under eighteen. I talked about the benefits many teenagers have found in various sorts of games—not realizing that the producers were running images from a gory first-person shooter game on the screen as I spoke. When I watched the tape later and heard myself saying, "I know of many kids who thrive in the gaming culture" as bullets blew through skulls and blood went flying, I was appalled at my own words.

Nothing sets off our revulsion like explicit gore. Nothing triggers our worries about how our kids may turn out than watching them gun down real-looking people on screen. It's understandable that hypotheses suggesting that video games are training our children to be killers have garnered tremendous publicity, even though the evidence doesn't support them. It's understandable that the Joint Statement on the Impact of Entertainment Violence on Children would expect "that they may be significantly more harmful" than other media. It's understandable that when we learned that the boys who attacked their classmates at Columbine High School were heavy players of shooter games, we assumed the games had helped make them killers.

But when concerned adults condemn entertainment that millions of well-adjusted young people love and insist is perfectly good for them, we owe it to the young people—and ourselves—to learn more about it. When I launched my exploration of bloody video games I felt as though I were taking a journey into one of the darkest recesses of contemporary youth culture. But the more I got to know those games and the people who played them, the less I saw to fear. Ultimately I've come to feel that video games are the least powerful and least dangerous of all forms of entertainment violence.

5 When we encounter something new, we try to understand it in terms of other things already known to us. In a powerful book, *On Killing,* U.S. Army psychologist Dave Grossman described operant conditioning methods used during the Vietnam War that resembled some of today's video games and revealed that some military units are now using those same video games to train soldiers. He argued well for the effectiveness of using animated but human-looking targets, the rapidity of a game, and instant rewards for quick

shooting as tools to desensitize soldiers to the human dimension of what they were doing—and he asserted that video games are doing precisely the same thing to our kids.

There are problems with Grossman's argument, however. Effective conditioning requires structured application and a well-controlled environment, which is scarcely what gamers are experiencing when they're fiddling with a video game in their own rooms or messing around an arcade with hundreds of other kids. Grossman frequently quotes B. E Skinner, who developed operant conditioning, but doesn't mention one of the essential human truths that Skinner himself acknowledged: our reactions, unlike those of dogs or rats, are profoundly affected by the feelings, thoughts, and meanings that we assign to the stimuli in our environments. All the military training Grossman described takes place in an authoritarian environment in which the soldiers know full well that the purpose of the game is to make them better killers; they generally want to cooperate (especially in a volunteer army), and every message they hear is, "Kill for your country." What our kids are doing with their video games is playing, and they know it. Games have always been a part of military training, and nearly all competitive games have a warlike subtext. Wellington said that the Battle of Waterloo "was won on the playing fields of Eton," but cricket and rugby haven't turned subsequent generations of Etonians into killers. Just because shooter games remind us of real shooting and military training doesn't mean that kids experience them as such when they play, any more than they experience plastic army men or chess pieces as real warriors.

After a decade of these games being played by millions of kids, Grossman and other critics have provided no evidence of the effects they have predicted. Certainly video games haven't had any significant impact on real-world crime. "The research on video games and crime is compelling to read," said Helen Smith, forensic psychologist, youth violence specialist, and author of *The Scarred Heart.* "But it just doesn't hold up. Kids have been getting less violent since those games came out. That includes gun violence and every other sort of violence that might be inspired by a video game." The contemporary style of the first-person shooter game hit the market with *Castle Wolfenstein* in 1991; *Doom* and *Quake,* still by far the best-sellers of the genre, followed in 1992. The peak of shooter-game play by teenagers was from approximately 1992 to 1995, by which time the games' sales had dropped, and they'd gone from being the fad of the moment to one of many genres in the industry. Violent crime dropped during those years. We've now had time for those millions of game players to reach adulthood, and the generation of "killer kids" predicted by the games' critics never materialized.

"There's no connection between video gaming and violence in the profiles of the kids I see," noted Smith. "In fact, the lower-income kids who make up the great majority of violent kids usually don't have any interest in games—and they couldn't afford the hobby even if they did." Both her practice and her survey show that extremely angry and violent kids often show interest in violent music, Web sites, and movies, but rarely in video games. "I don't discount the influence some media may have on very hostile young people," she concluded. "But there just doesn't seem to be any connection with games."

A few studies of adolescents have found a correlation between heavy video game use and various sorts of delinquent behavior. Among teenagers, unemployed boys who aren't great academic achievers are more likely to amuse themselves with video games; unemployed boys who aren't great academic achievers are also more likely to misbehave. Kids who work for high grades, play sports, do community work, and have jobs often play *Quake,* too, but they don't have the time to show up as "heavy users" in a correlative study. Several laboratory studies have recorded increases in aggression in young people after playing video games. Those studies, however, have had the subjects play for limited times, usually fifteen minutes, and then stop abruptly—a situation guaranteed to frustrate anyone in a highsuspense, high-adrenaline game. And the readings have been taken immediately after the kids have finished, when their arousal is as heightened as it would have been at the end of any competitive or exciting experience. The research process itself may create the reactions it measures.

10 Then there's Columbine. The planned, systematic way in which Dylan Klebold and Eric Harris attacked and slaughtered their schoolmates made it the most horrific of all the teen rampage shootings. We needed an explanation for it, and the discovery that Klebold and Harris loved these as yet little-known shooter games provided one. The boys apparently reprograrnmed their copy of *Doom* to simulate the slaughter they were planning and used the game to practice for it. Those hours upon hours spent shooting imaginary foes very likely made it easier for them to make their terrible fantasies real. But some perspective is needed.

Based on the data of Dr. James McGee, an authority on the "classroom avenger," there have been sixteen rampage shootings at schools by adolescents in recent years, involving eighteen boys. Only at Columbine, the thirteenth of the rampages, did the perpetrators turn out to be heavy game players. A few other boys liked shooter video games to one extent or another, though less, in every case, than they liked target shooting with real guns. Most of the shooters showed no interest in games at all. Other elements were much more common to the eighteen boys: bullying by peers, hostility with or dissociation from parents, suicidal threats, and fascination with news coverage of earlier rampage shootings show up among all of them. Several shared a preoccupation with Adolf Hitler or other symbols of historical violence, certain angry rock songs and violent movies, and real weapons. Klebold and Harris's costumes and rhetoric were unlike any in the games they played, but they owed an obvious debt to earlier school shooters (especially the first nationally publicized shooter, Barry Loukaitis of Moses Lake, Washington) and to right-wing extremists The news and history seem to have been far deadlier influences on them than the unreality *of Doom.*

Significantly, Loukaitis and other early school shooters were fascinated by the many earlier workplace rampages of adult men. In fact, school shooters resemble adult rampage shooters in nearly all important respects: demographics, personality types, the pattern of perceived slights and escalating grudges leading to the incidents, fascination with media notoriety, and even the sorts of comments made during and after the shootings. School shootings appear to be a case of teenagers imitating their elders. Those adult rampaging killings, who have erupted periodically since the late 1970s, have never been linked to video games.

Like the Beatles song that Charles Manson claimed inspired him to murder or the poetry that Timothy McVeigh quoted to justify his bombing of the Oklahoma City federal building, shooter video games have sometimes been plucked and twisted by troubled souls to give some shape to the rages within them. Sometimes they seem to help such people contain their rage. Sometimes they aren't powerful enough, and they may become part of a rehearsal for murder and suicide. But to condemn them because they lend themselves so easily to such terrible uses is to fail to understand their place in the lives of modern teenagers.

Helen Smith's principal objection to theorists who try to link video games to real-life crime is the same as mine: "They're not listening to the kids." Critic Dave Grossman asked in one chapter title, "What Are We Doing to Our Kids?" But not once did he ask the kids, "What are you doing?" He has viewed garners not as imaginative people using a mechanical toy but as cyborgs whose reactions are determined by the machine. "In video arcades," he wrote, "children stand slackjawed but intent behind machine guns and shoot at electronic targets. . . . " I don't know what arcade Grossman went to, but it would take a Zen master to play a video game slack-jawed. What gamers describe to me as the "video game face" is quite the opposite: twisted by tooth-gnashing, jaw-jerking, and occasional open-mouthed suspense. More experienced gamers may be tense and stoic, but they are viscerally, emotionally engaged in competition, choosing to devote their leisure time, money, and a great deal of effort to becoming better at a game. Most contemporary gamers are also involved in social and intellectual processes far more complex than merely playing in an arcade.

15 In talking to gamers visiting the annual Game Designers' Expo in Silicon Valley, reading the research, and playing the games myself, I've been struck by how different the video game world is from my preconceptions. The games are becoming remarkably creative. All the successful first-person shooter games now allow users to design their own "maps" in which the battles will take place, to create new "levels" with customized backgrounds and challenges, and to choose their own "skins," the physical appearance of their game selves. One teenage gamer led me through a communal tournament fought in the land of Oz by two Nazis, a cowboy, a mercenary, a teddy bear, and a loaf of bread. Although the basic story line remains the same— the player has to find his way through labyrinthine structures and fight off ambushing opponents to reach a distant goal—gamers are essentially scripting their own adventures.

According to Dr. Mihaly Csikszentmihalyi, a leading authority on adolescent development and the originator of the concept of "flow states," any media experience that demands activity, interaction, control, and emotional stimulation is far more constructive than a passive experience like watching television. Traditional forms of entertainment, such as storytelling, puppet plays, and live musical performances, challenge children to more vital intellectual and emotional states by requiring that they bring more imagination and more of their own psychic contents to comprehending material than do the electronic media, which typically supply prepackaged information. Csikszentmihalyi noted that the simpler video games, "those that involve primarily piling up as many cadavers as possible," offer more than television, but not much more. "However, the newer, more complex video games," he said, "give players worlds to explore and decisions to make that can stir some of the emotions of discovery. They may prove to be very valuable forms."

I experienced those emotions of discovery when I had a young player lead me through a level of *Quake 3.* We picked our way through the claustrophobic corridors of an abandoned castle, vigilant every moment to the possibility of ambush—although the attacks were far from constant, leaving us more time to dread them than to relieve the suspense in action—when suddenly we came to a staircase. We shot our way through one more pair of zombies and raced upward to freedom. Stepping through a door to the battlements of the castle, where the black stone suddenly fell away to reveal a vast sunset, filled me with an elation of freedom and courage. I wanted nothing more than to plunge into the next level.

Gaming is also becoming an increasingly social activity. Gamers talk and e-mail incessantly about strategies and shortcuts they've discovered, plan communal tournaments, pass around copies of *PC Gamer* magazine, and invite friends over to see their new games. Although "heavy gamers" may stick to their own esoteric cliques, most gamers are part of adolescent society and use games as icebreakers and bonding mechanisms. Most gamers now prefer not to play alone against the computer but against other gamers by way of multiplayer consoles or Internet-based games that can include dozens of players at once. The video game, at this point, becomes an athletic competition for kids who may not be able to throw far or run fast. Its players aren't cyborgs being conditioned by a machine but competitors assessing their own and their opponents' skills: who's quicker, who knows the "map" better, who can strategize most intelligently? Afterward there's usually a lot of talking or e-mailing about how the tournament played out and why. Gaming isn't a complete social life, but it can be a vital piece of one, especially for kids who don't fit well into other juvenile cliques.

Not surprisingly, then, gaming is also becoming a steadily less male-dominated world. "Heavy gamers" are more likely to be male, but among preteens, nearly as many girls as boys own and play video games—even the more violent games. As Dr. Jeanne Funk's focus groups with children suggest, girls tend to like violent games less than boys, and they prefer to use the word "action" for what boys call "violence," but they commonly play even the gorier shooting and fighting games in social situations. Unlike some violent music and movies, video games generally don't appeal to the more aggressive teenagers. As one game-industry marketer put it, "Heavy gamers are nerds. There are some borderline tough kids who also game, but the real bad-asses look down at this as kid stuff. Gamers are reasonably bright but not big achievers, hang with other gamers and don't like to attract too much attention. They can be socially clueless, selfabsorbed, and arrogant, but one of the main reasons they disappear into the gaming world is that they want to avoid real-life trouble."

20 Perhaps, then, it should have surprised me less than it did to learn that the extreme violence and realistic gore that disturbs us so much really doesn't matter much to the gamers. Studies show that if a gamer is given a choice between a gory game that doesn't challenge his skills and a non-gory one that does, he'll usually choose the challenge over the gore. Some of the best-selling first-person shooter games, such as *Goldeneye* with James Bond, feature bloodless violence in old-time Hollywood style. The ultraviolent games now account for less than 10 percent of the game market, and industry surveys show that few gamers specialize in them but typically play a wide variety of types. One fourteen-year-old gamer I talked to listed his five favorite games as *Quake 3, Half-Life, Starcraft* (science-fiction strategy), *The Legend of Zelda: Ocarina of Time* (humorous adventure), and *Tony Hawk Skateboarding.*

"Gore is at best a tertiary appeal of shooter games," said Dallas Middaugh, an editor of many books about gaming and a gamer himself. "Game play is by far the most important element—the difficulty, the strategy required, the complexity of variations, the suspense. Next comes the overall environment and appearance of the game world. Gore just adds a bit to the realism and visual impact."

Some game designers have tried to cash in on the negative, but lucrative, publicity that bad taste brings. One, *Soldier of Fortune,* successfully stirred up controversy with its sadistic portrayals of Americans attacking Vietnamese and Latin American villages, thus glorifying some of our most haunting atrocities. After a flurry of publicity, however, it faded in the marketplace. One adult gamer told me, "It wasn't challenging enough. Your opponents were too weak. It was all shock value, and gamers resent that." The shooter games that have remained successful are more fantastical and less vicious, and pit the player against more overwhelming odds. In *Half-Life*, the player is an innocent scientist who has to fight his way through hundreds of invading aliens and soldiers sent by a corrupt government. In *Quake 3*, he is a normal human battling a legion of zombies. These games are not about slaughtering victims but about killing monsters. . . .

The danger of these games is that by enabling people to immerse themselves so completely in play, they may make it hard to climb back out. The typical video-gamer plays only five or six hours a week, and the activity most often sacrificed in favor of gaming is television watching. But there are gamers who play five or six hours a day, who sacrifice their social lives and school performance and every other constructive activity. This seems to be most true of fantasy role-playing games, in which players become unique characters on the Internet and participate in long adventures and relationships with other gamers. But among standard video games, the first-person shooter games seem more likely than most to take the place of some gamers' real lives. They create such a viscerally compelling but controllable reality that the quiet tensions and messy ambivalence of reality can become increasingly unbearable by contrast. Gamers tell me about going into a "tournament" with the intention of passing a few minutes and finding that two hours have suddenly gone by. Some take that as a reminder to manage their time more consciously. Others go back in at the first opportunity.

"Some of my adolescent patients speak of being 'addicted' to video games," said Lynn Ponton." I don't like to use the word addiction, but it is habitual behavior. They use video games to contain their anxiety. And the games will do that for them for quite a while. But with time they can also desensitize them. The players need more and more stimulation to contain their anxieties, which not only keeps them from dealing with the causes of their anxiety but can actually increase their anxieties."

Psychiatrist Nancy Marks has also seen patients who seem to play video games instead of living. "For many people it's a way of avoiding the real existential issues, the angst, of life," she said. "They may try to deal with their pain and anxiety through the surrogate selves of these games, but there's really no way to work through significant issues in a game, not unless someone is sitting there talking to you about what you're doing in the game and what that might mean about your real life. These games can be constructive as long as the players know they're playing and come back to real life. But some people forget that this is just play."

Too often we just dismiss gamers, let them retreat into isolation, or chase them away by worrying too much about their gaming. Doctors Ponton and Marks both have stressed the power of communication. Ponton has advocated trying to play the games occasionally with the kids, which she does with both her daughters and her patients. "I don't usually last long at the games," she confessed. "But beating mom or Dr. Ponton makes them feel good in its own way and can ease some of the barriers between us." If a parent can't stand to play the game, just being available can help young people resurface. If a teenager disappears into his room for too many hours at the expense of the rest of life, consider moving the game console into the family room. "Sometimes," Ponton said, "it can be helpful to young people just to have a parent nearby, reading or balancing the checkbook."

When parents aren't available, teachers, friends, or any interested party can help habitual gamers integrate their fantasies with real life just by communicating with them about the games. Simply talking about the games calmly and respecting young people's passion for them, whether that means discussing them in schools or putting them in public places, will help open the door for gamers to connect more meaningfully with society at large. I contrast Jimmy, the boy from Pennsylvania who felt so ostracized by his teachers' reactions to his games, with Richard, the Quaker youth worker playing *Quake 3* at a public conference. Fear and hostility can make any entertainment problematic; communication and empathy can help make any entertainment constructive.

We are frightened by the images we see in the games, and so we become frightened of the people who love them, which makes us shove those people further from us and induces them to play the games more often and in greater isolation. Because the hobby looks bizarre to us, we seek evidence of its effects in bizarre events. "It's true that crime rates in general have gone down," said New York State Senator Michael Balboni in the course of his campaign for video-game regulation. "But according to a detective on the New York City Police Force I was speaking to, certain types of crimes are up. Beheadings are up. Burnings are up. These are the types of violence portrayed in these games. Is this a coincidence?" The question is a misdirection. Horrific, sadistic crimes have been with us for centuries, many of them perpetrated by adolescents. The 1924 Leopold and Loeb case, in which two wealthy young men murdered a younger boy mostly just to prove they could get away with it, sparked debates about the new generation of soulless youth and the pernicious influence of movies, jazz, and liberal education. But from the distance of time, it's clear that the cruelty of those two boys did not reflect any trend or pattern. There is no evidence to support the fear that video games have increased the amount or changed the nature of crime anywhere.

We are troubled by the idea of repetition. We fear that if kids do something over and over again in play they're more likely to replicate it in life. But the evidence suggests that repeated play is usually a good tool to diminish the power of their thoughts and feelings, not to strengthen them. We're also troubled by the thought of kids playing actively with disturbing images. But the example of video games suggests that kids' ability to write their own "scripts" and build their own "maps" gives them more control over those images. This is why I feel that the Joint Statement may have had it exactly backward when it suggested that video games "may be even more harmful" than other media. There do seem to be cases of movies and songs exacerbating young people's aggression or providing them scripts for acting out, but not games. Because games are so obviously artificial, so completely the player's tool, they are the medium least capable of inspiring any powerful emotion beyond the thrills of the playing itself. If they condition children to do anything, it's only to play more—which may be their one real pitfall.

30 Even if video games have inspired some acts of real violence, trying to prevent such incidents by restricting access to the games is an absurd and potentially dangerous idea. As the examples of alcohol, tobacco, and drugs have shown us, trying to restrict access usually means that the young people most fascinated with them will still get them, but they'll have to be covert in their use. They won't be able to work them into an open social life, won't discuss them with their parents, and will be even more likely to disappear into their rooms with them. They'll see themselves as outlaws just by playing the game. Already branding themselves "bad kids" because they play a forbidden game, they'll have been pushed one step closer to allowing themselves to do something really bad. What's true of the older forms of entertainment violence is true of this unsettling new one. All of us—parents, teachers, policymakers, children—will benefit not from more control but from more understanding.

When one of my articles was published, a reader responded: "My husband and I were at the Cliff House in San Francisco and I saw an Asian teenager playing that video game in which the player is supposed to destroy a peaceful Southeast Asian village. I wanted to jerk the controls out of his hands and ask him if he had any idea what he was doing! Didn't he know what messages this was sending him about his own history, about his own culture, about the cost of violence in the world?"

I answered that I understood; I came of age politically abhorring the Vietnam War, and I find glorification and trivialization of it appalling. But I pointed out that there's an arrogance, too, in thinking that a middle-aged white person's noblest response is to jerk the controls out of the boy's hands. That kid knows more about being a teenager and an Asian–American in contemporary America than we ever will. The only message jerking the controls from him will send is that adults don't care what he likes or why. Instead, we should ask the kid why he wants to play that game. I don't know what he would say, but we should ask. And I believe something good will come from the asking alone.

Notes

334 "It's understandable that . . . . "*Joint Statement on the Effects of Entertainment Violence on Children,* Congressional Public Health Summit, July *26,* 2000.

334 "In a powerful book . . . ." Lt. Col. Dave Grossman, *On Killing* (Boston: Little, Brown, 1995).

335 "Effective conditioning requires . . . ."B. F. Skinner, *About Behaviorism* (New York: Random House, 1976).

335 "Games have always been a part . . . ." See J. Huizinga, *Homo Ludens: A Study of the Play Element in Culture* (London: Routledge and Kegar Paul, 1949).

335 "After a decade of these games . . . ." See Jonathan L. Freedman *Media Violence and Its Effect on Aggression: Assessing the Scientific Evident?*(Toronto: University of Toronto Press, 2002).

335 '"The research on video games . . . .'" For more on Helen Smith' data, see her *The Scarred Heart: Understanding and Identifying Kids Who Kill* (Knoxville,Tenn.: Callisto, 2000).

335 "The contemporary style of the . . . ." Steven Poole, *Trigger Happy Video Games and Entertainment Revolution* (London: Fourth Estate, 2000) and data from International Digital Software Association (http://www.idsa.org).

336 "A few studies of adolescents . . . ." Craig A. Anderson, *Violent Video Games Increase Aggression and Violence,* testimony at U.S. Senate Committee on Commerce, Science, and Transportation hearing on "The Impact of Interactive Violence on Children," April 9, 2001; and Freedman, *Media Violence and Its Effect on Aggression.*

336 "The planned, systematic way . . . ."E. Pooley, "Portrait of a Deadly Bond," *Time* (May 10,1999).

336 "Based on the data of . . . ."James P. McGee, "The Classroom Avenger," *Forensics Journal* 4 (1999); and Caren D. DeBernardo and James P. McGee,

"Preventing the Classroom Avenger's Next Attack," *Center for School Mental Health Assistance Newsletter* (Fall 1999).

337 '"In video arcades . . . .'" Grossman, *On Killing,* p. 314.

337 "The games are becoming remarkably . . . ." See also Poole, *Trigger Happy;* and J. C. Herz, *Joystick Nation: How Video Games Ate Our Quarters, Won Our Hearts, and Rewired Our Minds* (Boston: Little, Brown, 1997).

337 "According to . . . ." Mihaly Csikszentmihaly, *Flow: The Psychology of Optimal Experience* (New York: Harper and Row, 1990); and Mihaly Csikszentmihaly and Reed Larson, *Being Adolescent* (New York: Basic Books, 1984).

338 "Gaming is also becoming an increasingly . . . ." Poole, *Trigger Happy;* Steve L. Kent, *The Ultimate History of Video Games* (Rocklin, Calif.: Prima, 2001); and data from International Digital Software Association (http://www.idsa.org).

338 "Not surprisingly, then, gaming . . . ." See Jeanne B. Funk, "Girls Just Want to Have Fun," paper submitted to *Playing by the Rules: The Cultural Policy Challenges of Video Games,* conference at the University of Chicago, 2001 (Durham, N.C.: Duke University Press, in press). See also Heather Gilmour, "What Girls Want: The Intersections of Leisure and Power in Female Computer Game Play," in *Kids' Media Culture,* ed. Marsha Kinder (Durham, N.C.: Duke University Press, 1999).

339 "Studies show that if . . . ." Poole, *Trigger Happy; Herz, Joystick Nation;* and data from International Digital Software Association (http://www.idsa.org).

340 '"It's true that crime rates . . . .'" Fox News Channel, August 4, 2000.

341 "The 1924 Leopold and Loeb . . . ." Michael E. Parrish, *Anxious Decades: America in Prosperity and Depression, 1920–1941* (New York: W. W. Norton, 1994).

Reflect & Write

- ❑ Locate Jones's thesis statement. Why do you think he placed it there? How does he prepare the reader for it in the previous section?
- ❑ Look carefully at how Jones deals with opposing arguments. Is he respectful of differing opinions? How does he manage to represent their arguments without undermining his own claims?
- ❑ Do you find Jones's argument to be persuasive? How does your own experience with video games support or contradict his claims?
- ❑ **Write.** Jones published *Killing Monsters* in 2000, before games like *Modern Warfare 2* and *God of War 3,* with their high definition, multiplayer experience, took violent gaming to the next level. Write an opinion piece in which you update his argument: support, refute, or qualify his claims, taking into account the current gaming experience.

■ **Daniel Terdiman** *specializes in writing about technology and Internet culture, and has contributed articles to the* New York Times, Salon.com, Time *magazine, and* Wired. *He has been a game development advisor for the BBC and NPR's* Talk of the Nation. *In 2006, he was part of a CNET news team that won an online journalism award from the Society of Professional Journalists for its series* Taking Back the Web. *The article that follows first appeared in the April 22, 2004, edition of* Wired.

Playing Games with a Conscience

Daniel Terdiman

At first, the game looks like so many other first-person shooters: cross hairs aiming missiles at a raft of enemy targets.

But *September 12th* isn't like other games. Because when a missile shot at Arab terrorists kills an innocent bystander in the game's fictional Afghani village—and it's nearly impossible not to—other villagers run over, cry at their loss and then, in a rage, morph into terrorists themselves.

"The mechanics of the game are about this horrible decision, whether to do things, to take actions that will inevitably kill civilians," says Noah Wardrip-Fruin, co-editor of *First Person,* a collection of essays about the relationship between stories and games.

Indeed, *September 12th* has a point to make: that our actions have consequences, and that we should try to understand why other people take to arms. As Wardrip-Fruin puts it, the goal of the game is to develop in the player "empathy for the people who will become terrorists out of that experience, of having seen innocent people killed."

5 Earlier this week, the Simon Wiesenthal Center issued its annual report looking at websites and online games that promote hate, racism and anti-Semitism.

The report seeks to raise awareness about how hate groups are exploiting technology to spread their message, says Mark Weitzman, director of the center's Task Force Against Hate.

Such use of technology "teaches us that there always have been people in our society that will use whatever means is available to send out a message of hate," Weitzman says. "Our concern is how to deal with it."

He points to games like *Concentration Camp Manager, Ethnic Cleansing, Ghettoopoly* and others as examples of games put out by extremist groups.

"There's suicide-bombing games, (and) the full range taken from today's headlines," says Weitzman. But "you won't find them advertised, especially because some of them are rip-offs of legitimate games. I don't think the people at Monopoly would be very happy about *Ghettoopoly.*"

10 But rather than focus on games that disseminate messages of hate, Wardrip-Fruin, *September 12th* designer Gonzalo Frasca and Persuasive Games founder Ian Bogost would prefer that people instead consider games that foster understanding and tolerance of other cultures.

"I think that what is essential is allowing players to freely experiment within a virtual environment and encourage them to discuss what they play with their peers," says Frasca. "*September 12th* carries its own humanistic message, but I think that eventually, it would be even better if players would be able to use games as small laboratories for exploring—and contesting—their own beliefs."

Bogost says there are a growing number of games that promote positive messages and mutual understanding. For example, he thinks that *Real Lives 2004* does a good job of helping players see what it would be like to experience life as a member of another culture.

"You're taking on the role of another person who is not you," says Bogost. "Maybe (it's) a person from rural India. You're implicating yourself in all the trials or tribulations or difficulties that you might not think of."

Another game Bogost likes is *Civilization III*, because of the way it makes players work together, regardless of race or religion.

15 To Wardrip-Fruin, it's just as important to look at how a game is built as it is to look at a game's message.

"It's important to think about the structure of the game," he says, "not just from these hate sites, but from mainstream publishers, if we're going to understand these issues."

He thinks that hate groups are doing no more than exploiting a style of game—for example, first-person shooters—for their own purposes.

"If you think about what these people are doing on these hate sites, they're taking a set of well-understood game mechanics that are about hating someone—about hating the Germans during World War II—and finding them and killing them," Wardrip-Fruin explains. "So it's very easy to just slap (on) the image of the group you hate. I would argue the message is the same: Find the group you hate and go and kill them."

Frasca agrees.

20 "Keep in mind that a lot of commercial games—following the Hollywood tradition—use token enemies like Arabs (and) Vietnamese," he says, "which are shot in these games without the players thinking twice about the ideological message that these games carry. Lots of people start thinking about this when, say, Hezbollah launches an anti-Israel game, but there are plenty of anti-Arab games that are available at Wal-Mart at $39.95."

Still, that's not to say that all violence discourages mutual understanding.

"I do not think that killing virtual people is wrong, though—it is a lot of fun, indeed," Frasca says. "But virtual killing is totally different from real killing. As long as we can make that difference within a critical attitude, the situation does not need to be problematic."

But Frasca also says there are countless games that promote neither hate nor violence.

Wardrip-Fruin concurs, and says open-ended simulation games like *The Sims* do a very good job of encouraging constructive thought in game players.

25 "It's very hard to imagine one that is about hating some ethnic or religious other," he says. "I'd say that the fundamental thing about a computer game is the structure of what you do as a participant, and the structure of something like *SimCity* or *The Sims* is about understanding a system, and trying to make it grow in the way you want it to grow."

Frasca goes so far as to say that some massively multiplayer games, even ones involving violence, help players understand each other better.

"Online games such as *EverQuest* foster cooperation between players from all over the world," he explains. "Even if there can be language barriers that can interfere with the communication, *EverQuest* allows players to work together based on their skills, without focusing on their gender, age, nationality (or) religion."

According to Bogost, there is a bright future for games that promote mutual tolerance and understanding.

But right now, says Frasca, games with such agendas are few and far between.

30 "Games for tolerance are (in) their infancy," he says. "But I think they have a great potential because games always allow you to be in somebody else's shoes and viewing the world through their eyes. And that is the essential requirement for tolerance: Understanding that other people have different realities that may not be the same (as) ours."

Reflect & Write

- ❑ What is the argument made by this article? How does Terdiman's selection of which games to mention and which descriptions to develop factor into the construction of this argument?
- ❑ At one point in the article, Terdiman mentions that Gonzalo Frasca suggests that even violent multiplayer games have their positive side. Do you agree with this assertion? Why or why not?
- ❑ **Write.** Draft a response to the Terdiman piece that argues for the benefits of venting "hate" online through gaming. You might choose to develop the position offered by Chris Kaye in the October 2004 issue of *Esquire*. In his article, "Joystick Jihad," he wrote, "Casting our enemy as the villain [in video games] can be as lucrative as a Halliburton contract in an oil-rich war zone (and a hell of a lot more fun)" (p. 114).

■ *The following screenshots are taken from games linked through the Website for* **Games for Change**, *an organization devoted to using persuasive games to produce "real world impact." These are "serious games," or games with an agenda, which, by definition, means that they are designed to argue a specific position about issues as varied as the environment, human rights, and world hunger.*

Screenshots: Games for Change

FIGURE 11.11. This screenshot from *Ayiti: The Cost of Life* shows how the game invites the player to help the Guinard family to make choices about schooling, work, community, and leisure to help them thrive in their homeland, Haiti.

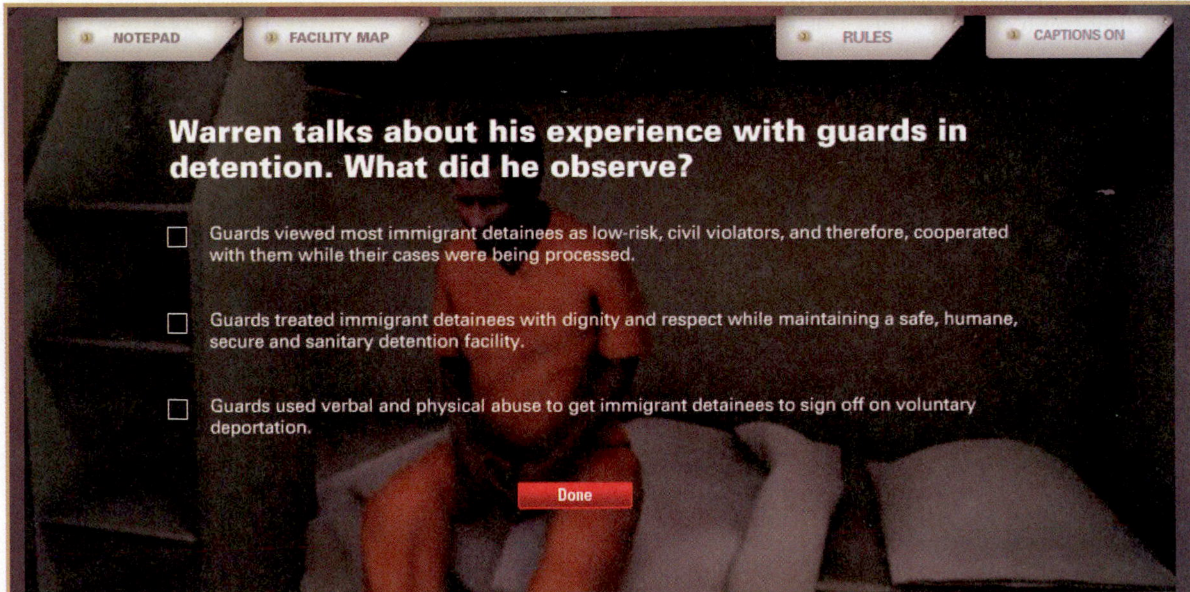

FIGURE 11.12. *Homeland Guatanamo* takes the player inside the Guantamo Bay facility in the role of a reporter investigating a "questionable" death of an inmate being held there.

FIGURE 11.13. As part of the *Energyville* game, players must leverage energy resources to successfully power a futuristic city.

Reflect & Write

- ❑ Examine the interface provided by each game. Is the player invited in through a "God view" (looking down from above)? Does the player seem to be given a more direct, first-person perspective? How might that angle affect game play?
- ❑ How does the color palette of the game set the mood for the game play?
- ❑ Are the graphics realistic? Cartoonish? How might that affect the message of the game? How would changing the graphics to be more realistic or more cartoonish alter that message? Why do you think the designers made that choice?
- ❑ **Write.** Play one of these games by visiting Games For Change, linked through the *Envision* Website. Write an analysis of the game that answers the following questions: Who is the intended audience? How can you tell? What type of game is it (i.e., shooter game, role-playing game, strategy game, simulation game)? How does this design choice determine the argument the game makes? What is that argument? To what extent is the game driven by *pathos*? By *ethos*? By *logos*?

  www.pearsonhighered.com/envision/347

Seeing Connections
Review the rhetorical appeals (*pathos*, *logos*, and *ethos*) in Chapter 2.

PERSPECTIVES ON THE ISSUE

1. Keeping Zoe Flower's and Sheri Graner Ray's arguments in mind, write out a series of questions and interview female gamers in your class or dorm to discover the way women play and the reasons they do so. Present your findings to the class.
2. The October 2004 issue of *Playboy* magazine featured several female avatars in provocative poses. Draft a letter to *Playboy* magazine in the persona of a female avator (e.g., Lara Croft from *Tomb Raider*, Rayne from *Blood Rayne,* or Faith from *Mirror's Edge*) declining the offer to appear in the magazine. Create an argument that engages some of the issues of gender, gaming, and identity that have been explored by the authors of the articles you have read in this chapter.
3. Visit the *Kuma/War*, *America's Army,* and *Full Spectrum Warrior* Websites, linked through the *Envision*. Website. Analyze the argument of each site and how each uses visual rhetoric to create an argument. What distinguishes the recreational game sites (such as *Kuma*) from the military-funded sites (such as *America's Army*)—both in terms of the visual and textual elements? www.pearsonhighered.com/envision/348a
4. Visit your local toy or electronics store or an online store such as Amazon.com and browse the computer games designed for young children. How many games seem to be targeted toward a specific gender? Are there any "pink" games? Which games seemed to be targeted toward a general audience? To what extent does the visual rhetoric of the packaging reinforce gendered gaming?

FROM READING TO RESEARCH

1. The images from Robbie and Spaight's book *Alter Ego* contained in this section create their own argument about what that book is "about" and what that book says about gaming avatars. Find a copy of the book at your library or local bookstore and select four to five alternate examples. Photocopy them, and then arrange them in a short booklet to make your own argument about gamer identity. Exchange these new booklets with a partner and discuss how each of you used evidence and arrangements differently to support your own individual argument.
2. Visit some online games directed at girls, such as those found at *Everything Girl*, *American Girl*, and *The Adventures of Josie True*, linked through the *Envision* Website. Spend time playing the games and studying the multimedia representations of girls in those games. Now compose one of the following three texts: an article for a newspaper about the state of gaming for girls; an op-ad for a parenting magazine; or an article for a girls' magazine. Showcase your work for the class and discuss your rhetorical choices and how they would have been different had you chosen one of the other two options. www.pearsonhighered.com/envision/348b
3. Research console war games from the 1980s such as Atari's *Battlezone* and then research more contemporary war games (*Modern Warfare 2; Bad Company*). Examine secondary sources (scholarly articles, gaming reviews); also draw on primary sources such as screenshots, walk throughs (often available on YouTube), or your own game play. Drawing on your observations and your evidence, write a research paper comparing military games then and now that makes a strong claim about the evolution of this genre.
4. Working in groups, research an important issue and develop a stance your topic might be campus-based (workers rights, alcohol on campus, student fees), local (tax increases, community recycling, school redistricting), or national (human rights violations, global poverty, global conflict). Conduct field research about this issue by interviewing members of the community. Draft a storyboard for an online game designed to persuade viewers to your point of view. Prepare a pitch for a fictional governing board in which you argue for the effectiveness of your game in effecting positive social

change. Be sure in your pitch to include the following: who the game will reach; how players will access the game; what the rhetorical features of the game are in terms of design and content; and why this form of interactive media would be an effective persuasive tool.

WHO OWNS POPULAR CULTURE?

What exactly is "copyright" and how does it shape our culture? Can we think of "copyright" as similar to the notion of property—or how people own certain things such as land and houses? How can we connect this notion to books, or music, or movies? At what point can we use existing works as inspiration for our own creative work, and to what extent can we appropriate material to produce fresh, innovative cultural texts? In a technological read-write culture, where software like iMovie and Adobe Photoshop invites us to create and customize our own expressive texts, where do we draw the line between fair use of original material and copyright infringement?

The complicated relationship among regulation, creativity, and culture is the focus of this section. Underlying the debate over copyright lies the concern that what is being regulated by legislation is not just individual content, but culture itself. In fact, Lawrence Lessig and others argue that culture itself is formed precisely by a "remixing" of established texts—that is, old images, songs, and films are revisited and incorporated to create new culture. Everywhere around us, we see this process of remixing becoming mainstream: Disney remixing Japanese *sentai* TV shows into the kid hit *Power Rangers* for a U.S. audience; DirecTV repurposing scenes from *Aliens, Dukes of Hazzard, Ferris Bueller's Day Off,* and *Back to the Future* to advertise its high definition offerings; and Gwen Stefani adapting the lyrics and melody from the classic *Fiddler on the Roof* song, "If I Were a Rich Man," to suit her own point of view. Culture literally is revised and remade every day.

This process was never more apparent than during the 2008 U.S. presidential election, where supporters of Barack Obama demonstrated the power of remix culture in making persuasive arguments in favor of their candidate. Case and point is the most iconic symbol of the Obama presidential campaign: the Barack Obama "Hope" poster (Figure 11.14). Designed by artist Shepard Fairey, the red, white, and blue stencil portrait was based on a photograph taken by Associated Press freelance photographer Mannie Garcia. The political and historical significance of the "Hope" poster found it a place in the Smithsonian Institute's National Portrait Gallery; its derivative nature landed it in court, with Fairey countering the Associated Press's demand for compensation with his own suit to declare the poster a fair use of the original photograph.

While the "Hope" poster resulted in a legal tug of war, another popular Obama campaign remix demonstrated the power of the mash-up without the proprietary complications. Produced by Black Eyed Peas member will.i.am and directed by Jesse Dylan, the "Yes We Can" music video pairs footage from Obama's concession speech after the 2008 New Hampshire Democratic primary with footage of famous musicians, artists, and actors reciting passages from that speech as lyrics. The very composition of the video suggests a powerful parallel between the then-candidate and his supporters visually as well as aurally by splicing the footage, collage-style, so that they occupied the

FIGURE 11.14. The famous Barack Obama "Hope" poster was designed by artist Shepard Fairey, but based on a photograph by Manny Garcia.

same frame. The key phrase itself is a remix of sorts, an English translation of "Sí, se puede," the 1972 slogan of César Chávez and the United Farm Workers. Released on Dipdive.com on February 2, 2008, the viral video quickly spread across the Internet. This grassroots mash-up garnered a 2008 Emmy Award, and although the official Obama campaign was not involved in producing the video, the slogan "Yes We Can" rapidly rose to prominence as a secondary slogan for the campaign.

This extended example gives us insight into a new way of creating and reshaping popular culture that is all around us. In this section, we'll investigate the limits and possibilities of how culture itself is created. We'll consider the intentions behind copyright regulation, then turn to the ways that such regulation is consistently tested and repurposed by cultural texts that remix, mash up, and remaster old material into new, exciting creations. After completing these readings, you should have a greater understanding of the complexities of this issue and its implication for your own use and production of cultural texts.

Reflect & Write

- ❑ Which strikes you as the more powerful argument for Barack Obama's candidacy, the "Hope" poster or the "Yes We Can" video? Why?
- ❑ What is it about the photograph used in the poster that makes it such a powerful argument? How does the caption work in collaboration with the picture? Why do

you think the artist chose to modify the photograph rather than use the photograph itself as his central image? What does he gain through his modification?

- ❑ **Write.** Watch the full "Yes We Can" video, linked through the *Envision* Website. Now write a short rhetorical analysis of the video that takes into account the style, arrangement, and delivery of the argument by looking at elements such as pacing, composition, integration of sources, and voice-over and music.
www.pearsonhighered.com/envision/351

Seeing Connections
Review the Prewriting Checklist on page 145 for strategies for analyzing a short film.

This excerpt is taken from Bound by Law? Trapped in a Struggle She Didn't Understand, *a comic book produced by the Duke Law School's Center for the Study of the Public Domain. This 53-page visual argument was developed by* **Keith Aoki**, *the Philip H. Knight Professor of Law at the University of Oregon School of Law, a specialist in intellectual property law and author of* Seed Wars: Cases and Materials on Intellectual Property and Plant Genetic Resources; **James Boyle**, *one of the founders of the Center for the Study of the Public Domain, a board member of Creative Commons, the William Neal Reynolds Professor of Law at the Duke Law School, and author of* Shamans, Software and Spleens: Law and the Construction of the Information Society; *and* **Jennifer Jenkins**, *Director of the Center for the Study of the Public Domain and a specialist in intellectual property and copyright infringement.* Bound by Law? *follows a documentary filmmaker through the process of understanding the implications of copyright restrictions for her intended film on New York City.*

Excerpt: Bound By Law?

Keith Aoki, James Boyle, and Jennifer Jenkins

FIGURE 11.15–11.20. These pages from *Bound By Law?* use comic book form to explore issues of intellectual property and copyright.

FIGURE 11.16. Here the main character ask a question after examining a number of texts she wants to include in her documentary.

FIGURE 11.17. The protagonist's face and body become boxed in by the cartoon lines as she faces the seriousness of copyright law.

FIGURE 11.18. In this panel, the artists layout a grid explaining different types of copyright restrictions.

FIGURE 11.19. The showcase of evidence, depicted in word and image, relies on research.

FIGURE 11.20. Here the cartoon evokes other famous drawings to bring home the point of its argument.

Reflect & Write

- ❏ Why do you think that these law professors chose to write their explanation of fair use in comic book form? Do you think this was a successful choice? Why or why not?
- ❏ Which panel or sequence of panels struck you as most effectively accomplishing the comic book's purpose? What elements of these panels make them particularly effective?
- ❏ How are point of view, persona, and stance reflected in this set of panels? What is the significance of the choice of characters? What roles do they serve in relation to the audience and the overall purpose of the text?
- ❏ **Write.** Choose one panel from those contained above and perform a rhetorical analysis in which you examine how rhetorical strategies of arrangement, style, and invention are used to produce an argument. Write up your analysis, being sure to include reference to specific visual detail.

■ **Michael Eisner,** *former-CEO of the Walt Disney Company, delivered this address to Congress on June 7, 2000, as part of the Internet Caucus Speaker Series. This program, sponsored by the Internet Education Foundation, was designed to allow leading members in the business community to share with Capitol Hill their ideas about the "Opportunities Facing the Internet."*

Address Before Members of the United States Congress

Michael Eisner

Thank you, Senator Hatch, for that kind introduction. You have been a leader in public-policy with regard to the Internet in particular and entertainment industries in general. We are grateful for your leadership.

I also want to thank Senators Leahy and Burns, and Congressmen Hyde, Conyers, Goodlatte and Boucher for hosting today's lunch. And, a thank you to Jerry Berman of the Internet Education Foundation for his assistance.

What's more, I want to thank all of you for being here today. You comprise the busiest audience on earth. I realize that each of you has tremendous demands on your time as you go about the business of running our country.

Because you are all such busy men and women, I am not here simply with my mouse ears on to sing the praises of our company. Rather, I'd like to talk about a much wider issue beyond Disney. . . one that directly affects the future of all of the entertainment companies, the future of all consumers and even the future of our nation's balance of international trade.

5 I realize that there are great risks when one attempts to speak so much about the future. I am reminded of a story you may have heard about a notice posted on a college bulletin board. It read: "This evening's meeting of the Clairvoyance Society has been canceled due to unforeseen circumstances."

However, I am willing to accept the risks of talking about the future because the implications of my subject today, I believe, will be undeniably enormous in the century that stretches before us.

And, that subject is: the protection of intellectual property in the digital age.

But, talk alone isn't adequate to cover this issue. After all, intellectual property encompasses more than just words—it's about art, music and imagery as well. So, I figured I would be doing a disservice by just delivering the usual 20-minute speech. What's more, if it is true that a picture is worth a thousand words, how many words are *ten thousand* pictures worth? Actually, not just pictures, but dramatically original computer-generated images.

Enough words. Let me show you.

10 [VIDEO - Opening of *Dinosaur*, freeze-framing abruptly as the pterodactyl is flying over herds of dinos]

O.K., let's stop right there. As you have probably figured out, you've just seen the first few minutes of our new film, *Dinosaur* which has already grossed more than $100 million in the U.S. But, I did not show it to you out of a shameless urge to promote our product—though I'm sure you and your families would enjoy going to see it this weekend, playing at a theater near you.

The debate over intellectual property often gets buried in jargon. The term "intellectual property" itself is obtuse legalese that sounds like a euphemism for the jar holding Albert Einstein's brain.

So, I thought I'd try and move away from the jargon and simply show you what the debate is all about—a piece of authentic intellectual property.

Of course, intellectual property is a rather wide-ranging category that covers everything from piano songsheets to computer software. But ultimately, it is about the work of the human imagination, such as what you see here on the screen.

15 What is now urgently needed is the implementation of a legislative, economic and technological environment that will foster creativity and encourage the legitimate use of all those silicon chips to create more flights of fancy like this. Otherwise, the same technology that enabled our artists to create these incredible images could also make them go away.

[Screen goes to black]

This is the perilous irony of the digital age.

Thanks to computer technology, filmmakers have been able to take us to incredible places in the last few years. They have hurled us into the heart of a tornado, they have invited us on board the Titanic, they have rocketed us to a galaxy far, far away. And today, they enable us to walk among the dinosaurs.

But, unfortunately, just as computers make it possible to create startlingly pristine images, they also make it possible to create startlingly pristine copies.

20 To fully appreciate the extent of this dilemma, I believe it's instructive to take a brief dino tour of the history of American cinema.

[VIDEO - *The Lost World*]

This was one of the first Hollywood blockbusters—*The Lost World*, made in 1924. It may look crude today, but back then it was magic to audiences who had little idea how the filmmakers were able to seemingly bring dinosaurs back to life.

[VIDEO - *"King Kong"*]

In 1933 came *King Kong,* which made a giant leap in special effects—and, of course, it added sound, which allowed audiences to hear the incessant screaming of Fay Wray.

25 [VIDEO - Fay Wray in King Kong's paw screaming]

[VIDEO - *Godzilla*]

The next landmark film on this dino tour was *Godzilla* in 1954. *Godzilla* may have spawned any number of cheesy sequels, but the first one set a new standard in the depiction of scaly monsters, and entranced and terrified audiences from Tokyo to Tacoma.

[VIDEO - *Jurassic Park*]

In 1993, as I'm sure you all remember, *Jurassic Park* came along. This film raised the dino bar even higher by utilizing the creative power of the computer to seamlessly integrate completely authentic-looking dinosaurs in a live-action film. I might add that we have received legal clearances to show you all this terrific copyrighted intellectual property of our competitors.

These dinosaur movies offer just one slice of the progression of our industry. I could just as easily have tracked the evolution of any number of other genres—gangster movies, from Cagney to Coppola . . . comedies, from Chaplin to Carrey. . . adventures, from Fairbanks to Ford . . . romances, from Hepburn & Tracy to Ryan & Hanks.

As you may have noticed, none of the films I've referred to came from The Walt Disney Studios. This is completely intentional. Our studio has a proud history, but we have hardly cornered the market on creating great intellectual property. For a variety of reasons, an incredible array of talent came to Southern California and built what were rightly called "dream factories," thereby inventing an industry. Throughout the century, this industry acquired ever-increasing importance to the entire American economy, since the products it produced were embraced by people across the nation and around the world.

To appreciate just how important, consider the significance of America's copy right-related industries, which include motion pictures, television, home video, music, publishing and computer software. In 1977, these industries added $160 billion to the U.S. economy, or roughly 3.6% of GDP. In 1997, this figure had grown to nearly $530 billion, representing 6.3% of GDP.

This growth is all the more significant when you consider that a tremendous amount of these revenues are generated overseas. In just six years—from 1991 to 1997—the foreign sales and exports of copyright-related industries nearly doubled from $36 billion to $66 billion. As a result, foreign sales from copyright industries are now greater than almost every other industry category, including such major exporters as the automotive industry and the agriculture industry. Earlier this year, the U.S. experienced its greatest foreign trade imbalance ever. Imagine how much worse the situation would have been without the positive impact of our content-based industries.

We now need to ensure that the necessary steps are taken to make sure that the success story of American intellectual property during the 20th century is not undermined during the 21st. At a time of burgeoning trade deficits, we must act to assure the security of one of America's few positive trade assets.

To give you an idea of what's really at stake, allow me to return to prehistoric times. We left off the *Dinosaur* clip with this shot.

[VIDEO - Freeze frame of pterodactyl flying over dinos]

Even being held in freeze frame for you to scrutinize, this looks like an impeccable aerial shot following a pterodactyl as it flies over a herd of dinosaurs. Unfortunately, we weren't able to find any real dinosaurs to star in the film—and if we had, I understand they're terribly hard to train. So, we had to digitally birth them ourselves, bit by bit.

It took more than four years, and it required the invention of proprietary technologies.

First, we had to shoot the live-action backgrounds. To do this, we designed something we called a "dino cam."

[VIDEO - Dino cam at work]

As you can see here, it is a camera suspended by cables that are attached to two 70-foot towers. This allowed us to make extremely fluid tracking and crane shots that could quickly go from the height of a 50-foot brachiosaur down to the eye level of a lemur. Our camera team spent 18 months taking the dino cam to a range of locations that included Australia, Jordan, Venezuela, Hawaii, Western Samoa—and even so far as the Los Angeles County Arboretum in exotic Arcadia.

Of course, there was no point to the "dino cam" if there were no dinos. So, we built our own digital animation studio back in Burbank and filled it with an extraordinary team of computer animators.

[VIDEO - Dinosaur production montage to illustrate the following]

These animators first created digital skeletons to better understand how dinosaurs were engineered.

Then they layered on musculature so their creations could move realistically.

Then there was the skin. Not only did it have to look completely real, but it had to have a sense of mass and weight that would convincingly relate the tremendous size of these animals.

Then our animators took on another challenge that was completely unknown in the Cretaceous Era. Our dinosaurs would talk. So, each dinosaur needed to be designed in such a way that it could convincingly mouth words.

All of this resulted in a tremendous amount of data that had to be processed. So, we built what we called a "render farm." This "farm" was a room full of computers running 24 hours a day to crunch all those billions of zeros and ones.

To give you some sense of the detail that went into the film, let's look again at one brief shot.

[VIDEO - Dinosaur running through the water amidst giant dinosaur legs, then freeze frame]

Let me build that scene for you step by step.

[VIDEO - "Build" to illustrate the points]

First the dino cam filmed a tracking shot across a pond.

Then we added the brachiosaurs in the background.

Next, we created rough animation of the youthful dinosaur.

Then we introduced the final animation of the dinosaur along with a flock of birds flying and the giant legs of some more brachiosaurs.

Next, we inverted all of these images in order to show their reflections in the water.

In order to make it look like the dinosaur is really interacting with the water, we added splash and ripple effects.

60 Finally, we composited all of these elements to produce the finished scene.

[VIDEO - Run the finished sequence]

This is one magic trick where even once you know how it was done, it still dazzles.

I'll resist the temptation to go on and on about the countless ingenious tricks that our animators and technicians devised to make this film, because my point isn't to promote the film. My point is that we have created a movie that took four years to make, during which 45 million megabytes were crunched—or enough data to fill 70,000 CDRoms—all to generate the necessary data for an 80-minute film—which, were it to get in the wrong hands, could be compressed onto a single DVD disk in a matter of minutes and instantaneously put on the Internet while the film is still in the theaters.

In other words, this film represents the flesh and bones—or, in this case, scales and bones—of that highfalutin legalistic term, "intellectual property." And, it is all put in jeopardy by an old-fashioned everyday term—"piracy."

65 But, in this context, I'm not talking about the comical characters sailing the high seas at the Pirates of the Caribbean. Rather, I'm talking about an underground of secretive and sequestered Pirates of Encryption—the hackers who shamelessly assert that anything they can get their hands on is legally theirs.

You may be familiar with the recent controversy over a company called *iCrave.com*, which claimed the right to pluck television signals off the air and stream them on the Internet for all the world to see. You may also be aware of software programs like Napster, Wraptster, Freenet and Gnutella, which allow college kids to build vast music collections on the hard drives of their lap top computers without ever buying a single CD.

These Internet programs enable the piracy of intellectual property. Their use is rapidly escalating, with a potential impact on our culture and our economy that is comparable to other Internet-related issues that many of you have expressed concerns about—such as cyber-security, credit card security and the safety of your children's web surfing.

There is no question that the Internet is an exciting and dynamic new force in commerce and entertainment. But so were, in their time, radio and television. And they had to play by the same boring old rules involving copyright infringement.

Today's Internet pirates try to hide behind some contrived New Age arguments of cyberspace, but all they are really doing is trying to make a case for Age Old thievery. When they hack a DVD and then distribute it on the web, it is no different than if someone puts a quarter in a newspaper machine and then takes out all the papers, which, of course, would be illegal and morally wrong.

70 The pirates will argue that this analogy is unfair, maintaining that all they're doing is cracking a digital code. But, by that standard, it would be justifiable to crack a bank code and transfer the funds from someone else's account into your own. There's just no way around it—theft is theft, whether it is enabled by a handgun or a computer keyboard.

The piracy of intellectual property takes all forms. I don't know if any of you have ever seen one of the videotapes for sale on the sidewalks of many major cities. Here's what they can look and sound like.

[VIDEO - Pirated scene from *Tarzan* in which the visuals are blurry and shaky, the sound is muffled and echoy]

As you can see, these tapes are barely watchable. But, they crop up with alarming speed—videos of *Dinosaur* have already been seen on the streets of Malaysia. Now look at the same scene from *Tarzan* as it could be downloaded directly off the Internet.

[VIDEO - Excellent quality scene from *Tarzan*]

75 Instead of one bad quality videotape for sale on the street, we could soon be talking about unlimited numbers of high quality copies available on the Internet. And, new technology is making it faster and easier for users to download this kind of material.

The Internet pirates who produce these contraband copies have found some odd bedfellows in the intellectual community and in industry.

Social critics, like Esther Dyson, have spoken out against traditional copyright protection on the web. Ms. Dyson once listed the "new rules" of the Internet and went on to say, and I quote, that "Chief among the new rules is that 'content is free'." I must say that I find this assertion interesting, since at the bottom of Ms. Dyson's newsletter, one can clearly read that it is copyrighted—and, as her subscribers can attest, her newsletter is most certainly not free.

Regrettably, Ms. Dyson is not alone in this self-serving hypocrisy. The same scholars and companies who advocate a "content is free" philosophy scrupulously protect their own intellectual property with copyrights, trademarks and patents. Just yesterday, it was reported that Napster is taking legal action against a punk rock group that has been selling t-shirts, hats and bumper stickers featuring the Napster logo. Apparently, they don't find copyright infringement so virtuous when they're the ones being infringed upon.

I find it especially remarkable when Internet hardware companies refuse to protest piracy—because I believe they are acting against their own long-term interests. This is because the Internet needs content—and it needs more of it every day.

80 The fact is that nobody signs up for the Internet because of the elegance of its routers. Nobody logs on because of the micro-chip inside. No, they use the Internet in ever-growing numbers because of the content. Right now, that content is largely information. But, increasingly, it will also be entertainment. The growth of bandwidth will increasingly make possible full video experiences. But, this expansion of Internet entertainment will stall if the creators of the content cannot enjoy the full rights of ownership of that content.

It does not take a CPA to figure out that a movie like *Dinosaur* does not come cheap. However, it is an investment worth making if there can be substantial reward in success. But, if this reward is allowed to be pirated away, then the creative risktakers will put their energies elsewhere, and the Internet will become a wonderful delivery system with nothing wonderful to deliver.

One of the fallacies of the intellectual property debate is that it's really just a conflict between the pro-technology members of the "New Media" against the anti-technology members of the "Old Media." As I hope I made clear with the discussion of *Dinosaur*, this characterization couldn't be more wrong. At Disney we embrace technology. And we always have.

Throughout his career, Walt Disney recognized new technology as the friend of the storyteller. He kept pushing the envelope with the first sound cartoon, the first color cartoon, the first use of the multi-plane camera, the first use of stereophonic sound, and the development of robotics for his theme parks. Walt was also almost alone among movie studio chiefs in the 1950s when he recognized television as a new opportunity and not a threat.

At Disney today, we are not only seizing the tremendous possibilities offered by technology in movies, as with *Dinosaur*—we are also active participants in the expansion of the Internet with our GO.com family of sites, such as Disney.com, ESPN.com, ABCNews.com, ABC.com and Family.com. And, we believe we are helping to pioneer the convergence of the Internet with television through the development of Enhanced TV, which allows viewers to become active participants in the programming, accessing stats during a football game, playing against the contestants on "Millionaire" and guessing the winners on the Oscars.

85 We intend to continue to pour resources into the Internet—but not if this requires surrendering the rights to things we own.

Just as our society is beginning to address other security threats posed by the Internet, we must address the security of copyrights. With this in mind, our company is undertaking a wide-ranging strategy to make the Internet truly secure for intellectual property. This strategy consists of five main elements.

First of all, we are turning to our representatives in Washington with both defensive and offensive requests. And, we do so clear in the understanding that this issue has fundamental roots in our nation's Constitution. Intellectual property rights are really no different from ordinary property rights. If you own something, you expect the government to respect your right to keep it from being stolen.

On defense, we ask the Congress to refrain from mandating a compulsory license for redistribution of creative works over the Internet. There are numerous factors that make compulsory licensing ill suited to a global medium like the Internet.

On offense, we ask you to begin to explore with us legislation that would assure the efficacy of technology solutions to copyright security. As we seek to develop measures such as watermarking, we need the assurance that the people who manufacture computers and the people who operate ISP's will cooperate by incorporating the technology to look for and respond to the watermarks. This same mandate could be part of the solution to a host of other Internet security issues as well.

90 The second element of our strategy to protect intellectual property is to work with governments around the world to respect our rights. We are actively involved in the Global Business Dialogue on E-Commerce, and our company is serving as chair of the Intellectual Property Work Group. The Internet is international. The issues involving it cannot be viewed with a myopic American eye. Instead, we must think and act globally.

The third element is education. Most people are honest and want to do the right thing. But they can't do the right thing if they don't know that they're doing a wrong thing. I am always amazed when I walk the streets of New York and stroll past an open fruit stand. Thousands of people go by each day respecting the fact that if they want an apple they need to pay for it, even though it would be incredibly easy to just take it. When it comes to the Internet, most people simply aren't aware that the same issues apply. According to a recent *Newsweek* cover story, college kids are simply oblivious to the legal and moral implications of downloading copyrighted material off the Internet. Working with Jack Valenti and the MPAA, we are advocating a more aggressive campaign to make people aware of intellectual property rights on the Internet, in much the same way as the FBI warning at the front of videotapes.

Fourth, we believe that the entertainment industry as a whole—and I mean all the companies with a stake in the e-future—should take meaningful technological measures. To an extent, piracy is a technical problem and must be addressed with technical solutions. The studios, broadcasters and record companies—working in cooperation with the technology companies—need to develop innovative and flexible watermarking or encryption systems that can stay one step ahead of the hackers.

The fifth and final of our initiatives is economic. History has shown that one of the best deterrents to pirated product is providing legitimate product at appropriate prices. In the music industry, we have already seen that most people will gladly pay fair prices for legally-produced product even when it can be easily reproduced and unlawful copies can be easily acquired. I am certain that the same person who pays a reasonable price for an apple at his local fruit stand will pay a reasonable price for a video on his local hard drive.

To be sure, none of these measures represents a silver bullet that will stop piracy in its tracks. But, that's o.k. Markets are messy, and, over time, these initiatives will be refined and new ones will emerge. But, there first needs to be a recognition and a commitment—in government, in industry and among the general populace—that theft will not be tolerated in any form—whether it's someone shoplifting in a store or downloading on the Net.

95 All we need is for this basic rule of society to be acknowledged and enforced in the cyber world as it is in the real world. If this can be achieved, then the possibilities of the Internet—for communication, for education, for entertainment and for commerce—will be as limitless as the lightspeed at which it has brought the world together.

Indeed, as long as intellectual property rights are adequately protected, then I firmly expect that the pirates will be defeated and the entertainment industry will not go the way of the dinosaur.

[VIDEO - Pick up the *Dinosaur* clip where we left off]

Rather, like our digital pterodactyl, we will continue to take wing and fly on toward new creative horizons, to the benefit of our industry, our audience and our nation.

Thank you very much.

Seeing Connections

For strategies for incorporating multimedia into your own presentations, see page 205 in Chapter 9.

Reflect & Write

- ❑ How does *ethos* figure into Eisner's argument? Cite passages as evidence.
- ❑ Consider the way in which Eisner uses examples to increase the persuasiveness of his argument. What do you think about his choice of multimedia examples? How does this reflect an awareness of his audience and of the *kairos* of his argument? Was his use of these examples a successful or less successful choice? Why?
- ❑ After his series of video clips, he points out, "As you may have noticed, none of the films I've referred to came from The Walt Disney Studios." Why is this an important point to make for his argument? Would his argument have been strengthened or weakened if he had limited himself to examples from his own studio? Why or why not?
- ❑ Eisner spends a lot of time detailing the process of making one scene from the Disney movie *Dinosaur.* Why do you think he decided to spend time doing this? How does this support his argument?
- ❑ How does Eisner's tone shift as he moves past his example to discuss Internet "pirates"? Does this tone shift undermine or reinforce his argument?
- ❑ Look at the structure of Eisner's argument. How does his introduction work in conjunction with his conclusion? How does the speech come full circle?
- ❑ **Write.** Draft a response to Eisner's argument in the persona of a person who advocates the exchange of free content—including movie downloads—on the Internet.

■ *This article originally appeared in* Shift, *a magazine devoted to issues related to digital culture.* **Bret Dawson** *has written several articles on digital culture, including articles on digital money and one on data mining and invasion of privacy.*

The Privatization of Our Culture

Bret Dawson

A few days after airplanes crashed into the World Trade Center, the nephew of a friend of a friend had his fourth birthday party. In classic fourth-birthday-party style, there was cake and ice cream, pin-the-tail-on-the-donkey and a loot bag for each guest when it was time to go home. There was a piñata, too, a big one shaped like Bart Simpson.

Most of the grownups there chose not to play pin-the-tail-on-the-donkey or tag or hide-and-seek, and instead stayed in the kitchen, far from the piñata, sipping coffee and chatting nervously about What This World Is Coming To. These were the days, remember, when CNN was still showing the 767-hits-tower footage on a five minute rotation, the days when you couldn't turn on the TV without seeing fireballs erupting and skyscrapers collapsing and panicked office workers jumping to their deaths. You remember the fear, the horror, the sick panic of the teens of September. You do, don't you?

As the mood grew darker in the kitchen, one of the party guests wandered in, bored of hide-and-seek and curious what everybody was talking about.

"Oh," the little interloper guessed, "all those people in New York who got sick."

5 Around the kitchen, the grownups nodded wistfully.

"I've been wondering about something about that," the four-year-old continued. "When the bad men stole those airplanes, where was Batman?"

The little kids in your own life, be they your siblings or your children or the nephews and nieces of your friends' friends, were all talking a lot about Batman last autumn, wondering where he and Spider-Man and the Flash were when the terrorists struck, wondering why the men in tights have forsaken us. Maybe you've wondered the same thing.

I think I have the answer. Batman was unavailable to the panicked citizens of NY on 9/11, was MIA in that hour of great need, because he is private property. Because he is private property and his owners are keeping him on a Los Angeles soundstage, where he is filming TV commercials for the OnStar concierge service, available on selected General Motors cars and other fine automobiles.

This essay is not about terrorism. It is not about little kids who say the darndest things. Neither is it terribly concerned with why a man in a cape and a rubber mask with pointy ears failed to save the day on September 11. So what is the point? Here is a convenient thesis statement for you: The discoveries, eureka-moments, fables, characters, songs and jokes that form the only common ground we share as citizens—the set of ideas collectively known as "The West"—are now the property of a few multinational corporations. Our entire culture has fallen into private hands, taking with it our right to tell our stories, our right to keep our personal lives personal, even our right to heal our sick. THIS SUCKS. THIS IS VERY BAD.

10 It need not be the end, however. Not if we as citizens, as Westerners, as participants in our own culture, can find the will and the resolve to reclaim what is ours.

Ours is a culture steeped in the art of make-believe. From the moment kids are old enough to watch the Teletubbies, they spend their waking hours soaking in a hot bath of wonder and whimsy, of magical stories full of amazing things that never happen in real life. We teach children to believe in Santa Claus and the Easter Bunny and Jack Frost and Monsieur Lactose (who causes tooth decay), and they do believe, and their excited musings and speculations about what really goes on at the North Pole delight us endlessly. A few years later, with a little more experience and a little more wisdom, the kiddies toss out make-believe about Santa and the Tooth Fairy and M. Lactose as "babyish."

But here is what these older, wiser kiddies do not toss out: Batman, Pokémon, Barbie, *Rugrats, Crash Bandicoot, The Lion King,* "It's Not Easy Being Green," "C is for Cookie," *The Powerpuff Girls, Sailor Moon,* Mario, Hello Kitty, *Metal Gear Solid, Enterprise, Buffy, Dawson, Felicity, Smallville*, "D'oh," Zoom Zoom, "Oh, for God's sake, Niles!" Master of Puppets Master Of The House Master Of My Domain, Etc.

This is not a bad thing all by itself, this lifelong attachment to the Neighbourhood of Make-Believe, and it is not a bad thing because it is making somebody rich. It is a bad thing because it means most of the thoughts passing through your head at any given moment are private property, subject to the whims and desires and litigious controls of the companies that own them.

During the big Harry Potter media pigout late last year, you probably heard a lot about the battle over internet domain names between Harry's pubescent fans and the meanies at Warner Bros. In case you didn't, here's how it went:

1. Fans of the books start Potter fan sites.
2. WB buys Potter film/merchandise rights.
3. WB begins aggressive lawyerly campaign to take possession of domain names with connections to Potter—most notably fifteen-year-old Claire Field's harrypotterguide.co.uk.
4. Field and her father raise media stink.
5. Sensing potential P.R. nightmare à la McLibel, WB backs off, saying it will leave noncommercial fan sites alone—for now.

15 Ah, a victory for little people the world over, right? Sure, provided you only cared about preserving your ability to praise somebody else's intellectual property on your website, and also provided you never, ever hoped to earn a living on the strength of those efforts.

No matter what you make of boys who fly on broomsticks, Harry Potter is a big big part of early twenty-first-century culture, a part too large for any but the most dogged of us to avoid. What Claire Field and all the other Pottersite proprietors were doing was merely what kids and grownups have been doing for as long as people have been telling stories: They were taking a tale that spoke to them, holding it close and making it their own.

A little historical context here: The Brothers Grimm did just that with Rapunzel and Snow White and Rumpelstiltskin and earned a hearty living at it. King James I did that when he decreed that the current crop of English bibles was a little lacking and it was time for a new edition. Ditto for the children who kept "Ring Around the Rosie" alive since the Plague. Robin Hood, Punch and Judy, Jesus Christ of Nazareth—they and many thousands of others have all had their stories edited and retold and re-tooled as their host culture evolved and changed over the years. That was the prerogative of the people who lived surrounded by those ideas, who went to sleep singing those songs. Well, we still live surrounded by ideas and we still go to sleep singing songs, but all those ideas and songs belong to companies with Big Expensive Lawyers.

The Potter flap ended because some of those Big Expensive Lawyers threw some kids a bone, not because anybody recognized the kids' right to play in their own sandbox. The distinction is important.

When napster finally went dark last summer, hardly anybody in the music industry did a victory dance. Oh, the famous internet song-trading service had finally been brought to heel, and the Ricky Martin MP3s were no longer flowing the way they once had, but the music still wanted to be free. On the Gnutella network, through spiffy new applications like BearShare and LimeWire, on a new service from Holland called KaZaA, on Morpheus and URLBlaze and OpenNap, people were shaking their bon bons like never before.

20 A lot of smartypants media types thought this was hilarious, that the public was showing Lars Ulrich and the RIAA who was boss, and that from now on we'd all make as many copies of "Enter Sandman" as we frickin' pleased, thank you very much. The war for free tunes was not over, however, and it is still not over today. As experiments with copy-protected CDs blossom and wilt, the legal resolve of the record companies and the music publishers hardens with every report of falling sales and every retail bankruptcy.

That legal resolve is now downright steely, as in gigantic, coconut-sized steel balls. Witness the Recording Industry Association of America's recent contribution to the War On Terrorism—a proposed amendment to the USA Act that would allow copyright holders to hack into private computers and delete illicit tunes and videos and pictures. The version that got the President's signature was blissfully free of that particular dingleberry, but the RIAA is unbowed, vowing to seek similar authority as legislative opportunities present themselves.

What are we really talking about here? We are talking about an industry, or a collection of industries, that produces and sells something called content. Here are some examples of content:

1. *Seinfeld*
2. Windows XP
3. *Men Are From Mars, Women Are From Venus*
4. *Star Wars Episode II: Attack of the Clones*
5. *"Sweet Caroline,"* by Neil Diamond

In other words, songs, movies, TV shows, software and all that. These are products that by their very nature are well suited to digital production and distribution. They may be sold in physical form (on CDs or DVDs or what have you), but at heart they are merely patterns of information, easily copied from one medium to another and one hard drive to another.

Napster, and by extension the Internet itself, so frightened the people who owned all this content because it threatened to leave them without a way to make their customers actually, you know, pay for the products they watched and listened to. Everybody, even those with MP3 collections numbering in the six-digit range, can understand that fear. There are billions and billions of dollars at stake, and all the aforementioned smartypants media blather notwithstanding, copyright owners are not going to say, "OK downloaders, you win; the new Slipknot record's on us."

25 Here is what they're going to say instead: "You. Downloader. We see you have made yourself a copy of the new Slipknot record. Give us money now or we will erase it." They will say this because they will have the ability to say it, because they will find a way to protect their valuable assets from freeloaders.

If song-swapping cannot be stopped at the server level or the network level, it will be stopped by snooping. (What's that you got there on your hard drive, fella? You paid for that?) It will be stopped by shoot-first-ask-questions-later litigation. It will be stopped by the creeping development of new pay-for-play media. It will be stopped by networked hardware that never plays a song or a movie without first getting clearance from a permission server. It will be stopped because money talks, because nobody with pockets that deep facing threats that great ever says "Uncle." It will be stopped because intellectual property is the real estate of the twenty-first century.

What does this mean for you? Consider how much of your life, your worktime and your playtime involves interacting with IP products, with software and media and information and entertainment. Now consider what it would mean to have your every move through that digital swamp tracked and recorded, all in the name of enforcing copyright. It would mean the Viacoms and the Disneys and the News Corporations of the very near future would own great volumes of information about your comings and goings, enormous databases full of your private life.

This is not a life anyone in the Western world can opt out of, remember. Choosing to avoid computers, music, television or movies brands you a crank, an eccentric. Avoiding all of them and still participating in society at large is completely out of the question.

On October 16, 2001, the Canadian government placed an order for $1.5 million of fluoroquinolone antibiotic with Apotex, a drug manufacturer specializing in generic equivalents of brand-name medications. Exactly what happened in the days before and after that order was placed is still the subject of dispute, but here is an approximation:

1. Anthrax infects several people in the U.S. Panic ensues.
2. Canadian government officials approach Bayer AG (Cipro patent-holder) for assurances that there will be enough fluoroquinolone-class antibiotic to go around.
3. Bayer allegedly cannot supply the number of tablets requested.
4. Canadian government officials approach Apotex, placing an order for a generic Cipro-equivalent, in knowing violation of the Bayer patent.
5. Bayer cries foul.
6. Public dustup ensues, with much disagreement over who offered how many pills when. Opposition makes hay with Health Canada's decision to break law of the land.
7. Deal reached. Bayer agrees to make its own pills available with forty-eight hours notice, and everyone agrees that if Bayer cannot deliver, the Apotex ones will stop the gap. Agreed-upon cost: about $1.30 per tablet, a discount over the regular price.
8. The media finds something else to pay attention to. Nobody mentions that generic Cipro is available in Colombia and Guatemala for about five cents a pill.

30 Cipro, which is generically known as ciprofloxacin, is protected by U.S. patent #4,670,444. What this means is that for the next couple of years (protection expires in 2003 in the U.S., 2004 in Canada), Bayer—along with any licensees it chooses to designate—has a monopoly on this now-famous antibiotic. Nobody else is allowed to run the string of chemical reactions described in the patent document, nobody else is allowed to manufacture products incorporating that chemistry, and certainly nobody else is allowed to sell any of it. Bayer owns the idea itself, the information, the A-leads-to-B-leads-to-C instruction set.

And even when panic is at an all-time high, even when innocent letter carriers are dying of hemorrhagic lung failure and nobody knows how big the whole deal could get, the company can still insist in public discourse that its patent will not be frickin' violated, thank you very much, and no one on the board of directors will lose a moment's sleep worrying about armed revolution.

Last October, a private entity's right to own ideas went head-to-head with a nation's right to use an idea to save its citizens from death by melting lung tissue. Guess which one prevailed?

In her neo-prog classic no logo, Naomi Klein wrote that "when we try to communicate with each other by using the language of brands and logos, we run the very real risk of getting sued."

True enough. But the ugly truth, the one we really need to talk about, is that everyone who lives in the West does that all day every day. We can't communicate any other way.

Here, in keeping with the spirit of this essay, is an unauthorized dance remix of a few paragraphs from pages 177–8 of the hardcover version of *No Logo*:

Many alleged violators of copyright are not trying to sell a comparable good or pass themselves off as the real thing. When I write a hot, dirty, porn story featuring Captain Kirk . . . with Mr. Spock . . . and post it on my website, I am not pretending to be Paramount Pictures, UPN, the estate of Gene Roddenberry or anybody but myself.

As branding becomes more expansionist, however, a competitor is anyone doing anything remotely related, because anything remotely related has the potential to be a spin-off at some point in the synergistic future. It also has the potential to seep into the public domain, where ordinary citizens will swap it and reshape it and republish and retell it. Lord knows, if enough people find themselves hollering and writing "Hello, Newman!" and "D'oh!" and "Motion to suppress!" at each other without legal interference, we're going to get the idea that it's generally OK for us plebes to talk to each other in our own mother tongue, the language of the media culture into which we were born.

And then just imagine what might happen: Mom 'n' Pop costume stores could stitch Batman Halloween capes without seeking or receiving the blessing of DC comics. Teachers could ask their students to write stories about Ash Ketchum and Team Rocket and Pikachu, could offer Pokémon Trainer badges for achievement prizes, could legitimately engage children in the lively, subtle, endlessly nuanced culture they live in. Competing publishers could produce mildly or wildly different editions of the same books, could bring familiar characters to unfamiliar situations and vice versa.

Artists will always make art by reconfiguring our shared cultural languages and references, but as those shared experiences shift from firsthand to mediated, a new set of issues raises serious questions about out-of-date definitions of freedom of expression in a branded culture. But artists are just the tip of it.

Yes, the underlying message of copyright bullying is that culture is something that happens to you, something you buy at the Virgin Megastore or rent at Blockbuster. But culture is more than that, all the efforts of armies of brand managers notwithstanding. Culture may begin as something you buy at the Virgin Megastore or rent at Blockbuster, but it only flowers into its true form when people turn those movies and tunes into conversations and ideas and personal, life-changing moments.

35 OK, enough already. This is not just about fancypants loft-dwellers making art about how media-soaked our society is. This is about our right to communicate with each other as citizens in the language we know best. It is about being able to say a ditzy pal is "being totally Phoebe," and know the choice of words is legitimate. It is about being able to call Bill Clinton "the teflon President" without a capital "T," about being able to say "velcro" without adding "brand fastener." It is about the important weight of trivial turns of phrase, about stories and jokes and ideas. It is about exactly the same things that unite people and ignite struggles the world over.

All our archetypes are private property. We should make them public again.

Here, then, is a manifestic closing for you.

A powerful movement is building even now, of people uniting to oppose the bullying thuggery of multinational corporations and their brands. This is generally a pretty good idea, as sweatshops are bad and so is environmental degradation and collusion with evil anti-democratic governments. Ugly corporate behaviour should be exposed and the people responsible should be shamed and fined and jailed.

But consider the real source of corporate power, the insidious force that allows and empowers all that ugly behaviour. It is copyright and trademark and patent. It is intellectual property. It is the exclusive right to emblazon a swoosh on a shoe, the exclusive right to call a sandwich a "Big Mac," the exclusive right to tell stories about the characters we care about, the exclusive right to produce certain kinds of fluoroquinolone-class antibiotics.

If anyone could open a restaurant and put up a big sign with golden arches on it and serve two-all-beef-patties-special-sauce-lettuce-cheese-pickles-onions-on-a-sesame-seed-bun, how much longer do you suppose there would still be a McDonald's Corporation to get up to no good around the globe?

If anyone with a sewing machine could put the Tommy Hilfiger blue-red-white icon on a shirt, how much longer do you suppose the original Hilfiger would be around to outsource his production to Southeast Asia?

If anyone could turn Batman into a hero or a rogue or a terrorist, if anyone could rewrite the story of his secret origin, if anyone could don the cape and the cowl, how much longer would our culture remain in private hands?

Let's not be any more naïve than we have been already. Copyright will not go away in our lifetime. Neither will trademarks and neither will patents. But consider this: As new technologies undermine the business models of the big intellectual property owners, those big intellectual property owners are seeking new ways to defend and enlarge their turf, and *this is not a done deal.* New and odious bits of IP statute and regulation are showing up in our legislatures and our Parliaments all the time, but they can be stopped, the same way anything else ugly and stupid can be stopped.

They can be stopped by vigorous and sensible public debate, by people who know their culture is under seige and who are committed to helping their fellow citizens understand. This is not pretty or simple, but making law and influencing public policy have never been pretty or simple. Our culture is private because the law has allowed it to become so, and the law can begin to swing the pendulum back, but making it so will require a delicate and persistent effort in the backrooms, in the courts, and in the streets.

They can be stopped by large and small acts of civil disobedience, by the willful and deliberate and unauthorized use of those precious trademarks in media large and small—on your school notebook, on your website, on your TV show. Eventually, they'll lose their power, becoming as generic and empty and valueless as "Kleenex" and "Aspirin" and "Thermos" have become.

They can be stopped by encouraging and supporting those public officials who understand something is wrong. On that score, the Cipro affair showed much promise, inasmuch as it was about a government department screwing up the nerve, just for a moment, to say to hell with your precious property rights.

They can be stopped if we dare to stop them, if we dare to take our archetypes and our icons and our superheroes and make them our own once more.

Batman *can* save the day, really he can, if only we have the courage to write that story.

So go ahead.

Just do it.

Because you're worth it.

Zoom zoom.

Reflect & Write

- ❑ Why does Dawson start his article with a birthday party, 9/11, and Batman? Did this opening make his argument stronger or weaker? Why?
- ❑ How would you characterize Dawson's voice? Find at least three instances where he constructs this voice through word choice, structure, or tone. How does the type of *ethos* he constructs as an author affect the way in which you receive his argument?
- ❑ Consider the examples that Dawson uses: Harry Potter, Napster, Apotex. Why do you think that he selected these examples? How did he anticipate they would render his argument more convincing? Was he correct?
- ❑ What was your reaction to reading Dawson's "unauthorized dance remix" of the paragraphs from Naomi Klein's *No Logo*? Did the fact that it was a remix detract from its persuasiveness as a piece of evidence? Did Dawson's experimentation with the form he was discussing increase his overall persuasiveness? Explore the implications of this particular "quotation."
- ❑ Look at the three "If anyone" examples toward the end of the article. Why are these important questions to ask at this point in the essay?
- ❑ Examine the final sentences of the article. Do they provide an effective capstone to the discussion? Why or why not?
- ❑ **Write.** Draft an analysis of Dawson's writing style. Include your answer to any of the "Reflect" questions above, and develop your essay around a solid thesis statement.

■ Revelations *is a non-profit* Star Wars *fan film produced and released on a very small budget by Panic Struck Productions. All of the artists who worked on the film were volunteers.*

Movie Poster: Revelations

Panic Struck Productions

FIGURE 11.21. This movie poster advertises the *Star Wars* fan-produced film, *Revelations.*

Reflect & Write

- ❏ Nowhere on the *Revelations* poster is the phrase *Star Wars* prominently displayed. Looking at the poster quickly, did you associate it with the *Star Wars* franchise? Why or why not?
- ❏ What aspects of the posters have been specially chosen to try to "brand" it as a *Star Wars* film? Consider the selection and arrangement of visual rhetoric.
- ❏ Compare this poster with an official poster for one of the official *Star Wars* films. Are there any differences that announce this poster as a "remix"?
- ❏ **Write.** Draft your plan for a remixed poster of a popular film. Include political figures and a strong argument about contemporary culture in your sketch.

Lawrence Lessig *is a professor of law at Harvard Law School and a founding board member of Creative Commons, an organization devoted to developing alternative licensing to encourage more productive sharing of authored works. He is one of the leading figures in copyright and intellectual property debates. In keeping with his stance on sharing and read-write (RW) culture, his most recent book,* Remix: Making Art and Commerce Thrive in the Hybrid Economy *(2009), from which this selection is taken, is available as a free Creative Commons licensed download.*

Remixed: Media

Lawrence Lessig

For most of the Middle Ages in Europe, the elite spoke and wrote in Latin. The masses did not. They spoke local, or vernacular, languages—what we now call French, German, and English. What was important to the elites was thus inaccessible to the masses. The most "important" texts were understood by only a few.

Text is today's Latin. It is through text that we elites communicate (look at you, reading this book). For the masses, however, most information is gathered through other forms of media: TV, film, music, and music video. These forms of "writing" are the vernacular of today. They are the kinds of "writing" that matters most to most. Nielsen Media Research, for example, reports that the average TV is left on for 8.25 hours a day, "more than an hour longer than a decade ago." The average American watches that average TV about 4.5 hours a day. If you count other forms of media—including radio, the Web, and cell phones—the number doubles. In 2006, the U.S. Bureau of the Census estimated that "American adults and teens will spend nearly five months" in 2007 consuming media. These statistics compare with falling numbers for text. Everything is captured in this snapshot of generations:

> Individuals age 75 and over averaged 1.4 hours of reading per weekend day and 0.2 hour (12 minutes) playing games or using a computer for leisure. Conversely, individuals ages 15 to 19 read for an average of 0.1 hour (7 minutes) per weekend day and spent 1.0 hour playing games or using a computer for leisure.

It is no surprise, then, that these other forms of "creating" are becoming an increasingly dominant form of "writing." The Internet didn't make these other forms of "writing" (what I will call simply "media") significant. But the Internet and digital technologies opened these media to the masses. Using the tools of digital technology—even the simplest tools, bundled into the most innovative modern operating systems—anyone can begin to "write" using images, or music, or video. And using the facilities of a free digital network, anyone can share that writing with anyone else. As with RW text, an ecology of RW media is developing. It is younger than the ecology of RW texts. But it is growing more quickly, and its appeal is much broader.

These RW media look very much like Ben's writing with text. They remix, or quote, a wide range of "texts" to produce something new. These quotes, however, happen at different layers. Unlike text, where the quotes follow in a single line—such as here, where the sentence explains, "and then a quote gets added"—remixed media may quote sounds over images, or video over text, or text over sounds. The quotes thus get mixed together. The mix produces the new creative work—the "remix."

5 These remixes can be simple or they can be insanely complex. At one end, think about a home movie, splicing a scene from *Superman* into the middle. At the other end, there are new forms of art being generated by virtuosic remixing of images and video with found and remade audio. Think again about Girl Talk, remixing between 200 and 250 samples from 167 artists in a single CD. This is not simply copying. Sounds are being used like paint on a palette. But all the paint has been scratched off of other paintings.

So how should we think about it? What does it mean, exactly?

However complex, in its essence remix is, as Negativland's Don Joyce described to me, "just collage." Collage, as he explained,

> [e]merged with the invention of photography. Very shortly after it was invented . . . you started seeing these sort of joking postcards that were photo composites. There would be a horse-drawn wagon with a cucumber in the back the size of a house. Things like that. Just little joking composite photograph things. That impressed painters at the time right away.

But collage with physical objects is difficult to do well and expensive to spread broadly. Those barriers either kept many away from this form of expression, or channeled collage into media that could be remixed cheaply. As Mark Hosler of Negativland described to me, explaining his choice to work with audio,

> I realized that you could get a hold of some four-track reel-to reel for not that much money and have it at home and actually play around with it and experiment and try out stuff. But with film, you couldn't do that. It was too expensive . . . . So that . . . drove me . . . to pick a medium where we could actually control what we were doing with a small number of people, to pull something off and make some finished thing to get it out there.

With digital objects, however, the opportunity for wide-scale collage is very different. "Now," as filmmaker Johan Söderberg explained, "you can do [video remix] almost for free on your own computer." This means more people can create in this way, which means that many more do. The images or sounds are taken from the tokens of culture, whether digital or analog. The tokens are "blaring at us all the time," as Don Joyce put it to me: "We are barraged" by expression intended originally as simply RO. Negativland's Mark Hosler:

> When you turn around 360 degrees, how many different ads or logos will you see somewhere in your space? [O]n your car, on your wristwatch, on a billboard. If you walk into any grocery store or restaurant or anywhere to shop, there's always a soundtrack playing. There's always . . . media. There's ads. There's magazines everywhere. . . . [I]t's the world we live in. It's the landscape around us.

10 This "barrage" thus becomes a source. As Johan Söderberg says, "To me, it is just like cooking. In your cupboard in your kitchen you have lots of different things and you try to connect different tastes together to create something interesting."

The remix artist does the same thing with bits of culture found in his digital cupboard.

My favorites among the remixes I've seen are all cases in which the mix delivers a message more powerfully than any original alone could, and certainly more than words alone could.

For example, a remix by Jonathan McIntosh begins with a scene from *The Matrix*, in which Agent Smith asks, "Do you ever get the feeling you're living in a virtual reality dream world? Fabricated to enslave your mind?" The scene then fades to a series of unbelievable war images from the Fox News Channel—a news organization that arguably makes people less aware of the facts than they were before watching it. Toward the end, the standard announcer voice says, "But there is another sound: the sound of good will." On the screen is an image of Geraldo Rivera, somewhere in Afghanistan. For about four seconds, he stands there silently, with the wind rushing in the background. (I can always measure the quickness of my audience by how long it takes for people to get the joke: "the sound of good will" = silence). The clip closes with a fast series of cuts to more Fox images, and then a final clip from an ad for the film that opened McIntosh's remix: "The Matrix Has You."

Or consider the work of Sim Sadler, video artist and filmmaker. My favorite of his is called "Hard Working George." It builds exclusively from a video of George Bush in one of his 2004 debates with John Kerry. Again and again, Sadler clips places where Bush says, essentially, "it's hard work." Here's the transcript:

> Sir, in answer to your question I just know how this world works. I see on TV screens how hard it is. We're making progress; it is hard work. You know, it's hard work. It's hard work. A lot of really great people working hard, they can do the hard work. That's what distinguishes us from the enemy. And it's hard work, but it's necessary work and that's essential, but again I want to tell the American people it's hard work. It is hard work. It's hard work. There is no doubt in my mind that it is necessary work. I understand how hard it is, that's my job. No doubt about it, it's tough. It's hard work which I really want to do, but I would hope I never have to—nothing wrong with that. But again I repeat to my fellow citizens, we're making progress. We're making progress there. I reject this notion. It's ludicrous. It is hard work. It's hard work. That's the plan for victory and that is the best way. What I said was it's hard work and I made that very clear.

15 Usually, the audience breaks into uncontrolled laughter at "I would hope I never have to—nothing wrong with that," so people don't hear the rest of the clip. But by the end, the filter Sadler has imposed lets us understand Bush's message better.

Some look at this clip and say, "See, this shows anything can be remixed to make a false impression of the target." But in fact, the "not working hard" works as well as it does precisely because it is well known that at least before 9/11, Bush was an extremely remote president, on vacation 42 percent of his first eight months in office.The success of the clip thus comes from building upon what we already know. It is powerful because it makes Bush himself say what we know is true about him. The same line wouldn't have worked with Clinton, or Bill Gates. Whatever you want to say about them, no one thinks they don't work hard.

My favorite of all these favorites, however, is still a clip in a series called "Read My Lips," created by Söderberg. Söderberg is an artist, director, and professional video editor. He has edited music videos for Robbie Williams and Madonna and, as he put it, "all kinds of pop stars." He also has an Internet TV site—soderberg.tv—that carries all his own work. That work stretches back almost twenty years.

"Read My Lips" is a series Söderberg made for a Swedish company called Atmo, in which famous people are lip-synched with music or other people's words. They all are extraordinarily funny (though you can't see all of them anymore because one, which mixed Hitler with the song "Born to Be Alive," resulted in a lawsuit).

The best of these (in my view at least) is a love song with Tony Blair and George Bush. The sound track for the video is Lionel Richie's "Endless Love." Remember the words "My love, there's only you in my life." The visuals are images of Bush and Blair. Through careful editing, Söderberg lip-synchs Bush singing the male part and Blair singing the female part. The execution is almost perfect. The message couldn't be more powerful: an emasculated Britain, as captured in the puppy love of its leader for Bush.

20 The obvious point is that a remix like this can't help but make its argument, at least in our culture, far more effectively than could words. (By "effectively," I mean that it delivers its message successfully to a wide range of viewers.) For anyone who has lived in our era, a mix of images and sounds makes its point far more powerfully than any eight-hundred-word essay in the *New York Times* could. No one can deny the power of this clip, even Bush and Blair supporters, again in part because it trades upon a truth we all—including Bush and Blair supporters—recognize as true. It doesn't assert the truth. It shows it. And once it is shown, no one can escape its mimetic effect. This video is a virus; once it enters your brain, you can't think about Bush and Blair in the same way again.

But why, as I'm asked over and over again, can't the remixer simply make his own content? Why is it important to select a drumbeat from a certain Beatles recording? Or a Warhol image? Why not simply record your own drumbeat? Or paint your own painting?

The answer to these questions is not hard if we focus again upon why these tokens have meaning. Their meaning comes not from the content of what they say; it comes from the reference, which is expressible only if it is the original that gets used. Images or sounds collected from real-world examples become "paint on a palette." And it is this "cultural reference," as coder and remix artist Victor Stone explained, that "has emotional meaning to people. . . . When you hear four notes of the Beatles' 'Revolution,' it means something." When you "mix these symbolic things together" with something new, you create, as Söderberg put it, "something new that didn't exist before."

The band Negativland has been making remixes using "found culture"—collected recordings of RO culture—for more than twenty-five years. As I described at the start, they first became (in)famous when they were the target of legal action brought by Casey Kasem and the band U2 after Negativland released a mash-up of Casey Kasem's introduction of U2 on his Top 40 show. So why couldn't Negativland simply have used something original? Why couldn't they re-record the clip with an actor? Hosler explained:

> We could have taken these tapes we got of Casey Kasem and hired someone who imitated Casey Kasem, you know, and had him do a dramatic re-creation. Why did we have to use the actual original . . . the actual thing? Well, it's because the actual thing has a power about it. It has an aura. It has a magic to it. And that's what inspires the work.

Reflect & Write

- ❑ How does Lessig redefine writing for the Internet age? Where do images and music factor into this new definition of writing? What is the relationship of new media writing to more traditional modes of writing?
- ❑ What is Lessig's idea of a powerful remix? In this case, what is the remix's relationship to its original texts?
- ❑ How does Lessig use examples to prove his point? Which, in your opinion, is the most powerful example he uses to underscore his points about remixes? Why?
- ❑ **Write.** During his "Free Culture" lecture series, Lessig often would speak at length about how "Creativity and innovation always build on the past," a point he develops further in his work on Remix Culture. Find three examples of remixes and write a brief essay, drawing on these examples, that explains how old images (and other texts) can be used to create new culture.

In February 2010, 17-year-old German novelist Helene Hegemann was accused of plagiarizing material from the novel Strobo *in her debut coming-of-age novel,* Axolotl Roadkill. *To the surprise of many, rather than denying the claims, Hegemann admitted to taking "about a page" from* Strobo, *defending herself from the charge of stealing by saying that "there is no such thing as originally anyway; there's only authenticity." In the following article, senior writer* **Laura Miller** *ponders the Hegemann incident as evidence of a possible generational shift in how creativity and authorship are defined. This article originally appeared in the February 16, 2010, edition of* Salon.com.

Plagiarism: The Next Generation

Laura Miller

Recent plagiarism accusations against the 17-year-old author of a German novel feel like déjà vu all over again, with one key distinction: Helene Hegemann, who wrote the best-selling tale of drugging and clubbing, "Axolotl Roadkill," is defending the practice, telling one German newspaper, "I myself don't feel it is stealing, because I put all the material into a completely different and unique context and from the outset consistently promoted the fact that none of that is actually by me."

Hegemann lifted as much as a full page of text from an obscure, independently published novel, "Strobo," by a blogger known as Airen. Another German blogger, Deef Pirmasens, was the first to point out the passages from "Axolotl Roadkill" that are said to be largely duplicated from "Strobo," with small changes. Despite the uproar caused by this revelation, "Axolotl Roadkill" has been selling better than ever and has been nominated for the $20,000 fiction prize at the Leipzig Book Fair. "Obviously, it isn't completely clean but, for me, it doesn't change my appraisal of the text," a jury member and newspaper book critic told the New York Times, explaining that the jury knew about the plagiarism accusations when it selected the novel for its short list. "I believe it's part of the concept of the book."

Plagiarizing journalists like the recently fired Gerald Posner (currently providing the occasion for ecstasies of self-righteousness over at Slate) could never pull off such a justification. Novelists and other artists, however, are always boasting about how much they "steal," as Robert McCrum pointed out in the Guardian a few weeks ago. How, then, can they wax indignant when other writers lift their work? "There's no such thing as originality anyway, just authenticity," Hegemann pronounced in a statement to the press. (Jim Jarmusch, incidentally, said virtually the same thing, and he probably got it from somebody else.) When the admirably game McCrum posted a quick follow-up take on the Hegemann affair, he prompted a heated conversation about copyright and its validity in the Information Age.

5 To this conundrum, Hegemann has added a heaping dollop of generational special pleading, and the story has prompted teachers to offer multiple examples of students who don't seem to understand what plagiarism is or that it's wrong. Kids these days, this Cassandra-ish line of reasoning goes, have unfathomably different values, and their elders had better come to terms with this because children are, after all, the future. You can't tell them anything! It's as if people under 25 have become the equivalent of an isolated Amazonian tribe who can't justly be expected to grasp our first-world prohibitions against polygamy or cannibalism—despite the fact that *they've grown up in our very midst.*

Count me among those who think that most plagiarism scandals are overblown—a classic example being the novelist Ian McEwan, who replicated in "Atonement" a few phrases from a memoir he used as historical research for that novel. What smells off in this instance is precisely Hegemann's claim to be using her borrowings to advance a cutting-edge concept of artistry. The daughter of an avant-garde dramatist, she says she practices "intertextuality" and explains, "Very many artists use this technique . . . by organically including parts in my text, I am entering into a dialogue with the author."

This would be more plausible if Hegemann had acknowledged from the beginning that she'd included work from other writers in "Axolotl Roadkill," but by all indications, she did not. (Granted, it's hard for me to substantiate this for myself since I don't read German and can't compare Hegemann's novel to Airen's.) Some copyright critics have pointed out that, thanks to "Axolotl Roadkill," "Strobo" is now enjoying a sales boost, proving that "remixes" can be a rising tide that lifts all boats. However, it took Pirmasens' plagiarism accusation to bring Airen's involuntary "contribution" to "Axolotl Roadkill" to the public's attention. If Hegemann intended to enter into a dialogue with Airen, she took pains to make it look like a monologue. If she viewed the writing itself as collaborative, she suppressed any urge to share those handsome royalty checks.

McEwan, who *did* credit the out-of-print nurse's memoir he used as a source for "Atonement," could at least argue that what he incorporated from that source was only a tiny portion of a very different and substantively original work. Hegemann has already, and rather stupidly, cut herself off from that option by declaring that she intended to write a collaboration from the very beginning, only she just forgot to mention it before this. How innovative is "Axolotl Roadkill"? Again, it's difficult for the Anglophone observer to say for sure, but since both "Axolotl Roadkill" and "Strobo" recount life among the youngest participants in Berlin's wild club scene, Hegemann's claim to be presenting the material in a "completely different and unique context" seems a stretch.

And—please!—how much longer can very young writers publish novels depicting anomie, drug use and casual sex among their peers and *still* provoke wonder among their elders? It happens every few years, from the apotheosis of "Less Than Zero" to the sensation of Nick McDonell's "Twelve," yet every new iteration is treated like some shocking, never-before-imagined exposé, when, really, only the playlist changes. With suspicious frequency, the enthusiasm for "Axolotl Roadkill" seems to boil down to just this strain of titillated astonishment. You can't blame other 17-year-olds for finding it incredibly daring and fresh, but as for us adults—shouldn't we know better?

Reflect & Write

- ❑ What is Miller's stance on the Hegemann case? What argument does she make in her article?
- ❑ How does Miller's own experience and perspective color the argument? How do you see evidence of this rhetorical stance in her word choice, tone, and examples?
- ❑ What is the purpose of Miller's last paragraph? What is the effect of ending with a question?
- ❑ **Write.** Do you think that this case reflects a generational divide? Write a brief response to Miller in which you clarify the "next generation's" stance on copyright, sharing, and creativity.

Seeing Connections
To delve further into the question of intellectual property and the ethics of documentation, see Chapter 9.

As the covers that follow suggest, both in the music and literary worlds, the practice of remixing materials has become increasingly well recognized, although still occasionally contested.

Remix Covers

FIGURE 11.22. The cover of DJ Danger Mouse's *Grey Album* visually represents the album's musical remix of the Beatles' *White Album* and Jay-Z's *The Black Album*.

FIGURE 11.23. Released in 2009, *Pride and Prejudice and Zombies* chose for its cover design a deliberate remixing of the classic cover for the Jane Austen novel.

Reflect & Write

- ❑ How does each cover reflect the fact that the work is a mash-up or remix? Consider how contrast, arrangement, style, color, and characters impact the argument.
- ❑ What are the differences in design between the two covers? How do these differences reflect on the types of texts that they represent?
- ❑ DJ Danger Mouse was served with a cease-and-desist notice for the *Grey Album*, while Seth Grahame-Smith's novel quickly earned a spot on the *New York Times* best-seller's list. What differs between these two texts that might account for their radically divergent receptions?
- ❑ **Write.** Choose a musical mash-up that you like. Now design a cover for it that reflects the way that it combines different artists and musical styles. Share your cover art with the class.

Seeing Connections
Review strategies for analyzing cover images by looking at the Prewriting Checklist for Chapter 5 (page 112).

Bill Werde *is the Editorial Director for* Billboard. *Previously, he served as the Associate Editor for* Rolling Stone *and also had contributed articles to the* Washington Post, *the* Village Voice, Wired *magazine, and the* New York Times. *This article was first published in the* Times *on June 7, 2004, a few days after the release of* Harry Potter and the Prisoner of Azkaban, *the third installment in the* Harry Potter *film series.*

Hijacking Harry Potter, Quidditch Broom and All

Bill Werde

On Friday night *Harry Potter and the Prisoner of Azkaban* sold out theaters all over the globe. But in a makeshift screening room in a Brooklyn warehouse, more than 75 filmgoers paid $7 each to watch the first film in the series, *Harry Potter and the Sorcerer's Stone.* Sort of.

On the screen *The Sorcerer's Stone* played as it was released by Warner Brothers. But the original soundtrack, dialogue and all, was turned down and replaced by an alternate version created by a 27-year-old comic book artist from Austin, Tex., named Brad Neely. He calls his soundtrack "Wizard People, Dear Reader," and it is one more breach of the media industry's control of its products.

With Mr. Neely's gravelly narration, the movie's tone shifts into darkly comic, pop-culture-savvy territory. Hagrid, Harry Potter's giant, hairy friend, becomes Hagar, the Horrible, and Harry's fat cousin becomes Roast Beefy. As imagined by Mr. Neely, the three main characters are child alcoholics with a penchant for cognac, the magical ballgame Quidditch takes on homoerotic overtones, and Harry is prone to delivering hyper-dramatic monologues. "I am a destroyer of worlds," bellows Mr. Neely at one point, sending laughter reverberating through the warehouse Friday night. "I am Harry" expletive "Potter!"

Mr. Neely, a fan of the series, created his alternate soundtrack last summer after joking about the notion with friends in an Austin nightspot. "Usually those kinds of jokes just die in the bar," he said. This time Mr. Neely burned his creation to CD, sent copies to friends and gave some to local video rental stores; several bundled his soundtrack with rentals of *The Sorcerer's Stone.*

5 The alternate soundtrack did not receive much attention until March, when it was shown at the New York Underground Film Festival. The festival's director, Kendra Gaeta, received a gift from her boyfriend weeks before the festival: a painting by Mr. Neely, who threw in a CD of his Potter narration. "It was just so funny," she said.

Among those attending that festival was Carrie McLaren, whose Web site, Illegal-art.org, functions as an online museum for copyright-infringing art.

Ms. McLaren has since offered the huge digital file of "Wizard People" for download and raved about the soundtrack on her site.

"We think Neely has crafted an as of yet unnamed new art form," she wrote, "one everyone should experience for themselves."

There is a brief history, at least, to alternative soundtracks. Woody Allen's 1966 movie *What's Up, Tiger Lily?* substituted Mr. Allen's comic dialogue and descriptions for the soundtrack of a bad Japanese spy movie. But while Mr. Allen bought the rights to the original film and distributed his new version in theaters, subsequent ventures in the digital era, like Mr. Neely's, have taken liberties without permission and let the Web take care of distribution.

10 In 2001, for example, an anonymous *Star Wars* fan was so displeased with the helium-voiced character Jar Jar Binks in *Star Wars, Episode I: The Phantom Menace* that he recut the film, removing the character, a stunt that became known as "the Phantom edit."

George Lucas, the creator of *Star Wars,* initially was intrigued by the alternative version of the film. But when bootleg copies began selling at comic book conventions, and other edited versions began to trade online, his firm, Lucasfilm, sent letters to the news media indicating that it viewed such projects as copyright infringement.

A spokewoman at Warner Brothers said that the studio was unaware of "Wizard People, Dear Reader" and declined to comment further.

It is not clear that Mr. Neely's soundtrack violates the studio's copyright. Jonathan Zittrain, co-director of the Berkman Center for Internet and Society at Harvard Law School, said that while the copyright holder retains the rights to derivative works, it was possible "Wizard People" was protected under the rules that allow "fair use" of copyrighted works for purposes like criticism, comment and news reporting.

"The long-term strategic threat to the entertainment industry is that people will get in the habit of creating and making as much as watching and listening, and all of a sudden the label applied to people at leisure, 50 years in the making—consumer—could wither away," he said. "But it would be a shame if Hollywood just said no. It could very possibly be in the interest of publishers to see a market in providing raw material along with finished product."

Mr. Neely has not let the lack of legal clarity stop him from making plans to perform the "Wizard People" soundtrack live at an Austin theater July 23 through 25, as well as one night each in Seattle, Portland and Olympia, Wash., in August.

He is also working on his next project, a similar concept with a different style. The films need to have a lot of action, he said. "I'm thinking maybe *Jurassic Park*."

Reflect & Write

- ❑ At one point, Bill Werde describes "Wizard People, Dear Reader" as "one more breach of the media industry's control of its products." Does Werde overall seem critical of the consumer remixing of popular movies? Why or why not?
- ❑ How does the Woody Allen example function in the article? Does it support the contention that consumers like Brad Neely should be able to remix film or does it undermine it? How?
- ❑ Look at the sources that Werde uses. What additional sources or quotations might Werde have included to make his argument more persuasive? What would these sources contribute to the article?
- ❑ **Write.** Listen to part of "Wizard People, Dear Reader," linked through the *Envision* Website, and then write a film review of this movie version of *Harry Potter* that makes clear your position on the issue of cultural remixing. www.pearsonhighered.com/envision/381

COLLABORATIVE CHALLENGE

In "Hijacking Harry Potter," Bill Werde describes the way in which one person "customized" Harry Potter to produce his own multimedia experience. Working with a small group, choose a short video clip—a commercial, a segment of a televised speech, a portion of a TV show—that you can replay either using a VCR, DVD player, or the Internet. Watch it with the sound off and then script your own remix narration for it. Share your remix with your class, either reading your narration live or playing a recorded version to accompany the clip.

PERSPECTIVES ON THE ISSUE

1. Re-read Michael Eisner's address to Congress. Is it a successful argument? Discuss how he might have rescripted this argument if he discovered that he would have no multimedia capabilities during his presentation. How might he make his argument into a cartoon like *Bound by Law*?
2. Look up the original paragraphs from Naomi Klein that Bret Dawson remixed in "The Privatization of Our Culture" and compare the two. To what extent does Dawson "remix" these paragraphs? What impact does it have on Klein's argument? How should such "remixes" be used in articles and formal arguments?
3. Some critics have likened the remixing of cultural texts to a return to something more like oral or folk-tale tradition, where stories were continually shared, adopted, and transformed by multiple tellers. Do you agree with this assessment? If so, why do you think this return to a more oral-based tradition is so threatening to so many people? Write a blog entry in which you work through this assertion and its ramifications for contemporary culture.
4. Search the Web for a fansite or visit a bookstore to find a fan magazine devoted to a particular film or TV show (for instance, *Lost, Glee*, *Star Trek*, or *Star Wars*). Examine one piece of fan fiction that generates its narrative from the characters and/or setting of the original. Now write an analysis in which you argue for the role of fan-produced texts in the spread—or the crippling—of American popular culture.
5. Consider the case of Helene Hegemann that Laura Miller describes in her article. Drawing on your understanding of their arguments advanced in their essays, how do you think Lawrence Lessig and Bret Dawson would interpret this case? Review the Dialogue of Sources section from Chapter 5, and write a fictitious dialogue between these authors in which they discuss the Hegemann case. Use paraphrases or direct quotes from their articles as appropriate.

FROM WRITING TO RESEARCH

1. For many years, Lawrence Lessig was famous for presentations based on his book *Free Culture*. Watch the Flash version of Lessig's "Free Culture" presentation online through the link on the *Envision* Website. Pay special attention to the relationship between his script and his PowerPoint slides. In groups, construct a list of observations about the rhetorical strategies that govern Lessig's use of PowerPoint. How does he use them to further his argument? How does this differ from other PowerPoint presentations you have seen? Now together redesign these observations into an oral and multimedia presentation in which you use the same strategies as Lessig did to present your argument. Deliver your presentation to your class and afterward talk about your own reactions to using visual and oral rhetoric in this way. www.pearsonhighered.com/envision/382
2. Do some field research on the illegal downloading of media from the Internet (such as music, film, television shows, software) by conducting a series of interviews and surveying your classmates and professors on the issue. Either narrow your focus to one type of media or focus more broadly on the ethics of the issue as a whole. Refer to Chapter 5 for advice on field research. Once you have compiled your data, create a multimedia presentation, complete with information graphics, in which you convey your findings and your argument about this issue to your class.
3. Find three examples of "remix" culture and write a brief essay that explains how old images (and other texts) can be used to create new culture. In what ways do your examples support or refute the claim that "culture always builds on the past"?

Visit www.pearsonhighered.com/envision for expanded assignment guidelines and student projects.
Visit www.mycomplab.com for additional general writing and research resources.

CHAPTER 12

Marked Bodies

When you look at the photo of the woman in Figure 12.1, what do you see? What catches your eye? Is it her direct gaze? Her lip piercing? Her ornate tattooing? How does she choose to mark herself—and how does her body thereby operate as a rhetorical text? Finally, how did you begin to draw conclusions about her identity based on your reaction to or interpretation of the markings on her body?

When we look at bodies as visual texts in society, we often participate in a social process of reading people according to certain social categories: as male or female, young or old, rural or urban, and from a certain race, class, or culture.

But how much do people shape the way they are viewed in society by choosing certain ways to present themselves visually—how do they mark their bodies? What happens if someone walks into a job interview wearing sweatpants or gives a formal presentation in a three-piece suit? How is the choice of clothing or jewelry or tattoos a matter of claiming identity, trying to shape the way bodies are viewed by others?

FIGURE 12.1. A woman asserts her identity by marking her body with piercings and body art.

In this chapter, we'll explore the rhetoric of bodies in society and how identity is shaped by the way people read visible signs and the way people use signs to construct identities. In other words, we will consider how bodies are both marked by culture and marked by their own choices (such as when people make rhetorical choices to change what society thinks of their identity through physical appearance, clothing, or adornment).

Marking in this way is linked to "looking." Often, we do not even have control over how we are looked at: others may interpret our bodies as markings that place us in a certain social group, race, age, or lifestyle choice. Many times in response, we—like the model in Figure 12.1—use our bodies purposefully to change the way we are looked at. We try to mark our bodies with signs of our identities, to announce who we are, our affiliation with a particular group or religion, our sexual orientation, and sometimes even our political stance. Hair-styles, piercings, clothing choices, tattoos, toned abs, or even painted toenails: these choices all constitute ways we "mark" ourselves in relation to our culture—or try to change the way we are "looked at" by remaking the signs of our identities. In this way, we may deliberately mark our bodies to show our membership in certain communities, such as religious groups, sports groups, even groups determined through shared experiences, such as the many groups of New York City firefighters who "marked" their bodies with similar tattoos commemorating the colleagues they lost in the 9/11 terrorist attacks.

In the pages that follow, we will examine different ways that bodies are marked in contemporary culture. In "Imagining the Ideal Body," we'll investigate the debate over body shape, race, and ideal beauty; in "Fashion Statements," we'll look at how people literally mark their bodies as a way of establishing their identity—such as when we write on an arm or leg with a beautiful ornate tattoo to signal membership in a certain community or just to change the way we are looked at, or when we wear a religious t-shirt or a head scarf in order to show the world our arguments about ourselves. In these instances, fashion works as argument; it changes the way we look and are looked at. It marks the body, and it makes a mark upon culture.

In all these examples, the body becomes a form of visual rhetoric, an argument about our identity: who we are, where we belong, and how others might read us. As you read the articles and write your own arguments about the marked bodies in this culture, you might begin to think more broadly about the way bodies function as visual rhetoric—in advertising, in places of worship, and in the ebb and flow of our daily lives.

IMAGINING THE IDEAL BODY

FIGURE 12.2. Stylized to resemble a fashion magazine photo, this image captures the costs of cultural idealization of feminine beauty.

What defines beauty? Who determines today's standards of "attractiveness"? How does the visual rhetoric of advertisements, films, television shows, and fashion magazines shape our notions of the "ideal body"? And how are our own bodies marked by the constructions of body image we see everywhere across cultures?

Consider the image in Figure 12.2. How does the woman's face and body both evoke and parody ideas about beauty that come from magazines such as *Vogue, Glamour, Cosmo,* or *Marie Claire*? If you were to flip through one of these magazines and locate a conventional beauty ad, what aspects would be similar? Perhaps you might comment on the model's direct gaze into the camera, her tussled hair, her makeup-covered eyes, or her arms raised in a seductive pose. But then why does this model have bandages? What sort of visual argument is Figure 12.2 making about the ideal body, especially in contrast with a standard beauty image from a fashion magazine?

As you think about the typical fashion magazine ad, consider also how contemporary images about men make equally powerful arguments about male beauty. Locate an ad from a men's magazine such as *GQ* or *Men's Health,* or look at how men are represented in a popular television show such as *Grey's Anatomy.* How, in each case, are we influenced by the images we see in the media? Your analysis of these images can help you begin to formulate your argument about how visual representations construct social notions that we come to accept as "natural."

FIGURE 12.3. The words on this billboard from a poor neighborhood in Beijing, China, say "Illusion: Cosmetology Beauty Shop."

FIGURE 12.4. In this street scene in Beijing, China, women try to imitate the body image shown in billboards from their neighborhoods.

The normalizing of these distorted images of ideal beauty becomes even more problematic if we shift to a broader, international context. The Beijing billboard shown in Figure 12.3 displays the white face and red hair of a Caucausian model but is situated in one of the poorest and oldest neighborhoods of the Chinese capital. How does this advertisement argue for a particular construction of "ideal beauty"? What visual and verbal elements contribute to the ad's argument about female beauty? Now compare the billboard to the photo of a street scene taken a few blocks away (see Figure 12.4). In the photo, Chinese women watch a demonstration on how to achieve the standard of beauty shown in the billboard. That is, they seek to color their hair red and fashion themselves after the body image shown in the advertisement. How does this photo show the cause-and-effect relationship of images of beauty in the media upon people in particular communities?

Advertisers within the past few years have become savvier about audiences' growing resistance to prescriptive representations of body image. In 2004, Dove beauty products launched its Campaign for Real Beauty, whose goal was "to make more women feel beautiful every day by widening stereotypical views of beauty" (http://www.campaignforrealbeauty.com). The first series of Real Beauty ads featured real women rather than professional models and celebrated a type of female physique that traditionally has been considered "too big," "heavy," or otherwise "out of proportion" with the ideal. By 2006, Dove took its discussion to the Internet, releasing two viral videos that exposed and debunked stereotypes reinforced by the fashion industry: "Evolution," which uses time lapse photography to show the transformation of a real woman into a model; and "Onslaught," which critiques the ever-perpetuating images of beauty that bombard young girls today.

While Dove's campaign seems a laudable attempt at addressing the issue of body image, we'll learn that there's more complexity to the debate. Even with our increased awareness of the link between the media and body image, popular culture images, from ads for skin cream to toys such as Barbie and G.I. Joe, continue to shape our notions about ourselves, our physical appearances, and our self-esteem.

It is important to consider what happens to our sense of self when the body we are meant to strive for is represented by a model or doll that is overly thin, obviously Caucasian, or unrealistically sculpted. As the articles in this section suggest, these representations seem to affect people's attitudes toward eating disorders, drug abuse, self-esteem, and societal norms. In the pages that follow, we'll explore these issues and more as we look at body image across genders, races, and ages.

Reflect & Write

- ❑ How would you characterize the body image shown in Figure 12.2? Discuss the visual elements. What aspects evoke a more conventional fashion ad? Which aspects make you question fashion ads?
- ❑ Notice the visual elements of the billboard in Figure 12.3. How do these factors contribute to our notions of body image?
- ❑ Examine Figures 12.3 and 12.4. What elements are culturally or class specific? How is a particular standard of beauty created by the billboard?
- ❑ **Write.** Take a walk and look for billboards posters, or displays that present images of ideal beauty on your campus or in your community. Write a letter to your local newspaper analyzing the persuasive power of these images. Include photos of the images as evidence for your claim.

■ *Psychotherapist and writer* **Susie Orbach** *first became a leading participant in the discussion of women's body image issues with the publication of her 1978 book* Fat Is a Feminist Issue. *Since that time, she has both written and taught extensively on the issue of women's physical and emotional health and has appeared on numerous television and radio programs. This article recounts Orbach's involvement in the genesis of Dove's "Campaign for Real Beauty" and was originally published in the June 17, 2005, issue of* Campaign, *an online advertising, marketing, and public relations magazine.*

Fat Is an Advertising Issue

Susie Orbach

When O&M called Susie Orbach to ask her advice on Dove's campaign for real beauty, she jumped at the chance to turn advertising's often destructive relationship with women's body image on its head.

More than one million hits on the 'campaign for real beauty' website; pictures of women on billboards all over the UK that make you smile inside; a programme to deconstruct beauty ads going into secondary schools; a fund to raise girls' and women's self-esteem; mother-and-daughter workshops on self-image; a mission to change negative feelings women can have towards their bodies . . . and all this from a soap-cum-beauty company?

In January two years ago, Mel White of Ogilvy & Mather rang me. 'I'd like to book an hour of your time. Some of us working on the Dove brand have been worrying that beauty advertising has been damaging to women. We want to make sure we understand how, and what we might to do to change it.'

White was the global brand and category partner at O&M. She was part of a team spearheading an attempt to make a positive contribution to women's lives. 'We all—at Dove and the agency—are women of a certain seniority,' she said. 'We think we can make a difference, a positive impact on women's lives. Dove has never sold products on the basis of stoking up insecurity. But maybe we can go further. Can you help?'

5 Could I help? To hear that creative teams were now interested in investing their energy in strengthening women was extraordinary. Years of banging on the doors of clothing manufacturers, government, the food industry and advertising, to persuade them that by making fashion funkier and food more interesting they would increase sales, made this a dream meeting. I never thought the beauty industry would come asking. I was delighted. I was intrigued.

Could White be serious? Was this a bit of ethical window-dressing or a sincere endeavour? Could they change the grammar of beauty in an industry that had been so instrumental in promoting exclusivity? Was Dove really up for a genuinely radical transformation of the representation of women?

Would the creatives actually hear the dissatisfaction emanating from girls and women about the absolutely torturous standards of beauty they had either wittingly or unwittingly foisted on them? Could the art directors come up with some way to meet that dissatisfaction and make difference sexy, something the fashionistas could resonate with?

The first step was to persuade Unilever. Such a retool was going to take a lot of money and steady commitment. If the executives there could understand the difficulties their wives, mothers, lovers, sisters and daughters had with their own physical appearance, then maybe we had a chance. The change that the Dove team were advocating would require consciousness-raising throughout the agency and the business. The 400 or so people working on Dove would have to be behind it. This was not just a whoopee new campaign like any other.

On the advertising side, O&M assembled creative teams that knew the Dove brand and had done some of their best work on it. They also brought on board teams who did not know Dove, but who had previously done outstanding work on other accounts across the world.

10 The film O&M made for one of their first internal pitches featured the daughters of executives talking about their own bodies and the cute noses, freckles, hair and tummies they wanted to do away with or change. The poignancy of these little (and big) girls showing their dissatisfactions and their wish to be free of some of the most quintessentially adorable aspects of themselves was completely compelling. It's not possible to watch that three-minute DVD without reaching for a tissue. It was a testimony to the hurt and damage we were unintentionally doing to our daughters.

The film hinted at the longing these lovely girls had to be acceptable, to be pretty, to feel good about themselves.

That DVD and others made for internal Unilever and O&M purposes provided the opening through which I, as a psychotherapist, academic and political activist in the area of women's psychology, body image and eating problems, could now deliver the relevant clinical evidence. My writing, public speaking and research experience with thousands of women could provide the backbone to the Dove initiative, an initiative that had the potential to turn around the grief and distress that lurked inside so many girls' and women's physical experience of themselves.

I told Dove that the Harvard psychiatrist and anthropologist Anne Becker had found that three years after the introduction of TV into Fiji in 1995, 11.9% of adolescent girls were puking into the toilet bowl trying to change their Fijian build into one that resembled the Western images they were imbibing via their TV sets.

I told Unilever that just half-an-hour looking at a magazine could lower youngsters' self-esteem significantly. I told them that one in four college females has a serious eating problem and that most women wake up and feel their tummies to check how good or bad they've been the day before. Before they've even brushed their teeth, their critical selves are planning how punishing to be today.

15 I told them that without intending to, mums were passing on negative attitudes about their own bodies towards their infant girls, and that their daughters were now absorbing a shaky body sense that made them vulnerable to the blandishments of the market that purported to meet this distress while actually reinforcing it.

The women working on Dove knew how women's magazines had discreet cosmetic surgery ads in the back long before TV shows such as The Swan and Extreme Makeover came along. However expectant you felt before reading Vogue, Glamour, Cosmo or Marie Claire, you felt coshed by a mood depressant after it. And all the Dove women knew they weren't just victims of the image industries. In a sense, all of us women are complicit in these unrealistic representations of femaleness. In order not to feel entirely powerless inside a visually dominating landscape that represents beauty so narrowly, we play out our own beauty scripts inside it: not questioning it, but trying to meet it.

The psychoanalyst in me could try to explain how women's relationship to the beauty industry perfectly encapsulates the psychological essence of the abused. The victim, shunning that awful feeling of being exploited and to gain some self-respect, rejects the idea she is being used. Instead, she makes the job of appearing beautiful her own personal project. She is not being compelled to bind her feet, she does it willingly. It's the only way to be. She will involve herself in trying to look younger, skinnier, taller, bigger-breasted, smaller-breasted and making sure every surface is coiffed, painted, plucked, waxed, perfumed, moisturised, conditioned or dyed. Taking the job on for herself is her response to being targeted.

It is her refusal to, as it were, be done to.

That this can't bring women satisfaction works in the interest of the beauty industry. Having set up this relationship of insecurity, there is always another area to work on—and even if all enemies were banished, ageing would be waiting just around the corner.

20 Dove's mission was to reformulate this warped and damaging engagement with beauty and offer in its place something based not on impossibility, but on possibility. Daring and innovative, so far. But could they take the campaign through their company and into the public domain?

In May 1999, work coming out of the Women's Unit at the Cabinet Office showed eating problems and concern about the body was the number one issue for girls and women aged between 11 and 80. The UK Government held a Body Image Summit, under the leadership of Tessa Jowell and Margaret Jay. Research showed that the promotion of images of ever-skinnier, wan-looking but apparently need-free women who shoved attitude into the camera lens was creating serious (health and mental health) problems in the lives of girls and women.

The Body Image Summit included influential magazine editors, fashion designers and buyers who could have changed our narrow visual culture.

But the Summit programme collapsed at the first whiff of contempt in the media. The Government showed itself to be entirely pusillanimous, back-pedalling and equivocating at its own subsequent press conferences.

After my experience as a consultant to and keynote speaker at the Summit, I was now interested to see what the commercial sector could do. I didn't expect the same kind of inertia and collapse from business when the first criticism came along. But I also hadn't quite understood how considerable are the resources the business community can call on when it is serious.

25 I'd known that a significant part of a product's cost was spent on marketing and advertising, but I hadn't appreciated how much time, labour and money could go into the development of a brand. As my work with Dove developed, I began to feel increasingly hopeful about how we might begin to challenge the negative aspects of what I'd come to call the visual musak—the ersatz femininity—around us and to include diverse, vibrant, pleasing and sexy images of women of all sizes, ages and physical types.

One of my key objectives was to get across the idea that recent times have seen a widening, a democratising, of the idea that everyone could be beautiful. Triggered by Twiggy and then fully realised by the Kate Moss generation (as much because of their class backgrounds as their skinniness), beauty had moved from being the interest of the few to the aspiration of all girls and women. This was pretty positive stuff in itself. But the terms and the expansion of beauty faltered on a paradox. The industry was simultaneously promoting an anti-democratic ideal of beauty that was narrow (literally) and excluding. Everyone had to be thin, thinner, thinnest.

If Dove was going to turn around the limited, destructive aspects of the beauty and dieting industries, then it was going to have to produce bold, startling, appealing images of women in all their sumptuous variety that would swagger in and dent the visual field. Dove would have to find a way to meet women where they had trained their eyes to be—on those images of skinny, untouchable and yet needy sexy women—and touch them deeply and humorously enough to bring them to where I knew from my clinical practice they wanted to be: appreciated for their magnificent differences, their uniqueness, not their sameness.

Women have had enough of not finding themselves in the ads they look at. If Dove could get it right, other companies would be playing catch-up. And, of course, they did. Within months of the launch of the 'campaign for real beauty', Revlon hired Susan Sarandon as one of its faces. It was a vindication that not only had Dove and Ogilvy caught the zeitgeist, but others would follow and the aims of the campaign would be met not just by women flocking to their brand, but also by their competitors.

What impressed the most and continues to impress me is the commitment of the leadership team at Dove—Silvia Lagnado, Alessandro Manfredi, Erin Iles and Daryl Fielding and, of course, White. They're making the campaign work. Everyone doing Dove business now asks the questions I was brought in to help them confront in order to make the campaign effective. How does this marketing help women's and girls' self esteem? In what ways could it harm them? How does this product affect me? How do I want it to affect my daughter, my niece, my sister, my wife? How can I make a positive impact and turn the scourge of body hatred around? How can I be a global player in the beauty industry spreading good feelings about women's bodies rather than promoting insecurity?

30 How can I give girls and women a chance to enter into a new, contented relationship with their bodies?

These are deep, painful and complex issues. That's why they called in the shrink. But, as their performance so far shows, it is a really good start.

Reflect & Write

- ❑ In this article, Orbach chronicles the process she used to persuade Unilever, the makers of Dove beauty products, to embrace the Campaign for Real Beauty. How did Orbach and the O&M team deploy strategies of *pathos*, *ethos*, and *logos* to accomplish their goals? Consider the order in which they used these appeals. Why did they structure their patterns of persuasion in this way?
- ❑ How might Orbach be trying to make the same argument she makes to Unilever to the reader? In which paragraphs can you see places where she makes her case to both audiences?
- ❑ At one point, Orbach claims that in order to be successful at this campaign, Dove was going to have to "produce bold, startling, appealing images of women in all their sumptuous variety that would swagger in and dent the visual field." Look at the images from the Dove campaign, linked through the *Envision* Website. Has Dove accomplished this goal? What differences do you see between Dove's campaign, and advertisements produced by other beauty product companies? www.pearsonhighered.com/envision/389
- ❑ **Write.** Some might argue that the Campaign for Real Beauty is simply an *ethos* appeal to the consumer. Write an essay in which you argue this point, considering whether or not the campaign has the potential to enhance or detract from the popularity of Dove's products—or whether it will have no distinguishable effect overall.

John Riviello *is a graphic designer specializing in Flash animations. The screenshots below are from a movie that is part of Riviello's Website on body image issues and their relationship to the diet industry, fashion magazines, and consumers's self-perceptions.*

What If Barbie Was an Actual Person? A Flash Movie

John Riviello

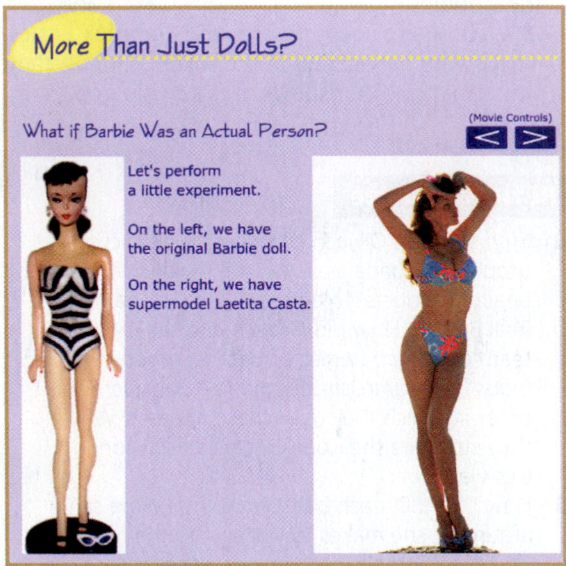

FIGURE 12.5. These screenshots from John Riviello's site juxtapose Barbie against a real model to demonstrate the differences between idealized versions of female beauty.

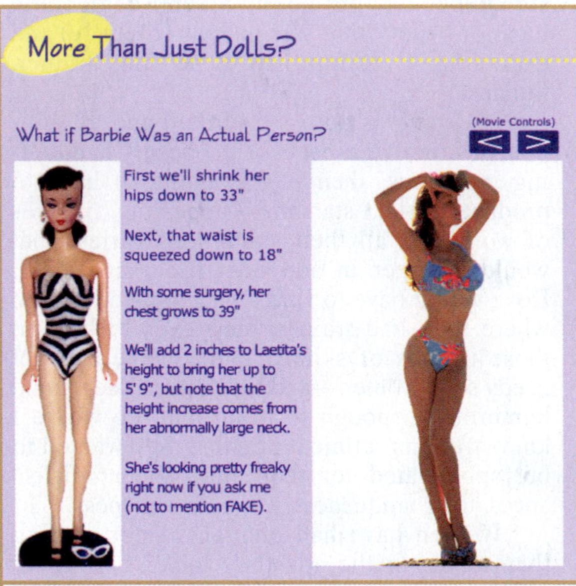

FIGURE 12.6. Riviello combines *pathos* and *logos* in this image by basing his striking visual modifications of the model's body in specific physical measurements.

Reflect & Write

Seeing Connections

For an alternative visual critique of Barbie, see the Body Shop Op-Ad on page 181.

- ❑ In his visual argument, Riviello pairs an image of a vintage Barbie with a photo of model Laetitia Casta. To argue his point, he both explains how he would transform Laetitia and then actually modifies her picture to reflect these alterations. What are the benefits of constructing his argument in this way? Why show both Laetitia and the Barbie? Is this an effective structure for the argument? Why?
- ❑ In the last frame (not shown), after Laetitia's eyes bulge cartoonishly in horror at her undersized feet, she disintegrates into a heap of dust, leaving us looking only at the vintage Barbie. To what extent is this an effective conclusion? What rhetorical appeals does it draw on?
- ❑ Visit the Flash animation itself, linked through the *Envision* Website. How does watching the animation change the effect of the argument demonstrated by the static images alone? What does the new media component add to the argument? www.pearsonhighered.com/envision/390

- ❑ **Write.** Riviello could have written his argument as an academic essay, but he chose instead to use a Flash movie to argue his point. Write an essay in which you move through the same process of argumentation that he does, but use a more academic style. What adjustments did you have to make to convert his argument? Is one more effective than the other? Why or why not?

■ *This poster is part of the* **National Eating Disorders Association***'s broader campaign to promote new programs and academic curricula designed to educate the populace about the dangers of eating disorders. This campaign produces a variety of visual arguments, some of which address the problems associated with anorexia and bulimia, and others which promote girls' positive self-image and a healthy relationship with food.*

2004 Get Real Campaign Ad

National Eating Disorders Association

FIGURE 12.7. This 2004 ad was featured as part of its "Get Real" campaign for National Eating Disorders Awareness Week.

Reflect & Write

- ❑ The first sentence of the copy below the image in this ad reads: "Girls with eating disorders can't see what's real." How does the image visually underscore this claim? What other images might the NEDA have used to visualize this claim?
- ❑ Look at the relationship between the text and image. Why is the ad laid out this way? What voices does the written text represent? How are those different voices portrayed visually?
- ❑ Now consider the visual elements of this hybrid composition. What is the function of the mirror? Of the bones? What is the effect of having the "real" girl be skeletal and the reflective image not?
- ❑ **Write.** Visit the "Obsession" and "Reality" Adbuster ads, linked through the *Envision* Website. Examine how they use different rhetorical strategies to make similar arguments. In each case, how are their purposes and their audiences different? Sketch out a design for your own parody poster to raise awareness among young girls about the dangers of eating disorders. Make it a hybrid composition by including both visual and written elements. Peer review your work with a partner before presenting it to the class.
  www.pearsonhighered.com/envision/391

Seeing Connections
The strategies for creating Op-Ads on pages 181–183 can provide guidance for designing an effective poster.

COLLABORATIVE CHALLENGE

The posters created by the National Eating Disorders Association primarily focus on body image issues and eating disorders experienced by young girls. Working as a group, identify body image problems facing boys in your community. Working in a team, create a poster (using both images and written text) aimed at addressing body image in young boys. Be sure to decide on your argument before drafting your poster: for instance, your poster could be designed either to promote positive body image or to call attention to male body image problems. Share your work with your class.

Susan McClelland *is an associate editor for* Maclean's, *a Canadian weekly newsmagazine, where this article appeared on August 14, 2000. She has also written an article on male body image, entitled, "The Lure of the Body Image: In Their Quest for the Beefcake Look, Some Men Try Extreme Measures," and has received several awards for investigative reporting.*

Distorted Images: Western Cultures are Exporting Their Dangerous Obsession with Thinness

Susan McClelland

When Zahra Dhanani was just seven years old, her four-foot frame already packed 100 lb.—so her mother, Shahbanu, put her on her first diet. "My mother, a fat woman, daughter of another fat woman, thought if I was skinny, different from her, I would be happy," says Dhanani. The diet, and many after, did not have the desired effect. By 13, Dhanani was sporadically swallowing appetite suppressants; at 17, she vomited and used laxatives to try to keep her weight under control. There were times when she wanted to die. "I had so much self-hate," recalls the 26-year-old Toronto immigration lawyer, "I couldn't look in the mirror without feeling revulsion."

The hate reflected more than just weight. "It was race," says Dhanani, who had moved with her family to Canada from East Africa when she was 4. "I was straightening my hair—doing anything to look white." Her recovery only began when, at age 19, she started to identify with women in other cultures. "I came to realize that there were people who revered large women of colour," says Dhanani, who now says she loves all of her 200 lb. She blames part of her earlier eating disorders on the images in western media: "When you have no role models to counteract the messages that fat is repulsive, it's hard to realize that you are a lovable human being."

Body image may be one of the western world's ugliest exports. Thanks to television, magazines, movies and the Internet, rail-thin girls and steroid-built beef-boys are being shoved in the faces of people all over the world. As a result, experts say, cultures that used to regard bulk as a sign of wealth and success are now succumbing to a narrow western standard of beauty. And that, in turn, is leading to incidences of eating disorders in regions where anorexia and bulimia had never been seen before. But body-image anxiety in ethnic cultures runs much deeper than weight. In South Africa, almost six years after the end of apartheid, black women still use harmful skin-bleaching creams in the belief that whiter is prettier. "We're seeing a homogenization and globalization of beauty ideals," says Niva Piran, a clinical psychologist at the University of Toronto. "It's white. It's thin. And the result is that people come to identify less with their own cultures and more with an image in the media."

In most cultures, bigger was considered better until the 19th century. "The larger a man's wife, the more he was seen as a good provider," says Joan Jacobs Brumberg, a professor of American women's history at Cornell University and author of *Fasting Girls: The History of Anorexia Nervosa*. That began to change during the Industrial Revolution, she says, as women in the United States and Great Britain began to see thinness as a way to differentiate themselves from the lower classes. By the 1920s, fat was seen as unhealthy. And in the burgeoning magazine, movie and fashion industries, the women depicted as being successful in love, career and finances were slim and almost always white.

5 Still, eating disorders are not a modern affliction. Records of women starving themselves (anorexia) date back to the medieval period (1200 to 1500). As Brumberg notes in *Fasting Girls*, during this time, a woman who did not eat was admired for having found some other form of sustenance than food, like prayer. Yet, until the last century, the number of women who fasted was low. But, particularly over the past 30 years, the number of anorexics and women who self-induce vomiting (bulimia) or use laxatives has increased dramatically. "It's generally this obsession with the body, constant weight-watching, that introduces a person to these behaviours," says Merryl Bear of the Toronto-based National Eating Disorder Information Centre. It was commonly believed, however, that sufferers came predominantly from white, middle- and upper-class backgrounds. Experts thought ethnic minorities were immune because of their strong ties to communities that emphasize family and kinship over looks alone.

Studies done in the United States with Hispanic, black and Asian college students, however, show that women who are alienated from their minority cultures and integrated into mainstream society are prone to the same pressures of dieting as their white counterparts. In a recent study of South-Asian girls in Peel, Ont., 31 per cent responded that they were not comfortable with their body shape and size. Fifty-eight per cent compared their appearance with others, including fashion models—and 40 percent wanted to look like them.

Some of the most compelling research comes from Harvard Medical School psychiatrist Anne Becker, who was in Fiji in 1995 when the government announced that TV, including western programs, would be introduced. "Fijians revere a body that is sturdy, tall and large—features that show that the body is strong, hardworking and healthy," says Becker. "Thinness and sudden weight loss was seen as some kind of social loss or neglect."

In 1998, Becker returned to Fiji and found that this had all changed. Her studies showed that 29 percent of the girls now had symptoms of eating disorders. Many said they vomited to lose weight. But what was most alarming were the girls' responses about the role of television in their lives. "More than 80 percent said that watching TV affected the way they felt about their bodies," Becker says. "They said things such as, 'I watched the women on TV, they have jobs. I want to be like them, so I am working on my weight now.' These teenagers are getting the sense that as Fiji moves into the global economy, they had better find some way to make wages and they are desperate to find role models. The West to them means success and they are altering their bodies to compete."

Cheryl McConney has felt the pressures to alter her body, too. The black 32-year-old native of Richmond Hill, Ont., co-hosts a daytime talk show on cable TV. And although it has not been difficult for her to get where she is in her career, she is concerned about how to navigate her next step. "Looking at Canadian television, I don't see many people who look like me on air," she says. At five-foot-five, and weighing about 145 lb., McConney has never been told she should lose weight. Still, in 1998, she went on a six-month, high-protein, low-carbohydrate diet, hoping to look better in front of the camera. She shed 20 lb. "I felt good. People in the studio thought I looked great, but it wasn't easy to maintain." Within a year, she had gained it all back.

10 For McConney, race has been more of an issue. An industry insider jokingly told her that she would do better if she dyed her hair blond. And just a few months ago, she was discouraged from applying for another on-air host position because of what the casting agents said they were looking for. "They wanted the 'girl next door' and 'peaches- and-cream' pretty, not chocolate and cream," says McConney, adding: "It was pretty clear some women were not invited to participate because of their skin colour." As to the girl next door part: "I said it just depends where you live."

While McConney says she is determined to make it on-air despite the barriers, Linda, who requested Maclean's not use her real name, may not be around to see her success. The 19-year-old—part South African and part East

Indian—has anorexia. She says trying to fit into a Canadian suburban community played a big role in her illness. "I was never proud of my different religion, different skin colour," she says. "I would put white baby powder on my cheeks just to make me look white." What alarms her now, Linda says, is that with her skin pale from malnutrition and her weight fluctuating between 75 and 85 lb., other young women often come up to her and say, "You look so good, I wish I looked like you." But she adds: "What they don't know is that my body is decaying. People glamorize eating disorders. But what it is is a lifetime of hospitalization and therapy." As long as the western media promote thinness and whiteness as the pinnacle of beauty, stories like Linda's will remain all too familiar.

Reflect & Write

- ❑ In this article, Susan McClelland addresses not only the way body image relates to thinness but also its relationship to different racial features and skin color. Do you agree that the media tends to model its ideal of beauty around a Caucasian standard? What evidence can you cite from your own observations to support your opinion?
- ❑ What rhetorical appeals does McClelland utilize in this article? *Pathos*? *Logos*? *Ethos*? Which does she use most prominently and which is most powerful in solidifying her argument?
- ❑ **Write.** Look at international or culturally targeted beauty magazines at your local bookstore or news stand. Select a few images or ads, and draft your own argument concerning how that magazine defines beauty. Does it seem reliant on white, Western standards? Does it offer new or alternative visions?

During the early twentieth century, **Charles Atlas**, *inspired by a statue of Hercules, started body building and within a few years became known as "The World's Most Perfectly Developed Man." He and partner Charles P. Roman founded Charles Atlas, Ltd., a company dedicated to selling the secrets of masculine health and fitness. His advertisements, including "Hey Skinny," "97 lb. weakling," and "The insult that made a man out of 'Mac'" (right), appeared in the back of numerous comic books and newspapers and continue to circulate as examples of vintage American advertising.*

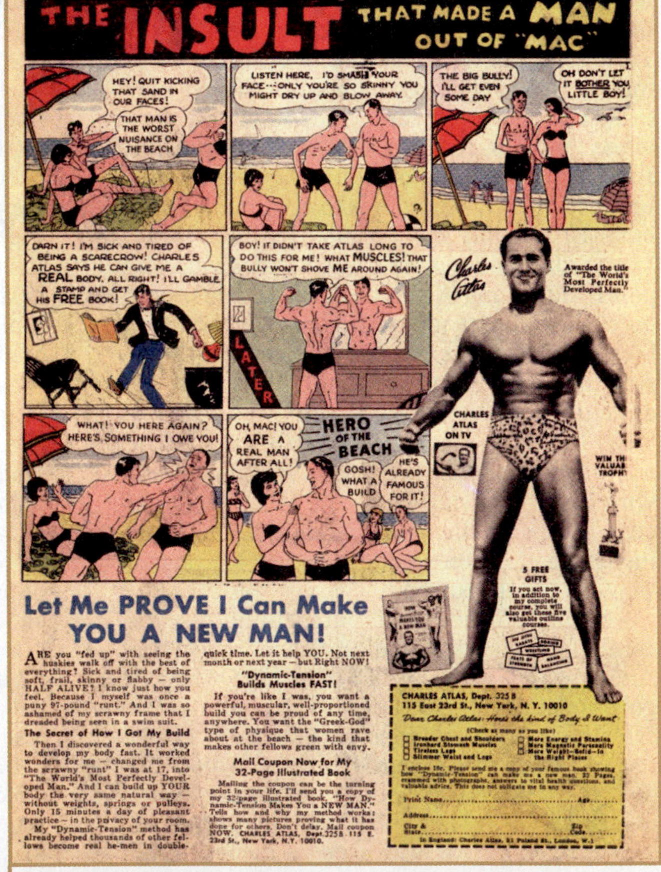

FIGURE 12.8. Blending cartoon and advertisement, this vintage Charles Atlas ad marketed a 32-page illustrated book designed to "make a man" out of the reader.

Reflect & Write

- ❑ How are *pathos*, *logos*, and *ethos* used in this advertisement to increase its persuasiveness?
- ❑ Visit the online Atlas archive linked, through the *Envision* Website and examine other similar ads. How do these ads use similar strategies to the one shown here? Are there any that make more effective arguments? What elements make those arguments more persuasive?
  www.pearsonhighered.com/envision/395
- ❑ Consider the issue of male body image. Although the Atlas ads are dated, can you find examples of similar pressures in contemporary culture? Where would you be most likely to find stereotypes of male body image? How do pressures about male body image compare to pressures about female body image?
- ❑ **Write.** Considering the pressures that face men and boys today in terms of body image, storyboard your own advertisement for a fictitious contemporary product or service that will make a "man" out of a modern-day "Mac."

Seeing Connections
See Chapter 2 to review how *pathos*, *logos*, *ethos*, and *kairos* function persuasively in arguments.

This landmark article, which investigates the relationship between boys' body image and action toys, first appeared in the International Journal of Eating Disorders *in 1999. The research later was featured in a key section of* The Adonis Complex *(2000), a book-length study of male body image.* **Harrison Pope** *and* **Amanda Gruber** *are professors of psychiatry at Harvard Medical School, and* **Robert Olivardia** *is a clinical instructor at the same institution.*

Evolving Ideals of Male Body Image as Seen Through Action Toys

Harrison G. Pope, Jr., Robert Olivardia, Amanda Gruber, and John Borowiecki

Abstract: **Objective:** *We hypothesized that the physiques of male action toys—small plastic figures used by children in play—would provide some index of evolving American cultural ideals of male body image.* **Method:** *We obtained examples of the most popular American action toys manufactured over the last 30 years. We then measured the waist, chest, and bicep circumference of each figure and scaled these measurements using classical allometry to the height of an actual man (1.78 m).* **Results:** *We found that the figures have grown much more muscular over time, with many contemporary figures far exceeding the muscularity of even the largest human bodybuilders.* **Discussion:** *Our observations appear to represent a "male analog" of earlier studies examining female dolls, such as Barbie. Together, these studies of children's toys suggest that cultural expectations may contribute to body image disorders in both sexes.* *© 1999 by John Wiley & Sons, Inc.* Int J Eat Disord 26: 65–72, 1999.

Key words: *male body image; male action toys; body image disorders*

Introduction

A growing body of literature has described disorders of body image among men. For example, such disturbances are frequently documented in men with eating disorders. In one study, college men with eating disorders reported a degree of body dissatisfaction closely approaching that of women with eating disorders, and strikingly greater than comparison men (Olivardia, Pope, Mangweth, & Hudson, 1995). Other studies of men with eating disorders have produced similar findings (Andersen, 1990; Schneider & Agras, 1987). Even in studies of male students without eating disorders, the prevalence of body dissatisfaction is often striking (Mintz & Betz, 1986; Drewnowski & Yee, 1987; Dwyer, Feldman, Seltzer, & Mayer, 1969). Body image disturbances may be particularly prominent in American culture. In a recent crosscultural comparison, groups of American college men reported significantly greater dissatisfaction with their bodies than comparable groups in Austria (Mangweth et al., 1997).

Another form of body image disturbance, also frequently affecting men, is body dysmorphic disorder (Phillips, 1991, 1997; Hollander, Cohen, & Simeon, 1993). Individuals with this disorder may develop obsessional preoccupations that their facial features are ugly, that their hairlines are receding, or that their penis size is too small—to name several of the more common presentations. Recently, we have described another form of body dysmorphic disorder found in both sexes, but probably more prevalent in men, which we have called "muscle dysmorphia" (Pope, Gruber, Choi, Olivardia, & Phillips, 1997). Individuals with muscle dysmorphia report an obsessional preoccupation with their muscularity, to the point where their social and occupational functioning may be severely impaired. For example, they may abandon important social and family relationships, or even relinquish professional careers, in order to spend more time at the gym (Pope et al., 1997). Many report that they refuse to be seen in public without their shirts on because they fear that they will look too small (Pope, Katz, & Hudson, 1993), Often they use anabolic steroids or other performance-enhancing drugs, continuing to take these agents even in the face of serious side effects because of persistent anxiety about their muscularity (Pope et al., 1993; Pope & Katz, 1994).

In many ways, muscle dysmorphia appears to be part of the "obsessive-compulsive spectrum" of disorders (Hollander, 1993; Phillips, McElroy, Hudson, & Pope, 1995). It is characterized by obsessional preoccupations and impulsive behaviors similar to those of classical obsessive-compulsive disorder. If this hypothesis is correct, it is natural to ask why modem American men with muscle dysmorphia would have developed this particular outlet for their obsessions, as opposed to a more traditional symptom pattern such as hand-washing or checking rituals.

One possible explanation for this phenomenon is that in our culture, the ideal male body is growing steadily more muscular. With the advent of anabolic steroids in the last 30 to 40 years, it has become possible for men to become much more muscular than is possible by natural means. Bodybuilders who won the Mr. America title in the presteroid era could not hope to compete against steroid-using bodybuilders today (Kouri, Pope, Katz, & Oliva, 1995). The public is exposed daily, in magazines, motion pictures, and other media, to increasingly—and often unnaturally—muscular male images. Some individuals, responding to these cultural messages, may become predisposed to develop muscle dysmorphia.

5 In an attempt to provide some quantitative data bearing on this hypothesis, we examined the physiques of American action toys over the last 30 years.

Methods

Action toys are small plastic figures, typically ranging from 3 3/4 in. to 12 in. in height, used by children in play, and frequently collected by adult hobbyists. Among the best known examples are the GI Joe figures, Star Wars and Star Trek characters, Superman, Spiderman, and Batman. Contemporary versions of these figures are readily available at toy stores and vintage figures may be purchased through a vast and well-organized collectors' market. Extensive reference works, such as the 480-page *Encyclopedia of GI Joe* (Santelmo, 1997), document the evolution of these figures over the years. We chose to study these toys because, unlike cartoon characters or movie stars, they can be readily physically measured, allowing accurate comparisons between figures of different eras.

We consulted with various action toy experts to ascertain toys which had been produced in various iterations by the same manufacturer over a period of 20 years or more. To obtain an objective index of the popularity of specific toys, we consulted the 1st through 15th annual sales surveys by *Playthings* magazine, published in the December issue of each year from 1983 to 1997 (*Playthings* magazine), to confirm that the toy had been among the 10 best-selling toy product lines in several years spanning the last two decades. We also required that the toy represent an actual male human being (such as a soldier or Luke Skywalker), rather than a nonhuman creature (such as Mr. Potato Head or the Teen-Age Mutant Ninja Turtles). Two toy product lines met all of these criteria: the GI Joe series manufactured by the Hasbro Toy Company since 1964 and the Star Wars figures manufactured by the Kenner Toy Company (a subsidiary of Hasbro) since 1978. We then purchased representative examples of these figures from different time periods. We also visited a branch of a large toy store chain and purchased additional examples of toys identified by store officials and by the most recent *Playthings* surveys as the most popular contemporary male action figures. Some of these latter figures, such as Batman and the Mighty Morphin Power Rangers, might not be considered completely "human," in that they possess powers beyond those of a real human being. Others, such as the X-Men, are mutants of human beings. However, they all possess essentially human bodies.

We then measured the waist, chest, and bicep circumference of all the figures and scaled these measurements using classical allometry (Norton, Olds, Olive, & Dank, 1996) to a common height of 1.78 m (70 in.).

Results

GI Joe

The action toy with the longest continuous history is GI Joe. The Hasbro Toy Company first introduced GI Joe as an 11 1/2-in. posable figure in 1964 (Santelmo, 1997). This figure continued without a change in body style as the GI Joe Adventurer in 1970 to 1973. It developed a new body style from 1973 to 1976 as the GI Joe Adventurer with kung-fu grip and lifelike body. In the late 1970s, production of the 11 1/2-in. figures was discontinued, being replaced by a series of 3 3/4-in. figures that was introduced in 1982. These smaller figures continued through 11 series over the next 10 years, eventually attaining a height of 4 1/2 in. and culminating in the GI Joe Extreme. This was a 5-in. figure

Table 1. Measurements of representative action toys extrapolated to a height of 70 in.

	Actual Measurements (in.)[a]				Extrapolated to Height of 70 in.[a]		
Toy. Date	Height	Waist	Chest	Biceps	Waist[b]	Chest[b]	Biceps[b]
GI Joe Land Adventurer, 1973 (with original body in use since 1964)	11.5	5.2	7.3	2.1	31.7	44.4	12.2
GI Joe Land Adventurer, 1975 (with new body introduced in 1974)	11.5	5.2	7.3	2.5	31.7	44.4	15.2
GI Joe Hall of Fame Soldier, 1994 (with body introduced in 1991)	11.5	4.8	7.1	2.7	29.2	43.2	16.4
GI Joe Extreme, 1998	5.8	3.0[c]	4.5[c]	2.2	36.5[c]	54.8[c]	26.8
The Gold Ranger, 1998	5.5	2.7	3.6	1.4[c]	34.4[c]	45.8[c]	17.8[c]
Ahmed Johnson, 1998	6.0	3.0	4.1	2.0	35.0	47.8	23.3
Iron Man, 1998	6.5	2.6	4.7	2.1	28.0	50.6	22.6
Batman, 1998	6.0	2.6	4.9	2.3	30.3	57.2	26.8
Wolverine, 1998	7.0	3.3	6.2	3.2	33.0	62.0	32.0

[a]Measurements estimated to the nearest 0.1 in.
[b]For comparison, the mean waist, chest, and biceps circumferences of 50 Australian soccer players, scaled to a slightly shorter height of 170.2 cm (67 in). were found to be 29.6 in., 36.3 in., and 11.8 in., respectively (19).
[c]These numbers are reduced by about 5% from actual measurments to compensate for the thickness of the figure's clothes and equipment.

(5.8 in. with knees and waist straightened) that was introduced in 1995 and is still available on the shelves of toy stores today. Meanwhile, the 11 1/2-in. figures were reintroduced in 1991 and continue to be manufactured to the present.

10 We purchased three representative 11 1/2-in. figures: a 1973 Adventurer with the original body in use since 1964, a 1975 Adventurer with the newer lifelike body, and a 1994 Hall of Fame figure. A photograph of these three figures appears in Figure 1 and their dimensions are shown in Table 1. Not only have the figures grown more muscular, but they have developed increasingly sharp muscular definition through the years. For example, the earliest figure has no visible abdominal muscles; his 1975 counterpart shows some abdominal definition; and the 1994 figure displays the sharply rippled abdominals of an advanced bodybuilder. The modern figure also displays distinct serratus muscles along his ribs—a feature readily seen in bodybuilders but less often visible in ordinary men.

FIGURE 1. GI Joe Sergeant Savage, 1982 (left); GI Joe Cobra Soldier, 1982 (middle); and GI Joe Extreme Sergeant Savage. 1998 (right) (Hasbro).

We also purchased several of the smaller figures for comparison—a 1982 Grunt, a 1982 Cobra soldier (GI Joe's archenemy), and a current GI Joe Extreme. As shown in Figure 1, the contemporary GI Joe Extreme dwarfs his earlier counterparts with dramatically greater musculature and has an expression of rage which contrasts sharply with the bland faces of his predecessors. Although the body dimensions of the earlier small action figures cannot be accurately estimated because of their layer of clothing, the GI Joe Extreme is more easily measured (see Table 1). If extrapolated to 70 in. in height, the GI Joe Extreme would sport larger biceps than any bodybuilder in history.

FIGURE 2. Luke Skywalker and Hans Solo, 1978 (left); Luke Skywalker and Hans Solo, 1998 (right) (Kenner).

Luke Skywalker and Hans Solo

A similar impression emerges upon examining the original (1978) versus the contemporary 3 3/4-in. figures of Star Wars characters Luke Skywalker and Hans Solo (manufactured by the Kenner Toy Company). As shown in Figure 2, Luke and Hans have both acquired the physiques of bodybuilders over the last 20 years, with particularly impressive gains in the shoulder and chest areas. Again, the clothing on these small plastic figures precludes accurate body measurements, so that they are not included in Table 1.

Modern Figures

Figure 4 [not shown here] depicts five more examples from the most popular contemporary lines of male action figures. As mentioned earlier, it might be argued that most of these characters are not entirely human, in that they possess powers beyond those of real people. Nevertheless, they are given fundamentally human bodies, but with musculature that ranges from merely massive to well beyond that of the biggest bodybuilders (Table 1).

Discussion

We hypothesized that action toys would illustrate evolving ideals of male body image in the United States. Accordingly, we purchased and measured the most popular male human action figures which have been manufactured over the last 30 years. On both visual inspection and anthropomorphic measurement, it appears that action figures today are consistently much more muscular than their predecessors. Many modern figures display the physiques of advanced bodybuilders and some display levels of muscularity far exceeding the outer limits of actual human attainment.

15 These findings, however, must be interpreted cautiously for several reasons. First, we found only two lines of male human action toys which fully met our criterion of long-term documented popularity. Thus, it might be argued that these particular toy lines happened to favor our hypothesis by chance alone. However, on the basis of our discussions with action figure experts, we believe that the examples analyzed here are representative of the overall trend of body image in male action toys over the last several decades. The other leading contemporary toys, shown in Figure 4 [not shown here], support the impression that this trend

toward a bodybuilder physique is consistent. The only notable exception to this trend is the Mattel Company's Ken, the boyfriend of Barbie. However, although the Barbie toy line overall has frequently ranked among the top 10 toy lines, Ken is but a small part of this market. Among boys in particular, Ken almost certainly ranks well below the popularity of the other male action figure discussed above (*Playthings* magazine).

Second, it is uncertain whether action toys accurately mirror trends in other media. It is our impression that comic strip characters, male models in magazines, and male motion picture actors have all shown a parallel trend toward increasing leanness and muscularity over the last several decades. However, more systematic studies will be required to confirm these observations.

Third, it is not clear to what extent these trends in toys, or parallel trends in other media, may be a cause or effect of an evolving cultural emphasis on male muscularity. Certainly, it would be premature to conclude that American men are prompted to develop disorders of body image purely as a result of boyhood exposure to muscular ideals of male physique. On the other hand, the impact of toys should not be underestimated. Male action toys as a whole accounted for $949 million in manufacturers' shipments in 1994 alone, with action figures accounting for $687 million of this total (*Playthings* magazine, 1995).

20 It should also be noted that similar theories have been advanced for many years regarding cultural ideals of thinness in women (Pope & Hudson, 1984; Cash & Pruzinsky, 1990). For example, one study found that both *Playboy* centerfold models and Miss America pageant contestants grew steadily thinner over the period of l959 to 1978 (Garner, Garfinkel, Schwartz, & Thompson, 1980). A recent update suggests that this trend has continued at least through 1988 (Wiseman, Gray, Mosimann, & Ahrens, 1992). Similarly, in the area of toys, the literature has documented the inappropriate thinness of modern female dolls (Norton et al., 1996, Pederson & Markee, 1991; Rintala & Mustajoki, 1992; Brownell & Napolitano, 1995). Indeed, one report has found that Mattel Company's Barbie, if extrapolated to a height of 67 in., would have a waist circumference of l6 in. (Norton et al., 1996)—a figure approaching the impossibility of our male superheroes' biceps.

In any event, these striking findings suggest that further attempts should be made to assess the relationship between cultural messages and body image disorders in both men and women.

The authors thank Erik Flint of Cotswold Collectibles, Whitbey Island, WA; Vincent Santelmo of the Official Action Figure Warehouse, New York, NY; and Jeff Freeman of the Falcon's Hangar, Auburn, IN, for their assistance in the selection and purchase of action toys and in the preparation of this manuscript.

References

Action figures duke it out. (1995). Playthings magazine, 93, 26–28.

Andersen, A.E. (Ed). (1990) Males with eating disorders. New York: Brunner Mazel.

Brownell, K.D., & Napolitano, M.A. (1995). Distorting reality for children: Body size proportions of Barbie and Ken dolls. International Journal of Eating Disorders, 18, 295–298.

Cash, T.F., & Pruzinsky, T. (Eds), (1990). Body images: Developments, deviance, and change, New York: Guilford.

Drewnowski, A., & Yee, D.K. (1987). Men and body image: Are males satisfied with their body weight? Psychosomatic Medicine. 49, 626–634.

Dwyer, J.T., Feldman, J.J., Seltzer, C.C., & Mayer, J. (1969). Body image in adolescents: Attitudes toward weight and perception of appearance. American Journal of Clinical Nutrition, 20, 1045–1056.

Garner, D.M., Garfinkel, P.E., Schwartz, D., & Thompson, M. (1980). Cultural expectations of thinness in women. Psychological Reports, 47, 483–491.

Hollander, E. (1993). Introduction. In E. Hollander, (Ed.), Obsessive-compulsive related disorders. Washington, DC: American Psychiatric Press.

Hollander, E., Cohen, I. J., & Simeon, D. (1993). Body dysmorphic disorder. Psychiatric Annals, 23, 359–364.

Kouri, E., Pope. H.G., Katz. D.L., & Oliva, P. (1995). Fat-free mass index in users and non-users of anabolic-androgenic steroids. Clinical Journal of Sport Medicine, 5, 223–228.

Mangweth, B., Pope. H.G., Jr., Hudson. J.I., Olivardia, R., Kinzi. J., & Biebl, W. (1997). Eating disorders in Austrian men: An intra-cultural and cross-cultural comparison study. Psychotherapy and Psychosomatics 66, 214–221.

Mintz, L.B., & Betz., N.E., (1986). Sex differences in the nature, realism, and correlates of body image. Sex Roles, 15, 185–195.

Norton, K.E., Olds, T.S., Olive. S., & Dank, S. (1996). Ken and Barbie at life size Sex Roles, 84, 287–294.

Olivardia, R., Pope, H.G., Jr., Mangweth., B., & Hudson, J.I. (1995). Eating disorders in college men. American Journal of Psychiatry, 152. 1279–1285.

Petersen, E.L., & Markee, N.L. (1991). Fashion dolls; Representations of ideals of beauty. Perceptual and Motor Skills, 73, 93–94.

Phillips, K.A. (1991). Body dysmorphic disorder. The distress of imagined, ugliness. American Journal of Psychiatry, 148, 1138–1149.

Phillips, K.A. (1997). The broken mirror. New York: Oxford University Press.

Phillips, K.A., McElroy, S.L., Hudson, J.I., & Pope, H.G., Jr. (1995). Body dysmorphic disorder: An obsessive-compulsive spectrum disorder, a form of affective spectrum disorder, or both? Journal of Clinical Psychiatry, 56 (Suppl. 4), 41–51.

Playthings. (1983–1997). New York: Geyer-McAlister Publications, Inc.

Pope, H.G., Jr., Gruber. A.J., Choi, P.Y., Olivadia. R., & Phillips. K.S, (1997). Muscle dysmorphia: An under-recognized form of body dysmorphic disorder. Psychosomatics, 38, 348–557.

Pope, H.G., Jr., & Hudson, J.I. (1984). New hope for binge eaters. Advances in the understanding and treatment of bulimia. New York: Harper and Row.

Pope, H.G., Jr., & Katz, D.L. (1994). Psychiatric and medical effects of anabolic-androgenic steroids. A controlled study of 160 athletes. Archives of General Psychiatry, 51, 375–382.

Pope, H.G., Jr., Katz. D.L., & Hudson. J.I. (1993). Anorexia nervosa and "reverse anorexia" among 108 male bodybuilders. Comprehensive Psychiatry, 34, 406–409.

Rintala, M., & Mustajoki, P. (1992). Could mannequins menstruate? British Medical Journal, 305, 1575–1576.

Santelmo, V. (1997). The complete encyclopedia to GI Joe (2nd ed.). Jola, WI: Krause Publications.

Schneider, J.A., & Agras, W.S. (1987). Bulimia in males: A matched comparison with females. International Journal of Eating Disorders, 6, 235–242.

Wiseman, C.V., Gray, J.J., Mosimann, J.E., & Abrens A.H. (1992). Cultural expectations of thinness: An update, International Journal of Eating Disorders, 11, 85–90.

Copyright of *International Journal of Eating Disorders* is the property of John Wiley & Sons Inc. and its content may not be copied or emailed to multiple sites or posted to a listserv without the copyright holder's express written permission. However, users may print, download, or email articles for individual use.

Reflect & Write

- ❑ Summarize the thesis in your own words. How does the historical examination of action toys provide powerful evidence about social norms for male body image? At the end of your summary, write a one-line response to the argument.
- ❑ How do the images work in conjunction with the written text to create a persuasive argument? What would be lost in terms of the argument's effectiveness without them? What is gained from viewing the visual rhetoric?
- ❑ How do the pressures facing boys differ from those facing girls? What can you add from your own experience in terms of how the media shapes body image standards along gender lines?
- ❑ Are the examples used in this article culturally specific? What kinds of toys or representatives of male bodies are common in different parts of the United States—in cities versus the countryside—or in different parts of the world?
- ❑ **Write.** This collaborative article was written for an academic audience. Draft a version of this article that could be published as a short opinion piece in a popular magazine. Include quotes from this article as if citing an interview.

Seeing Connections
Review Chapter 3's discussion of the canon of Style (page 53) and Chapter 8's discussion of levels of decorum (pages 168–169) to help you adapt the article for a popular audience.

COLLABORATIVE CHALLENGE

Together with two classmates, go to a toy store or visit one online and do your own survey of recent toys for boys. Look at Transformers, Rescue Heroes, Bionicles, and comic book heroes like Spiderman, Batman, and the X-Men. Also look at the Star Wars Clone Wars line and G.I. Joe toys. Write an essay in which you use your own observations on recent toys to either support, qualify, or refute the article's assertions about body image as projected through toy culture for boys. You might take digital photos of toys you find at the store and use them in your essay. Convert your writing to a presentation and share your work with the rest of the class, making sure each team member takes a turn in presenting part of the argument.

■ **Kim Franke-Folstad** *is a columnist for the* Rocky Mountain News, *where this article was originally published on May 24, 1999, in reaction to Harrison Pope's 1999 study on action toys and male body images.*

G.I. Joe's Big Biceps Are Not a Big Deal

Kim Franke-Folstad

Say it isn't so, Joe.

For years, I've been defending Barbie against accusations that she promotes an unrealistic body image for little girls.

And now it turns out good old G.I. Joe has been subjected to the same silly poking and probing, the same plastic-to-flesh measurement com-parisons and similarly ugly allegations that he's encouraging young boys to seek an artificially enhanced physique.

Will this foolishness never stop?

5 The latest bit of bicep bashing comes from Harvard psychiatrist Harrison Pope, who's apparently spent years studying hard-bodied action figures and how they affect the way males feel their real-life bodies should look.

Big, bulging and buff.

According to Pope's research, the plastic playthings are getting ever more muscle-bound, and young men are, too—often by abusing anabolic steroids.

The doctor says he can't be sure which came first: bulked-up toys or bulked-up boys. But, either way, when a G.I. Joe's bicep measurement translates to an impossible 26 inches for a real he-man, it could mean a dangerous trend.

Here we go again.

10 Barbie's bust is too big, her waist is too small, her arches (both foot and eyebrow) are unreasonably high. G.I. Joe's arms are too thick, his chest is too chiseled and the muscles in his massive thighs are ridiculously rippled.

So what?

They are toys. We all know that. That's why we stop playing with them before we get out of grade school.

Well, most of us, anyway.

Besides, if anything, I'm more comfortable with the freakish physiques of today's action figures than I was with the more realistic and appropriately proportioned appearance of my brother's G.I. Joe back in the 1960s.

15 Now, instead of sending a dog-tagged doll that looks like your next door neighbor's older brother into battle, it's more like you've dispatched a cartoon superhero. Of course bullets bounce off his chest and he's never afraid—he's not a man, he's a mutant with a crew cut and really great accessories.

Let's face it: Boys have wanted to bulk up—and do it quickly—since Charles Atlas promised he could transform any 90-pound weakling into a muscle man proud to stroll the beach in his Speedo. These days, young men (and not so young men) may be influenced by Mark McGwire's 19-inch biceps and the knowledge that he takes an over-the-counter testosterone booster. They may have noted the equally hunky Bill Romanowski's propensity for modeling EAS apparel. Or they could be checking out the bulging necks—and wallets—of popular professional wrestlers Goldberg and "Stone Cold" Steve Austin.

But a plastic doll?

Please. To suggest that even little boys measure manliness by taking a ruler to their G.I. Joes is comical.

And from here it looks as though the "real American hero's" musculature isn't the only thing being blown out of proportion.

Reflect & Write

- ❑ What is Franke-Folstad's argument in this article? Is it an effective rebuttal to Pope's claims? Do you find her argument convincing?

- ❑ Consider the author's voice. Does it try to be academic? Informal? Objective? Is this an effective choice for her argument?
- ❑ **Write.** Franke-Folstad does not include images in her article. Select an image or set of images (you can find them through a Google image search or by visiting a toy store and taking your own pictures with your digital camera) and write captions for them so that they function in support of her argument. Also consider where in the article you would place your visual rhetoric to maximize its persuasiveness.

PERSPECTIVES ON THE ISSUE

1. Visit the Love Your Body Day Website, linked through the *Envision* Website. Analyze the visual banner that runs along the top of the site. How does this make an effective visual argument for "Love Your Body"? Now compare this banner to the Dove Real Beauty Campaign, also linked through the *Envision* Website. What different strategies are used by each? Is one more successful than the other? If so, why? www.pearsonhighered.com/envision/404a
2. The National Eating Disorder Association poster featured in Figure 12.7 relies primarily on a pathos appeal to make its point. Conduct some research to locate further facts and statistics about anorexia in girls. Now, drawing on the lessons about visual arguments from Chapter 8, create an op-ad that relies on a *logos*-driven argument to make its point. Be sure to incorporate rhetorically purposeful images to substantiate and reinforce your argument.
3. Harrison Pope transformed his article, "Evolving Ideals of Male Body Image as Seen Through Action Toys" into a section of his book *The Adonis Complex* (NY: The Free Press, 2000). Locate this book in the library. Read pages 40–46 in *The Adonis Complex* and then write an essay in which you discuss the ways in which Pope developed the prose and content of his short piece into a longer research argument.
4. Follow the link on the *Envision* Website to the NPR transcript of "Cultural Differences Seen in Male Perceptions of Body Image," and also listen to the audio essay by following the link through the *Envision* Website. How does the audio version differ from the written transcript? Are the two pieces equally persuasive? Why or why not? www.pearsonhighered.com/envision/404b

FROM READING TO RESEARCH

1. Use a reference book such as Charles Goodrum and Helen Dalrymple's *Advertising in America* (NY: Harry N. Abrams Inc., 1990) or your own archival work with old magazines to get a sense of how magazines constructed ideals of beauty at a particular historical moment. Using specific examples from the advertisements and/or vintage magazine articles, write a persuasive essay that defines one of the foundations of beauty for that context.
2. What kinds of visual rhetoric might you design to address body image issues for women of different races and cultures? Research a body-image related topic for a specific population (for instance, skin bleaching among African-American women or eyelid surgery among Asian women), then mock up a public service media campaign (consisting of radio spots, print ads, and posters) designed to address this issue. Pitch your campaign to the class, making sure to be clear about your underlying claim about body image anxieties within that particular demographic.

FASHION STATEMENTS

Can we change the way people see us by purposefully altering our appearance through physical changes such as tattoos, piercings, or body art? Can we change how people look at us by deliberately putting on certain jewelry, clothes, or accessories? When we wear fashion, in many ways we seek to change the way we are seen by society. We use fashion to mark our bodies in a certain way and, in the process, we use visual markers to make a new argument about who we are. Sometimes this change is subtle: a tattoo hidden under clothes or a small cross around our necks. Other times, these visual signs stand as announcements to the world, such as when we wear a mohawk or certain clothes. In this way, we use fashion to make a statement about what we like, what we believe, where we belong, and how we think of ourselves in the world. As we'll learn in the pages that follow, fashion has long been used to make a statement about identity, values, and meaning in society. That is, fashion statements have served as arguments for centuries.

In this section, we'll start by considering how clothing and accessories are used to change the way the body looks. Specifically, we'll examine ways of using clothing fashion to make a statement about who we are, what we believe in, and how we want others to see us. Consider the woman in Figure 12.9. She wears a headscarf that matches her colorful outfit. She shops for jeans and shows a careful attention to style and the meaning of the clothes she wears. How does her choice of fashion shape the way we look at her? What if her headscarf and outfit were completely black? How would we look at her identity differently?

In the articles in this section, you'll see how clothing can function as a visible sign of our cultural and even religious values. In a time when audiences tune in regularly to the highly rated television *What Not To Wear* and log on daily to fashion blogs such as the Sartorialist, our everyday wardrobe choices are freighted with deep cultural significance. The decision to put on a yarmulke or a headscarf, a cross or an ankh, a pair of Uggs or Franco Sarto pumps, a suit and tie or university sweatshirt: each of these choices is a statement about how we define ourselves within a larger social context. The relationship between clothing and self-definition is clearly not a simple one. As the authors in this section show us, an examination of this topic prompts us to ask more complicated questions: To what extent does fashion tie to hegemony, the reinforcing of the dominant ideology? How is social acceptance or success equated or

FIGURE 12.9. Fashion and personal identity are strongly interrelated in this photograph of a young girl shopping for clothes.

FIGURE 12.10. In this fashion show, the model shows off not only her outfit but the body art tattooed on her neck as well.

mediated by dress code? How is religion complicated by commodification in the form Christian-themed T-shirts? These questions, and the recent debates over wearing religious jewelry or clothing in schools and countries across the globe, will be ones to explore.

But it is not only through clothing that we make our statements about our individual and cultural identity. In the middle of this section, we will move from how we clothe our bodies to how we modify them in the name of fashion. For instance, consider the model in Figure 12.10 walking down the runway at a fashion show. You might notice first the sleek lines of the white gown she wears, but most probably your eyes come to rest on the tattoo on her upper back. She wears her tattoo as an accessory, the same way she would a bracelet or necklace. What argument does the model make about her identity? Or, if it were a temporary tattoo, what argument would the fashion designer be making about his line? Additionally, how does the approval of the crowd in this photo support a shift in the cultural meaning of tattoos in society? How have tattoos and body art transformed from social stigma to status symbols now sported by celebrities from Johnny Depp to Angelina Jolie and 50 Cent?

By looking at body modification trends, both temporary and permanent—from hair straightening to tattooing and piercings—we will consider the very real way in which individuals remake themselves to create visual arguments about personal and cultural identity.

Reflect & Write

- ❑ How do the images shown here provide very different arguments about the values and cultures of the people?
- ❑ Analyze the elements of Figure 12.9. What elements surprise you? What aspects can you relate to? Knowing that this image is one in a series from a photo essay entitled "Looking Beyond the Veil," what argument do you think this image is trying to make about fashion, religion, and youth culture?
- ❑ As we see in Figure 12.10, women are increasingly choosing to mark their bodies through tattooing. Taking into account the rise of temporary tattoos, consider the way tattoos function as a fashion accessory and the statements they make.
- ❑ **Write.** When is a fashion statement a way of changing our understanding of religion or identity? Write an essay in which you argue your stance on this subject; be sure to provide concrete examples on the subject and use images wherever possible, whether those are photos you take yourself or find online.

■ **Pamela Abbott and Francesca Sapsford** *The following piece is an excerpt from Pamela Abbott and Francesca Sapsford's "Young Women and Their Wardrobes," which first appeared in the collection* Through the Wardrobe: Women's Relationships with Their Clothes. *In their research for the article, Abbott and Sapsford interviewed a group of 16-year-old women from a town in northern England who were all enrolled in year 11 of secondary school. Their interview questions focused on the girls' choices of what to wear, and they observed them at home, at school, and while shopping. One of Abbott and Sapsford's goals was to "give a voice to ordinary young women." In this section, they set up a theoretical framework through which to consider their primary evidence—the interviews with the girls.*

Clothing the Young Female Body

Pamela Abbott and Francesca Sapsford

Fashion plays a large part in a teenage girl's life. The media bombard her with advertisements for clothes and emphasize a particular image—the 'waif' look. Teenage magazines play an important part in shaping femininity. They are concerned with personal relationships (especially those with men), with physical appearance and with defining a particular form of beauty and style. Feature articles, advertisements and advice columns are all concerned with appearance and 'getting a man'. In these magazines, appearance and relationships to men define femininity. The teenage magazines such as Sugar and Bliss not only 'sell' the image but also promise that wearing certain clothes will attract young men. The promise is used as a tool to sell clothes to young women. However, Winship (1987) indicates that girls also get pleasure from fashion and she suggests that they interpret what the magazines say. Furthermore, girls don't have to be seen as dupes. They can think for themselves: Zoe (age 13) says 'I think it is a load of rubbish. You have the models that are skinny, but that's models. I don't think they say you should be this, you just get the ideas about clothes and what to look like.' (Quoted in article entitled 'Pure Bliss' in Young People Now, 30.07.96, p. 20).

Chua (1992) suggests that clothes have five functions:

1. They are chosen for a particular audience.
2. They are chosen for a particular event.
3. They are prefigured in preparation for the actual display.
4. The identity information forms a whole.
5. Once public, only limited modification is possible.

He makes a distinction between being in fashion and being in the vanguard of fashion. He argues that women wish to be in fashion; that is, they wish to be wearing what is seen as the norm. McCracken (1988) argues that clothing is the material of the visual representation of one's social worth. That is, from clothing one can infer things such as class, age and so on. In other words, clothing is a cultural category.

The consumption of clothes by young people is more than a need for clothes. Clothing is a statement. Clothes are acquired for their style, for their designer label, for the statements that they make about the wearer. Fashions are used and adapted by young women to make these statements. Young women also resist attempts to transform them and to make them conform. Here we can think about resistance to school uniforms and the attempt to transform school uniforms. Young women wear make-up to school when it is forbidden, wear jewelry which they then hide—for example earrings which they place their hair over—unacceptable shoes and short skirts in an attempt to resist conformity to the rules of the school. Often in doing so they become more alike in appearance.

Putting on clothes, make-up, or jewelry, and/or changing piercings are termed backstage activity (Goffman, 1971). The front stage, the display, is what we become when the body is adorned. For young women, part of growing up is learning how to present the female body—how to achieve femininity by fashioning the body. From magazines, themselves, female relatives and peers, young women learn how to invest in their looks, discipline their body, decorate and clothe it. This is achieved by cooperation and competition—and it is hard work. However, most young women cannot achieve the 'ideal'—the ideal is white, youthful, able-bodied and slim. As Hill-Collins (1990) has indicated 'Judging white women by their physical appearance and attractiveness to men objectifies, but their white skin and straight hair privileges them in a system in which part of the basic definition of whiteness is superior to black.' (p. 791).

Wolf (1991) argues that the 'beauty myth' undermines girls and women individually and collectively. She argues that young women must always be concerned about the presentation of self—about their appearance. The pressures that arise from the 'beauty myth' she suggests reduces young women's confidence and saps their energy and exposes them to dieting and cosmetic surgery. Young women, she argues, are looked at and objectified and controlled in the public sphere, and this control is exercised by boys/men, who are the final arbiters of what is desirable. Wilson, for example, suggests 'Even the bizarre can be fashionable and attempts to outrage or (as often happens) to be overtly sexual, or sexual in some different way, may nonetheless remain within stylistic boundaries of clothes that still express submissiveness to a boyfriend, even if they spell rebellion at home.' (1987, p. 24).

Clothes, then, are part of the way of adorning the body, and there are the 'right' clothes; girls have to learn clothing behaviour—to wear the right clothes. Clothes, adornment and conduct form a dress code, a code to which young women feel constrained to conform. However this does not mean that clothes are a disguise that hides the 'true nature' of the body/person, nor that young women are totally constrained by conforming to external pressure.

Goffman (1972) pointed to the social rules that provide appropriate body behaviour in public places and spaces and has also pointed to the performance or presentation of self. Mauss (1973, 1985) and Bourdieu (1986) have argued that clothing the body is an active process—a means of constructing and presenting the bodily self. Bourdieu (1984) has also indicated that the body is more than the clothes that adorn it. It is also ascribed ideologies of class, gender and race. As Craik (1994) indicates

> Women wear their bodies through their clothes. In other words, clothing does a good deal more than simply clothe the body for warmth, modesty or comfort. Codes of dress are technical devices which articulate the relationship between a particular body and its lived milieu—the space occupied by bodies, accented by bodily actions, in other words, clothes construct a personal habitat. (1994, p. 4)

We can conclude, then, that the body as a physical form is disciplined, and that appropriate behaviour includes conforming to a dress code. Fashion is prepackaged and is sold to a mass market, resulting in common identities. However, we are not totally controlled: we are actively involved in creating an identity to present, but within limits—what is acceptable as we play the fashion game.

Bourdieu (1984) refers to the concept of distinction—the ways that we use consumer goods to distinguish ourselves from others. Dress is a way of adding attraction, of constructing a self on a biological body, of presenting self to others in the way we wish to be seen. Young women get pleasure from fashion, from choosing clothes and from adorning the body.

The ways in which bodies are fashioned through clothes, make-up and demeanour constitute identity, sexuality and social position. In other words, clothed bodies are tools of self-management (Craik, 1994, p. 46).

Young women have to learn to become consumers—to become able to construct a self-identity through clothes, body-decorating and piercing. However, the clothes that are available are limited and women continue to be judged by their appearance. This means that young women tend to invest time and effort into managing and constructing their bodies. Part of becoming a woman for girls is to learn how to adorn their bodies, to love clothes and to be concerned about fashion and style. Furthermore, for young women, style gives meaning, validation and coherence to their group identity—it defines who is part of the group and who is external to the group. It is a visible expression of the individual belonging to a group. Clothing is part of tribalism and of social status and, in that sense, can be seen as opposed to individuality. The group recognizes itself and is recognized by others, so it is both a statement and relational and is part of display. It can also be related to hostility and to conflict, defining those who are members and those who are not and constructing one's identity within conflicting groups. An example would be the clothing of the mods and rockers, which not only identified separate groups, but groups in conflict.

Reflect & Write

- ❑ Why is it important for Sapsford and Abbott to establish a scholarly framework before moving to the interviews with the girls? What does this section contribute to the larger argument? What would a section of first person accounts provide? How would the two work in conjunction with one another?
- ❑ Go back and look at the opening selection again with a highlighter in hand. Mark the sections in which the authors make their own claims as opposed to quoting from or referring to other scholarship. To what extent do they spotlight their own argument in relation to their sources?
- ❑ As the headnote indicates, the primary research for this article was done in England. Do you think the conclusions drawn by the authors are specific to British girls? How do clothing mores translate to young women across cultures?
- ❑ At the end of this section, the authors refer to clothing as a form of "tribalism" that helps construct group identity. Their example are "mods and rockers." What alternate examples from your own experience might you give to prove this point? Discuss how you might develop a subsequent paragraph that extends and explores your example.

Seeing Connections

Look at "Spotlight on Your Argument" (page 121) for a discussion of how to develop your authorial stance in persuasive writing based on research.

- ❑ **Write.** The authors provide short summations of many theoretical positions, such as Chua's five functions of clothes, Wolf's beauty myth, and Craik's idea of clothed bodies as "tools of self-management." Choose one of these positions and write a personal essay in which you use a narrative of your own personal experience to either support or refute that position. Be sure to take time not only to tell your story but also to get at the cultural meanings behind your clothing choices or experience.

This how-to photo spread from the UK fashion magazine Fabulous *updates American author John Molloy's classic Dress-for-Success advice for a twenty-first-century female audience.*

Dress for Success

By Gok

FIGURE 12.11. This British magazine spread offers readers fashion advice on dressing effectively for different professional contexts.

Reflect & Write

Seeing Connections
See page 28 to review strategies of argumentation.

- ❑ What strategies of argumentation do the editors use in composing this argument about how to dress for success? Is this a successful rhetorical choice for their purpose? Why or why not?
- ❑ What gender, race, and class assumptions are present in this visual argument? In what other ways are the women's bodies "marked" than those highlighted by the text?

- ❑ What elements of this layout seemed representative of the fashion magazine genre? How might this visual argument be produced differently if it had been part of a Macy's clothes catalog? A career counselor's handout? A homeless women's shelter?
- ❑ To what extent do you agree with the advice given here? Identify elements of this argument that would—and wouldn't—work if it used in relation to your current context and rhetorical situation.
- ❑ **Write.** Create your own dress-for-success visual argument: How to Dress for Success at your college. Identify three different contexts in which you would need to Dress for Success (a rush event, dinner with faculty, a class presentation) and then delineate the different components of a formula for successful attire. Use photographs that you take yourself of you or your friends as visual examples, and when you are done, share your work with your class.

Artist and T-shirt designer Rob Dobi graduated from the Rhode Island School of Design and has provided graphic designs for clients as varied as Green Day, Blink-182, Eminem, Pearl Jam, Teen People, Warner Brothers, and Atari. His work includes a line of conceptual art–based tees (Fullbleed.org), the Fall Out Boy poster series, a photographic collection of abandoned spaces in the Northeast (newenglandruins.com), and illustrations for Harper Collins's Everybody Hurts: An Essential Guide to Emo Culture. *In the online graphic, "How To Dress Emo," he provides gendered guidelines for attaining the Emo look.*

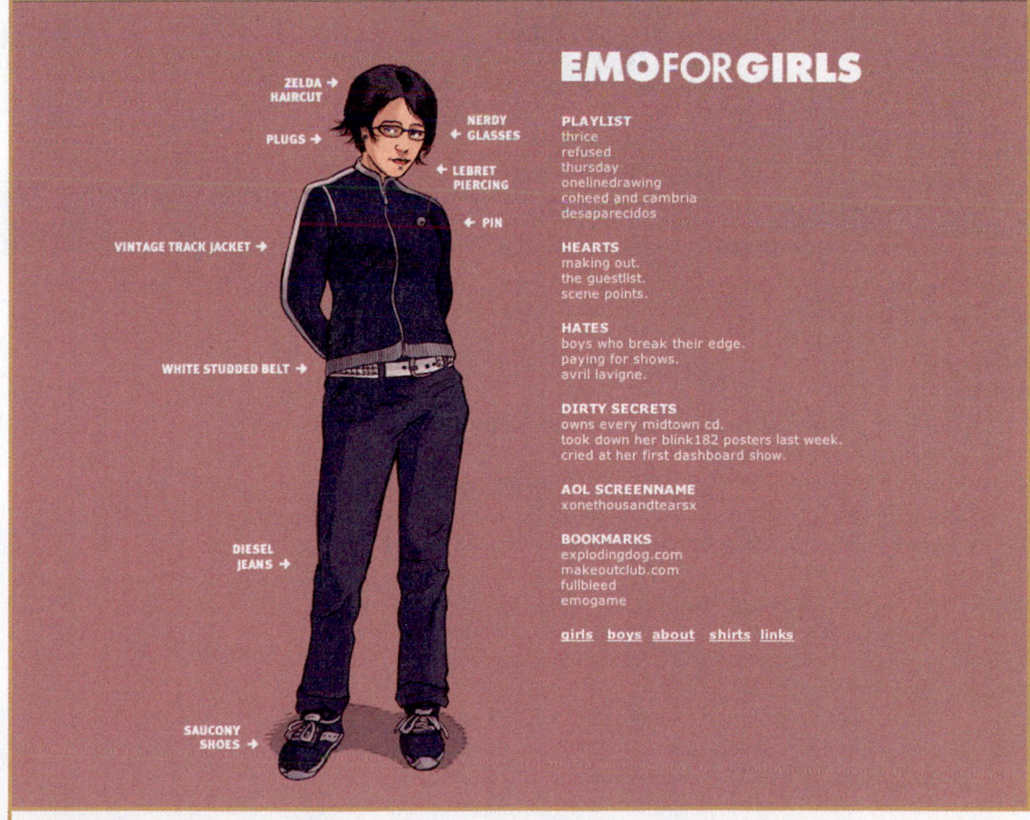

FIGURE 12.12. Rob Dobi's "Emo for Girls."

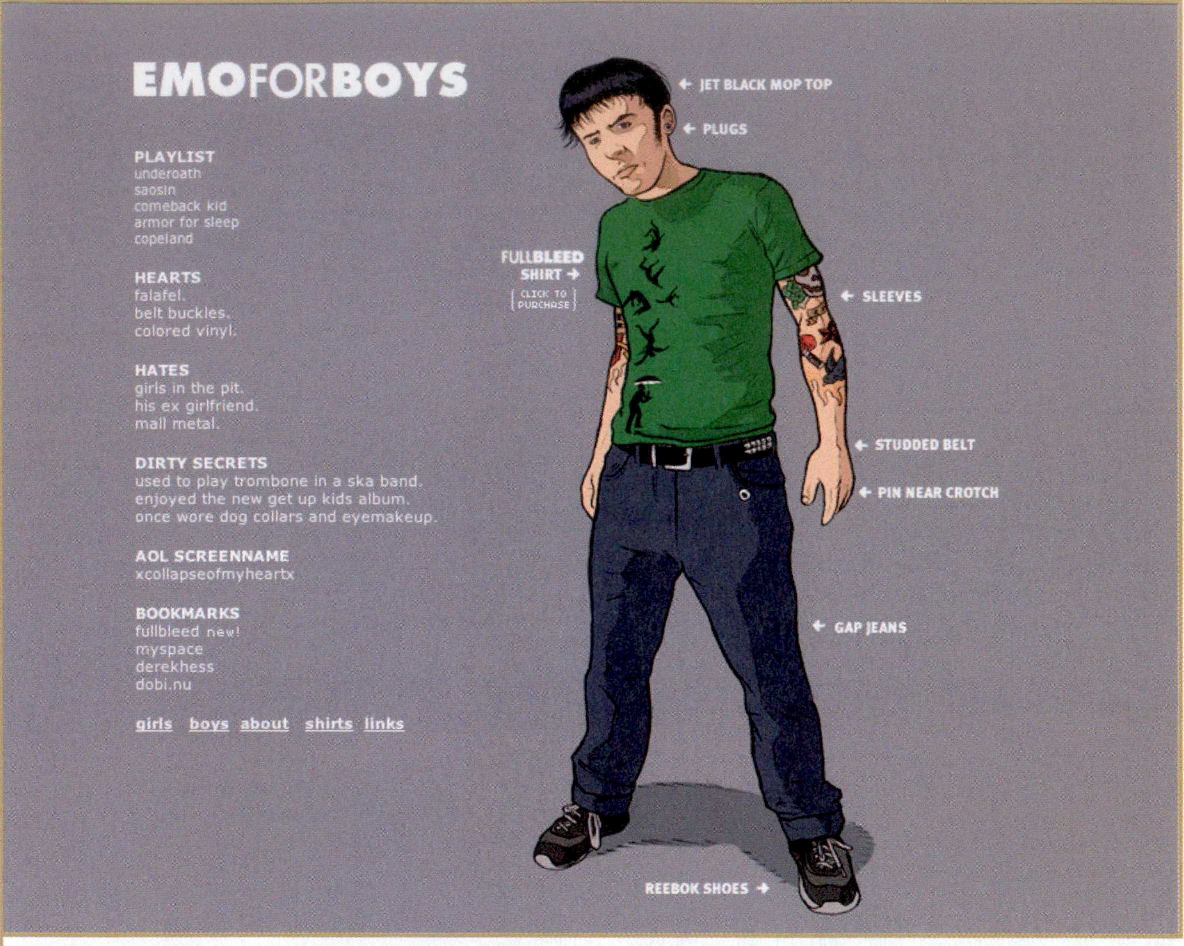

FIGURE 12.13. Rob Dobi's "Emo for Boys."

Reflect & Write

- ❑ How do the images define Emo? How is contemporary popular and consumer culture tied into the definition of Emo-wear?
- ❑ This artist decided to structure his visual argument around definition. How would he have had to change the composition of his argument if he had used the strategy of process as the principle organizing structure for a set of instructions for how to dress Emo?
- ❑ Notice how the definition for being Emo extends beyond wardrobe choice. In what ways is technology used as an "accessory" for constructing a cultural identity as Emo?
- ❑ Do you agree with these constructions of Emo? What would you add or change based on your own experience?
- ❑ **Write.** Construct your own visual definition or instructions for "How To Dress ___," based on the subculture of your choice (i.e., "How To Dress Goth," "How to Dress Couture." "How to Dress like a College Student"). If you want, use photographs you take yourself as part of your visual composition.

Ruth La Ferla *writes articles on fashion for the* New York Times, *where this article originally appeared on March 29, 2005.*

Wearing Their Beliefs on Their Chests

Ruth La Ferla

Source: *The New York Times.*

Late last week, Trapper Blu, a ski and snowboarding instructor from Wanship, Utah, dropped in with his family at Christopher's, a T-shirt shop in Greenwich Village, and tried on a shirt emblazoned with an image of Jesus and the slogan "Put Down the Drugs and Come Get a Hug." "I would wear this, you bet," Mr. Blu, 23, said, scrutinizing his reflection in the mirror. "The shirt is funny," he added, as he tweaked the brim of his cowboy hat, "but it doesn't make fun of Jesus or anything."

A few blocks south at Urban Outfitters, part of a youth-oriented chain that sells T-shirts along with shag rugs, coffee mugs and multitiered hippie skirts, Jurek Grapentin, visiting from Germany, looked on as a young friend of his examined a shirt printed with a rosary entwined with the words "Everybody Loves a Catholic Girl."

"It's a nice message," Mr. Grapentin, 22, said. "Catholic people most of the time can be so traditional in their thinking. To me this looks more new, more in."

Mr. Blu and Mr. Grapentin are among the legions of the faithful, or the merely fashionable, who are increasingly drawn to the religious themes and imagery—portraits of saints, fragments of scripture—that have migrated in recent months from billboards and bumper stickers to baseball caps, T-shirts, flip-flops and even designer clothing. Such messages are being embraced by a growing number of mostly young people, who are wearing them as a testament of faith or, ironically, as a badge of hipness.

5 "There is no question, religion is becoming the new brand," said Jane Buckingham, the president of Youth Intelligence, a trend-forecasting company. "To a generation of young people eager to have something to belong to, wearing a 'Jesus Saves' T-shirt, a skullcap or a cabala bracelet is a way of feeling both unique, a member of a specific culture or clan, and at the same time part of something much bigger."

There was a time when such symbols were worn discreetly and were purchased mostly at gift shops or Bible stores. Now, emboldened perhaps by celebrities like Ashton Kutcher and Paris Hilton, who are photographed brandishing spiritual messages on shirts and caps, aspiring hipsters and fashion groupies as well as the devout are flaunting similar items, which are widely available at mass-market chains and online.

A casual survey of the Internet last week, including mainstream marketers like Amazon.com, turned up T-shirts, bowling bags, belt buckles and dog tags by the hundreds bearing messages like "Inspired by Christ," "Give All the Glory to God," "I <heart> Hashem" (a Hebrew term for God), "Moses Is My Homeboy" and "Buddha Rocks."

Plastic tote bags and tank tops bearing images of Jesus and the saints stock the shelves of drugstore and cosmetics chains like Walgreens. Some items have worked their way up the fashion chain to stores like Atrium, a New York sportswear outlet popular with college students, which offers polo shirts with images from the Sistine Chapel; and Intuition, a Los Angeles boutique that sells rosaries, cabala bracelets and St. Christopher medals as fashion jewelry.

Come fall, members of the fashion flock, at least those with pockets deep enough, will find chunky sweaters that read "Jesus Loves Even Me" from Dsquared, a label that only a season earlier traded in fashions stamped with obscene images and slogans; a Derek Lam blanket wrap embroidered on the back with a torso-length cross; and Yves Saint Laurent coats and evening dresses seeded with ecclesiastical references.

10 Fashions with spiritual messages are just the latest expression of religion as a pop phenomenon, one that has steadily gained ground with consumers since the best-selling "Left Behind" series of novels, based on a fundamentalist Christian interpretation of apocalyptic prophecy, turned up on bookshelves, and "The Passion of the Christ" became a box-office hit. Their popularity arrives at a time when faith-based issues, including school prayer and the debate over the definition of life, are dividing Americans, a rift reflected to some degree among those who wear the new fashions.

Tanya Brockmeier, 19, another German visitor browsing last week at Urban Outfitters, wears a cross and sees nothing amiss in wearing a religious-theme T-shirt, "so long as it looks modern," she said. "These things are a way of showing my faith." But Larry Bullock, 41, treasures a T-shirt with an image of Jesus as a D. J. Mr. Bullock, the general manager of the Civilian, a gay club on Fire Island, N.Y., was brought up as a Roman Catholic. "But for me," he said, "wearing this shirt is a way of mocking the rhetoric that goes on over religion, which I think is just ridiculous."

The commodification of religious faith "is born of a consciousness that any religious movement, to stay viable, has to speak the idiom of the culture," said Randall Balmer, a professor of American religion at Barnard College in New York. Dr. Balmer also observed that airing one's religious views in public, which would have been regarded as unseemly or even presumptuous 20 years ago, has become acceptable. "We live in a multicultural, pluralistic environment," he said, "and acknowledge implicitly that individuals have a right to differentiate themselves. In fact, there is cachet in that."

Whatever is driving the popularity of message-driven merchandise, it is generating robust sales. Last year sales of apparel and accessories at Christian bookstores and gift shops reached about $84 million, according to the Christian Booksellers Association, a trade association of retailers. Teenage Millionaire, the Los Angeles-based makers of the "Jesus Is My Homeboy" T-shirt, a million of which have been sold, reported $10 million in sales last year, up from $2 million three years ago.

The Solid Light Group of Columbus, Ohio, which sells T-shirts with legends like "Jesus Rocks," does not disclose sales figures but is projecting a 40 percent increase from a year ago. "Ours has become a mainstream business," said Debbie Clements, a sales manager of the company. "It won't be too much longer before you see more designers in the secular marketplace doing religious fashions."

15 Chris Rainey, the director of marketing for Kerusso, a company in Berryville, Ark., that sells wristbands that say "Live for Him" and T-shirts with messages like "Dead to Sin, Alive to Christ," maintains that his wares make faith seem relevant. "We're just doing what a lot of churches have started to do, using marketing to reach a new generation," he said.

Still, the concept of religion as a wearable commodity rankles some consumers. "I would not wear clothing with a religious message," said Megan Schnaid, 27, a New York University graduate student from Los Angeles. "I'm not used to putting my faith on such loud display."

Many retailers, too, balk at selling fashions with an aggressively religious bent. Aurelio Barreto, who runs a Southern California chain of five stores called C28 (a reference to the biblical verse Colossians 2:8), recalled that when he first tried to sell his Not of this World line of tank tops and hoodies to secular stores at California malls, he was shown the door. "I was told, 'There is no way we will buy this,' " "Mr. Barreto said." 'We're not going to have God in here.' "

Michael Macko, the men's fashion director of Saks Fifth Avenue, who viewed the Dsquared collection in Milan last winter, said he was somewhat taken aback. "Hmm, I thought, 'Religion as a fashion theme. That's a little different from corduroy or camel. How do we handle this?' "Undeterred, Saks bought the Dsquared line for its stores across the country. "We bought it as a fashion item, not as a moral statement," said Ronald Frasch, the chief merchant of Saks. "We sell crosses, and it's not a big step from crosses to sweaters."

Not surprisingly, some secular retailers stock religious-based paraphernalia because they are loath to miss an opportunity. "We don't just want all the punks and rockers to walk into the store," said Priti Lavingia, the owner of the T-Shirt Stop in Marino Valley, Calif., which carries the Not of This World line. "Maybe 20 percent of the people in this area are very religious," Ms. Lavingia said. "I want their business also."

Reflect & Write

- ❑ Why do you think some merchants view religious rhetoric on clothing so differently, as either an imposing moral statement or as a meaningless fashion trend? How does La Ferla's organization of quotes in this article—her choice to alternate diverse perspectives throughout the piece—offer a nuanced view on this issue? What additional perspectives might you want to add to this article?
- ❑ Compare this argument with Ruth La Ferla's August 19, 2001, article in the *New York Times* entitled, "Noticed; Religious, Rebellious or Chic, Crosses Are Forever." How has the trend of wearing religious symbols as jewelry or clothing changed in subsequent years? What rhetorical strategies does she use in this article to make her argument (for instance, quoting her interview sources, using concrete detail, ending with an implicit thesis)? Which piece is more persuasive?
- ❑ **Write.** Compose a narrative about the religious visual rhetoric you encounter in one week on campus or in your hometown. Include images as evidence.

COLLABORATIVE CHALLENGE

Find two partners for this activity. Together, read the article "Thousands protest head scarf ban: French parliament's lower house voted Tuesday to approve law," linked through the *Envision* Website. According to the CNN article, the protestors marched against a new French law banning all kinds of religious apparel in school, including Jewish skullcaps and large Christian crosses from public schools. The law received global criticism for infringing on religious freedom, and protesters in Paris carried banners marked "The veil, my voice," "Secularism: Shame," and "School is my right. The veil is my choice. France is my shelter." As a team, develop your own slogans for a rally to protest governmental regulations on wearing religion in school. Now, compose a speech from the school president defending the law's rationale. Use all three rhetorical appeals in both the slogans and the presidential speech. Share your work with the rest of the class and discuss what you learned from this exercise.

www.pearsonhighered.com/envision/415

Mary Is My Homegirl T-shirt

FIGURE 12.14. Religion meets teen culture in this "Mary Is My Homegirl" T-shirt.

Reflect & Write

- ❏ Analyze the photo in Figure 12.14. What elements catch your eye? How do the model's stance, expression, and body language contribute to the argument of the image?
- ❏ Compare the T-shirt in Figure 12.14 to the the Derek Lam blanket wrap with an embroidered cross that appeared on a fashion runway in New York, shown in Ruth La Ferla's article. Does featuring a cross in a fashion show or as part of t-shirt art signify a disrespectful use of the visual rhetoric of Christianity? Or is it a sign of importance of religious culture in the United States?
- ❏ If freedom of expression is considered a natural right for all Americans, then can freedom of expression through fashion also be considered a right? Discuss this question with regard to the religious t-shirt shown here.
- ❏ **Write.** Sketch your own t-shirt design that represents your religious stance. Then, draft a proposal to a manufacturing company. Explain the argument of your design and how you are trying to change the way people look at you through this article of clothing.

An Australian author, script writer, and poet, **Paul Mitchell** *has taught at Victoria University and the University of Melbourne. He has published two books of Poetry as well as* Dodging the Bull *(2007), a collection of short fiction. This article originally appeared in the June 1, 2005, issue of* BreakPoint, *an online journal that offers a Christian perspective on current fashion trends and news items.*

Faith and Fashion: The Power of T-shirt Evangelism

Paul Mitchell

Nineteen ninety-two marked the birth of the grunge look. Mudhoney and Dinosaur Junior t-shirts graced the backs of 20-somethings who, along with fuzzed up power chords, also discovered body piercing. The famous Nirvana t-shirts (featuring a baby swimming underwater in pursuit of a one-dollar bill on a hook) were *de riguer* for the rock set.

I was a young Christian at the time and eager to attend the Australian rockfest known as "The Big Day Out." Hundreds of bands would be playing for 12 hours under hot Melbourne skies that cooled off only slightly at night. But the big question for me was not which bands I would catch, it was what t-shirt I would wear. The crowd would be wearing t-shirts featuring rock, metal, and dance acts from around the world. How could I best demonstrate my devotion to Christ?

I had been reading a lot of authors from the Apophatic tradition (St. John of the Cross, etc.), so I considered wearing a plain white t-shirt. I figured that my absence of "idols" would demonstrate the foolishness of theirs'. But that idea, in a strongly visual culture, didn't have me reaching for my t-shirt drawer.

Next, I toyed with the idea of wearing a U2 t-shirt. Even though they wouldn't be playing at The Big Day Out, wearing their t-shirt was an obvious way to make a Christian statement. Besides, lots of people would be wearing t-shirts of bands that wouldn't be playing, I reasoned. But I left my U2 shirt folded up in the drawer—basically because they were too mainstream to wear to such an *alternative* rock fest. Also, a part of me wanted to make a stronger statement.

5 In the end, I settled on a Christian t-shirt. But even then, I didn't pick just any Christian shirt. You see, there were lots of Christian shirts in the early '90s. Some showed burnt toast popping out of toasters—an attempt to symbolize Hell. Others portrayed a single peaceful fish swimming in one direction while a school of piranhas swam in the other. Maybe it was because of my intellectual pride, but I decided against those types of shirts. Instead, I wore a white t-shirt which had a full color copy of a perhaps 17th century painting of the Crucifixion." (My "intellectual pride" didn't extend far enough to bother finding out who was the artist or in what century the work was produced.)

To my surprise, none of my non-Christian friends at The Big Day Out commented on my shirt. Neither did anyone in the crowd, even though I didn't see anyone else wearing a t-shirt like mine. I expected someone to say something, anything. But no one did.

What I was doing that day was what Christians have tried to do for centuries—make some kind of outward sign of their inner conversion, to show the world that yes, I'm *different*. Something has happened to me and I want you to see it. And I want you to see it because I want you to experience what I have experienced.

The ancient Jewish people had the sign of circumcision to show that they belonged to God. But early Christians were not so, well, in a period of history without anesthesia, "lucky" isn't quite the right word. Yet the desire to *show* our Christian faith to the world on our person hasn't abated. While nuns, priests, monks, and members of the ruling class in Anglicanism and Catholicism have always worn clothes that showed their Christian status, the rank and file in early Christendom had to make do with wearing crosses.

Then, in the late 20th century, along came the mobile billboard called the T-shirt. And almost since its inception, Christians have seen it as a way to both show and propagate their faith. Through text and the psychedelic styles of the 60s and 70s, the Jesus People movement continues to disseminate the evangelical message about the end of the world and the coming of Christ's reign.

10 The early 21st century, however, has seen the mainstream culture make a mockery of such t-shirts. For example, I've seen shirts with pictures of a '70s-looking Jesus or Mary figure accompanied by the words "Jesus is my Homeboy"

or "Mary is my Homegirl"—a spoof from the film *Saved*. (Sadly, I even know Christians who wear them.) Some shirts parody Christian concepts. One such shirt reads, "In case of rapture, please cheer." (This is supposed to be an antidote to the many t-shirts and bumper stickers that show the results of Christians being raptured, i.e., driverless cars crashing.)

We could say that the previous examples are typical of a culture that ignores God. Or we could view them as simply being an assault on sloganeering in general. After all, they're not unlike the shirts with a Nike swoosh and the words: "Sweatshops: Just Don't Do It." Such shirts clearly attack the ubiquitous advertising slogans propagated by multinational companies.

Spoof Christian t-shirts give the same message to Christendom that spoof advertising t-shirts give to big companies: we see through your propaganda, and your slogans have become meaningless and even offensive to us.

It's obvious that Christians will continue making t-shirts with 'turn or burn' Christian messages and non-Christians (maybe even Christians?) will continue making shirts that spoof them. One company, however, has a different approach to Christian fashion messages. Luke's T-shirts creates garments that integrate high fashion and color design with a picture of a lion and the words, Tribe of Judah. There's a refreshing subtlety to this kind of work, which neither spoofs nor overtly proselytizes. Instead, these t-shirts more closely mirror the parables Jesus so often used.

Christian sloganeering—which is, of course, not restricted to the fashion world—has become too similar to the world's omnipresent advertising slogans. Consequently, it has diminished its ability to grab people's attention. Advertisers are all too aware of this phenomenon. That's why they try numerous approaches to garner the attention of consumers who are deadened by the sheer number of slogans that confront them every day. The reality of t-shirts that spoof Christian slogans spells the end of this kind of approach to communicating the faith.

15 In the end, Christianity is not a brand—it's a relationship whose depth can't be reduced to slogans. Any attempt to do so will only make our faith appear thin and open to parody. To outwardly communicate our Christianity, we must use the oldest and best method—our love.

Reflect & Write

Seeing Connections
For further discussion of *ethos* and *kairos*, see Chapter 2.

- ❑ Consider Paul Mitchell's strategy: he begins his article first with *kairos*, or establishing the context, and moves to *ethos*, or introducing his experience as an appeal to authority. How does this strategy construct the tone for the piece and invite readers to consider his position? As he strategically integrates references to theology as well as contemporary culture, his article becomes a well-researched argument. What is the effect of this added material?
- ❑ Mitchell describes the t-shirt as offering "some kind of outward sign of . . . inner conversion" and yet, he warns, the t-shirt runs the risk of parody. Which way do you read the visual rhetoric of the t-shirt? How might others see it?
- ❑ **Write.** Compose a rebuttal to Mitchell in which you use his quotations and references but come to a different conclusion.

Persepolis, *a graphic novel by* **Marjane Satrapi**, *shares the story of a young girl's experiences growing up in Iran in the middle of the 1979 revolution, as an increasingly fundamentalist regime changed the way she experienced childhood. The part of the novel shown here demonstrates a change in the way girls had to dress for school. The author explains that she uses books to help people understand other cultures: "If people are given the chance to experience life in more than one country, they will hate a little less . . . That is why I wanted people in other countries to read* Persepolis, *to see that I grew up just like other children." Satrapi has published a sequel to* Persepolis, *(2003) as well as two other graphic novels:* Embroideries *(2005) and* Chicken with Plums *(2006).* Persepolis *was adapted into a feature film, which was nominated for an Academy Award in 2008.*

"The Veil," *Persepolis: The Story of A Childhood*

Marjane Satrapi

Reflect & Write

- ❏ What is the rhetorical stance of the main character with regard to wearing the veil?
- ❏ The author states that she wrote *Persepolis* because she was a pacifist; she wanted people "to see that I grew up just like other children." Analyze this scene for the commonalities depicted between the main character and children you know. How does Satrapi construct childhood in Iran as both similar to and different from growing up in America? What message do you think she is trying to convey in this part of the book?
- ❏ Satrapi asserts that "images are a way of writing." How is that true in this passage from her graphic novel? Make your case by citing concrete evidence from the text.
- ❏ **Write:** Emulate Satrapi's strategy of writing by storyboarding your argument through cartoons. Then compose a brief description of your project for a future audience.

FIGURE 12.15. This page from Marjane Satrapi's graphic novel *Persepolis*, provides a child's perspective on headscarves in Iranian culture.

Source: "The Veil," translated by Mattias Ripa & Blake Ferris, from PERSEPOLIS: THE STORY OF CHILDHOOD by Marjane Satrapi, translated by Mattias Ripa & Blake Ferris, copyright (c) 2003 by L'Association, Paris, France. Used by permission of Pantheon Books, a division of Random House, Inc.

This photograph, called "Rebellious Silence," is part of **Shirin Neshat***'s series,* Women of Allah *(1993–1997). In this picture, a woman is shown wearing a "chador" (a type of open cloak that covers the head), marking her as belonging to the Islamic religion. As you look at the photo, ask yourself: how does this image raise questions about identity, purpose, and audience? What might be the photographer's comment on her country, Iran?*

Women of Allah: Rebellious Silence

Shirin Neshat

Reflect & Write

- ❑ Despite not knowing the background of this Iranian woman, or what the writing on her face even says, what would you say is the argument of this strategically posed photograph?
- ❑ How does the presence of the gun in the photo change the argument? How does the woman's facial expression contribute to your interpretation?
- ❑ According to one photography critic, "the chador has an ambiguous character: on the one hand, it is a symbol of the masculine oppression and the violence, but, by another one, it is an identity sign, a resistance sample before the loss of traditions." How might you make multiple, perhaps conflicting, interpretations of this photo as a visual argument about gender, culture, and identity?
- ❑ **Write.** What does it mean to mark the body with tattoos in this way? Compose three captions for this image that reveal your argument. Write a short explanation of your reasons for composing the captions you did. What have you learned about fashion statements made of tattoo writing, clothing, and props such as guns?

Seeing Connections

Further consider the power of captions and titles by examining the examples of front page headlines found in Chapter 3 (pages 55–57).

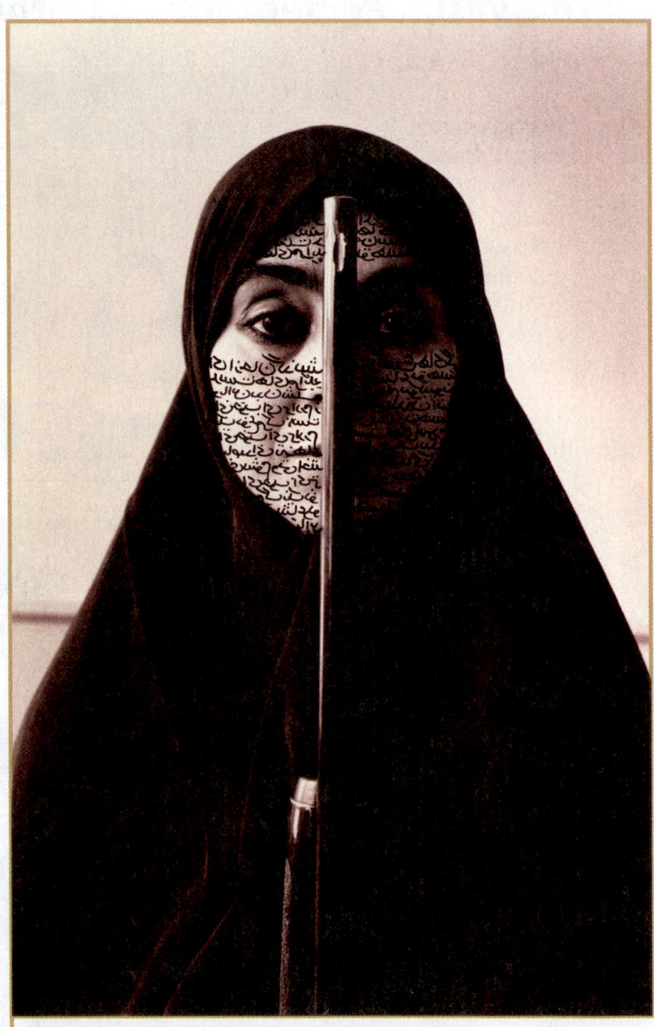

FIGURE 12.16. This dramatic photograph can be read as a strong cultural statement.

Source: "Rebellious Silence" by Shirin Neshat, 1994. B&W RC print and ink, 11x14 inches (photo taken by Cynthia Preston). Edition of 10+1AP. Copyright Shirin Neshat 1994. Courtesy Gladstone Gallery, New York (SN008).

Noted documentary photographer **Chris Rainer** *specializes in photographing indigenous people and natural wilderness throughout the world. In his words, "With my photography of the first people of our fragile planet, I hope to show spiritual traditions from our past in the present,—and become part of the process in some small way of helping preserve life for future generations." He has traveled extensively around the globe and has had his photographs featured in* Time *magazine,* Life, *the* New York Times, *the* Smithsonian, *and* National Geographic. *He is a contributing editor for the* National Geographic Traveler *magazine, a contributing photographer for* NGS Adventure Magazine, *and a correspondent on photography for NPR Radio's Day to Day Show. In this selection of photographs, published through the National Geographic Website, Rainer provides a vivid perspective on how tattoos, body markings, and piercings define identity for people around the globe.*

Tattoos, Piercings, and Body Markings

Chris Rainer

FIGURE 12.17. "Burning Man Festival, Nevada"

Elaborate religious tattoos adorn a man at the Burning Man festival in the Nevada desert. He is a follower of the Modern Primitivism movement, part of a subculture that includes extensive tattooing and piercing. Modern Primitivists believe body markings and other tribal traditions help reconnect them to the world and emphasize their own identity.

Called the Tribe, these men (gathered under the Golden Gate Bridge in San Francisco) are leaders of the local Modern Primitivism movement. The Tribe has a tattoo parlor that does only tribal marking. Several of the tattoo artists have traveled to Borneo and learned the craft from tribal masters.

FIGURE 12.18. "The Tribe, California"

The Maori culture has a long tradition of tattooing, which dated back centuries until the Europeans outlawed it in the 1800s. These Auckland men belong to the anti-European Black Power Group. Their tattoos are a combination of traditional Maori tattoo art, called *moko,* and symbols picked up from the U.S. Black Power movement of the 1960s.

FIGURE 12.19 "Maori Gang Members, New Zealand"

Reflect & Write

- ❏ In each case, how does the caption from the original photo essay explain or redefine the visual argument made by the photograph? How would the argument be different without the caption? What alternate sorts of captions could you imagine to accompany these images?
- ❏ How does background complement the focus on the individuals in these photographs? What does the setting add to the visual argument that might have been missing had Rainer photographed his subjects in a studio, against a white backdrop?
- ❏ How does Rainer's focus on tattoos as expressions of Primitivism underscore or contradict your own ideas about tattoos in contemporary culture?
- ❏ On his Website, Rainer states, "I believe photography plays a crucial role in helping sustain and revitalize cultures on the edge." How does this selection of photographs support this claim? Based on the selection here, what does it mean to be a "culture on the edge"?
- ❏ **Write.** Visit the complete collection of Rainer's "Tattoos, Piercings, and Body Markings" photos at the National Georgraphic Website, linked through the *Envision* Website. Write a paragraph that summarizes Rainer's argument about tattooing in the twenty-first century, using specific images as evidence. Remember: you do not need to refer to all the images, only to those that best support your argument. www.pearsonhighered.com/envision/423

■ **Josie Appleton** *This article was first published on July 9, 2003, in the British Internet magazine* Spiked. *Josie Appleton is a regular contributor to* Spiked *as well as Reason.com and is best known for her role as the head of the Manifesto Club's Campaign against Vetting, which argues for a "commonsense approach to child protection that recognizes the value of informal interaction between the generations." Her concern with personal freedoms clearly plays a role in her analysis of the body piercing project recounted below.*

The Body Piercing Project

Josie Appleton

The opening of a tattoo and piercing section in the up-market London store Selfridges shows that body modification has lost its last trace of taboo.

'Metal morphosis', nestled in the thick of the ladies clothing section, is a world away from the backstreets of Soho—where the company has its other branch. Teenagers, middle-aged women, men in suits and young guys in jeans flock to peer at the rows of tastefully displayed rings and leaf through the tattoo brochures.

Tattooist Greg said that he had seen a 'broad variety' of people: 'everything from the girl who turned 18 to the two Philippino cousins who just turned 40.' The piercer, Barry, said that a number of 'Sloanies' come for piercings (the most expensive navel bar retails at £3000, and there is a broad selection that would set you back several hundred pounds). A handful of women have even asked to be tattooed with the label of their favourite bottle of wine (1).

This is not just affecting London high-streets. According to current estimates, between 10 and 25 percent of American adolescents have some kind of piercing or tattoo (2). And their mothers are taking it up, too—in the late 1990s, the fastest growing demographic group seeking tattoo services in America was middle-class suburban women (3).

5 But while tattoos have been taken up by university students and ladies who lunch, more traditional wearers of tattoos—sailors, soldiers, bikers, gangs—find themselves increasingly censured.

In June 2003, the police rejected an applicant because his tattoos were deemed to have an 'implication of racism, sexism or religious prejudice' (4). The US Navy has banned 'tattoos/body art/brands that are excessive, obscene, sexually explicit or advocate or symbolise sex, gender, racial, religious, ethnic or national origin discrimination' and 'symbols denoting any gang affiliation, supremacist or extremist groups, or drug use' (5).

New-style tattoos are a very different ball-game to their frowned-upon forebears. While the tattoos of football supporters, sailors and gang-members tend to be symbols of camaraderie or group affiliation, the Selfridges brigade are seeking something much more individual.

For some, tattoos and piercing are a matter of personal taste or fashion. 'It's purely aesthetic decoration', said 37-year-old Sarah, waiting to get her navel pierced at Metal Morphosis. The erosion of moral censure on tattooing, and the increasing hygiene of tattoo parlours, has meant that body modification has become a fashion option for a much wider group of people.

For others, tattooing seems to go more than skin-deep. Tattoo artist Greg thinks that many of those getting tattoos today are looking for 'self-empowerment'-tattoos, he says, are about establishing an 'identity for the self'. As a permanent mark on your body that you choose for yourself, a tattoo is 'something no one will ever be able to take away from you', that allows you to say '*this is mine*'.

10 Seventeen-year-old Laura said that she got her piercings done because she 'wanted to make a statement'. When she turned 18, she planned to have 'XXX' tattooed on the base of her spine, symbolising her pledge not to drink, smoke or take drugs. 'It's not to prove anything to anyone else', she said: 'it's a pact with myself completely.'

Sue said that she had her navel pierced on her fortieth birthday to mark a turning point in her life. Another young man planned to have his girlfriend's name, and the dates when they met, tattooed on his arm 'to show her that I love her'—and to remind himself of this moment. 'The tattoo will be there forever. Whether or not I feel that in the future, I will remember that I felt it at the time, that I felt strong enough to have the tattoo.'

The tattoos of bikers, sailors and gang-members would be a kind of social symbol, that would establish them as having a particular occupation or belonging to a particular cultural subgroup. By contrast, Laura's 'XXX' symbol is a sign to herself of how she has chosen to live her life; Sue pierced her navel to mark her transition to middle-age. These are not symbols that could be interpreted by anyone else. Even the man who wanted to get tattooed with his girlfriend's name had a modern, personal twist to his tale: the tattoo was less a pact to stay with her forever, than to remind himself of his feelings at this point.

Much new-style body modification is just another way to look good. But the trend also presents a more profound, and worrying, shift: the growing crisis in personal identity.

In his book, *Modernity and Self-Identity* (1991), sociologist Anthony Giddens argues that it is the erosion of important sources of identity that helps to explain the growing focus on the body (6). Body modification began to really take off and move into the mainstream in the late 1980s and early 1990s. At around this time, personal and community relationships that previously helped to provide people with an enduring sense of self could no longer be depended upon. The main ideological frameworks that provided a system to understand the world and the individual's place in it, such as class, religion, or the work ethic, began to erode.

15 These changes have left individuals at sea, trying to establish their own sense of who they are. In their piercing or tattooing, people are trying to construct a 'narrative of self' on the last thing that remains solid and tangible: their physical bodies. While much about social experience is uncertain and insecure, the body at least retains a permanence and reliability. Making marks upon their bodies is an attempt by people to build a lasting story of who they are.

Many—including, to an extent, Giddens—celebrate modification as a liberating and creative act. 'If you want to and it makes you feel good, you should do it', Greg tells me. Websites such as the Body Modification Ezine (BMEzine) (7) are full of readers' stories about how their piercing has completely changed their life. One piercer said that getting a piercing 'helped me know who I am'. Another said that they felt 'more complete . . . a better, more rounded and fuller person' (8). Others even talk about unlocking their soul, or finally discovering that 'I AM'.

But what these stories actually show is less the virtues of body piercing, than the desperation of individuals' attempts to find a foothold for themselves. There is a notable contrast between the superlatives about discovering identity and Being, and the ultimately banal act of sticking a piece of metal through your flesh.

Piercings and tattoos are used to plot out significant life moments, helping to lend a sense of continuity to experience. A first date, the birth of a child, moving house: each event can be marked out on the body, like the notches of time on a stick. One woman said that her piercings helped to give her memory, to 'stop me forgetting who I am'. They work as a 'diary' that 'no one can take off you' (9).

This springs from the fact that there is a great deal of confusion about the stages of life today. Old turning points that marked adulthood—job, marriage, house, kids—have both stopped being compulsory and lost much of their significance. It is more difficult to see life in terms of a narrative, as a plot with key moments of transition and an overall aim. Piercings and tattoos are used to highlight formative experiences and link them together.

20 Some also claim that body modification helps them to feel 'comfortable in my own skin', or proud of parts of their body of which they were previously ashamed. The whole process of piercing—which involves caring for the wound, and paying special attention to bodily processes—is given great significance. By modifying a body part, some argue that you are taking possession of it, making it truly yours. 'The nipple piercings have really changed my relationship to my breasts', one woman said (10).

This is trying to resolve a sense of self-estrangement—the feeling of detachment from experiences, the feeling that your life doesn't really belong to you. One young woman says how she uses piercing: '[It's been] done at time when I felt like I needed to ground myself. Sometimes I feel like I'm not in my body—then its time.' (11)

But piercing is trying to deal with the problem at the most primitive and brutal level—in the manner of 'I hurt therefore I am'. The experience of pain becomes one of the few authentic experiences. It also tries to resolve the crisis in individual identity in relation to my breasts or my navel, rather than in relation to other people or anything more meaningful in the world.

Many claims are made as to the transformative and creative potential of body modification. One girl, who had just had her tongue pierced, writes: 'I've always been kind of quiet in school and very predictable. . . . I wanted to think of myself as original and creative, so I decided I wanted something pierced. . . . Now people don't think of me as shy and predictable, they respect me and the person I've become and call me crazily spontaneous.' (12)

Others say they use modification to help master traumatic events. Transforming the body is seen as helping to re-establish a sense of self-control in the face of disrupting or degrading experiences. One woman carved out a Sagittarius symbol on her thigh to commemorate a lover who died. 'It was my way of coming to terms with the grief I felt', she said. 'It enabled me to always have him with me and to let him go.' (13)

Here the body being modified as a way of trying to effect change in people's lives. It is the way to express creativity, find a challenge, or put themselves through the hoops. 'I was ecstatic. I did it!', writes one contributor to BMEZine. Instead of a life project, this is a 'body project'. In the absence of obvious social outlets for creativity, the individual turns back on himself and to the transformation of his own flesh.

Body piercing expresses the crisis of social identity—but it actually also makes it worse, too. Focusing on claiming control over my body amounts to making a declaration of independence from everybody else.

People with hidden piercings comment on how pleased they were they had something private. One says: 'I get so happy just walking along and knowing that I have a secret that no one else could ever guess!' Another said that they now had 'something that people could not judge me for, and something that I could hide'. Another said that her piercing made her realise that 'what other people say or think doesn't matter. The only thing that mattered at that moment was that I was happy with this piercing; I felt beautiful and comfortable in my own skin. . . . They remind me that I'm beautiful to who it matters . . . **me**.' (14)

Body modification encourages a turn away from trying to build personal identity through relationships with others, and instead tries to resolve problems in relation to one's own body. When things are getting rough, or when somebody wants to change their lives, the answer could be a new piercing or a new tattoo. There is even an underlying element of self-hatred here, as individuals try to deal with their problems by doing violence to themselves. As 17-year-old Laura told me: 'You push yourself to do more and more. . . . You want it to hurt.'

This means that the biggest questions—of existence, self-identity, life progression, creativity—are being tackled with flimsiest of solutions. A mark on the skin or a piercing through the tongue cannot genuinely resolve grief, increase creativity, or give a solid grounding to self-identity. For this reason, body modification can become an endless, unfulfilling quest, as one piercing only fuels a desire for another. All the contributions to BMEZine start by saying how much their life has been changed—but then promptly go on to plan their next series of piercings. 'Piercing can be addictive!', they warn cheerily.

30 Body modification should be put back in the fashion box. As a way of improving personal appearance, piercing and tattooing are no better or worse that clothes, makeup or hair gel. It is when body modification is loaded with existential significance that the problems start.

Notes

[1] 'Ladies who lunch get a tattoo for starters', *The Times*, 18 June 2003.
[2] 'Body piercing, tattooing, self-esteem, and body investment in adolescent girls', *Adolescence*, Fall 2002.
[3] See The Changing Status of Tattoo Art, by Hoag Levins.
[4] Police reject tattooed applicant, BBC News, 16 June 2003.
[5] Navy draws a line on some forms of body piercing, ornamentation, tattoos, *Stars and Stripes*, European edition, 29 January 2003.
[6] *Modernity and Self-Identity: Self and Society in the Late Modern Age*, Anthony Giddens, Polity Press, 1991. Buy this book from Amazon (UK).
[7] See the Body Modification Ezine.
[8] Quoted in *Body Modification*, (ed) Mike Featherstone, Nottingham Trent University, 2000.
[9] Quoted in *Body Modification*, (ed) Mike Featherstone, Nottingham Trent University, 2000.
[10] Quoted in *The Body Aesthetic*, (ed) Tobin A Siebers, University of Michigan Press, 2000.
[11] Body Piercing in the West: a Sociological Inquiry, by Susan Holtham.
[12] My Beautiful Piercing, on BMEnzine.
[13] *The Customised Body*, by Ted Polhemus and Housk Randall, 2000.
[14] All from the Body Modification Ezine.

Reflect & Write

- ❑ Do you agree with Appleton's opening claim that "body modification has lost its last trace of taboo"? Why or why not?
- ❑ How does Appleton argue that piercings and other body modifications reflect on the individual's self-identity? Find a specific passage in the article where she makes a strong claim about this relationship.
- ❑ How does Appleton balance primary and secondary research? Does she prioritize one more than the other? What effect does this have on her argument?
- ❑ Look at Appleton's conclusion and her claim that "Body modification should be put back in the fashion box." Did you see suggestions earlier in the essay that her argument would head in this directions? Find specific examples from the earlier paragraphs that either anticipate—or contradict—this final pronouncement.
- ❑ **Write.** If you were the editor of a magazine intending to publish Appleton's piece, what visual rhetoric would you suggest including to support the argument? Write a

memo to your magazine's research department to detail the types of visuals that you would like them to find to accompany your republication of this article. Note where in the article each image should go as well as how each image would work to reinforce the particular point being made at that point in the essay.

PERSPECTIVES ON THE ISSUE

1. Compare the recent controversies over Christian t-shirts in America, in which Christians themselves find the shirts potentially offensive as disrespectful visual rhetoric, against the debates over headscarves in France, where government officials are telling religious students not to make themselves visible as such in schools. What are the similarities between these issues? Where do the parallels end? Can there be a blanket policy for wearing markers of religion in public? Does it depend on context, audience, and the argument of the rhetoric itself? How does the visual rhetoric of attire that merges religious and nationalist rhetoric make a persuasive argument?
2. Visit and study the Religious Tolerance log of news events concerning religious clothing and jewelry in schools, linked through the *Envision* Website. How does this list provide evidence for the way students choose to wear clothing that suggest their arguments on an issue? Pick examples from the list and discuss them in relation to the articles by LaFerla and Mitchell. Then write a report naming instances of people at your school using fashion to convey a strong political or religious message. If you want, you can convert your report into a blog. Add hyperlinks to indicate your research and photographs wherever you can.
www.pearsonhighered.com/envision/428a
3. In an article entitled "Wearing your Religion," published in *The News-Star* (June 3, 2005), a newspaper in northeastern Louisiana, writer Magin McKenna seems to offer an objective report on a new trend in wearing religious icons on t-shirts. Yet what do her research findings reveal about the differences between American and European markets, or about the predominance of certain religions? Compare these t-shirts with the racial t-shirts printed (and then recalled) by Abercrombie & Fitch, linked through the *Envision* Website.
www.pearsonhighered.com/envision/428b
4. Based on your study of the images in this chapter, consider how the tattoo as a visual mark has transformed as the body bearing it has changed with time? How does the gender of the tattooed body carry great importance—for firefighters, for biker culture, for the Iranian woman with a gun, and for the examples of tattooed bodies throughout history?
5. Explore the subcultures of extreme body modification such as nail art, body piercing, and branding. How are responses to such visual rhetoric on the body shaped by cultural values and shared beliefs?

FROM READING TO RESEARCH

1. Pamela Abbott, Francesca Sapsford, and the editors of *Fabulous* magazine target young women in their discussion of clothing and identity. How does media attention to these same issues affect young men? Using examples from contemporary popular culture (magazines, celebrity culture), as well as interviews and ethnographic research modeled on that of Abbott and Sapsford, research this question and write a report that identifies how fashion trends inscribe identity for the young men.

Seeing Connections
See the *At a Glance* Box on page 107 for strategies for composing and conducting effective surveys.

2. Historical inquiry into global cultures will bring you new perspectives on tattoos as an important cultural ritual. Go to your library and locate two issues of *National Geographic* to find their images and create a photo essay in which you match these examples of tattooed bodies to examples in your own community: Alexandra Boulat, "Bold strokes of saffron mark a woman in Zaouia Ahansal," *National Geographic* (January 2005); "A Yemini woman displays the handiwork of a local artist who uses dye made from henna plants and a paint called khidab," *National Geographic* (February 2005). Now apply the argument from one of the scholarly pieces in this case study to the issue of henna. Analyze the issue from a historical perspective using your research and looking at temporary henna tattoos used in wedding ceremonies and parties, on boardwalks, and in traditional cultures. How does henna have a similarly rich and complex history in terms of what it means to mark the body in this way? Conduct a research paper on this issue and compose your own contribution to scholarship.
3. According to the Anti-Defamation League, "Religious messages on T-shirts and the like may not be singled out for suppression. Students may wear religious attire, such as yarmulkes and head scarves, and they may not be forced to wear gym clothes that they regard, on religious grounds, as immodest." See "Religion in the Public Schools," Anti-Defamation League, linked through the *Envision* Website. Consider the fact that some students see putting on an athletic uniform as an imposition on their religious or cultural values. How might you make an argument to defend students who seek to avoid wearing such visual rhetoric on their bodies? Conduct a survey of your peers in college or in your community. Then, using the survey results along with your reading in this chapter, develop a research paper on this issue. Craft a thesis and make your argument with ample references to your sources.
www.pearsonhighered.com/envision/429

Visit www.pearsonhighered.com/envision for expanded assignment guidelines and student projects.
Visit www.mycomplab.com for additional general writing and research resources.

CHAPTER 13

Sports and Media

When we see sports on television or covered in our favorite magazine, are we just viewers enjoying the show of athletics or does the media shape our experience of sports in some way? Why are certain sports favored by certain cultures? What role does the media have in shaping these choices? Who gets to be represented in sports coverage?

We'll tackle some of these questions in the pages that follow. We come to agree with scholar Paul Mark Pederson, who has suggested, "Sport and mass media are inextricably linked together in a symbiotic relationship. These two institutions rely on each other—the mass media sell sport and sport sells the mass media."

FIGURE 13.1. Track star Michael Johnson poses on part of the American flag for a cover of the *Time* special issue on the 1996 summer Olympics.

We can see this relationship represented in Figure 13.1, the *Time* magazine cover with which we open this chapter. The Olympics as a modern spectacle speaks to the power of spectatorship, the sporting arena, and the way the media brings international events back to the fans across the world. The picture itself presents a convergence of many of the themes that we explore in this chapter: the glorifying of both Michael Johnson's performance and his physique as an athlete, as he stands proud atop his pedestal; the international context of the Olympics offset by the patriotism of this staged photo; and the way that sports help shape our collectively held notions about race and masculinity. We'll examine these issues and many more, exploring questions about sports, identity, culture, gender, race, and how the media shapes our very experience of watching the games we love to see.

ENGINEERING A BETTER ATHLETE

From classical times, the image of the athlete has been one used to represent perfection in human form. Take, for example, the lost sculpture *Discobolus* (Figure 13.2), dated at around 450BC, which captures Greek sculptor Myron's idea of physical prowess and athleticism. Caught in the moment before releasing the discus, this athlete epitomizes *rhythmos*, a combination of balance and harmony, and *symmetria*, in his perfectly proportioned torso and limbs. In motion yet in stasis, *Discobolus* speaks to the potential for athletic greatness that is emblematized by the perfect physical form.

Even centuries later, we continue to idealize the athlete's capabilities through his appearance. Brawny arms, chiseled abs, muscular calves, strong pectoral muscles: these continue to be the standard against which many measure our athletes. But today we must question these ideals. Are these the markers of physical perfection, the visible results of the successfully trained athlete? Or are they something else, perhaps the end result of a performance enhancement practice—herbal cocktails, illegal stereoids, high-tech training regimens, or even gene doping—used to bolster the body's natural abilities? And does it matter? As science continues to advance into the field of sports, we find ourselves at an ethical crossroads. While most agree that steroid use constitutes a type of cheating, many are unsure of how to assess the use of perfectly legal enhancements, such as sleeping at high altitudes or in oxygen-rich tents or competing in technologically sophisticated smart suits. What do sports actually test? How can we be sure that all athletes are performing on a level playing field?

FIGURE 13.2. Myron's *Discobolus* embodies the classical definition of idealized athleticism.

These questions have wracked a sports industry now battered by drug abuse scandals that have led to severe consequences on many levels. Once-revered sports like baseball have been defamed, and, even at the Olympics, officials spend more time and money testing athletes for illegal and potentially dangerous performance-enhancing chemicals than they do judging events. In the most extreme cases, the quest for physical perfection and maximum performance has led to the death of star athletes, like baseball prospect Steve Bechler who died after using chemicals he believed would help improve his game.

To complicate matters, the quest for top athletic performance—and the achievement of perfection it suggests—is often a passion embraced by more than the players on the field or the runners on the track. Trainers, team owners, coaches, parents, pharmaceutical companies, and even national leaders all have a stake in the accomplishment of sports figures. As Mike Sokolove writes in his article for this chapter, "A whole subculture of athletes—and the coaches and chemists who are in the business of improving their performances—is eager for the latest medical advances." The newest methods of changing athletic looks and acts are found not only in bottles of Xenadrine or chemicals such as the human growth hormone erythropoietin (EPO), but they are also located within such technological advances as the Speedo LZR Racer suit, genetically engineered food, and nonstick spike sport shoes.

In the articles that follow, you'll be challenged to think about what is at stake in the quest to engineer the perfect athlete. We'll consider, with Steven Shapin, whether "steroid use is the natural consequence of the hyper-competitiveness and performance anxiety of our entire culture," and we'll ponder with Kieron Murphy the consequences of using chemistry to bioengineer the next great athlete. We'll study how standards of masculinity shape decisions for some athletes, such as Dominican baseball hopefuls, to take veterinary steroids, and how witnessing their sports heroes succumbing to steroid abuse affects the younger generation of athletes.

Reflect & Write

- ❑ Does *Discobolus* reflect your ideas of the perfect athletic form? Which athlete or sport would you choose to represent in your own sculpture of *rhythmos* and *symmetria*? Why?
- ❑ If you had to rework the sculpture to reflect athletes in the steroid age, what changes would you make?
- ❑ **Write.** Imagine that you have been asked to provide input on a museum exhibit on The Ideal Athlete that includes *Discobolus* as one of its showcase pieces. Write a memo to the curator in which you suggest a focus (time period, athletes) or even pieces of art (posters, sculptures, etc.) that you think would work well with Myron's sculpture to make an argument about the perfect athlete. Be sure to include rationale for your choices.

■ *In 2008, director* **Christopher Bell** *premiered* Bigger, Stronger, Faster, *his documentary about anabolic steroid usage, at the Sundance Film Festival. Focusing principally on the steroid use of Bell himself and his two brothers, the film questions the inconsistency with which Americans address the issue of performance-enhancing drug usage. In particular, the film looks at the generation that grew up idolizing sports and action heroes such as Hulk Hogan, Arnold Schwarzenegger, and Barry Bonds (all of whom have admitted steroid usage sometime during their sports careers), asking the question: "When you discover that your heroes have all broken the rules, do you follow the rules, or do you follow your heroes?"*

Bigger, Stronger, Faster*

FIGURE 13.3. This theatrical release movie poster was chosen as the cover image for the DVD release.

FIGURE 13.4. An alternate version of the theatrical release poster relies on slightly different strategies to appeal to moviegoers.

Official Movie Synopsis

In America, we define ourselves in the superlative; we are the biggest, strongest, fastest country in the world. We award speed, size, and above all else winning at sport, at business and at war. Metaphorically we are a nation on steroids. Is it any wonder that so many of our heroes are on performance enhancing drugs?

From the producers of *Bowling for Columbine* and *Fahrenheit 9/11* comes a new film that unflinchingly explores our win-at-all-cost culture through the lens of a personal journey. Blending comedy and *pathos*, BIGGER, STRONGER, FASTER* is a collision of pop culture, animated sequences and first-person narrative, with a diverse cast including US Congressmen, professional athletes, medical experts, and everyday gym rats.

At its heart, this is the story of director Christopher Bell and his two brothers, who grew up idolizing muscular giants like Hulk Hogan, Sylvester Stallone, and Arnold Schwarzenegger, and who went on to become members of the steroid-subculture in an effort to realize the American dream. When you discover that your heroes have broken all the rules, do you follow the rules, or do you follow your heroes?

Reflect & Write

Seeing Connections
See Chapter 3, page 58, for strategies for crafting an effective position paper.

- ❑ Consider the compositional differences between the two movie posters. How does the choice of background, the depiction of sports figures, the placement of the title, and the use of color and symbols influence the argument that each poster makes? How does the asterisk function differently in each? How does each poster draw on *pathos*, *ethos*, and *kairos* in making its argument?
- ❑ Look carefully at the movie synopsis, taken from the official *Bigger, Stronger, Faster** Website. What is the "argument" that this pitch makes, beyond "buy tickets to see this movie"? In what context does the synopsis ask its audience to consider the movie? What is the effect of ending the synopsis with a rhetorical question?
- ❑ The film producers selected Figure 13.3 to serve as the cover image for the theatrical release and to provide the visual accompaniment to the synopsis on the official Website. Analyze that image in relation to the written summary. Why do you think they chose this image over the one shown in Figure 13.4? What argument could you make for the second image being the better choice?
- ❑ **Write.** Both posters ask the question, "Is it Still Cheating if Everyone's Doing It?" Write a brief 400–600 word position paper in which you answer that question in relation to performance-enhancing drug usage, taking into account the conflict that *Bigger, Stronger, Faster** addresses: the responsibilities of athletes as role models in contemporary sports culture. For added challenge, watch the film, and then write your essay using examples from the film to inform your answer.

CREATIVE PRACTICE

Visit the *Bigger*, *Stronger*, Faster* Website, linked through the *Envision* Website. Using the skills you developed in Chapter 5 (see pages 101–103), consider how this site works to develop a specific argument about the film. Be sure to look at each of the pages linked from the tab horizontal menu.

Some questions to consider:

- The "Trailers and Clips" page contains four different windows into the film. Why do you think the producers chose these four clips? Knowing that viewers are most likely to watch them in order (left to right), why do you think they arranged them this way?
- How is the "Press" page designed to increase the film's ethos? What is the effect of highlighting some quotes at the top and then linking additional reviews at the bottom of the page?
- What photographs would you have anticipated would have been included on the "Photos" page? To what extent do the ones actually showcased there correspond to your expectations? What do these photos add to the site's overall argument? Why include photos at all?
- Look at the "Research" page. What information is provided? What does it suggest about the project? About the audience? About the level of scholarship behind the movie?

Write up your analysis as a one- to two-page essay that looks at how these elements contribute to the overall effectiveness of this site as an argument and marketing tool.

http://www.pearsonhighered.com/envision/434

In recent years, the All-American image of baseball has been tarnished by repeated accusations of steroid use and doping among its players. This visual reading compiles a range of responses by cartoonists to the debate about the role of doping in professional baseball.

Political Cartoons: Steroids and Baseball

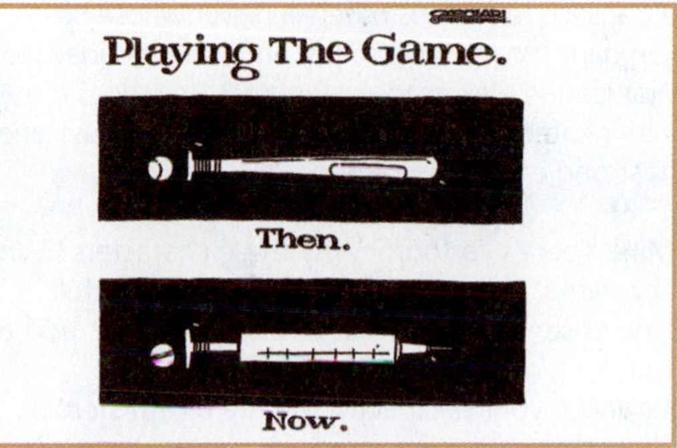

FIGURE 13.5. James Casciari's cartoon uses a then-and-now comparison in its argument about the recent change in "equipment" used by baseball players.

Source: James Casciari/Scripps Howard News Service.

FIGURE 13.6. Gary Varvel reworks a classic Peanuts scenario in this 2005 cartoon about baseball and steroids.

Source: By permission of Gary Varvel and Creators Syndicate, Inc.

FIGURE 13.7. In this 2009 cartoon, Mike Keefe depicts fan reaction to the Manny Ramirez steroid scandal.

Reflect & Write

- ❑ How does each cartoonist's rhetorical style provide an argument about the visible effects of steroids and performance-enhancing drugs? Notice the alterations to the body presented in each cartoon.
- ❑ How does James Casciari use both visual and verbal strategies of argument to suggest the way "the game" has changed? What does he mean through this play on words and images?
- ❑ What argument is made about influence in the Charlie Brown cartoon by placing in Snoopy's hands a book about Jose Canseco (a famous baseball player whose best-selling book, *Juiced: Wild Times, Rampant 'Roids, Smash Hits, and How Baseball Got Big*, claimed that 85 percent of major league players took steroids)? How does the book, together with Snoopy's steroid-inflated body, offer a perspective on cause and effect? Is Charlie Brown's comment strong enough in response? How might you rewrite the bubble?
- ❑ How does symbolism operate in Mike Keefe's cartoon? Why these characters? Why these props? Why this setting? Why names the speech bubble instead of a full, declarative sentence? What does the observer, peeking in through the door, add to the visual argument?
- ❑ **Write.** Draft a short position paper about your perspective on the recent steroid abuse scandals in sports. Having done so, convey the same argument—but this time by sketching a cartoon. Now exchange essays and cartoons with a classmate and discuss the ways the different media affected the composition and the reception of your argument.

Seeing Connections
Review the Prewriting Checklist at the end of Chapter 1 for ideas about how to use elements such as character, setting, composition, captions, layout, and imagery to convey your argument in your cartoon.

■ *"Clean Up Hitters" originally appeared in the April 18, 2005, issue of the* New Yorker. *Although it begins as a book review of Jose Canseco's eye-opening expose* Juiced: Wild Times, Rampant 'Roids, Smash Hits, and How Baseball Got Big, *social historian* **Steve Shapin** *expands his argument to provide a historical context for the controversy and to demonstrate the complexities behind the medical and ethical implication of steroid use. Shapin is the Franklin L. Ford Professor of the History of Science at Harvard University.*

Clean Up Hitters: The Steroid Wars and the Nature of What's Natural

Steven Shapin

One young man leads another to a toilet stall, cautiously looking around to make sure they're not being observed. Then he has him lower his trousers so that he can get at his buttocks. What follows is a matter of enormous public interest. Years later, President George W. Bush makes a speech condemning it. Congressional hearings are held to investigate it and to frame public policy.

It is the summer of 1988; the toilets are in the home locker room of the Oakland Athletics; and Jose Canseco is injecting Mark McGwire with anabolic steroids. Or so Canseco recounts in "Juiced: Wild Times, Rampant 'Roids, Smash

Hits, and How Baseball Got Big" . . . . "It was really no big deal," Canseco writes. "We would just slip away, get our syringes and vials, and head into the bathroom area of the clubhouse to inject each other." By the late nineteen-nineties, according to Canseco, teammates were pairing off together in bathroom stalls with such regularity that it became an object of clubhouse drollery: "What are you guys, fags?"

Anabolic steroids are synthetic variants of such naturally occurring hormones as testosterone. They're called anabolic because they work in "constructive metabolism," during which simple materials provided to the gut or the bloodstream are built up into complex living tissue. Among the main effects that athletes want is a boost of skeletal muscle mass, and anabolic steroids help you get big fast. Canseco says he started doing anabolic steroids and growth hormone in 1985—the first baseball player to use steroids "in a serious way," he claims—and he put on twenty-five pounds of solid muscle in just a few months. More followed. McGwire grew massive, too, and he and Canseco became known as "the Bash Brothers."

Canseco explains that oil-based anabolic steroids require a large-gauge needle, so you have to be careful where you inject yourself. If you're a baseball player, you don't want to use your quad or calf muscles, because it may hamper your running, or your shoulder muscles, because you're doing a lot of throwing and catching. That leaves the buttocks. It takes a lot of practice to be able to do it yourself; when you start out, you need a little help from your friends. Once you become more accomplished, you can inject yourself, and then you'll want to become "an ambidextrous injector," he says, "because you definitely are going to want to hit both sides of your glute." (If you keep hitting the same spot, he warns, "it can get nasty.") Steroid use, as Canseco tells it, is itself a form of athleticism. Different steroids do different things: if you want just to build muscle mass, one sort will do; if you want to run fast, there are steroids to increase your fast-twitch muscle fibres. The congeries of bodybuilding substances Canseco claims to have used includes Deca-Durabolin, Winstrol, Equipoise, and Anavar, as well as human growth hormone. He delightedly recalls that early in his steroid-fuelled career he was dubbed "the Natural."

5 Canseco writes that steroid use is no big deal, but he's wrong. President Bush made the remarkable decision to use his 2004 State of the Union address to denounce its dangers ("The use of performance-enhancing drugs like steroids in baseball, football, and other sports is dangerous, and it sends the wrong message—that there are shortcuts to accomplishment, and that performance is more important than character"). The U.S. Anti-Doping Agency sees it as a threat to sportsmanship ("Deterring the use of drugs in sport is necessary to preserve the integrity of sport in the United States"). The National Institute on Drug Abuse is alarmed at a range of irreversible side effects associated with steroid use by bodybuilding adolescents. There are fans who now wonder, say, whether there should be an asterisk by Barry Bonds's home-run record. And, of course, it's a criminal offense to possess anabolic steroids without a valid prescription.

Among the justifications for banning these substances are their side effects. For males, these may include breast development, atrophied testicles, and reduced sperm count, as well as baldness, severe acne, jaundice, tremors, an enlarged prostate, problems in liver and kidney function (with the possibility of tumor formation), hypertension, elevated risk of stroke and heart attack, and mood swings—the enhancement of masculine aggressiveness popularly known as "'roid rage." When administered to adolescent bodies still in the course of development, steroids may cause permanently stunted growth; their use has been implicated in some teen-age suicides. Sentiment against steroid use also flows from a widespread sense of fair play and equity. The ideal of the level playing field translates broadly into the belief that all competitors should come to play with normal bodies, functioning normally.

So it may come as a surprise that "Juiced" celebrates steroid use as part of a new era of "clean living" in baseball, driving out alcohol, cocaine, marijuana, and even amphetamines—the "greenies" that Jim Bouton wrote about in "Ball Four," back in 1970. With the "trend toward better fitness that came with steroid use," Canseco maintains, "you saw bigger, stronger, faster, and *healthier* athletes, instead of those raggedy, run-down, pot-bellied ball players of previous eras." Steroid use among athletes has clearly aroused national passions, but passionate arousal isn't the ideal frame of mind for reasoned debate. Are the medical and moral evils of steroids in competitive sport really so unambiguous?

Nothing in "Juiced" suggests that Canseco was using steroids under a physician's care, or even on a doctor's advice. He seems to have had himself periodically checked out by doctors, but that's all. He was, instead, part of the great civic tradition condensed in the old motto "Every man is his own physician." Canseco learned the techniques of steroid use by noticing how his own body reacted to the chemicals, and adjusting dosages and combinations accordingly. Yet steroid use also belongs to the history of mainstream modern medicine, and John Hoberman's excellent "Testosterone Dreams: Rejuvenation, Aphrodisia, Doping" . . . tells much of the story of how and why steroids came to the pharmacy shelves.

In the late eighteen-eighties, a septuagenarian French physiologist named Charles-Edouard Brown–Sequard announced that he had been rejuvenated—and had the arc of his urine lengthened—by injecting himself with extracts from the sex glands of a dog and a guinea pig. Brown-Sequard's "organotherapy" created a considerable market for these crude extracts, and by the nineteen-tens the transplant of animal testicles and testicular extract was heralded as a treatment for homosexuals, who could thereby achieve an "energetic and manly aspect." But the real breakthrough came with the artificial production of androgenic and estrogenic hormones in the nineteen-thirties, especially the synthesis of testosterone in 1935. In testosterone, the medical profession saw hopes for restored virility and vigor, the extension of life, the cure for a range of disease, the management or elimination of sexual deviance, and enhanced performance in a variety of life functions. That year, *Newsweek* declared that the hormone could prevent "premature sterility and feminine characteristics in men."

10 In a familiar pattern, the transformation of previously "natural" features of human life into diseases marched in step with the trade in hormones: one medical historian calls them "drugs looking for diseases." Testosterone has, in recent years, been prescribed for "the andropause"—the decline in testosterone levels supposedly suffered by many men over sixty-five—and for women who consult doctors for low libido. Elder sex is completing the transition from deviance to embarrassment to a chemically assisted new normal. It's the pharmaceutical version of "If you build it, they will come," and you can find a parable to this effect in "Juiced." Canseco says that when he joined the Texas Rangers he introduced Rafael Palmeiro to steroids, and Palmeiro's newfound prowess on the field led to a lucrative deal to endorse Viagra.

So there has always been the thinnest of lines between medical augmentation and medical restoration. Is the task of the physician to maintain and restore normal function? If so, what is to count as normal? Or is it to enhance and release the full range of human potential? Hoberman plausibly predicts that "the future of testosterone drugs will evolve within the contest between a wide-open medical ethos—one that approves medical interventions to enhance a range of life functions"—and our traditional sense that a well-lived life follows a natural trajectory from birth to death and that aging is a fate, not a disease."

Hormonal therapies lie right at the heart of these tensions, along with the chemical dosing of rambunctious kids, gastric-bypass surgery, and the more exotic forms of infertility medicine. Hoberman worries that "physicians who cater to patients' demands that are motivated by vanity or social fashion diminish the stature of practitioners by making them as much beauticians as healers." But who is to judge what pain is suffered by the obese or the wrinkled, not to mention the parents of aggressive and inattentive children? And who has the right to say which conditions you must live with and which you may mobilize the resources of chemical or surgical art to avoid?

The notion of what is normal—and, therefore, of what physicians may seek to restore and what they should leave untouched—isn't arbitrary, but neither is it unambiguous. A recent celebration of the biotechnological future, Ramez Naam's "More than Human: Embracing the Promise of Biological Enhancement" . . . points out that athletes' use of injectable erythropoietin (epo) to boost their red-blood-cell count, and thus their endurance, may come to be replaced by some sort of gene therapy—a once-and-for-all introduction of the genes allowing individuals to produce a higher level of red blood cells as long as they live. Is it an unnatural result when it's produced by your own undrugged body?

When anti-doping organizations condemn steroids as a threat to the "integrity" of sport, they take a view about what should count as artificial enhancement and what as legitimate treatment. So it's worth noting that anabolic steroids not only helped Canseco turn into a home-run-hitting monster but also, he says, allowed him to recuperate from a series of back surgeries which could otherwise have ended his career. "I was on steroids and growth hormone," he recounts of his third surgery, "so I guess they accelerated the natural healing process."

15 There's overwhelming evidence that professional cycling, and particularly the Tour de France, is a chem lab on wheels, but even here the line between the augmentative and the recuperative use of drugs is deeply unclear. Scaling the Alpe d'Huez is painful, and rebounding from *hors categorie* climbs to ride the next day calls for extraordinary recuperative powers. Is it unethical for a doctor to assist cyclists in managing that pain and restoring that extraordinary version of "normal" function which allows them to do their job? Physicians who make their living doing so can plausibly see themselves as healers. Spectators following the Tour de France seem to understand that. Even at the height of the doping revelations of 1998, the public continued to show their support for the cyclists. And one reason they did so was, as Hoberman says, "their appreciation of the physical ordeal the riders had to endure. Many ordinary people who depended on cigarettes, caffeine, or alcohol to make it through their days had no trouble sympathizing with men whose suffering could be read on their drawn and haggard faces."

In one way or another, we've always been juiced. When coffee and tea were new in the Western world, they were seen as powerful (and often dangerous) mind- and body-altering substances. The historical anthropologist Alan Macfarlane has recently argued for a causal link between the rise of British tea-drinking and the burst of physical energy that accompanied the Industrial Revolution. Opiated artists and coke-stoked musicians inspire both a tragic sense of damaged lives and a widespread appreciation of their chemically modified imagination and chemically managed psychic pain. And what do we say about the socially transformative effects of the steroidal birth-control pill? Do we put an asterisk next to the sexual revolution?

So the notion of the natural doesn't resolve the baseball issue; nor does the notion of harm or the notion of proper medical practice. The right question to ask is whether steroid use among competitive athletes is *fair*. To be sure, the definition of what's fair (as opposed to what's cheating) isn't any less contestable than the notion of what's normal. Nothing but shifting cultural preference lies behind our view that Lance Armstrong is not cheating if he sleeps in a pressure chamber to boost his red-blood-cell count but would be cheating if he used epo; or our view that it's all right to use methylxanthines (the stimulants in coffee) but not ephedra. These are ethical matters, and although ethical judgments are historically changing and culturally variable, the conventions express who we are and what we value. We can't live without them. It's possible to imagine a future in which the medically supervised and regulated juicing of athletes will become the norm. (Even then, "natural" athletics would undoubtedly continue as a specialty taste, comparable to the organic-foods section in the supermarket.) But it's impossible to imagine any competitive sport or social practice in which some forms of advantage-seeking aren't defined as cheating and sanctioned accordingly. To complain that the rules are contingent and somewhat arbitrary is beside the point: games are the celebration of such rules. That's what makes them games.

It's a matter of debate what damage "proper" steroid use might cause to baseball players and other athletes, as is the precise extent of current use. Hoberman maintains that steroid use is the natural consequence of the hyper-competitiveness and performance anxiety of our entire culture, and, if he's right, steroids are the price we pay for the spectator goods we demand. I suspect the matter is more complicated than that. The public is perfectly aware that the demand for performance creates the conditions for cheating in sport, as it does for fraud in science or in bookkeeping. But at the same time much of the public holds cheaters accountable for succumbing to competitive pressure. We've now decided that steroid use crosses the line. Yes, we're the ones who drew that line, and we could have drawn it somewhere else. But what of it? To understand all is still not quite the same as to forgive all.

Reflect & Write

- ❑ How effective is the opening scene as an introduction to the article's main argument? What kind of issues does the scene between two men in a bathroom raise? What are the logical fallacies in connecting sexuality, masculinity, and legality for an article on steroid use?
- ❑ "Steroid use, as Canseco tells it, is itself a form of athleticism," writes Shapin. Analyze this claim. Do you agree? What evidence does Shapin use to support it?
- ❑ The voice of Shapin as author emerges clearly in paragraph 5; what do you make of this tone shift? How does he support his rhetorical stance through appeals to *ethos*, *logos*, and *pathos* consecutively?
- ❑ **Write.** Compose a response to Shapin's argument that supports, advances, or contests his claims. Use direct quotes from the article to support your position; be sure to use proper MLA parenthetical form in doing so.

Seeing Connections
Review Chapters 6 and 7 for suggestions about integrating and citing quotations effectively.

COLLABORATIVE CHALLENGE

Together with three or four classmates, design a brief survey or interview questionnaire to conduct on your campus or in your community concerning doping in professional sports. You might decide to interview coaches, players, parents, and community or school leaders. Based on your reading in this chapter so far, what key questions might you ask? How do each of these groups perceive the situation of performance-enhancing drugs? Analyze rhetorically the answers you receive to determine your community's stance. Write a report based on the interviews and quote from people you interview. Present your findings to the class.

■ **Michael Sokolove** *is a contributing writer for the* New York Times *and the author of* The Ticket Out: Darryl Strawberry and the Boys of Crenshaw *(2004). A longer version of this article was originally published in the Sunday, January 18, 2004, edition of the* New York Times Magazine. *Two days later, during his State of the Union address, President Bush called for stronger measures to curtail the use of performance enhancers in baseball.*

Drug in Sport: The Shape to Come

Michael Sokolove

On a brisk day last December, I was led through a warren of red-brick buildings on the campus of the University of Pennsylvania in West Philadelphia and then up to a fifth-floor molecular physiology laboratory. I had come to visit some mice—and to take a peek at the future of sport.

I had heard about these mice, heard them called 'mighty mice', but I was still shocked at the sight of them. There they were in several small cages, grouped with normal mice, all of them nibbling on mouse chow pellets. The mighty mice looked like a different animal. They were built like cattle, with thick necks and big haunches. They belonged in some kind of mouse rodeo.

The Penn researchers have used gene therapy on these mice to produce increased levels of IGF-1, or insulinlike growth factor-1, a protein that promotes muscle growth and repair. They have done this with mice before birth and with mice at four weeks old. A result has been a sort of rodent fountain of youth. The mice show greater than normal muscle size and strength and do not lose it as they age. Rats altered in the same fashion and then put into physical training—they climb little ladders with weights strapped to their backs—have experienced a 35 per cent strength gain in the targeted muscles and have not lost any of it 'detraining', as a human being will when he quits going to the gym.

To H. Lee Sweeney, chairman of Penn's department of physiology, and Elisabeth Barton, an assistant professor, the bizarre musculature of their lab specimens is exciting. This research could eventually be of immense benefit to the elderly and those with various muscle-wasting diseases.

5 'Our impetus, going back to 1988, was to develop a therapy to stop people from getting weak when they get old,' Sweeney explained. 'They fall and injure themselves. We wanted to do something about that.'

Barton has the broad shoulders and athletic build of the competitive cyclist and triathlete she once was. 'You see children with muscular dystrophy and their parents are just so broken up because it's so sad,' she said. 'You see grandparents who can't get out of bed. These are the people this is for.'

But the Penn team has become acutely aware of a population impatient to see its research put into practice—the already strong, seeking to get stronger still. Sweeney gets their emails. One came from a high-school football coach in Pennsylvania not long after Sweeney first presented his findings at a meeting of the American Society for Cell Biology. 'This coach wanted me to treat his whole team,' he said. 'I told him it was not available for humans, and it may not be safe, and if I helped him we would all go to jail. I can only assume he didn't understand how investigational this is. Or maybe he wasn't winning, and his job was on the line.'

Other calls and emails have come from weightlifters and bodybuilders. This kind of thing happens often after researchers publish in even the most arcane medical and scientific journals. A whole subculture of athletes—and the coaches and chemists who are in the business of improving their performances—is eager for the latest medical advances.

Sweeney knows that what he is doing works. The remaining question, the one that will require years of further research to answer, is how safe his methods are. But many athletes don't care about that. They want an edge now. They want money and acclaim. They want a pay-off for their years of sweat and sacrifice, at whatever the cost.

10 'This was serious science, not sports science,' Dr. Gary Wadler, a United States representative to the World Anti-Doping Agency, said when I spoke to him about the Penn experiments. 'As soon as it gets into any legitimate publication, bingo, these people get hold of it and want to know how they can abuse it.'

Sweeney's research will probably be appropriated before it is ever put to its intended medical purpose. Someone will use it to build a better sprinter or shot-putter.

There is a murky quality to sport at the moment. We are in a time of flux. The rules are ambiguous. Everything is a little suspect.

Months before the great slugger Barry Bonds was summoned before a grand jury in December to answer questions about his association with the Bay Area Laboratory Co-Operative, known as Balco, which has been at the center of a spreading drug scandal after the discovery of a new "designer steroid," tetrahydrogestrinone (THG), a veteran American sprinter named Kelli White ran the track meet of her dreams at the World Championships in Paris. She captured the gold medal in the 100-meter and 200-meter races, the first American woman ever to win those sprints in tandem at an outdoor world championship. In both events, the 5-foot-4, 135-pound White, a tightly coiled ball of power and speed, exploded to career-best times.

On a celebratory shopping trip on the Champs-Elysees, White, 26, glimpsed her name in a newspaper headline and asked a Parisian to translate. She learnt that she had failed a post-race drug test and that her medals and $120,000 in prize money were in jeopardy. Later, she acknowledged that she had taken the stimulant modafinil, claiming that she needed it to treat narcolepsy, but had failed to list it on a disclosure form. What she added after that was revealing, perhaps more so than she intended. 'After a competition,' she told reporters, 'it's kind of hard to remember everything that you take during the day.'

15 The THG scandal and the attention focused on Balco, which has advised dozens of top athletes (including White) on the use of dietary supplements, has opened the curtain on the fascinating cat-and-mouse game played between chemists and the laboratory sleuths who try to police them.

But White's statement exposed another, deeper truth: elite athletes in many different sports consume cocktails of vitamins, extracts and supplements, dozens of pills a day—the only people who routinely ingest more pills are Aids patients—in the hope that their mixes of accepted drugs will replicate the effects of the banned substances taken by the cheaters. The cheaters and the non-cheaters alike are science projects. They are the sum total of their innate athletic abilities and their dedication—and all the compounds and powders they ingest and inject.

A narrow tunnel leads to success at the very top levels of sport. This is especially so in Olympic non-team events. An athlete who has devoted his life to sprinting, for example, must qualify for one of a handful of slots on his Olympic team. And to become widely known and make real money, he or she probably has to win one of the gold medals that is available every four years.

The temptation to cheat is human. In the realm of elite international sport, it can be irresistible.

After White failed her drug test, the United States Olympic Committee revealed that five other American athletes had tested positive this summer for modafinil. Did they all suffer from narcolepsy? That would be hard to believe. More likely, word of modafinil and its supposed performance-enhancing qualities (perhaps along with the erroneous information that it was not detectable) went out on the circuit. It became the substance du jour.

20 For athletes, performance-enhancing drugs and techniques raise issues of health, fair play and, in some cases, legality. For the fans, the issues are largely philosophical and aesthetic. On the most basic level, what are we watching, and why? If we equate achievement with determination and character, and that, after all, has always been part of our attachment to sport—to celebrate the physical expression of the human spirit—how do we recalibrate our thinking about sport when laboratories are partners in athletic success?

Major League Baseball seems to have decided that the power generated by bulked-up players is good for the game in the entertainment marketplace. The record-breaking sluggers Mark McGwire and Sammy Sosa have been virtual folk heroes and huge draws at the gate. Their runs at the record books became the dominant narratives of individual seasons. But the sport is much changed. 'Muscle baseball' is the near opposite of what I and many other fans over 30 were raised on, a game that involved strategy, bunting, stolen bases, the hit-and-run play—what is called 'little ball.'

Professional basketball is not generally suspected of being drenched in steroids and other performance enhancers. But anyone who has seen even a few minutes of old games, from, say, 20 years ago, is immediately struck by the evolution of players' physiques. Regardless of how it happened, today's NBA players are heavier and markedly more muscled and the game is tailored to their strengths. It is played according to a steroid aesthetic. What was once a sport of grace and geometry-athletes moving to open spaces on the floor, thinking in terms of passing angles-is now one primarily of power and aggression: players gravitate to the same space and try to go over or through one another.

But it is sports that have fixed standards and cherished records that present fans with the greatest conundrum. If what's exciting is to see someone pole vault to a new, unimaginable height—or become the 'world's fastest human'—how do we respond when our historical frame of reference is knocked askew by the suspicion, or known fact, that an athlete is powered by a banned substance?

But in elite sport, the substances themselves are murky. Because America's $18 billion-a-year (£10bn) dietary-supplement industry is (at best) loosely regulated, some items on sale at ordinary health food shops could well be tainted by steroids or growth hormones. The United States Food and Drug Administration only banned ephedra last month, long after the herbal stimulant was blamed for numerous serious health problems, along with the sudden death last year of Steve Bechler, a Baltimore Orioles pitcher.

25 The whole situation cries out for a dose of clarity, but the closer you look, the fuzzier the picture. Start with the line between what's legal and illegal when it comes to enhancing performance. The line, already blurry, is likely over time to disappear entirely. I visited a US swimmer last September as technicians sealed up his bedroom, after which they installed equipment that reduced the amount of oxygen in his room and turned it into a high-altitude chamber. This is a common and legal training method that Ed Moses, America's best male breaststroker, said he hoped would increase his count of oxygen-carrying red blood cells. A whole team of long-distance runners sponsored by Nike lives in a much more elaborate simulated high-altitude dwelling in Portland, Oregon. The desired effect of the so-called 'live high, train low' method—sleep at altitude, train at sea level—is the same as you would get from taking erythropoietin, or EPO, which increases red-blood-cell production and is banned in sports.

Two other US swimmers, in the lead-up to the Olympic Games in Sydney, were on a regimen of 25 pills a day, including minerals, proteins, amino acids and the nutritional supplement creatine, an effective but not necessarily safe builder of muscle mass. Much of the mix may well have been useless, but athletes tend to take what's put in front of them for fear of passing up the one magic pill.

'I like to think we're on the cutting edge of what can be done nutritionally and with supplements,' the swimmers' coach, Richard Quick, said then as his athletes prepared for the 2000 Games. 'If you work hard consistently, with a high level of commitment, you can do steroid-like performances.' One of his swimmers, Dara Torres, who increased her bench press from 105 pounds to 205 pounds and swam career-best times at the age of 33, said at the time that her goal was to 'keep up with the people who are cheating without cheating.'

And who are the cheaters? Everyone else. One primary motivation to cheat is the conviction that everyone else is at it. To draw the often arbitrary lines between performance enhancing and performance neutral, between health endangering and dicey but take it at your own risk—to ensure that sport remains 'pure'—a vast worldwide bureaucracy has been enlisted.

At the lowest level are those who knock on the doors of athletes in their homes and apartments in the United States and Europe and in the mountain villages of Kenya and at the training sites in China and demand 'out of competition' urine samples. Higher up on the pyramid are the laboratories around the world chosen to scan the urine (and blood) of elite athletes for the molecular signatures of any of hundreds of banned substances. At the top of the drug-fighting pyramid are the titans of international sport—the same people who often cannot see to it that a figure-skating competition is fairly judged.

30 Nearly every drug that is used by athletes to boost performance started out as a therapeutic miracle. Steroids are still prescribed for men with serious testosterone deficiencies. Aids patients and others with muscle-wasting conditions are dosed with steroids.

Until the mid-Eighties, people suffering from severe anaemia, as a result of chronic renal failure or other causes, had to have frequent blood transfusions. The development of recombinant human erythropoietin was a godsend. Instead of transfusions, anaemics could get injections to boost their red-blood-cell count. But what would the effect of EPO be on a person with a normal or better than normal red-blood-cell count? What could it do for an already genetically gifted, highly trained endurance athlete? Just what you would expect: make a super-endurance athlete.

EPO swept the European professional cycling circuit, nearly destroying the sport. There were police raids, huge stockpiles of EPO confiscated from cyclists' hotel rooms, arrests, trials, wholesale suspensions of competitors. 'Each racer had his little suitcase with dopes and syringes,' a former doctor said about one incident. 'They did their own injections.'

EPO migrated to other endurance sports, including cross-country skiing, marathoning and orienteering. Inevitably, it showed its fatal flip side.

'In simplest terms, EPO turns on the bone marrow to make more red blood cells,' says

Dr Gary Wadler, the American delegate to the World Anti-Doping Agency. 'But there's a very delicate balance. You can have too much EPO. The body is a finely tuned instrument. It has feedback mechanisms to keep it in balance. What these athletes are often trying to do is get around the feedback, to trick their own bodies.'

35 Between 1989 and 1992, seven Swedish competitors in orienteering—that mix of running and hiking that is sometimes called 'cross country with brains'—died, apparently from heart attacks. Nearly all were in their twenties. As many as 18 Dutch and Belgian cyclists died under similarly mysterious circumstances between 1987 and 1990. 'At first they said it was some kind of virus, a respiratory virus,' Wadler says. 'But what kind of virus only knocks off the most fit individuals in their country? The autopsies were private. All the deaths were not definitively linked.' That it must have been EPO, he added, was obvious.

For weightlifters and competitors in the throwing sports of shot-put, javelin, discus and hammer, the performance enhancer of choice has long been steroids. Anabolic steroids (anabolic means tissue building) increase muscle mass and enhance the explosiveness needed for a wide range of other athletic endeavours: sprinting, jumping, swimming, serving a tennis ball, swinging a baseball bat, delivering a hit on the American football or rugby field. Their use is starkly high risk, high reward. Other side effects include liver tumours, impotence, breast enlargement and shrunken testicles in men and male sexual characteristics in women. (Some of the side effects for women include enlargement of the clitoris, deepening of the voice, facial hair and male-pattern baldness.)

If you want a peek at the future of performance-enhanced sport—at what drug-laced athletes can accomplish—look back to the mid-Eighties, the apex of East Germany's shameful and ruthlessly effective doping programme. The East Germans were not the only practitioners of extreme pharmacological sport, only the most flagrant and well organised. (East Germany is the only nation known to have systematically doped athletes, often minors, without their knowledge.)

Steroid usage works particularly well for women athletes, because they naturally make only a fraction of the testosterone that men produce. John Hoberman says: 'In the 1980s, what we saw was this new breed of monster athletes, particularly on the female side.'

Certain records from this heyday of unpoliced steroid abuse—particularly in sports in which raw strength is a primary requirement—suggest that performances were achieved then that are unlikely to be matched by a clean competitor. The top 14 men's hammer throws in history occurred between 1984 and 1988. In the women's shot-put, you must go all the way down to the 35th farthest throw in history to find one that occurred after 1988.

40 Until last April, the top 10 men's shot-put throws in history occurred between 1975 and 1990. Then, at a competition in Kansas, the American shot-putter Kevin Toth finally broke into that elite group. His distance, 22.67 meters, was the farthest that anyone had put the shot in 13 years. Six months later, Toth's name was among the first to surface in the Balco scandal. Published reports said he had tested positive for THG, the new designer steroid.

In women's sprinting in the 1980s, the star—and still the world-record holder in the 100m and 200m—was Florence Griffith-Joyner, Flo-Jo. Americans loved her style, her body-hugging track suits, her long and fabulously decorated nails, her ebullience. Elsewhere in the world, and even in the United States among those with a knowledge of track and field, Flo-Jo's exploits were viewed with more scepticism.

After Joyner died in 1998, at 38 (the cause was related to a seizure), a strange hybrid of a column appeared in the *New York Times* sports section. Written by Pat Connolly, who had coached Evelyn Ashford, the woman whose 100m record Joyner smashed, it was partly a tribute and partly a posthumous indictment. 'Then, almost overnight, Florence's face changed—hardened along with her muscles that now bulged as if she had been born with a barbell in her crib,' Connolly wrote. 'It was difficult not to wonder if she had found herself an East German coach and was taking some kind of performance-enhancing drugs.'

Flo-Jo had been a very good, but never a champion, world-class sprinter. Her 1988 performance in Seoul was—in the damning parlance of international sport—anomalous.

Baseball is rarely thought of in the context of hammer throwing, shot-putting or women's sprinting. But in terms of anomalous performance, baseball is potentially East Germany in the 1980s: a new frontier. Just as in the steroid-drenched days of Olympic sport, a deep suspicion has attached itself to baseball and its lenient testing programme, not least because of the grotesque, bloated appearance of some of the players.

45 The question of how many home runs it is possible to hit in one season is more open-ended than, say, the fastest possible time a person can achieve in the 100m. Factors such as the size of the ballpark, liveliness of the ball and skill of opposing pitchers affect the outcome. Nevertheless, a century's worth of experience amounted to a pretty persuasive case that around 60 home runs, for whatever combination of reasons, was about the limit.

In 1927, Babe Ruth slugged 60, which remained the record until 1961, when Roger Maris (in a slightly longer season) hit 61. But in 1998 McGwire of the St Louis Cardinals obliterated Maris's record by hitting 70 home runs.

Late in that season, a reporter snooping around McGwire's locker spotted a bottle of androstenedione, or andro, a substance usually described as a steroid 'precursor' that provides a steroid-like effect (and that is still unregulated in the major leagues). McGwire was forced to acknowledge that his strength was neither entirely 'God given' nor acquired solely in the weight room. But McGwire entered baseball already big and as a prodigious home-run hitter: he hit 49 in his first big-league season, a record for rookies. Contrast that with the career arcs of Barry Bonds and Sammy Sosa, which are unlike any in the game's long history. Bonds had never hit more than 46 home runs until the 2000 season and in most years his total was in the 30s. But at age 35, when players normally are on the downside of their production, he hit 49 home runs. The following season he turned into superman, breaking McGwire's record by hitting 73.

Bonds's totals in the next two seasons, 46 and 45, were artificially low because pitchers walked him a staggering 346 times. His new capabilities had thrown the balance between pitcher and hitter completely out of whack: the new Barry Bonds was too good for the game. He needed a league all of his own.

Sosa's progression was even more unusual. In his first eight major-league seasons he averaged 22 home runs, although his totals did steadily increase and he hit 40 in 1996, then a career high. He was selected an All-Star exactly once. Unlike Bonds, he was not considered among baseball's elite players.

50 Then in 1998, McGwire's record-breaking year, Sammy Sosa hit 66 home runs—six more than the great Babe Ruth had hit in his best season. Sosa wasn't done. The following year he hit 63, followed by seasons of 50, 64 and 49—the best five-year total in baseball history.

There is no evidence that Bonds and Sosa have used steroids, but that there is steroid use in baseball, at all levels, is undeniable. Ken Caminiti, voted the National League's most valuable player in 1996, admitted his own use in a *Sports Illustrated* article in 2002 and estimated that at least half the players in the big leagues built strength with steroids. The former slugger Jose Canseco has acknowledged steroid use. In a 2002 *USA Today* survey of 556 big-league players, 44 percent said they felt pressure to take steroids.

Last year, the *Washington Post* published a sad series of stories revealing that teenage prospects in the baseball-rich Dominican Republic, the source of nearly a quarter of all players signed to US professional contracts, are taking veterinary steroids to try to get strong enough to attract the interest of scouts.

Nobody has presented evidence that Sosa or Bonds has built home-run power chemically. And both vehemently deny it. Sosa's name has not surfaced in the Balco case and he has not testified before the grand jury. Bonds did testify in December but he has not been accused of any wrongdoing.

Bonds has acknowledged patronising Balco, which under Victor Conte, its founder, has specialised in testing athletes' blood to determine the levels of elements such as copper, chromium and magnesium and then recommending supplements. Experts I talked to say they consider Conte's theories medical mumbo jumbo, but he consulted dozens of top athletes, including Marion Jones, Amy van Dyken (an Olympic champion swimmer) and Bill Romanowski, a linebacker in the NFL with the Oakland Raiders. Jason Giambi of the New York Yankees was also a client and also testified before the grand jury.

55 The World Anti-Doping Agency—imperfect as it may be—is generally considered an improvement over the patchwork approach to drug

enforcement that preceded it. Created in 1999 at the World Conference on Doping in Sport in Lausanne, Switzerland, the agency was intended to bring coherence to anti-doping regulations and harmonisation among all the different nations and sports bodies expected to enforce them. In theory, it is the ultimate authority on matters of drugs and sport—looming over national Olympic committees and the national and international federations of all the individual sports and making it more difficult for those parochial interests to protect athletes caught doping.

Wada's medical committee devoted several years to compiling an impressively voluminous list of banned substances. But the role of Wada and its president, Dick Pound, is mainly bureaucratic and political. Wada can't slow science down—or influence a culture that hungrily pursues human enhancements of all kinds.

'All of these issues are going to be moot in 20 or 30 years,' says Paul Root Wolpe, a professor of psychiatry at Penn and the chief of bioethics at Nasa. 'We already are seeing a blurring of the line between foods and drugs, so-called nutraceuticals. In the future, it will be more common, accepted. We'll eat certain engineered foods to be sharp for a business meeting, to increase confidence, to enhance endurance before a race or competition.'

What I learnt during my visit to Lee Sweeney's lab at the University of Pennsylvania is that lifting his research for purposes of athletic enhancement is not from some sci-fi future. It's possible—now. Sweeney and his team know for sure they can build muscle mass and strength. Their next step as they try to determine if their methods are safe for humans will be to experiment on larger animals, most likely dogs with muscular dystrophy.

I asked Elisabeth Barton what would happen if some rogue nation or outlaw conglomerate of athletes asked her to disregard scientific prudence and create a human version of the mighty mice. Could she do it?

'Could I?' she answered. 'Oh, yeah, it's easy. It's do-able. It's a routine method that's published. Anyone who can clone a gene and work with cells could do it. It's not a mystery.'

Behind her, Sweeney nodded his head in agreement. 'It's not like growing a third arm or something,' he said. 'You could get there if you worked at it.'

There is a parallel from the past for the entire issue of performance-enhancing drugs, one tied to what was once another unwelcome substance in sports: money. Some casual followers of the Olympic movement may still not fully realise that nearly all of the participants are now paid professionals.

There never was any big announcement that the cherished concept of amateurism—athletes competing for the pure love of sport—had been discarded. But over time, the changed reality has been accepted. Top athletes profiting from under-the-table payments? The public didn't care, and the ideal of amateurism expired, outdated and unenforceable.

One of the last things Pound said to me indicated that he knows, too, that Wada's mission has an expiry date pending. Maybe genetic enhancements really won't work for athletes, he speculated. 'If you strengthen the muscle to three times its normal strength, what happens when you break out of the starting blocks? Do you rip the muscle right off the bone?'

Pound seemed to like the thought of this gruesome image. He paused, then extended the thought. 'That would be nice if that happened,' he said. 'It would be self-regulating.'

Reflect & Write

- ❏ Why does the article open and close with the image of "mighty mice"? Considering that "Mighty Mouse" was a popular cartoon character fifty years ago, how might the image reflect cultural attitudes toward doping athletes today?
- ❏ Sokolove claims that once a drug's benefits appear in "a legitimate publication," then people clamor for it. How might appearing in print validate a drug? Is this an effect of *ethos* or *logos*? What does the look of scholarly research contribute to the economic value and social cache for a drug product?
- ❏ Why does Sokolove consistently compare athletes taking drug, vitamin, and nutrition supplements to AIDS patients? How does this writing strategy affect his overall argument?
- ❏ **Write.** How have sports taken on a new set of visual stereotypes? Locate Sokolove's use of descriptions such as "heavier," "marked," "gruesome," "monster," "bulged," "grotesque," and "bloated," and write a rhetorical analysis as to how his choice of language contributes to his argument.

■ *In this July 7, 2008, article for the Montreal* Gazette, **Margaret Munro** *tapped into the popular and scientific controversy that had started in February of that year when Speedo released its new LZR racer swimsuit. Her article was prompted by the upcoming 2008 Beijing summer Olympics and questions over whether the LZR was in fact "the world's fastest swimsuit," as Speedo boasted, as well as the ethical considerations about using it in the international competition. Munro specializes in scientific and environmental topics and has won four national writing awards from the Canadian Science Writers' Association as well as a 2003 Michener Fellowship for Public Service Journalism.*

Dressing for Success at the Olympics; Is it 'Doping on a Hanger' or is it just a Swimsuit?

Margaret Munro

Canadian Olympian Brent Hayden has a Superman tattoo over his heart. And now he's got the suit to match.

Slick, black and skin-tight, it wraps and compresses Hayden's powerful body with a "corset-like grip." Tightly woven water resistant fabric "reduces muscle oscillation and skin vibration," and "ultra powerful" panels reduce drag.

Add it all up and the LZR Racer suit, according to manufacturer Speedo, increases "oxygen efficiency" by five per cent, makes starts, sprints and turns four per cent faster, and lessens "passive drag" by 10 per cent.

The LZR, pronounced 'laser,' has sent the swimming world off the deep end. The suit's been described as "doping on a hanger" and points to a growing and thorny problem of technology in sport, which will be front and centre in Beijing where fancy swimwear may be just one of the hi-tech wonders heading for the podium.

5 Along with the LZR, athletes in Beijing will be sporting javelins made of aluminum wrapped in woven carbon, riding highly specialized bikes and wearing new high-temperature clothing and event-specific shoes.

U.S. track star Jeremy Wariner, 400-metre gold medal winner, will slip on customized Adidas spike shoes. They feature "the first ever full-length carbon nanotubes reinforced plate" and spikes designed to compress on the track, the company says. This "allows Jeremy to push even better in the turn," said Mic Lussier, leader of the shoemaker's innovation team. Lussier's team worked with Wariner for two years on the spike shoes that "cater to the specific needs and the role of each foot." Then there is blade runner Oscar Pistorius. The double amputee sprinter from South Africa, who runs on carbon fibre blades, fought to compete against able-bodied athletes in a case that shone the spotlight on technological advantage. Pistorius was initially banned from competing by the International Association of Athletics Federation, which argued the blades gave him an advantage over able-bodied athletes—in effect making him super-abled. Pistorius got the ban overturned by the Court of Arbitration for Sport, although he ultimately failed to qualify for both individual and team events.

All of which gives a glimpse of where technology is taking the sporting world, said Larry Katz, director of the sport technology research laboratory at the University of Calgary.

With advances in sport science, artificial materials and nanotechnology, it may not be long before gear will be tailored to the individual athlete, says Katz.

"It might be possible to customize to the person's body weight, perspiration rate, and who knows what else," he says. "There is no limit to it." Heading into Beijing, the LZR stands out among the technological controversies for making such a huge pre-Olympic splash.

10 Thirty-eight world records have been set by athletes wearing LZRs since its debut in February, making it the must-have suit for Beijing.

Many athletes have dropped their sponsors' gear and plan to squeeze into LZRs, generating plenty of controversy and a lawsuit by one jilted company.

Speedo is racing to meet the demand for the suits that appear to deliver both a physical and psychological kick.

"I'm just happy we're in Speedo's camp," said Tom Johnson, head coach of Canada's Olympic swim team, which has a $2.5-million, eight-year sponsorship deal with the swimwear maker.

Hayden and his 26 teammates got their pick of more than 400 LZRs that arrived in Canada in July direct from the only factory, in Portugal, that makes them. Speedo will also hand $50,000 to any Canadian swimmer who wins gold in Beijing, $10,000 for silver and $5,000 for bronze.

It is hard to image improving on the athletes' incredible physiques, but Speedo claims the suits mould and compress the body into a sleeker, more hydrodynamic shape.

"The internal core stabilizer supports and holds the swimmer in a corset-like grip and helps them to maintain the best body position in the water for longer," said Speedo.

Thin panels embedded at strategic points "deliver optimum streamlined shape and drag reduction"—they also make breasts, penises and other superfluous bulges all but disappear. "Ultrasonically welded, bonded seams create a perfectly smooth yet flexible streamlined surface." Johnson says he was skeptical at first, noting that earlier versions of the sci-fi swimsuits have been around since 2000.

"My initial thought was 'This is just propaganda, it's not going to make a difference'," he said as he put his swimmers through the paces in the pool at the University of B.C.

But the LZR is widely seen as being in a league of its own.

"It caught everybody with their pants down," said Johnson—athletes, coaches and the Fédération Internationale de Natation, or FINA, which sets the Olympic swim rules. "I don't think even Speedo realized how good the suit was." Out of 42 world records broken since February, 38 were smashed by swimmers wearing the suit.

And often by a "significant margin," said Johnson. "You're looking at something like 3/10th to 4/10th of a second in the shorter races—that's pretty significant in a sports measured by hundredths of a second." Johnson's men's 400-metre medley relay team shaved three seconds off the Canadian record when they first shimmied into **LZRs** at the Olympic trials in April. "You feel like a race car," Joe Bartoch, of London, Ont., said after swimming his butterfly in record time.

Speedo's "Aqualab" team recruited experts in aerospace, engineering and biomechanics to help design the suit. They ran 3D body scans, involving some 400 elite athletes, got NASA to assess about 60 types of fabric in wind tunnels then tested the prototype suits on mannequins and swimmers.

The company has not made public data to back its claims the suit results in 10 per cent less passive drag than other suits, "five per cent better oxygen efficiency" and faster starts and turns. The data, say officials, are proprietary.

FINA has plenty of rules about what is allowed in the Olympic pool. No suits that increase buoyancy. No fins or webbed gloves. But it rejected calls this spring for a ban on the LZR that the Italian swim coach and others have described as the equivalent of "technological doping." FINA ruled there is no scientific proof the LZR provides an unfair advantage.

Katz, of the University of Calgary, says there is no question technology can give top athletes a real advantage—especially in short distance events, where 100th of a second can be the difference between winning and losing.

"Instead of being athlete against athlete, you're now in a situation where it's technology versus technology," said Katz. "That applies in a lot of the sports." The problem is that poorer countries and athletes are increasingly at a disadvantage because they cannot afford or get access to the latest high-tech gear and training techniques. "What you have now is 'have' countries and 'have-not' countries," said Katz.

Many nations, including Canada, are keen to use technology to help Canada win more medals. The $110-million Own the Podium program, financed by the federal government, sporting groups and private companies, includes "top-secret" projects "to give Canadian athletes 'the edge' in equipment, technology information and training." Researchers, including Katz, cannot discuss details of their projects, having signed confidentiality agreements as a condition of funding.

Brent Rushall, a retired sports scientist at San Diego State University and former psychologist for Canadian Olympic teams, is critical of the way costly sports gear is embraced, even when there is scant evidence it offers an advantage.

The current swimsuit craze is "a remarkable example of marketing of products without accountability for any claims," said Rushall. Swimmers and coaches have been "shamelessly" endorsing the LZR, he says.

"One is left with the impression that if the suit was thrown into a pool it would break a swimming world record on its own." As for the spate of world records set in the LZR, he says the same swimmers would likely have broken the records without the suit. "When the majority of world record breakers are required to wear Speedo equipment, it is not surprising that most of the new world records are produced by swimmers wearing a Speedo suit," says Rushall.

30 Johnson says the technological race in the pool is here to say, be it using new biomechanics techniques to shave precious micro-seconds off start times or suits that try to turn the body into torpedoes.

"It's the way of the world," said Johnson. "People are always looking for an edge."

Reflect & Write

- ❑ How does Munro's first sentence set the tone for the rest of the article? What expectations does it set up about the suit and her evaluation of it?
- ❑ To what extent does Munro integrate an interest in evaluating the role of technology in performance enhancement in general with her concern with discussing the specific example of the LZR? Does she achieve balance, or does one get more prominence than the other? Why do you think she steered the article in that direction?
- ❑ Why does Munro include Rushall's perspective in her article? Why did she put it at the end rather than at the beginning of her piece? How would her argument have changed if Rushall was featured earlier?
- ❑ **Write.** Having read Munro's article, do you feel that the LZR is the equivalent of "Doping on a Hanger"? Write a short response to this piece of at least 300 words in which you reflect on the LZR specifically and more broadly on performance-enhancing technology as a type of "doping" in contemporary sports culture.

■ *In this August 25, 2008, post from the Tech Talk blog on* IEEE Spectrum, **Kieron Murphy,** *one of the* Spectrum's *editors, uses the closing ceremonies of the 2008 Beijing Olympics to initiate a conversation about performance enhancement among athletes. His focus is the practice of "engineering" world-class athletes from childhood, touching on the alleged practice of "gene doping" among professional athletes.*

Engineering a Better Olympic Athlete

Kieron Murphy

Can a nation engineer premier Olympic athletes, as if they were automobiles or aircraft?

During the broadcast of the Closing Ceremony of the Summer Olympic Games in Beijing, NBC commentator Joshua Cooper Ramos took note of the progress the Chinese athletes have made in recent years and referred to

China's nationalized sports program as "an engineering project." Fellow commentator Bob Costas was quick to agree, pointing to the country's focus on developing elite athletes from early childhood while paying scant attention to the physical fitness of those of its children who do not show precocious potential as future Olympians.

Not surprisingly, China won the most gold medals (51) of the Games in Beijing. As with many things developed in a Communist state, those medals were the result of a good deal of planning and long-term follow up. Nationalized sports programs are nothing new in the Olympics. The Soviet Union dominated the Games for years with cradle-to-medal-podium training regimens. But China's athletics "engineering project" still raises questions about the fairness of big, state-controlled programs competing against those of smaller, free-market nations. In other words, were these Games fair for all? Probably not, but the world is not a perfect place.

The bigger question, though, lies implicit in the comments of the NBC commentators: Can a nation engineer premier Olympic athletes, as if they were automobiles or aircraft?

5 The answer to that appears to be yes. And there are fears now that unscrupulous administrators of sports programs in years ahead could use highly sophisticated methods to give their proteges enhancements that go well beyond those that come from selective recruitment and nationally subsidized training.

In the most controversial (and illegal) example, a practice called gene doping, the medical techniques used to manipulate genetic material for therapeutic purposes are subverted by corrupt physicians to enhance the physical makeup of athletes. In a report from the American Association for the Advancement of Science (see Strong New Measures Against Gene Doping in Sports Urged at Conference Co-Sponsored by AAAS), gene therapy researchers urged participants at a recent meeting of the World Anti-Doping Agency (WADA) held in St. Petersburg, Russia, to advocate for stricter attention to the threat of gene doping in sports.

Gene doping could be used to modify an athlete's own genes to increase muscle mass or boost red blood cell production, for example.

"Science has moved so quickly in gene therapy and because it moves so quickly, it makes the non-therapeutic use of these kinds of methods much more likely and much more imminent," Theodore Friedmann, a former president of the American Society of Gene Therapy, told conference attendees. "And the sooner it pops up in sport, the more likely it is to pop up in other areas."

The experts in illegal performance enhancements called for governments to legislate sanctions against those who might be tempted to tinker with the genetic material of athletes in order to boost their prowess. The experts also called on physicians to be more vigilant in looking for signs that competitors have been genetically enhanced.

10 So far, according to the scientists, no documented cases of gene doping in the world of sports have been uncovered yet. That does not mean that somewhere there isn't someone trying to do it. The reward is so great that it seems illogical to believe that some ambitious program wouldn't stoop to the level of trying to engineer a better athlete genetically.

It's one thing to selectively train a young person to become a talented competitor as an adult. It's quite another to try to build one through human chemistry.

Reflect & Write

- ❑ How does *kairos* factor into the way that Murphy designs his argument?
- ❑ Where do you find the strongest articulation of Murphy's argument? How does he compose and organize the rest of the essay to persuade the reader of the validity of his claim?
- ❑ What authorities does Murphy cite in his article? What other sources might he have cited to support his claim? How might that have altered his argument?
- ❑ Given that the *IEEE Spectrum* is the "flagship publication of the IEEE, the world's largest professional technology association" (*about IEEE page*), how does Murphy's piece either confirm or subvert your understanding of what writing for engineers looks like? Consider elements such as topic, structure, organization, voice, tone, and style. What does this tell you about the genre of writing for professional engineers?
- ❑ **Write.** Look at an article on the same topic, published by *Newsweek* two weeks earlier than Murphy's post (Jamie Reno, "Juice For Today's Athlete," August 11, 2008: linked through the *Envision* Website). Write a comparative analysis of the two pieces, assessing how the differences in rhetorical situation affected the composition of these pieces. Be sure to consider issues of audience, genre, structure, strategies of development, and style.
www.pearsonhighered.com/envision/451

■ **Andrew Tilin** *has contributed articles to numerous publications, including the* New York Times Magazine, Rolling Stone, *and* GQ, *and has served as a contributing editor to* Wired *and to* Business 2.0, *a magazine focused on business, technology and innovation. This article originally appeared in the September 2000 issue of* Wired.

Ready, Set, Mutate!

Andrew Tilin

Italian physicist Ciro Fusco thinks he knows exactly what could stop a muscled-up sprinter from winning gold at this month's Summer Games in Sydney, Australia—the spikes on his or her shoes, which have a tiny-but-measurable "glue effect" when they stab a track's surface. Fusco has spent the last four years studying such minutiae while developing adidas gear for the 2000 Olympics. He and a team of engineers used computer modeling to rethink the existing shape of track spikes; what emerged was a shallow Z-shaped cleat, made from a ceramic-aluminum alloy, that doesn't poke into the runway. Instead the shoe grabs the running surface and then easily lets go.

It all sounds a little obsessive, but at a time when jocks are maxing out the body's capabilities, micro-innovations can add up. "Athletes have reached certain physical limitations," says Fusco. "And now technology is optimizing their performance."

Of course, the five-ring brass gets nervous when it hears talk of enhancements beyond extra effort, pep talks, and Gatorade; they're forever scrambling to control technology's growing influence on sports. Witness the absence (due to tubing size restrictions) from Sydney's velodromes of the aerodynamic, carbon-fiber bikes that were rolled out four years ago in Atlanta, and the mandate given to

Speedo, in the name of fair play, to dole out its sleek new swimsuits to any competitor who wants one. As for drugs, notorious test-tube elixirs like human growth hormone and erythropoietin are coming under more scrutiny than ever. Nevertheless, International Olympic Committee officials have all but conceded that their ability to test for banned substances isn't reliable enough to catch everybody.

Which raises a point: It may be time to reexamine this whole athletic purity thing and say to hell with it. Within at least five years, elite athletes will be able to obtain genetic upgrades, injecting mutated nucleotide chains that stimulate the production of oxygen-toting red blood cells or increased musculature. Olympic officials might not be able to stop that either, so wouldn't it be better to make sure everybody, including those teensy badminton players from South Korea, gets a safe, reliable gene boost? (And while we're at it, could we put Flubber tips on the shuttlecocks to liven up the action?)

5 In celebration of this escalating pursuit of faster-higher-stronger, we've compiled a cutting-edge athlete's duffel of techno-enhanced clothing, equipment, and drugs that will help the world's athletes mine gold starting September 15 and running through the October Paralympics. After that comes some innovations for the future. Although these optimizers may take a while to debut, an Olympic year is the perfect time to recognize the spirit they represent: Screw purity—what we want is possibility.

Arrow Dynamic

To battle Sydney's 20-knot springtime gusts and enhance the accuracy of the venerable X10 arrow long used in archery competition, Easton Technical Products sought out technology from a Defense Department contractor that builds tank-killing shells. The new addition to the barrel-shaped, aluminum/carbon-fiber shaft is a tungsten tip that's 2.2 times denser than conventional steel. With more of the arrow's weight concentrated at the front, the upgraded X10 travels straighter in a crosswind.

Fuel Injection

Sports drugs now come in more blends than you'll find at Starbucks. With the threat of a new Olympic dope test that could detect EPO (the popular hormone that stimulates the formation of red blood cells and thereby increases aerobic capacity by up to 15 percent), endurance athletes have found a new way to boost the transport of oxygen to redlining muscles. The illicit concoction is a blood expander—an undetectable and experimental synthetic plasma that carries additional oxygen and was originally designed for people in need of transfusions. Problem is, the shelf life of these red-cell substitutes can be short, and they may have been responsible for trauma-patient deaths in clinical trials. "The artificial blood could cause an allergic reaction, get stuck in your kidneys, and cause them to fail," warns Don Catlin, an opponent of such tactics who directs UCLA's Olympic Analytical Lab.

Skin Trade

The most impressive of the new uniforms debuting Down Under is Speedo's intricately textured Fastskin. Following four years of development, the full-body stretch-nylon swimsuit is covered with tiny scales and sharklike, V-shaped ridges. Water literally breaks off the Fastskin, lowering hydrodynamic drag by 6 percent over conventional spandex. Meanwhile, adidas' One-Armed Throwing Suit for javelin and discus competitors, as well as shot-putters, has a Power Lycra sleeve that compresses the athlete's arm to heighten proprioception, or the awareness of where one's limbs are in space. And Nike's Swift Suit has golf ball-style dimples on the arms and legs to cut down runner-generated turbulence.

Thrust and Parry

Fencers' feet perform distinctly different tasks, so adidas designers concluded that fencing footwear should follow suit. The lead shoe (far right) is always pointing at the opponent and moving back and forth, so the rubber tread runs side to side for maximum traction. A generous helping of foam cushioning provides for softer landings during Zorro-style attacks. The rear shoe, positioned perpendicular to the lead shoe, is canted toward the arch, easily rolling inward when an athlete lunges forward.

Live High, Train Low

10 One big conundrum for endurance athletes is finding a way to sleep at high elevations (where

thin air prompts the body to produce more red blood cells) and train at sea level (where oxygen-rich air permits exercise at the greatest intensities). Solution: the Hypoxico Tent System. The collapsible tent can accommodate a queen-sized bed and is attached to a hypoxicator, or air-separation generator, that withholds enough oxygen molecules to simulate conditions up to 9,000 feet. Olympic race-walkers and cyclists have been snoozing between the nylon walls since late last year.

Internal Combustion

The night-before group spaghetti-feed has been delivered a death blow: Performance diets are now tailored to the requirements of individuals and their sports. It begins with a prick of the finger in the lab, where white blood cells are isolated and analyzed down to the DNA level. After testing the effectiveness of various nutrients on the cells, a nutritionist determines specific responsiveness to such things as carbs and protein, and builds a custom diet that can result in fewer injuries and better performance. "Athletes in the same event can have very different dietary needs," says Jeffrey Bland, a nutritional bio-chemist and president of Washington's Institute for Functional Medicine, which is attracting the doctors of Olympic cyclists and runners.

Spring Action

Some Paralympic runners will strap on Flex-Foot's latest Sprint-Flex III prosthetic, a carbon-fiber, bowed spring of a lower limb, to speed them down the track. Drawing on feed-back from athletes, designers at the Aliso Viejo, California, company built the Sprint-Flex III's toe about 2 inches longer than earlier models for increased ground contact and better stability when launching out of the blocks. Look for the 2.5-pound artificial shin to propel a 100-meter competitor under the previously unassailable 11-second barrier.

Coming Soon!

High Style

What athletes wear to future games will be considerably more than just a fashion statement. Record-breaking bodyware will carry chemicals that convert sweat into energy or trigger timed, in-body adrenaline releases. "Nanofactories will synthesize chemicals directly on the fabric," says Stephen Michielsen, a professor of textile and fiber engineering at the Georgia Institute of Technology in Atlanta. Another closet possibility: duds knitted with optical fibers to transmit an athlete's voice and physiological data (heart rate, for instance) to a coach pacing the sidelines.

Manmade Muscles

Researchers at MIT are growing tissue in their petri dishes that could make prosthetics more human and less contraption, adding developed calf muscle, for example, to an already powerful, energy-rebounding limb like the Sprint-Flex III. Genetic- and nerve-related hurdles, as well as circulation-system issues, are currently keeping manmade muscles from being as good as the real thing. But the big brains believe their cultured muscles can grow stronger with use, and run less on battery power than sugar water. "The idea is that machines will be somewhat like us," says Hugh Herr, the MIT project director and a double-below-knee amputee. "In my lifetime, I would love to feed my prosthetic ankles."

Contact Lenses

15 Talk about synchronized swimming: Goggles with heads-up displays will make sure athletes swim their race by the numbers. Inside the goggles' lenses, stroke rate, elapsed time, and other key data will be projected the way vital information is flashed onto a fighter pilot's windshield. In addition, a poolside computer would be fed physiological statistics via telemetry so coaches could analyze the numbers and send radio-communicated advice to swimmers wearing remote headsets attached to goggle straps. By the time athletes make a splash in Athens four years from now, they'll be able to get and give feedback with nary a pause between strokes.

Redefining Runway

Nike engineers are betting that a high heel, not a sneaker, will produce the fastest times. Observing that full-tilt runners never come down off the balls of their feet during the first 10 meters of a race, researchers hypothesize that if an athlete could continue for the next 90 meters using the same stride, records would be broken. "The foot needs to act as a lever so the power coming from the rest of your body doesn't vanish," says Tom Carleo, head of shoe development for Nike's Olympic runners. "We're trying to improve on natural locomotion." Swooshed pumps, with heels kept high by springs, could be prototyped within two years.

Turbo Tablets

Who says performance-enhancing pills have to mess with your chemistry? Already being used by astronauts and soldiers to avert overheating and dehydration, one disposable sensor capsule from Palmetto, Florida's HTI Technologies could be repurposed by solo endurance athletes and team players to measure everything from body temperature to heart rate. Readings from the ingestible devices are sent to a Polar receiver and displayed on a handheld telemeter. While still only theory, another concentrated tablet envisioned by physiologist Bob Murray, director of the Gatorade Sports Science Institute, could release carbohydrates over time, ensuring optimal performance.

Reflect & Write

- ❑ How does the author use tone, diction, and even humor in this piece? How does this tone differ from that of other pieces about performance enhancement you've read in this chapter?
- ❑ All the points in this piece are based on research; how is research deployed and represented here?
- ❑ What image of future Olympians does this article conjure up for you?
- ❑ **Write.** Choose one of the innovations mentioned above and develop a marketing campaign for that product. Identify a target audience and a means of distribution (radio ads? commercials? print ads? Web ads?) for your marketing. You might choose to roll out your marketing campaign at the 2012 Olympics in London. Draft one sample advertisement for this marketing campaign and share it with the class. Carefully consider how to use rhetorical appeals and your understanding of *kairos* and the rhetorical situation to make a persuasive advertisement. Write a reflection to accompany your ad in which explain which rhetorical strategies you used in your ad, which mode of delivery, and why these were effective choices for your rhetorical situation.

COLLABORATIVE CHALLENGE

The United States Anti-Doping Agency (USADA) houses several videos on its Website designed to educate kids about the use of steroids and performance-enhancing drugs. Either in class or in small groups in a computer lab, watch the videos that link from the *Envision* Website. What rhetorical choices are evident in the composition of these films? How are words and images used in combination? How is the USADA represented in the films? If you were to revise one of the videos, how would you do so? Together with your peers, storyboard two or three scenes that you would add into the film to make it more effective for its target audience. Present your group storyboard and rationale to the class.

www.pearsonhighered.com/envision/454

PERSPECTIVES ON THE ISSUE

1. One of the major issues presented by the readings in this section is articulated by Steven Shapin: "What is to count as normal?" His intent here is to understand what we consider "normal" athletic performance in a world of record-breaking athletes. Write your own response to this question, responding explicitly to quotations you take from the second half of Shapin's article as well as to points made in the article by Mike Sokolove.
2. When Michael Sokolove revised his *New York Times Magazine* article for publication in the *Observer Sports Magazine,* he cut the article by almost half. Locate the original article online or in the library. Then compare the two versions. What did Sokolove excise during revision? Did the revision change the content of his argument? Did it change the delivery of his argument? Is one version more persuasive than the other? Why?
3. Compare Andrew Tilin's piece against Michael Sokolove's piece for their different strategies of relying on research. Which article makes its iceberg of research most visible? Which one seems more academic and which more popular? Can you identify each author's rhetorical stance? Compare their use of descriptive language as well. Which article seems to you more persuasive about the issue of performance and perfection?

FROM READING TO RESEARCH

1. In his cartoon (Figure 13.7), Mike Keefe focuses in on the fans' reaction to the issue of doping in sports; similarly, in *Bigger, Stronger, Faster*,* Chris Bell likewise examines how steroid use among athletes influences their fans. Visit the *Envision* Website and read other popular reactions to scandals about performance-enhancing drugs in sports as varied as swimming, bicycling, and tennis. Now, using the At a Glance box on Conducting Interviews and Surveys in Chapter 5, craft some questions for your own primary research with sports fans in your community. Drawing on your primary and secondary research, write an opinion piece that makes a strong claim about how the practice of doping does—or doesn't—affect sports fans.
   www.pearsonhighered.com/envision/455
2. Relying not only on the knowledge you've gained in reading the articles for this chapter but also on additional research you conduct in the library, write a research paper about the veterinary steroids taken by young Dominican baseball hopefuls. Then, transform your paper into an op-ad. What governs the rhetorical choices you make in terms of design, image, color, and verbal accompaniment? Use your op-ad as a cover for your research paper on the baseball recruitment and training conditions in the Dominican Republic. Ask your librarian for help locating additional sources you might use in this written document.
3. What lies ahead for the future of sports? Will we ever return to an age of "purity"? How do we draw the line between synthetic chemicals, technological innovations in shoes and clothing, innovative training regimes, oxygen sleep chambers, and medical advancements? Craft an argument in which you take a stand on this issue. Use quotations from the articles in this chapter if you wish to respond to their arguments. In addition, draw on additional primary and secondary sources in your argument. Follow the Guidelines in Chapter 6 in order to craft your own perspective on this issue.

PLAYING AGAINST STEREOTYPES

Sports figures play many different roles in contemporary culture. These roles range from figures of physical perfection to embodiments of national pride; they span from representations of local identity to symbols of global community. For many viewers and readers, these figures become much larger than life.

How is the media complicit in this process? We'll see in the following pages that the media constantly projects images of athletes to the consumer public, whether from the glossy covers of magazines, in flashy TV ad campaigns, or even on giant posters plastered on the sides of buses, billboards, or in the corridors of malls. Too often images of sports celebrity remain flat and two-dimensional, even if scaled to poster size or projected in surround sound on a high-definition TV. That is, we tend to see not complex, fully developed individuals, but instead figures that feed into and perpetuate certain cultural stereotypes. So a key question emerges: how do sports—and in particular the media coverage of sports—both reinforce and dismantle such stereotypes?

We can see the complicated relationship between stereotype and media at work in Nike's famous 2004 "Tennis Instructor" commercial. In that ad, the tennis pro arrives to meet his class: a group of young teenage girls. As he starts the lesson, he flips his hair and walks among them, the girls looking adoringly after him. However, on the court, the situation changes radically. He gently tosses a ball to a young blond girl who catches it, tosses it in the air to serve it, and then changes suddenly into Serena Williams who drills the ball over the net. The pro blinks, then walks on, but the transformation repeats: all around him, the giggly young girls literally turn into Williams on the court, astounding him with their strong backhands and power returns. At the climax, he ducks to avoid a ball that narrowly misses hitting him in the head. As he stands up, we see the girls through his eyes: a group of Serena Williamses, all looking at him with concern (Figure 13.8). He blinks, confused (Figure 13.9), and in the final frame they have transformed back to their teenage selves (Figure 13.10), though mirroring the poses and attitude of the multiple Williamses a moment before. It is not just the tennis pro that is schooled in this commercial, it is the viewer. Do not make assumptions about athleticism based on stereotype, Nike cautions: great athletes come in all shapes and forms.

In the readings that follow, we'll look carefully at the complex media messages about sports and uncover how sports figures become subject to gender and race stereotyping by reading articles that examine sports coverage, advertising, and photojournalism in depth. You'll learn to turn a critical eye on all future media coverage of the sports you may love—and those that may be quite new to you. In the process, you'll have a chance to contribute your own responses to this ongoing debate about "Sports and Media."

Reflect & Write

- ❑ Look at the screenshots in Figures 13.8 and 13.10. What is the effect of having the girls mirror Serena in their final poses?
- ❑ Consider Figure 13.9 How does the casting and characterization of the tennis pro feed into stereotype?
- ❑ Most of the commercial is shown through the perspective of the tennis pro. How would it have been different if he had not been part of the story? What does having his perspective add to argument?
- ❑ Some feminists have argued that this commercial is problematic because the young girls are only motivated to their Serena Williams-esque greatness out of a desire to impress their male tennis instructor. Based on your understanding of the commercial, is this a justified critique? To what extent does this interpretation complicate the commercial's message about powerful women athletes?
- ❑ **Write.** Watch the full commercial, linked through the Envision Website. Pay particular attention to the musical score and use of sound, the pacing, and how the images of Serena are integrated. Write a rhetorical analysis of this commercial that takes into account how these elements contribute to the persuasiveness of the ad. www.pearsonhighered.com/envision/457

FIGURE 13.8. Nike's "Tennis Instructor" commercial uses clever cinematography to transform a class of young tennis players into a group of Serena Williamses.

FIGURE 13.9. The tennis pro from the commercial does a double take.

FIGURE 13.10. In the final frame of the commercial, the class transforms back into a group of young girls.

In this image from the ESPN photo essay "Anything You Can Do," photojournalist **Carlos Serrao** *captures high-jumper Jeff Skiba cresting the bar in his event. Skiba, who won a gold medal in the high jump during the 2008 Summer Paralympics, was the first amputee in history to clear the 7' mark in the high jump, a distinction he earned at the 2008 Asuza Pacific Invitational in Los Angeles. Skiba continues to train to qualify in hopes of qualifying for the 2012 Olympics.*

"Anything You Can Do"

FIGURE 13.11. "In the future, disabled athletes will be 'limited' only by how fast, high and far their man-made limbs can take them. For some, like high-jumper Jeff Skiba (above), the future is already here" (Adelson).

Reflect & Write

- How does this image play to stereotypes of athletes? How does it defy them? Consider the composition of the photo in your analysis, including perspective, layout, focus, and framing.
- How does this image become an image of ability instead of disability? How does its message differ from that which might be found in a photo focusing on Skiba stretching to prepare for his event?
- Consider the implications of the title "Anything You Can Do" in relation to the image and theme of this photograph. What does the title add to the impression made by the photograph?

- ❑ The caption included with this photo is from the original photo essay. What alternate caption would you put underneath this image? Draft it out. Now compare it to the original caption. How does that original caption differ or operate in dialogue with the one you constructed? How does that reflect a difference in interpretation? How does each shape the photo's argument for its audience?
- ❑ **Write.** Look at the complete photo essay "Anything You Can Do," linked through the *Envision* Website. Suggest an alternate arrangement for the nine photos included in that piece, and write a short preface to your revised photo essay about athletes, stereotypes, and differing abilities.
www.pearsonhighered.com/envision/459

Seeing Connections
Review the section on Arrangement in Argument in Chapter 3 (page 50).

■ **Thad Mumford** *has been involved in the television industry for over 30 years; as a writer and producer, his credits include work on* M.A.S.H., A Different World, *and* Coach. *In this article, first published in May 2004 in the* New York Times, *he invokes the concept of minstrelsy, a form of American entertainment from the nineteenth and early twentieth century characterized by actors painting their faces black with charcoal in order to perform comic skits in "blackface." A form of burlesque, minstrelsy or black vaudeville often relied on stereotypical racist portrayals of African Americans to depict them as lazy, naïve, superstitious, or clownish.*

The New Minstrel Show: Black Vaudeville with Statistics

Thad Mumford

There has never been a better time to be a black athlete. Moneywise, it is now a sum-of-zeros game. (If only my parents had seen the long-term value of studying Rod Carew's books on hitting instead of math and chemistry.) African-Americans have turned white football and basketball players into tokens. And while our representation in baseball continues its decline, the percentage of blacks who dominate the game continues to surge. The reign of Tiger Woods and the Williams sisters could lead to a time when country club athletic equipment will be on back order in Harlem's sporting goods stores.

Advertisers now line up to have black sports figures push their products, especially to the audience they covet, with near-liturgical zeal, 18-to-25-year-old white suburban males, many of whom are mesmerized by the idiomatic hip-hop jargon, the cock-of-the-walk swagger, the smooth-as-the-law-allows attire of their black heroes.

But there is a downside to all this. The unsayable but unassailable truth is that the clowning, dancing, preening smack-talker is becoming the Rorschach image of the African-American male athlete. It casts a huge shadow over all other images. This persona has the power to sell what no one should buy: the notion that black folks are still cuttin' up for the white man.

Any ethnic group that ever found itself on the periphery of equality and acceptance has had to create coping mechanisms. Some who were victimized by bigotry secretly mimicked the prejudicial perceptions of their oppressor with exaggerated, self-deprecating depictions of their behavior, their very private burlesque that gave them brief respites from their marginalization.

5 For African-Americans, burlesque as healing balm became the essential comedic ingredient of black vaudeville. Comics would strut and cakewalk through now classic routines that savagely lampooned minstrel shows, popular staples of mainstream vaudeville in which white performers in blackface and coily-haired wigs further dehumanized their own creation, the darkie prototype.

Black vaudeville would become a casualty of expanding educational opportunities that created an evolving black middle class with deep concerns that minstrel-like characterizations were degrading and would only perpetuate the accepted attitude that the Negro was the slap-happy court jester for whites.

But a variety of factors, in particular the canonizing of youth culture, the de-emphasizing of wisdom and the glorification of the boorishness inherent in America's look-at-me culture, has played a major role in putting black vaudeville back on the boards. The featured attraction? A number of black athletes.

When we see a wide receiver strut and cakewalk to the end zone, then join teammates in the catalog of celebratory rituals, which now feature props, or hear a cackling, bug-eyed commentator speaking Slanglish ("Give up the props, dog, they be flossin' now!"), we are seeing our private burlesque, out of context, without its knowing wink and satiric spine. Minus these elements, what remains is minstrel template made ubiquitous by Stepin Fetchit and the handful of black actors who worked in the early motion pictures.

But unlike the Stepin Fetchits, left with no alternative but to mortgage their dignity for a paycheck, who often suffered tremendously under the weight of tremendous guilt and shame, some of today's black athletes have unwittingly packaged and sold this nouveau minstrel to Madison Avenue's highest bidders, selling it as our "culturally authentic" behavior, "keepin' it real," as they say.

10 Nothing could be less real or more inauthentic. Or condescending. How can 38 million people possibly have a single view of reality or authenticity? But the athletes who have exhumed the minstrel's grave keep alive these shopworn condescensions.

"The danger of the domination of these one-dimensional images is that they deny the humanity and the intellectuality of an entire people, eliminating the possibility of them being taken seriously," said Dr. Harry Edwards, a professor of sociology at San Jose State who is a consultant to the National Football League.

White adults, whose knowledge of black life is generally limited to what they see in pop culture, take burlesque at face value. This reinforces what was considered culturally authentic, that black people are funny as all get-out.

But the athletes aren't the main culprits. That, of course, would be television, which has brought its two major contributions to American culture, sex and excess, to every sport. TV has erased the line that separated sports from entertainment and created a product that encourages the marketing of black burlesque. Call it athletainment.

"We now allow people to take the pride and dignity from our athletes by celebrating them when they play for the camera," said Al Downing, a veteran of 15 major league seasons, now doing public relations for the Los Angeles Dodgers.

15 It can be a dizzying ride. Today's African-American athletes have been handled like porcelain eggs from the moment it became clear that preparing for the next game was of greater significance than preparing for the SAT. Then once they become seven-and eight-figure Hessians, they are walled off from the real world, and all accountability, by management, agents and corporate sponsors, who are all blessed with fertile amounts of unctuousness ("You rule, bro!"). The word no has become a museum piece. As the football Hall of Famer Deacon Jones once said, "There's no school that teaches you how to be a millionaire."

But does this mean that athletes who feel the need to pay homage to every tackle with a dance step, who triumphantly crow in the face of opponents after monster dunks, should be excused for not knowing the line between exuberance and bad sportsmanship?

"I'm more impressed by someone like a Barry Sanders, athletes who do their jobs without having to show up the opposition," said Bill White, whose major league career spanned 13 years.

Issues of cultural identity are complicated, contradictory and complex. One person's ethnic burlesque is another's sense of cultural autonomy. Questions beget more questions. If we keep our burlesque private, are we capitulating to people who feel we should be ashamed of this behavior? Aren't there more appropriate times and places to have fun with our own stereotypes? But does regulating this behavior inadvertently marginalize those African-Americans trapped in burlesquelike worlds? Is there a possible connection between the actions of the white fan who cheers rabidly after sack dances on Sunday, then may be reluctant to grant bank loans for black businesses on Monday?

Those most vulnerable to this confusion are the children, far too many growing up with mangled notions of race, manhood and sports. Black athletes who take our burlesque public could tell them, in the lingua-slanga they share, that there is a difference between having style and actin' the fool. Or that reading and speaking proper English isn't a punk white-boy thing. Or that their chances of playing professional sports are extremely remote. So, if these children do have athletic ability, they should think of using it for one purpose, to get a free education.

20 They'd get their props. Because that's keepin' it real.

Reflect & Write

- ❑ What does Mumford mean when he writes that "the clowning, dancing, preening smack-talker is becoming the Rorschach image of the African-American male athlete"? Do you agree? Why or why not?
- ❑ Who, in Mumford's opinion, should bear partial responsibility for perpetuating the stereotypical image of the African-American athlete? How convincing is his argument? Explain your response.
- ❑ Toward the end of the article, Mumford questions, "If we keep our burlesque private, are we capitulating to people who feel we should be ashamed of this behavior?" What is your response to this question?
- ❑ **Write.** Thad Mumford begins his article with an appeal to *kairos*: "There has never been a better time to be a black athlete." Considering his article appeared in 2004, do you think that this claim still holds true? What stereotypes of the African-American athlete circulate now in the second decade of the twenty-first century? Do we still see examples of "ethnic burlesque" in sports? Write a response to Mumford's article in which you update his argument, taking into account specific athletes from a variety of sports in the news today and the way in which the media represents them.

A nationally recognized commentator on American popular culture, **Todd Boyd** *is a professor of Critical Studies at the USC School of Cinematic Arts. He has published widely on race, sports, hip hop culture, and the media, contributing articles to newspapers as varied as the* New York Times, *the* Chicago Tribune, *the* Boston Globe, *and the* Charlotte Observer. *Boyd also has published several books on his area of specialty, including* The New H.N.I.C.: The Death of Civil Rights and the Reign of Hip Hop *(2002);* Am I Black Enough for You?: Popular Culture from the 'Hood and Beyond *(1997); and* Young Black Rich and Famous: The Rise of the NBA, the Hip Hop Invasion, and the Transformation of American Culture *(2003), from which this excerpt is taken. Boyd also has appeared as an expert on popular culture on many news programs and has served as a commentator on ESPN and NPR's* News and Notes with Ed Gordon.

"Doin' Me": From Young, Black, Rich, and Famous

Todd Boyd

As the players in question get to be younger and younger, it is certain that the influence of hip hop will continue to reign supreme. Hip hop at this point is more than just the music that the players listen to on their ubiquitous headphones, in the same way that basketball is more than just another game. Hip hop is a way of life that best defines the worldview from which these contemporary players emerge.

Hip hop has always been about having an upward trajectory. An abiding sense of social mobility abounds. Basketball has become the way that many who are talented enough and fortunate enough get to experience that mobility. This is their opportunity to showcase their skills and become rich in the process. What angers and alarms so many is the fact that a lot of these players have no interest whatsoever in imitating the ways of mainstream White society. This is evident in the style choices favored by so many contemporary players. Cornrows have replaced the bald head. Long baggy shorts are de rigueur. Tattoos are the order of the day.

The exception to this is a player like Tim Duncan, he of West Indian descent. West Indians have often been considered as better able to assimilate into mainstream America than their African American counterparts; think Sidney Poitier and Colin Powell, for example. Duncan then seems to be a throwback, a player from a previous time whose fundamental style of play and extremely unassuming disposition make him stand out among a league of players deeply ensconced in the hip hop milieu. No matter how much attention is lavished on Duncan by approving league and media starmakers, he is the exception, not the rule. Hip hop–minded players dominate the game and the conversations around it.

Though Duncan may be a throwback, it is a player like Rasheed Wallace who to me epitomizes the idea of retro. Wallace alternates between cornrows and a nappy old-school 'fro, also in the signature shoe of the hip hop generation, the now vintage Nike Air force One. Wallace has also been a source of controversy throughout his tenure in the league. He was one of the first players that the league fined for wearing his shorts too long, for instance.

5 Obviously the length of someone's shorts has nothing to do with how he plays basketball. A player wearing long shorts does not in any way gain a competitive advantage over a player in shorter pants. As the length of all basketball shorts has gotten longer over time, the extremely long shorts are about style, and especially hip hop style. This is where the problem comes in. The NBA wants to control the players' image and suppress expression of this hip hop style on the court. The result is the enforcement of nonsensical rules about ultimately insignificant issues like the length of shorts.

John Stockton, the older White superstar of the Utah Jazz, continues to wear his shorts at the same length they were worn back in the old days. His especially "short shorts" are worn to make a statement that he is not like the younger Black players in the league. Stockton's shorts are like basketball's version of the Confederate flag; an attempt to hold on to an antiquated and outdated sense of the NBA in spite of the obvious changes that abound.

Many of the younger Black players in the league, like Rasheed Wallace, wear their shorts long to make an equally provocative statement: "This is our league, and we will do things in accordance with our culture." Early in the 2001–2002 season, several Black players, including Kobe Bryant and Shaquille O'Neal, were fined and told to make the length of their shorts conform to league standards.

Hip hop-minded players like Rasheed Wallace are constantly being criticized for other things as well. The media has tended to focus on Wallace's excessive number of technical fouls, of which admittedly there are many. Wallace's emotion on the court is a demonstration of his desire to play the game at a high level. No one knows what to do with a Black man who exhibits emotion though. Unlike others, Black men are not allowed to exhibit anything remotely approximating passion. It is too often misperceived as a violent threat. In this regard they seem to be caught in a frustrating catch-22. If someone is angry, they are too emotional. And if they are laid back, they are not angry enough.

This double standard was most clearly at work when Rasheed Wallace was called for a technical foul in a playoff game against the Lakers back in 2000. Wallace was charged with a technical for an "intimidating stare" pointed in the direction of referee Ron Garretson. Though Wallace's reputation of being given to outbursts preceded him, this call was ridiculous. The call was the equivalent of accusing Wallace of "reckless eyeballing," a Jim Crow charge often leveled against Black men when it was perceived that they had been looking at a White woman or looking in a way thought disrespectful to a White person.

10 Though players like Wallace have come to represent the majority of players in the league, they are often still being discussed and manipulated by people of another generation and from another disposition altogether. Gone are the days when Jackie Robinson broke the color line in baseball and Black athletes were simply content to be included. Things have now changed quite drastically. One cannot honestly discuss sports in American society without including the contributions of Black people as a primary part of that conversation. After several generations of prominent Black athletes, their significance in sports is very much like their significance in the music industry: unquestionable. These are two areas of the culture where Black people have not only excelled, but where they are the standard by which all others are measured.

This being the case, contemporary Black athletes feel no need to simply be content because they are being Included. Unfortunately, their inclusion on the athletic side of things often mirrors a relative exclusion in other realms of the sporting world. Many members of the mainstream media are White and of a different generation. They often want to impose the dictates of the past on the Black athletes of the present. They tend to have the same expectations of an Allen Iverson as they did of a Joe Louis. Allen Iverson did not grow up in the same world that Joe Louis did, and he has not had the same experiences either. So why should he be expected to think and act in the same way? Contemporary Black basketball players have a great deal of money at their disposal along with a great deal of visibility and power. Yet the people who tend to control the aspects of the game off the court—the media, the league—reflect these old ideas and expectations.

I have often found that the incongruity of these circumstances is best reflected in the term "role model." To me, this is a modern-day version of saying that someone is a "credit to their race," as they said about Joe Louis and others in the past. Role model is another way of saying to the young. Black, rich and famous, "Stay in your place, speak when spoken to, and do as you are told . . . be thankful for what you've got." In response, the young, Black, rich and famous raise an extended middle finger. This seems to have resulted in an impasse. The proverbial unstoppable force meets the immovable object.

What emboldens the young, Black, rich and famous is that they know they are the reason people are paying attention in the first place. They are the reason for being. This reflects a shift in power relations. This is not to say that Black basketball players run things, but they do have a say-so. They are the attraction and they are the straws that stir the drink. Like stars in Hollywood who draw people to their movies, these basketball players command the box office. When the media, the establishment, and those fans with their heads in the sand wake up, they will realize all of this too. You cannot force a Black square peg into a round White hole. You cannot draw White blood from a Black turnip. You can however turn the game of basketball into a global entertainment commodity, with Black players at the center of a new definition of what now constitutes America.

Reflect & Write

- ❑ In this section of his book, Boyd claims that hip hop is a way of life that defines the culture of basketball players; it is a style choice. How does he support this assertion? Point to specific evidence. Is he convincing?
- ❑ How does Boyd strategically use diction to convey his argument about Black basketball players? Which terms are most familiar to you?
- ❑ Why does Boyd provide a historical and contemporary perspective on the notion of the "role model"? What is his point? Do you agree with it?
- ❑ **Write.** What is Boyd's point about the length of shorts being a sign of race and cultural identity? Pick another item of clothing and compose a blog entry explaining how this clothing serves as visual rhetoric for a cultural group in your community.

■ *Called the "the best sportswriter in the United States" by veteran sports journalist Robert Lipsyte,* **David Zirin** *writes about the politics of sports for* Nation *magazine and the* Los Angeles Times *and is host of Sirius XM Radio's Edge of Sports Radio. He was named one of* UTNE Reader's *"50 Visionaries Who are Changing Our World" and was Press Action's Sportswriter of the Year in both 2005 and 2006. In this article, Zirin addresses the responsibilities that Major League Baseball has toward its Latin American–born players. This piece originally appeared in the November 14, 2005, edition of* The Nation.

Say It Ain't So, Big Leagues

Dave Zirin

In early October 30-year-old Mario Encarnación was found dead in his Taipei, Taiwan, apartment from causes unknown. His lonely death, with the lights on and refrigerator door open, ended a tragic journey that began in the dirt-poor town of Bani in the Dominican Republic and concluded on the other side of the world. In between, Encarnación, or "Super Mario," as he was known on the baseball diamond, was the most highly touted prospect in the Oakland A's organization, considered better than future American League Most Valuable Player Miguel Tejada. Tejada, also from Bani, paid the freight to bring his friend home from Taiwan. It's hard to imagine who else from their barrio could have managed to foot the bill.

Encarnación's death was not even a sidebar in the sports pages of the United States. A

30-year-old playing out his last days in East Asia might as well be invisible.

But he shouldn't be. As Major League Baseball celebrates its annual fall classic, the World Series, it is increasingly dependent on talent born and bred in Latin America. Twenty-six percent of all players in the major leagues now hail from Latin America, including some of the game's most popular stars, like David Ortiz, Pedro Martinez and Sammy Sosa. Leading the way is the tiny nation of the Dominican Republic. Just five years ago there were sixty-six Dominican-born players on baseball's Opening Day rosters. This year, there were more than 100. This means roughly one out of every seven major league players was born in the DR, by far the highest number from any country outside the United States. In addition, 30 percent of players in the US minor leagues hail from this tiny Latin American nation, which shares an island with Haiti and has a population roughly the size of New York City's.

All thirty teams now scout what baseball owners commonly call "the Republic of Baseball," and a number of teams have elaborate multimillion-dollar "baseball academies." The teams trumpet these academies. (One executive said, "We have made Fields of Dreams out of the jungle.") But unmentioned is that for every Tejada there are 100 Encarnacións. And for every Encarnación toiling on the margins of the pro baseball circuit, there are thousands of Dominican players cast aside by a Major League Baseball system that is strip-mining the Dominican Republic for talent. Unmentioned is the overarching relationship Major League Baseball has with the Dominican Republic, harvesting talent on the cheap with no responsibility for who gets left behind. Unmentioned is what Major League Baseball is doing—or is not doing—for a country with 60 percent of its population living below the poverty line. As American sports agent Joe Kehoskie says in *Stealing Home,* a PBS documentary, "Traditionally in the Latin market, I would say players sign for about 5 to 10 cents on the dollar compared to their US counterparts." He also points out that "a lot of times kids just quit school at 10, 11, 12, and play baseball full-time. It's great, it's great for the kids that make it because they become superstars and get millions of dollars in the big leagues. But for ninety-eight kids out of 100, it results in a kid that is 18, 19, with no education."

Considering both the poverty rate and the endless trumpeting of rags-to-riches stories of those like Sosa and Tejada, it's no wonder the academies are so attractive to young Dominicans. Most young athletes in the DR play without shoes, using cut-out milk cartons for gloves, rolled-up cloth for balls, and sticks and branches for bats. The academies offer good equipment, nice uniforms and the dream of a better life.

Sacramento Bee sportswriter Marcos Breton's book *Home Is Everything: The Latino Baseball Story* highlights the appeal of the academies: "Teams house their players in dormitories and feed their prospects balanced meals. Often it's the first time these boys will sleep under clean sheets or eat nutritious meals. The firsts don't stop there: Some of these boys encounter a toilet for the first time. Or an indoor shower. They are taught discipline, the importance of being on time, of following instructions."

The competition to get into the "baseball factories," as they are often referred to, is fierce. Sports anthropologist Alan Klein describes, in *Stealing Home*, the scene in front of one of the academies:

> Every morning you would drive to the Academy, you would see fifteen, twenty kids out there, not one of them had a uniform, they all had pieces of one uniform or another, poor equipment, they would be right at the gate waiting for the security people to open up the gates and they would go in for their tryout. If they got signed, they were happy. If they didn't get signed, it didn't even deter them for a minute; they would be on the road hitchhiking to the next location. And they would eventually find one of those 20-some clubs that would eventually pick them up. And if not, then they might return to amateur baseball.

Yet even the ones who make it through the academy doors often find themselves little more than supporting players in a system designed to help pro teams ferret out the few potential stars. As Roberto González Echevarría, a Cuban baseball historian who also appears in the documentary, says, "I take a dim view of what the major leagues are doing in the Dominican Republic with these so-called baseball academies, where children are being signed at a very early age and not being cared for. Most of them are providing the context for the stars to emerge; if you take 100 baseball players in those academies, or 100 baseball players anywhere, only one of them will play even an inning in the major leagues. The others are there as a supporting cast."

And little is done for those very select few who make it into a major league farm system to protect them from the likely fall to the hard concrete floor of failure.

Brendan Sullivan III, a pitcher who played five seasons for the San Diego Padres, told author Colman McCarthy, "Sure, they were thrilled to have gone from dirt lots to playing in a US stadium before fans and getting paychecks every two weeks. But once a team decides a Dominican won't make it to the big leagues, he is discarded as an unprofitable resource. That's true for US players, but at least they have a high school diploma, and often college, and thus have fallback skills. Most Dominicans don't. They go home to the poverty they came from or try to eke out an existence at menial labor in the States, with nothing left over except tales of their playing days chasing the dream."

Major League Baseball seems unconcerned and uninterested in the situation it has a central role in shaping. Boston Red Sox owner John Henry speaks of the "special relationship Major League Baseball has with the people of the Dominican Republic," but it's unclear whether he believes the Bosox and Major League Baseball have any responsibilities regarding the players they employ and the families left behind.

Al Avila, assistant general manager of the Detroit Tigers, whose father, Ralph, operated the Los Angeles Dodgers' Dominican academy for decades, told ESPN.com, "Baseball is the best way out of poverty for most of these kids and their families. They see on television and read in the newspapers how many of their countrymen have made it. For parents that have kids, they have them playing from early on. The numbers show that the dream is within reach. And even if they don't make it, these Dominican academies house, feed and educate these kids in English. They become acclimated to a new culture, which is always positive. At the very least, even if they don't make it as a player, they could get different doors opened, like becoming a coach."

The question we need to ask is, Does baseball have a broader responsibility to the Dominican Republic and these 10- and 11-year-old kids who think they have a better chance of emerging from desperately poor conditions with a stick and a milk-carton glove than by staying in school? Does the highly profitable Major League Baseball have any responsibility to cushion the crash landing that awaits 99.9 percent of DR kids with big-league dreams, or the 95 percent of players who are good enough to be chosen for the academy but are summarily discarded with nothing but a kick out the door? We can probably surmise where the family and friends of Mario Encarnación fall on this question.

The death of "Super Mario" went unnoticed in the US press with one exception, a heart-wrenching column on October 6 in the *Sacramento Bee* by his friend Marcos Breton, who wrote, "Mario wasn't a warped athlete like we've come to expect in most ballplayers. He was big-hearted, fun-loving, a good friend. . . . The pressure of succeeding and lifting his family out of poverty was a weight that soon stooped Encarnación's massive shoulders."

Should it have been his responsibility alone to shoulder such a burden?

Reflect & Write

- ❑ How does Zirin engage his audience in his topic from the beginning of the essay? Look at both the language he uses and the strategy of development. How might he have started the essay differently? How would that have changed the way that he constructed his argument?
- ❑ How does Zirin use *logos* in his essay? How does he use direct quotation? Where does he bring in these elements and to what effect?
- ❑ If there is a "villain" in this piece, who is it? Find specific passages in the article where Zirin creates this characterization.
- ❑ Look at the structure of Zirin's argument. How does he create a frame? How do his introduction and conclusion work together? What is the effect of that cooperation?
- ❑ **Write.** Take Zirin's argument and transform it into a 2–3 minute oral presentation designed to open up this question of responsibility to a very specific audience: Bud Selig, Commissioner of Baseball. How would you persuade him of the importance of this issue? Consider issues of arrangement, style, example, embodied rhetoric, and multimedia support in planning your presentation. Script your presentation in middle to high style.

As a public record of American sporting history, Sports Illustrated *has charted the rise of female athletes on its covers, featuring sports figures from Mary Lou Retton to Candace Parker. Its treatment of these "cover girls" reflects the conflicted attitude toward women in sports, as demonstrated in these examples featuring two tennis greats.*

Sports Illustrated Covers

FIGURE 13.12. This cover of *Sports Illustrated* from May 26, 2003, features a powerful photo of tennis great Serena Williams.

FIGURE 13.13. *Sports Illustrated* chooses a different approach in its cover photo of Anna Kournikova from the June 5, 2000, issue.

Seeing Connections

For a different vision of women in sports, see selections from Jane Gottesman's photo essay, *Game Face* (pages 51–52).

Reflect & Write

- ❑ Compare the way Anna Kournikova and Serena Williams are portrayed in each of their cover shots; observe both their facial expressions and their postures. How does the accompanying text resonate with these choices?
- ❑ If both of these covers are about female agency—showing strong, dominant women—how do the covers show this dominance in different ways?
- ❑ To what extent does an idea of gender or the female athlete influence the design of the cover? How does each one define what it means to be a woman in sports?
- ❑ **Write.** Compose a letter to the editor of *Sports Illustrated* and present your perspective on the covers, suggesting a layout, design, and caption for a cover featuring your favorite female athlete.

Produced by the ***Media Education Foundation****, a nonprofit organization specializing in providing educational resources designed to encourage media literacy,* Playing Unfair *(2003) is a short film designed to provide analysis of the role of gender in sports 30 years after Title IX legislation mandated equal privileges for female athletes. The film integrates short clips from media footage with commentary by three prominent media scholars: Mary Jo Kane from the University of Minnesota, Pat Griffin from the University of Massachusetts, and Michael Messner from the University of Southern California.*

Transcript: Playing Unfair

The Media Education Foundation

Introduction—The Best of Times and The Worst of Times

[News voice-over] *Is the American public ready to embrace professional women's teams and the image of a tough, physical, female athlete?*

MARY JO KANE: As we enter a new century, we are in what I call the Best of Times and the Worst of Times with respect to media representations of female athletes. There has been both widespread acceptance and movement of women in sport that was unheard of thirty years ago, and at the same time there's been an increasing backlash about their success and their presence.

MICHAEL MESSNER: I think not too long ago, it was very easy to equate athleticism, strength, physical power, with men, and by contrast to think about women as weak, as supportive for men, purely as sexual objects. Now that landscape has changed somewhat with the tremendous growth of girls, and women's sports.

[Sports commentator] *There's Rebecca Lobo with a jumper!*

MICHAEL MESSNER: Everybody has the opportunity to see strong, powerful, physically competent, competitive women and I think that really challenges that simple gender dichotomy that we used to take so much for granted.

PAT GRIFFIN: Sport is not just a trivial activity for fun. It has real, deep cultural meaning in this society. And I think that to challenge that meaning in terms of what it means to be a man in this culture, by inviting women in and acknowledging that women are also athletic and muscular and strong, is a real challenge to that cultural norm that we live in.

MARY JO KANE: There is a cultural assumption that I think persists even to this day, that because of the definition of masculinity and sport, part of the birthright of being male in this culture is owning sport. You own sport. As women move into this once exclusive domain of male power and privilege and identity, there's been a tremendous backlash, and a desire to push back, and either to push women out of sport altogether or certainly to contain their power within in and keep them on the margins.

Out of Uniform—The Media Backlash Against Female Athletes

MICHAEL MESSNER: If you just watch the sports news, and you just watched ESPN, and if you just picked up *Sports Illustrated Magazine* for your main print source of information about what's going on in the sports world, it would be easy to continue to conclude that there is no women's sports happening.

MARY JO KANE: Women are significantly underrepresented with respect to amount of coverage, even though women represent 40% of participants nationwide in terms of sport and physical activity. What all the studies indicate is they represent about 3–5% of all the coverage. So we give viewers a very false impression if you just rely on the media, that women simply aren't participating in sports in the numbers that they are.

MICHAEL MESSNER: Over the course of a decade that we were doing research on the coverage of women's and men's sports, our dominant finding was how much the coverage of women's sports had not changed. About 5% of the airtime was given to women's sports. In our most recent study, ten years later that had gone up to about 8%, which is still miniscule. I mean it's really a tiny increase in over a ten year period in coverage of women.

[NBC News] *They are very excited. The NBA playoffs have arrived and while the Knicks are dominating . . .*

MICHAEL MESSNER: You set the tone and make a statement about what's most important and what the key happenings of the day were with your lead story.

[NBC News] *a big night coming up in sports as the Islanders . . .*

10 MICHAEL MESSNER: What we found is almost always the lead stories were about men's sports. They put a lot more production value into the men's coverage. There's tape, there's graphics, there's interviews and so forth.

[ESPN promo] *June heats up on ESPN.*

MICHAEL MESSNER: When women do kind of peak into the frame, though, it's usually in ways that are mostly dismissive or disrespectful.

[ABC News Channel 7] *Finally, a hearty erin go braugh to my countrymen and-women out there, and in your honor we have a little Erin Go Bra-less.*

MICHAEL MESSNER: In our study, one of the longest stories that was done on the sports news for instance was on a female nude bungee jumper on St. Patrick's Day who had painted her body green and jumped off of a bridge and they did a very long story on this—on the sports—meanwhile ignoring all the sports women had been playing that day: a major golf tournament and so forth.

[ABC News Channel 7]
— That's wonderful; do we have to slow that down?
— That was amazing, I'll remember it forever.
— . . . And so will we.

MICHAEL MESSNER: Well we all know that news isn't totally objective, but it's supposed to be a picture of what happened today in the world.

MARY JO KANE: What we know in terms of the data is that women athletes are significantly more likely than male athletes to be portrayed off the court, out of uniform, and in these hyper feminized roles. The thing that we infrequently see is images of women athletes as athletes. I think we need to talk about why that is and who benefits from *not* seeing women athletes as athletes.

15 PAT GRIFFIN: Who's controlling the images that we see in the media, and I think particularly if you look at sports media, by and large, the decisions about what images are portrayed, what images are used, who gets coverage, are still made by men. They're part of a culture that sees women in a particular way. And so I think they prefer to see women athletes portrayed in a more feminine way, it's more comfortable.

MICHAEL MESSNER: When television does cover women's sports, they're most likely going to cover women's tennis, and during certain seasons and certainly during the Olympics, women's figure skating. There's a traditional equation of femininity with tennis and figure skating that makes some sports commentators more comfortable with covering them—they fit more in their own ideological frame about what women are supposed to look like and how they're supposed to act. There's still a tendency, we found, in the play-by-play coverage of tennis to call women athletes more often by their first names, as though there's some sort of familiarity that the commentator has with them.

[Tennis commentator] *. . . to counter Jennifer's return.*
[Tennis commentator] *. . . you just never know which Amelie's going to show up.*
[Tennis commentator] *. . . Monica, trying to hang on, but Serena's serve . . .*

MICHAEL MESSNER: And to call men athletes by their last name or by their last and first name.

[Tennis commentator] *. . . Cand Ruzesky takes the game . . .*
[Tennis commentator] *. . . Agassi, through to the semis, and coming off his French Open win.*

MICHAEL MESSNER: People who work in an office, the boss will call the secretary by her—or his, if it's a male secretary—first name, and the referent the other way is always "Mr." or "Mrs." or some title.

PAT GRIFFIN: I think what's going on is we still have a lot of cultural anxiety about strong women and what that means about them as women. And until we can sort of move much further, as a culture in opening up the boundaries for what we consider to be OK for girls and women in sport, we're always going to have that ambivalence there.

20 MARY JO KANE: As we went into the women's World Cup soccer, nobody knew who Brandi Chastain was. We knew who Mia Hamm was, but we didn't know who Brandi Chastain was. We know who she is now.

[Newscaster] World Cup hero Brandi Chastain, throws the first pitch—tank top, no sports bra.
[ABC News Channel 7] And uh, Brandi did keep her shirt on, but did take a sweater off, during warm-ups.
[ABC News Channel 7] It was announced Nike will exploit Brandi Chastain's strip tease by attaching her to a line of sports bras.

MARY JO KANE: It immediately got turned into "Brandi Chastain took her shirt off," rather than "what fabulous athletes these women are!"

MICHAEL MESSNER: How many times did we see images of Jenny Thompson actually swimming in *Sports Illustrated*? But when she posed for *Sports Illustrated* in that way, we saw her and now we know who she is.

MARY JO KANE: What got taken up in the press and the public discourse wasn't who Jenny Thompson was and what she'd accomplished as a great swimmer, an Olympic swimmer, but what did it mean to have Jenny Thompson take her shirt off?

[Montage of images of female athletes and non-athlete models]

MARY JO KANE: And the images that you see of women being physically powerful and strong and contrast that to the images of women athletes as little sex kittens, it's an enormous difference. And it is such a powerful contrast that I would argue that is exactly why those images are suppressed. Because sport is all about physical, emotional, and mental empowerment. And so what do you do with all these women who are becoming great athletes and learning the lessons of empowerment and self respect and pride that you get from participating in sport? How are you going to keep that force at bay? And one way that you do that is to do a very time honored and tested mechanism of keeping women's power at bay and that is to sexualize them, trivialize them, and marginalize them.

There are more and more images of women athletes that bear alarming resemblances to soft pornography. What you see is an emphasis, not on their athleticism and their athletic achievements, or their mental courage and toughness, but on their sexuality, their femininity, and their heterosexuality. So what better way to reinforce all of the social stereotypes about femininity and masculinity than to pick up *Sports Illustrated* or *Rolling Stone* or *Maxim* or *Gear* and see an image of a female athlete, not as strong and powerful but as somebody that you can sexualize and feel power over. I don't think that there's a more overt example of that these days than in the world of professional tennis in the image of Anna Kournikova. She has the most corporate sponsorship of any professional female athlete and it is not because of her athletic competence because she is as of this date, still has never won any singles tournament, let along a Major.

PAT GRIFFIN: What it says to me is that an athlete's sexual appeal quotient is much more important than her athletic ability quotient and her athletic accomplishment quotient. And it's very difficult to imagine the same kind of thing happening in men's tennis—a player who has never won a major tournament getting the kind of attention—media attention and endorsement in terms of money that Anna Kournikova gets. And I think that as long as that's possible, it really gives us a pretty good gauge of what are the important things in women's sports.

MICHAEL MESSNER: One of the new things over the last several years is there definitely is more media sexualization of men and men athletes in particular. Men are being viewed as sexy, mostly because of what they do. Of course they have to look good, but they're viewed as sexy primarily for what they're doing on the court or on the field, how good an athlete they are, how powerful they are, how they move when they play. Women are being viewed as sexy not for what they're doing on the court or for what they're doing on the field, but for how they look and what they wear off the field and how they pose off the field, and that's the key difference.

[ESPN: World's Sexiest Athlete] *The world's sexiest athlete? Anna Kournikova, hands down. Have you seen the billboard of it? That explains enough.*

Kournikova*: All athletes are entertainers. As long as people like what they're seeing, they're going to keep coming back, so I think that's good.*

Playing Along—Empowerment or Exploitation?

MARY JO KANE: It's not just how the media portray women athletes. It's how they are promoted and how they portray themselves. They simply feed into and keep the engine going of the way in which the media portray women athletes.

[Entertainment Tonight!: Brandi Chastain interview] *It was something that I'm glad I did and if it got attention for soccer, then good.*

MICHAEL MESSNER: Those are paradoxical images that both suggest empowerment for women and suggest that this media is still trying to frame women in conventionally sexualized ways. And I think that plays into very easily the idea that I, as an individual, need to feel empowered or do feel empowered by taking off my clothes and posing and getting myself into a major national magazine and maybe getting some endorsements.

PAT GRIFFIN: There are other women that I've talked to—young women—who see this in a real different way. They don't really see that as compromising or an expression of concern about how people see them. They just see that as—"that's just my individual way of expressing myself." And I think that certainly could be true for a certain number of them. But what I always want to say to them is it's important to look at the larger picture of pressures, that it's not just about individual choice. That if you look at how women athletes portray themselves, and how they're portrayed in the media, it's a part of a much larger cultural expectation. Is this the kind of image that we want young girls who are interested in sport to aspire to? Do we want them to think that in order to be respected as an athlete, they have to strip?

30 MARY JO KANE: And a very common retort is "what's wrong with being portrayed as feminine?" and "we want to be portrayed as well-rounded" and "there's nothing wrong with showing off our bodies. We're *proud* of our bodies." And on the surface, I think that all of those are very legitimate arguments. The problem that I have is that for women to show that they have strong and powerful bodies, it does not require them to take their clothes off. The way that those images get taken off is basically in terms of locker room titillation. It has absolutely nothing to do with men sitting around, saying, "Boy, I really respect them as fabulous athletes." It's about consuming their bodies for men's sexual pleasure. So that in no way empowers them or is done as an empowering image.

MICHAEL MESSNER: I don't think you'd have near the amount of controversy or debate if a woman occasionally decides to pose half-clothed in front of a camera for *Sports Illustrated* or something. But it's the dearth of coverage of women and the dearth of respectful coverage of women's athletics in those major media that makes those images stand out so much and be so controversial.

The Glass Closet—Homophobia in Sport and Sports Media

MARY JO KANE: Homophobia is in the bone marrow of women's athletics, you simply cannot get around it.

[ABC News] *Billie Jean King, the undisputed Queen of Tennis. Last Friday, facing what is certainly the most serious crisis of her career, thirty-seven year old Billie Jean admitted she had had a homosexual affair with her former secretary Marilyn Barnett.*

[NBC News] *Billie Jean King's contract to make television ads for ER Squibb Company is not being renewed. The New York Daily News quotes a company official as saying she was too strong a personality, that she was overpowering the product. He denied that the company's decision had anything to do with Mrs. King's disclosure of a lesbian relationship. The News says Avon Products is reviewing its connection with Mrs. King cautiously.*

MARY JO KANE: I think its pretty clear that if you're a female athlete and you want corporate sponsorship, you'd better project a wholesome image. And part of that wholesomeness is the assumption that you are not lesbian, that you are heterosexual. So you'll have a disproportionate number of images of women athletes with children, with boyfriends, with husbands, to clearly mark themselves as heterosexual.

PAT GRIFFIN: Sometimes I refer to that as sort of the protective camouflage of feminine drag that women athletes and coaches feel sort of compelled to monitor in themselves and in others. Certainly it's this need to reassure people—I'm an athlete, I may be a great athlete, but don't worry, I'm still a normal woman.

MARY JO KANE: The acronym for the professional golf tour is the LPGA, as in the Ladies Professional Golf Association and I think it has been widely known or feared for many years that the "L" stands for "lesbian." The LPGA and the women who've played in the Tour have taken great pains to distance themselves from that lesbian image and to again, very overtly and explicitly identify themselves as heterosexual.

[TV ad] *Hey Laura Baugh, UltraBrite toothpaste would like to proposition you.*

***Laura**: Right here? On national television?*

MARY JO KANE: Jan Stephenson who was a well-known professional golfer was part of an LPGA calendar—"we're professional golfers by day but we're really sexy gals by night." A disproportionate amount of the coverage given to Nancy Lopez who's one of the greatest golfers ever on the Tour was about her marriage to Ray Knight who's a professional baseball player with the Mets, and her role as a mother. There were lots of pictures of Laura Baugh when she was pregnant and playing on the Tour. The LPGA rarely gets any media coverage and yet there was a lot of media coverage around "is she going to be able to get through the round and the tournament and not go into labor?" The media or the corporate sponsors or the women athletes themselves specifically identify themselves with the role of wife and mother, which clearly marks them as heterosexual.

[ABC News] For Chris Evert this will be her nineteenth and last US Open.

MARY JO KANE: In the late 1980s, one of the greatest professional tennis players this country has ever produced, Chris Evert, announced her retirement. *Sports*

Illustrated chose to put her on the cover: "Now I'm going to be a full time wife." They chose to portray her as somebody who was giving up her career to become a full-time wife. On the inside, with the profile, they had a pictorial chronology of Evert's "career" in sport. This isn't in "Bride Magazine" or in "Heterosexual Magazine"—its in *Sports Illustrated,* talking about her retirement as being a professional tennis player, and yet the focus, certainly in terms of the visual images you were given, was of Chris Evert as a heterosexual wife and mother.

PAT GRIFFIN: The more we focus on women athletes as heterosexual and sexy and feminine, the more lesbians in sport become invisible. It's difficult enough in many cases to be a lesbian in sport, but to be held up against that standard that is not about me—that sense of being made to feel as if I must be invisible for the sake of women's sports, for the sake of not creating controversy—it's a huge pressure, and it keeps us from really dealing with some of the key issues in women's sports which have to do with heterosexism and homophobia.

[ABC News] *It has added to the torment she has long suffered, from the public acknowledgement of her homosexuality.*

Martina: *It's much easier being heterosexual, believe me. It's much easier pretending.*

PAT GRIFFIN: There are heterosexual women in sport who are very much threatened by the idea that someone might think that they're a lesbian, or would call them a lesbian. And lesbians in sport are very much concerned—and rightly so—about being discriminated against, if they're identified in sport. And you put that together and it really drives a wedge between women in sport. And that wedge serves a larger social function of keeping women from forming alliances to really further women's sport as a whole.

[Tennis commentator] *. . . I mean she came out and openly declared her sexuality and in team sports of course that would be suicidal—I don't mean that literally, but I mean it would be a very, very hard thing*

40 PAT GRIFFIN: I think it's amazing to me that in the WBNA, there is not one publicly out basketball player. And yet we know that there are many lesbians in basketball as there are in any sport. But none of them have felt personally safe enough, or I think another factor is feeling like the league itself, the women's basketball professional league, is safe enough to withstand the potential media scrutiny of acknowledging that there are lesbian players. You know, the weird thing is everyone knows there are lesbian players. So we have this strange sort of paradox of lesbians feeling that they need to hide, yet everyone knows that they're there—I often call it the "glass closet."

MARY JO KANE: The WNBA is very much aware that a large part of their fan base is lesbian. They're a new league, they are struggling to survive. So they certainly don't want to alienate any section of their fan base, especially one that's so prominent and loyal. On the other hand, they take great pains to market themselves as a family-friendly entertainment venue. And so because of homophobia and cultural stereotypes, we see that there's this contradiction on the one hand wanting to market yourself as family values entertainment, and on the other hand, what do you do with the fact that you have these lesbians in the stands?

MICHAEL MESSNER: There are stars that were put forward to promote the league, were positioned as the "girl next door," like Rebecca Lobo, a mother—Cheryl Swoops, or a fashion model—Lisa Leslie. And in doing that what they did was they pushed certain women forward as representing the league, who could exemplify what they saw as pretty conventional, heterosexual roles for women.

MARY JO KANE: I think the struggle is, how do you show athletic competence, athletic strength, athletic power—beating up and beating down your opponent—in ways that don't trigger cultural stereotypes about women athletes being too butch, being too manly, being too aggressive?

[Basketball Coach Pat Summit] *Get tough! Get tough!*

MARY JO KANE: In order for women athletes to be taken seriously as athletes, they have to be portrayed as competent, which in sports like basketball, by definition means being big, strong, tough, fast, powerful. You can't have one without the other, and yet to equate them means to challenge every stereotype and construction of femininity and masculinity we have in the culture.

Fair Play—Women Athletes in Action

45 PAT GRIFFIN: Masculinity and femininity are not natural things. You know, boys don't pop out of the womb with a football in their arm, and girls don't pop out with a doll. We have to be *taught* very carefully how we're supposed to act to conform to those artificial expectations of masculinity and femininity. And to the extent that sport is very gendered in this culture—its one of the ways that masculinity and femininity are taught.

MICHAEL MESSNER: One of the things that people haven't really talked about that much though is that having more images of powerful women, respectful coverage of women's sports, is also potentially very good for boys. Boys are growing up in a world where they're going to have women coworkers, women bosses—the foundations for their views of women are being laid during their childhood. If what they're seeing is a sea of imagery that still suggests to them that athleticism is to be equated entirely with men and masculinity and that women are there simply as support objects or as objects of ridicule or as sexual objects, that is helping to shape the images that boys have of women. I don't believe that there's a conspiracy in the media to say "let's not cover women's sports" or "lets make fun of women athletes," but I think that especially sports desks and sports news people have not caught on to the fact yet that the culture has changed.

PAT GRIFFIN: Well, I don't think any social change happens in a nice, smooth sort of step-by-step path, onward and upward. If you look at any social change movement, whether we're talking about the black civil rights movement, the women's movement in general, the gay, lesbian, bisexual, transgender movement—when there are changes, there's always a pushback. And so change sort of happens in that way, and I think that's what we're seeing here.

MARY JO KANE: All I'm asking is, turn the camera on, and let us see what it looks like when women participate in sports. And what we'll see is that they are terrific athletes who are enormously gifted and enormously committed to something that many people in this country love, and that's sport.

Reflect & Write

- ❑ What issues concerning sexuality and the female body are raised by this film transcript?
- ❑ How do the speakers raise concrete points of evidence concerning the media's unfair depiction of women in sports? Discuss the use of names, the framing, the tapes, the particular sports shown, the focus on clothes and on sexual preference. Which of these media infractions do you think has the greatest consequences? Why?
- ❑ Do you agree with the contention that the media representation of several female athletes verges on "soft porn"? Argue for both sides of this debate.
- ❑ **Write.** Draft a letter to *Sports Illustrated* from the perspective of Chris Evert, Rebecca Lobo, and Anna Kournikova. How would each woman respond to the arguments made by this film? Quote from passages in the transcript in your letter.

COLLABORATIVE CHALLENGE

Get into groups of three for this activity. Using at least three different examples of a single type of sports coverage (for instance, three news reports, three newspaper articles, or three articles in a sports-oriented magazine), explore how the amount and tone of coverage of women athletes reveal the relationship between gender stereotype and sports media. Pick two recent and concrete examples to prove your assertions. Compose a Multiple Sides feature article (following the guidelines in Chapter 3) and present your findings to the class.

■ *In this article,* Chicago Tribune *reporter* **Shannon Ryan** *discusses the WNBA's 2008 orientation for its new rookies: a make-over. This article first appeared in the May 4, 2008, issue of the* Chicago Tribune.

Banking on Beauty Trying to Expand Fan Base by Marketing Its Players, the WNBA for the First Time Offers Rookies Lessons in Fashion and Makeup

Shannon Ryan

As a skilled instructor guided them, the WNBA's new class of rookies spent part of their orientation weekend learning how to perfect their arcs.

The trainer demonstrated how to smooth out a stroke, provided an answer to stopping runs and showed them how getting good open looks can seem effortless.

It was not Lisa Leslie or another veteran teaching basketball fundamentals but a cosmetics artist brought in by the league last month to teach the rookies how to arc their eyebrows, apply strokes of blush across their cheekbones and put on no-smudge eyeliner to receive the right attention off the court.

As part of the rookies' orientation into life as professional athletes, the WNBA for the first time offered them hour-long courses on makeup and fashion tips. The courses, at an O'Hare airport hotel, made up about a third of the two-day orientation, which also featured seminars on financial advice, media training and fitness and nutrition.

"I think it's very important," said Candace Parker, the Naperville product who was the league's No. 1 draft pick out of Tennessee. "I'm the type who likes to put on basketball shorts and a white T, but I love to dress up and wear makeup. But as time goes on, I think [looks] will be less and less important."

In its 12th season, the WNBA is still working to become a more profitable league with an expanded fan base. The average attendance was 7,742 per game last season. The Sky averaged 3,709 over 17 home games in 2007, compared with the 21,987 fans the Bulls averaged for 41 home games this season.

Marketing players is perhaps more important than ever, and the WNBA realizes that it's still a tough sell.

"It's all contributing to how to be a professional," league President Donna Orender said of the orientation classes. "I do believe there's more focus on a woman's physical appearance. Men are straight out accepted for their athletic ability. That's reality. I think it's true in every aspect of the work force. This is all about a broader-based education."

Physical Education

Female athletes being promoted for or encouraged to enhance their physical attributes is nothing new.

Tennis player Anna Kournikova, who never won a professional singles tournament, was the poster woman for marketing her sexuality in lieu of her athletic credentials. But far more accomplished female athletes are also marketed on the basis of their appearance.

Tennis player Maria Sharapova was the second youngest woman to win Wimbledon in 2004, which prompted Sports Illustrated to put her on its cover wearing a white tennis outfit under the words "Star Power." She appeared in Sports Illustrated again in 2006, this time wearing a variety of string bikinis on a beach for the magazine's swimsuit edition.

Last month, race car driver Danica Patrick became the first woman to win an IndyCar event. She made a name for herself posing in FHM in a red bustier atop a yellow Mustang and by starring in provocative TV commercials for GoDaddy.com. One such GoDaddy commercial was rejected for airing during this year's Super Bowl.

Softball pitcher Jennie Finch, who plays for the Chicago Bandits, set an NCAA record with 60 consecutive victories in college at Arizona and won an Olympic gold medal in 2004. She wore gold again in '05, posing in a metallic bikini for Sports Illustrated.

Even this newspaper, during a five-day series of stories chronicling the origin of the Sky franchise, posed players in gowns with basketballs.

Susan Ziegler, a Cleveland State professor of sports psychology, said disparity in wages and media coverage between male and female athletes, along with a battle against perceived negative stereotypes, are factors in marketing female sports figures for their physicality rather than their athletic assets.

The WNBA, she said, seems to be becoming more image-conscious.

"No. 1 is, of course, the need for the image of WNBA players to be seen as real women," Ziegler said. "That comes from the lesbian homophobia that surrounds women in sports in general."

Ziegler has done extensive research on female athletes being sexualized through the media. Even with something as common as applying lipstick, promoting physical appeal can take away from the athletes' legitimacy, she says.

"Once you begin to worry about how the person looks as opposed to how she plays, you've crossed the line into dangerous play," Ziegler said. "We're not really focused on marketing them as athletes but as feminine objects."

The WNBA's New Face

Parker, whose appearance is considered as marketable as her basketball skills, could be just the boost the league needs to help its bottom line.

Before the draft, Los Angeles coach Michael Cooper was excited about the prospect of male fans being enticed to watch Sparks games.

"She's already changed the interest in the WNBA," Cooper said. "Hopefully we can get some of those single guys who only watch the NBA to come watch the WNBA."

Whether they are men is hard to say, but more people already are paying attention.

The Sparks sold seven times the number of season

tickets in the first week after the draft as they did last season, and individual game ticket sales are up 272 percent.

Parker's rookie salary (around $44,000) will be a fraction of what she will make from endorsing Adidas and Gatorade.

Adidas did not release terms of Parker's multiyear contract, but she is the primary female athlete promoting the sports apparel company's products.

"She's unlike any other athlete," said Travis Gonzalez, Adidas' head of global public relations for basketball. "You look at Candace and she's the first female to dunk in a college game, probably the best female player ever. On the other side, she's an attractive girl. She's a beautiful young lady and she has a savvy sense of fashion."

For marketers, that's the complete package.

Fighting for Airtime

A league like the WNBA receives a fraction of the air time and media coverage devoted to a typical men's league, so WNBA athletes have to take advantage of any exposure they're offered.

"All of our public impressions are so important because women are covered so much less than men," Sky President Margaret Stender said. "They may not get a second chance. They have to be ready for the opportunity."

The WNBA has extended its contract with ESPN, the first for a women's professional league, through 2016. The new ad campaign aims to reintroduce sports fans to the league while emphasizing the vast improvement in pace and play over the years.

The Sky said Friday that its advertising campaign for the coming season will feature top draft pick Sylvia Fowles dunking while a voice says, "Yeah, we raised our game."

Marj Snyder, chief of programming and planning for the Women's Sports Foundation, says the paucity of media coverage given women athletes results in misplaced priorities.

"The problem is if only 8 percent of the coverage is on women, and the vast majority of the time we're talking about who they're married to, what clothing they're wearing, what kind of parents they are, there's not much room left to say, 'What a great athlete,'" Snyder said.

The WNBA works to promote its players as well-rounded role models, Stender said.

Renee Brown, the WNBA's vice president of player personnel, said the league aims to show its players as "mothers, daughters, sisters, nieces and entrepreneurs" and their "womanhood" is important to promote the league.

"You're a woman first," Brown said. "You just happen to play sports. They enjoy dressing up and trying on outfits, where back in the day, everyone just wore sweats.

"Call it what you want. We're just celebrating their womanhood."

'Game Face'

Back at the rookies' orientation, a makeup artist from the Bobbi Brown cosmetic line lectured about "a pop of blush," "brown shimmer shadow" and "twilight no-smudge" eyeliner at the rookie orientation. Parker and her colleagues paid close attention, as if a coach were a drawing up a play.

"You don't want to be caught without your game face on," makeup artist Faith Edwards said as she applied foundation to Charde Houston of the Minnesota Lynx.

Other players took part in a fashion show, strutting in Gucci stilettos and fuchsia evening gowns for their fellow players while taking tips from a style editor for OK! magazine.

Alexis Hornbuckle, a rookie guard with the Detroit Shock, said she rarely wears makeup but will start thinking about it more now.

"Appearance is important, whether you're an athlete or not," Hornbuckle said. "Hey, you've got to play the game. That's life."

NBA rookies go through a similar orientation, although their off-court conduct is stressed far more than their wardrobe or physical appearance. League VP Brown attended the fashion and makeup sessions, trying on some beauty products herself, and said the classes were purely "educational."

"I find it interesting that a lot of players do not even know how to apply mascara," Brown said. "I think as they get into it, they love it. I don't think we can run from the fact that they're women. They're so much more than basketball players."

Ziegler has some advice on how the WNBA should market Parker.

"As a pure athlete," she said. "As the top athlete in the country. Leave it at that."

Reflect & Write

- ❏ How does the essay use deliberate word choice in its opening lines to play with its reader's expectations? What is the effect of misdirecting the reader in this way?
- ❏ Is Ryan critical of the WNBA's marketing strategy? How can you tell? Look at specific examples from the essay for evidence.
- ❏ What is the significance of the multiple examples that Ryan uses in her "Physical Education" section? What do they contribute to her overall argument?
- ❏ How might visual rhetoric be used to compliment the written argument? Consider how different types of images would affect the way the readers understood Ryan's points.
- ❏ **Write.** What Renee Brown is quoted as calling "celebrating their womanhood" some feminists might call "objectification." Take on the persona of a feminist sports critic and write a brief response to this article that discusses the WBNA's 2008 marketing strategy in terms of gender politics.

■ *During 2008, the WNBA released its "Expect Great" marketing campaign, designed to promote women's basketball. The spot transcribed below features Seattle Storm point guard Sue Bird offering her perspective on the WNBA experience.*

"Expect Great" Commercial

Sue Bird

[Opens with Sue Bird running down the court]

[Cut to Bird speaking]

BIRD: Do I like to win? Yeah.

[Cut to Bird on the court, making a basket]

BIRD: I'll hit that shot with your hand right in my face.

ANNOUNCER: . . . it's Sue Bird! . . .

[Cut to Bird speaking]

BIRD: Lose your man?

[Cut to Bird on the court]

BIRD: . . . And I'll make the pass for an easy basket.

FIGURE 13.14. A close-up of Sue Bird from the WNBA "Expect Great" commercial series.

FIGURE 13.15. This frame from the "Expect Great" commercial shows Sue Bird in action on the court.

ANNOUNCER: ***[unintelligible excitement]***

[Cut to Bird speaking]

BIRD: Foul me going up? Score the bucket . . .

ANNOUNCER: . . . That's aggressive Sue Bird!

BIRD: . . . and one.

[Cut to Bird on the court]

BIRD: And, yes, that was me flying past you on the break.

[Cut to Bird speaking]

BIRD: Do I like to win? [shaking head with a small smile]

[Cut to Bird on the court after a successful play]

[Cut to Bird speaking]

BIRD: Expect great.

Reflect & Write

- ❑ How does the commercial use a combination of imagery, sound, and spoken word to build on Sue Bird's *ethos* as an WNBA player?
- ❑ Consider the composition of this commercial in relation to the canon of Arrangement. How would a different arrangement of these elements have affected the power of this ad?
- ❑ What other ways might you design a commercial to advertise an organization such as the WNBA? What rhetorical appeals would you feature in that commercial? How would you feature them? Why do you think that the marketing team decided on the particular approach it took with the Sue Bird commercial?
- ❑ **Write.** Several "Expect Great" ads featured a very different rhetorical approach: they featured WNBA superstars (such as Candace Parker) ventriloquizing typical comments made by critics of women's basketball ("I'm sorry, but you couldn't pay me to watch women's basketball"; "What kind of future does that league have? None that I can see."). Many viewers did not catch the sarcasm involved and considered the campaign to be a failure. List out your own critiques of women's basketball and use them as the basis for a new script for a Sue Bird ad. How would you integrate that text with the "Expect Great" footage to produce an ad promoting the WNBA? Look at the Candace Parker commercial, linked through the *Envision* Website, for a model.
www.pearsonhighered.com/envision/480

PERSPECTIVES ON THE ISSUE

1. Consider the portrayal of African-American athletes in sport—for instance, Kevin Garnett, Michael Jordan, Kobe Bryant, LeBron James, or Serena Williams. What does each portrayal have in common with the others? How does each portrayal support or dismantle racial stereotypes? Gender stereotypes?
2. Compose a script in which you put into dialogue the arguments made by Boyd and Mumford. See the directions in Chapter 5 on the dialogue of sources. What would each writer have to say in response to the argument of the other? What new synthesis of perspective on race and stereotypes in sports might you come to through a conversation with these authors?
3. Compare the portrayal of tennis stars Anna Kournikova and Serena Williams on the *Sports Illustrated* covers and the way women athletes are featured in the *Playing Unfair* transcript. Write an essay in which you use these diverse representations as evidence for discussing the stereotypes and challenges facing women and girls in sports coverage today.
4. Visit *Sports Illustrated*'s cover archive through the links in the *Envision* Website, and look at the covers from a few years. Consider at different ways that athletes have been represented. Write an essay in which you analyze the stereotypes of femininity, masculinity, heterosexuality, ethnic identity, and race at work in these covers. Center your argument around how far the media has—or hasn't—come in its representations of athletes.
   www.pearsonhighered.com/envision/481

FROM READING TO RESEARCH

1. Choose an advertisement that features an African-American athlete. Use it as evidence to support, modify, or refute the arguments offered by Mumford or Boyd. First perform a rhetorical analysis of the ad or commercial. Then assess the images in context by using quotations from the articles in this chapter as secondary source support for your claims. You may also draw on additional primary and secondary source materials by consulting your library. See Chapter 5 for various kinds of research you might consult and Chapter 6 for strategies on incorporating sources in your writing.
2. Explore the importance of Title IX in the history of women's participation in sports and the consequent representations of gendered athletes. Conduct research on the topic and formulate your perspective into a research argument. You might want to interview coaches as well as athletic women from diverse generations to get a range of viewpoints on this issue. Construct a list of questions based on the issues raised by the film *Playing Unfair.* For added challenge, transform your research report into a script for a film, with your interviewees as the key players in your movie.

Visit www.pearsonhighered.com/envision for expanded assignment guidelines and student projects.
Visit www.mycomplab.com for additional general writing and research resources.

CHAPTER 14

Representing Reality

How do images represent reality? Can they really capture the "truth" of an event, or does a photograph actually work as a tool of persuasion? This chapter will explore a range of instances in which photography and ethics collide. We'll look at both domestic photographs, snapshots of American communities, and international perspectives, images taken at moments of crisis across the globe. In all these examples, we will encounter challenging questions about the ethics of photography: Who can take a photo? Who is captured by print? What does it mean to freeze identity in time and place? Can photos ever tell the truth? How are arguments made—about people, places, events, and history—through the snapping of a photo?

Consider the photograph in Figure 14.1, taken in the wake of the devastating 7.0 magnitude earthquake that hit Haiti on January 12, 2010, and caused 230,000 people to lose their lives. What is the argument of this photograph? Notice the posture of the woman standing in the destroyed street. In another context, this might seem to be an image of the ordinary, such as a woman holding her rosary after attending church. But what effect do the other photographic

FIGURE 14.1. Faith: An old woman prays with rosary beads near the national cathedral in ruins, with an international aid helicopter in the background on its way to the airport. James Nachtwey, "Haiti: Out of the Ruins," TIME.com. This photograph from a photo essay on the 2010 earthquake in Haiti juxtaposes the figure of an elderly woman holding a rosary in front of a damaged church as a relief helicopter flies away overhead.

elements have? How do the ravaged church and the military helicopter overhead transform this into an image of crisis? What is the line between these two categories? Now consider the written caption accompanying the photograph.

How do the words shape our interpretation of the meaning of the image? How do words and pictures combine to create a compelling argument about what happened in Haiti and how the people are responding? At the same time, consider the choices of the photographer, James Nachtwey. How does his rhetorical strategy of capturing one woman's plight humanize this massive catastrophe? What is the *pathos* effect of focusing on one person in an image? Now compare the photo in Figure 14.1 with the photo shown in Figure 14.2, in which Nachtwey shows a large group of people seeking refuge from the lack of water, shelter, food, and safety. Notice how they are crammed into a dump truck—how does capturing this vehicle transform our understanding, as an audience, of what happened in Haiti? It would be a very different argument to see a group of people on a bus. Photography, as visual rhetoric, offers a powerful way of shaping what we understand about our world. Through strategies of invention (choice of subject), arrangement of elements and composition, and style (black and white or color, cropping and effects), photography offers arguments about our world that allow us a glimpse into the reality of others even while it challenges what we think we understand as "representing reality."

In capturing a moment in time, the photographer makes an argument—about our lives and our realities. How we interpret such images will be the focus of this chapter.

FIGURE 14.2. Escape. Thousands have fled the ruins of Port-au-Prince. Some of these displaced people have left by overcrowded bus, some by foot, and others by dump truck. James Nachtwey, "Haiti: Out of the Ruins," TIME.com.

In looking at images, captions, and arguments about these representations of reality, we'll come to a deeper understanding of how the media shapes our understanding of reality, our lives, and our world.

Our first perspective on this issue will take a close look at seemingly simple photos: those moments when we see normal people living their lives. But we'll ask how the moment in time actually turns into an argument when we consider these images as visual rhetoric. Take, for instance, a family in America at the dinner table. If we saw a photograph of this family holding hands and saying grace, we might come to some conclusions about the religious practices of this racial group, class status, geographic location, or era in time. But what if we took a photo of the family at a moment of debate, or what famous photography critic Susan Sontag calls a "pessimistic perspective" such as when the father places his fist on the table or the child seems about to break into tears. Perhaps this could be a passing moment, but it would send a message to viewers about the lives of this family and their values, experiences, and identity. We'll ask questions about how images of the ordinary shape what we might know about the reality of the subject. As we'll learn from writer Patrick Cox, images do this by capturing identity, freezing it in time, and making an argument for the viewer. Lenore Skenazy calls these "Kodak moments," while Michael Williams and colleagues claim that such snapshots "help us understand who we were and who we are." With this in mind, we'll cover snapshots of the ordinary from history as well as from city streets and suburban lawns, before ending with a consideration of how new technologies such as Flickr and YouTube enable people to share personal images with a wider public and—in the process—author their own arguments about the visual rhetoric of what America is.

In the second part, we'll look at how images of crisis—moments of conflict, tragedy, horror, or devastation—seem to capture national or international moments in time in ways that convey fixed arguments about what is happening. In doing so, as Daniel Okrent tells us, they thereby persuade viewers to interpret a situation in a given light, often using the images of people far away in foreign lands to sell papers sensationally. But what if images of conflict and war can serve as testimony, as a form of witness, as famous photographer James Nachtwey argues? This section of the chapter will engage you in this debate. To do so, we will not only examine images of natural disasters but also images from wartime, perhaps one of the most fraught situations in which photography and ethics collide. Since the Civil War, war photography and photojournalism have evolved with changing technologies to include color images and film footage, political positions on how much the public can see, and ethical concerns over the morale, confidentiality, and consequence of war coverage. We'll look at the most recent form of photojournalism in war, what the military and the media call "embedded journalism"—the practice of assigning photographers to a military unit. We'll ask, with Jim Lehrer and David Leeson, how the position of the photographer shapes the reality he or she represents for a viewing audience. By the end of the chapter, you'll have examined issues in representing reality from amateur to professional modes, across history and our contemporary landscape, exploring how the ordinary can be extraordinary, and the foreign all too familiar.

SNAPSHOTS OF THE ORDINARY

Photography takes an instant out of time, altering life by holding it still.
—*Dorothea Lange*

FIGURE 14.3. In this photograph, Christian Smith uses three cameras to capture an "ordinary" pose through the three types of photographic viewers, representing the way many see life in America today.

Look at the photo in Figure 14.3. In many ways, it is the quintessential image of ordinary life in America today, a culture filled with technology toys: cameras, phones, computers. And yet, there is something rather extraordinary about this image, comprised through the view-finders of three distinct cameras. This photo, taken by Christian Smith, represents the way many see life in America today. The photo shows how technology that has become seemingly ubiquitous (for example, the camera, the Blackberry, the iPhone) can be used to distort, enhance, and shape reality, thereby using the ordinary to create the extraordinary. How many of your friends today spend time capturing photos of friends or keep updating their profile photos on Facebook? How do photographs provide a visual account of what life is like in America for not only your generation but also generations in the past? Clearly, our interpretation of this image is based in *kairos*, or our understanding of the craze in handheld digital recording devices so prevalent in our society today. As we read the text as a representation—or argument—about America in the current decade, we learn how photographs work to shape the story we can tell about our culture.

In this chapter, we will look at such images that seem to capture "ordinary" reality. As we do so, we will learn to see photographs as evidence for the arguments we can make about our society. As Patrick Cox asserts in his review of the *America 24/7* exhibit, "Photographs play an essential role in defining our character." We'll start with photographs that people take of themselves, their families, their communities, and their friends, such as the one in Figure 14.3. Then we'll study ways in which photography has been used to define American culture. As part of this analysis, we'll start by going down memory lane to consider what Lenore Skenazy calls the "Kodak moment" of childhood, when families were first able to record themselves and thereby shape how future generations would look at them: always in a good light. Then we'll consider what we mean by "America" through the photography exhibition *America 24/7: A Family Photograph Album*. Expanding out to consider the cultural work of images in writing what we think of as our history, we'll consider images and arguments from the photo essay *Who We Were: America in Snapshots* and contemplate how photos can be like folk songs. Then we will zoom forward to the present to analyze what the newest technologies in digital photography have made possible in terms of how we "write" our story today in images. This includes a video-opinion piece by YouTube scholar, Michael Strangelove. This section raises questions as to how we represent "ourselves," both throughout America's past and today as new technologies of Flickr, YouTube, and Facebook allow people to share photos of the ordinary and post them on the Web as representations of their everyday reality.

Reflect & Write

- ❏ What do you think is the context and circumstance for this creative photo?
- ❏ If you have created images like this yourself, what was your process of invention, arrangement, drafting, revising, and production?
- ❏ What argument does the photo make about the role of technology today?
- ❏ **Write.** Draft your own caption for this photo. What argument are you trying to make with your words?

■ **Lenore Skenazy**, *a columnist for the* New York Sun *and* Advertising Age, *has written widely on American popular culture, politics, and family life. As a writer, she is known for her humorous, often ironic style. Her articles have been reprinted in numerous publications, including the* Miami Herald, *the* Montreal Gazette, *and the* Detroit Free Press. *This article originally appeared in the* New York Daily News *on January 5, 2003, and was read on NPR in March 2003.*

Don't Smile for the Camera

Lenore Skenazy

A 2-year-old was visiting our home the other day—clinging, crying, demanding juice then milk, no, JUICE!—and frankly, we found him fascinating. We simply could not remember any time that our own kids, ages 4 and 6, had ever been that horrid.

Er, young.

The 2-year-old's parents looked a tad peeved at our amnesia, until my husband, Joe, figured out the source of our self-satisfaction: "We took our videos at all the wrong times."

Bingo. If you look at the video record of our kids (bring some No-Doz), you will find a twosome so sweet, they could actually rot teeth. But you won't find real life.

5 Here they are pretending to toboggan through our living room, after a double timeout (not shown).

Here they are dancing to a Beatles song—after a half-hour, untaped, of Joe trying to get the CD player working.

And ah, just look at them there, stirring the brownie batter—with the camera expertly snapped off the second one started screaming, "You're licking too much!"

No, our family looks pretty perfect on film, as must yours, because if there's one thing we have all learned, it is what constitutes a Kodak moment: It is the moment our life most conforms, however briefly, to the way we'd like it to be. And it is about as reliable a record as a souvenir postcard.

"All families want to be seen as happy, friendly and successful," says Dan Gill, a freelance photographer. "However, these Kodak moment pictures are a far cry from our daily lives."

10 Not only do we instinctively reach for the camera only when our kids are acting like the ones on "The Cosby Show," often we wait until far-flung relatives have assembled and the house is clean and the dog isn't sniffing anywhere embarrassing. In this way, we create our own mythology of a perfect family.

Mythology? Yes, that's what you'll find between the covers of most family photo albums, says Arthur Dobrin, professor of humanities at Hofstra University.

A little history, here: In the days before photography and the industrial revolution, cultures passed down their myths orally: We are the people of the trees! Our chief is the son of thunder, etc. Everyone learned the same story about their collective ancestors.

But with the advent of photography, families were suddenly able to record their own individual history: This is our very own grandfather. We descended from *him*.

"Very few cultures present themselves negatively," says Dobrin. And neither do very many photo albums. They can't! The family's identity depends on it.

15 So in our pictures, "Children are always laughing and smiling. We also photograph ourselves loving and hugging," says Dobrin—including those of us who don't hug much. And of course, we photograph our great successes: graduation, marriage, the 30-inch striped bass.

When something goes wrong—say, a breakup—many are the miffed who will snip the discarded spouse out of the picture. There—that never happened.

Likewise, you won't find many portraits of loved ones sick in the hospital, or even sitting on the couch, watching reruns. That's not the stuff of myth. That's the stuff of real life.

The stuff that slips away.

Kodak moments may make us feel proud of who we are and where we come from, but they do a disservice to memory. When we don't have pictures of the toy-strewn house, mom in her bathrobe, grandpa drinking his soup, the life we really lived disappears. By the time we want to remember it, we can't.

We have gained a Kodak moment and lost the story of our lives.

Reflect & Write

- ❑ How does Skenazy's style work? How appropriate is it to the argument?
- ❑ Skenazy uses the phrase "Kodak moment" a few times in her article. What does she mean by this phrase?
- ❑ Compare the scenes described in Skenazy's article with the photo in Figure 14.4. How does the image of the skateboarder in the sun differ from the descriptions of childhood in the article? What "life story" is captured by the photo? What story, to use Skenazy's words, is "lost" by the image?
- ❑ **Write.** Select a photograph that is representative of your own family. Do your photos support Skenazy's assertion about the Kodak moment? Write an essay responding to her argument; use your own photographs as evidence.

FIGURE 14.4. "Kodak moment" of a skateboarder in Union Square, New York City.

Twelve years in the making, Who We Were *takes a look back at American history through the lens of photography, revealing that amateur snapshots have been representing the reality of life in the USA since 1888, when Eastman created the first Kodak.* **Michael Williams**, **Richard Cahan**, *and* **Nicholas Osborn** *chose 350 images for the book, and their work portrays snapshots as perspectives on everyday life. The collection begins inside a surrey with the fringe on top and ends with the man walking on the moon. The power of amateur photographs, the authors tell us, is that "like folk songs, they are the annals of everyday life."*

Who We Were: A Snapshot History of America

Michael Williams, Richard Cahan, and Nicholas Osborn

You can argue that the first photograph ever taken was a snapshot. Joseph Nicéphore Niépce, after all, was not a professional photographer, but an inventor. And his first photo, the view from an upper-floor window looking toward the barn and courtyard of his French estate in 1826, was certainly a personal record. But the image, which took at least eight hours to expose, was anything but rapid. And the term snapshot, which derives from a hunter's quick, cocked, rifle shot, implies speed and spontaneity.

Because early photographs needed time and deliberation to catch a fleeting figure, we advance the calendar at least sixty years before we find the first real examples of photo snapshooters. Until the 1880s, picture takers were part chemist, part magician, and part artist. They needed to know how to mix and apply a smelly collodion chemical upon a glass plate before capturing an image, and then had to coax that image to life in a dark tent before the plate dried.

All that changed when amateur photographer George Eastman quit his bank job in Rochester, New York, determined to figure out a way to simplify the complex process of making a picture. His first step was to set up a small factory that manufactured dry plates, actually called gelatino-bromides, which did away with the gooey, wet plates and the need for a portable darkroom. Then he produces what he called "American film," a roll of flexible, transparent, light-sensitive paper that replaced wet and dry plates altogether.

Eastman next introduced an easy-to-use camera. He built a square, leather-covered wooden box and called it the Kodak. The Original Kodak, first available in 1988, and the Kodak No. 1 and No. 2, which soon followed, made photography doable for most Americans. At $25 the camera was not cheap, but it was remarkably convenient. With a fixed-focus lens, which meant no focusing was required, the first Kodaks took pictures at a speed of 1/25 of a second and came packed with photo material to make 100 photos—more pictures than most amateurs had ever seen. After completing a roll, America's new photographers sent the camera back to Eastman's factory. Ten days later, mounted prints and a freshly loaded camera returned. The snapshot was born.

5 Just about every history of American photography mentions George Eastman and the development of his early cameras. But few histories go beyond that. Few discuss the billions of snapshots that have been taken since the Original Kodak was introduced. Instead, they focus on America's great photographers—Alfred Stieglitz at the turn of the century and his colleagues like Edward Steichen, the

documentaries of the thirties such as Dorothea Lange and Walker Evans, and *Life* photojournalists such as Margaret Bourke-White and Gordon Parks.

Stieglitz, Steichen, and the major photographers who followed told big stories with big cameras. They dealt with big issues and took photographs backed by big ideas. They left the small stories to the rest of us. It is the snapshooters who create pictures we pass down. And it is the snapshooters who help us understand who we were and who we are.

* * * *

Photo amateurs, the makers of snapshots, have had a checkered reputation ever since they started taking pictures. "It is well known that amateurs have produced the best and most interesting pictures," wrote the *Chicago Tribune* in 1887. "They are found at both extremes; it must be confessed that the worst results are found in their hands. Professionals are conservative. They make no new moves. They take no risks involving expenditure of money on failures. They follow established rules, and make no mistakes. At the same time, they accomplish no brilliant successes."

Since the start of the snapshot years, photo experts—i.e. camera store clerks, photofinishers, professionals, and avid amateurs—have tried to drum in the dos and don'ts of shooting. Do place our subject in the middle of the frame; don't shoot into the sun. Do use an exposure meter; don't shake the camera. Americans, by and large, have ignored these rules—and thank goodness for that. They take pictures the way they want. No matter how many times they are told otherwise, they use a flash at night to photograph the Lincoln Memorial from blocks away, or trip the shutter before they are firmly set. The result: An inconsistent but wonderfully quirky look at America.

In spite (or perhaps because) of the omnipresence of the snapshot, amateur photography has been largely disregarded in the area of high art until the past few years. In 1943, New York's Museum of Modern Art held a two-month show with hundreds of snapshots culled from the files of the Eastman Kodak Company. Williard D. Morgan, director of the museum's photography division, called snapshots "the medium of the millions" and declared snapshots important folk art. But by the 1950s, the term snapshot was a dirty word in photo circles.

10 "Today even the most amateur photographer reels under a price-crushing blow if his pictures are referred to as snapshots or having a 'snapshot-ish' quality," wrote Dorothy Fields in a 1956 issue of *Popular Photography*. "Nowadays, photographers must have a Message, artistic appeal, stark realism, feeling of movement, unique cropping or an overabundance of flesh spilling out of a bikini to qualify as worthy of a niche in this higher echelon of The New Art."

Fields longed for the day when people simply took photographs just to make a record. Cameras, she wrote, had become too complicated with light meters, filters, and a choice of f-stops.

"In our mothers' day, a gathering of the clan, the first day of school, or just a Sunday picnic was the occasion for mom to bring out the trusty folding Kodak, or box Brownie, wipe the dust off the lens with the corner of her handkerchief (no fancy lens brush), check the little red film window (what happened to these?), back up the required ten or twelve feet (no range-finder problems), glance behind her to make sure the sun was over her shoulder, click the shutter, and record the scene for posterity," Fields wrote.

That's what Eastman had in mind when he wrote that his new invention would serve as a time capsule. "Photography is thus brought within the reach of every human being who desires to preserve a record of what he sees," he wrote. "Such a photographic notebook is an enduring record of many things seen only once in a lifetime and enables the fortunate possessors to go back by the light of his own fireside to scenes which would otherwise fade from memory and be lost."

Eastman saw the snapshot as a personal record. What he failed to see was the possibility that a huge collection of diverse snapshots could tell history. Even though almost all snapshots are taken for personal reasons, they contain data and evidence that tell about communities, towns, nations, even eras. Just about every photograph in this book was once a part of a family's possessions, taken by parents, uncles, and aunts. That does not make them truer or purer than commercial or artistic photographs, nor does it make snapshots more or less beautiful. What they do share, however, is an unpretentious spirit and an insider's view. They are ground-level pictures produced by anonymous people out to create a visual diary of their own lives. When put together, snapshots provide a photographic record of us all. Like folk songs, they are the annals of everyday life.

15 The digital snapshots of today are quite different from the film snapshots in this book. With cell phone cameras, digital point-and-shoot and single-lens reflex cameras, we fire at will, amassing hundreds of images of even a single event. Many of these images—what we consider our mistakes—are tossed away to the chagrin (and relief) of future historians. The photographic record that we now create is both remarkable and overwhelming. It tells of a new time in a new way.

The photographs in this book, of course, don't tell the whole story. This is just one rambling walk through the briar patch of what we call America. It is a celebration—not a blind celebration—of an America that can never be resurrected or recreated. It tells of decades when farmers had all winter to while away their time. It tells of a place where people sat on front porches, or prayed in their backyards. It's an America of loners and eccentrics, soldiers and hippies, Okies and cotton pickers. Not a better America. Not a worse America. But our America.

Reflect & Write

- ❑ Analyze the organizational strategies of this piece. What is the purpose of beginning with a narrative? How do the concrete details of Eastman's development process influence the way you might think about old-fashioned photographs? How does the narrative help build momentum toward the thesis?
- ❑ The essay offers the main argument that "It is the snapshooters who create pictures we pass down. And it is the snapshooters who help us understand who we were and who we are." Who is "we" in this thesis? How does the writing include the audience as part of its persuasive technique? By the end of the piece, do you agree with this argument?
- ❑ What do you learn about the value of amateur photography as a means of representing reality in the United States? Which points of evidence convinced you most? Did you identify with the comment about the annoying advice of "do's and don'ts"?
- ❑ Notice how the language changes when the authors introduce the concept of digital photography. What do you make of the terms "fire at will" and "tossed away"? How does this style compare to the "rambling walk" and "briar patch" style used to characterize older photographic methods? What might be the purpose in this linguistic shift?

❑ **Write.** Do you think Eastman was correct in stating that each photograph is a "time capsule" or "personal record"? Write out your answer based on events from your life, your family's past, and your community's heritage. Search out amateur photographs to use as evidence for your argument and construct a photo-story of your own.

■ *In this article,* **Patrick Cox** *introduces the photography exhibition,* America 24/7. *Cox specializes in twentieth-century American political, media, and social history with an emphasis on Texas and the Southwest. He is the Associate Director of the Center for American History at the University of Texas, Austin. He has authored a biography on the late U.S. Senator Ralph W. Yarborough and co-authored two books:* The House Will Come to Order *and* Profiles in Power. *This article originally appeared in the November 2003 issue of the* Digital Journalist, *a monthly online magazine focused on visual journalism.*

America 24/7: A Family Photograph Album

Patrick Cox

Americans have maintained a long love affair with their lives and images.

In *America 24/7,* Rick Smolan and David Elliot Cohen captured a remarkable series of images of the lives of everyday Americans during one week in May 2003. Instead of attempting to capture America's epic moment on film, the authors chose to select the digital photographs of professional and amateurs from around the nation. Americans at work and play, pictures of celebration and meditation, urban and rural landscapes the pages contain photos that portray the ideas and lives that represent the very fabric of our nation.

Photographs play an essential role in defining our character. In the modern era, films and television provide a popular format for news and entertainment. Most people will state that they obtain information and visual images from television and the movies. Yet every family in America maintains their own highly prized collection of photos of their family and their history. These are the most coveted of all family treasures. Early in my life, working as a young reporter at a newspaper, I interviewed the local volunteer fire department chief about residential fires. I don't remember much of the story, but one statement always stayed with me. When a person's home catches on fire, people always want to save their loved ones, their pets and their family photographs.

Photos of everyday life are treasures. I have hundreds of family photos and pictures in my personal albums—my exuberant daughter with her first car, my wife and I on a secluded beach in Mexico, my dogs in the back of the pickup truck, a scenic waterfall on a back trail at Yellowstone, childhood photos when we were all slim and trim, family shots with everyone squeezed in front of the Christmas tree (and trying to have everyone smile and keep their eyes open).

5 One of my favorite photos is an 8 × 10 black and white picture of two great gentlemen who befriended me as a young newspaper editor. Standing on the left is Chester Franklin, white hair with a cowboy hat, and on the right is Beven Varnon, balding with a white beard. They are standing next to Indian Rock on the Blanco River in Wimberley, a small town about 40 miles southwest of Austin. Both men are smiling as they have just finished some great tale. In my early career, these two men were the wise old sages and the guiding forces who helped steer me through treacherous waters of my formative adult years. Both are now deceased, but their image and influence is firmly embedded in my mind. But they are the people who represent the best in American ideas and values.

These are the images and ideas that are captured in *America 24/7.* As the authors state in the book, the product is a visual patchwork. This is not a glitzy version of a Hollywood personality venue that is often promoted as the image desired by Americans. And this is not a public relations production intended to show only the desirable, edited photos for marketing a corporate brand. The photos capture the true essence of American character and communities. Just like the family photo album, this includes pictures from everyday life and records a week of American history for posterity.

Reflect & Write

- ❑ Patrick Cox begins his article with a premise that "Americans have maintained a long love affair" with images. How does Cox connect this thesis to the idea of photos as treasures?
- ❑ Analyze the use of narration as an argumentative strategy—one discussed in Chapter 2—and consider the effectiveness of this writing technique for a review essay. How does the use of story reflect the decision of the exhibition editors to tell a story with pictures?
- ❑ **Write.** The editors of the exhibit, Rick Smolan and David Elliot Cohen, address the issue of equal representation in the following statement: "*America 24/7* is not intended to be fair. Not every state, race, religion—or photographer—is represented; nor is every point of view included. This is not a book for tourists or one created by a public-relations firm to explain America to the world. It's a visual patchwork, woven by Americans from every walk of life." Compose a response to this statement, based on your own experience with photographs.

Described as the largest collaborative photography exhibit in history, America 24/7 *collected photos from over 25,000 amateur and professional photographers to create a visual chronicle of everyday life in America.*

Visual Reading: Images from America 24/7

FIGURE 14.5. A snapshot into domestic life in Pinehurst, Georgia, shows Howard "Curly" Borders reading his evening paper. What argument does this visual representation make about life in the American South?

FIGURE 14.6. Alphanso "Chippy" Edwards looks out from the kitchen window in Hartford, Connecticut.

Reflect & Write

- ❑ How does each visual text—as a photographic reading—serve to produce a sense of America's identity in a particular way? What specific rhetorical elements shape the composition of the text? Use the checklist at the end of Chapter 3 to help you answer this question.
- ❑ Taken together, how do these images constitute parts of the American "family album"? What do they say about this "family"? What images do you think should be included here as well?
- ❑ How are race, gender, and social class constructed by these images? Compare Figures 14.5 and 14.6 in particular, which show two men, two windows, but very different arguments about "America."
- ❑ The captions reproduced for these photographs are part of the original exhibit. How do the captions work in conjunction with the images? The captions read as follows:

> Figure 14.5: "Pinehurst, Georgia: Howard "Curly" Borders loves old houses and old cars. He's restored both his prized '29 Buick and the 100-year-old Victorian house he shares with wife Elaine." Figure 14.6: "Hartford, Connecticut: When Alphanso "Chippy" Edwards, 60, started his restaurant, Chippy's, 20 years ago he was one of only a handful of African-America business owners in Hartford. Today his domain also includes the Laundromat next door." Figure 14.7: "Calexico, California: The 80-mile All-American Canal not only irrigates California's Imperial Valley, it's also a perfect swim spot along the Mexican border. Although climbing through the westernmost edge of the border fence from Mexico into America is technically illegal, on particularly hot days the Border Patrol tends to look the other way."

FIGURE 14.7. Boys dive into the 80-mile-long All-American Canal on a hot day on the California/Mexico border.

- ❑ Consider the information contained in each caption and the order in which that information is presented. How is style, word choice, and voice used to create a certain impression? Why do you think each caption begins with the geographic location? How do the captions contribute to pulling together the individual photographs into a unified exhibit and argument about *America 24/7*?
- ❑ **Write.** Review other photographs in the *America 24/7* exhibit. Choose three photographs and write your own review of their rhetorical elements and significance.

  www.pearsonhighered.com/envision/494

COLLABORATIVE CHALLENGE

As a group, conduct your own *America 24/7* project. Use a digital camera and take photographs of everyday people during the course of one week. Arrange your photos into a sequence that tells a story and add captions. Finally, compose a cover article as both an introduction and review essay, explaining your rhetorical choices as well as the argument of your final project. Present your group work to the class. For added challenge, use a film recorder to make a "director's cut" with a voice-over providing the rationale for your images and the arguments they make about your life and culture.

David Pogue's *regular columns for the* New York Times *often deal with technology and generational gaps, or at least with interpersonal issues concerning technology. An Emmy award–winning tech correspondent for CBS News, and a best-selling author of seven "for Dummies" books, Pogue contributes weekly comic tech videos to CNBC. He has an honorary doctorate in music from Shenandoah Conservatory, has spent ten years conducting Broadway musicals, and entertains his wife and children with magic tricks.*

Photo Sharing Even the Folks Can Handle

David Pogue

RECEPTIVENESS to new technologies often seems related to age. For example, more 13-year-olds than 63-year-olds understand phrases like "Waz ^?" and "N2MH." (In case you're over 13, those expressions are cellphonese for, "What's up?" and "Not too much here.")

So it was with pride that I watched my parents "get" the magic of digital photography after our family reunion last summer. On the final night, I treated them to a laptop slide show of our week together. They dug it.

So much, in fact, that my mom asked if I could make her some prints.

I smiled confidently. Here, I thought, was an opportunity to lead my folks even further into the modern realm. The Web is crawling with sites that are designed for sharing photos and ordering prints of them.

5 I posted mine on Flickr.com, the biggest of them all. I told Mom to peruse the pictures and click Order Prints for each one she wanted on paper.

Unfortunately, Flickr was the wrong tool for that job. The terminology is confusing—quick, what's the difference between a Photo Group, a Photo Set and a Photo Stream? Worse, it takes seven mouse clicks, two pop-up menus and two dialog boxes to order one print of one photo. My mom wound up spending hours on what should have been a 10-minute job.

A lot of families are gathering at this time of year—for graduations, picnics and barbecues. Maybe, by seeking a better photo-sharing site, I could spare other families the exasperation I put my mom through.

My dream photo site would be free; would impose no limits on photo size or quantity; would let you order a print with just one click; and would let you pick up the prints at a local drugstore instead of waiting for the mail.

(Some of these sites require you to upload one picture at a time, which is like mowing your lawn with toenail clippers. Therefore, my original wish list also included, "Must offer a mass-uploading program." But then Zach, my 16-year-old intern, told me that "everyone" just uses PictureSync, a free, elegant, effortless program that can batch-upload photos to any sharing service. Nice. It's at picturesync.net.)

10 After examining eight free photo-sharing sites, I discovered that each specializes in a different area. In other words, Flickr's clumsiness as a peruse-then-print store wasn't necessarily its fault; it was mine, for misunderstanding its talents.

Here's a rundown.

FLICKR.COM With 525 million photos posted so far, Flickr may be the largest photo site. But its strengths are social interaction and personal expression, like a visual blog. For example, 75 percent of Flickr photos have been made available for public browsing, commenting, downloading and subscribing. (On many rival sites, you couldn't make your photos public if you wanted to.)

Flickr's Groups concept lets complete strangers collaborate on theme-related collections. There are 300,000 such groups on Flickr: collections of Nikon photos, of macro (superclose-up) photos, and so on. (For a really good time, click the Groups tab and search for "stick figures in peril.")

SHUTTERFLY.COM This service is free, all right, and it offers unlimited storage. The slide shows are attractive, complete with crossfades and speed control. You can retouch photos, crop them, add borders and otherwise get them ready for ordering prints. As on Flickr, other members can submit their own photos to themed "collections" that you establish.

And, lordy, does this site make ordering prints easy. In fact, selling prints—and calendars, photo books, jewelry, greeting cards and so on—is Shutterfly's real mission; sharing photos online seems to be only an afterthought.

For example, you can view the thumbnails of only 12 photos at a time, no matter how big the browser window. Similarly, Shutterfly imposes a maximum photo-viewing size, and it's not so big.

Finally, the public can't view your photos—only people you invite can. That could be good or bad, depending on your point of view.

WEBSHOTS.COM This site is a hybrid of Flickr (public photos, comments, search box); Shutterfly (order prints, luggage tags, magnets, books); and Times Square (the free account is cluttered with ads). Webshots also caps your free storage at 1,000 photos, a limit that goes up by 100 for each month that you're a member. As on most of the services here, some limitations go away if you upgrade your account for $25 a year.

Webshots' specialty is sharing photos online; handy buttons let you send a photo by e-mail, link to it on your Web site, share it on Facebook.com and so on. The slide shows are awesome, complete with subtle zooming and panning—and you can link to or e-mail the slide shows, too.

Unfortunately, you can't just flag each photo for printing as it goes by. You must enter a special print-ordering mode, several pages deep, and choose from tiny thumbnails.

KODAKGALLERY.COM Kodak Gallery (formerly Ofoto.com) follows the Shutterfly model. It lays the gift-ordering features on thick, and is restrictive about photo sharing; for example, you can't share with the public.

On the other hand, you can pick up your prints an hour after ordering them at a CVS drugstore (although you pay 23 cents each instead of Kodak's 15). Flickr, Shutterfly and Snapfish also offer local pickup—at Target, for example.

Over all, both Shutterfly and KodakGallery are terrific.

PHOTOBUCKET.COM Photobucket stands out because it accommodates videos and Flash animations, not just photos. And you can embed your photos onto your pages at MySpace, Blogger, Friendster, Facebook and so on, which makes Photobucket even more Web-wired than Webshots.

Cheapskates like me, however, will be put off by the crushing limits of the free account. You can't post any photo larger than 1,024-by-768 pixels (smaller than 1 megapixel); there's a one-gigabyte storage ceiling; and no slide show can contain more than 10 pictures. You can do much better.

PICASA WEB ALBUMS (photos.google.com) Who knew that Google has its own photo-sharing site? (Then again, what kind of site doesn't Google offer these days?)

Picasa Web Albums is ad-free, simple to use and loaded with powerful features. For example, you can upload your photos to it directly from iPhoto (on the Mac) or Picasa (on Windows). And one click generates the necessary HTML codes to embed a photo or an entire slide show into your own Web site—sweet.

You're offered three thumbnail sizes when working with your albums. You can reorder the photos in an album or slide show just by dragging them. Slide shows are stunning and nearly full screen. You can order a print with one click; you can download the full-resolution originals; and both public sharing and commenting are available.

The only weirdness is that Google hands off printing to either Shutterfly or something called PhotoWorks (your choice). That's the only part of this service that doesn't feel utterly seamless.

YAHOO PHOTOS (photos.yahoo.com) Yes! Yes! This one's free, it's unlimited, it's got both public and private photo sharing, you can edit the pictures, and your audience can rate, tag or add comments to your photos. Slide shows are big and clear, and—yes!—there's a one-click Order Print button.

Unfortunately, Yahoo Photos is about to shut down. Having bought Flickr, Yahoo's executives figured there's no sense in running rival sites.

No! No!

SNAPFISH.COM Now we're talking. One click begins

a slide show, complete with speed slider, background-color control and a relatively huge photo size. Moms, dads and grads can flag the shots worth printing with a single click.

All the usual goodies are here: electronic sharing with family (although not with the public); editing and cropping tools; and a catalog of photo prints, posters, mugs and decks of cards. All of it is designed simply and clearly, making it impossible to get lost.

There are paid subscription options—to upload videos, for example—but the free account is everything a family shutterbug could desire. Storage is unlimited if you order something once a year.

The bottom line. Next time my mother wants to review my photos on the screen and order prints with one click, I'll use Snapfish or Kodak Gallery. And next time I just want my friends to be able to see and grab copies of my pictures online, I'll use Picasa Web Albums.

All three of these services are free, devoid of advertising, quick and technologically foolproof—no matter how old you are.

Correction: June 8, 2007

The David Pogue column in the special Circuits section on Tuesday, about Web sites for sharing and printing photos, incorrectly described a feature of one site, Kodak Gallery. While a user with a free or paid account can upload photos to the site (kodakgallery.com) and allow others to view them, the site does not allow others to download them. But it has a "Print@Home" feature that lets others print photos without downloading them.

Reflect & Write

- ❑ How does the writer immediately grab the reader's attention with a hook that offers funny insight on the generation gap around new photography technologies?
- ❑ Why might Pogue continue to use his informal tone throughout the piece, even when he moves from narration to "division and classification"?
- ❑ While the article seems to offer merely a summary of types of photo-sharing networks, what is the implicit argument about how our options for representing reality are changing? What might you add to this list?
- ❑ **Write.** Compose a letter to the editor of the *New York Times*. Share a story about how you taught a family member to bridge the digital divide and master control over photo-sharing. Or, divide and classify what new types of photographic representation you think might be possible in the future.

■ **Michael Strangelove** *is a lecturer in the Department of Communication at the University of Ottawa. He is the author of two books focused on media and society:* The Empire of the Mind: Digital Piracy and the Anti-Capitalist Movement *(2005) and* Watching YouTube: Extraordinary Videos by Ordinary People *(2010). Dr. Strangelove also maintains a comprehensive collection of articles about YouTube on Creative Commons and a blog about new media and digital culture. This video, narrated by Strangelove, offers a video-trailer for the thesis of his latest book.*

There Is No Shame in Watching YouTube

Michael Strangelove

There is no shame in watching "David after the Dentist," that "Numa Numa" guy, "Laughing Baby," the gay cross-dressing dude, the oh-so-fake lonely girl 15, or the Star Wars Kid.

We watch them because we see in them a little bit of ourselves.

We see our triumphs, our tragedies, our past, our future.

We make fun of our pets, our leaders, our friends, and ourselves.

And while we were watching, something magical happened: the world started watching along with us.

Watching YouTube: it's all about us.

We like to watch.

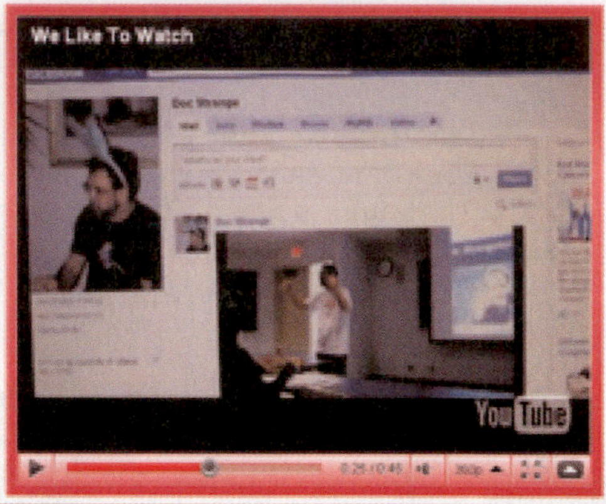

FIGURE 14.8. After a montage of YouTube's most played video, the author includes a screen shot showing his own photos and videos on facebook (Screenshot).

Reflect & Write

- ❑ How might this YouTube video represent a photo-trailer for the argument of Dr. Stangelove's book? Can a photomontage be a blurb? What changes in viewing the evidence as a series of still shots rather than as a written description? Compare Figures 14.8 and 14.9 in answering this question.
- ❑ How does the author use *pathos* expertly here? Notice how he begins with "there is no shame" and then moves to "something magical." What is the effect of this rhetorical strategy on you as a writer?
- ❑ Watch the complete 45-second movie linked through the *Envision* Website. Which videos do you recognize? How does the author "cite" them in this photo collection of screen shots? What additional videos would you cite as representing "ourselves" if you were to make a sequel to this video?
  www.pearsonhighered.com/envision/498
- ❑ **Write.** Compose a script for your own YouTube video as a photo-story about ordinary life. What videos would you include in your film? What would be your argument and thesis? Would you include representations of yourself as an author? Why or why not? In writing your script, you can either agree or disagree with the thesis of this short photo-story.

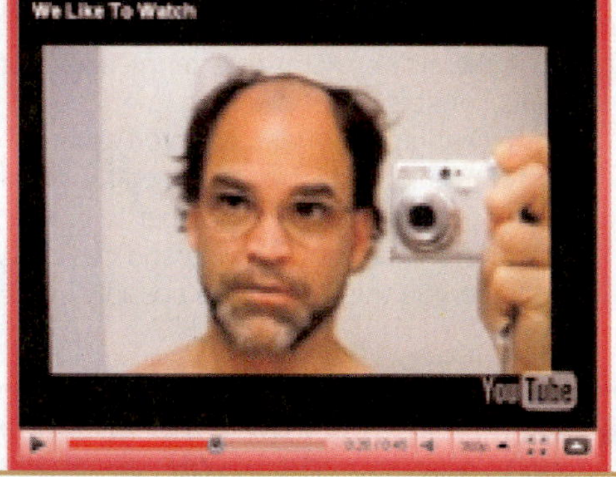

FIGURE 14.9. Author, self-portrait with a digital camera, filmed for YouTube (Screenshot).

COLLABORATIVE CHALLENGE

Visit the *Envision* Website and explore an online interactive multimedia feature on BBC, the *New York Times*, MSNBC, or I-Reports on CNN. How do these Websites and news sites feature photographs of everyday people? What arguments are being made about the countries, cultures, and people represented through inevitable selectivity? Compose an online photo essay or YouTube video with your comments on several choice examples of digitally captured identity through photo representation.
www.pearsonhighered.com/envision/498

PERSPECTIVES ON THE ISSUE

1. Return to the quotation from Dorothea Lange that opened this section: "Photography takes an instant out of time, altering life by holding it still." Assess this quotation now in light of the readings and photographs you've examined in this chapter. Compose an argument supporting or refuting the quotation and use specific evidence from the section materials to prove your thesis.
2. Compare the photographs of American life showcased in this chapter; what has changed over time in terms of subject matter, technique, and rhetorical elements of the image? What do such changes suggest about our changing cultural values as a society and our changing relationship with photography or the image? What do changing images suggest about how technology shapes our representations of reality?
3. What remains constant in looking at images of the ordinary across various media, from photographs to video blogs? What values, choice of subjects, or techniques of representing reality can you identify across media? Which readings make the most provocative points about this issue?
4. Analyze the point in Skenazy's article about strategic Kodak moments. How might you use this perspective to read the *America 24/7* review through another lens? How might you interpret Dr. Strangelove's YouTube video as a series of Kodak moments?

FROM READING TO RESEARCH

1. In an essay entitled "Photographing the Unfamous," writer Catherine Ryan asserts about the photographer Mary Ellen Mark:

   > From circus performers in India to street kids in Seattle, Mary Ellen Mark photographs people on the fringes of society—the "unfamous," as she calls them—to portray aspects of the world that many people never confront. She ultimately aims to show the common threads of humanity by photographing people of varying backgrounds.

   Conduct research on this photographer to see what Ryan means about the "unfamous." Visit Mary Ellen Mark's photography, linked through the *Envision* Website. Write up your own analysis of three images. Then compare Ryan's claim to another view on Mark's photography by reading the interview with Melissa Harris in *Aperture* (Winter 1997 n 146, p. 42–52), available in your library. Craft a Multiple Sides project (follow the directions in Chapter 3) representing the diverse views you have researched. Add your own framing perspective as editor of the collection for this research project.
   www.pearsonhighered.com/envision/499
2. Research the changing representations of women's roles in the media, from images in photographs you find on the news or in popular magazines (such as *People, Vogue, National Geographic, Elle*) to images on television shows (*Survivor, Extreme Makeover, American Idol*). What changes or trends do you see in representations of women? Conduct additional research into the representation of women's realities; look at the following texts for a starting point and then synthesize these views, along with your own rhetorical analysis of the images you find, in order to forge your research paper: John Berger, *Ways of Seeing;* John Tagg, *The Burden of Representation;* Marianne Hirsch, *The Familial Gaze;* and Amelia Jones, *The Feminism and Visual Culture Reader*.
3. Conduct the research project above but look at representations of masculinity, class, race, and American identity. Include additional visual representations of reality such as *Queer Eye for the Straight Guy, Everybody Loves Raymond,* and *The Jerry Springer Show.* Compose a rhetorical analysis of the texts you will study, and weave your research sources in as support for your argument. Follow the guidelines from Chapter 6 to help you draft your research paper. You might want to share it with a group of writers in class and exchange peer review feedback. When you are done, design a photo montage for the cover of your research paper. Present your work to the class.

IMAGES OF CRISIS

FIGURE 14.10. Two school children from Mercer Island, Washington, use images of suffering to solicit donations to raise money for victims of the 2004 tsunami in Southeast Asia.

I believe that photography can make a real connection to people, and can be employed as a positive agent for understanding the challenges and opportunities facing our world today.
—*David Griffin, Photo Director for National Geographic*

With the ubiquity of news coverage and global media today, we get our understanding of both local and world events from stories accompanied by powerful images. From the devastation in Haiti due to the 7.0 earthquake to the flooding of New Orleans to the 2004 tsunami disaster in Southeast Asia, we get a glimpse into the suffering of others through vivid photos, news films, blogs, and videos from those on the ground. In this way, images literally shape what it is possible for us to know about a crisis. Sometimes, looking at a particularly heart-wrenching image, we might wonder: What are the ethics involved in showing people caught in times of crisis, tragedy, pain, or suffering? Do the images accurately represent the reality of a situation or just show us one skewed view?

To begin to understand these questions, let's take the 2004 Indian Ocean tsunami as our first example. On December 26, 2004, when the natural disaster struck Southeast Asia, camera crews soon arrived to capture the devastation. Within hours, photographs of destroyed towns and coastal villages, ravaged tourist hotels, bodies of drowned victims, and grieving families swept like another tidal wave across streaming media, satellite news feeds, and newspapers worldwide. But in the wake of such media coverage emerged a tricky question of ethics—is it acceptable to use graphic representations of the affected countries and of the people who live there, even if the photos are used with the best intentions to help garner support for suffering people?

Consider the example in Figure 14.10, where two children use graphic photographs of the tsunami crisis to raise awareness—and money—to help the disaster victims. What do you make of the contrast between their smiling faces and the crisis-stricken people shown on their poster? The original caption for the photo celebrated their actions without considering the ethics of their capitalizing on the suffering of others:

> Eight-year-old twins Themio, left, and George Pallis of Mercer Island, Wash., already have delivered $5,660 to World Vision, an aid organization that focuses on children. Since then, fellow students have donated more.

Viewed through an ironic lens, it appears that to make their work possible, the children have used such horrific images without necessarily grappling with the issue of reproducing people's pain in photos for a specific cause. Now compare that photo to the one in Figure 14.11, in which a young child holds up a poster with the words, "Bake Sale for Haiti" on it, along with a smiling face and a cupcake. What are the ethics of not representing those who are suffering?

In this chapter, we will try to wrestle with the issue of representing global realities—often from times of crisis—through images. We'll ask, with Daniel Okrent, what it

FIGURE 14.11. This child's bake sale sign to raise money for victims of the 2010 earthquake catastrophe in Haiti does not use images of suffering, but the child is smiling.

means to raise international awareness through visual representation, and whether we have different standards for particular countries. We'll consider Bruce Jackson's letter to the editor wondering about our limits on decency and privacy. Then we'll study an opposing and powerful perspective by famous photographer James Nachtwey, who views photojournalism as a moral imperative, explaining: "I have been a witness, and these pictures are my testimony. The events I have recorded should not be forgotten and must not be repeated." Two views on the 1995 Oklahoma City bombing will help us explore the issue in more depth, and we'll consider the significance of what Mark Glaser calls "citizen paparazzi"—people who take photos with cell phones, such as happened after the July 2005 London terrorist bombings.

We will then turn to images of crisis during global conflicts and war. We'll consider a recent form of war photography that the military and the media call *embedded journalism*, in which access to shots are controlled by the military. This coverage stands as a dramatic change in terms of the kinds of images that news journalists provide the public. From an ethical standpoint, it may be as significant as the first color images depicting the war in Vietnam or the film footage that emerged soon after, through which audiences gained unparalleled access to what was happening on the other side of the world. Are such photographers able to see only part of the story? How can they represent the full reality of a situation? That is, can they offer the public a truly objective view or are they somehow now part of the military mission? And what happens when photographers stand aside in the face of true danger—when they refuse to save a life, pick up a gun, or help those who have been protecting them? What happens when photographers do become combatants? To address these questions, we'll end our readings with analysis from PBS's *NewsHour with Jim Lehrer* of the ways in which most representations of photojournalism in wartime reflect our changing attitudes about viewing—and experiencing—images of crisis.

Reflect & Write

- ❑ Analyze the rhetorical properties of the photo in Figure 14.10 and Figure 14.11. Look at the many complex elements: the boys' smiling faces, the grief-stricken faces of people in the newspaper photos. What are the various arguments made by each part of the image? How do the parts work together to create one comprehensive argument? Compare the image to the one of the child with the bake sale sign. What is the argument of that second image?
- ❑ Consider the context and circumstance for the photos. What can you tell about where each photo was taken and who the audience is? How does context influence an ethical interpretation of the photo?
- ❑ **Write**. Draft your own caption for one of the photos. Then write a letter to the editor explaining how your own caption offers a different perspective on the issue.

Daniel Okrent*'s article was published in the* New York Times *in the wake of the media blitz covering the 2004 tsunami tragedy. Okrent was the first public editor of the* New York Times*, and he has published several books, including* Last Call: The Rise and Fall of Prohibition. *He's also a baseball fan and the inventor of Rotisserie League Baseball, the best-known form of fantasy baseball.*

The Public Editor: No Picture Tells the Truth—The Best Do Better Than That

Daniel Okrent

Two Mondays ago, the scale of the Indian Ocean catastrophe was just emerging from the incomplete earlier reports (from a *Times* article the day before: a tidal wave had "killed more than 150 people in Sri Lanka"). By the 4:30 Page 1 meeting, picture editors had examined more than 900 images of devastation to find the one that would stretch across five columns and nearly half the depth of Tuesday's front page. Into a million homes came a grieving mother crouched beside the lifeless bodies of tiny children, and perhaps more horrifying, three pairs of feet extending from beneath a white sheet in an upper corner, suggesting the presence beyond the frame of row upon awful row of the tsunami's pitiless toll.

Many readers and at least a few members of *The Times*'s newsroom staff considered the picture exploitative, unduly graphic, and by its size and placement, inappropriately forced upon the paper's readers. Some felt it disrespectful of both the living and the dead. A few said *The Times* would not have published it had the children been white Americans. Boaz Rabin of Weehawken, N.J., wrote, "Lead with letters the size of eggs, use any words you see fit, but don't put a nightmare on the front page."

I asked managing editor Jill Abramson why she chose this picture. She said in an e-mail message that after careful and difficult consideration, she decided that the photo "seemed to perfectly convey the news: the sheer enormity of the disaster, as we learned one-third of the casualties are children in a part of the world where more than 50 percent of the population is children. It is an indescribably painful photograph,

FIGURE 14.12. One of many powerful photos included in Okrent's article.

but one that was in all ways commensurate to the event." When I spoke with director of photography Michele McNally, who believes the paper has the obligation "to bear witness" at moments like this, she had a question for me: "Wouldn't you want us to show pictures from Auschwitz if the gates were opened in our time?"

The surpassing power of pictures enables them to become the permanent markers of enormous events. The marines planting the flag at Iwo Jima, the South Vietnamese general shooting his captive at point-blank range, the young John F. Kennedy Jr. saluting his father's passing coffin: each is the universal symbol for a historical moment. You don't need to see them to see them.

5 But in every case, someone needs to choose them. Photo editors (*The Times* employs 40) and their colleagues make hundreds of choices a week. Stories may whisper with nuance and headlines declaim in summary, but pictures seize the microphone, and if they're good, they don't let go. In most cases, a story gets a single picture; major stories may get more, but usually only one on the front page itself—and that becomes the picture that stands for the event.

This won't make every reader happy. From last year's mail: "The picture hardly reflects the regular Turkish population." "I have never been a particular [fan] of Richard Grasso, but *The Times* should not prejudge his lawsuit by publishing photos that portray him as a monster." "I find it appalling and disgusting that you would print an Iraqi holding up the boots of one of our dead soldiers." "Why are we shown the pictures of tragically mutilated U.S. civilian contractors but not slain Iraqi children?" One reader felt that a picture of a smiling Jesse Jackson next to George W. Bush made it appear that Jackson had endorsed the president. Another believed that a photo of a dead Palestinian child in the arms of a policeman looked staged, as if to resemble the Pietà.

Richard Avedon once said: "There is no such thing as inaccuracy in a photograph. All photographs are accurate. None of them is the truth." In this Age of Fungible Pixels, when not every publication, political campaign, or advocacy organization follows the *Times* policy prohibiting manipulation of news photographs, I'm not even sure about the accuracy part. But the untruth—or, at least, imperfect truth—of any single photograph is inescapable. Some readers object to the way a picture is cropped, arguing that evidence changing its meaning has been sliced out of the frame. But meaning is determined long before that. A photographer points the camera here, then turns three inches to the left and snaps again: different picture, maybe a different reality. A photo editor selects from the images the photographer submits (should the subject be smiling? Frowning? Animated? Distracted?). The designer wants it large (major impact) or small (lesser impact). The editor picks it for Page 1 (important) or not (not). By the time a reader sees a picture, it has been repeatedly massaged by judgment. But it's necessarily presented as fact.

Last May, for an article considering whether Brazilian President Luiz Inácio Lula da Silva had a drinking problem, editors selected a seven-month-old file photo showing the president hoisting a beer at an Oktoberfest celebration. It may have been a sensible choice; drinking was the subject, and a picture of the president standing at a lectern would have been dull and disconnected. But any ambiguity in the article was steamrolled by visual evidence that may have been factual (da Silva once had a beer), but perhaps not truthful.

Even in the coverage of an event as photographically unpromising as a guy in a suit giving a speech, pictures convey judgment. When George J. Tenet resigned as C.I.A. director in June, a front page shot showed him looking down, biting his lip, possibly near tears; according to Bruce Mansbridge of Austin, Tex., at other moments during the broadcast of Tenet's speech, "he appeared quite upbeat." When Donald H. Rumsfeld visited Abu Ghraib in May, *The Times* showed him flanked by soldiers, striding through the grounds of the prison, as if (wrote Karen Smullen of Long Island) "Karl Rove must have said, 'What we really need now is a photo of [Rumsfeld] leading soldiers and looking earnest and determined and strong.'" Did Rumsfeld pause at any point and laugh at a joke told by a colleague, or bark at a reporter who asked him a difficult question?

10 Did any of these pictures tell the whole story, or just a sliver of it?

Mix a subjective process with something as idiosyncratic as taste and you're left with a volatile compound. Add human tragedy and it becomes emotionally explosive. The day *The Times* ran the picture of the dead children, many other papers led with a photograph of a grief-racked man clutching the hand of his dead son. It, too, was a powerful picture, and it's easy to see why so many used it. But it was—this is difficult to say—a portrait of generic tragedy. The devastated man could have been in the deserts of Darfur, or in a house in Mosul, or on a sidewalk in Peoria; he could have been photographed 10 years ago, or 10 years from now. His pain was universal.

But the picture on the front page of *The Times* could only have been photographed now, and only on the devastated shores of the Indian Ocean. My colleague David House of *The Fort Worth Star-Telegram* says, "In this instance, covering life means covering death." The babies in their silent rows were as real, and as specific, as the insane act of nature that murdered them. This picture was the story of the Indian Ocean tsunami of December 2004—not the truth, but a stand-in for the truth that will not leave the thoughts of those who saw it. *The Times* was right to publish it.

Reflect & Write

- ❑ What do you make of the writer's decision to use "I" in this article? How might it be a persuasive and effective tool here? What rhetorical appeal is at work?
- ❑ Compare the many historical examples Okrent mentions in his argument. How do they work together to offer coherence and depth for his thesis? Why might he have arranged them in the order he did?
- ❑ Visit the *Envision* Website and view the images Okrent originally included with his articles. How do these images speak to one another? What argument does each make about the conflict at hand and how do they work as a set? www.pearsonhighered.com/envision/504
- ❑ What are the ethical problems raised by the photos? Analyze their original captions and then the written explanations Okrent provided.
- ❑ **Write.** Draft your own captions for contemporary examples of ethically troubling photographs that you find for a recent conflict in the world today.

In this short letter to the editor, **Bruce Jackson** *raises a key point about the ethics of photojournalism.*

Letters to the Public Editor: "Some Words About Those Pictures"

Bruce Jackson

I agree with what you say about the impact and utility of the photograph of dead children that *The Times* used on the front page in its coverage of the tsunami. But why no similar photographs of dead and mutilated G.I.'s and civilians in Iraq, or of dead and mutilated Palestinians and Israelis?

The Times is choosing which dead are acceptable to show literally and which dead are to be shown by reference—for example, body bags or a blood-spattered vehicle or sidewalk.

Reflect & Write

- ❏ Not many words are needed to make a sharp and persuasive argument here. Restate the argument in your own words.
- ❏ What rhetorical strategies are used to make this concise yet effective argument? Consider the use of *pathos*, *ethos*, and *logos*.
- ❏ **Write.** Compose a response to both Okrent and to Jackson in which you offer a third perspective on the ethics of covering conflict in the media.

A graduate of Dartmouth College, **James Nachtwey** *became a photographer after seeing images from the Vietnam War and Civil Rights Movement. In a career spanning nearly 30 years, he has covered stories from the 1981 IRA hunger strike to the 2010 Haiti earthquake. His photographic essays examine conflict-ravaged places ranging from El Salvador to Somalia, South Korea to Sudan, Rwanda, Chechnya to the West Bank and Gaza, Afghanistan to the United States. He has been honored with dozens of awards, including the Martin Luther King Award, Robert Capa Gold Medal (five times), the World Press Photo Award (twice), Magazine Photographer of the Year (seven times), the International Center of Photography Infinity Award (three times), the Bayeaux Award for War Correspondents (twice), the Alfred Eisenstaedt Award, and the W. Eugene Smith Memorial Grant in Humanistic Photography. He is a fellow of the Royal Photographic Society, has an honorary doctorate of fine arts from the Massachusetts College of Arts, a founding member of VII and a photographer for* Time *magazine since 1984.*

Haiti: Out of the Ruins

James Nachtwey

"I have been a witness, and these pictures are my testimony. The events I have recorded should not be forgotten and must not be repeated."
—*James Nachtwey*

To witness the aftermath of the earthquake in Haiti is to be lost inside a waking nightmare. The markers on this mapless journey are the swarms of looters,

FIGURE 14.13. Nachtwey deliberately captures the suffering of children as a result of the Haiti earthquake in what he calls "testimony" to events that "should not be forgotten."

FIGURE 14.14. In this image called "Improved Hygiene," Nachtwey shows the resilience of people in Haiti. Here "a woman bathes herself in a makeshift camp in the central square next to a statue of Jean-Jacques Dessalines, a leader of the Haitian war of independence."

children with chopped-off limbs, cities fabricated of sticks and bedsheets, pulverized cathedrals, dogs circling the dead in the streets.

Most Haitians have always lived in a society constructed along a narrow ledge on a precipice above the abyss. The rich existed on the plateau above them, unseen in their black-windowed Land Cruisers. Higher still, as if levitating, was the immaculate, blinding white presidential palace—the secret desire of all despots—now crushed by the weight of its three Baroque domes. Where the ledge crumbled, the dead cascaded into oblivion. Where it held, people huddled closer, those with next to nothing suddenly with even less. They continue to endure their history—a crescendo of privation and hardship, matched by strength, pride and dignity. Their nation was born in the conquest of slavery; it has been shaped by poverty, struggle and faith.

The earth shrugged, Haiti collapsed, and the world responded. "Compassion fatigue" was exposed as the straw man of cynics and ad salesmen. Epic catastrophe was met with epic generosity, without benefit of untapped oil reserves or geopolitical gain. The U.N. is here in force, but the real united nations are the small NGOs from every corner of the planet that just showed up, flying by the seat of their pants. String their acronyms side by side, and they'd go halfway around the equator. Recite them, and you'd be speaking in tongues.

The Haitians are not just sitting back with their hands out. They're doing a lot of the heavy lifting—so humble in its nature, it seems invisible. Massive international relief supplies are transported by cargo ships, helicopters and C-130s. Haitians carry what they need on their heads. They dig survivors out of the wreckage by hand, not with big yellow machines. Everyone is doing what he or she can by whatever means available.

5 As a photojournalist, I've been involved in documenting the history of the past 30 years, and much of my work has focused on wars, conflicts and social injustice. It's been fueled by anger, driven by the belief that if people are informed, they will be inspired by compassion and will share a sense of outrage at violence, aggression and the unacceptable deprivation of fundamental human rights. Those issues are all man-made, and anger can jump-start the process of change. An earthquake is an act of nature. Tens of thousands die in a few minutes. Who is to blame? Regime change is not an option. How can anger be directed at the earth itself? Compassion is the ultimate motivation in a natural catastrophe. The challenge is to maintain it for the long haul, not allow it to die with the headlines.

Haitians have forged history, with a capital *H*. Slaves rose up to vanquish one of Europe's mightiest empires. Earthquakes reveal the power within the earth itself. But the spirit of the Haitian people is also a force of nature.

Virtually all the symbols of political power in a country synonymous with corruption have been erased. What will the Haitians write on the blank pages of a new chapter of their history?

Reflect & Write

- ❑ Notice how Nachtwey opens with a vivid account of what happened in Haiti. Analyze the arrangement of this piece and consider the writer's rhetorical choices. Why might he open by describing the scene in great detail? When does his personal "I" or *ethos* enter the argument? When is his call to action to the global community? When does he move from despair to anger to hope? What is the effect of these choices?
- ❑ How do these images serve as testimony? In what way do they help "write history" by capturing the spirit of the Haitain people?
- ❑ Study the captions provided by Nachtwey. How do they shape the story told by the image? How does Nachtwey view images of children differently from Okrent?
- ❑ **Write.** Compose a blog entry about this piece, commenting on what moved you most and what you view is the role of the photographer in the time of conflict.

■ **Charles Porter** *is a bank clerk and an amateur photographer; he captured the defining image of the Oklahoma City bombing in April 1995. His picture won a Pulitzer Prize. The selection here is a transcription of his account of taking the photo as told to BBC News, which published it on its Website on May 9, 2005.*

Tragedy in Oklahoma

Charles Porter

I am talking about two photographs that I took on 19 April 1995 from the Oklahoma City bombing.

One being of a policeman handing an infant to a fireman and the other of a fireman gently cradling this lifeless infant.

I have these images in front of me here, looking at them now, and there are things that strike me.

One is that the fireman has taken the time to remove his gloves before receiving this infant from the policeman.

The photo that won the Pulitzer Prize

5 Anyone who knows anything about firefighters know that their gloves are very rough and abrasive and to remove these is like saying I want to make sure that I am as gentle and as compassionate as I can be with this infant that I don't know is dead or alive.

And the second image is of this fireman just cradling this infant with the utmost compassion and caring.

He is looking down at her with this longing, almost to say with his eyes: "It's going to be OK, if there's anything I can do I want to try to help you."

He doesn't know that she has already passed away.

Spring Morning

And these images are in such contrast with the day.

10 It was such a beautiful, crisp, bright spring morning. And at 0902 it was just amazing.

First frame: The police officer hands the baby to the firefighter.

Our building shook and I looked out the window and saw this huge brown cloud of dust and debris and papers just flying in the air, and as I ran across towards the debris cloud, I turned this corner at the building and the street was covered with glass.

There were people on the street that were injured and bleeding, and there was a gentleman that was walking towards me who had taken his dress shirt off from the office building that he was in and had it to his head, and blood was dripping from that.

I just took my camera out and instinctively started taking pictures.

I ran to the front of the building and took some images of that, and as I ran back down the side, I noticed this ambulance where these firefighters were working on these people that were wounded and mortally wounded, and I noticed something out of the corner of my eye that was running across my field of vision.

15 I didn't know what it was, but I trained my camera on it and it was this police officer.

And as this policeman handed this infant to the fireman, I took one frame and then as the fireman is cradling this infant I took the second frame and that is exactly how these images came to be on 19 April 1995.

After I left I got my film developed and called a friend who was the head of photography at a local university.

I called him, and he said: "If you have images that have just happened, you need to go to somebody that wants to see them, like the Associated Press or somebody like that."

I looked the address up in the phone book, I got in my car. I drove over there. I knocked on the door and I went in and said: "Hi, I've got some images of what you're seeing on TV and wanted to know if you would like to look at them?"

Speechless

"Chills go over me just to think about the magnitude and the enormity of where that picture went."

20 Wendel Hudson, who was the AP photo editor at Oklahoma City at the time, picked them out immediately and said: "We'd like to use these." And I thought: "Wow!"

It went out on the AP wire, and not knowing exactly what the AP wire is, I go home and I honestly went home and told my wife: "You know what, I just took some images and they might be in the *Daily Oklahoma* tomorrow."

I go home about 1300. About 1320 I get this phone call from this lady and she says: "Hi, I am so-and-so from the *London Times* and I want to know if you are Charles Porter."

I said: "Yes I am, but how do *you* know who I am?"

She said: "Well I just received your image over the AP wire . . ."

And she proceeded to explain to me what the Associated Press wire was.

25 I said that I didn't know how to respond and she said, "Well sir, can I ask you one question?" And this is where it hit home: "Could I get your reaction and response to what your feelings are going to be, knowing that your image is going to be over every newspaper and every magazine in the entire world tomorrow?"

I was silent and speechless, and chills go over me just to think about the magnitude and the enormity of where that picture went and the impact that picture had at that time. It was beyond my scope of comprehension and understanding, way beyond.

Joe Strupp *is Associate Editor at* Editor & Publisher, *where this article appeared one month after the Oklahoma City bombing. Strupp writes on a number of controversial issues and has been an invited media commentator on* The O'Reilly Factor, The Fox Report, *Air America Radio, National Public Radio, Wisconsin Public Radio, Voice of America, and WPIX TV News in New York City. He has won two Jesse H. Neal Business Journalism Awards, the "Pulitzer Prize" of business journalism, and also contributes to Salon.com.*

The Photo Felt Around the World

Joe Strupp

Abstract: Bank clerk Charles H. Porter took a picture of a firefighter cradling a burned infant in his arms right after the Oklahoma City bombing, in OK, in Apr 1995. The photograph was sold to an AP state photo editor who sent it over the wires. Different newspapers discussed how they should use such an emotionally-charged picture, and, after its publication, many readers called to ask what happened to the baby. Other readers called to protest the picture's publication. However, most newspaper officials believed that it captured the tragedy of the situation in a wordless moment. The baby died the day after the picture was taken.

It sparked heated debate in several newsrooms, caused one veteran newspaper editor to cry, and, for most photo editors, became the focal front-page shot of the tragic April 19 bombing in Oklahoma City.

"It was the photo that was felt around the world," said Tommy Almon, the baby's grandfather.

President Bill Clinton even mentioned it in a televised address.

Ironically, however, the dramatic photo of firefighter Chris Fields cradling the badly burned body of infant Baylee Almon in his arms—which landed on numerous front pages the next day—was shot by a local amateur, developed at a one-hour photo shop, and nearly missed being distributed by the Associated Press.

5 Charles H. Porter IV, a 25-year-old Oklahoma City bank clerk, shot the picture of Fields holding the child, just moments after the bomb blast occurred.

He then sold the photo to AP state photo editor David Longstreath, who sent it over the wires.

"It was everything that was indicative of the bombing," said Longstreath. "It was one of those rare shots that gives the entire story, but in a way that words cannot."

Once Porter took the picture, and developed it with other bomb-blast photos, he still had nowhere to publish it. He initially took the shot to Dan Smith, a photographer at the University of Central Oklahoma, who knew Longstreath.

Longstreath said Smith called him and sent the photo over to AP to be considered. But, in the chaos that followed the explosion, Longstreath almost ignored the shot.

10 "My initial reaction when he sent it was that I was too busy," said Longstreath. "I looked at the roll he shot and took that frame. He took the rest of the roll and left that afternoon."

The infant, who had turned one-year-old the day before the explosion, was pronounced dead at the scene. The baby also was the subject of another widely distributed photo, which showed the infant being handed from police Sgt. John Avera to firefighter Fields, just moments before the Porter picture was taken.

Once it reached the AP nationwide photo wire, the shot of Fields holding the young baby became the subject of debate for several major newspapers, and the main front-page photo for many others.

The *Philadelphia Inquirer,* which played the picture on Page One the following day, made it the solo front-page art, except for a small, inside tease photo along the left column.

"That photo showed what happened better than anything I've seen," said Ashley Halsey, the *Inquirer's* national editor. "There wasn't a photo that better captured what happened there, so we decided to use it."

15 Halsey, a 27-year newspaper veteran, said he briefly discussed the decision to play up the

shot with fellow editors, but believed the tragic elements were important to the story.

"When you have an event that is this absolutely horrible, you will have this kind of photo," Halsey said. "It was deeply disturbing, but it best captured the tragedy."

Halsey said the photo sparked about a dozen phone calls from concerned readers the next day, including several who opposed its publication. But, he said, most agreed it was proper.

"It touched me very deeply because l have a child that same age," Halsey said. "After we put the paper to bed, I walked out to the parking lot and cried. I have never done that before."

Other editors, such as Morton Saltzman of the *Sacramento Bee,* chose not to print the photo, deciding it was inappropriate.

20 "We had a rather lengthy discussion about which photo to use on the front page, and we decided not to use it because we believed the baby was dead," said Saltzman, the *Bee*'s assistant managing editor for news. "We viewed it as a picture of a corpse, even though there was no information about the baby's condition. It was the most dramatic photo and very compelling, but we chose to go with a photo of a live child rather than a dead one."

For other newspapers, the decision to use the Porter photo or various others involving bloody victims also included lengthy discussions and compromises.

The *San Francisco Chronicle,* for example, published the firefighter photo, but did not use it as its main art. The *Chronicle* also took the unusual step of printing a short message to readers, warning them of the brutal pictures.

"There was a lot of discussion over that baby and firefighter photo, and everyone agreed that it had to be used because there were so many children who died," said Lance Iverson, the *Chronicle*'s picture editor. "But, at the same time, we didn't want to shock or offend anyone. We just wanted to tell the story and give a visual impression; that is why we ran it."

The response from readers about the baby's condition was so great, the *Chronicle* published a short story the next day explaining how the child had died.

25 "We got close to 100 phone calls asking what happened to the baby, and we had to report it was deceased," said Iverson. "We rarely get phone calls on photos; I can't recall the last time."

At the *New York Daily News,* where the shot of Avera handing the baby to firefighter Fields made Page One, executive editor Debby Krenek said the emotion of the shot made the decision easy.

"We thought it showed the gripping feeling of the situation," said Krenek. "We didn't think it was too harsh; there were a lot of other ones that we used inside that had blood running down shirts and on faces, but this was Page One."

Still, can a newspaper go too far in portraying such a tragic, bloody event as the Oklahoma City bombing? And did the dramatic firefighter/baby photo cross that line?

For Professor Tom Goldstein, dean of graduate journalism studies at the University of California at Berkeley, the answer is no.

30 "Newspapers are supposed to reflect the world, and that's what they did," Goldstein said. "There seems to be absolutely no doubt in my mind that those riveting photos should have been used, no doubt. It's not something that you necessarily want to look at during breakfast, but they are riveting."

Reflect & Write

- ❑ Both articles cover the same event—the ethical question of whether or not to publish a disturbing photo of a baby who later died as a result of the Oklahoma City bombing. What is the argument of each one? How does the first person testimony by Porter convey a different perspective than Strupp's more journalistic coverage? What rhetorical strategies are at work in each one?
- ❑ Porter's account ends with the offer of publication and Strupp's article takes up the debate among editors and officials about whether to publish. How does each one address a different audience? What is the *kairos* shaping each stance and the argument of each?
- ❑ Compare the styles of the two articles, noting rhetorical appeals, language, and even formality. How do these choices influence you as a reader?
- ❑ **Write.** Strupp's article mentions hundreds of calls and protests. Imagine that you are against the publication of this photo for ethical reasons. Write a letter to the editor and make your argument clear and sound.

Mark Glaser *is a freelance journalist, editor, and expert on online media and Weblogs. He writes a weekly column for* Online Journalism Review, *where this article appeared on July 13, 2005, five days after the London bombing. He also writes a bi-weekly newsletter for the Online Publishers Association. Glaser has written essays for Harvard's* Nieman Reports *and the Yale Center for Globalization, and he has appeared on National Public Radio and Minnesota Public Radio. Glaser has also written columns on the Internet and technology for the* Los Angeles Times, *CNET, and* HotWired, *and features for* the New York Times, Conde Nast Traveler, Entertainment Weekly, *and the* San Jose Mercury News. *He was the lead writer for the* Industry Standard's *award-winning "Media Grok" daily email newsletter, and was named a finalist for a 2004 Online Journalism Award in the Online Commentary category. He received a Bachelor of Journalism and Bachelor of Arts in English at the University of Missouri at Columbia, and he lives in San Francisco.*

Did London Bombings Turn Citizen Journalists into Citizen Paparazzi?

Mark Glaser

July 7, 2005, was one of the darkest days for London, as terrorists blew up three underground trains and a double-decker bus, killing scores and injuring hundreds. But out of that darkness came an unusual light, the flickering light from survivors such as Adam Stacey and Ellis Leeper as they shot the scene underground using cameraphones and videophones.

Like the tsunami disaster in Southeast Asia, the first reports came from people at the scene who had videocameras. In this case, the cameras were smaller and built into phones. But despite the day being a major breakthrough for citizen media—from Wikipedia's collective entry to group blogs such as Londonist's hour-by-hour rundown—it also brought out the worst in some bystanders.

A London blogger who identifies himself only as Justin and blogs at Pfff.co.uk, told his story of surviving the bombing on the train that exploded near Edgware Road. His harrowing account includes this scene as he finally comes out of the underground tunnel and into the fresh air: "The victims were being triaged at the station entrance by Tube staff and as I could see little more I could do so I got out of the way and left," he wrote. "As I stepped out people with cameraphones vied to try and take pictures of the worst victims. In crisis some people are cruel."

The next day, Justin reflected a bit more on the people outside who were trying to photograph the victims.

5 "These people were passers-by trying to look into the station," Justin wrote. "They had no access, but could have done well to clear the area rather than clog it. The people on the train weren't all trying to take pictures, we were shocked, dirty and helping each other. People were stunned, but okay. The majority of the train was okay as I walked from my carriage (the last intact one) down through the train I saw no injuries or damage to the remaining four or so carriages. Just people dirty and in shock. The other direction wasn't so pretty, but you don't need an account of this and what I saw, watching TV is enough."

While citizen media efforts became another big story, quickly picked up by the *Los Angeles Times* and *Wall Street Journal,* among many others, Justin was not so quick to exploit his story. In fact, his first impulse was not to watch any news accounts and not to give interviews to media outlets that wanted to glorify his situation.

I left a comment for him on his blog, asking him if he realized that all the people with cameraphones that day were helping to tell the story to the world. Was there a way they could tell that story in a more sensitive way?

"The news does hold a role and it's important for people to understand, comprehend and learn," Justin replied to me in another blog comment. "To ensure they're safe, systems and procedures change, that the world ultimately gets better. I don't even hold contempt really for the cameraphone people, but you must appreciate something else—were those people taking photos helping or were those people shocking the world? I've alluded to seeing [gruesome] things in the tunnel and carriage, but I've not documented them in any detail. I feel it is inappropriate and does not contribute to fact and information."

So far, gruesome images from the attacks haven't been widely distributed online or given a prominent place in Western media. That contrasts sharply with the response in the Spanish media after the Madrid train bombings on March 11, 2004, when bloody photos were on TV and in newspapers, according to a Reuters story.

The Best and Worst in All of Us

10 In fact, online news sources were at the top of their game on July 7 and beyond. The BBC Website experienced its most trafficked day ever on July 7 and was inundated with eyewitness accounts from readers—20,000 emails, 1,000 photos and 20 videos in 24 hours, according to editor and acting head of BBC News Interactive Pete Clifton.

"It certainly did feel like a step-change [on July 7]," Clifton told me via email. "We often get pictures from our readers, but never as many as this, and the quality was very high. And because people were on the scenes, they were obviously better than anything news agencies could offer. A picture of the bus, for example, was the main picture on our front page for much of the day."

The BBC and *Guardian* both had reporters' blogs that were updated as events unfolded, and group blogs such as BoingBoing and Londonist became instant aggregators of online information.

More surprising was the importance of alternative news sources such as Wikipedia and its useful entry created by volunteer hordes and the inundation of images on Flickr. Even across the pond, MSNBC.com experienced double its usual weekday traffic on July 7, with 10.2 million unique users, and set a record with 4.4 million users of streaming video that day.

Interestingly, both the BBC and MSNBC.com gave particular citizen journalists who survived a bit more room to tell their story on instant diaries set up for the occasion. The diarist on the BBC, a woman who would only identify herself as Rachel (previously just "R"), was not totally thrilled about becoming a media sensation herself.

15 "More journos phoned yesterday," Rachel wrote in one post. "I must have given my mobile to the stringer who was asking questions when I was wandering outside the hospital getting fresh air after being stitched still in shock. The *Mail* on Sunday and Metro wanted to send a photographer round! I said no way. I said I felt it was important to get witness statements out at the time as I was there and felt relatively untraumatized so I'd rather they spoke to me than shoved their mikes and cameras in the faces of those who were shell-shocked or more injured. Having done that I really do not want any more fuss. . . . I was incredibly lucky but I have no desire to become a 'Blast Survivor Girlie' one week on."

That naked impulse to tell a disaster story, glaring kleig lights and all, was once the province of mainstream and tabloid news organizations. But no longer. Now, for better and worse, our fellow citizens stand by, cameraphones in pockets, ready to photograph us in our direst times. Xeni Jardin, a freelance technology journalist and co-editor of *BoingBoing,* was aghast at the behavior of the citizen paparazzi at the scene described by Justin.

"It's like the behavior when you see with a car wreck on the highway," Jardin told me. "People stop and gawk. There's a sense that this is some sort of animal behavior that's not entirely compassionate or responsible. The difference here is that people are gawking with this intermediary device. I'm not sure if the people who did this were saying 'I've got to blog this and get it to the BBC!' But when everyone is carrying around these devices and we get used to this intuitive response of just snapping what we see that's of interest—as surreal and grotesque as that scenario sounds, I imagine we will see a lot more of that."

Jardin compared the behavior to the paparazzi that chased Princess Diana before her fatal car crash and noted that the ethical issues raised then are now applicable beyond just professional photographers.

"These are ethical issues that we once thought only applied to a certain class of people who had adopted the role of news as a profession," Jardin said. "Now that more of us have the ability to capture and disseminate evidence or documentation of history as a matter of course, as a matter of our daily lives—as a casual gesture that takes very little time, no money, not a lot of skill—those ethical issues become considerations for all of us."

Society Under Surveillance

20 Citizen paparazzi is not really a new concept, and the proliferation of cameras has continued unabated since the first point-and-shoot 35mm cameras took off right through cheap digital cameras. But while a few amateur photos might have made it into print magazines in the past, now the Internet is awash in photos and video taken by amateurs. As the term *citizen journalist* becomes part of mainstream thought—spurred on by Big Media outlets and startups—what role do these outlets play in spurring or reining in paparazzi behavior?

Dan Gillmor, founder of citizen media site Bayosphere, wrote in his landmark book *We the Media* about the proliferation of cameras in public spaces. "We are a society of voyeurs and exhibitionists," he wrote. "We can argue whether this is repugnant, but when secrets become far more difficult to keep, something fundamental will have changed. Imagine Rodney King and Abu Ghraib times a million. . . . Everyone who works, or moves around, in a public place should consider whether they like the idea of all their movements being recorded by nosy neighbors."

When I talked to Gillmor about the citizen paparazzi at the London bombing sites, he said he hoped that societies will eventually develop a zone of privacy for people in public places—but realistically didn't think it would happen.

"The line between an obviously important public event like what happened last week and public voyeurism is unclear," Gillmor said. "It's probable that there are pictures from last week floating around that are far too gruesome for any news organization to ever go near it. . . . In the end, we're going to have to develop new cultural norms, and I hope at some level that the more we wipe out the notion of privacy in a public space, the more I hope we end up with a kind of unwritten Golden Rule about privacy in public spaces and give people some space. I doubt it, but I hope people start to think about it."

Counterbalancing that was Gillmor's journalistic instinct, which said that news is news and is fair game for citizen journalists. "In a catastrophe, that's news, and I'm not going to tell people not to take photos of historic events," he said.

25 Jeff Jarvis, outspoken blogger at Buzzmachine and former president of Advance.net, trusts that normal folks using cameras will be more polite than paparazzi.

"The more I think about it, the more I do believe that most people will be more polite than paparazzi because they aren't motivated to get the picture no one else has to make a buck," Jarvis said via e-mail. "More reporters is merely more of what we have now. And believing in the value of news and reporting openness I think we need to see this as good. Are citizen journalists rude? Are professional journalists? Same question. Same answer."

Citizen journalism efforts are slowly coming out of beta, though there's room for more maturation in the relationship between contributors and media outlets. Andrew Locke, director of product strategy at MSNBC.com, said that his site made every effort to contact citizen journalists and pulled down contributions that didn't sit right with the editorial team.

"Jeanne Rothermich, who leads our small CJ team, has put a great deal of emphasis on fostering dialogue and partnership with individual citizen reporters," Locke told me. "We not only get more accurate information, but richer, more detailed accounts that we can share with the larger audience."

The advantage of the media sites over unmediated sources such as Flickr is that they can use the wisdom of photo and editorial staff to vet contributions and filter out insensitive or invalid material. But Locke says the next step for citizen media is more than just mentoring contributors.

30 "Over time, we want to turn those passing relationships into lasting bonds [with citizen journalists]," Locke said. "Once you have a real, ongoing relationship, then you can start sharing information and wisdom back and forth. You can develop a code of conduct that means something and can stick. It's not simply about us mentoring citizen journalists like cub reporters, it's about the community itself developing norms and standards of propriety. Yes, we'll always act as a gatekeeper, but once you're in the gate as a citizen journalist, you should be an empowered member of the storytelling community. We still have a long way to go, but for citizen journalism to grow to its full potential we have to get there."

Reflect & Write

- ❑ What might be Mark Glaser's purpose as a writer in linking this story to the 2004 tsunami in Southeast Asia? How does this strategy broaden the scope of his argument's significance?
- ❑ How do the integrated quotations work to increase the force of this argument? Consider the quotes by London Blogger Justin and the email response from BBC News Interactive's Pete Clifton. Why might the writer want to include such different sources? What can you learn about the power of field research as evidence in your writing from these examples?
- ❑ What larger questions of privacy are coming to light with the advent of new technologies? How is our visual world transforming? Answer by building on key passages from Glaser's article.
- ❑ **Write.** How does Glaser raise a key issue about the ethics of everyday people—not just of photojournalists? Do you think there should be an ethical code of conduct for cell phone camera users? Draft what such a code might look like.

Photos taken by members of the public during the London subway bombings in July 2005 pose a number of important questions about the roles and responsibilities of citizen journalists.

Visual Reading: Citizen Journalists Capture Images of Crisis

FIGURE 14.15. This image, taken with a train passenger's cell phone, captures the terror and confusion of the July 2005 bombing of the London underground.

FIGURE 14.16. This image, taken minutes after the London bombings, won the first Citizen Journalism award, which was sponsored by Nokia and the UK *Press Gazette.*

Reflect & Write

- ❑ Examine Figures 14.15 and 14.16. How do these two images—taken on the scene of the July 7, 2005, bomb attacks in London—serve as arguments for conflict in the international arena? That is, how do these images work as powerfully as words to tell a story, provide a perspective, and persuade the viewer to care?
- ❑ What ethical issues are involved in the taking of these photos at the scene of the conflict and in the publication of these images on the Internet?
- ❑ Consider the low resolution of the first image (taken from a cell phone) in comparison to the sharper images generally found in newsmagazines and newspapers. Does the context and *kairos* of that image make up for its difference in quality?
- ❑ Analyze the captions for the image as posted with the story, linked through the *Envision* Website.
www.pearsonhighered.com/envision/515
- ❑ **Write.** Draft new captions, reflecting on your interpretation of these images as visual arguments representing crisis or as statements on culture.

■ *In this interview, led by* **Terence Smith,** *experts in the field of media analysis, such as CBS anchor Dan Rather, and Defense Secretary Donald Rumsfeld discuss the evolution of photojournalism and the ethics of embedded journalism in particular. The interview has been taken from the March 22, 2003, edition of* NewsHour with Jim Lehrer.

War, Live

March 22, 2003

Terence Smith explores how the high-tech media equipment and the "embedding" of some 500 journalists with U.S. military units in Iraq has changed the way wars are covered.

TERENCE SMITH: If Vietnam was the living room war on American television, and the 1991 Desert Storm was the first satellite-fed real time war, this is the high-tech 21st century version.

CORRESPONDENT PETER ARNETT, in Baghdad: This is shock and awe, Tom, for the population of Baghdad.

High-tech Coverage

TERENCE SMITH: Familiar voices have been heard in the first few days such as that of veteran war correspondent Peter Arnett reporting for *National Geographic Explorer* and NBC.

His descriptions made this Operation Iraqi Freedom sound like what it is, a rerun of the first Gulf War, which he reported live from Baghdad for CNN. But this war is different.

While the military is using state-of-the art weaponry, like pilotless Predator drones, the media are employing some cutting-edge technology of their own.

5 On some networks, virtual view technology makes the battlefield look like a deadly version of a video game, and point of view or "tank cam" video gives viewers a sense of being aboard those armored units that rumble northward into Iraq.

Videophones made popular during the war in Afghanistan bring jerky but real-time images home.

Technology makes the coverage more current, but when the sirens warn of a possible missile-born gas attack, the reporting gets muffled.

CBS ANCHOR DAN RATHER: Hold that microphone up. That's it.

CBS CORRESPONDENT: All right.

"Embedding" Reporters with the Military

TERENCE SMITH: But technology is no protection against the very real dangers of war. An Australian journalist was killed today by a car bomb. And correspondent Terry Lloyd and a two-member crew from Independent Television News are missing after coming under fire near the southern Iraqi city of Basra. No American journalists have been wounded so far, but there have been some close calls on air.

CNN's Walter Rodgers was traveling with U.S. troops in northern Kuwait when shells from incoming enemy fire whistled overhead.

WALTER RODGERS: We just heard an incoming. What the hell!

TERENCE SMITH: The big difference in the coverage of this war is the arrangement under which some 500 reporters are embedded or assigned to travel with specific combat units.

10 TED KOPPEL: Any potential opposition as they can. . . .

TERENCE SMITH: ABC Nightline anchor Ted Koppel has been embedded with the U.S. Army Third Infantry Division. Some of the reporters embedded with troops have not been able to report for days because of the military's concerns about compromising operational security.

CORRESPONDENT: We can't get too specific on locations.

DEFENSE SECRETARY DONALD RUMSFELD: I think we're probably watching something that is somewhat historic.

TERENCE SMITH: Defense Sec. Donald Rumsfeld acknowledged the importance of the embedding process, but cautioned that the close-up view is not always complete.

15 DONALD RUMSFELD: And what we are seeing is not the war in Iraq; what we're seeing are slices of the war in Iraq.

We're seeing that particularized perspective that that reporter or that commentator or that television camera happens to be able to see at that moment, and it is not what's taking place. What you see is taking place, to be sure, but it is one slice, and it is the totality of that that is what this war is about.

Some Pitfalls of Embedded and High-tech Coverage

TERENCE SMITH: Syracuse University Professor Robert Thompson sees some potential pitfalls in the embedding process.

ROBERT THOMPSON: The danger to the embedding process is that when you are part of the troops that you're going in with, these are your fellow human beings. You are being potentially shot at together, and I think there is a sense that you become part of that group in a way that a journalist doesn't necessarily want to be.

20 TERENCE SMITH: Prof. Thompson argues that there are advantages and disadvantages to high-tech coverage.

ROBERT THOMPSON: The tyranny of the visual, those nights where all that bombing was going on, was so spectacular, was so interesting to see that it essentially blows everything else out of your brain.

Whatever analysis, whatever background, whatever context in history might be being reported tends to be overwhelmed by the fact that you so focus on these images, the likes of which we've never seen before.

TERENCE SMITH: As long as the media connection remains intact and the lights stay on in Baghdad, officials from both sides can engage in verbal combat. The Iraqi information minister made his case directly to the American viewing audience.

IRAQI INFORMATION MINISTER MOHAMMED SAEED AL-SHAHHAF: We have destroyed two of their helicopters. We have announced that yesterday. They said no. One of them has crashed. And the American warplanes have destroyed it in order not to be in the hands of the Iraqis. Well, this is silly. This is silly.

25 TERENCE SMITH: American and Arab networks have been sharing resources as well. When the shock and awe bombing began Friday, U.S. networks broadcast a live feed from Abu Dhabi Television or al-Jazeera Television, the pan-Arab satellite channel.

But as the war continues, strains are developing that may ultimately reduce coverage.

CNN PRODUCER INGRID FORMANEK: It just got very much more difficult to work in the days during the bombing. We were not allowed to use our satellite phones.

TERENCE SMITH: After months of reporting from Baghdad CNN's correspondent Nick Robertson and his crew were expelled this weekend by Iraqi authorities.

Reflect & Write

- ❏ Analyze the vivid language and word choice of Terence Smith as he describes the coverage provided by photojournalists. How do the words in this sentence create a striking image for the reader?: "On some networks, virtual view technology makes the battlefield look like a deadly version of a video game, and point of view or 'tank cam' video gives viewers a sense of being aboard those armored units that rumble northward into Iraq." What might be the purpose in using such visual language to set forth the scene for his listeners on this show? How does attention to his style help you as a writer decide which words might best mirror the content of your own argument?
- ❏ What is Smith's point about how technological advances have transformed the kinds of war coverage possible? Analyze more closely the argument he makes by isolating vivid passages.
- ❏ Defense Secretary Rumsfeld claims that "what we are seeing is not the war in Iraq; what we're seeing are slices of the war in Iraq." Why is this lack of what he calls "totality" a problem? Is such a totalitarian perspective ever truly possible even with the best technology?
- ❏ **Write.** What does Professor Thompson mean by "the tyranny of the visual"? Write a counterargument to his position in which you argue that high-tech coverage offers better visual access to the war than, say, embedded journalism.

COLLABORATIVE CHALLENGE

Building off the model of Terence Smith's "War, Live," roundtable on embedded journalism, collaboratively write a new interview, using research your group conducts on another historical period of war coverage. Your group might choose to research through Newseum's History of War Journalism accessible from the link below. Place your research sources as conversationalists in the interview, then enact the interview in a short skit in front of the class. Follow the example of the "Dialogue of Sources" from Chapter 5 to launch your group writing process.
www.pearsonhighered.com/envision/518

Photographer **David Leeson** *is well known for his impressive fieldwork and powerful photography. A staff photographer for the* Dallas Morning News *since 1984, Leeson has covered stories in 60 countries across the globe: from homelessness in Texas, to death row inmates across the U.S., the apartheid in South Africa, Colombia's drug wars, and the civil war in the Sudan. While on assignment in 2003, he was embedded with the Third Infantry Division in Iraq, a unit that saw a record 23 days of sustained army conflict. Leeson, along with his colleague Cheryl Diaz Meyers, was awarded a Pulitzer Prize for his work in Iraq. He has also won two Robert F. Kennedy Journalism Awards for outstanding coverage of the problems of the disadvantaged as well as a national Edward R. Murrow award, National Headlines award, and a regional Emmy for his videos and documentaries. The text on these pages represents photographer David Leeson's own descriptive captions for the four photos he took in Iraq.*

Visual and Verbal Reading Photographs and Stories

David Leeson

Body and Sole, Iraq

The shoes on the body of an Iraqi soldier killed as Army troops advanced north to Baghdad tell a story about a poorly equipped army. Almost all of the Iraqi dead—more than eight in this location—were wearing worn-out civilian-style shoes. Young soldiers came to view the bodies. A sergeant reminded them that 'this could be one of us' and that, for these war dead, 'their families will never know . . . they will just never come back home.'

FIGURE 14.17. David Leeson's photo of a dead man's shoes from Iraq is titled "Body and Sole."

Blank Stare

There was a tremendous firefight. Three soldiers died. I saw the blank stare of this wounded soldier as he passed by. I have no idea who he is. I never noticed his bandage until he filled the frame with my 200mm lens. It was his eyes I saw that day and remember.

FIGURE 14.18. In this photograph by Leeson, a soldier stares blankly out from a tank in Iraq.

Search Party

3rd Infantry Division soldiers from Fort Benning, Georgia, disembark from a Bradley Fighting Vehicle to surround a man who was stopped for suspicious activity somewhere in Iraq. An AK-47 automatic rifle and ammunition were found in the man's vehicle in which he traveled with another person.

This was my first "action" photo from Iraq. My video camera was still operational and I had to make a quick decision on which camera to grab first—my still camera or the video camera. I had made a commitment to place still photos above video in every reasonable circumstance so I made the photos as quickly as possible. As soon as I was satisfied that the still image was secured I switched to video and made very similar frames. The video from this scene became part of my documentary about the invasion.

The next day I learned that this image appeared on the front page of 43 newspapers nationwide and a video I had made the day before was aired on World News Tonight. My video camera succumbed to the dust not long after I made these final frames.

FIGURE 14.19. Leeson's photo of an American military unit arresting an Iraqi civilian appeared on the front page of 43 newspapers Leeson titled the photo "Search Party."

FIGURE 14.20. In "Taking the Plunge," Leeson captures a moment when soldiers relax through a swim in an irrigation pond in Iraq.

Taking the Plunge

(L to R) Spc. George Gillette and Spc. Robert Boucher with Task Force 2-69 Armor, 3rd Brigade Combat Team, 3rd Infantry Division from Fort Benning, Georgia, jump into an irrigation pond somewhere in Iraq. I had a goal to shoot at least one good photo each day—if possible. This image, part of the Pulitzer portfolio, was made near sunset on the drive to Baghdad. I had not made a single image all day. I was about to give up the idea that I would see anything worth shooting when I heard that soldiers were headed to some "pond" in the desert. The truth is I was very tired and was almost disappointed that I was going to have to grab my camera and follow. But, duty called and I went. Both of these soldiers stood on the side of the irrigation pond and discussed if they would get in trouble if they jumped.

I kept my mouth shut and watched. I knew if they jumped it would make a great photo but also knew that journalistic integrity meant that I could not enter into their decision-making process on whether to jump or not. Of course, they finally decided it was worth the risk and made the plunge. After making the photo—I jumped too. The water was very cold but after weeks without a bath it was a wonderful respite from the reality of war.

Reflect & Write

- ❑ How does each photographic text—as a visual reading—offer a specific perspective on the battle in Iraq and on war more generally? What specific rhetorical elements shape the composition of the text? Use the checklist at the end of Chapter 3 to help you answer this question.
- ❑ Look closely at the first photo, "Body and Sole." How might you analyze the various visual elements, including what kind of shoe you see. How do visual signs such as shoes provide readers with *context* about persona, nationality, economic status, and history? What kind of argument would a different set of shoes make on this Iraqi—expensive combat boots, religious slippers, or bare feet? How do the words of the photo's title shape your interpretation of the argument made by the photo?
- ❑ In the text for "Blank Stare," Leeson asserts that he "never noticed his bandage until [the soldier] filled the frame with my 200mm lens." How might the camera enable the photographer to see more details in times of war? How is the camera as a tool of photojournalism a vehicle for helping us see?
- ❑ Analyze the images from the perspective of a soldier. What is the argument about the reality of war from this angle of vision? What kind of writing would a soldier produce to explain what these photos mean? Write out that perspective in words.
- ❑ Consider how David Leeson's stories operate in conjunction with the images to produce a particular perspective on the war. How do his comments reshape your interpretation of the images? How do the images suggest different meanings without his stories about the images?

❑ **Write.** Compose your own response to David Leeson's narrative account of these images. Locate some images from war and create a photo essay.

■ *Best known for his work on the PBS series, the* NewsHour with Jim Lehrer, **Jim Lehrer** *has dedicated his life to the news, starting as a newspaperman in Dallas then eventually becoming an anchor on a local news show before moving into the national spotlight. CNN's Bernard Shaw has called him the "Dean of Moderators" because of his integral role in moderating more then ten debates by candidates in the last five presidential elections. Lehrer has won many awards for his work, including the 1999 National Humanities Medal. The selection included here is from the* NewsHour Extra, *a special Website created to help students understand important cultural and political issues.*

Pros and Cons of Embedded Journalism

NewsHour Extra with Jim Lehrer

A partnership between the military and the media has changed the nature of war journalism.

Journalists are experiencing unprecedented access to the battlefield thanks to a partnership between the military and the media that has embedded journalists within specific military units. The embedded reporters have to follow several agreed upon rules as they live with the soldiers and report on their actions.

New rules in a new arrangement

The new arrangement was formed out of meetings between the heads of news organizations and the Defense Department officials aimed at allowing journalists to report on war with the least possible danger.

Before joining their battalions, the embedded journalists had to sign a contract restricting when and what they can report. The details of military actions can only be described in general terms and journalists agreed not to write at all about possible future missions or about classified weapons and information they might find.

5 In addition, the commander of an embedded journalist's unit can declare a "blackout," meaning the reporter is prohibited from filing stories via satellite connection. The blackouts are called for security reasons, as a satellite communication could tip off a unit's location to enemy forces, the Pentagon explains.

Seeing a slice of the war

At the beginning of the experiment, U.S. Secretary of Defense Donald Rumsfeld called the embedding of journalists "historic," but cautioned that the close-up view is not always complete.

"What we are seeing is not the war in Iraq; what we're seeing are slices of the war in Iraq," he said.

"We're seeing that particularized perspective that that reporter or that commentator or that television camera happens to be able to see at that moment, and it is not what's taking place. What you see is taking place, to be sure, but it is one slice, and it is the totality of that that is what this war is about."

Thus far, editors of many large papers are pleased with the quality of journalism coming from embedded journalists, according to *Editor and Publisher* magazine. Susan Stevenson of *The Atlanta Journal-Constitution* said the embedded reporters give a "sense of immediacy and humanity" that make the stories very real. "From what a blinding sandstorm feels like to reporting how one of our embeds broke his unit's coffee pot, we're giving readers a better sense of the field."

How embedding can distort

10 However there have been instances when the embedded reporters transmitted inaccurate information. On Wednesday, embedded correspondents for several news organizations reported seeing a convoy of up to 120 Iraqi tanks leaving the southern city of Basra, and most news outlets reported a large troop movement.

The next day, a spokesman for the British military said the "massive movement" was really just 14 tanks.

Additionally, some journalism professors have warned that the embedding process can distort war coverage. Syracuse University Professor Robert Thompson warns, "When you are part of the troops that you're going in with, these are your fellow human beings. You are being potentially shot at together, and I think there is a sense that you become part of that group in a way that a journalist doesn't necessarily want to be."

Final results unknown

The results of the embedding experiment will not be known for some time. Bob Steele, from the Poynter Institute, an organization for journalists, says the access "has allowed reporters and photographers to get closer to understanding (the complexities of war), to tell the stories of fear and competence, to tell the stories of skill and confusion. I think that's healthy."

But, Steele cautioned that while "closeness can breed understanding," journalists must remain objective and not write about "we" or "our," but about "they."

15 "There's nothing wrong with having respect in our hearts for the men and women who are fighting this war, or respect for the men and women who are marching in the anti-war protests. The key is to make sure those beliefs don't color reporting," Steele said.

Reflect & Write

- ❑ How do the "new rules" set the contested parameters for a new form of photojournalism in war? That is, while this article might seem straightforward and informative, how does it actually offer a particular argument—the official version—on the proper form of photography for America's military engagements today?
- ❑ Looking closely at how the article uses both subheads and quotations, assess the writing in terms of both arrangement, or structure, and research depth. Why do

you think the author made these particular rhetorical choices? What is the effect of these choices on you as a reader?

- ❑ For the closing line of this article, the author relies upon a quotation by Bob Steele from the Poynter Institute, in which the ideal of objectivity is advanced: "The key is to make sure those beliefs don't color reporting." How does the quotation use visual discourse? What visual choices might a reporter make in presenting "colored" reporting? What does this mean? And how does the last subtitle destabilize the finality of that closing quotation?
- ❑ **Write.** Draft your own response to the article. Identify the central arguments made by each authority, and then compose two alternative perspectives on each argument. Include images that offer arguments for each of your own written texts, so that the visual and the verbal work in conjunction to convey your point of view for each response.

COLLABORATIVE CHALLENGE

Together with two or three classmates, compose a blog post in which you respond to several of the articles here; you might post your own code of conduct for photojournalists in the new century, or draft a set of guidelines for cell phone camera users. Include the photos that moved you most from this chapter and write new captions to show your understanding of the complex issues at stake in covering conflict.

PERSPECTIVES ON THE ISSUE

1. The articles in this chapter offer various contemporary perspectives on the question of whether or not—and how—to publish disturbing photographs of people who are dying, dead, or suffering. How do these debates differ from the controversy discussed by Nora Ephon in her article, "The Boston Photographs," reproduced in Chapter 3? What has changed since the 1970s? What remains constant despite decades of social change, an increasingly global media coverage, and seemingly greater sensitivity to suffering and death?
2. Mark Glaser raises crucial questions about privacy and human nature as he reflects on the many photos taken with camera phones in the wake of the 2005 London bombings. How is the question of privacy a key issue in each of the articles in this chapter, even if the writers don't mention it overtly? Pick three articles to discuss in formulating your answer. Draft your own position on privacy in an age of technological innovation.
3. The conflicts covered range from domestic tragedies, such as the New Orleans hurricane disaster and the Oklahoma City bombing, to international crises, such as the 2004 tsunami and the London bombings. How do media sources show a contextual bias depending on the given audience, the location of the writer, and the purpose of the article? What issues of cross-cultural rhetoric emerge from cross-cultural coverage of these events in both words and images?
4. Discussing "Search Party," Leeson explores the different kinds of photographs possible with different technological tools—the still camera and the video. How do still photos versus videos capture different aspects of an experience such as that in "Search Party"? In other words, are we shown only part of the story? How might more photos, or a video, shape a reader's opinion differently?

5. Compare Leeson's description of his own actions photographing the soldier's "blank stare" to photographer Stanley Forman's account of capturing a young woman falling off a fire escape as recounted in Nora Ephron's article (see Chapter 3). What is the relationship between the photographer as visual writer of moments in crisis and the visual text as one of many possible snapshots? How do the words of the photographers shape our own understanding of these texts as persuasive images and representations of reality?

FROM READING TO RESEARCH

1. Read Professor Paul Lester's book, *Photojournalism: An Ethical Approach* and famous critic Susan Sontag's article, "Regarding the Torture of Others," both available through the *Envision* Website. What arguments are shared between the writers? How might each one contribute to your understanding of the issues involved in photo ethics, both nationally and internationally? Using these sources as a starting point, compose a research-based argument in which you provide your own perspective on these questions. You might format your argument as a feature article modeled after Daniel Okrent's piece. Refer to Chapter 1 for strategies on developing a thesis and to Chapter 3 for a lesson on synthesizing multiple perspectives.
www.pearsonhighered.com/envision/524a

2. Locate photos from the Abu Ghraib torture and prisoner abuse scandal and conduct research into international human rights treaties in order to determine if the photos can be used as evidence of grave abuses. Read the coverage of the scandal—and the subsequent military trials—in order to shape your own research argument about photo ethics in times of war or military morals in an age of digital photography. For historical context, go to the *Envision* Website and read Dan Kennedy's article, "Witness to an Execution." In this provocative article, Kennedy tackles the complex issue of photojournalistic ethics, looking at cases from World War II to recent years.
www.pearsonhighered.com/envision/524b

3. Based on your reading of the articles in this chapter, how might you argue that the mode of photojournalism has changed over the years through developments in writing and communication technologies? Specifically, how do new technologies of writing and visual communication—such as blogs, video footage, multimedia reports, photo essays, and email—transform our understanding of the issues involved in combat reporting? How do independent photographers attempt to offer an alternative perspective on war by relying on new writing technologies such as blogs and digital photo essays? Conduct research on this topic and compose a photo essay to post online.

Visit www.pearsonhighered.com/envision for expanded assignment guidelines and student projects.
Visit www.mycomplab.com for additional general writing and research resources.

CHAPTER 15

Crossing Cultures

Today, America is still seen as a melting pot or salad bowl: a place where many cultures combine and cross over one another. Boundaries and borders are more fluid, and with ease of travel, globalization, and multicultural education, we now rarely think of culture in generic terms. Yet, there remain heated debates—in the news, in schools, and in our government—about what it means to cross cultures, whether that is people crossing into America (legally or illegally), or American culture moving outward, to cross over and influence countries and cultures around the world.

In this chapter, we'll first look inside America to consider how the country is a place of many cultures crossing borders, influencing language, food, recreation, music, and identity. Specifically, we'll examine the borderlands—the thin and troubled line between Mexico and America as well as the borders beyond America—where people seeking a better life travel precariously up from South America into Mexico. Articles by Hilary Hylton, Teresa Hayter, and Cynthia Gorney will provide controversial views on border crossing. An interview by Ted Robbins with "America's Toughest Sheriff" will offer one side of the story, while photo essays by Alex Webb and James Nachtwey will offer visual arguments about this journey and what it means to cross a border in order to seek a better life. Next, we'll broaden out to consider crossing cultures within the U.S.A. and ask: is racism on the rise? What about racism between and across minority groups? Michel Martin's argument on immigration will set up the op-ed about nativism by Ezra Klein. We'll also look at a dueling set of newspaper features on the benefits and dangers of increased immigrants crossing into America: Thomas Friedman and Stephen Steinlight will offer two contrasting views, leaving room for your own. Finally, this first section will look at how cultures intersect within America by considering the visual rhetoric of the Phoenix Suns, who made a visual argument about immigration by changing the words on their jerseys to "Los Suns."

Thus, the first part of this chapter looks at what it means to come to America, such as shown in Figure 15.1, in which a comic offers offers a visual rhetoric narrative about the European arrival to America and what that arrival changed in terms of the landscape of America.

FIGURE 15.1. The still images from the French film *Asterix Conquers America* show Mount Rushmore in the shape of Native American Indians before the Europeans arrived.

FIGURE 15.2. This image of American corporations circling the earth suggests diverse perspectives on crossing cultures: corporations either helping or strangling the globe.

Next, we'll take a look at how American culture travels outward. We'll focus on one of the most obvious signs of American culture crossing borders, in the form of McDonald's—or what scholar George Ritzer calls "McDonaldization." How does the seemingly simple set up of fast-food establishments across the globe actually work to change local customs, cultures, and values—even the very look of a country's national identity? Can the arrival of the Golden Arches and other aspects of American culture ever be a positive influence on a particular place?

The image in Figure 15.2 captures this controversy well, since it can be viewed as either a positive or negative argument about how companies such as McDonald's cross over into other cultures.

To start our discussion of these issues, we'll consider Mark Rice-Oxley's question of whether McDonald's, Disney, and Nike can endure as icons of wealthy Western society. Then, we'll move into exploring McDonald's as our case study—looking at articles from the Rutgers University newspaper through the views of Joseph Davicsin and Jeremy Sklarsky, before learning from George Ritzer why he fears the "McDonaldization" of the world, and exploring how Weblog writers and student activists respond to the visual rhetoric of McDonald's as perhaps *the* symbol of American culture. Randy James provides a compelling perspective, with a deferred thesis, about McDonald's across cultures, and finally we'll consider McDonald's own efforts at reaching out to diverse cultures across the globe through its "American Idol"–like competition called "Voice of McDonald's." As Stephanie Clifford argues in her well-researched piece, "While companies focus most of their marketing on persuading people to buy their products, internal marketing can also help their brands." We'll close our consideration of crossing cultures by looking at how McDonald's revamps its corporate image through new media-supported cultural events that connect people from all over the world in one big party.

As you delve into the complex issue of "crossing cultures" presented from many vantage points throughout this chapter, you can begin to shape your own argument about our changing world.

BORDERLANDS

In her famous book *Borderlands/La Frontera,* writer Gloria Anzaldua explains that while she is composing reflections about a real, physical border—the line between Texas and Mexico—for her, Borderlands are a more complex construct: "The actual physical borderland that I'm dealing with in this book is the Texas-U.S., Southwest/Mexican border. The psychological borderlands, the sexual borderlands, and spiritual borderlands are not particular to the Southwest. In fact the Borderlands are physically present wherever two or more cultures edge each other, where people of different races occupy the same territory, where under, lower, middle and upper classes touch, where the space between two individuals shrinks with intimacy."

This section takes as its theme the "Borderlands" as a space of cultures crossing over. We will look at readings and visual rhetoric about the movement of people (legal and illegal) into America and what that means both for "American culture" as well as for the lives of all those involved. We will study the debates over the "crossing" and the visual rhetoric used to categorize people in terms of belonging, exclusion, rights and crimes, hope and death. Along the way, you will have a chance to explore some of the most heated debates in America today, to question what you believe, and to learn the role of visual rhetoric and verbal argument in shaping a culture's values.

FIGURE 15.3. A road sign near the US-Mexico border, entitled "Caution" in this flickr photo by Penny Green.

To get started, look at the photo in Figure 15.3, which shows a sign found on the freeway in San Diego. What do you make of the figures? Does the stance and line of their bodies look like they are running? What do you make of the choice of hairstyle on the woman and the girl? How does this highway sign, located just inside the American border, speak to the tension and the trauma surrounding the Borderlands of America and Mexico?

Now consider the image in Figure 15.4. How does this image complicate a set of boundaries we might have in our minds about who constitutes an immigrant and what defines an American? This image, from the Library of Congress, reveals the shifting history of America through visual rhetoric. See if you can make out the words beneath or above the images of people who were all once consider "immigrants," crossing from one culture to another, shaping what we now consider to be "American identity."

In this section, we'll read many diverse arguments about crossing cultures, immigration, becoming an American, and breaking the law. You'll have a chance to question how we might define racism, what a journey across borders entails, and how you want to add your own voice to this important debate.

FIGURE 15.4. A visual representation of the history of immigration, from the Library of Congress Immigration Website.

Reflect & Write

- ❑ Analyze the visual rhetoric strategies of both images. Do they rely on stereotype or caricature? What rhetorical strategies are at work in each image? How do they confirm or refute your understanding of America's *ethos* as a nation?
- ❑ How might you revise Figure 15.4 to reflect "the changing face" of your own community?
- ❑ What third image would you add to this opening to indicate your current stance on Borderlands? If you are familiar with Gloria Anzaldua's book, what do you think she would add as an image to this opener?
- ❑ **Write.** Compose new captions for these images that reveal your argument about Borderlands based on your current thinking. When you are reading and responding to the sections in this part of the chapter, make a photo essay of the most moving pieces you read and make new captions for those pieces.

■ **Alex Webb** *is an award-winning photographer and the author of seven photography books. A graduate of Harvard, Webb also studied at the Carpenter Center for the Visual Arts. He joined Magnum Photos in 1976, around the same time he began photographing Mexico, the Caribbean, and the American South. His work has been exhibited across America and Europe. He writes of his art: "What does a street photographer do but walk and watch and wait and talk, and then watch and wait some more, trying to remain confident that the unexpected, the unknown, or the secret heart of the known awaits just around the corner." The photos on the following pages are part of a photo essay by Webb for a* TIME Special Report *on "The New Frontier/La Nueva Frontera."*

Life on the Border

Alex Webb

FIGURE 15.5. On the beach beside the border, a wall stretching out in the ocean, people take shelter from the heat under towels bearing the visual rhetoric of American cartoons.

FIGURE 15.6. Notice the way Webb captures the man caught between two cultures, literally standing between two visual signs of American commercialism, Pepsi and Aquafina, while the original caption locates the man next to Wal-Mart.

FIGURE 15.7. Families separated by the border reveal the deep emotional impact of immigration.

FIGURE 15.8. The visual signs of life on the borderlands reveal themselves in this photo of people kneeling for a make-shift mass.

Reflect & Write

- ❑ How do the photos provide an argument about what life is like for immigrants and their families on both sides of the border?
- ❑ What appeals tell the story most powerfully? The emotions or *pathos* of the boy by the fence? The logical comparison of Pepsi and water vending machines? Or the *ethos* or character of people practicing their faith by kneeling in the dirt?
- ❑ Discuss in small groups how you might develop your own photo essay about cultures in your community. What images would you include? What captions would you write to tell this story?
- ❑ **Write.** Compose your own captions for these images that show what you have learned about crossing cultures by studying these photos. Then, write an imaginary email to the photographer, Alex Webb, sending him your new captions and explaining to the photographer what you learned from his work.

Hilary Hylton *is a regular writer for* TIME *magazine. She has also authored the* Insiders' Guide to Austin, *now in its sixth edition. The article below is one of many* TIME *features on the U.S.-Mexico border. The flu scare hit in the spring of 2009, prompting fears that it would spread from Mexico to the United States.*

Calls to Shut U.S.-Mexico Border Grow in Flu Scare

Hilary Hylton

When the U.S. sneezes, Mexico catches a cold—so goes the old saying that is ironically being turned on its head as all eyes look south, afraid that the U.S. may be infected by what appears to be Mexican swine flu. But while public health and government officials on both sides of the border battle the outbreak, a virus of another sort is spreading across the Internet as anti-immigration groups use the imminent flu pandemic as an argument for closing the U.S.-Mexico border.

"Americans want our borders secured now more than ever," declared William Gheen, head of Americans for Legal Immigration. The North Carolina–based group is calling on the Obama Administration to shut down the southern border. "This latest in a series of health threats emanating from Mexico speaks loudly for border security, and the government's failure to respond accordingly should be a wake-up call for all Americans," Gheen said in a statement posted on the group's website.

Other groups like the California Coalition for Immigration Reform, the San Diego Minutemen and various Save Our State groups have joined the chorus, sending out a barrage of e-mails to supporters and engaging in Web chatter about the perceived threats from Mexico. The push has gained some traction in Washington, while being rejected, thus far, by the Administration. "The public needs to be aware of the serious threat of swine flu, and we need to close our borders to Mexico immediately and completely until this is resolved," New York Democratic Congressman Eric Massa, a member of the Homeland Security Committee, said earlier this week. Across the aisle, San Diego Republican Congressman Duncan Hunter suggested that all nonessential border traffic be shut down.

FIGURE 15.9. Anti-immigration demonstrators hold hand-painted signs and American flags during a rally.

But shutting down the almost 2,000-mile-long U.S.-Mexico border would be a disaster of a different sort. While anti-immigration groups focus on the impact of illegal entrants to the country, there is little attention paid to the goods that flow both ways: wheat (vital for production of the Mexican staple, tortillas) and other food commodities head south, while assembled goods made from U.S. components head back north. In that mix are some products that could be essential if the flu spreads. Dr. Carlos del Rio, chairman of the global health department at Emory University, wrote in a CNN op-ed, "In the event of a serious flu outbreak in this country, there would be a need for mechanical-ventilator deployments to hospitals. The national stockpile has sufficient ventilators, but the necessary circuits that are needed to operate them are not produced in the United States but in Mexico, so having them come across to this country is critical for taking care of critically ill patients in the United States."

5 "Half of the land-borne U.S.-Mexico trade comes through Laredo," says Keith R. Phillips, a senior economist with the Federal Reserve Bank of Dallas. Much of it heads north along Interstate Highway 35, through Austin, Dallas and on through the heartland. And it's not only the land ports along the border that are conduits for trade and travelers, Phillips points out. The Port of Houston has been one of the fastest-growing ports in the country, with a significant amount of trade from Mexico, and trade also flows into inland ports like Fort Worth's Alliance Texas Logistics Park. As residents of Midland, Texas, can attest, the constant rumble of freight trains coming up from Mexico's deep water ports on the Pacific Coast is further evidence of the deep economic relationship.

Before the flu epidemic emerged, both sides of the border were feeling the economic downturn—and the ripple effect was moving farther north. Phillips says the manager of a large outlet mall in San Marcos, 200 miles north of Laredo, Texas, told him that sales were down over the Easter holiday, traditionally a popular shopping time for Mexican tourists in Texas. But that slowdown would pale beside the impact of a border shutdown.

The first known flu fatality on the U.S. side of the border is emblematic of the problem posed by the symbiotic relationship. The 22-month-old boy who died of the flu in a Houston hospital had flown from Mexico City to Matamoros to visit relatives across the bridge in Brownsville. Many families, Phillips points out, have one foot in both countries. Managers for Mexican industrial plants on the border often live north of the river, while workers in the plants have family ties deeper inside Mexico and frequently head south.

The border is a crossing point, not a canyon, and just a brief look at the numbers offer an idea of how busy that crossing point is. In January and February of this year, some $16 billion in exports went south from the U.S., while some $21 billion of imports came north, according to the Texas Center for Border Economy and Enterprise Development at Texas A&M International University. In Brownsville alone, in the first two months of this year, there were 297,478 legal pedestrian crossings north and 284,662 legal southbound crossings. Personal-vehicle crossings were almost double that number. Almost 4 million passenger vehicles crossed each way between Texas cities and their sister communities in Mexico in the first two months of this year, while almost half a million trucks headed south in the same period and 370,000 headed north, according to the center.

Texas Governor Rick Perry says any talk of closing the border is "premature." Meanwhile, Perry has declared a state of emergency and called on the Federal Government for support—an irony, his opponents say, given his recent comments about secession. But Perry, cognizant of the economic importance of the border and the close relationship with Mexico, appealed again to Texas pride: "As Texans always do when facing a challenge: We prepare for the worst, we pray for the best. Working together, we will get through this challenge as well." But if the demands to close the border succeed, Texas would have not only a public health challenge on its hands; it would face a disruption in trade that would send an economic tsunami into the heart of America.

Reflect & Write

- ❑ How does the photograph accompanying the article set the *tone* for the article? Whose perspective is privileged in the photo? Who is the main audience for the written article?
- ❑ The third paragraph of Hylton's piece mentions "a barrage of e-mails" and other communications. How is writing used in the ongoing cultural conflict between the United States and Mexico? How is writing a political tool?
- ❑ When the piece turns to *logos* in the fourth paragraph, what happens to the focus of the article? Discuss the shift from people to things ("goods that flow both ways").

- ❑ How does Hylton effectively integrate her research sources into the article? What can you apply to your paper on immigration and cross-border controversies?
- ❑ Notice the powerful language of the last paragraph. What is the purpose for such emotional and lyrical phrases? What is the effect on you?
- ❑ **Write.** Watch the cited video of protests, available through the *Envision* Website. Then, write a script for your own argument on this issue. www.pearsonhighered.com/envision/533

■ **Teresa Hayter** *is a seasoned campaigner, activist, and author of several books including* Urban Politics, Aid as Imperialism, *and* The Creation of World Poverty. *Her latest is* Open Borders, *published by Pluto Press in 2000. This article covers the themes of why borders should be open for immigration by touching on topics such as national identity, the decline of nation-states, and how immigration boosts wealth.*

The New Common Sense

Teresa Hayter

Immigration controls are a cruel 20th-century aberration. Although they may seem like common sense, an unavoidable reality, in fact, in most countries they are less than 100 years old.

International migration, on the other hand, has always existed. Twice as many people migrated from Europe to the rest of the world as have come in the opposite direction. And since the current theory is that human beings originated in East Africa, every other part of the world is the product of immigration. All of us, the racists and the rest of us, are either immigrants or descended from immigrants.

Freedom of movement should be the new common sense. It is hard to see why people should not be allowed to move around the world in search of work or safety or both.

Within the European Union there are growing attempts to secure the principle of freedom for its citizens to live and work in any member country. Between the states of the US federation there are no restrictions on the movement of people. It would be considered an outrage if the inhabitants of a country were not free to travel to another part of that country to get a job there, or if they were not allowed to leave it. Indeed, it was considered an outrage when this happened in the former USSR.

5 The 1948 Universal Declaration of Human Rights asserts these rights. Yet the Universal Declaration is strangely silent on the question of the right to enter another country. Governments cling to what seems to be one of their last remaining prerogatives: their right to keep people out of their territories. Few people question the morality, legality or practicality of this right.

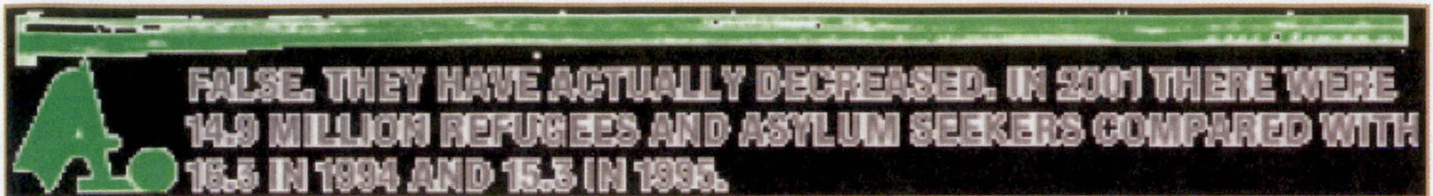

Nation-states in decline

Nation-states are the agents and enforcers of immigration controls and country boundaries. Most were themselves not fully established until the 19th century.

Now nation-states are supposed to be on the decline. International institutions such as the United Nations, the International Monetary Fund, the World Bank and the World Trade Organization attempt to control the actions of national governments. Economic power is concentrated in fewer and bigger corporations. These put pressure on governments to allow goods and capital to move freely around the world, unaffected by considerations of national sovereignty. Sometimes they also press governments to allow the free movement of people, in order to secure the labour they need for expansion. Yet by the 1970s many countries, especially in Europe but not in North America, had more or less ended the right of people to enter and work.

In theory, the right to gain asylum under the United Nations 1951 Geneva convention, within certain restrictive conditions, remains. But during the past 15 years or so, governments have increasingly failed to observe the spirit of this undertaking.

Governments claim—unjustly—that most asylum seekers are in fact 'economic migrants', migrating to better their economic situation. Incorrectly labelling them as 'illegal immigrants', they build a vast edifice of repression.

Immigration boosts wealth

10 Even if it were morally acceptable for the rich nations of the world to use immigration controls to preserve their disproportionate wealth, as the South African whites tried to use apartheid to preserve theirs, it is doubtful whether they achieve this purpose.

There is a mass of evidence to show that immigrants actually make a big contribution to the wealth and prosperity of the countries they go to. When asked after the IMF/World Bank meetings in Washington why he had raised upwards the estimates of his country's economic growth, British minister Gordon Brown said this was because net immigration was higher than expected. Economists have also suggested that the abolition of immigration controls would cause a doubling of world incomes.[1]

Immigration is not just good for the capitalists. It also improves both the job prospects and the wages and conditions of workers. Without immigration, sectors of industry would collapse or move abroad, with knock-on effects on other jobs. The US economy, especially its agriculture, building trades and services, is heavily dependent on immigrants, including those who have no legal permission to work.

Many industrialized countries—especially in Europe—have declining and ageing populations. Unless immigration is increased, there will not be enough young workers to pay taxes, keep the public sector and industry functioning and look after the old people.

On average immigrants contribute more in taxes than they receive in public services, studies in the US have shown. In Britain too the Home Office estimates that immigrants make a net contribution of $3.75. billion a year to public finances. The cost of immigration controls, on the other hand, is at least $1.5 billion a year, and rising.

National identity

15 Immigration controls are explicable only by racism. Those who defend them often refer to the need to 'preserve national identity'. National identity is hard to define. More or less every country in the world is the product of successive waves of immigration. Each new group of arrivals has tended to be vilified as unable to assimilate, prone to disease, crime and so on.

It is sometimes argued that the numbers migrating from poor countries to the rich countries of Europe, North America and Australasia would be larger and might 'swamp' local populations and cause severe social disruption.

Yet the few migrants and refugees who make it to the rich countries are exceptional people who have to have some money and a great deal of courage and enterprise. They come because there are jobs, or because they are in desperate danger. Few people want to uproot themselves and leave their families, friends and cultures and most of those who do so wish to return; immigration controls have the perverse effect of making this harder.

Contrary to predictions, the introduction of free internal movement within Europe did not lead to mass migration from the poor South to the richer North; on the contrary the authorities would like to have more rather than less labour mobility in the European Union. They also predict that the planned opening to the East will have a similarly limited effect on migration.

The existence of extreme world poverty and inequality does not cause mass migration, but rather the opposite. Most people in the Third World do not have a remote possibility of migrating. Economic development, where it occurs and especially of the skewed type which results from Western intervention, is more likely to cause an increase in migration than extreme poverty.

If the governments of the rich West really do wish to reduce the number of refugees in the world, including the tiny proportion who try to make it into their territories, there are things they should stop doing. For example they should not create refugees by selling arms in conflict zones or to repressive regimes.

Model for opening

As in apartheid, the apparatus of repression required to enforce immigration controls is becoming increasingly unsustainable.

The costs, the suffering, and the racism they engender are escalating. Sooner or later, immigration controls will be abandoned. The main issue is how much longer is the suffering to continue before they can be consigned to the dustbin of history?

Clearly it would not make much sense to campaign for immigration controls to be ended only in one country. Their abolition would need to be by agreement between the rich governments of the world.

A precedent for the opening of borders exists in the European Union. Those who worked for the abolition of European internal frontiers were animated not only by the interests of big business and free trade, but by an idealistic view of the future of Europe.

North American Free Trade Area (NAFTA) agreements provide only for the free movement of goods and capital. But president Fox of Mexico, who is a strong supporter of neo-liberal policies and also a friend of George Bush, is pressing for the free movement of labour to be included in the agreements, as the Wall Street Journal and sections of US capital have done for some time.

Abolition of borders implies complete freedom of movement for all, and the right to settle and work in a place of the person's choice, just as people can now do within countries. This in turn implies the abandonment not just of immigration controls, but of the whole apparatus of determining whether or not a person is entitled to refugee status.

Little would be gained by expanding quotas or agreements on 'burden sharing' and dispersal of those who some agency decided were 'genuine' refugees. Refugees themselves are best able to decide whether or not they need to flee; the presumption that this can be determined by immigration officials operating quotas is absurd. Those whose claims were refused would have to be kept out, which would mean the continuation of repression.

Some argue that the way ahead is to increase the number of work permits issued to employers to employ immigrants and that this would get rid of 'people smuggling'. However, either the number of permits issued would meet demand in which case controls would be unnecessary, or those who failed to migrate legally would continue to try to do so illegally.

In a more just world order, movements of capital would be democratically controlled to meet people's needs and to reduce inequalities. But people are not goods or capital—and they should be free to move. The attempt to limit this basic freedom leads to some of the worst abuses of human rights which exist in the world today. The abolition of immigration controls would mean a vast increase in freedom and prosperity for all of us.

[1] Free-market economists B Hamilton and J Whalley, *Journal of Development Economics*, 1984, quoted in Teresa Hayter's *Open Borders*.

Reflect & Write

- ❑ What is the argument and audience of this piece? How can you tell from the strong *pathos* language of the opening line? How is an audience addressed by the line, "All of us, racists and the rest of us, are either immigrants or descended from immigrants"? Now compare the opening to the closing lines. How does Hayter's argument offer a contrasting view to the piece by Hylton, even if the ostensible focus is different?
- ❑ What do the visuals add to this piece as a more popular article (see Chapter 8 on academic versus popular writing and conventions of document design)? Why might there be a Q box followed later by an A box? What does the footnote add to the piece in terms of *ethos?*
- ❑ Assess the article's emphasis on general social trends. How might the article be interpreted differently if it covered a series of case studies? What does this strategy of arrangement allow the writer to accomplish?
- ❑ **Write.** Update the article for today by adding another argumentative subject and section before the conclusion (that begins "Model for opening"). What would you want to add about racism, immigration, and national identity today as it relates to your community?

■ *After a career as an award-winning features writer for the* Washington Post, **Cynthia Gorney** *became a professor at the Berkeley Graduate School of Journalism in 1999. A frequent writer for the* New Yorker, National Geographic, Harper's, Sports Illustrated, *the* New York Times Magazine, Runners World, O: The Oprah Magazine, *and the* American Journalism Review, *Gorney is also the author of* Articles of Faith: A History of the Abortion Wars. *She attended the University of California at Berkeley; worked as a visiting Poynter Institute teacher, a newsroom writing coach, and an interviewer on public radio KQED-FM; and is a past recipient of the American Society of Newspaper Editors feature writing award. The excerpts below are taken from her national feature on Mexico's Other Border, accompanied by photos from Alex Webb.*

Mexico's Other Border

Cynthia Gorney

Jessenia and Armando López crossed the Suchiate River from Guatemala into Mexico on a hired raft of wood planks lashed to giant inner tubes.

The raftsman pegged them immediately as undocumented migrants and charged them ten times the usual fare, even though Jessenia thought she had disguised herself as a local lady by wearing platform shoes and carrying all her belongings in a homemaker's plastic shopping bag. She had managed to bathe and wash her clothes daily since they had left Nicaragua—in Mexico, Jessenia reminded her husband, thieves and officials identify migrants not only by their packs and caps and dirty walking sneakers, but also by the smell of their bodies on crowded buses. She put on makeup and perfume every morning, and dangling earrings. These were the rituals that gave her momentum, a certain degree of calm: launder, improve appearance, pray.

When they reached the Mexican side of the river, Armando unloaded the used mountain bicycle they had bought in Guatemala, and they waited while a uniformed soldier on the riverbank rifled indifferently through Jessenia's bag, explaining that he was looking for weapons or drugs. Then the soldier assessed them a ten-dollar bribe, and the Lópezes got on the bicycle and began to ride north.

Every year, hundreds of thousands of Central Americans cross illegally into Mexico—400,235, to cite one oddly precise estimate from the Mexican National Institute of Migration—along the country's southern border, which angles over 750 miles of river and volcanic slope and jungle at the top of Central America. Nobody knows exactly how many of those migrants are headed to the United States, but most put that figure at 150,000 or more a year, and the pace of illegal migration north has picked up dramatically over the past decade, propelled in part by the lingering aftermath of the 1970s and '80s civil wars in Guatemala, El Salvador, and Nicaragua. In depictions of this modern Latin American migration into the United States, the image of a great wave is often invoked, and Mexico's southern border today feels like the place in distant water where the wave first rises and swells and gathers uncontainable propulsive force.

5 Before the Lópezes left Managua, they had heard the counsel repeated now in certain poor neighborhoods of Central America: If you are leaving for El Norte, find Padre Flor Maria Rigoni in the city of Tapachula, 20 miles north of the border, because the first dangerous crossing you will make is not the one that takes you into the United States. It is at the southern Mexican border where the perils begin—the thugs, the drug runners, the extortionists in official uniforms, the police and migration agents who pack undocumented migrants into detention facilities before forcing them onto buses to be deported. The Tapachula migration station was recently rebuilt, to hold 960 migrants and process them more quickly; the southward-bound buses roll out every morning before dawn.

The Lópezes rode for hours in the 90-degree heat, Jessenia standing on blocks attached to both sides of the bicycle's rear wheel. She carried her shopping bag in the crook of her arm and kept her hands on Armando's shoulders as he pedaled, avoiding migration checkpoints by veering at intervals off the pavement and onto dirt paths. They had remarkably good luck. No one assaulted them with machetes or rifles or handmade pistols fashioned from PVC pipes stuffed with gunpowder; no one beat Armando and dragged Jessenia into the weeds; no one forced them to undress so that their body cavities and secret sewn-in clothing pockets could be examined for hidden money. No passing taxi driver decided to collect a payoff that day by alerting muggers or immigration officials that a vulnerable-looking couple was approaching on the road.

Toward the end of the afternoon Armando pedaled into the outskirts of Tapachula, rounded a curving downhill past an untended field of banana trees, and came to a stop at the wide red doors of the Casa del Migrante, where Padre Rigoni took them in.

Flor Maria Rigoni is a wiry 64-year-old Italian priest who speaks six languages, has a cascading gray beard, uses a thin mattress on the floor for a bed, and wears a wooden cross jammed like a holstered weapon into the belt of his cotton vestments. His Casa del Migrante is a nerve center, an improvised message and transit depot, and an international sanctuary. He first arrived in Mexico more than 20 years ago, dispatched from his previous posting among Italian migrants in Germany.

"Migration, for me, is where we really encounter the God of the Bible—the God of Abraham, of Exodus, of the great journey," he told me one day, in his Italian-accented Spanish, as we sat on worn couches in an open-air alcove where he receives migrants seeking advice or a blessing. At the entrance to the Casa's dining hall is a bronze statue of John Baptist Scalabrini, the 19th-century Italian bishop who founded the order to which Rigoni belongs. The pastoral mission of the Scalabrinians is the care of migrants; the missionaries run centers in 24 countries, including four in Mexico and one just across the Suchiate River in Tecún Umán, on the Guatemalan side of the raft crossing. Three of the Mexican Casas del Migrante—in Tijuana, Ciudad Juárez, and Tapachula—were built up by Rigoni.

10 One evening, three dozen migrants sat on the sidewalk just outside the entrance to the Casa, too hot to go inside. A rooster crowed, and the migrants talked in low voices and smoked cigarettes, which a vendor across the street was selling for 15 cents apiece. Several huddled around a pay phone, peering by flashlight at pieces of paper with area codes indicating Houston and Atlanta and Pittsburgh and Chicago.

There was a 19-year-old Honduran who wrote poems every night about leaving his beloved behind in order to cross the border into America; he was on his way, he had decided, to Los Angeles. There was a Nicaraguan construction worker on his way back to Santa Cruz, California, where he had lived for six years, until American immigration officials threw him out. There was a Guatemalan woman on her way to a sister in North Carolina; a Salvadoran couple, passing their swaddled baby back and forth in the darkness, on their way to cousins in Maryland they'd never met; and a 15-year-old Salvadoran boy who turned to me suddenly, after learning I was American, and asked, "You have streets there with three lanes on each side, right?" He nodded when I confirmed this was so and said he intended to fall in love in the United States.

On a map on the Casa's entrance wall, someone had attached a note containing distances, in kilometers. Tapachula to New York: 4,375. To Houston: 2,930. To Chicago: 3,678. Above the map was a warning poster about the hazards of the Texas and Arizona crossings—don't risk it, the desert temperatures can be fatal. I had seen no one so much as glance at the poster.

"Where are we going? We don't know," said Fernando Somosa, a lanky Nicaraguan boy with an enormous smile, punching the arm of his friend José Ramos, who had left their village with him four days earlier. "We're just going where the dollars are." Somosa was wearing a shirt he had bought secondhand in a market near his home; it had permanent-marker writing on it, in a loopy scrawl: "To Alyssa—Ur Super Cool! Meghan."

Jessenia López sat with her back against a boulder, her hair still damp from the shower. "Miami," she said, when I asked where she and Armando, a car mechanic and handyman, hoped

FIGURE 15.10. The visual rhetoric of immigrants resting their sleeping heads on the train track makes a powerful argument about the dangers of the journey for immigrants entering into Mexico from Central America.

to find work. "We have a friend there. We're carrying her phone number. But we haven't been able to reach her. We don't know what to do." She is 33 and Armando 29; they had left their three children—two teenagers and a baby—with her family in Managua. When Jessenia told me her baby was two years old, she began to cry, but she pressed her hand against her face and stopped. "I never in my life thought I was going to do this. It's just need that makes you do certain things."

Reflect & Write

- ❑ How does the narrative of Jessenia and Armando López draw the reader into the subject of the article? Why might Gorney decide to offer such personal stories? Which other people are most memorable to you from this piece?
- ❑ What is the purpose of describing the Casa's map? How does the visual rhetoric of the migration journey work to educate the reader of this relatively unknown history of crossing borders? What is the significance of the detail that the writer "had seen no one so much as glance at the poster"?
- ❑ Why do you think the writer saves the detail of Jessenia's children until quite late in the writing? What is the effect of this organization on you, the reader?
- ❑ How is the voice of the writer constructed? Notice words, phrases, comments, and also how the writer keeps in the shadows, as a recorder and an observer.
- ❑ **Write.** Interview someone from your own family or community about his or her journey. Did the family cross cultures from Europe or Asia? Did they suffer hardships along the way? What were the cultural values that brought them to America? Write up your notes in the form of a narrative, and include a strategic image such as the one shown in Figure 15.10.

■ *This story is the first of a three-part report by* **Ted Robbins,** *seasoned broadcast journalist for National Public Radio who covers the Southwest: Arizona, New Mexico, Nevada, West Texas, northern Mexico, and Utah. Previously Robbins worked for* The NewsHour with Jim Lehrer, *CBS News, NBC, and* USA Today. *Robbins also covered international stories in Mexico, El Salvador, Nepal, and Sudan. An Emmy award winner and recipient of the CINE Golden Eagle documentary award, Robbins went to the University of California at Berkeley and taught journalism at the University of Arizona for ten years.*

'America's Toughest Sheriff' Takes on Immigration

Ted Robbins

March 10, 2008 - STEVE INSKEEP, host:

Illegal immigrants may be flowing into much of the nation, but they're apparently fleeing Arizona. In fact, legal immigrants are leaving the state, too. Arizona has passed a series of laws restricting services and making it tougher to find jobs. So over the next three days, we're going to introduce you to three Arizona men influencing the debate over illegal immigration. One makes the laws, one is fighting those laws. We start with a man enforcing the laws at all costs.

Sheriff JOE ARPAIO (Maricopa County Sheriff): These demonstrators I've caught—to have placards, I'm a Nazi, KKK—but you know what, the more they go after me, the more I go in their face.

INSKEEP: Joe Arpaio of Maricopa County is dubbed America's Toughest Sheriff. NPR's Ted Robbins has his story.

TED ROBBINS: If you want to know the man his fans call Sheriff Joe, you might want to start at one of his jails, the place called Tent City. It's Joe Arpaio's most famous invention, a vast, open-air annex in south Phoenix that houses 2,000 prisoners. They live outside, sleeping on cots in hundreds of old canvas tents, in the broiling summer heat and the chilly desert winter. It looks like a Korean War-era Army camp. The idea is to make life tough and humiliating. Inmate Steven Pleasant(ph) models the sheriff's fashion creation, a black-and-white striped uniform usually worn over pink underwear.

5 Mr. STEVEN PLEASANT (Inmate at Tent City): Yeah, you've got pink thermals and black striped. . .

Unidentified male #1: Actually we're short on the thermals, we don't have any thermals yet. At 5 in the morning, we'll be there getting our bottoms.

ROBBINS: For food, the sheriff serves inmates green, as in fetid, bologna sandwiches. Sheriff Joe Arpaio's policies are either innovative or a throwback to harsher times. Either way, his tactics and his colorful personality have kept him in the news pretty much since he took office in 1993.

Sheriff ARPAIO: Everything I do is publicized. When I go to the toilet, they publicize it. You do know that. So, I'm being a little sarcastic, but it shows whatever I do, they pretty well publicize it, especially if it's controversial.

ROBBINS: What the sheriff doesn't say is that he often seeks that publicity, even calling a news conference recently in a central Phoenix parking lot to announce ahead of time a crime-suppression operation.

10 Sheriff ARPAIO: I want everybody to know about this. Maybe they won't be violating the laws if they knew that we're going to catch them.

ROBBINS: He says it's to catch all criminals, but the headline on the sheriff's news release narrows it down a bit. It says illegal immigrant arrests expected. Illegal immigrants are Joe Arpaio's latest target, especially in this neighborhood. For months, it's been the sight of protests over day laborers, often illegal immigrants, who line the streets looking for work.

Sheriff ARPAIO: If we come across any illegal aliens during the course of this operation, they will be arrested and put in jail.

ROBBINS: Arrested using another of the sheriff's innovations. He's taken a state law intended for human smugglers and used it to arrest any illegal immigrant for smuggling themselves. His is the only agency in the state using the law that way.

Ms. AMY COON (Sheriff's Deputy, Maricopa County, Arizona): Juan.

15 ROBBINS: Down at the county jail, which houses prisoners from a number of jurisdictions in the Phoenix area, Arpaio employs one more tactic. When someone is booked on any charge, they are taken to a row of computers hooked into the Federal Immigration and Customs Enforcement, or ICE, database.

Ms. COON: What's the first three of your social security?

Unidentified Male #2: (unintelligible) six–O–one.

Ms. COON: Of what country are you a national or citizen of?

20 Unidentified Male #2: United States.

ROBBINS: Sheriff's Deputy Amy Coon is one of 160 Maricopa County Sheriff's deputies trained to enforce federal immigration law. The sheriff says since last May, more than 7,000 illegal immigrants have been detained for ICE this way. According to the agreement with ICE, prisoners are only supposed to be held on immigration charges if they were arrested for something else first. But on this night, at least one illegal immigrant was arrested for simply being a passenger in a car that was stopped. Arpaio justifies his practices.

Sheriff ARPAIO: We put the holds on them so they won't be released back to the streets. We do that since the cops will not do it.

ROBBINS: That was a dig at the Phoenix Police Department, which has a policy of not asking citizenship on arrest—an immigrant-friendly policy now under review because public opinion has turned against immigrants. And if there's one thing Sheriff Joe Arpaio is sensitive to, it's public opinion. Michael Lacey is executive editor of Phoenix New Times, an alternative weekly paper. He says the sheriff wasn't always so gung-ho on arresting illegal immigrants.

Mr. MICHAEL LACEY (Executive editor, Phoenix New Times): He's got a very famous quote about he wasn't gonna be busting corn vendors or getting Mexicans out on the street looking for work, and that there were real criminals out there. But he discovered that there were votes in going after Mexicans, and he switched his policy 180 degrees.

25 ROBBINS: New Times may be the only media outlet Arpaio won't talk to.

Sheriff ARPAIO: What's the New—is that that porno magazine you're talk—the weekly paper they have to give away free?

ROBBINS: It's the paper that has relentlessly attacked the sheriff's policies for years, pointing out millions of dollars the county has paid to former inmates or their families over mistreatment charges and publishing the sheriff's home address for a story on his real estate deals. That got Lacey and his co-publisher arrested last fall along with an order to hand over the e-mail addresses of everyone who visited the paper's Web site. The order and the charges were dropped. Lacey and New Times are suing the sheriff and the county attorney.

Mr. LACEY: What made them think they could get away with it is because they have been gradually getting away with it for years here. Okay. You begin with prisoners. Okay. Then you move on to Mexicans, then you move on to editors and reporters.

ROBBINS: Arpaio's opponents, like civil rights activist and former Democratic state legislature Alfredo Gutierrez, say Joe Arpaio is out of control.

30 Mr. ALFREDO GUTIERREZ (Civil Rights Activist): This sheriff is a sad clown but unfortunately, he's a sad clown with horrible power.

ROBBINS: But listen to one of the speeches he frequently gives, weaving his personal story with the issues, and you can see why Joe Arpaio keeps getting re-elected.

Sheriff ARPAIO: Born and raised in Springfield, Massachusetts, my mother and father came from Italy—legally.

(Soundbite of laughter and applause)

ROBBINS: This is the community center at Leisure World, a retirement community in conservative Mesa. And Joe Arpaio, himself 75 years old, is tapped into his audience.

35 Sheriff ARPAIO: We don't train our officers to speak Spanish to talk to them. They're in the United States of America, and they're in my jail, so they're gonna learn English.

(Soundbite of applause)

ROBBINS: These are the people who re-elect this sheriff, voters like Betty Wilson and Donna Kurr.

Ms. BETTY WILSON (Arpaio supporter and resident at Leisure World, Mesa, Arizona): I think he's wonderful. He's tough and puts those kids in jail.

FIGURE 15.11. Sheriff Arpaio portrays a "tough-guy" persona beside his van.

Ms. DONNA KURR (Arpaio supporter and resident at Leisure World, Mesa, Arizona): I think he's just down to earth and doing what he really needs to do.

ROBBINS: Sheriff Joe's approval ratings have been falling a bit, down from an astronomical 80 percent to somewhere in the 60s. But most analysts think he'll probably get elected for the fifth time in November.

Ted Robbins, NPR News.

(Soundbite of music)

Reflect & Write

- ❑ How does this radio transcript open with the very words of the sheriff to engage the listeners through *pathos*? What emotions are evoked with the references to Nazi and KKK?
- ❑ How do the sheriff's own words cast him in a certain light? Studying his rhetoric, do you agree with the description of him as "as sad clown but unfortunately, he's a sad clown with horrible power"? Compare his words with the visual rhetoric of him in Figure 15.11.
- ❑ What do the voices of the unidentified men in the piece add to the overall argument? How do their words paint a fuller picture of the reality of detention?
- ❑ Notice when the voice of Ted Robbins, the writer, enters. What is the significance of his editorial comment: "He's taken a state law intended for human smugglers and used it to arrest any illegal immigrant for smuggling themselves. His is the only agency in the state using the law that way"?
- ❑ **Write.** Compose a set of interview questions for a follow-up session with Sheriff Arpaio. Include your own voice as moderator. Then, compose an imaginary email to Ted Robbins and ask him what his perspective is on your draft work so far.

■ **James Nachtwey**, *whose photographs are also featured in Chapter 14, has won numerous awards for his work, which spans several decades and focuses on conflicts as well as war. A photographer for* TIME *magazine since 1984, Nachtwey contributed these images as part of a* TIME Special Report *on "The New Frontier, La Nueva Frontera."*

Caught Crossing

James Nachtwey

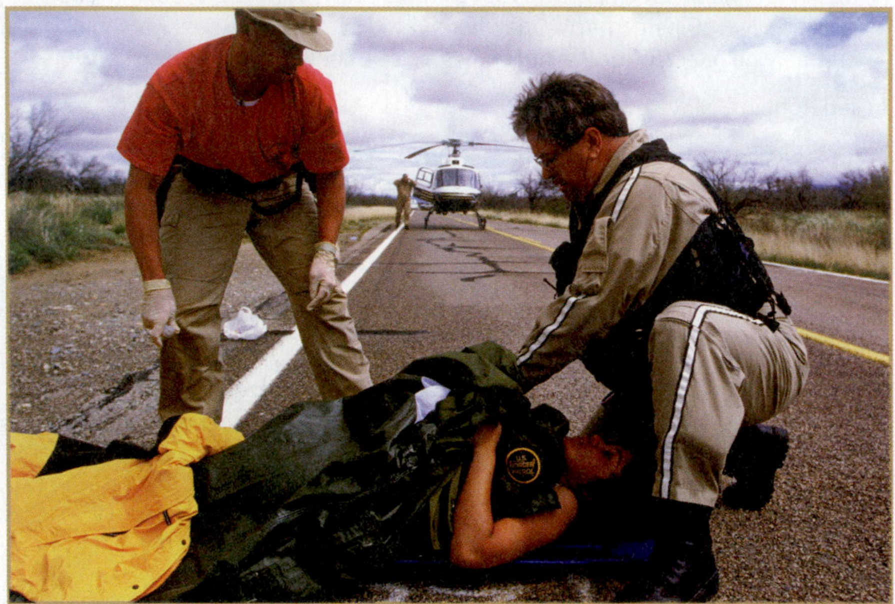

FIGURE 15.12. Lying across the road, literally in the cross path of the helicopter, is a woman deathly ill from the journey.

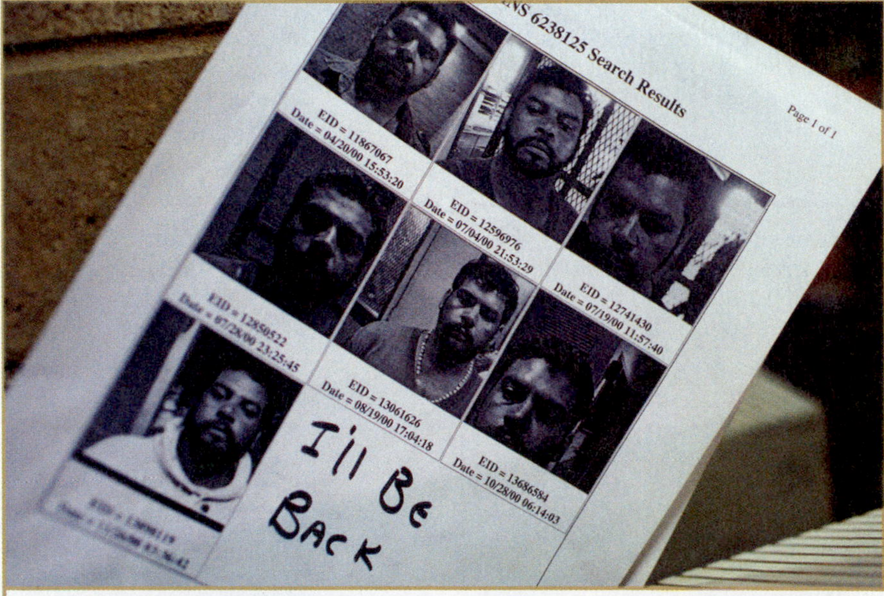

FIGURE 15.13. The immigrants caught and returned use writing to leave a message for the border patrol.

FIGURE 15.14. The visual rhetoric of the causalities of crossing mark this fence along the route.

Reflect & Write

- ❑ How do the three visual arguments provide another perspective on illegal immigration? What is the message of each photo and where do you find your sympathies falling in studying the elements and argument of each text?
- ❑ What is the function of the captions? How does the writing add to or detract from the power of the images? If you could change the captions, what would you write?
- ❑ Notice the compositional strategies of these visual arguments. What role do background and formal elements play in setting the *tone* as well as telling the story of the people in the images?
- ❑ Compare the photos by Nachtwey with those of Alex Webb, presented earlier in this chapter but taken from the same *TIME Special Report* on Borderlands. What is the specialty of each photographer? How do they "write" the story of immigration differently through their composition and selection of images?
- ❑ **Write.** Draft four or five research questions to pursue concerning photographer James Nachtwey in order to learn more about his work on this photo essay. What would you want to learn concerning his preparation, journey, and experience? Shape your questions around his method of capturing content and making an argument about this story. If you were to contact him, what might you tell him that you learned from his work?

■ *As a self-described journalist, woman of color, wife and mother,* **Michel Martin** *offers a regular one-hour daily public radio program called* Tell Me More. *An award-winnning journalist, Martin previously worked for ABC News and* Nightline. *Her subjects have ranged from U.S. embassy bombings in Africa to racial profiling and the aftermath of Hurricane*

Katrina, as well as covering September 11, the Anita Hill–Clarence Thomas controversy, and a critically acclaimed series "America in Black and White." Martin won an Emmy for her coverage of the international campaign to ban the use of landmines, and was a regular panelist on This Week with George Stephanopoulos. *Before ABC, Martin worked for the* Washington Post, *the* Wall Street Journal, Washington Week, *and* NOW with Bill Moyers.

With Immigration, Racism Knows No Borders

Michel Martin

I have a few words about the immigration mess.

That bill aimed at curbing illegal immigration just signed in Arizona has sparked outrage across the country. It makes it a state crime to be in the U.S. without proper authorization and steps up law enforcement aimed at identifying same.

Civil libertarians, religious leaders, immigrants-rights groups are all up in arms. Not to mention the president, who is—it's worth remembering—a former professor of constitutional law. All these people have sounded the same alarm: that the measure is fundamentally racist, because requiring law enforcement officers to act based on their suspicions will encourage *exactly* the kind of profiling that minorities, especially racial minorities, have been fighting against for decades.

Can I just tell you? It might be hard to see this at this moment, if you are one of the people who now see yourselves with a big bull's-eye on your back. But there's an upside, which is that Arizona's lawmakers have pushed the issue of immigration back to the front burner. It is also worth noting that this has happened without bloodshed, or at least a very great deal of it.

5 That's not to say that people have not already lost their lives needlessly in the absence of a rational and consistent approach to immigration. They have, including people crossing the border dangerously, the people charged with stopping them, and people, like that Arizona rancher who was mysteriously shot to death recently, who were just caught in the middle.

FIGURE 15.15. Racism isn't just black and white. A groundbreaking survey by New America Media found that African Americans, Hispanics and Asians in America have negative stereotypes about each other.

Still, all too often it seems that unpopular people cannot get the attention of policymakers until a lot of people die at once—there's some sort of incident (usually involving the police), it escalates, there's a riot. And everybody snaps to attention to resolve whatever issue has been sitting there in plain sight all along.

At least in this case, the political system *did* finally react, and President Obama, who is always being chided about putting too much on his plate, will presumably be able to turn his attention to yet another issue that really must be faced.

But there's something else that needs to be faced: Now that the issue has surfaced about how immigrants and black and brown people could potentially be treated based on their appearance, we need to also talk about how immigrants treat other people based on theirs.

I realize this is a sensitive issue—nobody likes being kicked when he or she is down—but progress depends on all sides being willing to speak honestly with each other about what they want and expect. And while immigrants-rights groups have been vocal about how they believe immigrants should be treated in this country, it is also true that Americans have a right to be vocal about what they expect from immigrants. One thing Americans have a right to expect is that immigrants will in fact make an effort to assimilate. Often this means learning English. On this score, the data are pretty clear that most immigrants will, and with a quickness.

10 But there's another matter that gets less attention and deserves more, which is whether immigrants will be called upon to surrender their *own* prejudices—regarding race, skin color, sexual orientation and religious preference.

A groundbreaking survey by New America Media in December 2007 offered a window into what I am talking about. It was a comprehensive survey of African-Americans, Hispanics and Asians in America, and it found that all of these groups have negative stereotypes about each *other.*

For example, majorities of each group said they preferred doing business with white people above all others. Significant percentages of Hispanics and Asians said they are afraid of blacks, and significant percentages of non-Asians said Asians had no respect for people unlike themselves.

There's more, but you get the point.

This isn't to say that all immigrants are carrying around retrograde racial and cultural attitudes, far from it. And it's worth pointing out that some prejudices are within the group—blacks look down on other blacks; people from one part of the world often have very strong feelings about others from other countries in the same region, often because of historic national tensions. And there has always been a fine line between appreciating one's own culture, and shunning those who don't share it.

15 My purpose is simply to point out that part of the dialogue of the new beginning ought to include a reminder that just as politics are supposed to stop at the water's edge, so should centuries of the kind of racial and ethnic baggage that Americans have spent generations fighting to put behind us.

Reflect & Write

- ❑ Why might the writer begin with "I" and a short, one-line sentence? How does this opening suggest her *ethos* or credibility as an established writer? Notice then how she builds more authority by naming all those other people who are also "fired" up about immigration.
- ❑ How does the writer make use of low style or casual language? Underline the phrases that move you most. How are some of the phrases very visual ("see yourselves with a big bull's eye on your back" or "kicked while down")?

- ❑ What is the impact of turning to *logos*, in this case statistics and evidence about the survey of minority group stereotypes about each other? What happens to the scope of the argument as a whole? What do you think is the writer's closing point?
- ❑ **Write.** Draft a response to Michel Martin with your perspective on minority group stereotypes and racism in America today. Be sure to choose your own language level, select your evidence, and make your point clear.

■ *Since* **Thomas L. Friedman** *joined the* New York Times *as a columnist in 1981, he has won three Pulitzer Prizes for commentary and international reporting (from Lebanon and Israel). He has authored several best-selling books including* The World is Flat: A Brief History of the 21st Century, *which won the inaugural Goldman Sachs/Financial Times Business Book of the Year award,* From Beirut to Jerusalem, *which won the National Book Award,* The Lexus and the Olive Tree, *which won the 2000 Overseas Press Club Award, and* Longitudes and Attitudes: The World in the Age of Terrorism. *Friedman received a B.A. degree in Mediterranean studies from Brandeis University, a Master of Philosophy degree in modern Middle East studies from Oxford, and the honorary title, Order of the British Empire (OBE), by Queen Elizabeth II.*

America's Real Dream Team

Thomas L. Friedman

Went to a big Washington dinner last week. You know the kind: Large hall; black ties; long dresses. But this was no ordinary dinner. There were 40 guests of honor. So here's my Sunday news quiz: I'll give you the names of most of the honorees, and you tell me what dinner I was at. Ready?

5 Linda Zhou, Alice Wei Zhao, Lori Ying, Angela Yu-Yun Yeung, Lynnelle Lin Ye, Kevin Young Xu, Benjamin Chang Sun, Jane Yoonhae Suh, Katheryn Cheng Shi, Sunanda Sharma, Sarine Gayaneh Shahmirian, Arjun Ranganath Puranik, Raman Venkat Nelakant, Akhil Mathew, Paul Masih Das, David Chienyun Liu, Elisa Bisi Lin, Yifan Li, Lanair Amaad Lett, Ruoyi Jiang, Otana Agape Jakpor, Peter Danming Hu, Yale Wang Fan, Yuval Yaacov Calev, Levent Alpoge, John Vincenzo Capodilupo and Namrata Anand.

No, sorry, it was not a dinner of the China-India Friendship League. Give up?

O.K. All these kids are American high school students. They were the majority of the 40 finalists in the 2010 Intel Science Talent Search, which, through a national contest, identifies and honors the top math and science high school students in America, based on their solutions to scientific problems. The awards dinner was Tuesday, and, as you can see from the above list, most finalists hailed from immigrant families, largely from Asia.

Indeed, if you need any more convincing about the virtues of immigration, just come to the Intel science finals. I am a pro-immigration fanatic. I think keeping a constant flow of legal immigrants into our country—whether they wear blue collars or lab coats—is the key to keeping us ahead of China. Because when you mix all of these energetic, high-aspiring people with a democratic system and free markets, magic happens. If we hope to keep that magic, we need immigration reform that guarantees that we will always attract and retain, in an orderly fashion, the world's first-round aspirational and intellectual draft choices.

This isn't complicated. In today's wired world, the most important economic competition is no longer between countries or companies. The most important economic competition is actually between you and your own imagination. Because what your kids imagine, they can now act on farther, faster, cheaper than ever before—as individuals. Today, just about everything is becoming a commodity, except imagination, except the ability to spark new ideas.

If I just have the spark of an idea now, I can get a designer in Taiwan to design it. I can get a factory in China to produce a prototype. I can get a factory in Vietnam to mass manufacture it. I can use Amazon.com to handle fulfillment. I can use freelancer.com to find someone to do my logo and manage my backroom. And I can do all this at incredibly low prices. The one thing that is not a commodity and never will be is that spark of an idea. And this Intel dinner was all about our best sparklers.

Before the dinner started, each contestant stood by a storyboard explaining their specific project. Namrata Anand, a 17-year-old from the Harker School in California, patiently explained to me her research, which used spectral analysis and other data to expose information about the chemical enrichment history of "Andromeda Galaxy." I did not understand a word she said, but I sure caught the gleam in her eye.

My favorite chat, though, was with Amanda Alonzo, a 30-year-old biology teacher at Lynbrook High School in San Jose, Calif. She had taught two of the finalists. When I asked her the secret, she said it was the resources provided by her school, extremely "supportive parents" and a grant from Intel that let her spend part of each day inspiring and preparing students to enter this contest. Then she told me this: Local San Jose realtors are running ads in newspapers in China and India telling potential immigrants to "buy a home" in her Lynbrook school district because it produced "two Intel science winners."

10 Seriously, ESPN or MTV should broadcast the Intel finals live. All of the 40 finalists are introduced, with little stories about their lives and aspirations. Then the winners of the nine best projects are announced. And finally, with great drama, the overall winner of the $100,000 award for the best project of the 40 is identified. This year it was Erika Alden DeBenedictis of New Mexico for developing a software navigation system that would enable spacecraft to more efficiently "travel through the solar system." After her name was called, she was swarmed by her fellow competitor-geeks.

Gotta say, it was the most inspiring evening I've had in D.C. in 20 years. It left me thinking, "If we can just get a few things right—immigration, education standards, bandwidth, fiscal policy—maybe we'll be O.K." It left me feeling that maybe Alice Wei Zhao of North High School in Sheboygan, Wis., chosen by her fellow finalists to be their spokeswoman, was right when she told the audience: "Don't sweat about the problems our generation will have to deal with. Believe me, our future is in good hands."

As long as we don't shut our doors.

Reflect & Write

- ❑ Why might Friedman begin with a question? How does this engage your interest?
- ❑ Notice how he next offers an entire paragraph of names before turning to a humorous comment and another question: "No, sorry, it was not a dinner of the China-India Friendship League. Give up?" How do these opening strategies establish his *persona* as a writer?
- ❑ What is the effect of naming people such as "Namrata Anand, a 17-year-old from the Harker School in California" and "Alice Wei Zhao of North High School in Sheboygan, Wis"? How does naming people bring the writing alive to you as a reader? Does it work as a tool of persuasive writing?

- Discuss his point that "In today's wired world, the most important economic competition is no longer between countries or companies. The most important economic competition is actually between you and your own imagination." What is your response to this claim? What examples do you see from your life?
- **Write.** Draft your own perspective on this issue and send it to the *New York Times* as an op-ed. Try to imitate Friedman's writing strategies, but use examples from your community and build your argument to support your own argument.

Stephen M. Steinlight *is a fellow at the Center for Immigration Studies. He is also currently a fellow at Timothy Dwight College, Yale University. For more than six years he was the Director of National Affairs at the American Jewish Committee and for two years served as a senior fellow at the AJC. Steinlight is co-editor of* Fractious Nation: Race, Class and Culture in America at the End of the Twentieth Century.

Thomas L. Friedman: Foe of Open-Borders and 'Comprehensive Immigration Reform'?

Stephen M. Steinlight

Though Thomas Friedman's *New York Times* column "America's Real Dream Team" squandered a teachable moment, copping out by failing to offer an explicitly political condemnation of America's current immigration policies and the unending campaign for "comprehensive immigration reform," he indirectly demolished both.

That he did so while declaring himself a "pro-immigration fanatic" isn't a contradiction, nor does his deep genuflection towards immigration appear to be a sop to his publishers. His enthusiasm is authentic, but the immigration he's endorsing is of a kind that never figures in any of the tediously repetitive *Times* editorials in favor of open borders. The immigration Friedman wants–"legal," "orderly," resulting in America's attracting and retaining "the world's first-round aspirational and intellectual draft choices"–can actually be seen as consonant with the Center for Immigration Studies' advocacy of a "pro-immigrant policy of lower immigration" predicated on the national interest. In "America's Real Dream Team," Friedman reveals himself to be a passionate advocate of that vision—even while his message is substantially neutered by the role he's created for himself as the nation's leading journalistic paradigm inventor who is simultaneously naïve about, dismissive of, or simply afraid to confront the political implications of his own "future talk."

The variety of immigration over which he rhapsodizes–which he claims is key to maintaining America's world leadership–bears no resemblance to that endorsed by the president or the weird conglomeration of usual suspects and special interests: a hefty cross-section of our fiscal and financial elite, mainstream media and "newspapers of record," foundation-bankrolled cadres of immigrant activists, the Hispanic and Black Congressional Caucuses, the most exploitative employers in the corporate service sector, ethnic identity extremists, Big Religion with its posturing morally purblind post-American clerics, among others.

In fact, it's axiomatic that immigration Friedman-style is wholly antithetical to current immigration policy and "comprehensive immigration reform"–which begins with amnesty, though that's an instrumentality, not remotely an end in itself. The core component of "comprehensive immigration reform" is an exponential increase in what will become legal immigration triggered by amnesty in conjunction with extended family reunification. If passed, it won't result in a "pathway to citizenship" for a mere 11 million illegal aliens, but in the immigration of tens of millions of uneducated less-skilled foreigners, connected to the 11 million often by fraudulently alleged family ties.

5 This cataclysmic immigration will come overwhelmingly from oligarchic Latin American cultures with chasm-like divides between the rich and the poor, with oppressive, rigid class systems that give their citizenry, particularly their own poor, little access to learning or the means or motivation to pursue the life of the mind. It will result in the importation of a vast less-skilled demographic that is the inverse of Friedman's "Real Dream Team." According to data from the Pew Hispanic Center, some 30 percent of immigrants from Mexico have not finished 9th grade; some 62 percent lack high school diplomas. Conscious decisions to promote and preserve ignorance have been taken by corrupt undemocratic oligarchies to preserve their stolen wealth and power. Similarly, their complicity in illegally exporting millions of their own less-educated citizens to the United States reduces pressure on the steam cooker of potential social unrest at home, while the billions sent back by the exported poor provides just enough in a society with relatively low economic expectations to avert a potentially revolutionary situation.

Friedman wrote his paean to the benefits of immigration by the "best and brightest" as a result of having attended an award ceremony for high school kids from across the U.S., the children of legal immigrants, mostly from Asia, who were finalists in the 2010 Intel Science Talent Search. Unlike the 40 finalists, a high proportion of the children of today's legal and illegal less-skilled immigrants from Mexico and Central America have parents with very low levels of education, and the parents' education attainment is one of the best predictors of a child's success. The result is that many children from Latin American immigrant families are dropping out of school and socializing downward. While Hispanics once had the highest rate of intact families of any group, the native-born children and grandchildren of Hispanic immigrants have rates of out-of-wedlock births second only to those in the African-American community, one of the principal causes and symptoms of the crises that beset the black community. Nearly half of Hispanic immigrant families use at least one federal welfare program, and the education system is not providing a basis for upward social mobility. In our knowledge-based, post industrial society it is unlikely that the immigrants who come here from Mexico and Central America will provide many of the finalists for the Intel Talent Search for generations; meanwhile we can predict inverse outcomes: high rates of academic failure, functional illiteracy in two languages, welfare dependency, out-of-wedlock births, and disproportionate rates of incarceration.

I can already hear the accusation that Friedman is guilty of pro-Asian racialism or celebrating "model minorities," but those charges would be nonsensical. The winners weren't chosen on affirmative action bases. The finalists competed in a national contest that identifies the top U.S. high school students in science and math, and the 40 winners were selected on the basis of the quality of thinking they employed in solving scientific problems. Friedman, who believes the future belongs to democratic, free-market societies that place a high premium on the life of the mind and intellectual aspiration, came away reassured: "Gotta say, it was the most inspiring evening I've had in D.C. in 20 years. It left me thinking, "If we can just get a few things right–immigration, education standards, bandwidth, fiscal policy–maybe we'll be O.K."

There's no argument these criteria are critical, even essential to maintaining American world leadership and Exceptionalism. But the Panglossian optimism, breezy confidence, and bizarre sense of relief that accompanied Friedman home from the event seem frighteningly misplaced. When he cites "getting immigration right," and "making it orderly" and adds, "This isn't complicated," one wonders whether he inhabits the same universe as 300 million other Americans.

It is astoundingly unrealistic, even oddly childish, to opine that getting immigration right is no big deal. An epic political struggle has thus far achieved nothing more than preventing America's political and fiscal elite–who have it totally wrong–from taking the nation over Niagara Falls. That we have thus far prevented America from succumbing to "comprehensive immigration reform" by defeating three legislative incarnations is our only consolation. Fighting and winning desperate rearguard actions is no minor achievement, but such actions stave off defeat rather than deliver victory. We remain on the defensive.

5 If Thomas L. Friedman chose to use his influential voice–one especially resonant among liberal Americans–to help them understand how radically different is the immigration he advocates from the sort being pushed by the cynical, greedy, or ethnically chauvinist "comprehensive reform" crowd, he might actually make a difference. But to do that he would have to descend from the mountaintop from which paradigm-creators prognosticate and enter the gritty political fray. In "Politics and the English Language" George Orwell reminds us "all issues are political issues." One would have thought Thomas Friedman would recognize that's true even of his dreams for America's future.

Reflect & Write

- ❑ How does Steinlight provide an *ad hominem* attack on both Friedman and the *New York Times* more generally? Do you think this is an effective rhetorical strategy? (See Chapter 2 for a discussion of the *ad hominem* fallacy)
- ❑ Notice the shifts in style in the writing, from very low or casual to quite intellectual. Why might the writer shift style to make certain points? Paraphrase what the writer might mean by this line: "But the Panglossian optimism, breezy confidence, and bizarre sense of relief that accompanied Friedman home from the event seem frighteningly misplaced."
- ❑ What is the value of raising a question in the title? How does the writer answer it (or not) by the end of the piece?

❑ **Write.** Write a commentory to Steinlight, addressing the points made in Friedman's most recent article "America's Real Dream Team," and including your own view on immigration. Peer review your work in class, or even debate it.

■ **Lexington** *is a regular columnist for* The Economist. *He also keeps a blog, called "Lexington's Notebook," posting opinions about "America's political fray."*

The Hub Nation

Lexington

Immigration places America at the centre of a web of global networks. So why not make it easier?

FIGURE 15.16. A visual representation of our changing international connections.

IMMIGRANTS benefit America because they study and work hard. That is the standard argument in favour of immigration, and it is correct. Leaving your homeland is a big deal. By definition, it takes get-up-and-go to get up and go, which is why immigrants are abnormally entrepreneurial. But there is another, less obvious benefit of immigration. Because they maintain links with the places they came from, immigrants help America plug into a vast web of global networks.

Many people have observed how the networks of overseas Chinese and Indians benefit their respective motherlands. Diasporas speed the flow of information: an ethnic Chinese trader in Indonesia who spots a commercial opportunity will quickly alert his cousin who runs a factory in Guangdong. And ties of kin, clan or dialect ensure a high level of trust. This allows decisions to be made swiftly: multimillion-dollar deals can sometimes be sealed with a single phone call. America is linked to the world in a different way. It does not have much of a diaspora, since native-born Americans seldom emigrate permanently. But it has by far the world's largest stock of immigrants, including significant numbers from just about every country on earth. Most assimilate quickly, but few sever all ties with their former homelands.

Consider Andres Ruzo, an entrepreneur who describes himself as "Peruvian by birth; Texan by choice". He moved to America when he was 19. After studying engineering, he founded a telecoms firm near Dallas. It prospered, and before long he was looking to expand into Latin America. He needed a partner. He stumbled on one through a priest, who introduced him to another devout IT entrepreneur, Vladimir Vargas Esquivel, who was based in Costa Rica and looking to expand northward. It was a perfect fit. And because of the way they were introduced—by a priest they both respected—they felt they could trust each other. Their firm now operates in ten countries and generates tens of millions of dollars in annual sales. Mr Ruzo wants the firm, which is called ITS Infocom, to go global. So although he and Mr Vargas Esquivel natter to each other in Spanish, they insist that the firm's official language must be English.

Trust matters. Modern technology allows instant, cheap communication. Yet although anyone can place a long-distance call, not everyone knows whom to call, or whom to trust. Ethnic networks can address this problem. For example, Sanjaya Kumar, an Indian doctor, arrived in America in 1992. He developed an interest in software that helps to prevent medical errors. This is not a small problem. Perhaps 100,000 Americans die each year because of preventable medical mistakes, according to the Institute of Medicine. Dr Kumar needed cash and business advice to commercialise his ideas, so he turned to a network of ethnic Indian entrepreneurs called Tie. He met, and was backed by, an Indian-American venture capitalist, Vish Mishra. His firm, Quantros, now sells its services to 2,300 American hospitals. And it is starting to expand into India, having linked up with a software firm there which is run by an old school chum of one of Dr Kumar's Indian-American executives.

5 Ethnic networks have drawbacks. If they are a means of excluding outsiders, they can be stultifying. But they accelerate the flow of information. Nicaraguan-Americans put buyers in Miami in touch with sellers in Managua. Indian-American employees help American consulting firms scout for talent in Bangalore. The benefits are hard to measure, but William Kerr of the Harvard Business School has found some suggestive evidence. He looked at the names on patent records, reasoning that an inventor called Wang was probably of Chinese origin, while some called Martinez was probably Hispanic. He found that foreign researchers cite American-based researchers of their own ethnicity 30-50% more often than you would expect if ethnic ties made no difference. It is not just that a Chinese boffin in Beijing reads papers written by Chinese boffins in America. A Chinese boffin in America may alert his old classmate in Beijing to cool research being done at the lab across the road.

Network effects

In Silicon Valley more than half of Chinese and Indian immigrant scientists and engineers report sharing information about technology or business opportunities with people in their home countries, according to AnnaLee Saxenian of the University of California, Berkeley. Some Americans fret that China and India are using American know-how to out-compete America. But knowledge flows both ways. As people in emerging markets innovate—which they are already doing at a prodigious clip—America will find it ever more useful to have so many citizens who can tap into the latest brainwaves from Mumbai and Shanghai. Immigrants can also help their American employers do business in their homelands. Firms that employ many ethnic Chinese scientists, for example, are more likely to invest in China and more likely to do so through a wholly owned subsidiary, rather than seeking the crutch of a joint venture, finds

Mr Kerr. In other words, local knowledge reduces the cost of doing business.

Immigration provides America with legions of unofficial ambassadors, deal-brokers, recruiters and boosters. Immigrants not only bring the best ideas from around the world to American shores; they are also a conduit for spreading American ideas and ideals back to their homelands, thus increasing their adoptive country's soft power.

All of which makes the task of fixing America's cumbersome immigration rules rather urgent. Alas, Barack Obama has done little to fulfil his campaign pledge to do so. With unemployment still at nearly 10%, few politicians are brave enough to be seen encouraging foreigners to compete for American jobs.

Reflect & Write

- ❑ How does the drawing in Figure 15.16 establish the argument for the article? Can it be seen as a visual abstract for the writer's main point about immigrants as a "conduit for spreading American ideas and ideals back to their homelands"?
- ❑ Although there is only one subhead in this piece, how does it unite the two parts of the argument and propel the writer's thesis forward?
- ❑ Assess the tone and stance by looking at word choice, sentence length, and specific examples. What passages work best for you as a reader?
- ❑ **Write.** Develop a letter to *The Economist* describing "networks" in your own community, or observations you have had of immigration conduits. Feel free to include drawings or photos as visual rhetoric.

■ **Ezra Klein** *writes a blog for the* Washington Post *on subjects ranging from economic policy, to collapsing banks, to cap and trade, to health care reform. Klein has appeared as a guest on CNN, MSNBC, NPR, and C-SPAN, and he previously served as an associate editor at the* American Prospect. *He also contributes to the group food blog the Internet Food Association.*

Nativism Doesn't Appear To Be on Much of a Rise

Ezra Klein

There's been plenty of overheated rhetoric and creative paranoia on display this year, but nativism has been, to me, the dog that didn't bark. The Tea Parties haven't been very focused on immigration, and while abortion and socialism both became major issues during health-care reform, fears that the bill would cover illegal immigrants (it won't, incidentally) never became a marquee issue.

But in the *American Prospect*, Gabriel Arana suggests that the situation has worsened for immigrants, even if it's been a quiet deterioration: "Since the 2006 protests, membership in anti-immigrant groups has increased 600 percent," Arana reports. "The number of these groups has also risen from around 40 in 2005 to over 250 today." He also notes that most of the moderate Republicans who once seemed friendly to immigration reform have abandoned the issue, with Sen. John McCain being the most visible example.

Is that evidence of broader shifts in public opinion, though? The polling I can find—and there's not that much of it—paints a cheerier picture. A CNN poll asked whether respondents would like to see the number of illegal immigrants in the country increased or decreased. Between 2006 and 2008, "decreased" got between 65% and 69% In October of 2009, it got . . . 73%. An increase, but nothing catastrophic.

Perhaps more on point, a *Washington Post* poll asked "Would you support or oppose a program giving illegal immigrants now living in the United States the right to live here legally if they pay a fine and meet other requirements?" At various points in 2007, support for this ranged from 48% to 59%. In April of 2009—which was well into the recession—support hit 61%.

5 I wouldn't draw any overly firm conclusions from these numbers. But they don't paint a picture of nativism on an unchecked rise. And perhaps that's to be expected. People blame this recession on Wall Street. Illegal immigrants, love 'em or hate 'em, aren't at the forefront of people's minds.

FIGURE 15.17. Demonstrators hold a rally for Immigration Reform at the Capitol, strategically using the nation's visual rhetoric with posters and with flags.

Reflect & Write

- ❑ How does Klein argue that immigration isn't really a core issue for our country right now despite media rhetoric? Notice how he begins with *kairos*, or attention to right time and place, by naming other current political controversies.
- ❑ Who is the intended audience? How can you tell this from expressions such as "to me, the dog that didn't bark"? What does he mean by "nativism"?
- ❑ How does his turn to *logos*—the *Washington Post* poll in particular—serve his overall argument about the prominence of immigration on the nation's mind? What is his argument about this issue?
- ❑ **Write.** Take the point of view of one of the people shown in the photo and write a blog response to Ezra Klein offering a strong argument about rhetoric, media, and immigration. Be sure to comment on the visual rhetoric of the photo as evidence.

This article was posted on National Public Radio as part of "The Two-Way" news blog. **Frank James** *included a video, available for view through the* Envision *Website, with a multimedia version of this story.*

Phoenix (Los) Suns Wade Into Immigration Fight

Frank James

Corporations tend to be risk-averse, especially when it comes to wading into issues as controversial as Arizona's new law meant to crack down on illegal immigration.

But that hasn't stopped the NBA's Phoenix Suns from entering the fray. The team's managing partner, Robert Sarver, publicly criticized the new law and reportedly had the support of all the players on the team.

The team didn't stop there. On Wednesday evening, the team plans to have its players wear jerseys bearing its name in Spanish—Los Suns—during their playoff game against the San Antonio Spurs.

It's in part to mark Cinqo de Mayo, the Mexican holiday, and partly to show solidarity for Hispanics, many of whom believe the law will be used to racially profile even those who are in the U.S. legally.

FIGURE 15.18. Screen shot of multimedia version of this story, available through the *Envision* Website. www.pearsonhighered.com/envision/557

5 The Arizona Republic reports:

> The gesture, which came with the blessing of the NBA and the league's players union, reflects Sarver's belief that passing Senate Bill 1070 was not "the right way to handle the immigration problem, Number 1," he said. "Number 2, as I read through the bill, it felt to me a little bit like it was mean-spirited, and I personally just don't agree with it."
>
> Arizona sports teams and events have become targets for protests and calls for boycotts since SB 1070 was signed into law by Gov. Jan Brewer on April 23.
>
> The law makes it a state crime to be in Arizona without proper documents and requires local police to check the legal status of suspected undocumented immigrants.
>
> Sarver's decision is the first time a state sports entity has taken a public stand on the law, which is scheduled to go into effect in about 90 days.

> 10 "We think it's appropriate what the Suns are doing," NBA Commissioner David Stern told nba.com in Orlando.
>
> The players union applauded the Suns' move, saying in a statement Tuesday that Arizona's new law is "disappointing and disturbing."

Again, one of the most noteworthy aspects about all of this is that the businesses, especially those that rely on public image, tend to not want to take stands that could be unpopular with some of their customer base.

And several polls indicate that a majority of Americans support the Arizona law which suggests that the Suns could be spitting into the wind to a degree.

A message on the Suns' Planet Orange discussion board underscores why most for-profit concerns attempt to give political matters a wide berth:

> 15 As a former Suns and NBA fan, I would suggests you go all the way and call yourselves "Los Soles", move to Tucson or better yet Nogales! What gives you the right to get involved in Arizona politics? you are all "mercenaries" you follow the money wherever they take you. this issue is for Arizonans, and they have spoken 70% of us did! you are so out of touch with reality from your super mansions, your range rovers, and surrounded by people kissing your collective arses! I used to watch your games for sheer entertainment, no longer will nor would I support your endorsers. By the way Mr Sarver; you should really issue free tickets to all the illegal aliens who wants to attend the play-off games, you will have the arena pretty full in no time, ah but not revenue, except from burritos and nachos! If you don't like our laws, pack up and get out, life will go on in Arizona without you! Adios

Also, some observers believe the jerseys should really say Los Soles, to be accurate. But as some have noted, maybe that was too uncomfortably close to "lost souls."

Reflect & Write

- ❑ How does the visual rhetoric of sports shirts introduce an argument about immigration into the public in a way that is very different from an op-ed or article in a journal? What do you think of this strategy?
- ❑ The article focuses on the "public image" of the NBA's Phoenix Suns. What do you learn about the team's persona and perspective from this story?
- ❑ Contrast the writing from the *Arizona Republic* to that of the Suns' Planet Orange discussion board. How do the grammar errors and exaggerated *pathos* of the discussion board writer paint that author in a particular light?
- ❑ **Write.** Watch the multimedia story through the *Envision* Website and then write up your own account of this event. You can interview people in your school to quote their opinions and get practice integrating sources. www.pearsonhighered.com/envision/558

PERSPECTIVES ON THE ISSUE

1. Compare how Hilary Hylton and Teresa Hayter integrate research sources differently into their pieces. In some ways, their arguments are opposing. How does the strategic reliance on evidence in the form of research help each one make her points persuasively? What can you learn and apply from their examples to your own paper on immigration and cross-border controversies?
2. Compare the views of Thomas Friedman and Stephen Steinlight on immigration's benefit to the American economy. What are their perspectives? Who builds *ethos* more effectively? Which writing strategies do you admire more? How convincing is each argument? How can you read the Lexington piece as a third perspective on this issue? Now, write your own article as a fourth response to this issue. Be sure to quote from all the previous pieces and also to use evidence or case studies from your own life or community.
3. Which pieces in this section seem to be in direct conversation with each other? What do you think James Nachtwey or Michel Martin would say in response to the piece by Ted Robbins? How is Ezra Klein's piece another view on the issue presented by Cynthia Gorney through narrative reporting and by Alex Webb through a photo essay? Which pieces move you most? Which persuade you intellectually? What can you learn from these different writing strategies?
4. Examine the visuals in this first part of the chapter. How do they tell the story of immigration or reveal the controversies covered by the articles? In small groups, reorder the images to make a different argument about crossing borders.
5. How effective is the visual rhetoric protest of the Phoenix Suns? Identify how your sports team could launch a protest about a similar controversy at your campus. What would be the argument and the impact?

FROM READING TO RESEARCH

1. Research the CNN op-ed mentioned by Hilary Hylton in her article. Then, go to Daryl Cagle's cartoon site (linked through the *Envision* Website) and locate political cartoons about "swine flu" and the fear of Mexico-U.S. cross-cultural contamination. Use this material in writing your own op-ed, with images.
www.pearsonhighered.com/envision/559a
2. Follow the links through the *Envision* Website and study all three of Ted Robbins's pieces in his series on immigration: the interview with Salvador Reza, "'America's Toughest Sheriff' Takes on Immigration," and "The Man Behind Arizona's Toughest Immigrant Laws." What do you learn from examining multiple sides of this issue? How does each person provide his stance on immigration?
www.pearsonhighered.com/envision/559b
3. Working in groups, locate the additional photo essays posted as part of the *TIME* Special Report on "The New Frontier, La Nueva Frontera," linked through the *Envision* Website. Examine the photos as well as the interactive map on the main page. How do these texts form visual arguments? Now, conduct some field research (using the strategies outlined in Chapter 5). Interview people in your community who have experienced "Borderlands" of any kind. Take photos (with their permission) and make careful notes in quoting from them about their lives and perspectives on crossing cultures. Assemble your materials into your own photo essay and present your work to the class or post it online.
www.pearsonhighered.com/envision/559c

MCDONALDIZATION

FIGURE 15.19. This security guard in Bejing, China, hardly "loves" his job working for McDonalds. © Photo by Laird J. Rawsthorne.

In many ways, McDonald's and the Golden Arches have become visual rhetoric signs of how American culture moves across cultures and borders. As the American-based fast-food chain McDonald's has continued to expand globally, it has been met with celebration and with protests. The readings in this section take a look at McDonald's as a case study of U.S. culture moving outward, to reach international customers and bring with it a little bit of the American way of life—including food, work practices, and cultural events such as "American Idol."

Consider the image in Figure 15.19. A security guard in Beijing, China, holds on to an umbrella displaying the trademark visual rhetoric of McDonald's exported from America: the Golden Arches in their child-like yellow script, the lowercase slogan "i'm lovin' it" with its American slang, and the red and yellow colors of the corporation. Yet the expression on the man's face provides another argument: it tells the story of globalization, or how cultures across the world inherit the fast food and culture of America in a way that does not always live up to the media hype or stimulate growing economies. This disparity between appearance (or visual rhetoric promise) and reality (or the true condition of cultures and people's lives) is exactly the issue we will explore in this section on "McDonaldization."

What's at stake in this issue is that McDonald's sells more than food; it creates what blog columnist Paul Feine calls "McCulture," or a way of life that it exports to various countries around the world. This is often very good for the nation, Feine argues, in terms of bringing hygiene, nutrition, and entertainment for children, among other benefits. But critics of McDonald's, such as George Ritzer, see McCulture as a threat to human creativity. As we'll learn, Ritzer contends that McDonald's sells a "false image" of world unity through shared food preferences. Ritzer coined the term *McDonaldization* to mean "the process by which the principles of the fast-food restaurant are coming to dominate more and more sectors of American society as well as the rest of the world" (*The McDonaldization of Society*, p.11).

FIGURE 15.20. Entitled "Umm–Mao–Mao," this photo posted on Flickr makes a spoof argument about the culture of McDonald's.

A spoof image on how McDonald's has come to take over the world can be seen in Figure 15.20. Here, the familiar Mickey Mouse ears of Disney are imposed on China's former communist ruler, Chairman Mao. This photo, from the original McDonald's restaurant in Des Plaines, Illinois, might be seen as a visual argument that all the fast-food stores are imposing a similar diet and culture on places around the world.

But not all responses to McDonald's are filled with such good humor. The image in

Figure 15.21 could be seen as a visual rhetoric argument of protest against McDonald's. If placed within a blog entry or analyzed in an essay, this photo could be seen to make a powerful counter-statement to the seemingly joyous culture that McDonald's attempts to create with its own marketing campaigns. Here, we see the famous Golden Arches, but they are laying in shambles in the middle of the parking lot, and even half of the famous name is missing. This visual argument reflects the way in which the symbol of an international fast-food store might become a marker of ineffective cultural crossing—or how a company could fail to reach people's hearts and wallets.

FIGURE 15.21. This image captures much anti-McDonald's energy through simple composition and layout.

This dichotomy of views is, perhaps, the crux of the debate: when another restaurant opens across the globe with the Golden Arches on top, do we see McDonald's as the example of an American company exporting Western looks, values, poor eating habits, and economic practices including heavy consumerism and use of natural resources? Or do we see a model of international development that shows respect for local cultures, customs, and practices? We'll address these questions in the pages that follow. We'll also look at how McDonald's as a corporation works hard to design visual rhetoric for its restaurants, its ad campaigns on billboards, and even its Internet identity.

Reflect & Write

- ❑ Look closely at the three different photos capturing an aspect of McDonald's as a global company. How does each one make an argument about the corporation's *ethos*? What other rhetorical strategies are at work in each image?
- ❑ Why do you think are there no people actually eating the food in these visual arguments? What does that tell you about how the cultural force of McDonald's is so much more than merely being a restaurant?
- ❑ How are American cultural values, fashions, and musical trends reproduced—or not—in the images here? Do a Google search for McDonald's images and compare your results.
- ❑ In small groups, go online to the McDonald's homepage, select another country from the pulldown menu, and analyze the visual rhetoric strategies you find there. Compare the visual rhetoric there to the images from Flickr reproduced here in this introduction. How does the company construct a persona for itself in the digital world? What types of Web marketing would you expect the company to use when launching a franchise in specific countries? What do you make of representing a country in this way and trying to win audiences through this visual rhetoric?
- ❑ **Write.** Draft a letter to McDonald's explaining your comparison of Flickr photos to the marketing on the McDonald's Website. Use specific visual evidence from the images you have studied, and make your argument about the cultural reception of McDonald's based on what you have studied so far. When you are done working through the readings in this section, return to your letter and add an addendum with your new thinking on this issue.

Mark Rice-Oxley *is a correspondent for the* Guardian *and the* Christian Science Monitor, *where this article appeared on January 15, 2004. He has written stories on British manners and the "Gross National Happiness Index"; he performed the role of* David Copperfield *at the West Yorkshire Playhouse.*

In 2,000 Years, Will the World Remember Disney or Plato?

Mark Rice-Oxley

Down in the mall, between the fast-food joint and the bagel shop, a group of young people huddles in a flurry of baggy combat pants, skateboards, and slang. They size up a woman teetering past wearing DKNY, carrying *Time* magazine in one hand and a latte in the other. She brushes past a guy in a Yankees' baseball cap who is talking on his Motorola cellphone about the Martin Scorsese film he saw last night. It's a standard American scene—only this isn't America, it's Britain. US culture is so pervasive, the scene could be played out in any one of dozens of cities. Budapest or Berlin, if not Bogota or Bordeaux. Even Manila or Moscow.

As the unrivaled global superpower, America exports its culture on an unprecedented scale. From music to media, film to fast food, language to literature and sport, the American idea is spreading inexorably, not unlike the influence of empires that preceded it. The difference is that today's technology flings culture to every corner of the globe with blinding speed. If it took two millenniums for Plato's "Republic" to reach North America, the latest hit from Justin Timberlake can be found in Greek (and Japanese) stores within days. Sometimes, US ideals get transmitted—such as individual rights, freedom of speech, and respect for women—and local cultures are enriched. At other times, materialism or worse becomes the message and local traditions get crushed. "The US has become the most powerful, significant world force in terms of cultural imperialism [and] expansion," says Ian Ralston, American studies director at Liverpool John Moores University. "The areas that particularly spring to mind are Hollywood, popular music, and even literature." But what some call "McDomination" has created a backlash in certain cultures. And it's not clear whether fast food, Disney, or rock 'n' roll will change the world the way Homer or Shakespeare has.

Cricket or basketball?

Stick a pin in a map and there you'll find an example of US influence. Hollywood rules the global movie market, with up to 90 percent of audiences in some European countries. Even in Africa, 2 of 3 films shown are American. Few countries have yet to be touched by McDonald's and Coca-Cola. Starbucks recently opened up a new front in South America, and everyone's got a Hard Rock Café T-shirt from somewhere exotic. West Indian sports enthusiasts increasingly watch basketball, not cricket. Baseball has long since taken root in Asia and Cuba. And Chinese young people are becoming more captivated by American football and basketball, some even daubing the names of NBA stars on their school sweatsuits. The NFL plans to roll out a Chinese version of its website this month. Rupert Murdoch's satellites, with their heavy traffic of US audiovisual content, saturate the Asian subcontinent. American English is the language of choice for would-be pop stars in Europe, software programmers in India, and Internet surfers everywhere.

America's preeminence is hardly surprising. Superpowers have throughout the ages sought to perpetuate their way of life: from the philosophy and mythology of the ancient Greeks to the law and language of the Romans; from the art and architecture of the Tang Dynasty and Renaissance Italy to the sports and systems of government of the British. "Most empires think their own point of view is the only correct point of view," says Robert Young, an expert in postcolonial cultural theory at Oxford

University. "It's the certainty they get because of the power they have, and they expect to impose it on everyone else."

5 Detractors of cultural imperialism argue, however, that cultural domination poses a totalitarian threat to diversity. In the American case, "McDomination" poses several dangers.

First, local industries are truly at risk of extinction because of US oligopolies, such as Hollywood. For instance in 2000, the European Union handed out 1 billion euros to subsidize Europe's film industry. Even the relatively successful British movie industry has no control over distribution, which is almost entirely in the hands of the Hollywood majors.

Second, political cultures are being transformed by the personality-driven American model in countries as far-reaching as Japan and the Philippines.

Finally, US domination of technologies such as the Internet and satellite TV means that, increasingly, America monopolizes the view people get of the world. According to a recent report for the UN Conference on Trade and Development, 13 of the top 14 Internet firms are American. No. 14 is British. "You have to know English if you want to use the Internet," says Andre Kaspi, a professor at the Sorbonne in Paris.

A main problem is that culture is no longer a protected species, but subject to the inexorable drive for free trade, says Joost Smiers, a political science professor at the Utrecht School of the Arts. This means that it is increasingly difficult for countries to protect their own industries. France tries to do so with subsidies, while South Korea has tried quotas. Such "protectionist" tactics meet with considerable US muscle, Dr. Smiers says. "America's aggressive cultural policy . . . hinders national states from regulating their own cultural markets," he says. "We should take culture out of the WTO."

10 Another danger, detractors say, is the consolidation of the communications industry into a few conglomerates such as AOL-TimeWarner, Disney, and News Corporation, which means that the "infotainment" generated for global consumption nearly always comes from an Anglophone perspective. "You can't go on with just three music companies organizing and distributing 85 percent of the music in the world," says Smiers. "It's against all principles of democracy. Every emotion, every feeling, every image can be copyrighted into the hands of a few owners."

American, with a twist

A backlash is being felt in certain places. In Japan, locals have taken US ideas like hip-hop and fast food, and given them a Japanese twist, says Dominic al-Badri, editor of *Kansai Time Out.* In Germany, there is still strong resistance to aspects of US pop culture, though there is an appetite for its intellectual culture, says Gary Smith, director of the American Academy in Berlin. In France, resistance is growing partly because of frustrations over the Iraq war—but partly because Americanization is already so advanced in the country, says Mr. Kaspi.

He notes one interesting anecdotal sign of US influence—and the futility of resistance. France has repeatedly tried to mandate the use of French language in official capacities to check the advance of English. "But most of the time, the law is impossible to apply, because if you want to be understood around the world you have to speak English," Kaspi says.

In the Philippines, even the best US ideals have caused complications. "The pervasive American influence has saddled us with two legacies," notes respected local commentator Antonio C. Abaya. "American-style elections, which require the commitment of massive financial resources, which have to be recouped and rolled over many times, which is the main source of corruption in government; and American-style free press in which media feel free to attack and criticize everything that the government does or says, which adds to disunity and loss of confidence in government."

Meanwhile, for all the strength of the US movie industry, sometimes a foreign film resonates more with a local audience than a Hollywood production—and outperforms it. For instance, Japan's "Spirited Away" (2001) remains the top-grossing film in that country, surpassing global Hollywood hits like "Titanic." In addition, British TV has influenced and served up competition to US shows, spawning such hits as "Who Wants to Be a Millionaire?", "The Weakest Link," and "American Idol."

1,000 years from now

15 So how much good does American culture bring to the world? And how long will it last? Ian Ralston cautions against sweeping dismissals of US pop culture. British television may be saturated with American sitcoms and movies, but while some are poor, others are quite good, he says. "British culture has always been enriched by foreign influences. In some ways American culture and media have added to that enrichment." Others note that it is not all one-way traffic. America may feast largely on a diet of homegrown culture, but it imports modestly as well: soccer, international cuisine, Italian fashion, and, increasingly, British television.

As to the question of durability, some experts believe US domination of communication channels makes it inevitable that its messages will become far more entrenched than those of previous empires. "The main difference now in favor of American culture is the importance of technology—telephone, Internet, films, all that did not exist in ancient Greece or the Mongol empire," Kaspi says. "American influence is growing, it's so easy to get access to US culture; there are no barriers. "Disney is known worldwide now," he adds. "Plato is more and more unknown, even in Greece."

But not everyone thinks American culture will stand the test of time. "It remains to be seen whether the Monkees and Bee Gees are as durable as Plato," says Professor Young, with a dab of irony. "Let's have another look in 4,000 years' time."

Reflect & Write

- ❑ How does this article immediately engage your interest as a reader with its two particularly vivid opening paragraphs? Discuss the detailed names in the opening and how they relate both to globalization and to what Mark Rice-Oxley calls "McDomination"?
- ❑ How does the writer both construct an audience and create a unique persona through word choice? What word choices make this article targeted at a specific demographic? What is your response to the author's stylistic choices?
- ❑ How does the article integrate quotations as research and as appeals to authority? What is the effect of this rhetorical strategy on you as a reader? What is the effect of this on the writing as a text?
- ❑ What organizational structure does this article employ? Return to Chapter 6 to review the various strategies of arrangement.
- ❑ How does this article itemize its arguments logically? Map out the strategies of rebuttal, concession, and qualification. What do you make of the last line?
- ❑ **Write.** Compose a narrative about visual rhetoric of globalization or crossing cultures in the community around you. What instances of globalized culture strike you as having "staying power"? Be as detailed as Rice-Oxley in naming specifics. Turn your writing into a photo essay, using images you take or from the Web, and share your work with others.

■ *This article, by* **Qui Jianghong**, *appeared in the June 1, 2004, edition of the* China Daily, *an English-language newspaper published in China. Sometimes called the "Window to China," the* China Daily *and its Website (chinadaily.com.cn) are dedicated to providing the world with information about China and its role in the international community.*

KFC and McDonald's: A Model of Blended Culture

Qui Jianghong

CEOs of America Tricon Global Restaurants, the group that owns KFC and Pizza Hut, promotes Traditional Peking Chicken Roll at a KFC restaurant in Shanghai.

At present, there are more than 1,000 KFC restaurants in China, and they are increasing at annual rate of 200. A new KFC restaurant opens every other day. Western counterpart McDonald's also continues to expand its premises.

Having arrived on the mainland in the early 1990s, McDonald's has more than 600 restaurants in nearly 100 cities. Although there have been fewer golden arches in America, its native country, in the past two years, China's McDonald's have grown at a rate of 100 restaurants per year.

The total income of fast food restaurants in China now stands at 180 billion yuan RMB, and KFC and McDonald's account for eight percent. What kind of magic has brought them such success in China? How do they sustain growth rates? Their standardized business operation apart, the key is excellent intercultural management.

Western Fast Food Chinese Style

5 Alluring the captious customers is a hurdle every foreign fast food restaurant must clear. The novelty of these fast food restaurants initially won many customers. Although cheap and commonplace in America, at the time the Chinese government's opening-up policy was newly enacted, fast food was exotically foreign enough to whet Chinese people's curiosity about the outside world. Managers took advantage of this by charging the relatively high prices of 10 yuan for a hamburger, and 5 yuan for a Coke.

By the mid-1990s, there were 100 fast food restaurants around Beijing; the convenience, efficient service, comfortable environment, pleasing music and jovial atmosphere garnered fans. Office workers enjoyed grabbing a quick bite on their way to work, and friends enjoyed relaxing over a Coke. However, certain eagle-eyed managers noticed that some people never dropped in when they passed by. Some customers complained that fast food was not as good as their Chinese cuisine, and that it lacked variety. McDonald's and KFC restaurants were almost empty during the traditional celebrations of Spring Festival and Mid-autumn Festival, while Chinese restaurants were heaved and bustled.

The reason? Cultural differences. Fast food restaurants like KFC and McDonald's are distinct American brands. Differences between China and US politics, economics, social development and ideology became obstacles to international enterprises operating in China. Corporate culture could not be understood or accepted here, especially in the restaurant field, where culture plays a crucial role.

So the solution was to adapt: when in Rome, do as the Romans. Deep-rooted in the Chinese consciousness is the traditional culture of food and drink that features color, fragrance, flavor and variety. Fast food simply does not compare. Now that curiosity had faded, people returned to their own more extensive cuisine. Under such circumstances, the only way out was to combine the two different cultures. Fast food restaurants have been learning to absorb elements of Chinese culture.

10 Since the summer of 2001, KFC has introduced many Chinese items onto their menus. Preserved Sichuan Pickle and Shredded Pork Soup was one of the first. Consumers felt their traditions were being respected when they could taste Chinese cuisine at a foreign restaurant. The soup proved a success, and Mushroom Rice, Tomato and Egg Soup, and Traditional Peking Chicken Roll were soon added to the menu. KFC also serves packets of Happy French Fry Shakes that contain beef, orange and Uygur barbecue spices.

Not content to lag behind, McDonald's Vegetable and Seafood Soup and Corn Soup were introduced, and the company worked to modify the restaurants' design. During the 2004 Spring Festival, McDonald's on Beijing's Wangfujing Street attracted many people with a traditional Chinese look, decorating their interiors with paper-cuts of the Chinese character Fu (Happiness), magpies and twin fishes, all auspicious symbols.

Inter-cultural Management Mode

KFC and McDonald's have absorbed the Chinese cultural elements of showing respect, recognition, understanding, assimilation and amalgamation, while maintaining the substance of the Western culture of efficiency, freedom, democracy, equality and humanity. This inter-cultural management mode, with American business culture at the core, supplemented by Chinese traditional culture, provides reference for international enterprises which need to adjust, enrich and reconstruct their corporate culture to enhance local market flexibility.

There are, however, certain conditions essential to inter-cultural management mode. On the objective side, there must be similarities in environment in order for the two cultures to connect and synchronize. KFC and McDonald's embody an accommodation of the fast tempo of modern life: a product of development and a market economy. Their resultant speed and efficiency are only meaningful in countries with a market economy. China's rapid economic development offered the environmental conditions corresponding to fast food culture. Services offered by fast food chains express their full respect for freedom, an American value, as well as the psychological statement of Chinese open-mindedness that yearns to understand and experience the Western lifestyle. Two cultures proactively crashed, connected, and assimilated. KFC and McDonald's use the localization strategy to re-express American business culture, with profound traditional Chinese cultural emblems, catering to local customs on the basis of standardized management.

Reflect & Write

- ❑ Notice the heavy reliance on *logos* in this article. What might be the reason for using so many statistics, facts, and dates in presenting this argument about the integration of McDonald's into Chinese culture?
- ❑ Summarize the argument of this essay. What side of the globalization debate is represented here? How is this argument different from the one by Rice-Oxley?
- ❑ Who is the audience for this essay? What details and descriptions suggest this to you? What aspects of the writing would need to change in order to address a different audience?
- ❑ **Write.** Copy down the menu of a fast food restaurant in your college town, one that is very different from the food in your home town. How do menus create a visual representation of the cultural community?

■ *The two pieces that follow appeared in Rutgers University's newspaper, the* Daily Targum, *in October 2002. The* Targum *ran the first piece, written by 2001 Rutgers graduate* **Joseph Davicsin**, *in its October 16 edition; "Globalization or McDonaldization?" appeared in response the following day. Its author,* **Jeremy Sklarsky**, *was a first-year student at Rutgers at the time.*

The Daily Targum: Two Opinions on McDonaldization

Corporations Leave Small Business Behind

Joseph Davicsin

Three months ago, a coffee shop opened on Church Street—where the used CD store "Tunes" was—called Basic Elements. This shop

Globalization or McDonaldization?

Jeremy Sklarsky

I am writing in response to Joseph Davicsin's commentary about international corporations conquering the world and eliminating "mom and offered homemade beverages and food at prices comparable to similar chain stores. I say "offered" because, as of recently, the place has flown the coop like so many boiler room scams. I later saw the proprietors at Starbucks doing espresso shots and mumbling Wicca chants at the Cranium board game. Basic Elements deserved a hell of a lot more than it was given—a crappy side street with little visibility, despite being right near the Court Tavern (which I know for a fact that you frequent because I can never get a square foot of space to stand on when I'm in there), irregular hours—which is understandable in a quality place run by two people (you can't expect Walmart)—and most of all, our apathy.

Our apathy is linked largely to globalization, which is trying to unite the planet in blanket sameness so that you can experience a thrill at the notion of shopping at a Gap in Prague and eating at a McDonalds in India. Now, something in your mind should tell you there's something wrong with going to a McDonalds in India. The idea of going abroad is to experience new things outside your microcosm. But alas, the success of these businesses in pandering their crack all over the world has gotten people comfortable with this sameness. We stick to the chains because they're familiar, convenient and plowed into our faces on a regular basis. When you get that taste of mocha, you're hooked and nothing else seems to matter.

Of course, if it were simply laziness and chemical brainwashing causing the underdogs to fail, it would be easier to rectify, but life is never that simple. There's also the notion of capital to think of. Corporations like Starbucks have enough money to keep their prices relatively the same no matter where you go, so there's not only uniformed coverage, but also uniformed prices. The same cannot be said of the localized stores because they have less coverage and really need the extra money to stay alive, forcing them to increase their prices to compete. This delegates them to the "fine arts" category in which only the wealthy can indulge, resulting in an even split between cheap and prevalent and expensive and exclusive, with the midways—i.e. the moderately priced Basic Elements—getting squished in the ever-shrinking gap. Our culture becomes the following: Either you go to McSystem for pop" establishments. Davicsin's comments exemplify some of the most commonly held misperceptions about globalization and corporations.

Globalization is not an enemy. It is an international, socioeconomic-political system. Due to advances in information technology, the rise of a postindustrial economy and the collapse of the bipolar Cold War world, a system has arisen in which the interests of individuals and governments around the world are intertwined. The overlap of people's interests has led to increased global cooperation. It can even be argued that the motivation for acts of international terrorism like Sept. 11 is actually a categorical rejection of the globalization system. The young men who crashed airplanes into the World Trade Center were born and raised in some of the countries that are the least globalized.

Globalization is not trying to "unite the planet in blanket sameness." Actually, quite the contrary is true. Take McDonald's, a notorious symbol of globalization, for example. McDonald's was not introduced into foreign countries in order to push American cultural hegemony over the rest of the world. McDonald's was mostly imported into foreign countries by nationals of those countries that wanted to make some profit—not as a part of a master plan to make everyone American. McDonald's is just a company that wants to make money. It isn't part of a "conspiracy of American corporations to take over the world."

Furthermore, a quick trip to the McDonald's Web site will put to rest anyone's fears that Ronald and friends are trying to undermine the culture of a local population. In Italy, McDonald's serves Mediterranean salads. Japanese customers can get teriyaki burgers. In Israel there are several kosher McDonald's restaurants, and in Mexico burritos are served. These are just a few examples of when McDonald's has actually changed itself to fit into the local culture. In India, the country that Davicsin used in his column as an example, consumers can get McDonald's sandwiches made with mutton and chicken instead of beef, as McDonald's recognizes the importance of the dietary laws in Indian religions and cultures. McDonald's has also initiated many community service programs. In Saudi Arabia, it was the first chain restaurant to sponsor a campaign to increase seatbelt awareness.

victuals or spend exorbitant amounts of cash on the trendier French fry.

5 Then, of course, there's the small matter of demand, and that's when convenience takes precedence. Anyone who still reads out there will have little hope of finding a Recto & Verso when the majority only cares about getting textbooks and spirit clothing. The alternative is Barnes and Noble. If you want a real alternative you have to walk the world over to Pyramid Books in Highland Park, which, judging by the abundance of romance novels infesting their shelves, leads me to believe that they too are trying desperately to stay afloat.

Countless fables tell of local pizza places rejecting the system, but are they really? Or are they just biding their time before Burger King offers pizza for breakfast? They too seem to be getting increasingly gimmicky (check out King's Pizza and the ultimate tax write-off that is their wide-screen TV) and streamlined (toppings ranging from tortellini to ecstasy). There are still a few locales, like Noodle Gourmet, that do solid business on their own two legs, but it's not enough. What we need to do is alternate our habits a little. Back to coffee—like Café 52? I know you do because I see you bastards flood it every Monday night for the free music, then try West End on alternate nights. Spread out! Balance the pros and cons of each place and try to find a niche in one when the other doesn't meet your needs. But above all, give newer places your undivided attention because they may not be around long enough without you. Show the smaller places that there's a need for them and that quality need not mean pricey. And don't let companies know where you're going, lest they turn that into a trend as well. Be as random as a chaos pendulum.

5 A McDonald's in every country? Sounds good to me. Thomas Friedman, columnist for *The New York Times,* recently put forth a theory—which has been proven—that states that no two countries with a McDonald's has gone to war with each other since McDonald's arrived in their countries. In Friedman's own words, people in countries that have developed an economy at the level needed for McDonald's to be successful would rather "wait in line for burgers instead of in line for gas masks."

Davicsin refers to corporations as though they are some supernatural enemy imposed upon us by some external forces. Where did they get all of their money? And why are they so successful? A chain like McDonald's or Starbucks Coffee has had so much success for one simple reason: They are just better than the "corner shop." But chances are, if a local store can make a lower-priced product of higher quality, it will thrive. Take another corporation—Pizza Hut. Pizza Hut just isn't that good. Result? There are hundreds of individually owned pizza parlors around America. We shouldn't, however, support every local pizza place just for the sake of fighting corporations—that's just silly.

I'm not suggesting globalization or corporations are perfect—they are far from it. Many Third World countries would probably be better off if the World Bank or IMF behaved better. And corporations could probably afford to pollute a little less and pay their workers a little bit more. But that's really not the issue. The point is that globalization is not a choice. The real question is how everyone is going to act in order to benefit from its existence. If local coffee shops wish to thrive in the globalization system, they'd better be damned good, otherwise Starbucks will run them out of business—and for good reason. Consumers deserve to consume good products. If the only reason to go to a local burger joint is to prevent the domination of McDonald's, then I'll have another Big Mac.

Reflect & Write

- ❑ Map out the points of each argument. How does each writer use concrete examples and structure his perspective through carefully chosen rhetorical appeals?
- ❑ Davicsin emphasizes the necessity of what he calls "visibility" and small establishments. How does his language create a favorable image for local stores in contrast to his disparagment of "blanket sameness" across the globe?

- ❑ How does Sklarsky structure his rebuttal? What points does he choose to refute and do you follow the logic of his conclusion? Which piece is more persuasive to you, and why?
- ❑ **Write.** Draft a response to both pieces, synthesizing and advancing beyond the debate between Joseph Davicsin and Jeremy Sklarsky. Be certain to quote passages from both in your own article. Where might you publish your composition?

■ *Professor of Sociology at the University of Maryland,* **George Ritzer** *has published extensively but is best known for his "McDonaldization thesis." He has published numerous books, including* The McDonaldization of Society *5 (2008) and* The Globalization of Nothing 2 *(2007),* Enchanting a Disenchanted World *(2005), and several edited volumes on* Sociology and Social Theory. *This interview was conducted by One-Off Productions in February 1997.*

Interview with George Ritzer

One-Off Productions

You have described the McDonaldised society as a system of "iron cages" in which all institutions come to be dominated by the same principle. So what sort of world would you like us to be living in ?

Well, obviously (laughter) . . . a far less caged one. I mean the fundamental problem with McDonaldised systems is that it's other people in the system structuring our lives for us, rather than us structuring our lives for ourselves. I mean, that's really what McDonald's is all about. You don't want a creative person clerk at the counter—that's why they are scripted. You don't want a creative hamburger cook—you want somebody who simply follows routines or follows scripts. So you take all creativity out of all activities and turn them into a series of routinised kinds of procedures that are imposed by some external force. So that's the reason why it is dehumanising. Humanity is essentially creative and if you develop these systems that are constraining and controlling people they can't be creative, they can't be human. The idea is to turn humans into human robots. The next logical step is to replace human robots with mechanical robots. And I think we will see McDonaldised systems where it is economically feasible and technologically possible to replace human robots with non-human robots. I'd like to see a society in which people are freed to be creative, rather than having their creativity constrained or eliminated.

To what extent do you think McDonald's threats of lawsuits and censorship are an attempt to control their public image?

Well, I think they are certainly not the first or alone in trying to control the public image that they have, and of course their public image has been very important to them. I suppose it could be related to the control idea, you are accustomed to controlling everything else so why not try to control that public image.

How important is McDonald's image?

Well, the fact is of course that they are producing what everybody else produces—there is very little to distinguish the McDonald's hamburger from anybody else's hamburger, except maybe the special sauce or something like that. Basically they have to manufacture a sense of difference and a lot of that manufacture has to do with the fun and the colours, the clowns and the toys, and the squeaky clean image.

How much duplicity do you think there is going on here in terms of the image McDonald's presents?

I think there is a duplicitousness about McDonald's in the sense that it wants to portray an image of children and happy employees and one big joyous happy family and everyone having a good time. I think that American corporations in various ways try to create a duplicitous image, a false image. I mean that's what, in a sense, successful capitalism is about it's "WE ARE THE WORLD" and a number of major companies have tried to do essentially the same thing.

5 *You say very rightly that it's not just McDonald's—but why do you think that you, and Helen and Dave, and other people keep choosing McDonald's as the one to pick on?*

They are the icon and McDonald's is chosen by critics because it stands for a variety of things. I mean, from my point of view, it stands for efficiency and predictability. For other people it stands for America and America's influence throughout the world, so it gets picked up as a positive model. Although all of these things are virtues, the problem is that they are taken to such extraordinary lengths by McDonald's that they end up producing all kinds of irrational consequences so that the irrationalities outweigh the rationalities.

Do you go as far as to say that McDonald's represents capitalism?

Well it's a funny kind of capitalism that McDonald's represents because after all capitalism—American capitalism—for generations was the symbol of the huge smoke-stack industry, steel and automobiles . . . but it is not the automobile industry that represents America around the world now it is McDonald's and Disney and Coca Cola.

Do you think going into McDonald's, particularly in other countries, is more like entering the Western Dream than just buying a product?

It's not just that you are buying a product—you are buying into a system. In the 1940s there was a big flap in France over what was called a Coca Colonisation. The French were very upset about the coming of Coca Cola to France. They felt it threatened the French wine industry, it threatened the French way of life. But that was just the influx of an American product—what we have here is the influx of an American way of life, which is to trivialise eating, to make it something that is fast, make it something that's to get done and over with.

But it's striking to me that the last time I was in Paris the Parisians appeared to have embraced this kind of fast food phenomenon. You have developments of fast food croissanteries where this model French way of life—the croissanterie—has been reduced to fast food. French bread is more and more treated on a fast basis rather than lots of local bakeries baking their own distinctive kind, so if the French succumb to this in the realm of food then it strikes me that there is little that is safe from the expansion of this process.

The significance here is not buying the big Mac, it's buying the system, buying the whole package and being part of America, that's the key.

Do you think this process is ever going to be reversed?

Well the caged imagery suggests that there is an inevitability to it. Clearly, all the trends are in the direction of the greater spread of McDonald's or greater spread of the process of McDonaldisation. And there is certainly plenty of room for it to expand into other cultures, and there are still many cultures which are completely or relatively completely unaffected.

But there are also always counter-reactions, there are also always all sorts of things that are coming up from the people that represent innovations and creations. I mean you are not going to get innovations and creations from McDonaldised systems. Those innovations and creations—those non-McDonaldised ways of doing things—are going to well up from the people. But what makes me most pessimistic is that anything that's any good, anything not successful, some entrepreneur or organisation is going to come along and make great to rationalise it, make great to McDonaldise it, trivialise it, they are going to turn it into a system—a cash counter—and generate money. There is nothing that seems to be immune to this process, no aspect of life that seems to be immune to it. It's difficult to think of things that can avoid the process.

Does it mean that it is appealing to some fundamental call of human nature?

Well, sociologists don't believe in human nature. You never say human nature to a sociologist because if it was human nature that really mattered, then sociologists would be out of business. I think that there are a variety of things that people need at some level, like some degree of efficiency in their lives and some degree of predictability. What McDonald's has done is pick up on those and transform them into a system. I don't think people need the level of efficiency that McDonald's provides for them or want that level of efficiency . . . it's not something that is innate.

Another sort of pessimistic aspect to this is that you have children born into this McDonaldised world, you have people being trained, being lured into the system by the commercials and the toys and the clowns and the bright lights. They are trained that this is the way you eat, this is the way a hamburger should taste, this is how a French fry should taste, salty-sweet. These are the standards and so you if try to say to people of this generation "well look, this is not really how a hamburger should be, here is a home cooked hamburger" they will likely turn their nose up and say "well, that doesn't taste like . . . "

There are really, it seems to me, only two groups that historically have been critics of the process of McDonaldisation. They are the people who were born before the process and knew a different way of life and then were stunned by the development of McDonaldisation, or people from non-McDonaldised cultures who see this influx and are able to react. But once that generation that was born before McDonaldisation dies off, and once all these other cultures are McDonaldised, well where is the opposition going to come from . . . from children who have been trained by McDonald's or gone to McDonald's schools and done everything that they had to do from one McDONALD'S SYSTEM AFTER ANOTHER?

Obviously McDonalds and related corporations are spending billions of dollars to socialise children into this system so that this becomes their standard.

One of the basic premises of McDonald's is to focus on quantity, low price (or what appears to be low price) and large quantities of things and inevitably what suffers when you emphasise quantity is quality so they are serving what is at best mediocre food.

10 *But why do you think that Dave and Helen are able to criticise the process?*

You see I don't think that England is as McDonaldised as the U.S.A. In Europe you have some degree of McDonaldisation but nothing to the degree that this process has proceeded in the U.S. So there would be examples of people in other cultures who, because of the nature of that culture and the large number of non-McDonaldised aspects of that culture, would be sensitised to it. I think fewer and fewer Americans are sensitised to it, question it. I mean they don't know anything else, you are going to go and eat you go to fast food restaurant and eat. You mentioned the French cuisine and I think one of the trends in the future of McDonaldisation is the McDonaldisation of higher-up restaurants, of haute cuisine. You already see sort of middle range restaurants and restaurant chains in the U.S. now. Red Lobster or a chain like that is selling fairly upscale food but you now see signs that some elegant restaurants are trying to move in the direction of developing chains. So the challenge is going to be how do you McDonaldise a system by retaining quality because all McDonaldised systems have sacrificed quality. It's the process that's the problem here.

Do you think that the issue should be broadened to include more than just the specific case of McDonald's?

Yeah, see for me it's that they've set in motion something which is so much bigger than they are, that this process is so much broader than what they are. In fact, McDonald's could disappear tomorrow, or could go out of business tomorrow and this process would continue on. You might have to give it a different name but the process would continue, I mean the process has a history long before McDonald's. In Weber's theory of rationalisation and in Weber's model was the bureaucracy, the German bureaucracy, and we're living in an extension, a massive extension of that process with a new model in the fast food restaurant. The fast food restaurant, or McDonald's could disappear but that process will be transformed into some new form.

Is there a 1984/Brave New World kind of element to this?

The Brave New World/1984 image is one of centralised control. What McDonaldisation means for me is kinds of microsystems of control or whole systems of microsystems of control. Actually Michel Foucault, the French post-structural theorist, talked about these micropolitics of control, micromechanisms of control and I think that what's being set in place here is not an iron cage, but innumerable mini iron cages and there are so many of them and they're so widely spaced throughout society that the iron cages envisioned here is one where you simply have your choice of which cage to enter but there's nothing but cages to go to.

What effects does a McDonaldised society have its people?

I think that McDonald's has a profound effect on the way people do a lot of things I mean it leads people to want everything fast, to have, you know, a limited attention span so that kind of thing spills over onto, let's say, television viewing or newspaper reading, and so you have a short attention span, you want everything fast, so you don't have patience to read the *New York Times* and so you read McPaper, you read *USA Today.* You don't have patience to watch a lengthy newscast on a particular issue so you watch CNN News and their little news McNugget kinds of things so it creates a kind of mindset which seeks the same kind of thing in one setting after another. I see it in education where you have, in a sense, a generation of students who've been raised in a McDonaldised society, they want things fast, they want idealic nuggets from Professors, they don't want sort of slow build up of ideas, you gotta keep them amused, you gotta come in with the Ronald McDonald costume and quip a series of brilliant theoretical points or else they're going to turn you off. It's quite amazing what they've done, what they've undertaken here.

What do you think of what Helen and Dave are doing?

I think that clearly, from very small beginnings, they've created a worldwide movement here, worldwide attention, and have laid the basis for a real potential threat to McDonald's and the process of McDonaldisation. We talked about this earlier, the possibility of bringing together these disparate groups and I think that McDonald's has got to devote, I mean if they want to prevent this from occurring, they've got to devote some attention to how to diffuse and strategically keep apart these oppositional forces that seem likely to come together, to focus on it as a negative force. I mean if there really comes to be a time where McDonald's is viewed as this evil force in the world by a significant number of people, then that becomes a real threat to the organisation. But again I want to point out that even if McDonald's disappeared tomorrow, even if they closed their doors because of the McLibel trial the process would continue apace.

15 *Do you eat at McDonald's?*

Only when I'm in the iron cage and it's the only alternative. I mean, you do find yourself in the United States in a situation especially when you're on the highways now where there is no place to go other than a fast food restaurant. One of the big developments on American highways is that virtually all of the rest stops have been taken over by the fast food chains and so if you're driving on the highway and you wanna eat you're gonna eat in a fast food restaurant.

There is no alternative unless you get off the highway and then all of the restaurants that are immediately off the highway are going to be fast food restaurants too, so you've got to search quite a bit to avoid eating in a fast food restaurant. So occasionally you just find yourself now in the States where that's your only alternative and of course again that's the ultimate iron cage. I mean, when the whole society's like that, where you just cannot find any kind of alternative, you just throw up your hands and say "ok, I'm gonna eat this way, I'm gonna do things this way".

Reflect & Write

- ❑ How does George Ritzer introduce quite an innovative angle into the debate over McDonald's with his opening points on "dehumanizing" robot conditions? Does he make this argument successfully?
- ❑ Ritzer's focus on McDonald's "public image" takes into account the toys, the Website, and the commercials. What do you learn about the power of visual rhetoric from this interview?
- ❑ What argument is Ritzer making about historical shifts? How different is the "automobile industry that represent[ed] America around the world" compared to "McDonald's and Disney and Coca Cola"? What's at stake in terms of cultural values?
- ❑ When Ritzer brings in foundation texts—such as Weber's model and Foucault—what happens to the depth of his argument? How do such references transform his *ethos* as a writer?
- ❑ How does Ritzer make use of the cage image in this piece? How does he apply his focus on McDonald's to the news and society more broadly? Do you find these applications effective?
- ❑ **Write.** Compose your assessment of the conclusion. What other questions would you like to ask this author?

■ *In this humorous and narrative-based essay,* **Paul Feine** *discusses the power and fearsome aspects of the McDonald's empire but concludes that Americans both at home and abroad just cannot live without the Golden Arches. Feine is Director of Innovation for the Institute of Humane Studies at George Mason University. He published this piece in aworldconnected.org, a project housed in that institute, committed to promoting conversations about how to achieve a free, peaceful, and prosperous world. Feine originally posted this article on his blog, A World Connected, and it has since been republished in a number of readers and anthologies.*

McBastards: McDonald's and Globalization

Paul Feine

On a recent trip to Paris with my family, I was standing inside a McDonald's restaurant gazing out at the street as my wife ordered Le Happy Meal for our two-year old. My son at the time was happily tugging away at my hair from his perch in his baby backpack (one of the most significant technological innovations in recent history, to my mind).

We hadn't traveled to Paris with the intention of eating at McDonald's, but we were looking for a quick fix for our hungry little boy, and McDonald's represented a cheap alternative to the more traditional cafés. Typical Paris cafés are not only far more expensive, but as previous experience made clear, they tend to be filled with Parisians who are less than charmed by the presence of toddlers.

As I pondered the differing cultural attitudes toward children and stared out onto the busy Paris street, my gaze rested on an elderly French man, whom I instantly categorized as quintessentially French, complete with black beret, long black trench coat, and a cane. The man hobbled by the entrance to McDonald's, stopped, turned to look inside, spat loudly, and sneered "bastards," or its rough equivalent in French.

I sipped my coffee, which was very good (Café Jacques Vabre, I learned later), while our son used his pommes frites as a ketchup delivery device and my wife drank from bottle Evian. We both chuckled as I shared with her image of the authentic anti-McDonald's activist I had just witnessed.

McWhipping Boy

5 As the symbol for cultural imperialism and multinational corporate greed, McDonald's takes a lot of heat. McSpotlight, the anti-McDonald's website, for instance, boasts over one million hits per month. Critics demonize McDonald's for its unabashed pursuit of profits, its disregard for nutritional value and the environment, and the way it panders to children.

Most recently, McDonald's has been condemned for systematically seeking to addict naïve youngsters to its fatty fare, just like its evil older brothers in the cigarette business. In fact, crusading public interest lawyer John Banzhaf (whose van sports a license plate with a shortened version of "sue the bastards") is suing McDonald's in an attempt to hold them responsible for fast food addicts' health problems.

Indeed, though this multinational giant controls 43% of the US fast food market, McDonald's avarice seems to have no bounds. As Nick Gillespie of *Reason* magazine points out, "McDonald's is so desperate for customers that it's held prices essentially constant over the past two decades, while boosting portion sizes (burgers, fries, and drinks are all bigger than they used to be), expanding its menu, and building elaborate play structures for kids while simultaneously throwing increasingly sophisticated toys at them."

As anyone with small children knows, safe and secure McDonald's Playlands can be a dream come true, especially when you're stuck inside on a rainy day with kids who desperately need to burn some energy. Tiny plastic toys are received with as much delight as any large plastic toy they might have received last Christmas and, it must be emphasized, they're free.

Maybe, just maybe, McDonald's, in its unwavering pursuit of profits, has figured out the secret to succeeding in business—you've got to give the people what they want.

FIGURE 15.22. This McDonald's locates itself inside a mall, inviting children to sit on the bench next to Ronald.

FIGURE 15.23. This photo reveals the consistent "McCulture" of each store, in terms of the trademark colors and golden arches.

McCulture?

10 Okay, maybe McDonald's is fine for the US. Perhaps we're too value conscious, gluttonous, and superficial to care that our landscapes are littered with gleaming arches that have already polluted our bodies and our minds. But surely the same cannot be said for other societies around the world. Isn't it true that places that still have truly authentic dining experiences should be protected from the barbaric McHordes that are clamoring at their gates?

Golden Arches East, a recent book edited by James Watson, seeks to gain a better grasp on how McDonald's is affecting Asian culture. The results of this inquiry are in many ways surprising. For instance, one essay tells the story of an unintended and unanticipated consequence of McDonald's invasion of Hong Kong—the rest rooms in the city became cleaner.

Before the first McDonald's opened up in the mid-1970s, restaurant restrooms in Hong Kong were notoriously dirty. Over time, the cleanliness standards of McDonald's were replicated by other restaurants eager to out-compete the increasingly popular restaurant.

In Korea, McDonald's established the practice of lining up in an orderly fashion to order food—the traditional custom, it seems, was to mob the counter.

When the first McDonald's was opened in Moscow, it was necessary for an employee to stand outside the McDonald's with a blow horn in order to explain to those in the queue that the smiling employees were not laughing at them but, rather, were pleased to serve them.

15 Moreover, and in contradistinction to the widespread assumption that McDonald's is having an implacably homogenizing effect on global culture, *Golden Arches East* is filled with examples of the pains McDonald's takes to appeal to the unique local tastes and customs of people around the world. My own experience with the decidedly leisurely attitude of McDonald's employees in southern Spain further attests to McDonald's ability to adapt to the local culture.

Is It True That No Two Countries with McDonald's Have Ever Gone to War?

Long before I'd enjoyed the Andalucian version of McDonald's, I traveled to Belgrade, in what was then Yugoslavia, and I must admit that I was ecstatic to see a sign for a recently opened McDonald's. I'd just spent a couple of months consuming nothing but souvlaki, salad, and Ouzo in Greece, and the very thought of Quarter-Pounder and a Coke made my mouth water.

My traveling buddy and I proceeded to wait in line for more than an hour and, as I stood happily munching on a french fry that brought back sweet memories of childhood Sunday-after-church treats, I looked across a sea of dark haired Yugoslavians into the eyes of two beautiful, blonde, obviously American women (actually it turned out they were Canadian nurses, but who am I to complain?). Absurdly, we waved to each other and fought through the crowd to greet one other like dear old friends. The memory of that day in Belgrade still brings a smile to my face.

Although you often hear people say it, it's not quite true that no two countries with McDonald's have ever gone to war—both the US and Serbia, for example, had McDonald's during the conflict between the two nations. But even if McDonald's isn't a kind of multinational for-profit god of peace, McDonald's does provides cheap food, decent coffee, and free entertainment for kids, not to mention a salad-in-a-cup for health-conscious parents.

Around the world, this increasingly popular symbol (like it or not) of America is encouraging healthy competition—competition that, in many cases, is leading to improved sanitation standards and civility. And sometimes, just sometimes, McDonald's even brings people together and creates a few smiles . . . just like its commercials say it does.

20 The bastards.

Reflect & Write

- ❑ Why might Paul Feine begin his article with a first person narrative? How does this writing strategy help engage his audience and construct his own persona?
- ❑ What role do visual stereotypes play in this piece? Notice the description of the French man, the characterization of cigarette companies, and even the playland imagery used to depict McDonald's. How do you respond as a reader?
- ❑ What do you learn about the research Feine conducted to write this article? What new knowledge do you have about McDonald's in Asia based on his writing here?
- ❑ Notice the turn in the argument. What do you make of the sudden shift in his thesis? Do you agree with his view or not?
- ❑ **Write.** Write your own travel narrative about encountering McDonald's—either in your community or on recent trips away from home. Be sure to include subtitles that indicate your argument much as Paul Feine did for his piece. You might include images and turn this into a blog post.

■ *A regular writer for Time.com,* **Randy James** *specializes in stories that often focus on popular culture. His recent pieces have included the top ten controversial cartoons (*Aladdin *ranked first), Tiger Woods's alleged mistress, the adultery scandal on the Appalachian Trail, Serena Williams's anger issues, and White House party crashers. James also writes quite serious pieces, such as his coverage of the elections in Iraq, Arab extremist groups in Somalia, and the cultural history of Hanukkah.*

A Brief History of McDonald's Abroad

Randy James

Since its founding in 1948, McDonald's has grown from a family burger stand to a global fast-food behemoth, with more than 30,000 locations in 118 countries. Those nations, however, are about to have their ranks reduced by one: the Golden Arches are pulling up stakes in

Iceland this week, and Icelanders pining for a Big Mac and large fries will soon be going hungry. The global chain says it is shuttering its three stores in the capital, Reykjavik, citing the collapse of the local economy and the high cost of imports. The closures aren't a first for the company: McDonald's has pulled out of Bolivia, Jamaica and a handful of other countries due to poor sales. But the setback is decidedly unusual for the world's largest fast-food chain. **(See the 10 worst fast food meals.)**

Dick and Mac McDonald opened their eponymous burger stand in 1948 in San Bernardino, Calif. Under the guidance of Ray Kroc, a onetime milkshake-mixer salesman wowed by the restaurant's success, McDonald's franchises grew swiftly: by the end of the 1960s, there were more than 1,000 across the U.S. The first international franchise opened in 1967 in British Columbia, and was followed by another in Costa Rica later that year. From there, the chain spread steadily: over a six-month period in 1971, Golden Arches popped up on three new continents, as stores launched in Japan, Holland and a suburb of Sydney. A Brazilian McDonald's opened in 1979, bringing Ronald McDonald to South America for the first time. McDonald's reached its sixth (and, barring a sub-Arctic drive-thru, final) continent in 1992, with the opening of a restaurant in Casablanca, Morocco. Four years later, the company heralded the expansion into its 100th nation, Belarus, and claimed to be opening a new restaurant somewhere in the world every three hours. **(See the top 10 bad beverage ideas.)**

By the end of 2008, McDonald's had grown to 31,967 locations in 118 countries. Of those, only about 14,000, or 45%, were in the U.S. With 58 million daily customers worldwide, McDonald's are now so ubiquitous around the globe that *The Economist* publishes a global ranking of currencies' purchasing power based on the prices charged at the local Mickey D's, dubbed the Big Mac Index. That's not to say that every nation carries the same menu items: choices vary widely depending on location. The biggest seller in France after the Big Mac is a mustard-topped burger called Le Royal Deluxe. Some Asian locations serve fried shrimp in a Big Mac roll, while McDonald's in India don't serve beef at all, relying instead on burgers made from veggies, rice and beans. Brazilian McDonald's offer baked banana pies for dessert. **(Read "Not Everyone Is Lovin' Japan's New McDonald's Mascot.")**

Not everyone in the world has been happy to greet Ronald McDonald when he moves to town. Many see the corporate juggernaut as a symbol of American economic and cultural chauvinism, and European nations in particular have viewed American-style fast food as an insult to their cherished national cuisines. Bermuda banned all fast-food restaurants to squelch a McDonald's planned for the island. A French farmer, Jose Bove, became something of a national hero in 1999 after he and a band of activists destroyed a McDonald's under construction to protest globalization and "bad food." The next year, a bomb detonated in a French McDonald's, killing a 27-year-old employee. No one claimed responsibility. **(Read "Supersizing Europe: The McDonald's Stimulus Plan.")**

5 But regardless of whether you like their food or their policies, McDonald's is still widely seen as one of the true vanguards of peaceful globalization. After 14 years of discussions with the Kremlin, the Soviet Union's first McDonald's opened in Moscow in

FIGURE 15.24. An employee of McDonald's serves a meal in Seoul, South Korea. Notice all the visual rhetoric persuading the customer which product to buy through over-bombardment of images.

1990—a move credited with helping thaw Cold War tensions. Columnist and author Thomas Friedman has asserted that nations with McDonald's locations do not go to war with each other—the so-called Golden Arches Theory of Conflict Prevention—although that thesis notably collapsed in the case of the 2008 war between Russia and Georgia. There are other signs that overseas resentment of the burger giant has softened. A McDonald's is slated to open in November in a shopping area beneath one of France's most treasured cultural meccas—the Louvre—but the news has hardly caused a stir in the City of Light. Bank employee Laurent Mortin told the *New York Times* he didn't have a problem with the American import: "It's more of a real lunch than eating a sandwich in the street, and it doesn't take as much time as sitting in a restaurant."

Reflect & Write

- ❑ While the title of this piece suggests that it is only a "history," the article actually moves to a strong and powerful argument in the closing paragraphs. What is the thesis of the piece? What strategies of argumentation from Chapter 2 does James use to convince the reader? What can you learn about writing choices from this example of a "deferred thesis"?
- ❑ Along with a deferred argument, the article also switches in tone. Pick out words that reveal the writer's rhetorical stance in this seemingly objective report.
- ❑ How does the writer incorporate research effectively? Discuss both the obvious hyperlinks (posted in bold and parenthesis and available through the *Envision* Website) as well as the research sources named in the piece. Find four examples of field research (interviews with specific people), one example of a newspaper secondary source, one example of a magazine secondary source providing foundational background evidence, and one example of a scholarly authority (hint: there is an interview with that authority included elsewhere in Chapter 15). www.pearsonhighered.com/envision/579
- ❑ **Write.** This article provides an excellent overview of how McDonald's has expanded internationally, reaching out across cultures. Taking the research and information from this article, transform it into a dialogue of sources (see Chapter 5 for directions). Focus on the issue of adaptation, beginning with the imagined words of Dick and Mac McDonald to the words of people protesting or celebrating how the company changes its offerings for Asian, Indian, French, American audiences. Rewrite the material from this article by "giving voice" to each of the multiple perspectives conveyed in this piece. Then, conclude with your own opinion as moderator on the Golden Arches behemoth: is it a positive or negative force of globalization across cultures?

■ **Stephanie Clifford** *writes for the the* New York Times *as a reporter focusing on advertising, media, and marketing trends. Writing on the cutting edge, her recent articles have included pieces on newspapers, Web revenues, Google ad strategies, and "Billboards that Look Back." She has also worked as a writer and reporter for* Inc. *magazine,* Business 2.0 *in San Francisco,* Time, Life, *and* Real Simple. *A graduate of Harvard, Clifford served as executive editor of the* Harvard Crimson *before launching her career as a writer.*

Burnishing a Brand by Selecting an 'Idol'

Stephanie Clifford

While companies focus most of their marketing on persuading people to buy their products, internal marketing can also help their brands. These days, many customers care about how companies treat employees.

That's the thought behind an "American Idol"-style competition called Voice of McDonald's. Now in its third iteration, the competition gives McDonald's employees from around the world a chance to sing at a giant trade conference—complete with vocal coaching and judging from stars like Ne-Yo—and win a $25,000 top prize.

"We know that customer perceptions about your employment brand do have some impact in terms of people's decisions to frequent certain restaurants or retail establishments," said Rich Floersch, chief human resources officer for McDonald's.

Entrants submit audition videos. Professionals from the music industry select 30 semifinalists, and the public is encouraged to vote on which 12 singers should make the finals.

"We wanted to be able to really leverage this concept that McDonald's is known for, which is opportunity," Mr. Floersch said. "Our employees can become entrepreneurs and end up owning stores, or come up through the ranks in the company." Twenty of the 50 top executives, including the chief executive, James Skinner, began as restaurant workers, he said.

Each Voice of McDonald's finalist wins a trip, with a guest, to the McDonald's Worldwide Convention in Orlando, Fla., in April. It's a giant trade show and networking event, with 15,000 franchisees, employees and vendors who pay their own way to rub elbows.

The convention has 800,000 square feet of exhibit space, where the Ukrainians can check out what's new on the Brazilian menu, and the Japanese can show off their cellphone-ordering technology to the franchisee from Liechtenstein.

"It's all geared to, how do you run better restaurants, how do you contemporize your brand or your operating system, what's new about the new menu items," Mr. Floersch said.

The Voice competitors, once in Orlando, get full "Idol"-like training and styling, including hair and makeup, wardrobe, choreography and vocal coaching. Their final performances are before those 15,000 attendees, backed by a 50-piece orchestra. Judges include people in the music industry, and usually a celebrity (Ne-Yo participated two years ago).

This year, there were 10,500 entries—China had the most, followed by Japan—which vocal coaches narrowed to 30 semifinalists. The semifinalists had to pick from among a list of Sony Music songs that McDonald's had licensed to use, leading to employees like Weijie Wu from China, Jesus Miguel Molinares Espinoza from Peru and Franz Carl Guerrero from Canada all letting lose with versions of "Stand By Me" with a variety of accents.

Using Facebook, Twitter, YouTube and international social-media sites like Russia's VKontakte, McDonald's asked the public to vote. There were 685,000 votes this year, versus the 46,000 from the last competition two years ago.

This year, only two Americans made it to the 12-person final—and they were both from towns about a half-hour's drive from each other in Michigan.

Fatima Poggi, a 17-year-old senior at Pinckney Community High School in Pinckney, Mich., had been working part time at McDonald's for a year and a half, handling the front counter and drive-through window. Ms. Poggi moved to the United States from Peru at age 10, and didn't speak English. Now, in addition to the McDonald's job and school, she performs lead roles in community theater musicals like "Aida" and "Aladdin," and performs in events and contests around the country.

FIGURE 15.25. Eddie Davenport and Fatima Poggi were among 12 finalists in the Voice of McDonald's contest. The photo shows the way the company is trying to create an "American Idol"-like environment.

"The owner found out I was singing around the area," Ms. Poggi said, "and he talked to me about the competition that they were going to be having."

15 For Ms. Poggi's semifinal song, she chose "Alone" by Heart. Her homemade video is dramatic, showing Ms. Poggi, in knee-high leather boots, strutting on a train track, interspersed with scenes of her emoting on a dock.

Ms. Poggi is the youngest finalist ever in the competition, and the oldest ever, 50-year-old Eddie Davenport, is from Stockbridge, Mich., just west of Pinckney.

Mr. Davenport moved to Michigan from North Carolina several years ago. After spending some time as a youth minister, he got a job at McDonald's as a secondary maintenance man at two area restaurants. He works 24 hours a week, doing jobs like filtering the frying oil and washing windows. Mr. Davenport has retinitis pigmentosa, a degenerative eye disease. "Because of the vision, I couldn't see how to do the registers and things like that. Mopping the floor is pretty easy," Mr. Davenport said.

His semifinal submission is simple: showing him with a microphone, in front of a wall, singing Babyface's "When Can I See You Again."

Last week, Mr. Davenport arrived at work at 4:45 a.m. as usual, and was rearranging some stock items when he was called out front. He found his wife, a video crew, and a McDonald's representative, who told him he had made the finals.

20 He was thrilled, especially since he thought he was running out of time—Voice of McDonald's happens only every two years, and he may not be able to see, or work at McDonald's, long enough for the next event.

"Honestly, I felt like this is my last shot, because the deterioration of my vision for the last year has been so severe that if it continues the way that it has been going, I don't really feel that I would be able to work here actively two years from now to try again," he said.

Mr. Floersch, who will be in the audience at the April competition, said it was an important part of positioning McDonald's as a good employer, especially since it needed 1.6 million workers worldwide. "We want to make sure that we have an employment brand that is compelling, that draws people to the organization," he said.

Reflect & Write

- ❑ How does the "internal marketing" campaign of "Voice of McDonald's" use *pathos* to change the corporate persona of the company? What is the argument about the *ethos* of the company worldwide?
- ❑ Examine the paragraph describing the McDonald's Worldwide Convention in Orlando, Florida. How is this event a miniature version of globalization? How does Clifford use specific in using examples to give the reader a visual of what happens at the convention?
- ❑ Consider the full "Idol"-like training and styling described in the article. How is the corporation using *kairos* in order to ride the cultural wave of popularity for the show "American Idol" and use this to bring people together under a revamped image of McDonald's as sponsor? How is this rhetorical strategy different from or similar to McDonald's other community outreach efforts, such as scholarships and charity work through the Ronald McDonald House?
- ❑ Why might the article turn to the story of Mr. Davenport in the second half? What is the effect on you as a reader of this organizational strategy?
- ❑ **Write.** Given that McDonald's uses social media like Facebook, YouTube, Twitter, and international social-media sites for the "Voice of McDonald's" competition, write up a entry to post on one of these sites, describing how your view of McDonald's has changed by reading this article. You can write a song to post on YouTube, post a Facebook entry, or write a concise and compelling Twitter feed that conveys your argument about McDonald's.

PERSPECTIVES ON THE ISSUE

1. What type of writing or persuasion do you find most compelling? Mark Rice-Oxley's researched article? The competing *Daily Targum* op-eds? The interview with George Ritzer? The blog position piece by Paul Feine? How do the visual and written texts both contribute positions on the issue of McDonald's in the world theater?
2. How do specific texts use strategies of visual persuasion, whether through embedding images as evidence in the text or through evoking visual aspects of culture? When you are done discussing each text, pick two of the articles that seem most rich to you and write a rhetorical analysis comparing them.
3. Compose an opinion essay or blog in response to one of the conversations about McDonald's you have encountered here. Send your short article to the campus newspaper or post it on a blog site.
4. Compare the argumentative strategies used by Feine, James, and Clifford. How do two of them employ overt thesis statements near the beginning of their pieces while one uses a "deferred thesis" near the end? Which writing strategy works best in your opinion? Now, compare the tone of each one. How do the choices of slang, statistical evidence, narrative, and visual rhetoric work to convey the argument and persona of each piece? Taking as your subject the persona of McDonald's in your own town, write up an article about it, making an argument about the company's persona and presence, using the writing strategies of the article you like best.

FROM READING TO RESEARCH

1. Conduct a Google search to locate more images of McDonald's abroad in order to create a research-based photo essay. You might want to include images of protests against McDonaldization such as in Figure 15.2, depictions of deforestation, or images of families enjoying time together in the restaurant. Or, you could use cartoons such as the one in Figure 15.1. Your selection of images will necessarily shape your group's argument on the issue. Together with your team members, organize these images into a photo essay to convey your argument about McDonald's abroad. You might record quotes from the articles above and use them as audio evidence or research sources in your photo essay.
2. Use your research skills from Chapters 5 and 6 to locate articles on the debate over EuroDisney. How, according to your research, does seemingly innocuous visual culture in the form of cartoons, magic castles, family rides, and popcorn potentially threaten national languages and traditions? Applying your skills in visual production from Chapter 8, design an op-ad to convey your research-based argument about Disney's influence internationally.
3. What other corporations use "internal marketing" strategies such as the "Voice of McDonald's" contest sponsored by McDonald's? Research this issue by investigating the major coporations depicted in Figure 15.2 of this chapter (the logos company names surrounding the earth): you might research Coca-Cola, ExxonMobil, Microsoft, Marlboro, or even a news network such as CNN. Be sure to find primary and secondary source evidence to help you develop a research-based argument about this issue. Convert your findings into a visual argument and share your work with the class.

Visit www.pearsonhighered.com/envision for expanded assignment guidelines and student projects.
Visit www.mycomplab.com for additional general writing and research resources.

Works Cited

CHAPTER 1

Aristotle. "Rhetoric." *The History and Theory of Rhetoric.* By James A. Herrick. Boston: Allyn & Bacon, 1998. Print.

Diamond, Matthew. "No Laughing Matter: Post-September 11 Political Cartoons in Arab/Muslim Newspapers." *Political Communication* 19 (2002): 251–72. Print.

Holkins, Jerry. "The Hipness Threshold." *Penny-Arcade.* Penny Arcade Blog, 12 Mar. 2004. Web. 22 June 2006.

Marchetto, Marisa Acocella. *Cancer Vixen: A True Story.* New York: Knopf, 2006. Print.

Marlette, Doug. "I Was a Tool of Satan." *Columbia Journalism Review* (Nov./Dec. 2003): 52. Web. 22 June 2006.

McCloud, Scott. *Understanding Comics.* New York: HarperPerennial, 1993. Print.

Villanueva, Victor Jr. *Bootstraps: From an American Academic of Color.* Urbana, IL: National Council of Teachers of English, 1993. Print.

CHAPTER 2

Bowen, Laurence, and Jill Schmid. "Minority Presence and Portrayal in Mainstream Magazine Advertising: An Update." *Journalism and Mass Communications Quarterly* 74.1 (2004): 134–46. Print.

Stevenson, Seth. "You and Your Shadow." *Slate.com.* Slate, 4 Mar. 2004. Web. 7 June 2006.

Twitchell, James B. *Adcult USA.* New York: Columbia UP, 1996. Print.

——. "Listerine: Gerard Lambert and Selling the Need." *Twenty Ads That Shook the World.* New York: Three Rivers Press, 2000. 60–69. Print.

CHAPTER 3

Booth, Wayne. *The Rhetoric of Fiction.* Chicago: University of Chicago Press, 1961. Print.

Curtis, James. "Dorothea Lange, Migrant Mother, and the Culture of the Great Depression." *Winterthur Portfolio: A Journal of American Material Culture* 21 (Spring 1986) 1–20. Print.

Dunn, Geoffrey. "Photographic License." *San Louis Obispo Times.* San Luis Obispo (CA) Times, 17 Jan. 2002. Web. 11 June 2006.

Ephron, Nora. *Scribble, Scribble: Notes on the Media.* New York: Knopf, 1978. Print.

Frank, Robert. *The Americans.* New York: Grove Press, 1959. Print.

Gottesman, Jane. *Game Face.* NewYork: Random House, 2001. Print.

CHAPTER 5

Zimbardo, Philip G., Ann L. Weber, and Robert L. Johnson. *Psychology: Core Concepts.* 4th ed. Boston: Allyn & Bacon, 2003. Print.

CHAPTER 6

Blast, Joseph. "Gorgeous Propaganda, Frightening Truth." *Heartland Perspectives.* Heartland.org, June 2006. Web. 11 June 2006.

Lamott, Anne. *Bird by Bird: Some Instructions on Writing and Life.* New York: Anchor, 1995. Print.

Rasch, David. "How I Write Interview." *Stanford Writing Center.* Stanford University, 17 Nov. 2003. Web. 17 Nov. 2003.

Schulte, Bret. "Saying it in Cinema." *U.S. News and World Report.* U.S. News, 28 May 2006. Web. 20 April 2010.

CHAPTER 7

Chicago Manual of Style. 16th ed. Chicago: University of Chicago Press, 2010. Print.

American Psychological Association. *The Concise Rules of APA Style.* Washington, DC: American Psychological Assoc. 2009. Print.

Cone, Justin. "Building on the Past." JustinCone.com. n.d. Web. 27 June 2006.

Modern Language Association. *MLA Handbook for the Writers of Research Papers.* 7th ed. New York: Modern Language Association, 2010. Print.

American Psychological Association. *Publication Manual of the American Psychological Association.* 6th ed. Washington, DC: American Psychological Association. 2010. Print.

Council of Science Educators. *Scientific Style and Format: the CSE Manual for Authors, Editors and Publishers,* Seventh Edition. Reston, VA: Council of Science Educators in cooperation with the Rockefeller University Press, 2002. Print.

CHAPTER 8

Adbusters Culturejammer Headquarters: Journal of the Environment. Web. <http://www.adbusters.org>.

Agee, James. Foreword. *Let Us Now Praise Famous Men.* Boston: Houghton Mifflin, 1969. Print.

Allard, William Albert. "Solace at Surprise Creek." *National Geographic* (June 2006). Print.

Cicero. *De Inventione.* Trans. H. M. Hubbell. Cambridge, MA: Loeb Classical Library, 1949. Print.

Greenfield, Laura. *Girl Culture.* San Francisco, CA: Chronicle Books, 2002. Print.

Levy, Matthew. "A Rescue Worker's Chronicle." University of Maryland Baltimore County. November 2001. Web. 9 June 2010.

Ross, Carolyn, and Ardel Thomas. *Writing for Real: A Handbook for Writing in Community Service.* New York: Pearson Longman, 2003. Print.

CHAPTER 9

Burton, Gideon. *Silva Rhetoricae: The Forest of Rhetoric.* Humanities. Brigham Young University. Updated 26 February 2007. Web. 9 June 2010.

Ingleman, Kelly. "Delivery." *Rhetoric Resources at Tech.* Georgia Institute of Technology. Web. 20 October 2006.

CHAPTERS 10–15

For source citations for readings in Chs. 10–15, see the Credits on pp. 585–590.

Credits

Images

Page 1: Abhed Omar Qusini/Reuters. 2: © 2009 Nate Beeler, Washington Examiner, and PoliticalCartoons.com.
Figure 1.2: The Advertising Archives.
Figure 1.3: AP/Wide World Photos.
Figure 1.4: © Tribune Media Services, Inc. All Rights Reserved. Reprinted with permission.
Figure 1.8a, Figure 1.8b: Excerpted from Cancer Vixen. © 2006 MARISA ACOCELLA MARCHETTO. Cartoonist Marisa Acocella Marchetto tells the story of her triumph over breast cancer in her celebrated memoir Cancer Vixen (Knopf) www.marisamarchetto.com.
Figure 1.15: © 2009 Nate Beeler, Washington Examiner, and PoliticalCartoons.com.
Figure 2.1: Alyssa J. O'Brien, 2006
Figure 2.2: Courtesy of RUSK PROFESSIONAL HAIRCARE.
Figure 2.4: © Chevron Corporation and used with permission.
Figure 2.5: The Procter&Gamble Company. Used by permission.
Figure 2.6: Courtesy of Volkswagen of America, Inc.
Figure 2.7: The Advertising Archives.
Figure 2.8: General Motors Corp. Used with permission. GM Media Archives.
Figure 2.9: Courtesy of Ford Motor Company.
Figure 2.10: Alyssa J. O'Brien, 2006.
Figure 2.11: Image courtesy of The Advertising Archives.
Figure 2.12: Image Courtesy of The Advertising Archives.
Figure 2.13: Image Courtesy of The Advertising Archives.
Figure 3.1: AP/Wide World Photos.
Figure 3.2: Margaret Bourke-White/Time&Life Pictures/Getty Images.
Figure 3.3: Library of Congress.
Figure 3.4: Library of Congress.
Figure 3.5: Todd Heisler/Polaris Images
Figure 3.6: Bettmann/Corbis.
Figure 3.7: "Triathlon Start" Harvey's Lake, Pa., 1994. Photograph by Mark Cohen.
Figure 3.8: "By a Nose" Philadelphia, Pa. Norman Y. Lono, 1980.
Figure 3.9: "Girl on a Swing" Pitt Street, NYC, 1938. Photograph by Walter Rosenblum.
Figure 3.10: AP/Wide World Photos.
Figure 3.12: Courtesy of Deseret Morning News Archives.
Page 61: AP/Wide World Photos.
Figure 3.13: Abhed Omar Qusini/Reuters.
Figure 3.14: Courtesy Boston Herald.
Page 73: TM&Copyright © 20th Century Fox. All rights reserved/Courtesy Everett Collection.
Figure 4.1: Patrick Broderick/Modern Humorist.com.
Figure 4.2: Hoover Institution Archives Poster Collection.
Figure 4.3: Courtesy National Archives 513533.
Figure 4.4: Courtesy National Archives 516102.
Figure 4.5: Courtesy National Archives 514597.
Figure 4.7 top right: Library of Congress.
Figure 4.7 bottom right: The Art Archive/Musee des 2 Guerres Mondiales Paris/Dagli Orti.
Figure 4.7 bottom left: Image Courtesy of The Advertising Archives.
Figure 4.7 top left: Courtesy National Archives 513533.
Figure 4.8 top right: Library of Congress.
Figure 4.8 bottom right: The Art Archive/Musee des 2 Guerres Mondiales Paris/Dagli Orti.
Figure 4.8 bottom left: Image Courtesy of The Advertising Archives.
Figure 4.8 top left: Courtesy National Archives 513533.
Figure 4.9: Library of Congress.
Figure 4.10: Courtesy of Micah Ian Wright&AntiWar-Posters.com.
Figure 4.11: © 2003-WHITEHOUSE.ORG.
Figure 4.12: Courtesy of Steve Horn.
Figure 4.13: Courtesy of Micah Ian Wright&AntiWar-Posters.com.
Page 84: Office of Global Communications. http://www.psywarrior.com/afghanleaf08.html.
Page 85: Courtesy of National Archives 513533.
Figure 5.1: ArcticNet-NCE/Time&Life Pictures/Getty Images.
Figure 5.2: Cover text only from SCIENCE Vol. 311, No. 5768 (24 March 2006). Reprinted with permission from AAAS. Photo: Nevada Wier/Corbis.
Figure 5.3: Time&Life Pictures/Getty Images.
Figure 5.4: Steve Bronstein/The Image Bank/Getty Images.
Figure 5.5: Rocket Blitz from the Moon by Chesley Bonestell. Bonestell Space Art.
Figure 5.6: Time&Life Pictures/Getty Images.
Figure 5.9: Stem Cells, March 2006 cover © AlphaMed Press.
Figure 5.10: Courtesy of the Yale Scientific Magazine.
Figure 5.11: © Vincent Chen 2009.
Figure 6.1: Courtesy of Universal Studios Licensing LLLP.
Page 171: Warner Bros./Photofest.
Figure 6.3 top: TM&Copyright © 20th Century Fox. All rights reserved/Courtesy Everett Collection.
Figure 6.3 middle: TM&Copyright © 20th Century Fox. All rights reserved/Courtesy Everett Collection.
Figure 6.3 bottom: TM&Copyright © 20th Century Fox. All rights reserved/Courtesy
Everett Collection.
Figure 6.4: © Lions Gate/Courtesy Everett Collection.
Figure 6.5: © Paramount/Courtesy Everett Collection.
Figure 7.1: Building on the Past by Justin Cone.
Page 167: AP/Wide World Photos.
Figure 8.1: Courtesy of the author.
Page 172 left: Danjaq/Eon/UA/Keith Hamshere/The Kobal Collection.
172 right: Paramount/Icon/Andrew Cooper/The Kobal Collection.
Figure 8.6: Reproduced with the kind permissions of The Body Shop International, plc.
Figure 8.7: Courtesy www.adbusters.org
Figure 8.8: Courtesy of the author.
Figure 8.13: Courtesy of the author.
Figure 9.1: AP/Wide World Photos.
Page 193 left, right: AP/Wide World Photos.
Page 193 center: Paramount Classics/Photofest
Figure 9.2: Reuters/Stefan Wermouth/Landov.
Figure 9.3: AP/Wide World Photos.

Figure 9.4: Official White House Photo by Pete Souza.
Figure 9.17: Bettmann/Corbis.
Figure 9.18: Topham/The Image Works.
Figures 10.1 & 10.2: Roy Gumpel
Figure 10.3: author supplied
Figure 10.4: ©Magnolia Pictures/Courtesy Everett Collection
Figure 10.5: Laura Thai
Figure 10.6: Ping Yee, Singapore
Figure 10.7: Su-Lin Lee
235: AP/Wide World Photos
Figure 10.8: Courtesy of the Author
Figure 10.10: © 2008 Corn Refiners Association. Ryan Robinson Photography.
Figure 10.11: © Peter Menzel/from the book Hungry Planet, What the World Eats by Peter Menzel&Faith D'Aluisio/www.menzelphoto.com
Figure 10.12: © Peter Menzel/from the book Hungry Planet, What the World Eats by Peter Menzel&Faith D'Aluisio/www.menzelphoto.com
Figure 10.13: © Peter Menzel/from the book Hungry Planet, What the World Eats by Peter Menzel&Faith D'Aluisio/www.menzelphoto.com
Figure 10.14: © Peter Menzel/from the book Hungry Planet, What the World Eats by Peter Menzel&Faith D'Aluisio/www.menzelphoto.com
Figures 10.18 & 10.19: Reprinted from: AN INCONVENIENT TRUTH by Al Gore. Copyright © 2006 by Al Gore. Permission granted by Rodale, Inc. Emmaus, PA 18098.
265T: Courtesy of TerraChoice Inc.
265C: Courtesy of TerraChoice Inc.
265B: Courtesy of TerraChoice Inc.
266T: Courtesy of TerraChoice Inc.
266C: Courtesy of TerraChoice Inc.
266B: Courtesy of TerraChoice Inc.
Figure 11.1: John Eder/The Image Bank/Getty Images
Figure 11.2: cartoonbank
Figure 11.3: Courtesy of Randall Munroe. Reprinted with permission.xkcd.com
Figure 11.6: Courtesy of the author
Figure 11.7: Self Portrait; Pighed Stonecutter by Mark Stephen Meadows
Figure 11.8: Robbie Cooper, from Alter Ego: Avatars and their Creators, Chris Boot Ltd
Figure 11.9: Robbie Cooper, from Alter Ego: Avatars and their Creators, Chris Boot Ltd
Figure 11.10: Robbie Cooper, from Alter Ego: Avatars and their Creators, Chris Boot Ltd
Figure 11.14: AP/Wide World Photos
Figure 11.23: Quirk Books
Figure 12.1: WireImageStock/Masterfile Corporation
Figure 12.2: Brand X Pictures/Fotosearch
Figures 12.3 & 12.4: 2 images supplied by authors
Figure 12.7: Courtest National Eating Disorders Association
Figure 12.8: Advertising Archives
Figure 12.9: Kate Brooks/Polaris Images
Figure 12.10: Fernanda Calfat/Getty Images
Page 413: The New York Times
Figure 12.14: Arely D. Castillo/The News-Star
Figure 12.15: "The Veil," translated by Mattias Ripa & Blake Ferris, from PERSEPOLIS: THE STORY OF CHILDHOOD by Marjane Satrapi, translated by Mattias Ripa & Blake Ferris, copyright (c) 2003 by L'Association, Paris, France. Used by permission of Pantheon Books, a division of Random House, Inc.
Figure 12.16: "Rebellious Silence" by Shirin Neshat, 1994. B&W RC print and ink, 11x14 inches (photo taken by Cynthia Preston). Edition of 10+1AP. Copyright Shirin Neshat 1994. Courtesy Gladstone Gallery, New York (SN008).
Figures 12.17, 12.18, & 12.19 (3images): Chris Rainer
Figure 13.1: Time & Life Pictures/Getty Images
Figure 13.2: Vanni/Art Resource, NY Museo Nazionale Romano (Palazzo Massimo alle Terme), Rome, Italy
Figures 13.3 & 13.4: Courtesy Magnolia Pictures
Figure 13.5: James Casciari/Scripps Howard News Service
Figure 13.6: By permission of Gary Varvel and Creators Syndicate, Inc.
Figure 13.7: © 2009 Mike Keefe, The Denver Post, and PoliticalCartoons.com
Figures 13.8, 13.9, & 13.10 (3 images): Advertising Archives
Figure 13.11: Carlos Serrao/Beauty & Photo
Figure 13.12: Walter Iooss, Jr./Sports Illustrated
Figure 13.13: AP Images/Sports Illustrated
Figure 14.1: James Nachtwey
Figure 14.2: James Nachtwey
Figure 14.3: Courtesy of Authors
Figure 14.4: William Hoiles
Figure 14.5: Courtesy of Rich Addicks
Figure 14.6: Courtesy of Marc-Yves Regis I
Figure 14.7: Peggie Peattie/The San Diego Union-Tribune/ZUMA Press
Figure 14.10: Elaine Thompson/AP Images
Figure 14.11: Jenny Vorwaller
Figure 14.12: Daniel Okrent/AP
Figures 14.13 & 14.14 (2 images): James Nachtwey
p507: Charles Porter/ZUMA Press
p508: Charles Porter/ZUMA Press
Figure 14.15: Image taken by Al=dam Stacey.
Figure 14.16: This work is licensed under a Creative Commons License; Scoopt.com
Figures 14.17, 14.18, 14.19, & 14.20 (4 images): David Leeson/The Dallas Morning News
Figure 15.1: Courtesy asterix.co.nz
Figure 15.2: Courtesy Axel Feuerberg
Figure 15.3: Amy Koller
Figure 15.5: Alex Webb/Magnum Photos
Figures 15.6 & 15.7 (2 images): Alex Webb/Magnum Photos
Figure 15.8: Alex Webb/Magnum Photos
Figure 15.9: Justin Sullivan/Getty
Figure 15.10: Alex Webb/Magnum Photos
Figure 15.11: A. T. Willett
Figures 15.12 & 15.13 (2 images): James Nachtwey
Figure 15.14: James Nachtwey
Figure 15.15: iStock
Figure 15.16: Kevin Kallaugher
Figure 15.17: Jason Reed/Reuters/Landov
Figure 15.19: Laird J. Rawsthorne
Figure 15.20: Andrew Kitzmiller
Figure 15.21: Stephen Morton/Bloomberg News/Getty
Figure 15.22: Najlah Feanny/Corbis
Figure 15.23: Ramin Talaie/Corbis
Figure 15.24: Chung Sung-Jun/Getty
Figure 15.25: Adam Bird

Text

Aoki, Keith, James Boyle, Jennifer Jenkins. Reprinted from "Bound by Law" available online at http://www.law.duke.edu/cspd/comics/, by Keith Aoki, James Boyle and Jennifer Jenkins, copyright © 2006. Used by permission.

Appleton, Josie. "The Body Piercing Project" by Josie Appleton, © July 9, 2003. Reprinted by permission of Spiked-online.com, www.spiked-online.com.

Banim, Green&Guy. From *THROUGH the WARDROBE: Women's Relationship with their Clothes* by Maura Banim, Eileen Green&Ali Guy, © 2001. Reprinted by permission of Berg Publishers, an imprint of A&C Black Publishers Ltd.

Boyd, Danah. "Social Network Site Taste Test: MySpace or Facebook?" from *White Flight in Networked Publics? How Race and Class Shaped American Teen Engagement with MySpace and Facebook.* Reprinted by permission of the author.

Boyd, Todd. "Doin' Me" from *Young, Black, Rich&Famous: The Rise of the NBA, The Hip Hop Invasion and the Transformation of American Culture* by Todd Boyd. Copyright © 2003. Reprinted by permission of the author.

Cahan, Richard, Nicholas Osborn,&Michael Williams. From "Who We Were: A Snapshot of America" by Richard Cahan, Nicholas Osborn and Michael Williams. Used by permission of the authors.

© 2005–2010 Chevron Corporation. Used with permission.

Clifford, Stephanie. "Burnishing a Brand by Selecting and Idol" from *The New York Times,* December 24, 2009. Copyright © 2009 *The New York Times.* All rights reserved. Used by permission and protected by the Copyright Laws of the United States. The printing, copying, redistribution, or retransmission of the Material without express written permission is prohibited.

Cloud, John. "Eating Better Than Organic" from TIME, March 2, 2007. Copyright © 2007, *Time* Inc. All rights reserved. Reprinted by permission.

Collier, Paul. "Put Aside Prejudices" from *New York Times Room for Debate,* October 26, 2009. Reprinted by permission of the author.

Cooper, Robbie. "Alter Ego: Avatars and Their Creators" © 2007. Used with permission of the author.

Coro, Paul. "Phoenix Suns 'Los Suns' jerseys making a statement," THE ARIZONA REPUBLIC, May 5, 2010. © *The Arizona Republic.* Used with permission. Permission does not imply endorsement.

Cox, Patrick. "America 24/7: A Family Photograph Album" from THE DIGITAL JOURNALIST, November 2003. Reprinted by permission of the author.

Davicsin, Joseph. "Corporations Leave Small Business Behind," THE DAILY TARGUM, October 16, 2002. Reprinted by permission of the *Daily Targum.*

Dawson, Bret. "The Privatization of Our Culture" from SHIFT (2002). Reprinted by permission of the author.

Delucchi, Mark A., Mark Z. Jacobson. "A Path to Sustainable Energy by 2030." Copyright ©2009 Scientific American, a division of Nature America, Inc. All rights reserved. Reprinted with Permission.

Diamond, Jared. "Will Big Business Save the Earth?" THE NEW YORK TIMES OP-ED, December 6, 2009. Copyright © 2009 *The New York Times.* Reprinted by permission.

Dobi, Rob. "How to Dress Emo Boy" and "How to Dress Emo Girl" from www.robdobi.com. Reprinted by permission of Rob Dobi.

"Do No Harm: The Coalition of Americans for Research Ethics." Screen shot from http://www.stemcellresearchy.org/. Reprinted by permission Do No Harm: The Coalition of Americans for Research Ethics.

Ephron, Nora. "The Boston Photographs." Reprinted by permission of International Creative Management, Inc. Copyright © 1978 by Nora Ephron.

Feine, Paul. "McBastards: McDonald's and Globalization" as appeared on AworldConnected.org. Reprinted by permission of the author.

Flower, Zoe. "Getting the Girl, The Myths, Misconceptions and Misdemeanors of Females in Games." Reprinted from www.1UP.com, January 2005, Copyright © 2005. Reprinted with permission of 1 UP.com. All rights reserved.

Foley, Jonathan "The Third Way" from *New York Times Room for Debate,* October 26, 2009. Reprinted by permission of the author.

Franke-Folstad, Kim. "G.I. Joe's Big Biceps are Not a Big Deal," ROCKY MOUNTAIN NEWS, May 24, 1999. Reprinted by permission of *Rocky Mountain News.*

Friedman, Thomas. "America's Real Dream Team" from *The New York Times,* March 21, 2010. © 2010 *The New York Times.* All rights reserved. Used by permission and protected by the Copyright Laws of the United States, The printing, copying, redistribution or retransmission of the Material without express written permission is prohibited.

Glazer, Mark. "Did London Bombings Turn Citizen Journalists into Citizen Paparazzi?" from ONLINE JOURNALISM REVIEW, July 13, 2005. Reprinted by permission.

Gore, Al. Nobel Peace Prize acceptance speech by Al Gore. ©The Nobel Foundation 2007. Reprinted by permission.

Gorney, Cynthia, "Mexico's Other Border" © 2008. National Geographic Images. Reprinted with permission.

Gottesman, Jane. Screen shots from the online version of *Game Face,* found at http://washingtonpost.com/wp-srv.photo.onassignment.gameFace/. Reprinted by permission of Game Face Productions.

Graner Ray, Sheri. "What if the Player is Female?" from GENDER INCLUSIVE GAME DESIGN: EXPANDING THE MARKET 1e by Sheri Graner Ray. ©2004. Reprinted with permission of Delmar Learning, a division of Thomson Learning: www.thomsonrights.com Fax 800-730-2215.

Hayter, Teresa. "The New Common Sense" by Teresa Hayter, NEW INTERNATIONALIST, October 1, 2002. Reprinted by permission of the *New Internationalist.*

Hylton, Hilary. "Calls to Shut U.S.-Mexico Border Grow in Flu Scare," TIME Magazine, April 29, 2009. Copyright © 2009, *Time* Inc. All rights reserved. Reprinted by permission.

Lessig, Lawrence. "R.W, Revived" from REMIX: MAKING ART AND COMMERCE THRIVE IN THE HYBRID ECONOMY by Lawrence Lessig. Copyright © 2008 by Lawrence Lessig. Used by permission of the Penguin Press, a division of Penguin Group (USA) Inc.

Jackson, Bruce. Letter to the Public Editor: "Other Voices: Some Words About Those Pictures" sent by Bruce Jackson, Buffalo, January 9, 2005. Published January 16, 2005 in THE NEW YORK TIMES. Reprinted by permission of Professor Bruce Jackson.

James, Frank. "Phoenix (Los) Suns Wade Into Immigration Fight." ©2010, NPR®, News blog by NPR's Frank James was originally published on the Two-Way, NPR's News Blog on NPR.org on May 5, 2010 and is used with the permission of NPR. Any unauthorized duplication is strictly prohibited.

Jianghong, Qui. "KFC and McDonald's—A Model of Blended Culture" CHINA TODAY, June 1, 2004. http:/www.chinatyoday.com. Reprinted by permission of *China Today.*

Johnson, Geoffrey. "Marking Earth Day Inc." THE NEW YORK TIMES, OP-ED, April 22, 2004. Copyright © 2004 *The New York Times.* Reprinted by permission.

Johnson, Steven. "How Twitter Will Change the Way We Live," TIME, June 5, 2009. Copyright © 2009, *Time* Inc. All rights reserved. Reprinted by permission.

Jones, Gerald. From *Killing Monsters* by Gerald Jones. Copyright © 2003 Perseus Books Group. Reprinted by permission.

Klein, Ezra. "Nativism Doesn't Appear to be on Much of a Rise" by Ezra Klein, *The Washington Post,* March 30, 2010. ©2010 *The Washington Post.* All Rights reserved. Used by permission and protected by the Copyright Laws of the United States. The printing, copying, redistribution, or retransmission of the Material without express written permission is prohibited.

Kluger, Jeffrey. "How America's Children Packed on the Pounds," TIME Magazine, June 12, 2008. Copyright © 2008, *Time* Inc. All rights reserved. Reprinted by permission.

Kolbert, Elizabeth. "Can America Go Green" by Elizabeth Kolbert, *New Statesman,* June 19, 2006. © *New Statesman* Ltd. All rights reserved. Reprinted by permission.

La Ferla, Ruth. "Wearing Their Beliefs on Their Chests" by Ruth La Ferla, from *The New York Times.* © 2005 *The New York Times.* All rights reserved. Used by permission and protected by the Copyright Laws of the United States. The printing, copying, redistribution, or retransmission of the Material without express written permission is prohibited.

Leeson, David. *Photographs and Stories.* © March 2005. Reprinted by permission of the author.

Lehrer, Jim. "Pros and Cons of Embedded Journalism," *NewsHour Extra,* March 27, 2003. © 2003 MacNeil/Lehrer Productions. Reprinted by permission.

Lexington. "The Hub Nation" by Lexington, THE ECONOMIST, April 22, 2010. © 2010 *The Economist Newspaper Limited,* London. Reprinted by permission.

Lomborg, Bjorn. "Inconvenient Truths for Al Gore" by Bjorn Lomborg in Project Syndicate © 2006-09-05. Reprinted by permission of Project Syndicate, www.project-syndicate.org.

Marlette, Doug. "I Was a Tool of Satan." Reproduced from *Columbia Journalism Review.* November/December 2003. © 2003 by *Columbia Journalism Review.*

Martin, Michel. "With Immigration, Racism Knows No Borders" © 2010, NPR®, News commentary by NPR's Michel Martin was originally broadcast on NPR's "Tell Me More® on May 3, 2010, and is used with the permission of NPR. Any unauthorized duplication is strictly prohibited.

Meadows, Mark Stephen. I AVATAR: CULTURE AND CONSEQUENCES OF HAVING A SECOND LIFE, "Auto Portraits" p. 106, © 2008 Mark Stephen Meadows. Reproduced by permission of Pearson Education Inc.

McClelland, Susan. "Distorted Images: Western Cultures Are Exporting Their Dangerous Obsession with Thinness," *Maclean's Magazine,* February 22, 1999. Reprinted by permission of *Maclean's Magazine.*

Media Education Foundation. Transcript of documentary film "Playing Unfair" (2002) with Mary Jo Kane, Pat Griffin and Michael Messner, produced by Media Education Foundation. Reprinted with permission.

Miller, Laura, "Plagiarism, the Next Generation". This article first appeared in Salon.com, www.salon.com, an online version remains in the Salon archives. Reprinted by permission.

Mir-Hossein Mousavi Khameneh message to the Iranian people as posted on Twitter. Reprinted by permission.

Mitchell, Paul. "Faith and Fashion: The Power of T-Shirt Evangelism" by Paul Mitchell from *BreakPoint,* June 1, 2005, reprinted with permission of Prison Fellowship, www.breakpoint.org.

Morozov, Evgeny. "Slacktivism to Activism." Copyright © 2009. Reprinted with permission of the author.

Mumford, Thad. "The New Minstrel Show: Black Vaudeville with Statistics," THE NEW YORK TIMES, May 2004. © 2004, *The New York Times.* Reprinted by permission.

Munro, Margaret. "Dressing for Success at the Olympics: Is it 'Doping on a Hanger' or is it just a Swimsuit?" Reprinted with the express permission of CAN-WEST NEWS SERVICE, a CanWest Partnership.

Newzcrew. Screen shot from Ayiti: The Cost of Life in http:/www.ayiti.newzcrew.org/globalkids/. Used with Permission.

Murphy, Kate. "First Camera, Then Fork" from *The New York Times* © 2010 *The New York Times.* All rights reserved. Used by permission and protected by the Copyright Laws of the United States, the printing, copying, redistribution or retransmission of the material without express written permission is prohibited.

Murphy, Kieron. "Engineering a Better Athlete" by Kieron Murphy, posted on DiscoveryNews.com on February 3, 2010. Courtesy of Discovery Communications. LLC.

NIH Stem Cell information hosted by the National Institute for Health of the U.S. government. (http://stemcells.nih.gov)

Obama, Michelle. "Let's Move" launch speech by Michelle Obama. February 9. 2010.

The Onion. "MySpace Outage Leaves Millions Friendless." Reprinted with permission of THE ONION. Copyright ©2010, by ONION, INC., www.theonion.com. [COMP: Type must be at least 9 pts for this one entry]

Orbach, Susie. "Fat is an Advertising Issue" by Susie Orbach. Reproduced from CAMPAIGN MAGAZINE with the permission of the copyright owner, Haymarket Business Publications Limited.

Okrent, Daniel. "To The Public Editor: No Picture Tells the Truth—The Best Do Better Than That" by Daniel Okrent, *The New York Times*, January 9, 2005. Reprinted by permission of the author.

Patel, Raj. "When Cheap Water and Oil Disappear" by Raj Patel from *The New York Times Room for Debate*, October 26, 2009. Copyright © 2009 by Raj Patel. Reprinted by permission of International Creative Management.

Pew Internet&American Life Project. "Social Media and Young Adults 'Summary of Findings'" from PEW INTERNET AND AMERICAN LIFE PROJECT © 2010, www.pewinternet.org. Reprinted by permission.

Phoenix Suns. From Sun's Planet Orange Discussion Board, NPR blog, "Phoenix, Los Suns, Wade into Immigration Fight," May 5, 2010.

Pogue, David. "Photo Sharing Even the Folks Can Handle," *The New York Times*, June 5, 2007. Copyright ©2007 *The New York Times*. All rights reserved. Used by permission and protected by the Copyright Laws of the United States, the printing, copying, redistribution or retransmission of the material without express written permission is prohibited.

Pollan, Michael. "When a Crop Becomes King" THE NEW YORK TIMES OP-ED, July 19, 2002. Copyright © 2002 *The New York Times*. Reprinted by permission.

Pope Jr., Harrison, Robert Olivardia, Amanda Gruber, John Borowieki. "Evolving Ideals of Male Body Image As Seen Through Action Toys" from the *International Journal of Eating Disorders*, July, 1999, Vol. 26, No. 1.

Porter, Charles. "Picture Power: Tragedy in Oklahoma," BBC NEWS ONLINE, May 9, 2005. Reprinted by permission of the author.

Randy, James. "McDonald's Abroad," TIME Magazine, October 28, 2009. Copyright © 2009, *Time* Inc. All rights reserved. Reprinted by permission.

Rice-Oxley, Mark. "In 2000 years, Will the World Remember Disney or Plato?" Reproduced with permission from the January 15, 2004 issue of the *Christian Science Monitor* (www.CSMonitor.com). © 2004 *The Christian Science Monitor*.

Ritzer, George. "McLibel-Two Worlds Collide." Interview with George Ritzer, February 1997, from the documentary *McLibel*. Reprinted by permission of Spanner Films Ltd., www.spannerfilms.net.

Riviello, John. "More than Just Dolls" from WHAT IF BARBIE WAS AN ACTUAL PERSON? A flash movie by John Riviello. Reprinted with permission.

Robbins, Ted. "America's Toughest Sheriff Takes on Immigration" © 2008, NPR®, News report by NPR's Ted Robbins was originally broadcast on NPR's Morning Edition® on March 10, 2008, and is used with the permission of NPR. Any unauthorized duplication is strictly prohibited.

Ryan, Shannon. Banking on Beauty: Trying to expand fan base by marketing its players, the WNBA for the first time offers rookies lessons in fashion and makeup from Chicago.

Schulte, Bret. "Saying it in Cinema." www.usnews.com/usnews/newsarticles/060605/05warming,b,htm, © 2006, in *U.S. News*.

Screenshot from http://www.homelandgitmo.com/ (A Breakthrough Campaign, © 2008.) Reprinted by permission.

Shapin, Steven. "Clean Up Hitters: The Steroid Wars and the Nature of What's Natural," from *The New Yorker* © April 18, 2005. Reprinted by permission of the author.

Shiva, Vandana. "The Failure of Gene-Altered Crops" from *New York Times Room for Debate*, October 26, 2009. Reprinted by permission of the author.

Silverblatt, Art. "Twitter as Newspeak" by Art Silverblatt, *St. Louis Journalism Review*, September/October 2009. Reprinted by permission.

Skenazy, Lenor. "Don't Smile for the Camera," *Daily News*, January 5, 2003. Copyright © *New York Daily News*, L.P. Used with permission.

Sklarsky, Jeremy. "Globalization or McDonaldization," THE DAILY TARGUM, October 17, 2002. Reprinted by permission of the *Daily Targum*.

Smith, Terrance. "War, Live," The News Hour with Jim Lehrer, March 22, 2003 © 2003 MacNeil/Lehrer Productions. Reprint by permission.

Sokolove, Michael. "Drug in Sport: The Shape to Come" by Michael Sokolove, THE NEW YORK TIMES MAGAZINE, January 18, 2004. © 2004 Michael Sokolove. Reprinted by permission of *The New York Times Syndication Sales Corp*.

Steffen, Alex. "On Earth Day" by Alex Steffen as appeared in worldchanging.com, April 21, 2006. © 2006. Reprinted by permission.

Steinlight, Steven. "Thomas L. Friedman: Foe of Open Borders and Comprehensive Immigration Reform" by Steven Steinlight, Curious Times Op-ED, March 26, 2010. Reprinted by permission of the Center for Immigration Studies.

Stevenson, Seth. "You and Your Shadow: The iPods are mesmerizing. But does your iPod think it's better than you?" Reprinted by permission from *Slate*. 3/2/2004 Issue.

Strangelove, Michael. "There is No Shame in Watching YouTube" http://www.strangelove.com/blog/2010/03/there-is-no-shame-in-watching-youtube/. Reprinted with permission of Dr. Michael Strangelove, Google and FaceBook.

Strupp, Joe. "The Photo Felt Around the World," *EDITOR&PUBLISHER*, May 1995, © Nelson Business Media, Inc. Reprinted by permission.

Terdiman, Daniel. "Playing Games with a Conscience," *Wired News*, April 22, 2004. Reprinted by permission of the author.

TerraChoice. "The Seven Sins of Greenwashing." Reprinted by permission of TerraChoice.

TheTruth.com. "Crazyworld" screen shot from http://www.thetruth.com. Reprinted by permission of the American Legacy Foundation.

Thompson, Clive. "I'm So Digitally Close To You" by Clive Thompson. Copyright © 2008 Clive Thompson. Reprinted by permission of Featurewell.com, on behalf of the author.

Tilin, Andrew. "Ready, Set, Mutate!" from WIRED, September 9, 2000. Reprinted by permission of the author.

Tribune, © 2008 *Chicago Tribune.* All rights reserved. Used by permission and protected by the Copyright Laws of the United States. The printing, copying, redistribution, or retransmission of the material without express written permission is prohibited.

Wan, Gok. From *Dress for Success* by Gok Wan, Copyright ©2008. Reprinted by permission of HarperCollins Publishers Ltd.

Werde, Bill. "Hijacking Harry Potter, Quidditch Broom and All" from *The New York Times.* © 2004 *The New York Times.* All rights reserved. Used by permission and protected by the Copyright Laws of the United States, The printing, copying, redistribution or retransmission of the material without express written permission is prohibited.

WNBA. The WNBA Identifications reproduced herein are used with the permission from WNBA Enterprises, LLC © 2010 WNBA Enterprises, LLC All Rights Reserved.

"What's Wrong With the Body Shop." From the Beyond McDonald's pages at http://www.McSpotlight.org.

Zirin, Dave. "Say It Ain't So, Big Leagues" by Dave Zirin. Reprinted with permission from the November 14, 2005 issue of *The Nation.* For subscription information, call 1-800-333-8536. Portions of each week's *Nation* magazine can be accessed at http://www.thenation.com.

Index